Lecture Notes in Computer Science   11806

More information about this series at http://www.springer.com/series/7410

Xiaofeng Chen · Xinyi Huang ·
Jun Zhang (Eds.)

Machine Learning
for Cyber Security

Second International Conference, ML4CS 2019
Xi'an, China, September 19–21, 2019
Proceedings

Editors
Xiaofeng Chen
Xidian University
Xi'an, China

Xinyi Huang
Fujian Normal University
Fuzhou, China

Jun Zhang
Swinburne University of Technology
Hawthorn, VIC, Australia

ISSN 0302-9743   ISSN 1611-3349 (electronic)
Lecture Notes in Computer Science
ISBN 978-3-030-30618-2   ISBN 978-3-030-30619-9 (eBook)
https://doi.org/10.1007/978-3-030-30619-9

LNCS Sublibrary: SL4 – Security and Cryptology

This Springer imprint is published by the registered company Springer Nature Switzerland AG
The registered company address is: Gewerbestrasse 11, 6330 Cham, Switzerland

Preface

The Second International Conference on Machine Learning for Cyber Security (ML4CS 2019) was held in Xi'an, China during September 19–21, 2019. ML4CS is a well-recognized annual international forum for AI-driven security researchers to exchange ideas and present their work. This volume contains papers presented at ML4CS 2019. The Program Committee also invited seven distinguished researchers to deliver their keynote talks. The keynote speakers were Elisa Bertino from Purdue University, USA; Qiang Yang from Hong Kong University of Science and Technology, SAR China; Michael Pecht from University of Maryland, USA; Zheng Yan from Xidian University, China; Feifei Li from University of Utah, USA; Xuemin Lin from University of New South Wales, Australia; and Jaideep Vaidya from Rutgers University, USA.

The conference received 70 submissions. Each submission was reviewed by at least three Program Committee members. The committee accepted 23 regular papers and 3 short papers to be included in the conference program. The proceedings contain revised versions of the accepted papers. While revisions are expected to take the referees comments into account, this was not enforced and the authors bear full responsibility for the content of their papers.

ML4CS 2019 was organized by the School of Cyber Engineering, Xidian University. Furthermore, ML4CS 2019 was sponsored by the State Key Laboratory of Integrated Service Networks (ISN) and National 111 centre of Mobile Internet Security (China 111 project No. B16037), Xidian University. The conference would not have been such a success without the support of these organizations, and we sincerely thank them for their continued assistance and support.

We would also like to thank the authors who submitted their papers to ML4CS 2019, and the conference attendees for their interest and support. We thank the Organizing Committee for their time and effort dedicated to arranging the conference. This allowed us to focus on the paper selection and deal with the scientific program. We thank the Program Committee members and the external reviewers for their hard work in reviewing the submissions; the conference would not have been possible without their expert reviews. Finally, we thank the EasyChair system and its operators, for making the entire process of managing the conference convenient.

September 2019

Xiaofeng Chen
Xinyi Huang
Jun Zhang

ML4CS 2019

The Second International Conference on Machine Learning for Cyber Security

Xi'an, China
September 19–21, 2019

Sponsored and organized by

State Key Laboratory of Integrated Services Networks (ISN)
National 111 Center for Mobile Internet Security

General Chairs

Xinbo Gao	Xidian University, China
Hui Li	Xidian University, China
Jianfeng Ma	Xidian University, China

Technical Program Chairs

Xiaofeng Chen	Xidian University, China
Xinyi Huang	Fujian Normal University, China
Jun Zhang	Swinburne University of Technology, Australia

Steering Committees

Jonathan Oliver	Trend Micro, USA
Jun Zhang	Swinburne University of Technology, Australia
Ian Welch	Victoria University of Wellington, New Zealand
Wanlei Zhou	Deakin University, Australia
Islam Rafiqul	Charles Sturt University, Australia
Ryan Ko	Waikato University, New Zealand
Iqbal Gondal	Federation University, Australia
Yang Xiang	Swinburne University of Technology, Australia
Vijay Varadharajan	The University of Newcastle, Australia

Publicity Chairs

Jianfeng Wang	Xidian University, China
Yuexin Zhang	Swinburne University of Technology, Australia

Technical Program Committees

Ammar Alazab	Balqa Applied University, Jordan
Man Ho Au	The Hong Kong Polytechnic University, SAR China
Elisa Bertino	Purdue University, USA
Arcangelo Castiglione	University of Salerno, Italy
Liqun Chen	University of Surrey, UK
Xiaofeng Chen	Xidian University, China
Long Chen	New Jersey Institute of Technology, USA
Robert Deng	Singapore Management University, Singapore
Changyu Dong	Newcastle University, Australia
Christian Esposito	University of Napoli Federico II, Italy
Elena Ferrari	University of Insubria, Italy
Jinguang Han	Queen's University Belfast, UK
Weili Han	Fudan University, China
Debiao He	Wuhan University, China
Qiong Huang	South China Agricultural University, China
Xinyi Huang	Fujian Normal University, China
Christian D. Jensen	Technical University of Denmark, Denmark
Shouling Ji	Zhejiang University, China
Hai Jiang	Arkansas State University, USA
Georgios Kambourakis	University of the Aegean, Greece
Elif Kavun	The University of Sheffield, UK
Ayesha Khalid	Queen's University Belfast, UK
Miroslaw Kutylowski	Wroclaw University of Technology, Poland
Jin Li	Guangzhou University, China
Kuan-Ching Li	Providence University, China
Qi Li	Tsinghua University, China
Jing Liu	Xidian University, China
Siqi Ma	CSIRO, Australia
Flix Gmez Mrmol	University of Murcia, Germany
Weizhi Meng	Technical University of Denmark, Denmark
Jonathan Oliver	Trend Micro, USA
Lei Pan	Deakin University, Australia
Javier Parra-Arnau	Universitat Rovira i Virgili, Spain
Javier Pastor-Galindo	University of Murcia, Germany
Yongli Ren	RMIT University, Australia
Goce Ristanoski	Data61, Australia
Fabio Scotti	University of Milan, Italy
Chao Shen	Xi'an Jiaotong University, China
Willy Susilo	University of Wollongong, Australia
Qiang Tang	Luxembourg Institute of Science and Technology, Luxembourg
Qiang Tang	New Jersey Institute of Technology, USA
Vijay Varadharajan	The University of Newcastle, Australia
Athanasios Vasilakos	Lulea University of Technology, Sweden

Ding Wang	Peking University, China
Huaxiong Wang	Nanyang Technological University, Singapore
Shi Wei	Caleton University, Canada
Xuetao Wei	University of Cincinnati, USA
Ian Welch	Victoria University of Wellington, New Zealand
Qianhong Wu	Beihang University, China
Liang Xiao	Xiamen University, China
Peng Xu	Huazhong University of Science and Technology, China
Shouhuai Xu	University of Texas, USA
Guoliang Xue	Arizona State University, USA
Laurence T. Yang	St Francis Xavier University, Canada
Yong Yu	Shaanxi Normal University, China
Moti Yung	Columbia University, USA
Zhihui Zhan	University of Science and Technology of China, China
Fangguo Zhang	Sun Yat-sen University, China
Jun Zhang	Swinburne University of Technology, Australia
Leo Yu Zhang	Deakin University, Australia
Mingwu Zhang	Hubei University of Technology, China
Rui Zhang	Chinese Academy of Sciences, China
Zonghua Zhang	Institut Mines-Tlcom (IMT) Lille Douai, France
Xi Zheng	Macquarie University, Australia
Yao Zheng	University of Hawaii at Manoa, USA
Haojin Zhu	Shanghai Jiao Tong University, China
Tianqing Zhu	University of Technology, Australia

Additional Reviewers

Biwen, Chen	Song, Qipeng
Chen, Haoyu	Wang, Chuntao
Dibaei, Mahdi	Wang, Zi-Jia
Li, Dawei	Yang, Yaxi
Li, Jianyu	Yang, Yi
Li, Na	Zhang, Huang
Li, Shunpeng	Zhang, Jiani
Li, Ximing	Zhang, Xiaoyu
Liu, Zhengqiu	Zhang, Yunru
Ma, Sha	Zhong, Lin
Pattaranantakul, Montida	Zhong, Qi
Peng, Cong	

Contents

Network Data Collection, Fusion, Mining and Analytics for Cyber Security

Zheng Yan[1,2]([⊠]) [iD]

[1] State Lab of ISN, School of Cyber Engineering,
Xidian University, Xi'an 710071, China
zyan@xidian.edu.cn
[2] Department of Communications and Networking,
Aalto University, 02150 Espoo, Finland

Abstract. Cyber security has become the most crucially important topic for safeguarding national and personal safety. Achieving cyber security depends not only on defense technologies, but also the technologies to detect and discover cyber intrusions, threats and attacks. Herein, network data plays an essential role. However, network data for security detection (i.e., security-related data) normally features big data characters. How to collect and process them in an efficient, effective and precise way becomes a big challenge towards network security measurement. In this article, I will introduce the current research results of my research team in terms of adaptive network data collection in heterogeneous networks, data fusion and compression for highly efficient network intrusion detection and economic data storage, a method of application-layer tunnel detection with rules and machine learning, as well as data mining and analytics on opinions posted in the website for retrieving trust information and generating reputation. Working on security-related network data collection, fusion, mining and analytics, we make efforts to collect and process as few as possible data in a context-aware manner, but achieve as accurate as possible security detection results.

Keywords: Data collection · Data fusion · Data mining · Data analytics · Cyber security · Machine learning

1 Introduction

Cyber security has become the most crucially important topic for safeguarding national and personal safety. Achieving cyber security depends not only on defense technologies, but also the technologies to detect and discover cyber intrusions, threats and attacks. Herein, network data plays an essential role. However, network data for security detection (named security-related data) normally features big data characters. How to determine the target security-related data for sampling, effectively collect useful data and process them in an efficient, economic and precise way becomes a big challenge towards network security measurement [1–5].

In this article, I will introduce the current research results of my research team in terms of adaptive network data collection [6–8], data fusion and compression for highly

© Springer Nature Switzerland AG 2019
X. Chen et al. (Eds.): ML4CS 2019, LNCS 11806, pp. 1–5, 2019.
https://doi.org/10.1007/978-3-030-30619-9_1

efficient network intrusion detection and economic data storage [9–13], a method of application-layer tunnel detection with rules and machine learning [14], as well as data mining and analytics on opinions posted in website for retrieving trust information and generating reputation [15, 16]. Working on security-related network data collection, fusion, mining and analytics, we make efforts to collect and process as few as possible data in a context-aware manner, but achieve as accurate as possible security detection results.

2   Adaptive Network Data Collection

The network security is usually reflected by some relevant data that can be collected in a network system. By learning and analyzing such data, called security-related data, we can detect the intrusions to the network system and further measure its security level [5]. Clearly, the first step of detecting network intrusions is to collect security-related data. However, in the context of 5G and big data, there are a number of challenges in collecting these data due to the heterogeneity of network and ever-growing amount of data. Therefore, traditional data collection methods cannot be applied into the next generation network systems directly [7, 8], especially for security-related data.

We designed and implemented an adaptive security-related data collector based on network context in heterogeneous networks [6]. The proposed collector solves the issue caused by heterogeneity of network system by designing a Security-related Data Description Language (SDDL) to instruct security-related data collection in various networking contexts based on a number of thorough surveys [1–4]. SDDL specifies what kind of data should be collected in which way and at what place based on the detection of networking context. SDDL also marks the tags about data processing methods and the target attacks that the data can be used for detection. By integrating the SDDL with network context detection, the proposed collector can flexibly collect data at any network nodes with context awareness in a large-scale heterogeneous network. In addition, by introducing adaptive sampling algorithms, data collection efficiency can be further improved and the volume of the collected data can be reduced with the insurance of data collection precision. Performance evaluation based on a prototype implementation shows the effectiveness of the adaptive security-related data collector in terms of a number of pre-defined design requirements.

3   Network Intrusion Detection Based on Reversible Sketches

With the continuous increase of network scale, the growth of network traffic brings great challenges to the detection of DDoS flooding attacks and amplification attacks. Incomplete network traffic collection or non-real-time processing of big-volume network traffic will seriously affect the accuracy and efficiency of attack detection. Recently, sketch data structures are widely applied in high-speed networks to compress and fuse network traffic. But sketches suffer from a reversibility problem to make it difficult to reconstruct a set of keys that exhibit abnormal behaviors due to the irreversibility of hash functions.

In order to address the above challenges, we first design a novel Chinese Remainder Theorem based Reversible Sketch (CRT-RS). CRT-RS is not only capable of compressing and fusing big-volume network traffic but also has the ability of reversely discovering the anomalous keys (e.g., the sources of malicious or unwanted traffic). Then, based on traffic records generated by CRT-RS, we propose a Modified Multi-chart Cumulative Sum (MM-CUSUM) algorithm that supports self-adaptive and protocol independent detection to detect DDoS flooding attacks and amplification attacks [9, 10]. The performance of the proposed detection method is experimentally examined by several open source datasets. The experimental results show that the method can detect DDoS flooding attacks and amplification attacks with efficiency, accuracy, adaptability, and protocol independability. Moreover, by comparing with other attack detection methods using sketch techniques, our method has quantifiable lower computation complexity when recovering the anomalous source addresses, which is the most important merit of our method.

4 Application-Layer Tunnel Detection with Rules and Machine Learning

Application-layer tunnels are often used to construct covert channels in order to transmit secret data, which is often applied to raise network threats in recent years. Detection of abnormal application-layer tunnels can assist identifying a variety of network threats, thus has high research significance. However, existing methods, such as feature signature-based detection, protocol anomaly-based detection and behavior statistics-based detection suffer from such drawbacks as high false positive rate, low efficiency, invalid for encrypted tunnels, low identification rate and poor real-time performance.

For overcoming the above problems, we explored application-layer tunnel detection and proposed a generic detection method by applying both rules and machine learning [14]. Our detection method consists of two parts: rule-based domain name filtering regarding Domain Generation Algorithm (DGA) and a machine learning based generic feature extraction framework for tunnel detection. We employed a trigram model to design rule-based DGA domain name filtering, which can identify tunnels with obvious features for reducing the amount of data that need to be further processed in machine learning-based detection. Therefore, our method can greatly improve efficiency and real-time performance of tunnel detection. In terms of machine learning, we proposed a generic feature extraction framework by combining multiple detection methods, supporting network layer, transport layer and application layer and performing multiple statistical and security-related features extraction for tunnel detection. Thus, our method can ensure high accuracy with low false positive rate. We tested the effectiveness of the proposed method by conducting experiments on commonly used Domain Name System (DNS), Hyper Text Transfer Protocol (HTTP) and Hypertext Transfer Protocol Secure (HTTPS) tunnels. Experimental results showed that our proposed method is more generic and efficient compared with other existing works.

5 Fusing and Mining Opinions for Reputation Generation

The Internet provides a convenient platform for people to freely share their opinions on any entities. The opinions expressed in natural languages carry the subjective attitudes and preferences of humans. They represent the public perspectives on entities, thus impact user decisions and behaviors in some way. Therefore, opinions have been recognized as useful and valuable pieces of information for reputation generation. Fusing and mining opinions offer a promising approach to extract trust and reputation information and track public perspectives. However, we are still facing a number of problems [15]. First, few existing studies on reputation generation are based on opinion fusion and mining. Second, an important issue that was neglected in the past research is the degree of relevance between opinions. Third, there is still a lack of a comprehensive method for reputation visualization in order to effectively assist user decision. Forth, a serious issue of online shopping reputation management system gives rise to a problem called "all good reputation". Such strong positive bias impacts buyers to make a wise decision.

In order to overcome the above problems, we propose a novel reputation generation approach based on opinion fusion and mining [15]. In our approach, opinions are filtered to eliminate unrelated ones, and then grouped into a number of fused principal opinion sets that contain opinions with a similar or the same attitude or preference. By aggregating the ratings attached to the fused opinions, we normalize the reputation of an entity. Meanwhile, various types of recommendations can be generated based on relationships among opinions. To offer sufficient reputation information to users, we also propose a new way of reputation visualization. It shows the details of opinion fusing and mining results, such as the normalized reputation value, principal opinions with popularity and other statistics. Experimental results coming from an analysis of big real-world data collected from several popular commercial websites in both English and Chinese demonstrate the generality and accuracy of the proposed approach, especially the effectiveness of opinion filtering for reputation generation. A small-scale real-world user study further quantifies the user acceptance of the developed reputation visualization method. In the sequel, this implies that the proposed approach can be applied in practice to generate reputation.

6 Conclusion

Network data is the foundation for finding potential risks of networks in order to trigger defense mechanisms. In this article, I summarized our recent research results on network data collection, fusion, mining and analytics for cyber security. Efficiency and accuracy are crucial requirements of data collection and processing. On this aspect, we focus on researching effective methods to collect and process as few as possible data in a context-aware manner, but achieve as accurate as possible security detection results.

Acknowledgement. This work is sponsored by the National Key Research and Development Program of China (Grant 2016YFB0800700), the NSFC (Grants 61672410, 61802293 and U1536202), National Postdoctoral Program for Innovative Talents (grant BX20180238), the

Project funded by China Postdoctoral Science Foundation (grant 2018M633461), the open grant of the Tactical Data Link Lab (Grant CLDL- 20182119), and the Key Lab of Information Network Security (Grant C18614).

References

1. Jing, X.Y., Yan, Z., Pedrycz, W.: Security data collection and data analytics in the internet: a survey. IEEE Commun. Surv. Tutorials **21**(1), 586–618 (2019)
2. Xie, H.M., Yan, Z., Yao, Z., Atiquzzaman, M.: Data collection for security measurement in wireless sensor networks: a survey. IEEE Internet Things J. **6**(2), 2205–2224 (2019)
3. Liu, G., Yan, Z., Pedryczc, W.: Data collection for attack detection and security measurement in mobile ad hoc networks: a survey. J. Netw. Comput. Appl. **105**, 105–122 (2018)
4. He, L.M., Yan, Z., Atiquzzaman, M.: LTE/LTE-a network security data collection and analysis for security measurement: a survey. IEEE Access **6**(1), 4220–4242 (2018)
5. Yan, Z., Zhang, Y.Q., Choo, R.K.K., Xiang, Y.: Editorial: security measurements of cyber networks. Secur. Commun. Netw. **2018**(6545314), 3 (2018)
6. Lin, H.Q., Yan, Z., Fu, Y.L.: Adaptive security-related data collection with context awareness. J. Netw. Comput. Appl. **126**, 88–103 (2019)
7. Lin, H.Q., Yan, Z., Chen, Y., Zhang, L.F.: A survey on network security-related data collection technologies. IEEE Access **6**(1), 18345–18365 (2018)
8. Zhou, D.H., Yan, Z., Fu, Y.L., Yao, Z.: A survey on network data collection. J. Netw. Comput. Appl. **116**, 9–23 (2018)
9. Jing, X.Y., Yan, Z., Liang, X.Q., Pedrycz, W.: Network traffic fusion and analysis against DDoS flooding attacks with a novel reversible sketch. Inf. Fusion **51**, 100–113 (2019)
10. Jing, X.Y., Zhao, J.J., Zheng, Q.H., Yan, Z., Pedrycz, W.: A reversible sketch-based method for detecting and mitigating amplification attacks. J. Netw. Comput. Appl. **142**, 15–24 (2019)
11. Yan, Z., Liu, J., Yang, L.T., Pedrycz, W.: Data fusion in heterogeneous networks. Inf. Fusion **53**, 1–3 (2020)
12. Ding, W.X., Jing, X.Y., Yan, Z., Yang, L.T.: A survey on data fusion in Internet of Things: towards secure and privacy-preserving fusion. Inf. Fusion **51**, 129–144 (2019)
13. Li, G.Q., Yan, Z., Fu, Y.L., Chen, H.L.: Data fusion for network intrusion detection: a review. Secur. Commun. Netw. **2018**(8210614), 16 (2018)
14. Lin, H.Q., Liu, G., Yan, Z.: Detection of application-layer tunnels with rules and machine learning. In: The 12th International Conference on Security, Privacy and Anonymity in Computation, Communication and Storage (SpaCCS2019), Atlanta, USA, July 2019
15. Yan, Z., Jing, X.Y., Pedrycz, W.: Fusing and mining opinions for reputation generation. Inf. Fusion **36**, 172–184 (2017)
16. Liu, D., Yan, Z., Ding, W.X., Atiquzzaman, M.: A survey on secure data analytics in edge computing. IEEE Internet of Things J. **6**(3), 4946–4967 (2019)

Malicious Web Request Detection Using Character-Level CNN

Wei Rong[(✉)], Bowen Zhang, and Xixiang Lv

Xidian University,
266 Xinglong Section of Xifeng Road, Xi'an 710126, Shaanxi, China
rw_rongwei@126.com

Abstract. Web parameter injection attacks are common and have put a great threat to the security of web applications. In this kind of attacks, malicious attackers can employ HTTP requests to implement attacks against servers by injecting some malicious codes into the parameters of the HTTP requests. Against the web parameter injection attacks, most of the existing Web Intrusion Detection Systems (WIDS) cannot find unknown new attacks and have a high false positive rate (FPR), since they lack the ability of re-learning and rarely pay attention to the intrinsic relationship between the characters. In this paper, we propose a malicious requests detection system with re-learning ability based on an improved convolution neural network (CNN) model. We add a character-level embedding layer before the convolution layer, which makes our model able to learn the intrinsic relationship between the characters of the request parameters. Further, we modify the filters of CNN and the modified filters can extract the fine-grained features of the request parameters. The test results demonstrate that our model has lower FPR compared with support vector machine (SVM) and random forest (RF).

Keywords: Malicious detection · Injection attacks · CNN · Embedding · Deep learning

1   Introduction

Tons of communications happens through protocol like HTTP/HTTPS today, in which a client can initiate a web request and send it to the web server. A web request usually carries some parameters input by users. Figure 1 shows the request parameters in GET method that is one of HTTP methods. However, such ordinary protocols or methods can lead to great threatens, that many attackers use this part to pass their malicious code to the webserver.

In fact, web application attacks are common in attack incidents against web servers. According to the recent report of Alert Logic [2,3], 73% of the attack incidents in the past 18 months are web application attacks and these attacks affected 85% of its customers. Akamai (a Content Delivery Network service provider) also demonstrated that hackers had launched 47,417,828 web

© Springer Nature Switzerland AG 2019
X. Chen et al. (Eds.): ML4CS 2019, LNCS 11806, pp. 6–16, 2019.
https://doi.org/10.1007/978-3-030-30619-9_2

a request parameter

```
GET http://localhost:8080/index.jsp?param1=v1&param2=v2&param3=v3 HTTP/1.1
User-Agent: Mozilla/5.0 (compatible; Konqueror/3.5; Linux) KHTML/3.5.8 (like Gecko)
Pragma: no-cache
Cache-control: no-cache
Accept: text/xml,application/xml
Accept-Encoding: x-gzip, x-deflate, gzip, deflate
Accept-Charset: utf-8, utf-8;q=0.5, *;q=0.5
Accept-Language: en
Host: localhost:8080
Cookie: JSESSIONID=F563B5262843F12ECAE41815ABDEEA54
Connection: close
```

Fig. 1. The request parameter in an HTTP header

attacks aiming at Akamai servers in just 8 days, between November 8, 2017 to November 15, 2017 [4]. Within all web attacks, code injection attacks account for a large proportion. By injecting some malicious codes into the parameters of HTTP requests, attackers can employ HTTP requests to accomplish their attacks against servers. This type of attacks is called parameter injection attacks, which is a growing concern to the security of web service and require web service providers to build an efficient mechanism to detect code injection attacks.

Existing countermeasures against web parameter injection attacks are usually referred as Web Intrusion Detection Systems (WIDS), which includes signature-based detection and anomaly-based detection [17]. With signature-based detection, the server needs to maintain a library of malicious symbols that distinguish an injection attack from normal web requests. When it receives a request, the server searches the request parameters to see if they contain a malicious symbol, and web requests containing a malicious symbol will be considered as attacks. This signature-based detection usually performs very well on the known attacks that contain distinct symbols. However, a tiny change on the injected codes will hide the symbols and disable such method. Obviously, signature-based detection cannot find unknown new attacks. As for anomaly-based detection, the server needs to train a math model which can characterize normal web requests and filter most abnormal web requests. Compared with signature-based detection, this type of WIDS is able to discover some unknown new attacks. Unfortunately, the FPR (false positive rate) of anomaly-based detection is high in practice.

Besides the high FPR, the model of anomaly-based detection lacks the ability of re-learning since it is a constant model. In fact, earlier anomaly-based detection system collects all training data once and then generates a constant model. Earlier anomaly-based detection systems take the sample with abnormal data structures as an attack. Thus, it can detect some unknown attacks. However, when the data structure of an attack is similar with a normal one, an anomaly-based detection system is incapable of finding such attack. The reason is that an anomaly-based WIDS cannot update its model in time.

In this paper, by using CNN we build a model for detecting parameter injection attacks in terms of web applications. In our model, we add a character-embedding layer before the convolutional layers. The parameters within a request is first fed into the character-embedding layer, by which they will be transformed into feature vectors that are then put into a traditional CNN along with their labels. The output of CNN is a prediction demonstrating if the request is a malicious attack or not. Unlike all previous models, our system is dynamic and has the ability of re-learning. That is to say, the model can be restored when there is some new data that it has never seen before. Our system is not only able to find unknown new attacks, but also able to extract features of the malicious query automatically, instead of maintaining a feature library like the signature-based detection method. Since our model can extract both normal features and malicious features, it has lower FPR than anomaly-based detection model which only learns normal features.

The main contributions of this paper are as follows:

We build an improved CNN model in order to detect malicious web requests. In this model, we add a character-level embedding layer before the convolution layer aiming to digitize a character sequence. Different from the normal digitization, character-level embedding is able to learn the hidden similarity of characters in web requests. In the convolution layer, considering the one-dimensional data structure, we design vertical filters to extract features from character sequence.

Based on the improved CNN model, we present an online learning system which has re-learning ability. That is, the model can be updated in time when there are some unknown new attacks. Therefore, it can adapt to the changing attack methods.

2   Related Work

2.1   Malicious Request Detection

Malicious request detection has been an active research area, and various malicious request detection systems have been proposed. They provide solutions for some specific type or multiple types of malicious requests. For example, reference [9,14,16] showed us their solution to SQLI attack, which is one of the most common malicious requests. Reference [14,16] trained a Support Vector Machine (SVM) model to detect SQLI attacks. Joshi and Geetha [9] detected SQLI attacks using the Naive Bayes machine learning algorithm. Reference [9,14] created feature vector of string by the tokens of sql-query strings and feed these vectors into the SVM-Train process to generate a model. Uwagbole and Buchanan [16] created feature vectors by a hashing procedure called Feature hashing. But these methods of creating feature vectors cannot reflect the relationship between words. On the other hand, models of these papers are constant models that are hard to be updated when there are some new form of SQLI attacks. Dong and Zhang [7] proposed an adaptive system based on SVM for detecting malicious queries in web attacks. This system focused on 4 most frequent types of web-based code-injection attacks. The model of this system can be updated by some new queries periodically. But it does not pay attention to the local features which have an important impact on the final detection result.

2.2 Convolutional Neural Network

In recent years, neural networks (NNs) have been successfully applied in many areas. To some extent, malicious web request detection is a special kind of text classification problem. NNs have achieved great success in text classification area. For example, Kim [10] applied CNNs to sentence classification and Shibahara et al. [15] applied CNNs to url sequence, which is similar to parameter string focused in this paper. Kim [10] proposed a special CNNs named TextCNN. TextCNN converts word sequence to a matrix that CNNs are able to process through embedding layer. Shibahara et al. [15] proposed an Event De-noising CNN (EDCNN). The input of EDCNN is more than just url sequence. They use one-hot representation to denote the categorical features which contain city corresponding to the IP address, TLD and country corresponding to the IP address. In conclusion, CNN performs very well in these text classification problem, therefore it is possible to solve the malicious web request detection problem using CNN.

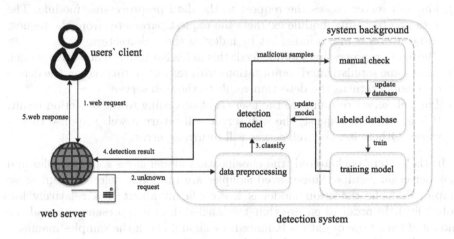

Fig. 2. System overview

3 Proposed System

In this section, we will present the proposed system detecting malicious web request and give its details.

3.1 System Design

Our system receives the parameters of the web request as input, and outputs the detection results. As shown in Fig. 2, the system includes five modules including

Lowercase letters	a	b	c	d	e	f	g	h	i	j	k	l	m	n	o	p	q	r	s	t	u	v	w	x	y	z
Uppercase letter	A	B	C	D	E	F	G	H	I	J	K	L	M	N	O	P	Q	R	S	T	U	V	W	X	Y	Z
Digital	0	1	2	3	4	5	6	7	8	9																
Special characters	;	,		:	/	=	%	&	@	!	*	(	)	{	}	[	]	>	<	?	'	\	.	_	|	+
	-	`		"	#	$	~	^																		

Fig. 3. Characters list

data preprocessing, classification model, manual check, labeled database and training model.

Before running our system, we need some labeled samples to train an initial detection model. As illustrated in Fig. 2, the system works as follows:

(1) A client sends a web request with some parameters to the web server.
(2) The web server passes the request to the data preprocessing module. The data preprocessing module extracts the request parameter from the request and converts it into a index list by indexing these characters.
(3) The data preprocessing module feeds this index list into the detection model.
(4) After some sophisticated computations with respect to this vector, the detection model returns the detection result to the web server.
(5) The web server responds to the user client according to the detection result. If it is a benign request, the web server will return a web response that it wants. Otherwise, the web server will return an error.

In the system background, the classification model saves some samples and their detection results. These saved samples are randomly selected from those samples that the detection model is less confident about (has relatively low probability). In order to ensure that the labeled data is representative and the amount of each type of data is balanced, we should check the samples manually before adding them into the labeled database. When the system finds that the labeled database has changed, it will train a new detection model based on the old model by using the changed database. Then, system updates its detection model with the new model. In this way, the model can get the re-learning ability and adapt to the change of web attacks.

In this system, the detection task is mainly completed by the detection model. The details of the detection model will be given in the next subsection.

3.2   Detection Model

Aiming to analyze web request parameters, we build an improved CNN model. Using character embedding, we make the model learn by itself to digitalize characters according to its tasks. Then, the improved CNN extracts features of request parameters and gives the detection results by the output layer.

Character Representation. A request parameter is a character sequence which contains three types of characters, i.e. letters, digitals and special characters, see Fig. 3 for details. There are 95 characters in total. We convert character sequences into index lists by indexing these characters. However, the character index cannot reflect the relationship between the characters in a specific context. For example, the character '=' is not associated with the character '&' in normal texts. As shown in Fig. 4, in the context of web request parameters, they play a similar role which as a separater. This similarity cannot be represented by index numbers.

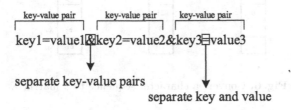

Fig. 4. The two characters '=' and '&' in a request parameter

Regarding this problem, we use character-level embedding in our model to learn the hidden similarity between characters in web request parameters. The idea of character-level embedding comes from the word embedding used in NLP [6].

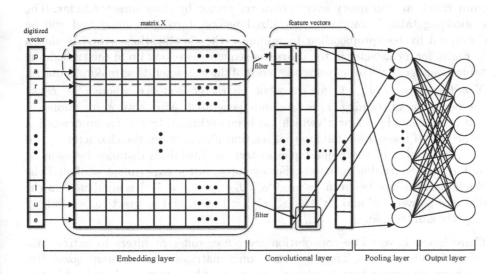

Fig. 5. Model architecture

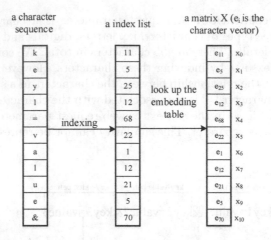

Fig. 6. Convert a character sequence to a matrix X

Model Architecture. The model architecture, shown in Fig. 5, is a deep neural network we used in our demo system. It mainly consists of four parts: the embedding layer, the convolution layer, the pooling layer and the output layer.

Embedding Layer: The embedding layer converts a index list into digital matrix and then feeds it to the convolution layer. Let $e_i \in \mathbb{R}^k$ be the k-dimensional vector corresponding to the i-th character in the character list. Here, i denotes the index of a character. Then, we get an embedding table $E = \left(e_0, e_1, e_2, ..., e_{94}\right)^T$, from which we can query every character vector by the character index. The embedding table is randomly initialized before starting training and will be optimized by backpropagation to minimize the classification error. As shown in Fig. 6, for a character in the character sequence, we look up in the embedding table E and get a vector e_i using the index of the character, thus making a matrix $X = \left(x_0, x_1, x_2, ..., x_{n-1}\right)^T$ for the whole character sequence, where $x_i^T \in E$. At the beginning of training, x_i is randomly generated. After several iterations, x_i will be replaced by a new x_i^* which has been optimized by the backpropagation algorithm. If there are some internal relationships between the character c_a and the character c_b in the request parameter, the Euclidean distance between x_a^* and x_b^* will be smaller relatively. For example, in the experiment we found the Euclidean distance between '=' and '&' ($L_2(x_4^*, x_{10}^*) = 7.8$) is smaller than the distance between 'a' and '&' ($L_2(x_6^*, x_{10}^*) = 10.09$), and in practice '=' and '&' play the similar role.

Convolution Layer: The convolution layer uses different filters to extract different feature vectors. The filters are some matrices with different sizes. But these matrices must have k columns, where k is the column of E in Embedding layer. It should be noted that the difference in size only lays in rows. Unlike CNNs applied in image recognition, the filters in our model can only be moved vertically. Because we want our CNN model to learn the relationship between characters, and every row of the matrix X represents one character. In our model, we set the width of filters equal to that of matrix X to ensure the indivisibility of each character. Let y be one of the output feature vectors and F be a filter. Then the output feature vector y is computed as:

$$y_i = Relu(\sum_{r=0}^{L-1}\sum_{c=0}^{k-1} F_{r,c}X_{i+r,c})$$

where y_i denotes i-th value and F has L rows and k columns. Relu (Rectified Linear Units) function is a popular activation function in the field of deep learning, which is proposed and applied in reference [11]. When we use n different filters F, we will get n feature vectors y in convolution layer and these vectors may have different lengths.

Pooling Layer: Pooling is a commonly used method in the field of deep learning. Pooling layer outputs n results, where n denotes the amount of filters in convolution layer. In our system, we use max pooling to calculate the outputs. The output is derived as $z_i = max_{0 \leqslant t \leqslant l-1}(y_t^i)$, where l denotes the length of feature vector y in convolution layer. This pooling layer is used to reduce the amount of parameters and the computation in our network and hence to control overfitting.

Output Layer: The output layer outputs the classification results. The length of the output vector is the number of the classes. The output vector is computed as $y_j = Softmax(\sum_{i=0}^{n-1} w_{i,j}z_i)$, where n denotes the length of the output vector of previous layer, w denotes weights of this layer and the function Softmax is computed as $Softmax(x_j) = \dfrac{e^{x_j}}{\sum_i e^{x_i}}$. In order to improve the generalization ability of our model, we can also add dropout regularization in this layer. If we use dropout in this layer, z_i we get from the previous layer has a 50% probability of being zero. The summation of all output values of this layer is 1 and the output values are all non-negative. Therefore, an output value represents the probability of belonging to a specific class.

To sum up, the embedding table, the filter matrices and the weights of every layer are what we need to train, and they will be optimized by backpropagation algorithm to minimize classification error.

4   Test and Evaluation

4.1   Dataset

In our experiment, we build our dataset through crawling from internet or extracting the data we need from other datasets [1,8]. Then we merge them into one dataset. There are 5 types of data samples we chose in our dataset: Benign request, SQL injection (SQLI), Remote File Inclusion (RFI), Cross-Site Scripting (XSS) and Directory Traversal (DT). However, the amount of each category is extremely unbalanced. In order to keep the relative balance between each category, we set a threshold for the amount of each category. When the

Table 1. Composition of dataset

Category	Number of samples	Proportion
Benign request	2000	46.49%
SQLi	472	10.97%
XSS	720	16.74%
RFI	599	13.92%
DT	511	11.88%
SUM	4302	100%

number of samples in one category is greater than this threshold, we will randomly sample this category to limit the number of samples to this threshold. Table 1 displays the composition of the dataset we use finally.

4.2   Test Environment

We implement our architecture in Python 3.5.3 using Tensorflow [5]. The operating system we use is Ubuntu 17.04. We also use some of Python's third-party libraries, scikit-learn [13] and numpy.

Table 2. Performance of each model

Model	Indicators	Benign request	DT	RFI	SQLi	XSS	FPR
RF	Recall	99.62%	99.99%	99.58%	99.99%	99.65%	0.38%
	Precision	99.99%	98.58%	99.57%	99.53%	100%	
SVM	Recall	99.87%	99.53%	98.25%	98.52%	99.99%	0.13%
	Precision	99.12%	99.53%	99.98%	99.53%	100%	
CNN	Recall	99.95%	100%	100%	100%	100%	0.02%
	Precision	100%	100%	99.83%%	99.79%	100%	

4.3   Evaluation

We implement a demo classifier for malicious requests detection using the model shown in Fig. 5. In the training process, we shuffle all training samples and divide them into several batches. Then the samples of each batch are used to optimize embedding table and weights of every layer. The process that we use one batch of samples to optimize these parameters is one step. So we can optimize these parameters by all batches step by step. Figure 7 shows how our model is optimized step by step and demonstrates the sum of softmax cross entropy and L2 regularization [12].

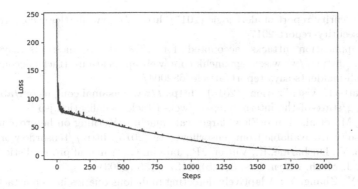

Fig. 7. Train process

In order to compare with the traditional model, we add two control group. We chose Random Forest (RF) and SVM as the control group. The model from control group converts character sequences into sparse matrix through TF-IDF algorithm. We calculate precision and recall rate [18] for every category and FPR (we choose malicious samples as positive samples) for each model. Therefore for one model we have one FPR and 5 pairs of precision and recall rate to calculate. The results of our model against other two models are listed in Table 2. Our model distinctively reduces FPR from 0.38% in RF and 0.13% in SVM to 0.02%. We attribute this to the character-level embedding layer and the modified filters of CNN. We believe that the limited improvement in the recall and precision rate of our model is due to the limitations of the dataset, which is highly unbalanced and small in quantity. Therefore, there is reason to believe that better results will be achieved when it comes to practical issues, where more high quality data is accessible. In addition, only one convolution layer is used in our demo system considering the limitation of our dataset, we believe more advanced features can be extracted if we use deeper networks on bigger dataset.

5 Conclusion

We proposed a malicious requests detection system with re-learning ability based on an improved CNN model. Compared with two other traditional model: SVM and RF, our model pays more attention to the extraction of the local feature in the request parameters. Specifically, we add a character-level embedding layer and modify the filters of CNN to extract the local feature in the request parameters. The results show that our improved CNN model outperforms traditional models on test datasets, while the performance in more practical applications remains to be tested.

References

1. WAF malicious queries data sets. https://github.com/faizann24/Fwaf-Machine-Learning-driven-Web-Application-Firewall

2. Cloud security report of alert logic (2017). https://www.alertlogic.com/resources/cloud-security-report-2017/
3. Web application attacks accounted for 73% of all incidents says report (2017). https://www.scmagazineuk.com/web-application-attacks-accounted-for-73-of-all-incidents-says-report/article/682004/
4. Web attack visualization (2018). https://www.akamai.com/uk/en/about/our-thinking/state-of-the-internet-report/web-attack-visualization.jsp
5. Abadi, M., et al.: TensorFlow: large-scale machine learning on heterogeneous systems, software available from tensorflow. org (2015). http://tensorflow.org
6. Bengio, Y., Ducharme, R., Vincent, P., Jauvin, C.: A neural probabilistic language model. J. Mach. Learn. Res. 3(Feb), 1137–1155 (2003)
7. Dong, Y., Zhang, Y.: Adaptively detecting malicious queries in web attacks. arXiv preprint arXiv:1701.07774 (2017)
8. Gimnez, C., Villegas, A.P., Marañón, G.Á.: HTTP data set CSIC 2010 (2010)
9. Joshi, A., Geetha, V.: SQL injection detection using machine learning. In: 2014 International Conference on Control, Instrumentation, Communication and Computational Technologies (ICCICCT), pp. 1111–1115. IEEE (2014)
10. Kim, Y.: Convolutional neural networks for sentence classification. arXiv preprint arXiv:1408.5882 (2014)
11. Nair, V., Hinton, G.E.: Rectified linear units improve restricted Boltzmann machines. In: Proceedings of the 27th International Conference on Machine Learning, ICML 2010, pp. 807–814 (2010)
12. Ng, A.Y.: Feature selection, L1 vs. L2 regularization, and rotational invariance. In: Proceedings of the Twenty-First International Conference on Machine learning, p. 78. ACM (2004)
13. Pedregosa, F., et al.: Scikit-learn: machine learning in python. J. Mach. Learn. Res. 12, 2825–2830 (2011)
14. Rawat, R., Shrivastav, S.K.: SQL injection attack detection using SVM. Int. J. Comput. Appl. 42(13), 1–4 (2012)
15. Shibahara, T., et al.: Malicious URL sequence detection using event de-noising convolutional neural network. In: 2017 IEEE International Conference on Communications (ICC), pp. 1–7. IEEE (2017)
16. Uwagbole, S.O., Buchanan, W.J., Fan, L.: Applied machine learning predictive analytics to SQL injection attack detection and prevention. In: 2017 IFIP/IEEE Symposium on Integrated Network and Service Management (IM), pp. 1087–1090. IEEE (2017)
17. Wikipedia contributors: Intrusion detection system – Wikipedia, the free encyclopedia (2018). https://en.wikipedia.org/w/index.php?title=Intrusion_detection_system&oldid=844776879#Detection_method. Accessed 13 June 2018
18. Wikipedia contributors: Precision and recall – Wikipedia, the free encyclopedia (2018). https://en.wikipedia.org/w/index.php?title=Precision_and_recall&oldid=845527433. Accessed 13 June 2018

A LBP Texture Analysis Based Liveness Detection for Face Authentication

Zhiqiong Yang$^{(\boxtimes)}$, Qiuheng Li, Yan Li, and Zilong Wang

School of Cyber Engineering, Xidian University, Xi'an, China
yzq568@163.com

Abstract. Face authentication systems are becoming more and more prevalent, but it has an intrinsic vulnerability against the media-based face forgery (MFF) where adversaries display photos or videos containing victims' faces to deceive face authentication systems. Liveness detection is an important defense technique to prevent such attacks. In this paper, we propose a practical and effective liveness detection mechanism to protect the face authentication system against the MFF-based attacks. Our approach send the challenge to the user in random and the camera capture the response as a video. The Local Binary Pattern (LBP) is a widely used descriptor in texture analysis due to its efficiency. We utilize δ-LBP, a LBP variant, to detect the expression frame from the video. Additionally, We improve the original LBP by using proper sampling radius in different subareas of a facial image and apply the approach in extracting the facial texture feature from the expression frame as a histogram. Our method detects the MFF-based attacks by measuring the consistency between the LBP histogram and the real facial texture feature. To demonstrate its effectiveness, We collect real-world photo data and video data from both legitimate authentication requests and the MFF-based attacks. The experiment results show that it can detect the MFF-based attacks with an accuracy of 96.45%.

Keywords: Face authentication · Media-based face forgery ·
Liveness detection · Local binary pattern

1 Introduction

Face authentication is a promising method which has been widely applied in user authentication as it requires no user memory while providing a higher entropy for identifying users [1]. Unfortunately, human faces can be easily captured and reproduced from social networks, which makes face authentication system vulnerable to attacks. Most existing face authentication systems, such as Facelock-Pro [2], have an intrinsic weakness against the media-based face forgery (MFF) where an adversary forges or replayes a photo/video containing a victim's face to circumvent face authentication systems.

To defend against such attacks, liveness detection has been proposed to distinguish between legitimate face of live users and the forged face [3,4]. Crucial to

© Springer Nature Switzerland AG 2019
X. Chen et al. (Eds.): ML4CS 2019, LNCS 11806, pp. 17–28, 2019.
https://doi.org/10.1007/978-3-030-30619-9_3

such methods are challenge-response protocols, where sensors send the challenges to the user who then makes responses according to the displayed instructions in real time. The responses are subsequently captured and verified to distinguish that whether they come from a real human being or other forged face. Typical challenges consist of blinking, smiling and other facial expressions.

In this work, we propose a liveness detection mechanism based on challenge-response and local binary pattern to protect face authentication system against the MFF-based attacks. The local Binary Pattern was first proposed by Ojalain in 2002 [5], which is invariant to monotonic gray-value changes and has low computational complexity, to extract local texture feature information. Our system make sensors generate a dispalayed instruction as challenge randomly, like blinking, smiling and other facial expressions. Then the camera can capture the response from the user as a video. The system mainly consists of three components:expression frame detection, facial feature extractor from this frame and liveness classifier. In the first step, a LBP variant called δ-LBP is proposed to detect the expression frame from the video. δ-LBP with selection of the proper value of δ is helpful to detect the contour of the face image, so that we can utilize δ-LBP to detect the expression frame. In the second step, we imporve the original LBP by using proper sampling radius in different subareas of a facial image. The current LBP operators, which adopt a fixed sampling radius for all pixels in the facial image to extract facial texture feature, ignore the fact that different subareas have different local gray-value distributions [9]. It is reasonable that small sampling radius should be assigned to the fast-changing subarea while big sampling radius should be assigned to the smoothly distributed subarea. Therefore, we can use the enhanced LBP with different sampling radius to extract facial texture feature and draw the corresponding LBP histogram. Finally, we send the LBP histogram to the liveness classifier and find out whether the facial texture feature is from a real live user.

We conduct a user study to validate the proposed liveness detection mechanism. We collect real-world photo data and video data from both legitimate authentication requests and MFF-based attacks. Our experimental results show that FaceLBP can detect MFF-based attacks with an accuracy of 96.45%.

2   Related Work

Various liveness detection techniques for face authentication have been proposed in the literature. In this section, we discuss differences between our method and those relevant studies.

Our method is a challenge-response protocol, which require interactions with users in real time. Pan et al. proposed a liveness detection technique based on blinking [10]. A popular face authentication software called VeriFace, asked users to rotate their heads so as to verify the liveness [11]. Unfortunately, Attackers can use videos containing the required human reactions to deceive those systems. Our method can detect such video-based attacks effectively because the texture feature of a real live user is obviously different between the feature of the fake face.

Our approach can also be categorized as a texture analysis method according to the classification in Chakraborty's survey [12]. The traditional methods in this category mainly use various descriptors to extract features of images and pass features through a classifier to obtain the final result. For example, Matta et al. used the local binary patterns extracted from a single image to determine the liveness of a user [13]. Compared with our method, random challenges provide a stronger security guarantee. IDAIP team took a facial video as input and the local binary patterns from each extracted frame in the video in order to build a global histogram for the video. The liveness of face is determined based on the global histogram [14]. It's time-saving that our method detect the expression frame from the video and extract the facial texture feature from this frame instead of taking local binary patterns of each frame. Besides, we imporve the LBP operator with proper sampling radius of different subareas of a facial image, which reduces the computational complexity.

Besides above methods, there is another technique named multimodal based liveness detection approache, which take face biometrics and other biometrics into account in user authentication. For instance, Rowe et al. proposed a multimodal based technique which requires a camera and a finger print scanner to fuse face authentication and fingerprint authentication together [15]; Wilder et al. took facial thermogram from an inferred camera and face biometrics from a generic camera in authentication process [16,17]. Compared with our method, multimodal approaches need more hardware sensors.

3   Background

3.1   Face Authentication

As one of the most prevalent biometric-based user authentication, face authentication verifies a claimed identity of a user by checking the user's facial features extracted from the user's facial photos or videos. A typical architecture of face authentication system is illustrated in Fig. 1 [18]. It is divided into three parts: sensors, liveness detection module and face recognition module. Sensors comprises a camera and other auxiliary hardwares. When the user commences the authentication process, the liveness detection module is initiated and sends generated parameters to sensors (Step 1). Subsequently, the sensors generate challenges according to the received parameters and deliver them to the user (Step 2). After receiving the challenges, the user make corresponding responses. The sensors capture such responses and encode them (Step 3). In real time, the sensors send the captured responses to the liveness detection module (Step 4). The liveness detection module gathers all decoded data and checks whether the user is an actual human being. If so, the liveness detection module selects some faces among all the responses and sends them to the face recognition module to determine the identity of the user (Step 5).

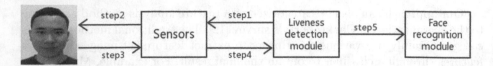

Fig. 1. A typical face authentication system

3.2 Media-Based Face Forgery Attacks

The media-based face forgery (MFF) attacks mean that an adversary can forge users' face biometrics based on photos or videos containing their faces and the adversary can display the forged face biometrics to deceive face authentication systems [20]. We can divide the MFF attacks into two categories according to the types of media. There are traditional media and digital media. Traditional media means that attacker use the paper photos to forge faces. Digital media refers that attackers display the video containing the user's face to circumvent the system. Face authentication systems are inherently vulnerable to the MFF attacks, because it cannot distinguish if the input facial photo or video is from a live user or from pre-recorded photo or video of the same user. As shown in Fig. 1, The liveness module is designed for protecting face authentication system from the MFF-based attacks, including the photo-based attack and the video-based attack. The liveness detection module aims at differentiating between legitimate face biometris that are captured from a live user and the face biometrics forged by adversary from the user's facial photos or videos.

4   Design Overview

Our method verifies the liveness of a face against MFF-based attacks by measuring the consistency between the LBP histogram and the real facial texture feature. It mainly consists of three modules which are Expression Frame Detection (EFD), Facial Feature Extractor (FFE) and Liveness Classifier (LC), which is shown in Fig. 2. Firstly, the sensors generates a challenge randomly and send it to the user. The challenge is the displayed instruction on the screen which require the user to make corresponding facial expressions. Our challenge consists of five facial expressions. They are blinking, smiling, nodding, opening mouth and shaking head. Then the camera captures the response as a video. After that, the EFD module takes the video as an input and detects the expression frame. With the detected frame, The FFE module extracts the facial texture feature by enhanced LBP with different sampling radius and draw the LBP histogram. At last, the LC module utilizes a classification algorithm to distinguish a real face from a forged face in MFF-based attacks.

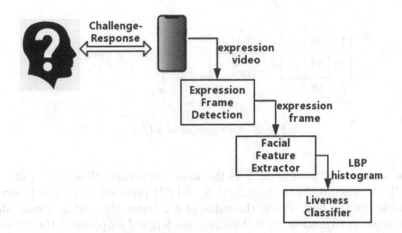

Fig. 2. The components of our method

4.1 Expresssion Frame Detection

The expression video shows a successive process of the facial expression from the onset state, the apex state to the offset state [6,7]. Onset indicates the time from the start of the expression episode to the peak of the facial movement. Apex is defined as the amount of the time when the expression is held at the peak and finally, the offset is the time from the fading of the expression until it stops [8]. The expression frame is defined as the frame in the video with a maximum expression state in the apex. Usually, a given video contains a lot of frames, and it is unreasonable to consider every frame to recognize the expression in the video because of two reasons. The first one is that extracting the facial feature of every frame is time-consuming. The second one is that other frames in the video contain too much noise which is caused by various emotions. Therefore, it's of great importance to detect the expression frame.

We can detect the expression frame by concentrating on the contour of the face. One weakness of the original LBP is that it is sensitive to noise. To solve this problem, δ-LBP was proposed by Lu et al. to find the edge of the target more conveniently [19]. δ-LBP can reduce the impact of noise and computational burden, and the 8-bit binary δ-LBP code of the central pixel is defined as follows:

$$\delta - LBP_c = \sum_{p=0}^{7} s(g_p - g_c)2^p$$

$$s(z) = \begin{cases} 1 & z \geq \delta \\ 0 & z < \delta \end{cases}, \delta \geq 0 \tag{1}$$

where s(z) is the threshold function, g_c and $g_0,...,g_7$ denote respectively the gray values of the center pixel and its 8 neighbor pixels. Figure 3 shows an example of δ-LBP.

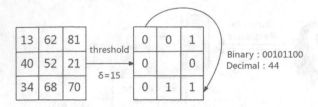

Fig. 3. An example of δ-LBP

The selection of parameter δ is the most important. When the value of δ is small, the texture image obtained by δ-LBP presents more subtle texture information of the face. When the value of δ is large, the texture image shows more contour information of the face because larger δ emphasizes the difference between the surrounding pixels and the central pixel. Figure 4 shows the texture image using δ-LBP with different values of δ.

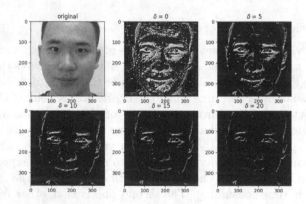

Fig. 4. Examples of texture image using δ-LBP with different δ

As illustrated above, δ-LBP with smaller δ can reflect more subtle texture information of the face, and δ-LBP with larger δ can present contours of the face. However, the value of δ can not be increased without limit. The contour of the texture image with δ = 20 seems a little blurrier than the contour of the texture image with δ = 15. So the selection of δ is the most crucial part in this method. We constantly adjust the value of δ in the experiment and finally we determine it as 15.

Let's take an example where the challenge is blinking. The first step is to extract all the frames from the video, as shown in Fig. 5. Then we can use δ-LBP operator to detect the expression frame. According to the definition above, the expression frame has the maximum expression state so that the difference between the expression frame and the initial frame is the biggest. δ-LBP help us to reflect the contour of the eyes so that we can find out that frame6 is the expression frame of blinking. Then we send this frame to the Facial Feature Extractor module.

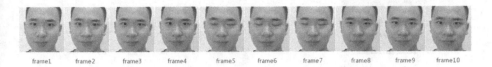

frame1   frame2   frame3   frame4   frame5   frame6   frame7   frame8   frame9   frame10

Fig. 5. All the frames of blinking

4.2   Facial Feature Extractor

The expression frame received from the Expression Frame Detection module shows the maximum expression state which has the most obvious facial feature. We use LBP with different sampling radius to extract the facial texture feature. Traditional LBP operator use fixed radius to extract the facial texture feature of the whole face, which ignores the fact that different central pixels actually have different local gray-value distributions and the proper sampling radius should be different for pixels. It is reasonable that small radius should be assigned to the fast-changing facial area while large radius should be assigned to the smoothly distributed facial area.

Generally, gradients can be used for getting information about changes of a subarea of images. The gradient of the image is equivalent to the difference between 2 adjacent pixels. Therefore, we can utilize gradient to evaluate local gray-value distribution of each pixel. Small gradient value indicates that this pixel has a smooth local distribution while big gradient value means that this pixel is in a fast-changing local area.

We divide the expression frame into 4*4 subareas, as shown in Fig. 6. The area containing important organs of the face, like eyes or mouth, should have smaller sampling radius because the value of pixels in the subarea change fast. Other slow-changing subareas can have bigger sampling radius. In this way, we draw the histogram from LBP value of each subarea and integrate them as a feature histogram, as shown below. The x-coordinate of the histogram has $256*16 = 4096$ components, and the y-coordinate of the histogram means the number of every component. Then we deliver the histogram to the Liveness Classifier module.

4.3   Liveness Classifier

After the Facial Feature Extractor module outputs a LBP histogram of the expression frame, the Liveness Classifier module takes histogram as an input and uses a classification algorithm to determine whether the histogram is taken from a real face or a forged face from the MFF-based attacks. There are several ways to discriminate the similarity of the obtained histogram features, such as Histogram intersection (Pyramid Match Kernel), Chi square statistic, and so

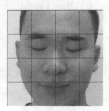

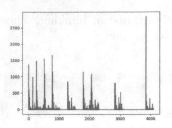

Fig. 6. 4*4 subarea   **Fig. 7.** Feature histogram

on. In this case, we directly calculate the "distance" between the histograms to determine whether they are from the same real face. Let the histogram of the image to be matched be $S_{i,j}$, and the histogram of the known image be $M_{i,j}$ where i $= 1, 2, ..., 16$ represents the number of subarea, j is the value of a column in the histogram in the subarea. Then the similarity of the two images Δ is

$$\Delta = \sum (S_{i,j} - M_{i,j})^2 \tag{2}$$

After calculating the value of Δ, we are supposed to complete a binary classification task. We have to consider how to properly set the threshold of Δ to minimize the cost of classification errors. The cost caused by different types of classification errors are different. For example, the cost caused by recognizing a fake face as a real face is significantly greater than the cost caused by recognizing a real face as a fake face. In this section, we use a parameter E called cost-sensitive error rate to help us find out the value of threshold. Let 0 and 1 respectively denote the real faces class and the fake faces class. Then $cost_{01}$ means the cost caused by recognizing a real face as a fake face and $cost_{10}$ means the cost caused by recognizing a fake face as a real face. Obviously, the value of $cost_{10}$ is greater than the value of $cost_{01}$. Both $cost_{00}$ and $cost_{11}$ mean no cost. Let D^+ and D^- respectively denote the set of real faces class and the set of fake faces class, then the cost-sensitive error rate E is defined as follows:

$$
E = \frac{1}{m} \left(\sum_{x_i \in D^+} \mathbb{I}(f(x_i) \neq y_i) \times \text{cost}_{01} \right.
$$
$$
\left. + \sum_{x_i \in D^-} \mathbb{I}(f(x_i) \neq y_i) \times \text{cost}_{10} \right) \tag{3}
$$

where m denote the number of faces in class, x_i denote the face to be detected. Function $f()$ can be recognized as a detection function. When our method detects the face correctly, we can get $f(x_i) = y_i$. And $\mathbb{I}(\cdot)$ is an indicator function, where $\cdot$ is True and False, the values are 1 and 0 respectively. By minimizing the value of the cost-sensitive error rate, we can find out the value of the threshold of Δ. In the Liveness Classifier module, If the calculated value of Δ less than or equal to the threshold, the two images are considered to come from the same real live face.

5 Data Collection and Experiment

5.1 Data Collection

Our user study involves 48 participants, including 29 males and 19 females with the age range between 20 and 32. We choose an indoor place with normal light as our data collection environment. The device for taking photos and recording videos is the iphone7 front camera. The challenge consists of 5 facial expressions, which are blinking, smiling, nodding, opening mouth and shaking head. Our data is divided into two parts. They are legitimate face dataset and the MFF-based attacks dataset. In the first part, we record the process that users make facial expressions according to the random challenges as a video which is about 3 s long. The distance between the user and the camera is 30 cm. In the second part, we collect the MFF-based attacks dataset. It consists of the photo-based attack dataset and the video-based attack dataset. We take 5 photos for each participant with 30 cm distance and 240 photos are obtained totally. We divide these photos into two parts in random, half of which are printed on A4 paper and the other half of which are printed on photographic paper. As for the video-based attack dataset, we play the video we recorded before and we record the process as a new video. The distance is set as 40 cm in order to make the size of faces in the front camera and the face size in the original video basically the same. Finally, we get 165 segment videos as the video-based attack dataset.

5.2 Experiment

In this section, we fist present the settings of our experiments, then we evaluate the performance of our method against the MFF-based attacks. In the expression frame detection module, we select a proper value of δ. The larger the value of δ, the lower of the dimension of δ-LBP. But if δ is outside a certain range, the contour of the face will become blurry. Finally, we set the value of δ as 15 by adjusting it in the experiment. In the facial feature extractor module, we set the number of sampling points around the central pixel as 8. The value of sampling radius depends on the gradient value of each subarea. The bigger the value of sampling radius, the less time it takes to draw a histogram, as shown in Table 1. The subareas containing important organs of the face, like eyes or mouth, should have small sampling radius, because the gradient of the area is large. And in other subareas where the gradient is small can have big sampling radius. We can not only reduce computational complexity but also improve recognition accuracy. At last, we respectively set the value of small radius and large radius as 2 and 10. In the liveness classifier module, we divide all value of Δ from both real faces and fake faces into two groups in random. One group is used for training to get the threshold, and the other group is used to test accuracy. In the training group, the maximum value of Δ from real faces has overlapping interval with the minimum value of Δ from fake faces. We select multiple thresholds at regular intervals in this interval and classify test data with each threshold. After calculating the cost-sensitive error rate, we choose the threshold which has the minimum error rate. Repeating the above steps 20 times, we select the intermediate value of the threshold interval with the highest frequency as the final threshold. The value of the threshold is 1380000.

Table 1. The relationship between radius and time

Radius (pixel)	2	5	10	15
Time (s)	3.81	3.77	3.39	3.18

By analyzing the experimental data, We find out that our method is efficient in detecting the MFF-based attacks. Our approach achieves the accuracy of 96.45% against the MFF-based attacks. We also conduct an experiment about using original LBP with fixed sampling radius in feature extraction module and compare it with our method. The accuarcy of using fixed sampling radius is only 91.13%, which is shown in Fig. 8

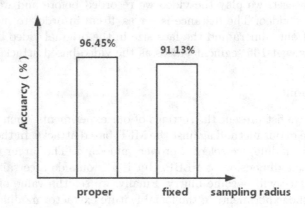

Fig. 8. Accuracy of two methods against the MFF-based attacks

6   Conclusion

In this paper, we propose an effective and practical liveness detection mechanism for face authentication to prevent MFF-based attacks. Our approach can effectively detect the MFF-based attacks by measuring the consistency between the LBP histogram and the real facial texture feature. Experimental results prove that our method is efficient.

Acknowledgment. The work was supported in part by NSFC under Grant 61802289, 61671013. We thank those anonymous reviewers for their insightful comments. We also want to thank those participants for providing their face data in our experiment.

References

1. O"Gorman, L.: Comparing passwords, tokens, and biometrics for user authentication. Proc. IEEE **91**(12), 2021–2040 (2003)
2. Facelock Homepage. http://www.facelock.mobi/facelock-for-apps. Accessed 20 May 2019
3. Bao, W., Li, H., Li, N., Jiang, W.: A liveness detection method for face recognition based on optical flow field. In: 2009 International Conference on Image Analysis and Signal Processing, pp. 233–236. IEEE, Taizhou (2009)
4. Kahm, O., Damer, N.: 2D face liveness detection: an overview. In: 2012 BIOSIG - Proceedings of the International Conference of Biometrics Special Interest Group (BIOSIG), pp. 1–12. IEEE, Darmstadt (2012)
5. Ojala, T., Maenpaa, T., Pietikainen, M., Viertola, J., Kyllonen, J., Huovinen, S.: Outex-new framework for empirical evaluation of texture analysis algorithms. In: 16th International Conference on Pattern Recognition, ICPR 2002, vol. 1, pp. 701–706. Quebec, Canda (2002)
6. Kotsia, I., Buciu, I., Pitas, I.: An analysis of facial expression recognition under partial facial image occlusion. Image Vis. Comput. **26**(7), 1052–1067 (2008)
7. Yeasin, M., Bullot, B., Sharma, R.: Recognition of facial expressions and measurement of levels of interest from video. IEEE Transact. Multimedia **8**(3), 500–508 (2006)
8. Ding, Y., Zhao, Q., Li, B., Yuan, X.: Facial expression recognition from image sequence based on LBP and Taylor expansion. IEEE Access **5**, 19409–19419 (2017)
9. Pan, Z., Wu, X., Lu, Z.: Recognition of facial expressions and measurement of levels of interest from video. Expert Syst. Appl. **120**(2019), 319–334 (2018)
10. Pan, G., Sun, L., Wu, Z., Lao, S.: Eyeblink-based anti-spoofing in face recognition from a generic webcamera. In: 2007 11th IEEE International Conference on Computer Vision, vol. 1, pp. 1–8 (2007)
11. Lenovo Homepage. http://en.wikipedia.org/wiki/VeriFace. Accessed 17 May 2019
12. Chakraborty, S., Das, D.: An overview of face liveness detection. Int. J. Inf. Theory **3**(2) (2014)
13. Määttä, J., Hadid, A., Pietikäinen, M.: Face spoofing detection from single images using micro-texture analysis. In: 2011 International Joint Conference on Biometrics (IJCB), pp. 1–7. IEEE, Washington (2011)
14. Chakka, M.M., Anjos, A., Marcel, S., et al.: Competition on counter measures to 2-D facial spoofing attacks. In: 2011 International Joint Conference on Biometrics (IJCB). IEEE, Washington (2011)
15. Rowe, R.K., Uludag, U., Demirkus, M., Parthasaradhi, S., Jain, A.K.: A multispectral whole-hand biometric authentication system. In: 2007 Biometrics Symposium, pp. 1–6. IEEE, Baltimore (2007)
16. Ghiass, R.S., Arandjelovic, O., Bendada, H., Maldague, X.: Infrared face recognition: a literature review. Comput. Sci., 1–10 (2013)
17. Wilder, J., Phillips, P.J., Cunhong, J., Wiener, S., Shode, P.G.: Comparison of visible and infra-red imagery for face recognition. In: International Conference on Automatic Face & Gesture Recognition, pp. 182–187. IEEE, Killington (1996)

18. Tang, D., Zhou, Z., Zhang, Y., Zhang, K.: Face flashing: a secure liveness detection protocol based on light reflections. In: 2018 Network and Distributed Systems Security (NDSS) Symposium, San Diego (2018)
19. Shan, L.U., Jinhua, Y., Bo, Z., Jinquan, Z.: Infrared target detection based on LBP. J. Changchun Univ. Sci. Technol. (Nat. Sci. Ed.) **32**(1), 22–24 (2009)
20. Li, Y., Li, Y., Yan, Q., Kong, H., Deng, R.H.: Seeing your face is not enough: an inertial sensor-based liveness detection for face authentication. In: 22nd ACM SIGSAC Conference on Computer and Communications Security, pp. 1558–1569. ACM, Denver (2015)

A Survey on Deep Learning Techniques for Privacy-Preserving

Harry Chandra Tanuwidjaja, Rakyong Choi, and Kwangjo Kim$^{(\boxtimes)}$

School of Computing, Korea Advanced Institute of Science and Technology (KAIST),
291 Gwahak-ro, Yuseong-gu, Daejeon 34141, Korea
kkj@kaist.ac.kr

Abstract. There are challenges and issues when machine learning algorithm needs to access highly sensitive data for the training process. In order to address these issues, several privacy-preserving deep learning techniques, including Secure Multi-Party Computation and Homomorphic Encryption in Neural Network have been developed. There are also several methods to modify the Neural Network, so that it can be used in privacy-preserving environment. However, there is trade-off between privacy and performance among various techniques. In this paper, we discuss state-of-the-art of Privacy-Preserving Deep Learning, evaluate all methods, compare pros and cons of each approach, and address challenges and issues in the field of privacy-preserving by deep learning.

Keywords: Secure Multi-Party Computation ·
Homomorphic encryption · Trade-Off ·
Privacy-Preserving Deep Learning

1 Introduction

The invention of machine learning, *i.e.*, Artificial Intelligence (AI) brings a new era to human life. We can train a machine to do decision making like human beings. In general, machine learning consists of training phase and testing phase. In order to get better result by using machine learning, huge dataset is required during the training phase. There is a trend to utilize machine learning in the field of social engineering [1], image recognition [2], healthcare service [3], *etc*. In order to get a satisfying result in machine learning, one of the main challenges is the dataset collection. Since the data will be scattered upon individuals, lots of efforts to collect them are required.

Sensitive users tend to reluctantly submit their private data to a third party. A risk of data leakage will happen due to compromised server-side, e.g., when

This work was partly supported by Indonesia Endowment Fund for Education (LPDP) and Institute for Information & communications Technology Promotion (IITP) grant funded by the Korea government (MSIT) (No. 2017-0-00555, Towards Provable-secure Multi-party Authenticated Key Exchange Protocol based on Lattices in a Quantum World).

X. Chen et al. (Eds.): ML4CS 2019, LNCS 11806, pp. 29–46, 2019.
https://doi.org/10.1007/978-3-030-30619-9_4

we use cloud computing. Users choose not to store their confidential data in cloud because they worry about that somebody can look at their private data. In order to convince users for their data security and privacy, an approach to use privacy-preserved data is required to input training process in deep learning. For this, the data sent to server must be encrypted and it should be kept encrypted during the training phase, too. The challenge here is to modify the current deep learning technique, so that it can process encrypted data. In this paper, we will discuss state-of-the-art of Privacy-Preserving Deep Learning (PPDL) techniques, evaluate them, compare pros and cons of each technique, and suggest the issues and challenges in PPDL.

The remainder of this paper is organized as follows: Sect. 2 discusses classical privacy-preserving technology in brief. We examine the original structure of Neural Network and modification needed for privacy-preserving environment in Sect. 3. Section 4 presents state of the art of PPDL techniques. Furthermore, Sect. 5 discusses about the analysis of the surveyed methods. Finally, conclusion and future work are provided in Sect. 6. The main contribution of this work is to give detailed analysis about state-of-the-art of PPDL method and show which method has the best performance based on our metrics described on Sect. 4.

2   Classical Privacy-Preserving Technology

Privacy-preserving technique is classified as a special tool that enables the processing of encrypted data [4]. The importance of privacy-preserving technique is to enable computation on data, without revealing the original content. So, it can ensure the privacy of highly confidential data. Directive 95/46/EC [5] on the protection of individuals with regard to the processing of personal data is a European Union directive that regulates the processing of personal data based on human rights law. The directive states that *"[The data] controller must implement appropriate technical and organizational measures to protect personal data against accidental or unlawful destruction or accidental loss, alteration, unauthorized disclosure or access, in particular where the processing involves the transmission of data over a network, and against all other unlawful forms of processing."* The goal of privacy-preserving is based on this regulation.

2.1   Homomorphic Encryption

In 1978, Rivest *et al.* [6] questioned whether any encryption scheme exists to support the computation on encrypted data without the knowledge of the secret information. For example, the textbook RSA encryption supports multiplication on encrypted data without its private secret key and we call such a system as multiplicative Homomorphic Encryption (HE). Likewise, we call a system as an additive HE [7] if it supports addition on encrypted data without its secret key.

Fully Homomorphic Encryption (FHE) means that it supports any computation on encrypted data without the knowledge of the secret key, *i.e.*, for any operation o and two plaintexts m_1, m_2, $Enc(m_1) \ o \ Enc(m_2) = Enc(m_1 \ o \ m_2)$.

It was remained as an interesting open problem in cryptography for decades till Gentry [8] suggested the first FHE in 2009.

Afterwards, there are a number of research on HE schemes based on lattices with Learning With Errors (LWE) and Ring Learning With Errors (Ring-LWE) problems [9–13] and schemes over integers with approximate Greatest Common Divisor (GCD) problem [14,15]. Early work on HE was impractical but for now, there are many cryptographic algorithm tools that supports HE efficiently such as HElib, FHEW, and HEEAN [16–18].

HE can be applicable to various areas. For example, it can improve the security of cloud computing system since it delegates processing of user's data without giving access to the original data. It is also applicable to machine learning methods for encrypted data by outsourcing computation of simple statistics like mean and variance of all original data.

2.2 Secure Multi-Party Computation

The concept of secure computation was formally introduced as secure two-party computation in 1986 by Yao [19] with the invention of Garbled Circuit (GC). In GC, all functions are described as a Boolean circuit and an oblivious transfer protocol is used, to transfer the information obliviously.

Then, Goldreich et al. [20] extended the concept to Secure Multi-Party Computation (MPC) in 1987. The purpose of MPC is to solve the problem of collaborative computing that keeps privacy of a user in a group of non-trusted users, without using any trusted third party.

Formally, in MPC, for a given number of participants, $p_1, p_2, \cdots, p_n$, each has his private data, $d_1, d_2, \cdots, d_n$, respectively. Then, participants want to compute the value of a public function f on those private data, $f(d_1, d_2, \cdots, d_n)$ while keeping their own inputs secret.

Compared to HE schemes, in secure MPC, parties jointly compute a function on their inputs using a protocol instead of a single party. During the process, information about parties' secret must not be leaked.

In secure MPC, each party has almost no computational cost with a huge communication cost, while the server has a huge computational cost with almost no communication cost in HE scheme.

To apply secure MPC to deep learning, we must handle the cost of calculating non-linear activation functions like sigmoid or softmax since its cost during training is too large.

2.3 Differential Privacy

Differential privacy was first proposed by Dwork et al. in 2005 [21], to treat the problem of privacy-preserving analysis of data.

From the definition in [22], a randomized function $\mathcal{K}$ gives ϵ-differential privacy if for all datasets D_1 and D_2 differing on at most one element, and for all $S \subseteq Range(\mathcal{K})$,

$$\Pr[\mathcal{K}(D_1) \in S] \geq \exp(\epsilon) \times \Pr[\mathcal{K}(D_2) \in S]$$

Differential privacy deals with the case that a trusted data manager wants to release some statistics over his/her data without revealing any information about the data. Thus, an adversary with access to the output of some algorithm learns almost the same information whether user's data is included or not.

Applying differential privacy, there are a number of researches on machine learning algorithms like decision trees, support vector machines, or logistic regressions [23–25].

3 Deep Learning in Privacy-Preserving Technology

This section describes the original structure of deep learning technique and the modification needed for privacy-preserving environment.

3.1 Deep Neural Network (DNN)

Activation Layer. Activation layer, as shown in Fig. 1, decides whether the data is activated (value one) or not (value zero). The activation layer is a nonlinear function that applies mathematical process on the output of convolutional layer. There are several well-known activation function, such as Rectified Linear Unit (ReLU), sigmoid, and tanh. Since those functions are not linear, the complexity becomes really high if we use the functions to compute the HE encrypted data. So, we need to find a replacement function that only contains multiplication and addition. The replacement function will be discussed later.

Pooling Layer. Pooling layer, as shown in Fig. 2, is a sampling layer whose purpose is to reduce the size of data. There are two kinds of pooling: max and average poolings. In HE, we cannot use max pooling function, because we are not able to search for the maximum value of encrypted data. As a result, average pooling is the solution to be implemented in HE. Average pooling calculates the sum of values, so there is only addition operation here, which is able to be used over HE encrypted data.

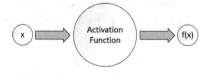

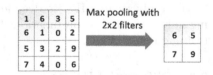

Fig. 1. Activation layer   Fig. 2. Pooling layer

Fully Connected Layer. The illustration of fully connected layer is shown in Fig. 3. Each neuron in this layer is connected to neuron in previous layer, so it is called fully connected layer. The connection represents the weight of the feature like a complete graph. The operation in this layer is dot product between the value of output neuron from the previous layer and the weight of the neuron. This function is similar to hidden layer in Neural Network. There is only dot product function that consists of multiplication and addition function, so we can use it over HE encrypted data.

Dropout Layer. Dropout layer, which is shown in Fig. 4, is a layer created to solve over-fitting problem. Sometimes, when we train our machine learning model, the classification result will be too good for some kind of data, which shows bias to the training set. This situation is not good, resulting in huge error during the testing period. Dropout layer will drop random data during training and set the data to zero. By doing this iteratively during the training period, we can prevent over-fitting during the training phase.

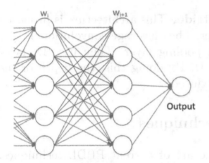

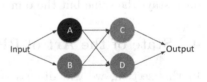

Fig. 3. Fully connected layer   **Fig. 4.** Dropout layer

3.2 Convolutional Neural Network (CNN)

CNN [26] is a class of DNN, which is usually used for image classification. The characteristic of CNN is convolutional layer whose purpose is to learn features which are extracted from the dataset. The convolutional layer has $n \times n$ size, which we will do dot product between neighbor values in order to make convolution. As a result, there are only addition and multiplication in convolutional layer. We do not need to modify this layer as it can be used for HE data, which is homomorphically encrypted.

3.3 Modification of Neural Network in Privacy-Preserving Environment

Batch Normalization Layer. Batch Normalization (BN) layer was proposed by Ioffe and Szegedy [28]. The main purpose of BN layer is to fasten the training process by increasing the stability of NN. This layer receives the output from activation layer, then do re-scaling process, resulting in a value between zero and one. BN layer computes the subtraction of each input with the batch mean value, then divides it by the average value of the batch.

Approximation of Activation Function. There have been several researches [4, 29, 30] to do polynomial approximation for activation function. Some well-known methods include numerical analysis, Taylor series, and polynomial based on the derivative of the activation function. Numerical analysis generates some points from ReLU function, then uses the points as the input of approximation function. Taylor series uses polynomials of different degrees to approximate the activation function.

Convolutional Layer with Increased Stride. This architecture is proposed by Liu *et al.* [30] to replace the pooling layer. They leverage convolutional layer with increased stride as a substitution of pooling layer. They use BN layer between the fully connected layer and ReLU. By doing this, the depth of the data stays the same but the dimension is reduced.

4 State of the Art of PPDL Techniques

In this section, we will discuss state of the art of current PPDL techniques. We divide PPDL method into three: HE-based PPDL, Secure MPC-based PPDL, and Differential Privacy-based PPDL. Figure 5 shows the classification of privacy-preserving method, to the best of our knowledge. The methods are divided into classical and Hybrid PPDL. Classical privacy-preserving method does not contain any deep learning technique, whereas Hybrid PPDL is the combination of classical privacy-preserving method with deep learning. In this paper, we focus on Hybrid PPDL technique since the classical privacy-preserving technique has been already outdated.

In order to compare the performance of each surveyed paper, we use five metrics including accuracy, run time, data transfer, Privacy of Client (PoC), and Privacy of Model (PoM). Figure 6 shows the metrics for surveyed PPDL works in this paper. Accuracy means the percentage of correct prediction made by PPDL model. Run time is the time needed by the model to do encryption, sending data from client to server, and doing classification process. Data transfer is the amount of data transferred from client to server. PoC means that neither the server or any other party knows about client data. PoM means that neither the client or any other party knows about the model classifier in server. We measure the average of accuracy, run time, and data transfer of each method. Then, we set

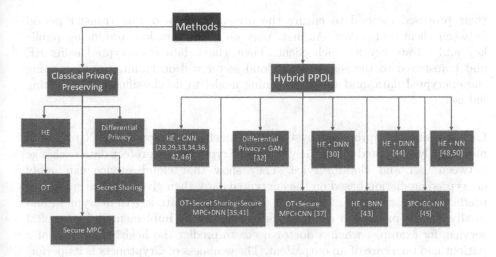

Fig. 5. Classification of privacy-preserving (PP)

the average value as the standard. If the accuracy value is higher than average, it means that the accuracy of the proposed method is good. Furthermore, if the run time and data transfer are lower than average, it means that the run time and data transfer of proposed method are good. We take the comparison data from the respective papers as we believe it is the best result that is possible to achieve. We do not re-execute their codes since not all of the codes are open to public. We focus our paper to Hybrid PPDL method which combines classical privacy-preserving with various deep learning practices.

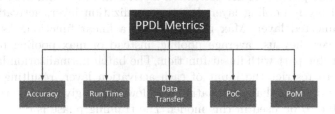

Fig. 6. Metrics for surveyed PPDL works

4.1 HE-Based PPDL

In this section, we discuss PPDL method that leverages HE to ensure the privacy of the data.

ML Confidential [31], developed by Graepel *et al.*, is a modified CNN that works on HE scheme. They use polynomial approximation to substitute non-linear activation function. They use cloud service based scenario, and utilize their proposed method to ensure the privacy of data during transfer period between client and server. At first, they do key generation, producing public key and private key for each client. Then, client data is encrypted using HE and transferred to the server. The cloud server will do training process using the encrypted data, and use the training model to do classification on testing dataset.

Cryptonets [34], proposed by Gilad-Bachrach *et al.*, applies CNN to homomorphically encrypted data. They propose Cryptonets to protect data exchange between user and cloud service. They show that cloud service can apply encrypted prediction based on the encrypted data, then give back the encrypted prediction to user. Later, a user can use his own private key to decrypt it, and finally get the prediction result. This scheme can be implemented for hospital service, for example, when a doctor needs to predict the health condition of a patient and take care of an outpatient. The weakness of Cryptonets is its performance limitation on the number of non-linear layer. If the number of non-linear layer is large, which we can find from deeper Neural Network, the error rate will increase and its accuracy drops.

PP on DNN [35], proposed by Chabanne *et al.*, is a privacy-preserving technique on DNN. For the methodology, they combine HE with CNN. Their main idea is to combine Cryptonets [34] with polynominal approximation for activation function and batch normalization layer proposed by Ioffe and Szegedy [28]. They want to improve the performance of Cryptonets, which is only good when the number of non-linear layer in the model is small. The main idea of this paper is changing the structure of regular Neural Network that consists of convolutional layer, pooling layer, activation layer, and fully connected layer into convolutional layer, pooling layer, batch normalization layer, activation layer, and fully connected layer. Max pooling is not a linear function. As a result, in pooling layer they use average pooling, instead of max pooling to provide the homomorphic part with linear function. The batch normalization layer gives contribution to restrict the input of each activation layer, resulting in stable distribution. Polynomial approximation with low degree gives small error, which is very suitable to be used in this model. The training phase is done using the regular activation function, and the testing phase is done using the polynomial approximation, as a substitution to non-linear activation function. Their experiment shows that their model achieves 99.30% accuracy, which is better than Cryptonets (98.95%). The pros of this model is its eligibility to work in Neural Network with high number of non-linear layers, but still gives accuracy more than 99%, unlike Gilad-Bachrach *et al.* [34] approach that experiences accuracy drop when the number of non-linear layers are increased.

CryptoDL [29], proposed by Hesamifard *et al.*, is a modified CNN for encrypted data. They change the activation function part of CNN with low degree polynomial. This paper shows that the polynomial approximation is indispensable for Neural Network in HE environment. They try to approximate three kinds of activation function; ReLU, sigmoid, and tanh. The approximation technique is based on the derivative of activation function. Firstly, during training phase, CNN with polynomial approximation is used. Then, the model produced during the training phase is used to do classification over encrypted data. The authors apply their method to MNIST dataset [41], and achieve 99.52% accuracy. The weakness of this scheme is not covering privacy-preserving training in deep Neural Network. They use the privacy-preserving for classification process only. The pros of this work is it can classify many instances (8,192 or larger) for each prediction round, unlike Rouhani et al. [40] that classifies one instance per round. So we can say that CryptoDL works more effective compared to DeepSecure [40].

PP All Convolutional Net [30], proposed by Liu et al., is a privacy-preserving technique on convolutional network using HE. They use MNIST dataset [41] that contains handwritten number. They encrypt the data using HE, then use the encrypted data to train CNN. Later, they do classification and testing process using the model from CNN. Their idea is adding batch normalization layer before each activation layer and approximate activation layer using Gaussian distribution and Taylor series. They also change the non-linear pooling layer with convolutional layer with increased stride. By doing this, they have successfully modified CNN to be compatible with HE, and achieve 98.97% accuracy during the testing phase. We can see that the main difference between regular CNN and modified CNN in privacy-preserving technology is the addition of batch normalization layer and the change of non-linear function in activation layer and pooling layer into linear function.

Distributed PP Multi-Key FHE [39], proposed by Xue et al., is a PPDL method using multi-key FHE. They do some modification to conventional CNN structure, such as changing max pooling into average pooling, adding batch normalization layer before each activation function layer, and replacing ReLU activation function with low degree approximation polynomial. Their method is beneficial for classifying large scale distributed data, for example, in order to predict the future road condition, we need to train Neural Network model from traffic information data which are collected from many cars. The security and privacy issue during data collection and training process can be solved using their approach.

Gazelle [43], proposed by Juvekar et al., is a new framework for PPDL. They combine HE with GC to ensure privacy in Prediction-as-a-Service (PaaS) environment. The goal of this paper is to facilitate a client to do classification process without revealing his input to the server and also preserve the privacy of model classifier in server. They try to improve the encryption speed of HE using Single Instruction Multiple Data (SIMD). They also propose new algorithm to accelerate convolutional and matrix vector multiplication process. Finally, Gazelle is also able to switch protocol between HE and GC, so it successfully combines secret-sharing and HE for privacy preserving environment. For the deep learning part, they leverage CNN that consists of two convolutional layers, two ReLU layers as activation layers, one pooling layer, and one fully connected layer. In order to ensure the privacy of the Neural Network model, they hide the weight, bias, and stride size in the convolutional layer. Furthermore, they also limit the number of classification queries from client to prevent linkage attack. The experiment shows that Gazelle fully outclasses another popular technique such as MiniONN [42] and Cryptonets [34] in terms of runtime.

TAPAS [44], proposed by Sanyal *et al.*, is a new framework to accelerate parallel computation using encrypted data in PaaS environment. They want to address the main drawback of HE to do a prediction service, which is the large amount of processing time required. The main contribution here is a new algorithm to speed up binary computation in Binary Neural Network (BNN). The algorithm firstly transforms all data into binary. Then, it computes the inner product by doing XNOR operation between encrypted data and unencrypted data. After that, they count the amount of 1's from the result of previous step. Finally, they check whether two times of the counted amount is bigger than the difference between the number of bits and the bias. If yes, then they assign value 1 to activation function and if no, they assign −1 to the activation function. They also show that their technique can be parallelized by evaluating gates at the same level for three representations at the same time. By doing this, the time needed for evaluation step will be improved drastically. They compared their approach with and without parallelization. The result shows that using MNIST dataset, non-parallel process needs 65.1 h while the parallelized process only takes 147 s to complete.

FHE DiNN [45], proposed by Bourse *et al.*, stands for Fast HE Discretized Neural Network technique, which is used for PPDL. They want to address complexity problem in common HE technique when it is used in Neural Network. The deeper the network is, the higher the complexity, resulting in more computational cost. They use bootstrapping technique to achieve linear complexity to the depth of the Neural Network. When we compare to standard Neural Network, there is one main difference, the weight, bias value, and the domain of activation function in the proposed method needs to be discretized. They use sign activation function to limit the growth of signal in the range of −1, 1, showing its characteristic of linear scale invariance for linear complexity. The activation function will be computed during bootstrapping process, in order to refresh neuron's output. They successfully show that BNN can accomplish accuracy close to regular NN by gaining more network size. During the experiment, FHE-DiNN achieves more than 96% accuracy in less than 1.7 s. Overall, the processing time of FHE-DiNN is much faster than Cryptonets [34], but their accuracy is slightly worse (2.6% less).

E2DM [47], proposed by Jiang *et al.*, stands for Encrypted Data and Encrypted Model, which is a PPDL framework that performs matrices operation on HE system. E2DM encrypts a matrix homomorphically, then do arithmetic operations on it. The main contribution of E2DM is less complexity needed during computation process. It has $O(d)$ complexity to do dot product between two encrypted $d \times d$ matrices, instead of $O(d^2)$ complexity. They leverage CNN with one convolutional layer, two fully connected layers, and a square activation function. During the experiment, they use plain text whose size is less than 212 and can predict 64 images during one circle of processing. E2DM achieves 20 fold latency reduction and 34 fold size reduction compared to Cryptonets [34]. They also show that compared to MiniONN [42] and Gazelle [43], E2DM has less bandwidth usage because it does not require interaction between protocol participants.

As a summary, Table 1 illustrates the comparison of each HE-based PPDL method based on our metrics.

Table 1. Comparison of HE-Based PPDL techniques

Scenario	Proposed schemes	DL technique	Accuracy (%)	Run time (s)	Data transfer (Mbytes)	PoC	PoM
Cloud Service	ML Confidential [31]	DNN	Bad (95.00)	Bad (255.7)	–	Yes	No
	Cryptonets [34]	CNN	Good (98.95)	Bad (697)	Bad (595.5)	Yes	No
	PP on DNN [35]	CNN	Good (99.30)	–	–	Yes	No
	E2DM [47]	CNN	Good (98.10)	Good (28.59)	Good (17.48)	Yes	Yes
	PPDL via Additively HE [48]	CNN	Good 97.00	Good (120)	–	Yes	Yes
Image Recognition	CryptoDL [29]	CNN	Good (99.52)	Bad (320)	Bad (336.7)	Yes	No
	PP All Convolutional Net [30]	CNN	Good (98.97)	Bad (477.6)	Bad (361.6)	Yes	No
Content Sharing	Distributed PP Multi-Key FHE [39]	CNN	Good (99.73)	–	–	Yes	No
PaaS	Gazelle [43]	CNN	–	Good (0.03)	Good (0.5)	Yes	Yes
	Tapas [44]	BNN	Good (98.60)	Good (147)	–	Yes	Yes
	FHE-DNN [45]	DiNN	Bad (96.35)	Good (1.64)	–	Yes	Yes

PPDL via Additively HE [48], proposed by Phong *et al.*, is a PPDL system based on a simple NN structure. The author shows that there is a weakness in Shokri and Shmatikov paper [49] that leaks client data during training process. The weakness is called Gradients Leak Information. It is an adversarial method to get input value by calculating the gradient of corresponding truth function to weight and the gradient of corresponding of truth function to bias. If we divide the two results, we will get the input value. Because of that reason, Phong *et al.* propose their revised PPDL method to overcome this weakness. The key idea of is letting cloud server updating deep learning model by accumulating gradient value from users. However, actually there is a weakness too on this approach because it does not prevent attacks between participants. Proper authentication to participants should be done by the cloud server to prevent this vulnerability.

Secure Weighted Possibilistic C-Means (PCM) Algorithm for PP [50], proposed by Zhang *et al.*, is a secure clustering method to preserve data privacy in cloud computing. They combine C-Means Algorithm with BGV encryption scheme [12] to produce a HE based big data clustering on a cloud environment. The main reason of choosing BGV in this scheme is because of its ability to ensure correct result on the computation of encrypted data. They also address PCM weakness, which is very sensitive and need to be initialized properly. To solve this problem, the authors combine fuzzy clustering and probabilistic clustering. During the training process, there are two main steps: calculating the weight value and updating the matrix. In order to do it, Taylor approximation is used here, as the function is polynomial with addition and multiplication operation only.

4.2   Secure MPC-Based PPDL

In this section, we will talk about PPDL method that leverages Secure MPC to ensure the privacy of the data.

SecureML [36], proposed by Mohassel and Zhang, is a new protocol for privacy-preserving machine learning. They use Oblivious Transfer (OT), Yao's GC, and Secret Sharing. OT is a security protocol proposed by Rabin [37], in which the sender of message remains oblivious whether the receiver has got the message or not. Secret sharing becomes one of basic cryptographic tools to distribute a secret between parties since the introduction of secret sharing by Shamir [38] in 1979. For deep learning part, they leverage linear regression and logistic regression in DNN environment. They propose addition and multiplication algorithm for secretly shared values in linear regression. The authors leverage Stochastic Gradient Descent (SGD) method in order to calculate the optimum value of regression. The weakness of this scheme is that they can only implement a simple Neural Network, without any convolutional layer, so the accuracy is quite low.

DeepSecure [40], proposed by Rouhani *et al.*, is a framework that enables the use of deep learning in privacy-preserving environment. The authors use OT and Yao's GC protocol [19] with CNN to do the learning process. DeepSecure enables a collaboration between client and server to do learning process on cloud server using data from client. They do security proof of their system by using semi-honest, honest-but-curious adversary model. It has been successfully shown that the GC protocol keeps the client data private during the data transfer period. The cons of this method is its limitation of number of instance processed each round. They are only able to classify one instance during each prediction round.

MiniONN [42], proposed by Liu *et al.*, is a privacy preserving framework to transform a Neural Network into an oblivious Neural Network. The transformation process in MiniONN include the nonlinear functions, with a price of negligible accuracy lost. There are two kinds of transformation provided by MiniONN, including oblivious transformation for piecewise linear activation function and oblivious transformation for smooth activation function. A smooth function can be transformed into a continuous polynomial by splitting the function into several parts. Then, for each part, polynomial approximation is used for the approximation, resulting in a piecewise linear function. So, MiniONN supports all activation functions that have either monotonic range, piecewise polynomial, or can be approximated into polynomial function. During the experiment, they show that MiniONN beats Cryptonets [34] and SecureML [36] in terms of message size and latency.

Table 2. The comparison of secure MPC-Based PPDL techniques

Scenario	Proposed schemes	DL technique	Accuracy (%)	Run time (s)	Data transfer (Mbytes)	PoC	PoM
Cloud Service	DeepSecure [40]	CNN	Good (98.95)	Bad (10,649)	Bad (722,000)	No	Yes
Image Recognition	SecureML [36]	DNN	Bad (93.40)	–	–	No	Yes
PaaS	MiniONN [42]	NN	Good (98.95)	Good (1.04)	Good (47.60)	No	Yes
	ABY3 [46]	NN	Bad (94.00)	Good (0.01)	Good (5.20)	No	Yes

ABY3 [46], proposed by Mohassel *et al.*, is a protocol for privacy-preserving machine learning based on three-party computation (3PC). This protocol can switch between arithmetic, binary, and Yao's 3PC, depending on processing needs. The usual machine learning process works on arithmetic operation. As a result, it cannot do polynomial approximation for activation function. ABY3

can be used to train linear regression, logistic regression, and Neural Network model. They use arithmetic sharing when training linear regression model. On the other hand, for computing logistic regression and Neural Network model, they use binary sharing on three party GC. During experiment, they show that ABY3 outperforms MiniONN [42] by four order of magnitude faster, when it runs on the same machine. Table 2 summarizes the comparison of each Secure MPC-Based method.

4.3   Differential Privacy-Based PPDL

PATE [33], proposed by Papernot *et al.*, stands for Private Aggregation of Teacher Ensembles. PATE learning process consists of teacher phase and student phase based on differential privacy in GAN (Generative Adversarial Network) [27]. In PATE, firstly, during teacher phase, the model is trained using subset of data. Then, the student model will learn from the teacher model. The key of privacy is in teacher model [32], which is not made public. The advantage of this model is due to the distinguished model, when an adversary can get a hold on student model, it will not give them any confidential information. They also show that there is possible failure that reveals some part of training data to the adversary. As a result, notification to the failure is really important, aside from developing cryptography technique for privacy protection.

5   Analysis of the Surveyed Methods

After we have surveyed all papers mentioned above, we can see that E2DM [47] gives the best performance based on our metrics defined here. It is indicated by getting good accuracy, good run time, good data transfer, and ensure both PoC and PoM. E2DM is the only work that satisfies all parameters that we define, which indicates the best PPDL method for this time. Furthermore, from our analysis above, we believe that main challenge in privacy-preserving machine learning technique regards to the trade-off between accuracy and complexity. If we use high degree polynomial approximation for activation function, the accuracy will become better, but in cost for high complexity. On the other hand, low degree polynomial approximation for activation function gives low complexity with worse accuracy compared to high degree polynomial. Choosing correct approximation method for each privacy-preserving scenario is the main challenge here.

6   Conclusion and Future Work

In this paper, we have discussed state of the art of PPDL. We analyze the original structure of Neural Network and the modification needed to use it in privacy-preserving environment. We also address the trade-off between accuracy and complexity during the substitution process of non-linear activation function as the main challenge. An open problem regarding privacy-preserving machine learning technique is to reduce computational burden. How to divide the burden between a client and a server optimally, to get the best performance is a big challenge that needs to be addressed in the future. Another challenge is to ensure the PoC and PoM at the same time, while maintaining the computation performance. Ensuring the PoC and PoM requires two extra computation from client's and model's point of view, respectively. Our survey shows that only E2DM has successfully fulfill those requirements, even though its accuracy still lower than CryptoDL [29], DeepSecure [40], and MiniONN [42]. However, those three methods only satisfy one of PoC or PoM, not both of them. Achieving more than 99% accuracy with PoC and PoM properties becomes the main challenge of the future PPDL method. Lightweight PPDL with fast and cheap cost is also an interesting challenge for future work.

References

1. Lazer, D., Pentland, A.S., Adamic, L., Aral, S., Barabasi, A.L.: Life in the network: the coming age of computational social science. Science **323**, 721 (2009)
2. Nasrabadi, N.M.: Pattern recognition and machine learning. J. Electron. Imaging **16**, 049901 (2007)
3. Chen, M., Hao, Y., Hwang, K., Wang, L.: Disease prediction by machine learning over big data from healthcare communities. IEEE Access **5**, 8869–8879 (2017)
4. Zhang, D., Chen, X., Wang, D., Shi, J.: A survey on collaborative deep learning and privacy-preserving. In: IEEE Third International Conference on Data Science in Cyberspace, pp. 652–658 (2018)
5. Meints, M., Moller, J.: Privacy-preserving data mining: a process centric view from a european perspective (2004)
6. Rivest, R.L., Adleman, L., Dertouzos, M.L.: On data banks and privacy homomorphisms. Found. Secure Comput. **4**(11), 169–180 (1978)
7. Paillier, P.: Public-key cryptosystems based on composite degree residuosity classes. In: Stern, J. (ed.) EUROCRYPT 1999. LNCS, vol. 1592, pp. 223–238. Springer, Heidelberg (1999). https://doi.org/10.1007/3-540-48910-X_16
8. Gentry, C.: Fully homomorphic encryption using ideal lattices. In: Annual ACM on Symposium on Theory of Computing, pp. 169–178. ACM (2009)
9. Brakerski, Z., Vaikuntanathan, V.: Efficient fully homomorphic encryption from (Standard) LWE. SIAM J. Comput. **43**(2), 831–871 (2014)
10. Brakerski, Z., Vaikuntanathan, V.: Fully homomorphic encryption from ring-LWE and security for key dependent messages. In: Rogaway, P. (ed.) CRYPTO 2011. LNCS, vol. 6841, pp. 505–524. Springer, Heidelberg (2011). https://doi.org/10. 1007/978-3-642-22792-9_29
11. Gentry, C., Sahai, A., Waters, B.: Homomorphic encryption from learning with errors: conceptually-simpler, asymptotically-faster, attribute-based. In: Canetti, R., Garay, J.A. (eds.) CRYPTO 2013. LNCS, vol. 8042, pp. 75–92. Springer, Heidelberg (2013). https://doi.org/10.1007/978-3-642-40041-4_5
12. Brakerski, Z., Gentry, C., Vaikuntanathan, V.: (Leveled) Fully homomorphic encryption without bootstrapping. ACM Transact. Comput. Theory (TOCT) **6**(3), 13 (2014)

13. Clear, M., McGoldrick, C.: Multi-identity and multi-key leveled FHE from learning with errors. In: Gennaro, R., Robshaw, M. (eds.) CRYPTO 2015. LNCS, vol. 9216, pp. 630–656. Springer, Heidelberg (2015). https://doi.org/10.1007/978-3-662-48000-7_31

14. van Dijk, M., Gentry, C., Halevi, S., Vaikuntanathan, V.: Fully homomorphic encryption over the integers. In: Gilbert, H. (ed.) EUROCRYPT 2010. LNCS, vol. 6110, pp. 24–43. Springer, Heidelberg (2010). https://doi.org/10.1007/978-3-642-13190-5_2

15. Cheon, J.H., et al.: Batch fully homomorphic encryption over the integers. In: Johansson, T., Nguyen, P.Q. (eds.) EUROCRYPT 2013. LNCS, vol. 7881, pp. 315–335. Springer, Heidelberg (2013). https://doi.org/10.1007/978-3-642-38348-9_20

16. Halevi, S., Shoup, V.: Algorithms in HElib. In: Garay, J.A., Gennaro, R. (eds.) CRYPTO 2014. LNCS, vol. 8616, pp. 554–571. Springer, Heidelberg (2014). https://doi.org/10.1007/978-3-662-44371-2_31

17. Ducas, L., Micciancio, D.: FHEW: bootstrapping homomorphic encryption in less than a second. In: Oswald, E., Fischlin, M. (eds.) EUROCRYPT 2015. LNCS, vol. 9056, pp. 617–640. Springer, Heidelberg (2015). https://doi.org/10.1007/978-3-662-46800-5_24

18. Cheon, J.H., Kim, A., Kim, M., Song, Y.: Homomorphic encryption for arithmetic of approximate numbers. In: Takagi, T., Peyrin, T. (eds.) ASIACRYPT 2017. LNCS, vol. 10624, pp. 409–437. Springer, Cham (2017). https://doi.org/10.1007/978-3-319-70694-8_15

19. Yao, A.C.-C.: How to generate and exchange secrets. In: Foundations of Computer Science 27th Annual Symposium, pp. 162–167. IEEE (1986)

20. Goldreich, O., Micali, S., Wigderson, A.: How to play any mental game. In: Proceedings of the Nineteenth Annual ACM Symposium on Theory of Computing, pp. 218–229. ACM (1987)

21. Dwork, C., McSherry, F., Nissim, K., Smith, A.: Calibrating noise to sensitivity in private data analysis. In: Halevi, S., Rabin, T. (eds.) TCC 2006. LNCS, vol. 3876, pp. 265–284. Springer, Heidelberg (2006). https://doi.org/10.1007/11681878_14

22. Dwork, C.: Differential privacy. In: Bugliesi, M., Preneel, B., Sassone, V., Wegener, I. (eds.) ICALP 2006. LNCS, vol. 4052, pp. 1–12. Springer, Heidelberg (2006). https://doi.org/10.1007/11787006_1

23. Chaudhuri, K., Monteleoni, C., Sarwate, A.D.: Differentially private empirical risk minimization. J. Mach. Learn. Res. **12**, 1069–1109 (2011)

24. Kifer, D., Smith, A., Thakurta, A.: Private convex empirical risk minimization and high-dimensional regression. In: Conference on Learning Theory, pp. 1–25 (2012)

25. Jagannathan, G., Pillaipakkamnatt, K., Wright, R.N.: A practical differentially private random decision tree classifier. In: IEEE International Conference on Data Mining Workshops 2009, ICDMW 2009, pp. 114–121. IEEE (2009)

26. LeCun, Y., Haffner, P., Bottou, L., Bengio, Y.: Object recognition with gradient-based learning. Shape, Contour and Grouping in Computer Vision. LNCS, vol. 1681, pp. 319–345. Springer, Heidelberg (1999). https://doi.org/10.1007/3-540-46805-6_19

27. Goodfellow, I.: Generative adversarial nets. In: Advances in neural information processing systems, pp. 2672–2680 (2014)

28. Ioffe, S., Szegedy, C.: Batch normalization: accelerating deep network training by reducing internal covariate shift. arXiv:1502.03167 (2015)

29. Hesamifard, E., Takabi, H., Ghasemi, M.: CryptoDL: deep neural networks over encrypted data. arXiv:1711.05189 (2017)

30. Liu, W., Pan, F., Wang, X.A., Cao, Y., Tang, D.: Privacy-preserving all convolutional net based on homomorphic encryption. In: International Conference on Network-Based Information Systems, pp. 752–762 (2018)

31. Graepel, T., Lauter, K., Naehrig, M.: ML confidential: machine learning on encrypted data. In: International Conference on Information Security and Cryptology, pp. 1–21 (2012)

32. Abadi, M., Erlingsson, U., Goodfellow, I.: On the protection of private information in machine learning systems: two recent approches. In: Computer Security Foundations Symposium, pp. 1–6 (2017)

33. Papernot, N., Abadi, M., Erlingsson, U.: Semi-supervised knowledge transfer for deep learning from private training data. arXiv:1610.05755 (2016)

34. Gilad-Bachrach, R., Dowlin, N., Laine, K., Lauter, K., Naehrig, M., Wernsing, J.: Cryptonets: applying neural networks to encrypted data with high throughput and accuracy. In: International Conference on Machine Learning, pp. 201–210 (2016)

35. Chabanne, H., de Wargny, A., Milgram, J., Morel, C., Prouff, E.: Privacy-preserving classification on deep neural network. IACR Cryptology ePrint Archive (2017)

36. Mohassel, P., Zhang, Y.: SecureML: a system for scalable privacy-preserving machine learning, pp. 19–38 (2017)

37. Rabin, M.O.: How to exchange secrets with oblivious transfer. IACR Cryptology ePrint Archive, p. 187 (2005)

38. Shamir, A.: How to share a secret. Commun. ACM **22**(11), 612–613 (1979)

39. Xue, H., et al.: Distributed large scale privacy-preserving deep mining. In: IEEE Third International Conference on Data Science in Cyberspace, pp. 418–422 (2018)

40. Rouhani, B., Riazi, M., Koushanfar, F.: DeepSecure: scalable provably-secure deep learning. In: 55th ACM/ESDA/IEEE Design Automation Conference, pp. 1–6 (2018)

41. Deng, L.: The MNIST database of handwritten digit images for machine learning research. IEEE Signal Process. Mag. **29**, 141–142 (2012)

42. Liu, J., Juuti, M., Lu, Y., Asokan, N.: Oblivious neural network predictions via MiniONN transformations. In: Proceedings of the 2017 ACM SIGSAC Conference on Computer and Communications Security, pp. 619–631 (2017)

43. Juvekar, C., Vaikuntanathan, V., Chandrakasan, A.: GAZELLE: a low latency framework for secure neural network inference. In: 27th USENIX Security Symposium, pp. 1651–1669 (2018)

44. Sanyal, A., Kusner, M.J., Gascón, A., Kanade, V.: TAPAS: tricks to accelerate (Encrypted) prediction as a service. arXiv preprint, arXiv:1806.03461 (2018)

45. Bourse, F., Minelli, M., Minihold, M., Paillier, P.: Fast homomorphic evaluation of deep discretized neural networks. In: Shacham, H., Boldyreva, A. (eds.) CRYPTO 2018. LNCS, vol. 10993, pp. 483–512. Springer, Cham (2018). https://doi.org/10.1007/978-3-319-96878-0_17

46. Mohassel, P., Rindal, P.: ABY 3: a mixed protocol framework for machine learning. In: Proceedings of the 2018 ACM SIGSAC Conference on Computer and Communications Security, pp. 35–52. ACM (2018)

47. Jiang, X., Kim, M., Lauter, K., Song, Y.: Secure outsourced matrix computation and application to neural networks. In: Proceedings of the 2018 ACM SIGSAC Conference on Computer and Communications Security, pp. 1209–1222. ACM (2018)

48. Phong, L.T., Aono, Y., Hayashi, T., Wang, L., Moriai, S.: Privacy-preserving deep learning via additively homomorphic encryption. In: IEEE Transactions on Information Forensics and Security, pp. 1333–1345. IEEE (2018)

49. Shokri, R., Shmatikov, V.: Privacy-preserving deep learning. In: Proceedings of the 22nd ACM SIGSAC Conference on Computer and Communications Security, pp. 1310–1321. ACM (2015)
50. Zhang, Q., Yang, L.T., Castiglione, A., Chen, Z., Li, P.: Secure weighted possibilistic C-means algorithm on cloud for clustering big data. Inf. Sci. **479**, 515–525 (2019)

Quantifiable Network Security Measurement: A Study Based on an Index System

Guoquan Li[1], Yulong Fu[1(✉)], Zheng Yan[1], and Weilin Hao[2]

[1] School of Cyber Engineering, Xidian University, Xi'an, China
ylfu@xidian.edu.cn
[2] School of Electronic Engineering and Computer Science, Peking University, Beijing, China

Abstract. Security Metrics help network administrators master the security status and strengthen security management for many years. Recently, with the usages of many new techniques and network structures, the cyber attacks become complex and the security measurement has received more and more attentions. However, existing methods usually focus on one aspect of security and the indicators used are usually difficult to quantify, which makes it difficult to understand network security status in some real circumstance. In this paper, we consider the network system security from the perspective of attack and defense and the changes of external security environment to propose a comprehensive and quantifiable index system for network security measurement. We illustrate the corresponding theories and the usages of each selected indicators and we also complete the real-time security measurement in various attacks and defenses by using NS3 simulator. The simulation results verify the correctness and rationality of the proposed Security Measurement Index System.

Keywords: Security metric · Index system ·
Attack and defense confrontation · NS3 simulation

1 Introduction

The rapid growth of information technology promoted the development and the quality of computer networks, and also bring cyber attacks to users. Increasing cyber threats and hacker activities made the network environment become serious and became the headache of modern networks system. In order to relieve user's safety anxiety and accelerate the development and use of modern network technologies, a security measurement to the network is necessary. However,

National Key R&D Program of China (grant 2016YFB0800700), NSFC (grants 61602359 and 11571281), Fundamental Research Funds for the Central Universities (JB150115) and the 111 project (grant B16037).

existed rule-based or machine learning-based security measurement methods are passive, single-assist mitigations for specific security issues. These measures lack of systematic considerations, which may blindly add protective equipment, waste manpower and material resources, and can no longer meet the current network security needs [1]. In order to fully understand the network security status and effectively strengthen network security, network security metric has become a hot and difficult issue. Although some security metric standard have been established, many of them have some limitations and may lead to some issues.

Existed network security metric models, such as the National Institute of Standards and Technology (NIST) cyber security framework, the Common Criteria for Information Technology Security Assessment (CC), the Information Security Technology Framework (IATF) and the information security protection level (ISPL) are define the security measurement with standards or frameworks. These security standards or frameworks tend to focus on product or management, and indicators in them are not quantified. In addition, there are also some researchers conduct network risk assessments from the vulnerabilities [3]. Common methods include probability-based attack graph model, system evolution of Markov chain random representation, fault tree analysis and attack tree, etc. [4]. However, these existed methods only focus on the possible risks, they does not consider the changes of the network system's own detection and defense capability and the indicators used are usually difficult to quantify. In order to solve the problems mentioned above, in this paper, we propose a complete, dynamic, quantifiable and comparable index system for security measurement. Through the real-time measurement and calculation of security indicators, the dynamic changes of network status can be accurately described, and the internal causes of network status changes can be deeply reflected, so that security-enhanced decision support can be provided to security management.

The main contributions of this paper are listed as follows:

1. We propose a comprehensive, dynamic, quantifiable and comparable index system from the perspective of offense and defense for network security measurement.
2. We implement the multiple attack and defense modules in NS3 simulator.
3. We use the NS3 simulator to measure the network security status in real time, verify the rationality and correctness of the proposed index system.

The remainder of this article is organized as follows. Section 2 introduces the background knowledge and related work of security metric. A security index system is proposed and the weights were determined in Sect. 3. Section 4 completes the real-time measurement of the network status and verify the correctness and rationality of the index system based on NS3 simulator. Section 5 summarizes the whole article and points out the directions of future work.

2   Related Work

Security Measurement is important and many existed works has been done in the literature. Some authoritative and relatively new security standards, including Common Criteria for Information Technology Security Assessment (CC), Classified Protection of Information Security (CPIS), Network and Information Security Directive (NIS), National Institute of Standards and Technology (NIST) and Information Assurance Technical Framework (IATF) have defined their indicators for security evaluation. We strictly reviewed these indicators, and compare them against comprehensiveness, dynamics, quantification, objectivity, and comparability. The results of the comparison are shown in Table 1.

Table 1. Index system comparison

Standard	Comprehensiveness	Dynamics	Quantification	Objectivity	Comparability
CC	No	No	No	No	Yes
CPIS	Yes	No	Yes	No	Yes
NIS	Yes	Yes	No	No	Yes
NIST	Yes	Yes	No	No	Yes
IATF	Yes	Yes	No	No	Yes

Besides those published standards, private research on this problem are also contributed. In [6], the authors discuss the importance of network metric and believes that security metric should be characterized by certainty, simplicity, objectivity and repeatability. Then several commonly used metric method are introduced and the security metric work is introduced from the policy and economic aspects. However, this article only introduces the basic knowledge of network metric, and does not propose a specific metric scheme. Literature [7] proposes a hierarchical security threat metric model, including three levels of service, host and network, and quantifies the evolution of security risks of these levels based on IDS alarm and network bandwidth occupancy. The article proposes some threat risk calculation formulas, which can quantify the risk index of service, host and network in real time, and verify the correctness of risk index quantification through experiments. However, the article only considers the attack risks, and does not consider the changes in the network's own defense capabilities. In [8], the authors believe that the core of security metric is the result of an attacker using vulnerability to launch attacks and interact with defense. From the perspective of attack and defense confrontation, the metrics are divided into four categories: vulnerability indicator, defense indicator, attack indicator and status indicator. The index system proposed in the paper is relatively comprehensive, but just introduce the meaning of these indicators and lack quantitative calculation formulas.

Although the researches on security metric are plenty, but the existed results are single aspect, static and subjective, a comprehensiveness, dynamics and quantifiability security metric are always required.

3 Security Metric Index System

Building a quantifiable and relatively complete index system is the main purpose of our work. In order to solve the shortcomings of the existing index system, we propose a quantifiable, comprehensive, dynamic and universal index system from the perspective of offensive and defensive confrontation. As shown in Fig. 1, we consider network's own defense capability and threats caused by attack, vulnerability. In addition, the network performance anomaly index is proposed from the perspective of overall network communication performance. We describe the definition of all indicators in the proposed index system, and then the calculation and quantization formula of indicators will be given and the calculation results are normalized.

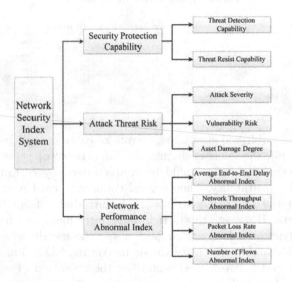

Fig. 1. Network security index system

3.1 Security Protection Capability

Threat Detection Capability. Threat Detection Capability (TDC) is a metric that measures the detection and monitoring efforts of devices such as IDS or monitoring audit system for cyber attack. Threat detection capability is related to threat detection intensity level (TDIL) and intrusion detection classification performance. These two indicators are described below.

Threat Detection Intensity Level. It describes the scope and effectiveness of attack detection by threat detection device. To best of our knowledge, mainstream attacks account for the majority of all attacks, such as DDoS, XSS, buffer overflow, etc. Therefore, successful detection of mainstream attacks contributes a lot to network security [9]. We use interval data to describe different levels of threat detection capability, as shown in Table 2.

Table 2. Hierarchical definition of threat detection intensity

Level	Capability	Threat detection intensity description
1	0	No threat detection device, no threats can be detected
2	0.3	Can only detect a few threats, the detection effect is poor
3	0.8	Can detect mainstream threats, the detection effect is good
4	1.0	Can detect most threats, the detection effect is very good

Intrusion Detection Classification Index. IDS is a network behavior classifier and its role is to identify threat behaviors [10]. Therefore, we can use traditional classification evaluation indicators in statistical learning to measure intrusion detection capability. The commonly used classification performance indicators include recall, precision and etc. Precision (P) indicates the correct proportion of the prediction in the positive samples, and recall (R) indicates the proportion of the true positive samples that are predicted as positive samples. P and R reflect the classification performance from different aspects, but sometimes there are conflicts [11]. To deal with this problem, we use F-Measure (F1) as the intrusion detection performance indicator. The formula for F1 is as follows.

$$F1 = \frac{2 * P * R}{P + R} \qquad (1)$$

Threat Detection Capability Calculation. The value of TDC is equal to the product of TDL and F1. The calculation formula is as follows.

$$TDC = TDL * F1 \qquad (2)$$

Where F1 is calculated based on the historical detection data of IDS. The TDC has no dimension and the value ranges from 0 to 1, so it is not necessary to normalize.

Threat Resist Capability. Threat Resist Capability (TRC) is a measure of the ability to block or mitigate threats. It can defend against cyber attacks, and prevent malicious behavior detected in time to ensure the network security. The devices with threat resistance mainly include firewall, anti-virus software, intrusion prevention system, and active defense technology [12]. TRC is related to the threat resist intensity level and the blocking ratio. And these indicators are described below.

Threat Resist Intensity Level. TRL measures the range and effect of security protection and preventing threat. To best of our knowledge, mainstream attacks occupy a large proportion, so the ability to defend against mainstream attacks is important for network defense capabilities. We use interval data to describe the ability of different threat level, and Table 3 gives the definition of threat strength level.

Table 3. Hierarchical definition of threat resist intensity

Level	Capability	Threat resist intensity description
1	0	No security measures to reach and prevent threats
2	0.3	Can only defend against few threats, the protection effect is poor
3	0.8	Can defend against mainstream threats, the protection effect is good
4	1.0	Can protect most threats, the protection effect is very good

Blocking Ratio. Blocking ratio (BR) is the ratio of the number of successful defending attacks to the number of hosts that are attacked. It can measure the efficiency of defense equipment. The formula is as follows.

$$BR = \sum_{n}^{i=1} \frac{Blk(i)}{En(n)} * 100\%, Blk(i) \in [0, 1] \tag{3}$$

Where n is the number of network device, Blk(i) is the degree to which the i-th device successfully blocked the attack, ranging from 0 to 1, and En(n) indicates the number of devices being attacked.

Threat Resist Capability Calculation. The value of TRC is equal to the product of BR and TRL. The calculation formula is as follows.

$$TRC = TRL * (BR_b * m_{br1} + BR_t * m_{br2}), m_{br1} + m_{br2} = 1 \tag{4}$$

Where BR_b is calculated according to historical data of the defense device, and BR_t is calculated in the current security metric period T. In order to prevent the security metric calculation error caused by the zero-day attack, the value of BR is the weighted sum of BR_b and BR_t. For real-time measurement of network status, we need to pay more attention to the current measurement period, so that $m_{br1} = 0.2$ and $m_{br2} = 0.8$. TRC has no dimension and the range of values is between 0 and 1, so it is not necessary to normalize.

3.2 Attack Threat Risk

Attack Severity. The Attack Severity (AS) measures the extent to which an attack is harmful to network. Traditional cyber risks involve three elements, namely threat, asset, and vulnerability [13]. The attack severity defined here fuse threat and asset, which can more comprehensively and accurately measure the degree of harm caused by attack to network resources. The calculation of the severity of the attack involves the attack severity level and the target asset importance level (TAIL). Their definitions are described below.

Attack Severity Level. Attack Severity Level (ASL) ranks the severity of an attack and visually shows the difference between different attacks. We determine the severity of the attack according to the attack classification and prioritization in the snort user manual. The snort manual divides the attack into three levels, namely high, medium, and low. In this paper, we use 3, 2, 1 to represent these three levels. The snort user manual already contains most of the attacks. For some attacks that are not involved, we give them the same severity level as the same type of attack.

Target Asset Importance Level. Successful implementation of a cyber attack must be done through the target of the attack. Different device or service may become target of intruder, such as router, firewall, and user data. The target asset importance level (TAIL) is determined by the target type. We classify TAIL into there levels, namely high, medium and low, represented by 3, 2 and 1.

Attack Severity Calculation. The severity of the attack is related to the type and the number of attack, and the importance of the target assets. The calculation formula is as follows.

$$AS = \sum_{m}^{i=1}(1 + k_i * cf_i) * r * 10^{ASL_i} * N_i * TAIL_i \tag{5}$$

Where m is the number of attack category, ASL_i is the severity level of the i-th attack, N_i is the number of occurrences of the i-th attack, and $TAIL_i$ is the asset importance level of the i-th attack's target. We use 10^{ASL_i} instead of ASL_i according to the literature [7]. In order to more accurately reflect the impact of attack and defense interaction on the network, we add the resist factor r to indicate that attacks are successfully resisted by defense. The value of r is 0.1 indicating that the attack is only 10% of the original when the attack is resisted. We divide attack into independent attack and coordinated attack, and their severity calculation methods are slightly different. Implementing an coordinated attack scenario requires multiple attack steps in sequence. And the attack that occurs later is more threatening, so we propose the attack correlation factor cf to more accurately describe the impact of attack. k_i is the number of attack steps before the i-th attack, and cf_i is the attack-related factor, indicating the degree of the collaborative attack threat increasing, the value of cf_i is 0.1.

Max-min and z-score normalization are not applicable because it is difficult to determine the maximum number of attacks based on historical statistics. To solve this problem, we choose the negative exponential function e^{-a*x} as the mapping function. It maps the indicator to between 0, 1 and is very close to the max-min mapping. Based on experience and historical data analysis, we take a equal to 0.005, a can be adjusted according to the actual size and status of network, so the formula of AS is normalized as follows.

$$AS' = e^{-a*AS} \tag{6}$$

Vulnerability Risk. The execution of the attack is inseparable from the exploitation of the vulnerability. These vulnerabilities and efforts to compromise these vulnerabilities are the most commonly collected data for understanding network security. Many researchers have conducted network risk assessment and analysis from the perspective of vulnerability analysis and have achieved many results. The risk caused by the vulnerability is a potential energy that can affect the network. Therefore, based on previous vulnerability risk assessment, we propose vulnerability risk (VR) indicator. VR is related to the vulnerability severity score and TAIL. The latter has been quantitatively analyzed in the previous section. Below we describe the vulnerability severity score.

Vulnerability Severity Score. CVSS is often used to measure the severity of vulnerabilities and help people determine their priority. It is mainly based on measurements in different dimensions, namely basic, temporal, and environmental measure. In CVSS, the vulnerability score is between 0 and 10 and the high score represents a very serious risk. Our vulnerability severity score (VSS) is based on the CVSS.

Vulnerability Risk Calculation. The value of VR is the product of VSS and TAIL. The calculation formula is as follows.

$$VR = \sum_{n}^{i=1} VSS_i * TAIL_i \tag{7}$$

Where n is the number of vulnerabilities, VSSi is the severity score of vulnerability i, and $TAIL_i$ is the asset importance of the device with vulnerabilities i. We use the negative exponential function e^{-b*x} as a mapping function to normalize the vulnerability risk. Based on the analysis of historical risk data, we take c equal to 0.005. The normalized formula for VR is as follows.

$$VR' = e^{-b*VR} \tag{8}$$

Asset Damage Degree. Intruders break the network and cause damages to the network, such as server crash, database leak, and router outage. Network damage directly affects network security and we propose the asset damage degree (ADD) to measure the degree of asset damage. The value of ADD is determined by TAIL, and the calculation formula is as follows.

$$ADD = \sum_{n}^{i=1} TAIL_i \tag{9}$$

Where i represents the i-th damaged target, and $TAIL_i$ is the severity of the damaged target. We use the exponential function e^{-c*x} as a mapping function to normalize. Based on the analysis of historical NDD data, we take c equal to 0.2. The normalization formula is as follows.

$$ADD' = e^{-c*ADD} \tag{10}$$

Network Performance Anomaly Index. In order to measure the network security status more accurately, we provide an overall research perspective by detecting abnormal changes in network communication performance. When applying the metric system to the actual network, we may encounter some unknown attacks. The metrics of attack and defense indicators will be deviated, and the network performance metric can slightly alleviate this deviation. We propose 4 indicators, including average end-to-end delay abnormal index (AEEDAI), network throughput abnormal index (NTPAI), packet loss rate abnormal index (PLRAI) and number of flows abnormal index (NFAI), which are described in detail below.

Average End-to-End Delay Abnormal Index. End-to-end delay refers to the time it takes for a packet to be sent from being received. Some attacks can be reflected in end-to-end delay changes, such as the router's routing table failure and server resource exhaustion. Average End-to-End Delay (AEED) refers to the average of all communication link delays across the network. AEEDAI indicates the extent to which AEED deviates from the normal range. The calculation formula is as follows.

$$AEEDAI = \frac{\|AEED - AEED_{norm}\|}{AEED_{max} - AEED_{norm}}$$

$$\|AEED - AEED_{norm}\| = \begin{cases} AEED - AEED_{norm}, other \\ 0, AEED - AEED_{norm} < 0 \end{cases} \tag{11}$$

Where $AEED_{norm}$ is the average threshold of AEED, and $AEED_{max}$ is the maximum threshold. We normalize AEEDAI using the exponential function e^{-d*x} as a mapping function. Based on the historical AEED data, we take the value of d as 0.005. The normalization formula for AEEDAI is as follows.

$$AEED' = e^{-d*AEDD} \tag{12}$$

Network Throughput Abnormal Index. Network throughput represents the actual maximum data transmission rate, mainly related to network congestion, storage mechanism and processor performance. The Network Throughput Abnormal Index (NTPAI) indicates the extent to which the network throughput deviates from the normal range. The calculation formula is as follows.

$$NTPAI = \frac{\|NTP_{norm} - NTP\|}{NTP_{norm} - NTP_{min}} \tag{13}$$

Where NTP_{norm} is the maximum throughput of the network, and NTP_{min} is the minimum threshold of NTP. We use max-min method to normalize NTPAI as shown below.

$$NTPAI' = \frac{NTPAI_{max} - NTPAI}{NTPAI_{max} - NTPAI_{min}} \tag{14}$$

Packet Loss Rate Abnormal Index. The packet loss rate (PLR) refers to the ratio of lost data packets to transmitted data packets. Many attacks can increase the packet loss rate, such as routing attacks and virus attacks. PLRAI is an indicator that we propose to measure the extent to which PLR deviates from the normal range. The calculation formula is as follows.

$$PLRAI = \frac{PLR - PLR_{norm}}{PLR_{max} - PLR_{norm}} \tag{15}$$

Where PLR_{norm} is the normal threshold of PLR, and PLR_{max} is the maximum threshold. We normalize PLRAI using the min-man rule as shown in Eq. 16.

$$PLRAI' = \frac{PLRAI_{max} - PLRAI}{PLRAI_{max} - PLRAI_{min}} \tag{16}$$

Number of Flows Abnormal Index. A flow is a classification of packet characteristic. In general, source destination IP, source destination port and protocol with the same data packet form a stream. The number of flow will fall within a normal range. If the number of flow changes greatly, it indicates that the network status changes. Therefore, we propose NFAI to measure the extent to which the number of flow deviates from the normal range. The calculation formula is as follows.

$$NFAI = \frac{\|NF - NF_{norm}\|}{NF_{max} - NF_{norm}} \tag{17}$$

Where NF_{norm} is the average number of flow, and NF_{max} is the maximum number of flow. We use the exponential function e^{-g*x} as a mapping function to normalize NFAI. Based on the historical data, we take g equal to 0.005. The normalized formula is as follows.

$$NFAI' = e^{-g*NFAI} \tag{18}$$

We propose four indicators based on commonly used network performance parameters to describe the degree of network performance anomalies. And these indicators can mitigate attack and defense metric errors caused by zero-day attacks. The threshold of the network performance indicators in this paper is determined by 30 experimental statistics.

Indicator Weight Calculating. There are many methods for determining indicator weights, such as Delphi, AHP, principal component analysis and entropy weight. The first two are subjective, but can can rely on expert experience. The latter two are relatively objective, but they are not applicable here, because different network configurations and changing network environments can result in unreliable statistics. In this paper, we use the AHP method to calculate the weight of all indicators.

4   Security Metric Simulation Implementation

In order to verify the rationality and correctness of the proposed index system, we use the NS3 simulator to achieve real-time measurement of network status. First, we need to build an enterprise network and configure network resources and vulnerability information. Then implement different attack and defense modules and build different network scenarios. Finally, the security indicators are collected and calculated in different scenarios, and the real-time network status value is obtained, and the rationality of the index system is judged according to the actual network status.

4.1   Build Network Scenario

Simulation Environment. We use the simulator NS3.25 to build the enterprise network. We use 101 nodes to simulate the equipment of the intranet, and 125 nodes are used to simulate the external network. Different subnets are connected through routers. The simulated network topology is shown in Fig. 2. We configure the resources in the enterprise network and list the vulnerability information as shown in Table 4.

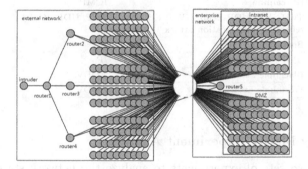

Fig. 2. Simulation network topology

4.2   Offense and Defense Module

In order to measure the impact of offense and defense on network, we add different strengths of attack and defense to the network scenarios in NS3. As NS3 simulator does not involve any security function, the implementation of the attack module is to use the attack principle to embed the attack function code in NS3. NS3 is more flexible than the actual network attack tools, and there is no limitation of system permission [14], so we can modify the kernel source code as needed. We implemented the attacks listed in Table 5, and also implemented different defense modules in NS3 to defense the attacks, including IDS and firewall, etc.

Table 4. Implemented defense module

Asset	TAIL	Quantity	System type	Vulnerability number	CVSS score
Router	3	1	MikroTik	CVE-2018-10070	7.8/10
switcher	3	2	Cisco IOS XE	CVE-2018-0165	6.1/10
				CVE-2018-0090	5.0/10
Database server	2	4	Windows	CVE-2018-2775	4.0/10
				CVE-2018-2769	4.0/10
Web server	2	1	Linux	CVE-2005-1110	7.5/10
Mail server	2	1	Windows	CVE-2004-2168	5.0/10
TFTP server	2	1	Windows	CVE-2001-1097	5.0/10
User host	1	10	Windows	CVE-2011-0514	5.0/10
User host	1	35	Windows	CVE-2013-1451	4.0/10
User host	1	6	Linux	CVE-2017-8779	7.8/10
User host	1	40	Linux	CVE-2008-5183	4.3/10

Table 5. Implemented attack module

Attack type	Dependent protocol
TCP-SYN, UDP, ICMP flood attack	TCP, UDP, ICMP
TCP-SYN, UDP port scan	TCP, UDP
IP scanning	ICMP
TCP-SYN, UDP-Echo, ICMP-Echo reflection amplification attack	TCP, UDP, ICMP
Botnet	Irc
IP spoofing	IP
Blackhole attack	AODV
Wormhole attack	AODV

4.3 Security Metirc Experiment Analysis

We designed two sets of experiments to analyze the network state changes in attack and defense confrontation. The attack strength level in the experiment refers to the snort user manual [15], and the defense strength level is determined by the number of defense device. Table 6 lists the attack severity levels and attack targets. Table 7 shows the defense equipment and defense strength. The security metric experiment is detailed below.

The Impact of Attack on Network Security. In order to measure the impact of attacks on network security, we need to fix the defense strength and then adjust the different attack strength. We first determined that the defense device is CRT-RS-IDS, blacklist and ACL, and then set up four different attacks. Table 8 lists five different offensive and defensive scenarios. "/" means no attacks occur.

Figure 3 show the changes in comprehensive indicators. In subgraph 1, we can find that the network status value exceeds 0.8 when the attack did not occur because the strength level of the defense is 3. When an attack occurs, the security status values in scenario 1 and 3 are drastically reduced because the protection

Table 6. Attack information used in the experiment

Attack type	Severity level	Attack target
IP spoofing	1	Combined with DDoS attack
UDP DDoS	3	TFTP server
UDP DoS	2	TFTP server
UDP port scanning	1	DMZ area server
TCP-SYN DoS	2	Mail server
IP scanning	1	Enterprise network equipment
TCP-SYN port scanning	1	DMZ area server

Table 7. Defense strength information used in the experiment

Defense	Defense strength level	Threat detection intensity level	F-measure
CRT-RS-IDS, blacklist, ACL	3	3	0.99
CRT-RS-IDS, BF-ICMP-DEFEND-DDoS, blacklist, ACL	3	3	0.99
CRT-RS-IDS, blacklist, ACL, IP-MAC binding	3	3	0.99
CRT-RS-IDS, BF-ICMP-DEFEND-DDoS	3	3	0.99
CRT-RS-IDS, blacklist	2	3	0.99

device cannot defend against DDoS or DoS attacks. The attacks in scenario 2 and 4 can be detected by CRT-RS-IDS and blocked by blacklist or ACL, so the security status value is slightly reduced. Subgraph 2 shows the impact of the attack on security capabilities. When no attack occurs, multiple defense devices make the network highly resistant. If the attack breaks through the defense, such as scenario 1 and 3, then the network will be damaged and security protection ability will decline. If the attack is successfully defended, the security protection capability is basically unaffected. Subgraph 3 shows the impact of an attack on the attack threat capability. The attack threat capability is less than 1 when no attack occurs, because the vulnerabilities cause the network to have a threat risk. We can find that the attack strength is directly proportional to the attack threat

Table 8. Implemented defense module

Defense	0–20 s	20–40 s	40–60 s	60–80 s	80–100 s
1	/	/	IP spoofing, UDP DDoS(A1)	/	/
2	/	/	UDP DDoS(A2)	/	/
3	/	/	IP spoofing, UDP DoS(A3)	/	/
4	/	/	UDP port scanning(A4)	/	/
5	/	/	/	/	/

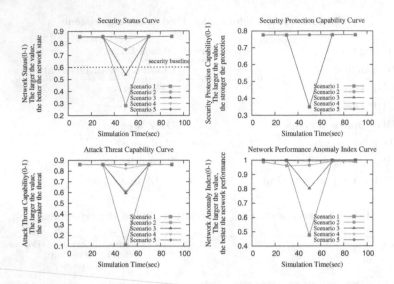

Fig. 3. The impact of attacks on network comprehensive indicators

capability from scenario 1, 2, 3 and 4. Subgraph 4 depicts the impact of attacks on network performance. When no attack occurs, the network performance anomaly index is very low, so the network communication performance is good. When an attack occurs, the attack that breaks through the defense has a large impact on the network performance, such as scenario 1 and 3, because the large amount of data generated in a short time causes the communication link and bandwidth to be occupied, resulting in an increase in network delay and PLR. When the attack is successfully blocked by the defense, the network communication performance is almost unaffected. In general, the measurement results can accurately reflect the real-time impact of different attacks on network status.

The Impact of Defense on Network Security. Figure 4 describes the impact of different defense strengths on comprehensive indicators. In subgraph 1, the network status value increases as the security level increases without attack. When there is no protection, such as scenario 5, the network security status is lower than the security baseline due to the risk of vulnerabilities. When an attack occurs, attacks can be successfully blocked by BF-ICMP-DEFEND-DDoS in scenarios 1 and 3, so network status value is not greatly affected. In other cases, the network is not effective against DDoS attacks with IP spoofing, and the network status value is below the security baseline. From subgraph 2, we can find that the security protection capability is directly related to the security defense strength. If the network defense can defend against the attack, the defense ability will not be affected, otherwise it will be seriously degraded, such as scenario 2 and scenario 4. In scenario 5, when there is no defense, the value of security protection capability is zero. Subgraph 3 shows that the attack threat capability depends not only on the strength of the attack, but also on the outcome of the attack and

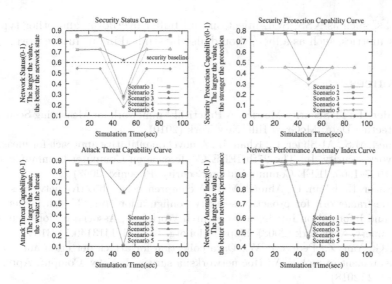

Fig. 4. The impact of defense on network comprehensive indicators

defense interaction. Subgraph 4 shows the impact of defense strength on network performance. Whether network performance is seriously affected depends on whether the current attack breaks through the defense, such as scenario 2 and 3. In general, the measurement results can accurately reflect the real-time impact process of different defenses on network status.

Combining the above analysis to compare the real state of the network with the values of the various comprehensive indicators, the accuracy and rationality of the indicator system can be verified.

5   Conclusion and Future Works

This paper describes the importance and necessity of security metric, and points out the deficiencies of metrics by analyzing and comparing existing security standards. In order to solve the problem that the existing index system cannot be quantified, we propose a quantifiable, comprehensive, dynamic and comparable network security index system through the perspective of attack and defense confrontation and calculate the index weight through AHP. The index system considers both the threat brought by the attack and the defense capability of the network itself. AHP can use the data collected in real time to ensure the reliability and accuracy of the measurement results, and reduce the computational difficulty and complexity. We also used NS3 simulator to test the proposed methods, the simulation results show the quantitability and dynamics of the indicator system, but also verify that the index system is accurate and comprehensive.

In the future, we need to take a more objective and appropriate weight calculation method to measure the network security status more accurately. More types of attacks, such as XSS, SQL injection and buffer overflows, and other types of network metrics, such as adhoc, should also be studied in our future work.

References

1. Hayden, L.: IT Security Metrics: A Practical Framework for Measuring Security & Protecting Data. McGraw Hill, New York (2010)
2. Ahmed, M.S., AI-Shaer, E., Khan, L.: A novel quantitative approach for measuring network security. In: The 27th IEEE Conference on Computer Communications, pp. 1957–1965. IEEE Communication Security, Phoenix (2008)
3. AI-Shaer, E., Khan, L., Ahmed, M.S.: A comprehensive objective network security metric framework for proactive security configuration. In: The 4th Cyber Security and Information Intelligence Research Workshop, Association for Computing Machinery, New York (2008). https://doi.org/10.1145/1413140.1413189
4. Liu, G., Yan, Z., Pedryczc, W.: Data collection for attack detection and security measurement in mobile Ad Hoc networks: a survey. J. Netw. Comput. Appl. **105**, 105–122 (2018)
5. Li, G.Q., Yan, Z., Fu, Y.L.: Data fusion for network intrusion detection: a review. Secur. Commun. Netw. **2018**, 1–16 (2018)
6. Atzeni, A., Lioy, A.: Why to adopt a security metric? a brief survey. In: Gollmann, D., Massacci, F., Yautsiukhin, A. (eds.) Quality of Protection. ADIS, vol. 23. Springer, Boston (2006)
7. Chen, X.Z., Zheng, Q.H., Guan, X.H.: Quantitative hierarchical threat evaluation model for network security. J. Softw. **17**(4), 885–897 (2006)
8. Pendleton, M., Garcia-lebron, R., Cho, J.H.: A survey on systems security metrics. ACM Comput. Surv. **49**(4), 62–96 (2016)
9. Jing, X.Y., Yan, Z., Pedryczc, W.: Security data collection and data analytics in the internet: a survey. IEEE Commun. Surv. Tutorials **21**(1), 586–618 (2018)
10. Lin, H.Q., Yan, Z., Zhang, L.: A survey on network security-related data collection technologies 2018, p. 1 (2018)
11. Jing, X.Y., Yan, Z., Pedrycz, W.: Network traffic fusion and analysis against DDoS flooding attacks with a novel reversible sketch (2018)
12. Hong, J.B., Yusuf, E.S., Seong, K.D.: Dynamic security metrics for measuring the effectiveness of moving target defense techniques. Comput. Secur. **79**, 33–52 (2018)
13. Abraham, S., Nair, S.: A stochastic model for security quantification using absorbing Markov chains. J. Commun. **9**, 899–907 (2014)
14. Li, G.Q., Yan, Z., Fu, Y.L.: A study and simulation research of blackhole attack on mobile AdHoc network. In: 2018 IEEE Conference on Communications and Network Security, pp. 1–6. IEEE Communication Security, Phoenix (2018)
15. Snort users manual. http://manual-snort-org.s3-website-us-east-1.amazonaws.com/snort_manual.html. Accessed 2018

CatraDroid: A Call Trace Driven Detection of Malicious Behaiviors in Android Applications

Cong Sun[1](✉) (iD), Jun Chen[1,2], Pengbin Feng[1], and Jianfeng Ma[1]

[1] School of Cyber Engineering, Xidian University, Xi'an 710071, China
suncong@xidian.edu.cn
[2] Tencent Technology (Shenzhen) Company Limited, Shenzhen 518057, China

Abstract. The explosive growth of Android malware has led to a strong interest in developing efficient and precise malware detection approach. Recent efforts have shown that machine learning-based malware classification is a promising direction, and the API-level features are extremely representative to discriminate malware and have been drastically used in different forms. In this work, we implement a light-weight classification system, *CatraDroid*, that recovers the semantics at call graph level to classify applications. CatraDroid leverages text mining technique to capture a list of sensitive APIs from the knowledge consisting of exploits databases, code samples, and configurations of codebases. It builds a complete call graph for Android applications and identifies call traces from entry methods to sensitive API calls. Using call traces as features, our classification approach can effectively discriminate Android malware from benign applications. Through the evaluation, we demonstrated that our approach outperforms the state-of-art API-level detection approach, with high-quality features extracted by efficient static analysis.

Keywords: Android · Malware detection · Machine learning · Classification · Call graph

1 Introduction

Malware has posed a great threat to the Android ecosystem. Detecting malicious behavior of Android applications is complicated by the nature of the component-based Android framework and the incomplete control and data flow implicated by the callbacks and runtime binding mechanism. Static analysis for Android applications usually address different approach to reconstruct the complete control flow and data dependence information [13,36] as the basis of malicious behavior detection. These efforts are likely to cause some performance issue. Machine learning-based malware detection is a promising approach to detect

---

C. Sun and J. Chen—The first two authors contribute equally to this work.

© Springer Nature Switzerland AG 2019
X. Chen et al. (Eds.): ML4CS 2019, LNCS 11806, pp. 63–77, 2019.
https://doi.org/10.1007/978-3-030-30619-9_6

Android malware because of the scalability and the flexibility to integrate diverse aspects of the characteristics from Android applications.

The greatest challenge of using machine learning-based malware detection is how to extract and select representative features for the malicious behaviors in Android applications. Many different feature categories have been considered, such as user permissions [30,32], API calls or relations [9,24,26,35,39], and more complicated semantic features [28]. Some efforts have combined different feature categories to build classifiers for discriminating complicated malicious behaviors [12,18].

API-level features are considered to be extremely representative and also easy to be extracted. A lot of features for malware detection are built upon API, e.g. the frequency of API calls [9], the code-block and package relationship of APIs [24], the similarity between API dependency graphs [39], data dependence paths starting from and leading to specific APIs [26], source-sink pairs of APIs [14], and some abstract correlations between APIs [35]. Some of these features are fine-grained to catch both the control flows and data dependencies to discriminate malicious behaviors. However, the scalability usually becomes an issue especially when the data flows are considered to specify the program semantics of applications.

In this work, we propose CatraDroid, a supervised learning-based approach that recovers the semantics of program at call graph level to classify Android applications and detect malware. Without constructing any data dependency as did in [14,26,39], our approach tracks through the call graph and finds out all the critical call traces leading from the entry methods to the sensitive API calls. The sensitive APIs are discovered by text mining for the keywords of well-established Android vulnerability descriptions, code samples, and the configurations of well-known codebases. In the learning phase, we build different classification models with these call traces and use them to predict the malicious behavior of unknown applications. We evaluated CatraDroid on 15733 distinct applications including 10880 malware, and the evaluation results revealed that our approach can outperform the state-of-art API-level detection approach on different classification models. The time cost of our static analysis is reasonable.

In summary, we make the following contributions:

1. We build a more comprehensive sensitive API list than the state-of-art approach using text mining on exploits databases, code samples, and configurations of codebases.
2. We construct the complete call graph for applications and identify call traces from entry methods to sensitive API calls as the fine-grained features for classifying Android applications and discriminating malware.
3. The evaluation results showed that CatraDroid outperformed the baseline approach in classification performance, demonstrated the quality of features, the comprehensiveness of sensitive API list, as well as the efficiency of our static analysis.

2 Related Work

Machine learning has been pervasively used in Android malware detection. In this area, API-related features have been addressed as one of the most critical features. These features can be extracted by either static or dynamic analysis.

In order to derive the API level features using static analysis, DroidAPIMiner [9] addresses the frequency of API calls and the package information issuing the API calls. For the critical APIs, a data flow analysis is performed to infer the real value of parameters. DroidSIFT [39] constructs the API dependency graph and queries the similarity scores between graphs to detect anomalies. Droid-Miner [38] uses two-tiered behavior graphs constructed with relations of either lifecycle methods or permission-related APIs to characterize malicious behaviors. DroidADDMiner [26] uses a build-in data-flow analysis to derive the API data dependence paths for generating the modalities and features. A similar principle was taken by MUDFLOW [14] to detect the abnormal data dependencies bridged by specific pairs of source-sink APIs. MalPat [35] uses permission information to decide the sensitivity of APIs and the correlations between them. The correlations between APIs are more abstract compared with the source-sink relations [14,33] and the relations built with the call traces in this work. Drebin [12] adopts API calls as one aspect of the features relevant to malicious attacks.

Another choice to derive API level features is dynamic analysis, usually based on sandboxing and profiling the sequence of critical system calls or API invocations. CrowDroid [15] uses the API call sequences in the Linux kernel as features. Dimjašević et al. [21] tracked the system calls as features to classify Android malware and extensively evaluated the quality of their heuristics-based feature encoding. DroidScribe [20] generates multi-level features, including pure system calls, Binder communication, and abstract behavioral patterns. It has demonstrated that the features at different levels are better in quality than the innocent features of system calls. MADAM [34] takes a similar multi-level approach to detect user's and device's anomaly based on the kernel-level system calls, application-level critical API calls, user-level activities, and package level metadata. Both dynamic monitoring and static assessment are used to capture these features. EnDroid [23] also combines system-level call sequences with many application-level dynamic features to develop effective malware detection. Droid-Cat [16] can profile a diverse set of dynamic features based on method calls and inter-component communication mechanism and use these features to categorize malware with high accuracy. One of the weaknesses of dynamic analysis-assisted approaches is that it is unsound and tend to miss critical features during profiling when the inputs are insufficiently fed or the configurations are inappropriately given.

3 CatraDroid

In this section, we propose CatraDroid, a call-trace driven approach to detecting Android malware. In general, the approach of CatraDroid is a three-phase learning-based classification:

1. We generate a list of sensitive APIs according to the knowledge base derived from online exploits databases, code samples, and configurations of well-known codebases with text mining technique.
2. We build a complete call graph over each reverse-engineered Android application, identify all the call traces triggered from the entry method and leading to some sensitive API call.
3. We encode the call traces into feature vectors and apply supervised-learning with different classifier models to discriminate malware from benign applications.

3.1 Sensitive API List Generation

Many Android APIs operate on sensitive data, e.g. contact list or SMS messages, or require different critical services, e.g. URL/database connections, HTTPResponse. These APIs with critical functionality tend to be exploited by attackers to conduct some malicious behaviors threatening user's privacy or system security. We call them sensitive APIs. In many API-based detection systems, the identification of sensitive APIs mainly relies on the supervision of experts or sandbox-based dynamic profiling. Both the domain-specific knowledge needed by the experts and the profiled call sequences are impacted by the scale of samples, and may have a significant bias. For example, TaintDroid [22] was reported to manually embed 62 sensitive APIs in 9 categories [37], while for FlowDroid [13], the number of sensitive sources and sinks is 224. Susi [33] takes a learning-guided approach to effectively identify and categorize sensitive APIs in the Android framework and applications, with a specific focus on the data flow dependencies.

   In this work, we propose to use text mining technique to identify the sensitive APIs for our call trace generation. In order to derive a comprehensive list of sensitive APIs, we first collect a set of features. The features include the Android-related literal descriptions that mention the potential malicious behaviors, sensitive functionalities, triggering inputs to vulnerabilities, from the Common Vulnerabilities and Exposures (CVEs) [5] and the Exploit Database [6], as well as the related code samples. We also collect the configurations of well-known codebases, e.g. [13,17,22,33,36], including the source and sink lists, callback lists, and taint wrapper lists. These descriptions, code samples, and configurations constitute the knowledge base of the malicious behaviors and vulnerabilities of the Android system and applications. Then, from these textual features, we extract the technical terms to build a set of keywords. For example, we can find some report that describes malware residing in app-readable/writable directories, exploiting dynamic loading classes or reflection mechanism to obtain the component instance to conduct malicious behaviors. In this case, we can extract at least keyword `reflect` and `ClassLoader` for identifying the sensitive APIs. To prune the set of keywords, we apply the algorithm of *term frequency-inverse document frequency* (TF-IDF) to rank the keywords and select a subset of more informative keywords for the sensitive API identification. Thirdly, we search the official online document of Android platform APIs [2] for these keywords. If the number of keywords presenting in the name and description of a specific API is greater than a threshold, we identify this API as a sensitive API. A list of sensitive APIs is generated in their method signatures, e.g. in Table 1, as critical inputs of the call trace identification.

In this step, we identify 647 sensitive APIs for the call trace identification. This list of sensitive APIs can cover all the sensitive APIs of TaintDroid, and is also more comprehensive than the critical API list of DroidAPIMiner, see Sect. 4.3 for details.

Table 1. Sensitive APIs w.r.t. `reflect/ClassLoader` derived from Android APIs

No	API Signature
①	<java.lang.reflect.Method.invoke(Ljava/lang/Object;[Ljavalang/Object;)Ljava/lang/Object;>
②	<java.lang.ClassLoader.loadClass(Ljava/lang/String;Z)Ljava/lang/Class;>
③	<dalvik.system.DexClassLoader(Ljava/lang/String;Ljava/lang/String;Ljava/lang/String; Ljava/lang/Object;)V>
	...

3.2 Call Graph Generation and Call Trace Identification

Previous API-based detection approaches usually require to distinguish between how the sensitive APIs are used in malicious verses benign applications. These approaches may not be precise enough because a lot of sensitive APIs that are found to be common in both benign and malicious apps may be pruned out. In contrast, the traces of either system calls or invocations to the critical APIs are more recognizable to distinguish the malicious behaviors from the normal executions of applications. However, the sandbox-assisted dynamic trace profiling takes a similar principle of must-analysis, and is incomplete to found all the traces related to malicious behaviors of the application. To mitigate such limitation, in this work, we propose to identify the traces leading to critical APIs, i.e. *call trace*, statically over a precise call graph of Android applications. This finc-grained feature will then be used in the learning-based malware classification.

In the first step, we propose to generate a precise call graph for Android applications. This is the prerequisite for identifying the call traces. Due to the event-driven characteristic of Android application lifecycle, the call graph generation is not straight-forward by starting from one specific entry. Instead, the Android application usually contains multiple entry methods. Each entry method, usually being some event handler, can receive events/callbacks from the Android system to support switchable execution contexts.

We present the call-graph generation algorithm in Algorithm 1. Firstly, we derive all the possible edge relations in *EdgeStore* from the bytecode of application. Each entity in *EdgeStore* is a tuple, whose first element mtd represents a method object for analysis, and the second element $callee_{mtd}$ is an ordered set of method objects that are invoked in the bytecode of mtd. $callee_{mtd}$ will be empty if *mtd* does not call other methods. Then we build the class hierarchy for the classes of the application. After that, we extract the component information from the manifest file of the application, including the path name of component n_c and the category of component τ_c. For each component, we traverse the class hierarchy to find the class object c, and search for all the lifecycle methods of the component or interface method of event listeners. We accumulate these methods into the set of entry methods, i.e. *Entries*. Starting from each entry method in *Entries* for code traversal, we perform a breadth-first search (BFS) over the *EdgeStore*. For each method *mtd* in the vertice worklist, if $\langle mtd, callee_{mtd} \rangle \in EdgeStore$, then we should add any $mtd' \in callee_{mtd}$ into the vertice worklist and add (mtd, mtd') into the edge worklist. Consequently, we generate a partial call graph by merging the results of the breadth-first search. Then we iterate on the interface methods of callback listeners found in the partial call graph, add them to *Entries*, update the partial call graph until no new entry method is added to *Entries*. The list of callback listeners we use is generated by using EdgeMiner [17]. From the callback methods of EdgeMiner, we obtain 3390 different callback listeners for use. Finally, for the implicit intents which are not directed by explicit `invoke` instruction, we add new edges to generate the final call graph.

Algorithm 1. Call Graph Generation for Android Application

1: $EdgeStore \leftarrow \{\langle mtd, callee_{mtd} \rangle \mid \forall mtd \in Classes(app)\}$
2: $T \leftarrow ClassHierarchy(app)$
3: $Comps \leftarrow \{\langle n_c, \tau_c \rangle \mid$ path name n_c and category τ_c of component class c extracted from `AndroidManifest.xml`$\}$
4: $Entries \leftarrow \emptyset$
5: **for all** $\langle n_c, \tau_c \rangle \in Comps$ **do**
6:      $c \leftarrow traverse(T, n_c)$
7:      $Entries \leftarrow Entries \cup getEntryMtd(c, \tau_c)$
8: **end for**
9: **for all** $entry_i \in Entries$ **do**
10:     $\langle V_i, E_i \rangle \leftarrow BFS(entry_i, EdgeStore, T)$
11: **end for**
12: $PartialCallGraph \equiv \langle V, E \rangle \leftarrow \bigcup_{entry_i \in Entries} \langle V_i, E_i \rangle$
13: Search $PartialCallGraph$, add interface methods of callback listener instances to *Entries* and iterate over Step 9 until *Entries* reaches fixpoint
14: Add edge for implicit intents

Then we identify all the call traces over the complete call graph. Each call trace is a directional path in the call graph. It starts from one of the entry methods, and ends at one invocation of a sensitive API identified in Sect. 3.1. We perform a depth-first search (DFS) from each entry method to see if there is any invocation to some sensitive API on each directional path starting at this entry method. If a path from the entry method *mtd* can lead to an invocation to sensitive API mtd', we use (mtd, mtd') to represent a sensitive call trace and add it to the set of call traces.

The method signature mtd and mtd' used to denote the node of call trace consist of some type information of the component class that implements the method. To build a reasonable granularity of features, we parse the manifest file again and use the category information τ_c to substitute the type information of component in the method signatures. The feature repository is then constructed after duplication eliminations of the call traces.

3.3   Learning-Based Malicious Behavior Detection

The call traces identified in Sect. 3.2 are used as the critical features to detect the malicious behaviors of Android malware. This is usually more precise than identifying the invoked sensitive APIs because malicious applications and benign applications usually target to different purpose and take different paths in the call graph to operate on the critical data and confidentialities. Then, our machine learning module uses the supervised learning technique for training the binary classifiers. We adopt four algorithms, kNN [10], Naive Bayes [25], SVM [19], and Random Forest [27], for the classification to decide if the performance of our approach is achieved by the classification models or the features.

For simplicity, our approach does not quantify the frequency of call traces to assign a rank score to each call trace. Instead, we apply the one-hot encoding to build the feature vector of each sample. After training the classifier, for any unknown application, we decompile the application for bytecode, extract its manifest file, build the call graph, identify call traces, generate its feature vector and input the feature vector to one of the classifiers for the malicious behavior prediction. For comparison, we find the Random Forest model is better in performance due to the results in Sect. 4.3.

4   Implementation and Evaluation

4.1   Implementation

Figure 1 depicts the implementation of CatraDroid. In the implementation of call graph generation, we firstly leverage the Apktool [4] and Dare [29] to derive the bytecode and the manifest file `AndroidManifest.xml`. We use IBM WALA [8] to implement the call graph generation and call trace identification. In the implementation of call graph generation, multiple-origin breadth-first search, as well as the callbacks and implicit intents, should be carefully addressed. In the call trace identification, substituting the type information of component with the category information τ_c is critical to control the granularity of features derived by the depth-first traverse on the call graph. The learning-based detection module is based on the built-in algorithms of `Scikit-learn` [31].

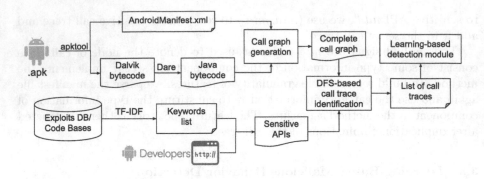

Fig. 1. Implementation of CatraDroid

4.2 Experimental Setups

The malware samples are collected from Drebin [12] and VirusShare [7], while the benign samples are collected from AndroZoo [11], whose benign samples are largely collected from Google Play. For the benign samples, a pre-processing step is applied to filter out all the benign samples that contain at least one invocation to sensitive APIs. After the pre-processing step, we collect 4853 benign applications and 10880 malicious applications (2647 from Drebin, 8233 from VirusShare) for the evaluation.

We use stratified 5-fold cross-validation to evaluate the performance of our approach. To measure the performance of classifiers we derived, we use four standard metrics *accuracy*, *precision*, *recall*, and *AUC*. *Accuracy* means the proportion of samples that are predicted correctly. *Precision* is defined as the proportion of correctly identified malicious apps to all classified malicious samples. *Recall* represents the ability to identify malicious apps correctly in all the malicious samples. These three metrics are defined based on the *true positive* (TP[1]), *true negative* (TN[2]), *false positive* (FP[3]), and *false negative* (FN[4]).

$$Accuracy = \frac{TP + TN}{TP + FP + TN + FN} \tag{1}$$

$$Precision = \frac{TP}{TP + FP} \tag{2}$$

$$Recall = \frac{TP}{TP + FN} \tag{3}$$

Because it will be more dangerous when we treat malware as a benign application, *recall* is usually more valuable than the false positive rate. The area under ROC curve (*AUC*) represents the probability that a classifier will rank

---

[1] TP: the number of malicious apps that are classified as malicious.

[2] TN: the number of benign apps that are classified as benign.

[3] FP: the number of benign apps that are misclassified as malicious.

[4] FN: the number of malicious apps that are misclassified as benign.

a randomly chosen malicious instance higher than a randomly chosen negative one. An area of 1.0 means a perfect classifier, while an area of 0.5 indicates a worthless classifier.

Our experiments are conducted on a workstation with $3.2\,\mathrm{GHz} \times 16$ Intel CPU, $64\,\mathrm{GB}$ RAM, and Linux 4.13.0-46-generic kernel (Ubuntu 17.10).

4.3 Experimental Results and Analysis

In this section, we present the experimental results on performance and more analysis on the characteristics of our approach to answering the following research questions (RQ1 – RQ4).

RQ1. Can our approach outperform the state-of-art approach?

In order to demonstrate the effectiveness of our approach, we compare our approach with DroidAPIMiner [9]. DroidAPIMiner uses static analysis to identify a variety of API-level features. These API features tend to be exploited by malicious applications more frequently than being used by benign applications. Supervised learning methods are applied to train some lightweight classifier for detecting the malicious behavior of Android applications. We use Androguard [1] to extract sensitive APIs and package-level information. Then we use Androwarn [3] to reimplement the parameter-level API feature extraction of DroidAPIMiner. From the invocations in smali code, we do a backward tracking to obtain the possible values of API parameters.

The comparisons of the different evaluation metrics are presented in Table 2. In our approach, the Random Forest model exhibits the best performance for all the metrics, with accuracy of 98.90%, precison of 99.38%, and recall of 95.83%. For DroidAPIMiner, the kNN model performs the best, with accuracy of 94.93%, precision of 91.79%, and recall of 92.13%. Although its precision is lower than SVM and Random Forest, it is still the best on F-measure. Because our approach is on higher dimensional feature spaces compared with DroidAPIMiner, the Random Forest model is a better choice for our approach. Meanwhile, SVM performs very well on deciding recall for both our approach and DroidAPIMiner.

Table 2. Performance comparison between CatraDroid and DroidAPIMiner (DAMiner for short)

Model	Accuracy (%)		Precision (%)		Recall (%)		AUC	
	DAMiner	Ours	DAMiner	Ours	DAMiner	Ours	DAMiner	Ours
kNN	94.93	90.11	91.79	94.61	92.13	84.44	94.28	94.49
Naive Bayes	88.20	94.31	93.75	95.71	67.22	92.15	81.03	92.12
SVM	94.27	95.60	96.77	97.45	84.12	94.08	88.72	98.73
Random Forest	92.83	98.90	96.02	99.38	80.10	95.83	91.43	99.37

In summary, the Random Forest model of our approach improves the kNN model of DroidAPIMiner on accuracy by 3.97%, on precision by 7.59%, and on recall by 3.70%. Our approach outperforms DroidAPIMiner on most of the classification models. It means the features of sensitive call traces in our approach make for the malicious behavior detection better than the frequency feature of critical APIs in DroidAPIMiner. Malware and benign applications tend to have different critical actions represented by the call traces.

RQ2. Are the sensitive APIs identified in Sect. 3.1 representative on the critical actions to distinguish malware from benign applications?

The list of sensitive APIs derived using NLP-based technique contains 647 sensitive APIs. In Fig. 2 we illustrate the number of sensitive APIs we identified in each specific package or library. On the other hand, DroidAPIMiner selects top 169 APIs that can mostly differentiate benign applications from malicious applications based on the usage frequency for evaluation. The numbers of APIs in each package or library are presented in Fig. 3. By comparing the two lists in detail, we find that except for some standard library package, e.g. `java.util`, `java.lang`, and `java.io`, our sensitive APIs can cover 80.4% of the critical APIs of DroidAPIMiner. Meanwhile, our approach falls short of identifying the critical APIs in `http`-related package. This is because in the CVEs and exploit database, we did not treat most of the `http`-related APIs or standard Java libraries as in the context of Android vulnerabilities. In contrast, the frequency and data flow relation captured by DroidAPIMiner are good at identifying critical APIs in these packages.

Our sensitive APIs list is more comprehensive than that of DroidAPIMiner. We extract more information from the exploits databases and configurations of codebases on malicious database access, Bluetooth connection, multimedia modules launching, near field communication, location data release, as well as the critical actions from many different system toolkits.

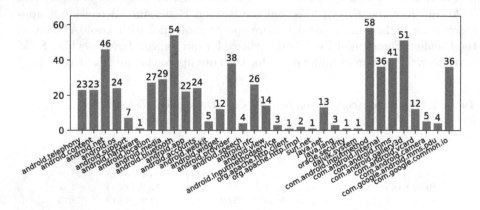

Fig. 2. Distribution of sensitive API number of CatraDroid

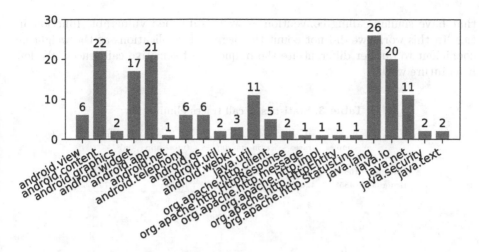

Fig. 3. Distribution of critical API number of DroidAPIMiner

RQ3. Does the set of call traces show sufficient diversity on malware and benign applications?

In the answer to RQ1, we know that the call traces we concern are generally more fine-grained than the frequency of sensitive APIs addressed by DroidAPIMiner. In order to illustrate the property of the call traces of an individual application, we introduce a new metric *internal repetition rate, (IRR)*:

$$IRR = \frac{Avg.\ No.\ call\ traces - Unduplicated\ Avg.\ No.\ call\ traces}{Unduplicated\ Avg.\ No.\ call\ traces} \tag{4}$$

The type information of the methods in call traces generated in Sect. 3.2 should be substituted with the category information τ_c. This procedure will lead to an in-app duplication elimination on call traces. Then when we build the feature space, all the call traces after in-app duplication elimination are merged together. In this procedure, the same call trace from different applications should only reserve one copy, which we called cross-app duplication elimination.

In Table 3 we show the statistics of the call trace elimination. In the malware in our data set, we find 931501 call traces before duplication eliminations. The maximal number for individual malware is 9909. After the in-app duplication elimination, there are 374331 call traces. The average number of call traces reduces from 85.6 to 34.4. The IRR for malware is 148.8%. In the benign applications in our data set, we find 424709 call traces before duplication eliminations. The maximal number of call traces for an individual benign application is 2996. After in-app duplication elimination, the number of call traces becomes 236146 and the IRR for benign applications is 79.9%. The difference in IRR reveals that malware uses more types of components in the same category to perform malicious actions. These components with different types should have a similar interface but different implementations. This reflects a reasonable way to implement malicious functionalities, e.g. with some inherited or third-party libraries that have similar calling convention as well-established vulnerable functionalities. In this work, we did not count the degree of duplications as the weighting coefficient to further differentiate the frequency of sensitive call traces. We left it as future work.

Table 3. Statistics of call traces elimination

Category	No. samples	No. call traces	No. call traces (in-app dupl. elim.)	No. call traces (cross-app dupl. elim.)	IRR
Malware	10880	931501	374331	60059	148.8%
Benigns	4853	424709	236146	49571	79.9%

Table 4. Time costs of each step of CatraDroid

Step	Reverse engineering	Call trace identification	RF classifier model training	Detection
Avg. time (s)	4.14	170.27	8763.35	1.35×10^{-4}

Then we show the difference on the set of call traces after two-phase duplication eliminations between malware and benign applications. We find 60059 call traces from malware after cross-app duplication elimination, and for benign applications, this number is 49571. The number of duplicated call traces between the two categories is 22828. The duplication rate is 26.3%. It indicates the call traces used by malware are greatly different from the call traces used by benign applications. The features we concern can well classify the calling conventions of both benign and malicious applications.

RQ4. Are the time costs reasonable for each step of our approach?

The static analysis over Android applications is generally a time consuming procedure. In this section, we have to figure out the average time cost by each step of our approach, especially the call graph generation and call trace identification, in order to estimate the time cost on any unknown application. The time costs of each step are listed in Table 4. Clearly, the time costs of reverse engineering and malware detection are ignorable. The average training time of Random Forest models is acceptable because this time cost is averaged on the cross-validation folds, instead of on application samples. The average time of call trace identification, including the call graph generation time, is 170.27 s. Generally, this time cost is positively correlated with the size of applications, i.e. 7.6 MB on average for the applications in our data set. In summary, the time cost of our approach is reasonable.

5   Conclusion

We presented CatraDroid, a supervised learning-based classification approach that detects malware using the semantics from the call graph of Android application represented by the call traces leading from entry methods to the sensitive API calls. We showed that our approach achieves higher classification performance than the state-of-art API-level malware detection approach with a more comprehensive sensitive API list. We also demonstrated the diversity of features and the efficiency of our static analysis.

Although we have evaluated our approach to be efficient, this kind of API-level malware classifications based on static analysis still confront some evasion attacks, e.g. code obfuscation to defeat the identification of sensitive API calls. It will be a benefit for the classification performance in the future to distinguish call traces of the third-party libraries from call traces of the standard libraries and user code. Also, we can quantify the frequency of sensitive call traces to derive more fine-grained features for discriminating malware.

Acknowledgment. Supported by National Natural Science Foundation of China (Grant No: 61872279), the China Scholarship Council (Grant No: 201806965002), the Key R&D Program of Shaanxi Province of China (Grant No: 2019ZDLGY12-06).

References

1. Androguard - Reverse engineering, malware and goodware analysis of android applications. https://github.com/androguard
2. Android platform APIs. https://developer.android.com/reference/packages
3. Androwarn - Yet another static code analyzer for malicious android applications. https://github.com/maaaaz/androwarn
4. Apktool. https://ibotpeaches.github.io/Apktool/
5. Common vulnerabilities and exposures (CVEs). https://cve.mitre.org
6. Exploit database. https://www.exploit-db.com/
7. VirusShare. https://virusshare.com/
8. WALA-T. J. Watson libraries for analysis. http://wala.sourceforge.net
9. Aafer, Y., Du, W., Yin, H.: DroidAPIMiner: mining API-level features for robust malware detection in android. In: Zia, T., Zomaya, A., Varadharajan, V., Mao, M. (eds.) SecureComm 2013. LNICSSITE, vol. 127, pp. 86–103. Springer, Cham (2013). https://doi.org/10.1007/978-3-319-04283-1_6
10. Aha, D.W., Kibler, D.F., Albert, M.K.: Instance-based learning algorithms. Mach. Learn. **6**, 37–66 (1991)
11. Allix, K., Bissyandé, T.F., Klein, J., Traon, Y.L.: AndroZoo: collecting millions of android apps for the research community. In: Proceedings of the 13th International Conference on Mining Software Repositories MSR 2016, pp. 468–471 (2016)
12. Arp, D., Spreitzenbarth, M., Hubner, M., Gascon, H., Rieck, K.: DREBIN: effective and explainable detection of android malware in your pocket. In: 21st Annual Network and Distributed System Security Symposium, NDSS 2014 (2014)
13. Arzt, S., et al.: FlowDroid: precise context, flow, field, object-sensitive and lifecycle-aware taint analysis for Android apps. In: ACM SIGPLAN Conference on Programming Language Design and Implementation PLDI 2014, pp. 259–269 (2014)

14. Avdiienko, V., et al.: Mining apps for abnormal usage of sensitive data. In: 37th IEEE/ACM International Conference on Software Engineering, ICSE 2015, pp. 426–436 (2015)
15. Burguera, I., Zurutuza, U., Nadjm-Tehrani, S.: Crowdroid: behavior-based malware detection system for Android. In: SPSM 2011, Proceedings of the 1st ACM Workshop Security and Privacy in Smartphones and Mobile Devices, Co-located with CCS 2011, pp. 15–26 (2011)
16. Cai, H., Meng, N., Ryder, B.G., Yao, D.: DroidCat: effective android malware detection and categorization via app-level profiling. IEEE Trans. Inf. Forensics Secur. **14**(6), 1455–1470 (2019)
17. Cao, Y., et al.: EdgeMiner: automatically detecting implicit control flow transitions through the android framework. In: 22nd Annual Network and Distributed System Security Symposium, NDSS 2015 (2015)
18. Chen, W., Aspinall, D., Gordon, A.D., Sutton, C.A., Muttik, I.: More semantics more robust: improving android malware classifiers. In: Proceedings of the 9th ACM Conference on Security & Privacy in Wireless and Mobile Networks WISEC 2016, pp. 147–158 (2016)
19. Cortes, C., Vapnik, V.: Support-vector networks. Mach. Learn. **20**(3), 273–297 (1995)
20. Dash, S.K., et al.: DroidScribe: classifying android malware based on runtime behavior. In: 2016 IEEE Security and Privacy Workshops, SP Workshops 2016, pp. 252–261 (2016)
21. Dimjasevic, M., Atzeni, S., Ugrina, I., Rakamaric, Z.: Evaluation of android malware detection based on system calls. In: Proceedings of the 2016 ACM on International Workshop on Security And Privacy Analytics, IWSPA@CODASPY 2016, pp. 1–8 (2016)
22. Enck, W., et al.: TaintDroid: an information-flow tracking system for realtime privacy monitoring on smartphones. In: 9th USENIX Symposium on Operating Systems Design and Implementation OSDI 2010, pp. 393–407 (2010)
23. Feng, P., Ma, J., Sun, C., Xu, X., Ma, Y.: A novel dynamic android malware detection system with ensemble learning. IEEE Access **6**, 30996–31011 (2018)
24. Hou, S., Ye, Y., Song, Y., Abdulhayoglu, M.: HinDroid: an intelligent android malware detection system based on structured heterogeneous information network. In: Proceedings of the 23rd ACM SIGKDD International Conference on Knowledge Discovery and Data Mining, pp. 1507–1515 (2017)
25. John, G.H., Langley, P.: Estimating continuous distributions in bayesian classifiers. In: UAI 1995: Proceedings of the Eleventh Annual Conference on Uncertainty in Artificial Intelligence, pp. 338–345 (1995)
26. Li, Y., Shen, T., Sun, X., Pan, X., Mao, B.: Detection, classification and characterization of android malware using API data dependency. In: Thuraisingham, B., Wang, X.F., Yegneswaran, V. (eds.) SecureComm 2015. LNICST, vol. 164, pp. 23–40. Springer, Cham (2015). https://doi.org/10.1007/978-3-319-28865-9_2
27. Liaw, A., Wiener, M., et al.: Classification and regression by randomForest. R News **2**(3), 18–22 (2002)
28. Meng, G., Xue, Y., Xu, Z., Liu, Y., Zhang, J., Narayanan, A.: Semantic modelling of Android malware for effective malware comprehension, detection, and classification. In: Proceedings of the 25th International Symposium on Software Testing and Analysis ISSTA 2016, pp. 306–317 (2016)
29. Octeau, D., Jha, S., McDaniel, P.D.: Retargeting Android applications to Java bytecode. In: 20th ACM SIGSOFT Symposium on the Foundations of Software Engineering (FSE-20), SIGSOFT/FSE 2012, p. 6 (2012)

30. Olejnik, K., Dacosta, I., Machado, J.S., Huguenin, K., Khan, M.E., Hubaux, J.: SmarPer: context-aware and automatic runtime-permissions for mobile devices. In: 2017 IEEE Symposium on Security and Privacy SP 2017, pp. 1058–1076 (2017)
31. Pedregosa, F., et al.: Scikit-learn: machine learning in Python. J. Mach. Learn. Res. **12**, 2825–2830 (2011)
32. Qu, Z., Rastogi, V., Zhang, X., Chen, Y., Zhu, T., Chen, Z.: AutoCog: measuring the description-to-permission fidelity in Android applications. In: Proceedings of the 2014 ACM SIGSAC Conference on Computer and Communications Security, pp. 1354–1365 (2014)
33. Rasthofer, S., Arzt, S., Bodden, E.: A machine-learning approach for classifying and categorizing Android sources and sinks. In: 21st Annual Network and Distributed System Security Symposium, NDSS 2014 (2014)
34. Saracino, A., Sgandurra, D., Dini, G., Martinelli, F.: MADAM: effective and efficient behavior-based Android malware detection and prevention. IEEE Trans. Dependable Secur. Comput. **15**(1), 83–97 (2016)
35. Tao, G., Zheng, Z., Guo, Z., Lyu, M.R.: MalPat: mining patterns of malicious and benign Android apps via permission-related APIs. IEEE Trans. Relia. **67**(1), 355–369 (2018)
36. Wei, F., Roy, S., Ou, X., Robby: Amandroid: a precise and general inter-component data flow analysis framework for security vetting of Android apps. In: Proceedings of the 2014 ACM SIGSAC Conference on Computer and Communications Security, pp. 1329–1341 (2014)
37. Wong, M.Y., Lie, D.: IntelliDroid: a targeted input generator for the dynamic analysis of android malware. In: 23rd Annual Network and Distributed System Security Symposium, NDSS 2016 (2016)
38. Yang, C., Xu, Z., Gu, G., Yegneswaran, V., Porras, P.: DroidMiner: automated mining and characterization of fine-grained malicious behaviors in Android applications. In: Kutyłowski, M., Vaidya, J. (eds.) ESORICS 2014. LNCS, vol. 8712, pp. 163–182. Springer, Cham (2014). https://doi.org/10.1007/978-3-319-11203-9_10
39. Zhang, M., Duan, Y., Yin, H., Zhao, Z.: Semantics-aware android malware classification using weighted contextual API dependency graphs. In: Proceedings of the 2014 ACM SIGSAC Conference on Computer and Communications Security, pp. 1105–1116 (2014)

Password Guessing via Neural Language Modeling

Hang Li[1,3], Mengqi Chen[2,3], Shengbo Yan[2,3], Chunfu Jia[2,3(✉)], and Zhaohui Li[2,3]

[1] College of Artificial Intelligence, Nankai University, Tianjin 300350, China
LeeJuly30@gmail.com
[2] College of Cyber Science, Nankai University, Tianjin 300350, China
cfjia@nankai.edu.cn
[3] Tianjin Key Laboratory of Network and Data Security, Nankai University, Tianjin 300350, China

Abstract. Passwords are the major part of authentication in current social networks. The state-of-the-art password guessing approaches, such as Markov model and probabilistic context-free grammars (PCFG) model, assign a probability value to each password by a statistic approach without any parameters. These methods require large datasets to accurately estimate probability due to *the law of large number*. The neural network, approximating target probability distribution through iteratively training its parameters, was used to model passwords by some researches. However, since the network architectures they used are simple and straightforward, there are many ways to improve it.

In this paper, we view password guessing as a language modeling task and introduce a deeper, more robust, and faster-converged model with several useful techniques to model passwords. This model shows great ability in modeling passwords while significantly outperforms state-of-the-art approaches. Inspired by the most advanced sequential model named *Transformer*, we use it to model passwords with bidirectional masked language model which is powerful but unlikely to provide normalized probability estimation. Then we distill Transformer model's knowledge into our proposed model to further boost its performance. Comparing with the PCFG, Markov and previous neural network models, our models show remarkable improvement in both one-site tests and cross-site tests. Moreover, our models are robust to the password policy by controlling the entropy of output distribution.

Keywords: Authentication · Password guessing · Neural network

1 Introduction

Passwords are the most widely used mode of user authentication, perhaps, it is because they are both easy to remember and to implement. Unfortunately, many users choose predictable passwords, making password crackable. Password

X. Chen et al. (Eds.): ML4CS 2019, LNCS 11806, pp. 78–93, 2019.
https://doi.org/10.1007/978-3-030-30619-9_7

guessing aims at cracking as many user passwords as possible with minimum guess numbers and can be used to simulate real-world attackers, so researches are interested in finding more effective password guessing models than brute force to accurately gauge password strength. In this work, we concentrate on *trawling offline guessing*, where an attacker has gained access to a leaked database of hashed passwords and tries to recover it.

Commonly used password guessing tools, such as John the Ripper [1] and HashCat [14], combine the dictionary attacks with many heuristics like *mixed letter* and *leet speak* to crack user passwords. Weir et al. [29] proposed the first probabilistic model called probabilistic context-free grammars (PCFG). They assumed that passwords could be divided into independent structures and calculated their probabilities separately. Ma et al. [19] and Dürmuth et al. [6] showed that Markov models that closely represent natural language could generate passwords efficiently. Beside those statistical approaches, Melicher et al. [20], Xu et al. [30] and Liu et al. [18] used neural network to extract passwords' feature and estimate their probabilities automatically. Although the neural network approaches seem to outperform statistic methods, none of them investigates in the connection between password guessing and language modeling. The architecture they used was a simple LSTM network and can be fully improved. We refer those models to the shallow neural network model since those models are shallow.

In this paper, we borrow ideas from language modeling to model and guess passwords because passwords with meaningful sequential characters can be regarded as short natural languages, which helps us study password guessing from a scientific perspective. For example, the frequencies of characters within passwords are actually quite different and this indicates that we are dealing with an unbalanced classification task. To completely make use of the neural network, we first introduce a carefully designed deep neural network, whose architecture is more effective and the performance is better in modeling passwords. Secondly, since the *Transformer* model shows great potential in language modeling, we introduce a bidirectional model trained with masked language task. Although it is powerful, it can't provide normalized probability for one password which is vital in password guessing. To handle this problem, borrowing idea from knowledge distillation [9, 27], we use the Transformer model as a teacher to guide the proposed model. This simple trick improves the efficiency of our model in some tests. We perform both one-site tests and cross-site tests to compare our deep model with state-of-the-art password guessing models, including Markov model, PCFG model, and shallow neural network model. Then we evaluate the performance of those models with Monte Carlo method [4]. The result shows that our deep model outperforms previous approaches in most cases.

In summary, the contributions of this paper are as follows:

- A deep neural network which guesses passwords more efficiently than previous approaches is introduced.
- The proposed model is adapted to fit password's nature that it belongs to natural language.

– A bidirectional language model is used to improve our deep neural network model.

The rest of this paper is structured as follows. We introduce some related works in Sect. 2, and describe the model design of our deep neural network model in Sect. 3. In Sect. 4, we evaluate our model and compare it to the state-of-the-art methods. Finally, in Sect. 5, we conclude the paper and discuss the future work.

2 Background and Related Works

Human-chosen text passwords are today's dominant mode of authentication. However, as is revealed in predecessor's work, the distribution of password space is far from being random, thus cracking passwords is much easier than users think. In this section, we first present an overview of recent development in password guessing area. Then, we briefly introduce some key concepts in language modeling.

2.1 Password Guessing

To accurately evaluate password strength, we need to develop effective password guessing models in case of underestimating the capacity of attackers. The state-of-the-art password guessing models can be mainly categorized as statistical models or neural network models.

PCFG Model. Probabilistic context-free grammars (PCFG) was introduced by Weir et al. [29] in 2009. The intuition behind PCFG is that passwords consist of independent template structures and each structure has different terminals. The probability of password is the probability of its structures multiplied by those of its terminals. For instance, "rockyou123" can be divided into two structures "L7", "D3" and "rockyou", "123" are the terminals of those structures. The terminals' probability of Digits and Special chars are obtained from the training set and those belong to Letters are obtained from natural language dictionary. Li et al. [17] improved the capacity of generalization to Chinese password databases by introducing Pinyin into the attack dictionary. [12] added keyboard patterns and multi-word patterns to the context-free grammars. However, traditional PCFG models as mentioned above use equal-weight dictionary to generate "L" field, so the actual distribution of passwords cannot be reflected. Ma et al. [19] experimentally proved that counting the terminals' frequencies of letters from the training set can improve guessing.

Markov Model. Markov model is the dominant approach for modeling language, and was first introduced into the area of password guessing in [23]. The core concept of Markov model is to predict the next character based on previous characters. The length of context characters used to predict the following character is called *order*. There are many variants of Markov models developed for password guessing [3,15]. Castelluccia et al. [3] proposed to use Markov models for evaluating password strengths. Ma et al. [19] concluded that, through empirical analysis, markov model was better suited for estimating password probability. They proposed end-symbol normalization and Laplace smoothing to improve the Markov model. An end-symbol normalization is a normalization approach that appends an end symbol c_e to every password so that the probabilities assigned to all passwords will add up to 1. Markov model with higher-order can utilize more contextual information for generating passwords, but it may lead to overfitting. Laplace smoothing is a kind of technique to alleviate overfitting, which smoothes the probabilities of passwords by adding δ to the count of each substring. We use markov model with end-symbol normalization and Laplace smoothing as another baseline.

Neural Network Model. The neural network is a computational model that mimics the structure and function of biological neural network which is broadly used to estimate or approximate functions. The neural network has made great achievements in the field of Natural Language Processing (NLP). Markov models can only utilize fixed-length context, while a long short-term memory (LSTM) network [11] can store the features learnt long ago. However, nobody had used a neural network model for password guessing until Melicher et al. [20] used LSTM network to extract passwords' feature and make predictions. Although the result was impressive, Melicher evaluated the result with restricted structures and limited data, so the result cannot be considered general [21]. Similar to Melicher, Xu et al. [30] also used a LSTM network to guess passwords, but the guess number was set to 10^{10} thus lack of comprehensive evaluations. Hitaj et al. [10] first introduced Generative Adversarial Networks (GAN) to password guessing, but their model required more guessing attempts to catch up with LSTM-based model. Liu et al. [18] combined PCFG rule with LSTM network and showed great improvement. However, they only tested their model at maximum guess number of 10^{12}. In trawling offline guessing scenario, the maximum of guess number is around 10^{16}, so the compare might not be convincing.

2.2 Language Modeling

Language modeling could be a fundamental task in natural language processing. Given a sequential data $x_{1:T} = \{x_1, x_2, \ldots, x_T\}$, the goal is to predict the joint probability $P(x_{1:T})$ which can be factorized as:

$$P(x_{1:T}) = P(x_1)P(x_2|x_1)P(x_3|x_2, x_1) \cdots P(x_T|x_{T-1} \ldots x_1).$$

Traditional N-gram language models use Markov assumption to simplify this complex conditional probability $P(x_T|x_{T-1} \ldots x_1)$ to $P(x_T|x_{T-1} \ldots x_{T-N})$ where N called *order*. The major drawback of traditional N-gram language models is the sparsity, which makes model provide imprecise probability estimation even with several smoothing techniques. Recurrent neural network (RNN) has shown its capacity in modeling sequential data, [16,21,32] used RNN-based models and achieved state-of-the-art results on various benchmarks. Since passwords can be viewed as short natural language, it's reasonable to apply advanced language modeling techniques to password guessing.

Perplexity. We need a metric to justify different language models' performance, *perplexity* is the most wildly used method. Perplexity is closely related to the joint probability $P(x_{1:T})$ and is given by:

$$PP(x_{1:T}) = P(x_{1:T})^{-\frac{1}{N}} = \sqrt[N]{\frac{1}{P(x_{1:T})}}$$

A well-performed model should assign low perplexity to passwords in test set. Calculating perplexity will only cost little time and is easy to parallel, however, the perplexity of password is infinity if the joint probability of password equal to 0, thus perplexity is applicable only for those models that assign a non-zero probability to each password. Due to this limitation, we only compare RNN-based models' perplexity.

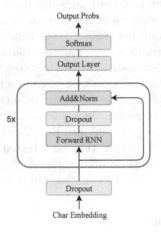

Fig. 1. The architecture of our neural network model.

3   Modeling Password with Neural Network

RNN-based models have shown great capacity in modeling neural language. Compared with statistical models, they are more robust and flexible because of their ability in extracting features. Beside the RNN model, several techniques have been applied to language modeling and might be helpful to guess passwords.

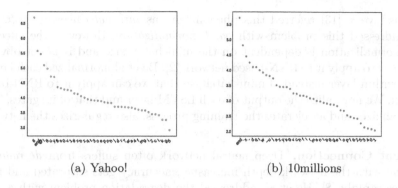

(a) Yahoo!   (b) 10millions

Fig. 2. The L_2 norm of output layer's weight. *end* means a specific token we add to each password's end.

3.1 Extended Deep LSTM Network

Mass of different experiments as Melicher et al. tested to verify their work, the base structure of the network was too simple and still had great potential for improvement. They merely stacked three LSTM layers with two fully connected layers. Although a deep neural network always works better than a wide but shallow neural network, stacking more layers onto a shallow neural network directly will undermine its performance because a plain deep neural network is hard to optimize [8]. Therefore, we craft the architecture of our model with a series of tricks improving the performance.

Normalize Output Layer's Weight. It's well-known that words in natural language corpus obey *the Zipf's Law*, that is, the frequencies of words are closely related to its rank. Similarly, different characters in passwords have different frequencies and the distribution is far away from a uniform distribution. Since we are doing a multi-step classification task, we would like to investigate the impact of this skewed distribution. Notice that the output layer is actually a linear transformation followed by a softmax function, denoting the output layer's weight as $W^{D \times V}$ where D is the output feature dimensionality and V is the vocabulary size, if we view each column of W as each character's vectorized representation, we can investigate the L_2 norm of each column. We train a LSTM network on Yahoo! and 10 millions, then plot the L_2 norm according to each column of output layer's weight, and the result is shown in Fig. 2, the L_2 norm also exhibits Zipf-like property. Recalling that there is a positive correlation between probability $P(c)$ and dot product $f \cdot w_c = \|f\| \|w_c\| \cos \theta$, characters with larger L_2 norm will get larger probability. We should diminish the impact of L_2 norm to get better feature representation f, a straightforward way is to normalize all characters' norm to 1, so that all characters are treated equally.

Layer Normalization. When networks going deep, they are hard to train because the distribution of each layer's inputs varies with the parameters of the previous layers. [13] referred this phenomenon as *internal covariate shift*, and they addressed this problem with *batch normalization*. However, the effect of batch normalization is dependent on the mini-batch size and it is not obvious about how to apply it to RNN-based network [2]. Ba et al. normalized each layer's inputs within layer instead of mini-batch, so that we can apply it to RNN-based network. We normalize the output of each LSTM layer and that of its gates. This trick stabilizes and accelerates the training process, also regularizes the network.

Shortcut Connection. Deep neural network often suffers from *degradation* problem: with the network depth increasing, accuracy gets saturated and then degrades rapidly [8]. He et al. addressed the degradation problem with a *deep residual learning* framework where layers directly connect with each other. The intuition behind the shortcut connection is that instead of hoping each layer directly fit a desired underlying mapping $\mathcal{H}(x)$, these layers are expected to fit a residual mapping $\mathcal{F}(x) = \mathcal{H}(x) - x$, enabling training a deep neural network. We add each layer's input to its activated output, this shortcut connection allows gradients to flow smoothly between layers.

Table 1. Information of leaked dataset

Name	Language	Number
Myspace	English	37144
phpbBB	English	184389
RockYou	English	14344391
Yahoo!	English	5376849
10 millions	English	10000000
clixsense	English	1628894

Table 2. Classification accuracy

(a) Training on phpBB	Myspace	Yahoo!	RockYou
bidirectional	57.75%	48.85%	50.79%
unidirectional	47.16%	38.64%	40.38%

(b) Training on RockYou	Myspace	Yahoo!	phpBB
bidirectional	68.40%	52.42%	59.60%
unidirectional	49.93%	38.92%	46.10%

Dropout. Deep neural networks with massive parameters are easy to overfit on training set. Hinton et al. [26] proposed *dropout* technique to prevent neural network from overfitting by randomly droping some connections between inputs and outputs. This approach forces network to learn robust features independent on specific units. We not only add dropout between LSTM layers but also employ dropout for the embedding layer [7]. Applying dropout to embedding layer can be quite different from the standard approach, while a special character will disappear within a single forward pass. This can be viewed as randomly delete some characters in a password, thus makes network robust. This simple approach yields good performance.

Control Output's Entropy. As different password sets may have different password policy, the training set distribution may vary from the test set. This means that we are overfitting on train set to some degree, so how to relieve this overfitting problem without suitable training set? An alternative way is to use a hyper-parameter T called *temperature* to control output's entropy. We denote the output layer's output logit as $Z = \{z_1, z_2, \ldots z_V\}$, the normalized probability is given by:

$$P(c) = \frac{e^{z_c/T}}{\sum_{i=1}^{V} e^{z_i/T}} \tag{1}$$

The different between Eq. 1 and standard softmax is that logit is divided by the temperature T. If $T \to 0$, $P(c)$ is approaching to an one-hot distribution with very low entropy, and if $T \to \infty$, $P(c)$ is approaching to an uniform distribution with high entropy, in other words, higher T correspond to higher entropy. So if the training set's policy is very different from the test set's, we should choose a higher T to get a smoother output distribution. By changing the temperature T, we can control the output's entropy, so that we can adjust to different password policies.

Combining these techniques, we build a deep neural network that is shown in Fig. 1. This model consists of five LSTM layers and one output layer. When generating passwords, the network takes the previous state s_{t-1} and character a_{t-1} as inputs in each time step t, outputs the probability of the next character by:

$$s_t = \text{MultiLSTM}(s_{t-1}, e_{a_{t-1}}), \tag{2}$$

$$g_t = \text{softmax}(\text{MLP}(s_t)/T), \tag{3}$$

$$p(a_t) \sim g_t. \tag{4}$$

Where $e_{a_{t-1}}$ is the embedding of the previous character, MultiLSTM means multi-layers LSTM transformation with layer normalization and shortcut connection, MLP denotes the output layer, and g_t is a distribution over alphabets from where the tth step's output character a_t is sampled. This deep neural network model converges much faster and guesses passwords more efficiently than Melicher's shallow model.

3.2   Improved with Bidirectional Language Model

Markov and neural network models use left-to-right unidirectional language model to model passwords. It is a natural approach since human always generate passwords from left to right. A Transformer encoder, modeling language based on jointly conditioned on both left and right context in all layers, is superior to the traditional model [5]. However, it can't provide normalized probability estimation for one passwords, So we need to find an alternative way to take advantage of the bidirectional model. A straightforward way is *knowledge distillation* [9, 27].

Bidirectional Language Model. Standard language models are unidirectional, which limits the choice of network architectures and severely restricts the ability of network to represent language. RNN-based model has provided a very elegant way of dealing with time sequential data that embodies correlations between data points. However, unidirectional language model can only use the information of tokens preceding the current token to represent it, while the future information also contribute to modeling the password. Many literatures improved the effect by bidirectional modeling the existing models, and some of them even obtained state-of-the-art results.

Transformer [28] is a model architecture relying entirely on an attention mechanism to draw global dependencies between input and output. It beats CNN and RNN-based models in Neural Machine Translation (NMT), Question Answering (QA), and other NLP tasks both in efficiency and performance. Devlin et al. [5] proposed a new language representation model called Bidirectional Encoder Representations from Transformer (BERT), which obtains new state-of-the-art results on eleven NLP tasks. Essentially speaking, BERT is just the implementation of Transformer under the bidirectional language model, which further proves the fact that bidirectional language models perform better than unidirectional models. BERT addresses the unidirectional constraints in standard language model by proposing a new objective, the "masked language model" (MLM), that trains the bidirectional model by randomly masking some percentages of the input characters and then predicting those masked characters based on their context. For instance, a password "password123" becomes "pass[mask]ord[mask]23" after masking, and the model is required to predict "w" based on the context of the first "[mask]" and predict "1" based on the context of the second "[mask]". This will force the model to involve rich contextual information. We leverage BERT to extract the characteristic representation of passwords, and the knowledge within is transferred into our password guessing model through knowledge distillation.

Knowledge Distillation. In an abstract sense, knowledge is a learned mapping from input vectors to output vectors [9]. In particular, when processing the language modeling task, the knowledge is the semantics contained in sequences. Knowledge distillation is a form of transfer learning, that uses a well-trained model as a teacher to train other child models by the predictions of the teacher model. The posterior probabilities (softmax output) generated by the teacher model are called "soft targets" while the one-hot targets used in traditional training objective are called "hard targets". In general, the teacher model is more complex and carefully trained (with exceptions, of course, such as [27]), so soft targets contain a lot of information in addition to pointing out the right categories. For example, the posterior probabilities generated by the teacher model such as $[0.08, 0.9, 0.02]$ preserve the rank information for non-target class, which indicates the second class is more similar to the first class than the third. However, even if the teacher model is well trained, its output is still not as discriminating as one-hot targets, thus the student model should be guided by both.

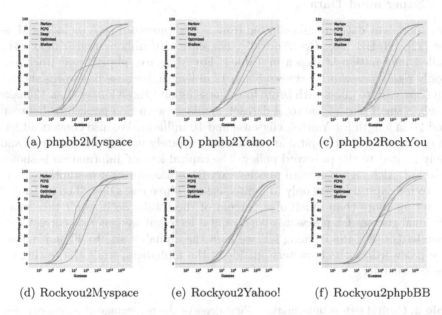

| (a) phpbb2Myspace | (b) phpbb2Yahoo! | (c) phpbb2RockYou |

| (d) Rockyou2Myspace | (e) Rockyou2Yahoo! | (f) Rockyou2phpbBB |

Fig. 3. Cross-site tests. *Markov* denotes the Markov model, *PCFG* denotes the PCFG model, *Shallow* denotes the shallow neural network model, *Deep* denotes our proposed deep neural network model and *Optimized* denotes our proposed deep neural network model optimized by the bidirectional language model.

In our work, BERT bidirectional language model introduced above is used as a teacher model to tutor and improve our crafted unidirectional language model. During the training process, the unidirectional model is not only guided by original one-hot deterministic targets, but also encouraged to minimize the Kullback-Leibler divergence between its softmax outputs and the soft targets generated by the bidirectional model. The objective function is given by:

$$\mathcal{L}(\theta) = \alpha \mathcal{L}_{\mathcal{S}}(\theta) + (1 - \alpha)\mathcal{L}_{\mathcal{H}}(\theta). \tag{5}$$

Where $\mathcal{L}_{\mathcal{H}}(\theta)$ is the cross-entropy between softmax outputs and one-hot target, $\mathcal{L}_{\mathcal{S}}(\theta)$ is the Kullback-Leibler divergence between softmax outputs and the soft targets, α is a hyper-parameter that makes a trade off between two functions.

4 Experiment and Evaluation

We perform a series of experiments to test our deep neural network model and compare it to state-of-the-art password guessing models. In this section, we first briefly describe our training and testing setting and then evaluate the results of our experiments.

4.1 Experiment Data

Our experiment data are all collected from leaked password sets, including Myspace [22], phpBB [24], RockYou [25], clixsense, 10 millions and Yahoo! [31], detailed information is shown in Table 1. For Myspace, phpBB and RockYou, we only retain passwords between 6 and 12 in length, because passwords shorter than 6 are easy to guess with brute force guessing and those longer than 12 make up only a small part of the total dataset, similarly we retain passwords between 6 and 20 in length for Yahoo!, clixsense and 10 millions. We also convert all letters to lowercase since capital letters are only a rarely part of all characters and closely related to the password policy. The capital letters' information is shown in Table 3. Although password policies vary from password set to another, users tend to use capital letters only in limited cases (Three cases described in Table 3 account for more than ninety-five percent of the total). So it won't take much additional guesses for passwords with capital letters if we generate correct lowercase letters. For the training set, we keep the alphabet size to 40 and remove those passwords with characters outside of the alphabets, while the testing set does not change.

Table 3. Capital letters' information. *First* denotes the percentage of passwords' first letter is in uppercase, *Last* denotes the percentage of passwords' last letter is in uppercase, *Fully* means the percentage of passwords whose all letters are in uppercase, *Total* corresponds to the percentage of passwords with capital letters, and *Total** corresponds to the percentage of all letters that are capitalized.

	Myspace	phpbBB	RockYou	Yahoo!
First	44.86%	65.45%	41.05%	79.16%
Last	2.04%	8.07%	1.96%	4.98%
Fully	52.27%	20.50%	55.87%	12.12%
Total	6.17%	8.15%	5.86%	27.90%
Total*	3.67%	3.91%	4.37%	9.48%

4.2 Evaluation

For the PCFG model, we follow [19] that all information are obtained from the training set. For the Markov model, we use 5-gram model for RockYou and phpBB, 4-gram model for Yahoo and 10 millions. Both models with end-symbol normalization and Laplace smoothing. For the shallow neural network model, we stack two fully-connected layer onto three LSTM layers. Our deep neural network model consists of two fully-connected layer and five LSTM layers, with techniques including dropout, layer normalization and shortcut connection. We prepare both cross-site tests and one-site tests for those five models to comprehensively evaluate their performance. The results are simulated with the Monte Carlo method [4]. We generate one million random passwords at a time and repeat the generating process ten times to provide accurate estimations.

The Capacity of the Bidirectional Model. Firstly, we want to see the capacity of the bidirectional model since it involves rich information. So we perform a classification task for both bidirectional and unidirectional models to compare their performance. We randomly mask some characters for each password in the testing set, and then the bidirectional model is excepted to predict those masked characters based on its bidirectional context while the unidirectional model will predict those based on its previous context. We use classification accuracy as the metric, and the result is shown in Table 2. It is clear that the bidirectional model beats the unidirectional model with a significant margin in every situation. We also find that the bidirectional model uses data more efficiently than the unidirectional model since when the training set changes from a small dataset phpBB to a large dataset RockYou, the accuracy of the unidirectional model improves 2.77% on Myspace and 0.28% on Yahoo!, while the improvement of the bidirectional model is 10.65% and 3.57% respectively.

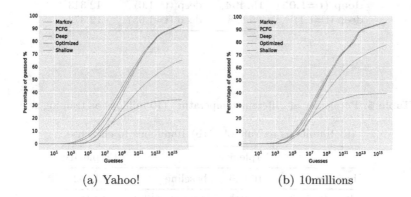

(a) Yahoo!   (b) 10millions

Fig. 4. One-site tests

Cross-Set Tests. We first evaluate those model on cross-set tests, this means that the training sets and test sets are from different password sets.

We choose a medium dataset phpBB and a large dataset Rockyou as our training sets, the result is shown in Fig. 3. When training on phpBB, the performance of statistic models are barely efficient in general, only the PCFG model outperforms shallow model before at around 10^{10} guesses when testing on Myspace, their performance on Yahoo! and Rockyou are much weaker than RNN-based models. Our proposed models are superior to other models with a huge margin, since phpBB is a medium dataset, and statistic models estimate probability by counting, which requires large training set to provide accurate results, our models show great robustness. When training on Rockyou, the statistic models improve much more than on phpBB. In Fig. 3(d) when testing on Myspace, our proposed models outperform the statistic model beginning at around 10^{11} guesses with a slender margin. In Fig. 3(e) and (f) when testing on Yahoo! and phpBB, our proposed models beat the PCFG model beginning at around 10^8 guesses and always outperforms the Markov model. The shallow model, however, underperforms the statistic models in many cases. This illustrates the effect of the techniques we use.

Table 4. Perplexity of different temperature (Yahoo! as training set)

(a) Yahoo! to 10millions		(b) Yahoo! to clixsense	
	Perplexity		Perplexity
baseline	16.014	baseline	14.048
deep (t=0.95)	15.565	deep (t=0.9)	12.316
deep (t=1.0)	15.503	**deep (t=0.95)**	**12.289**
deep (t=1.05)	**15.494**	deep (t=1.0)	12.313
deep (t=1.1)	15.528	deep (t=1.05)	12.373

Table 5. Perplexity of different temperature (10 millions as training set)

(a) 10millions to Yahoo!		(b) 10millions to clixsense	
	Perplexity		Perplexity
baseline	16.646	baseline	14.432
deep (t=0.95)	16.247	deep (t=0.95)	13.157
deep (t=1.0)	15.934	deep (t=1.0)	12.980
deep (t=1.05)	15.712	deep (t=1.05)	12.868
deep (t=1.1)	15.562	deep (t=1.1)	12.808
deep (t=1.15)	15.470	**deep (t=1.15)**	**12.792**
deep (t=1.2)	**15.425**	deep (t=1.2)	12.808

One-Site Tests. We then evaluate those models on one-site tests, this means that training and test sets come from a same password dataset (e.g., 80% for training and 20% for testing), as different websites may have different requirements for password formats. Guessing the passwords of a completely different websites is sometimes difficult to justify.

We test those models on Yahoo! and 10 millions which is longer and more complex than Myspace, phpBB and RockYou. Notice that the Markov model we use here is 4-gram instead of 5-gram because we find that 5-gram dictionary is extremely sparse and smoothing techniques are nearly out of work. The results are shown in Fig. 4, all the network based models outperform these statistic models, while in cross-site tests, the shallow network model underperforms statistic models in many cases. This means that the shallow network model is more likely to overfits. Our proposed model, even though with more parameters, is more general, supporting the effectiveness of techniques we use. We also notice that statistic models' performance dropped compare to cross-site tests, it's mainly because Yahoo! and 10 millions are more complex and longer passwords datasets than Myspace, phpBB and RockYou, while the performance of RNN-based models is consistent.

Impact of Password Policy. As we have mentioned above, if training set have different password policy from test set we may need a smooth output distribution, a hyper-parameter T is introduced to control the output's entropy. We use perplexity to evaluate result because Monte Carlo method is time-consuming, result is shown in Tables 4 and 5, baseline denotes shallow network model. It is clear that when we use 10 millions as training set, increasing T will directly decrease perplexity. Recalling that higher T corresponds to higher entropy, since 10 millions have quite different password policy from Yahoo! and clixsense, we could increase T to tackle the overfitting problem when the target set is different from the training set.

Those experiments show that the performance of statistic models heavily rely on size of training set and is not good at dealing complex passwords. RNN architecture shows potential but fall short in many cases, the techniques we used strongly improve RNN-based models' performance. It is worth noting that when the training set changes from phpBB to RockYou, the accuracy of the bidirectional model improves much more than the unidirectional model, but such improvement does not reflect in the guess-number graph, so the potential of the bidirectional model is not yet fully realized.

5   Conclusion

This paper describes how to build a deep neural network to model and guess human-chosen passwords and how to improve it with a bidirectional language model. We show that neural network based models are effective in guessing based on large dataset, and can be largely improved by many techniques such as layer normalization. Our proposed models could guess passwords more effective than the state-of-the-art models. Comparing with the PCFG and Markov model, our proposed models outperform them in both cross-site tests and one-site test. A simple trick called temperature is introduced to adjust from different password policy. We also show that the bidirectional language model is a more efficient way to model passwords comparing with left-to-right language model used in the Markov and neural network models. We use a simple technique called knowledge distillation to improve the performance of our deep neural network model and the improvement is significant at guesses of a low number yet not obvious in general. However, we believe in the potential of the bidirectional language model in password guessing, once we find a more applicable approach than knowledge distillation we would get a more powerful model, and we remain this in future works.

Acknowledgment. The authors are grateful to the anonymous reviewers for their constructive comments. This work was supported in part by the National Natural Science Foundation of China under Grant 61702399 and Grant 61772291 and Grant 61972215 in part by the Natural Science Foundation of Tianjin, China, under Grant 17JCZDJC30500.

References

1. John the ripper (1996). https://www.openwall.com/john/
2. Ba, J.L., Kiros, J.R., Hinton, G.E.: Layer normalization. arXiv preprint arXiv:1607.06450 (2016)
3. Castelluccia, C., Dürmuth, M., Perito, D.: Adaptive password-strength meters from Markov models. In: NDSS (2012)
4. Dell'Amico, M., Filippone, M.: Monte carlo strength evaluation: fast and reliable password checking. In: Proceedings of the 22nd ACM SIGSAC Conference on Computer and Communications Security, pp. 158–169. ACM (2015)
5. Devlin, J., Chang, M.W., Lee, K., Toutanova, K.: BERT: pre-training of deep bidirectional transformers for language understanding. arXiv preprint arXiv:1810.04805 (2018)
6. Dürmuth, M., Angelstorf, F., Castelluccia, C., Perito, D., Chaabane, A.: OMEN: faster password guessing using an ordered Markov enumerator. In: Piessens, F., Caballero, J., Bielova, N. (eds.) ESSoS 2015. LNCS, vol. 8978, pp. 119–132. Springer, Cham (2015). https://doi.org/10.1007/978-3-319-15618-7_10
7. Gal, Y., Ghahramani, Z.: A theoretically grounded application of dropout in recurrent neural networks. In: Advances in Neural Information Processing Systems, pp. 1019–1027 (2016)
8. He, K., Zhang, X., Ren, S., Sun, J.: Deep residual learning for image recognition. In: Proceedings of the IEEE Conference on Computer Vision and Pattern Recognition, pp. 770–778 (2016)
9. Hinton, G., Vinyals, O., Dean, J.: Distilling the knowledge in a neural network. arXiv preprint arXiv:1503.02531 (2015)
10. Hitaj, B., Gasti, P., Ateniese, G., Perez-Cruz, F.: PassGAN: a deep learning approach for password guessing. In: Deng, R.H., Gauthier-Umaña, V., Ochoa, M., Yung, M. (eds.) ACNS 2019. LNCS, vol. 11464, pp. 217–237. Springer, Cham (2019). https://doi.org/10.1007/978-3-030-21568-2_11

11. Hochreiter, S., Schmidhuber, J.: Long short-term memory. Neural Comput. **9**, 1735–1780 (1996)
12. Houshmand, S., Aggarwal, S., Flood, R.: Next gen PCFG password cracking. IEEE Trans. Inf. Forensics Secur. **10**(8), 1776–1791 (2015)
13. Ioffe, S., Szegedy, C.: Batch normalization: accelerating deep network training by reducing internal covariate shift. arXiv preprint arXiv:1502.03167 (2015)
14. Hashcat (2009). https://hashcat.net/oclhashcat/
15. Kelley, P.G., et al.: Guess again (and again and again): measuring password strength by simulating password-cracking algorithms. In: 2012 IEEE Symposium on Security and Privacy (SP), pp. 523–537. IEEE (2012)
16. Krause, B., Kahembwe, E., Murray, I., Renals, S.: Dynamic evaluation of neural sequence models. arXiv preprint arXiv:1709.07432 (2017)
17. Li, Z., Han, W., Xu, W.: A large-scale empirical analysis of chinese web passwords. In: USENIX Security Symposium, pp. 559–574 (2014)
18. Liu, Y., et al.: GENPass: a general deep learning model for password guessing with PCFG rules and adversarial generation. In: 2018 IEEE International Conference on Communications (ICC), pp. 1–6. IEEE (2018)
19. Ma, J., Yang, W., Luo, M., Li, N.: A study of probabilistic password models. In: 2014 IEEE Symposium on Security and Privacy (SP), pp. 689–704. IEEE (2014)
20. Melicher, W., et al.: Fast, lean, and accurate: modeling password guessability using neural networks. In: USENIX Security Symposium, pp. 175–191 (2016)
21. Merity, S., Keskar, N.S., Socher, R.: Regularizing and optimizing LSTM language models. arXiv preprint arXiv:1708.02182 (2017)
22. Myspace. https://www.myspace.com/
23. Narayanan, A., Shmatikov, V.: Fast dictionary attacks on passwords using time-space tradeoff. In: Proceedings of the 12th ACM Conference on Computer and Communications Security, pp. 364–372. ACM (2005)
24. phpBB. https://www.phpbb.com/
25. RockYou. https://www.rockyou.com/
26. Srivastava, N., Hinton, G., Krizhevsky, A., Sutskever, I., Salakhutdinov, R.: Dropout: a simple way to prevent neural networks from overfitting. J. Mach. Learn. Res. **15**(1), 1929–1958 (2014)
27. Tang, Z., Wang, D., Zhang, Z.: Recurrent neural network training with dark knowledge transfer. In: 2016 IEEE International Conference on Acoustics, Speech and Signal Processing (ICASSP), pp. 5900–5904. IEEE (2016)
28. Vaswani, A., et al.: Attention is all you need. In: Advances in Neural Information Processing Systems, pp. 5998–6008 (2017)
29. Weir, M., Aggarwal, S., De Medeiros, B., Glodek, B.: Password cracking using probabilistic context-free grammars. In: 2009 30th IEEE Symposium on Security and Privacy, pp. 391–405. IEEE (2009)
30. Xu, L., et al.: Password guessing based on LSTM recurrent neural networks. In: 2017 IEEE International Conference on Computational Science and Engineering (CSE) and Embedded and Ubiquitous Computing (EUC), vol. 1, pp. 785–788. IEEE (2017)
31. Yahoo!. https://www.yahoo.com/
32. Yang, Z., Dai, Z., Salakhutdinov, R., Cohen, W.W.: Breaking the softmax bottleneck: a high-rank RNN language model. arXiv preprint arXiv:1711.03953 (2017)

RETRACTED CHAPTER: A Cooperative Placement Method for Machine Learning Workflows and Meteorological Big Data Security Protection in Cloud Computing

Xinzhao Jiang, Wei Kong, Xin Jin, and Jian Shen[✉]

School of Computer and Software,
Nanjing University of Information Science and Technology,
Nanjing 210044, China
s_shenjian@126.com

Abstract. Cloud computing has proven to be a powerful paradigm in both academia and industry. A variety of meteorological applications using machine learning modeled as the workflows and meteorological big data have been accommodated in the meteorological cloud infrastructure. However, it still faces challenges to guarantee the execution enciency of the meteorological machine-learning workflows and avoid the privacy leakage of the datasets in a semi-trusted cloud. To tackle this challenge, a collaborative placement method (CPM) and a two-factor-based protection mechanism for machine-learning workflows and big data security protection is proposed. Technically fat-tree topology is leveraged to institute the meteorological cloud infrastructure. Then, the non-dominated sorting differential evolution (NSDE) technique is employed to realize joint optimization of data access time, energy efficiency and load balance. In terms of security protection, the proposed mechanism allows data owners (DOs) to send encrypted data to users through meteorological cloud server (MCS). The DOs are required to formulate access policy and perform cipher-text-policy attribute-based encryption (CP-ABE) on data. In order to decrypt, the users need to possess two factors that a secret key and a security device (e.g., a sensor card in meteorological application). The ciphertext can be decrypted if and only if the user gathers the secret key and the security device at the same time. Eventually, the experiment evaluates the performance of CPM.

Keywords: Meteorological big data · CPM ·
Machine-learning workflows · Load balancing · Two-factor protection ·
CP-ABE

1 Introduction

With the continuous accumulation of meteorological data, the computational complexity of performing the meteorological applications is growing rapidly. To

The original version of this chapter was retracted: The retraction note to this chapter is available at https://doi.org/10.1007/978-3-030-30619-9_28

ensure their performance, meteorological applications and the collected data from automatic meteorological observation station are often offloaded to the cloud for accommodation [1,2]. Traditionally, vast amounts of historical meteorological data are analyzed by the meteorological applications (e.g., weather prediction and hazard assessment) to obtain the valuable information. Nevertheless, due to the enormous volume and complexity of meteorological big data, the implementation efficiency of applications employing pure data analysis is greatly degraded, which is not conducive to improve the service quality of these applications. Fortunately, as an effective technology, machine learning improves the execution efficiency of meteorological applications by feeding several parameters into the single learning model directly, which could theoretically improve the accuracy of meteorological services by analyzing the abundant meteorological data [3,4]. In addition, there has been interest in applying workflow technology to build multiple meteorological services based on machine learning into automatic application instances. The meteorological machine-learning application is divided into multiple sub-tasks, and each node in the workflow has been responsible for every link of machine learning.

However, to improve the implementation performance of such meteorological machine-learning workflows, the internal relations between the massive meteorological data and the workflows requires to be analyzed. Accordingly, in order to respond to the access requests from geographically distributed machine-learning workflows in cloud infrastructure [5,6], it is particularly important to rationally distribute meteorological big data to individual storage nodes. However, the implementation performance of all the workflows can hardly be guaranteed just by distributively placing the data sets. Thus, it is of great importance for the meteorological department and the cloud service providers to properly schedule all machine-learning workflows and meteorological big data (including the workflow input data and generated intermediate data) to the cloud infrastructure, with the aim of reducing the average data access time for the machine-learning workflows [7,8]. Concomitantly, the energy consumption of cloud data centers is also rapidly increasing to accommodate the ever-increasing applications and data [9], especially the power generated by massive data transmission during the execution of workflow applications [10]. Currently, energy optimization has limited the sustainable development of cloud services to some extent, and become a primary problem with cloud data centers [11,12]. On the other hand, to guarantee the service quality, the stability and availability of cloud data centers also receives growing attention [13,14]. Load balance can enhance the reliability of the cloud data centers - a key measure for ensuring the service performance and minimize the probability of overloading or even downtime of a single node [15]. Therefore, while designing the placement method for the meteorological cloud, the energy consumption and load balance metrics should be considered.

Furthermore, along with the increasing scope of meteorological services, there also exists the privacy-leaking problem, since meteorological cloud may often involve confidential data [16]. When acquiring important public resources, for example, the staffs at the meteorological department read confidential documents (e.g., meteorological observation data), security device and secret key are essential for users. To prevent data being stolen, researchers mostly design single public key encryption schemes [17,18]. The key is generally stored in a private device or a trusted third party (TTP). If there is no malicious attackers, these secret key storage schemes are safe enough. Unfortunately, when being accessed with other equipment through the Internet, private devices and TTP are most likely to be attacked by illegal hackers, resulting in the secret key being stolen. But for all these, the users know nothing. In addition, let's consider the following two real-life work occasion: personal computers that store a user's secret key may be used by others in observatory, laboratories and offices, public computers in meteorological department that record user login information will be shared by different users. Under these circumstances, the secret keys are able to be compromised by some malicious attackers who use technical or non technical means. Therefore, single secret key encryption scheme no longer satisfies certain security requirements in meteorological applications, and the two-factor data protection mechanism arises at the historic moment [19].

With these observations, it remains challenging to achieve energy saving, balanced load distribution, high data acquisition efficiency for the implementation of machine-learning workflows and security protection in cloud environment. For replying this challenge, a collaborative placement method, called CPM, for machine-learning workflows and two-factor mechanism with security preservation are designed. Specifically, the key contributions are as follows.

- Fat-tree topology is introduced to institute the meteorological cloud infrastructure.
- The Non-Dominated Sorting Differential Evolution (NSDE) algorithm is leveraged to achieve the balanced placement strategies.
- Simple Additive Weighting (SAW) and Multiple Criteria Decision Making (MDCM) are employed to identify the most balanced data placement strategy.
- A two-factor-based data protection mechanism that utilizes CP-ABE and public key encryption is proposed.

2   Preliminary Knowledge

First of all, we introduce a fat-tree based meteorological cloud framework. Then, we manage in detail a real-world instance of the meteorological machine-learning workflows. Finally, we introduce the CP-ABE framework.

2.1   A Fat-Tree Based Meteorological Cloud Framework

Fat-tree topology is one of the most famous techniques to construct the cloud infrastructure, which is composed of three layers, including core layer, aggregation layer and edge layer [20]. The switches in the aggregation layer and edge layer form multiple pods to efficiently manage the switches and the physical nodes in the data center. Thus, fat-tree topology is employed to establish the meteorological cloud infrastructure, which provides high throughput transmission service for MCS' to ensure that the non-blocking network communication. In addition, there are multiple parallel paths between any two physical nodes, so the fault tolerance of network also performs good. Taking advantage of the fat-tree network, meteorological department distributes massive meteorological big data to MCS.

Figure 1 illustrates a fat-tree based MCS framework. In this framework, Pod i $(i = 0, 1, 2, \ldots, Z-1)$ manages all the physical nodes of the subordinate meteorological center. Specially, the Pod 0 mainly manages the compute nodes and storage nodes in the demilitarized zone (DMZ) and the lightning protection center. The Pod 1 mainly manages all the compute nodes and storage nodes in the information center which are the main master nodes for the MCS infrastructure.

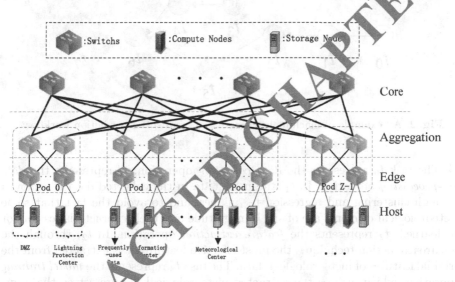

Fig. 1. A fat-tree based MCS framework

2.2 Machine Learning-Based Meteorological Workflow

Benefit from the workflow technology, the meteorological applications can be modeled as a variety of meteorological workflows, and the operations in a meteorological application are modeled as a series of tasks with prioritized relationships. Generally, the meteorological workflows mainly include the meteorological data Extract-Transform-Load (ETL) workflow, the special production workflow, the element forecasting workflow. However, for those element forecasting workflows that require high accuracy of forecasting, machine learning technology, with strong learning ability and predictive ability, gradually replaces some traditional forecasting methods, which is introduced into the process of meteorological element forecasting [21], e.g., short-term lightning forecasting, air pollution forecasting, precipitation forecasting, temperature forecasting, wind speed forecasting.

In addition, to improve the execution efficiency, the meteorological machine-learning workflows which consume large amounts of resources are offloaded to the MCS for accommodation. Figure 2 shows an example of a typical machine-learning workflow for wind speed prediction. In this workflow, all the operations are abstracted as a series of tasks, i.e., t_0 to t_7. Among them, the white nodes are the common tasks similar to those in traditional forecasting workflows, i.e., t_0, t_1, t_7. The gray nodes are the personalized machine-learning tasks, i.e., t_2, t_3, t_4, t_5, t_6. The specific description of these tasks is presented as follows.

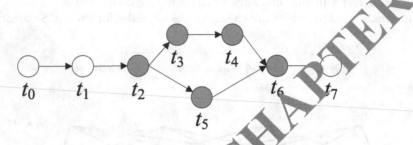

Fig. 2. An example of machine learning-based wind speed prediction workflow.

The task t_0 represents the *data collection* operation. t_1 represents the *data pre-processing* operation. In t_1, the noise data in the collected data is removed through clustering and regression techniques, and to avoid the fact that some meteorological elements are of small magnitude and their characteristics cannot be learned. t_2 represents the *feature extraction* operation. In t_2, through the feature extraction technique, the most effective feature set is extracted from the original features of meteorological data. The task t_3 represents the *model training* operation, which utilizes the extracted meteorological feature set as the input data of the "model training", and uses the "wind speed" corresponding to the feature set as the prediction result, and then trains the "wind speed prediction model" based on a large number of training samples [21]. t_4 is the *model validation* operation, which generally measures the accuracy of the model by "root mean square error". The task t_5 is the *model test* operation. To assess the generalization ability of the wind speed prediction model, t_5 tests the true prediction performance of the model by "cross-validation". The tasks t_6 and t_7 represent the *model determination* and *wind speed prediction* operation, respectively. The model with the smallest generalization error is selected as the final wind speed prediction model.

2.3   Ciphertext-Policy Attribute-Based Encryption

CP-ABE is a kind of cryptographic primitive for realizing one to many secure communication, where the DOs share data to specific users by constructing an access policy and embedding the policy into ciphertext. The most CP-ABE consists of following four algorithms.

$Setup(1^k)$. This algorithm takes a security parameter k as input. It outputs a public parameter PK and a master key MK.

$KeyGen(PK, MK, S)$. This algorithm takes public parameter PK, the master key MK and an attribute set S as input. It outputs a private key SK related to the attribute S.

$Encrypt(PK, M, \mathbb{A})$. This algorithm takes the public parameter PK, a message M and an access policy $\mathbb{A}$ as input. It outputs ciphertext CT such that only the user whose attribute set satisfies the access policy can decrypt.

$Decrypt(PK, CT, SK)$. This algorithm takes the public parameter PK, a ciphertext CT and a private key SK as input. If and only if the attribute set S of user satisfies the access policy $\mathbb{A}$, the algorithm can decrypt the message M successfully.

3   System Model and Formulation

In this section, we mainly formulate the data access model, energy consumption model, data access model, load balancing model and two-factor security protection model. Then a formalized goal function is defined.

3.1   Data Access Model

In the fat-tree network, suppose the task t_m and its required data d are placed on are v_i and v_j, respectively, then the relationship between node v_i and node v_j is presented by $\gamma_{i,j}$.

- If v_i and v_j are the same node, $\gamma_{i,j} = 0$;
- If v_i and v_j belong to the same edge switch, $\gamma_{i,j} = 1$;
- If v_i and v_j belong to the different edge switches in the same pod, $\gamma_{i,j} = 2$;
- If v_i and v_j belong to the different pods, $\gamma_{i,j} = 3$;

Assume that the number of physical nodes in meteorological fat-tree network is L, then the relationship of all nodes can be expressed as a two-dimensional array γ taking values in $\{0, 1, 2, 3\}$, and the size of the array γ is $L * L$. According to the relationship $\gamma_{i,j}$ between v_i and v_j, then the access time T_{ac} of task t_m for data $d(d \in \beta_m)$ can be expressed by

$$T_{ac} = \begin{cases} 0, & \gamma_{i,j} = 0 \\ 2 * d/B_{he}, & \gamma_{i,j} = 1 \\ 2 * (d/B_{he} + d/B_{ea}), & \gamma_{i,j} = 2 \\ 2 * (d/B_{he} + d/B_{ea} + d/B_{ac}), & \gamma_{i,j} = 3 \end{cases} \tag{1}$$

where B_{he} is the bandwidth between nodes and edge switch, B_{ea} is the bandwidth between the edge switch and the aggregation switch and B_{ac} is the bandwidth between the aggregation switch and the core switch.

The total data access time T_m of task t_m mainly includes the access time of task t_m for obtaining its required dataset β_m and the intermediate result data md_m. So the total access time T_m of task t_m is calculated by

$$T_m = \sum_{d \in \beta_m \cup md_m} T_{ac} \tag{2}$$

Then the access time T_{total} of all tasks in the meteorological application is calculated by

$$T_{total} = \sum_{m=0}^{M-1} T_m \tag{3}$$

where M is the number of tasks in the current meteorological application.

Finally, the average access time T_{avg} for all tasks is calculated by

$$T_{avg} = T_{total}/M \tag{4}$$

3.2 Energy Consumption Model

The energy due to the data extracting and accessing by the machine-learning workflows mainly refers to the energy generated by switches.

If the forwarding rate of the switch is r and the forwarding power of the switch is p, then the forwarding time t_{switch} of data d on a single switch is calculated by

$$t_{switch} = d/r \tag{5}$$

Denote the total amount of switches for v_j to access the datasets on v_i as $NS_{i,j}$. Then the energy generated by all the switches for accessing a dataset is calculated by

$$E_{switch} = NS_{i,j} * t_{switch} * p. \tag{6}$$

Consequently, the energy consumption E_m for t_m to extract all the input datasets is calculated by

$$E_m = \sum_{d \in \beta_m \cup md_m} E_{switch} \tag{7}$$

Finally, the total transmission energy consumption E generated by the switches for all the tasks is calculated by

$$E = \sum_{m=0}^{M-1} E_m \tag{8}$$

3.3   Load Balancing Model

The load balancing in the cloud is analyzed from two aspects, i.e., the load balancing of all the compute nodes and load balancing of all the storage nodes. In this paper, the load balancing metric is quantified by the variance value of the node utilization. Generally, the smaller the average utilization variance of all nodes, the more balanced the load on each node.

Assume that the size of the virtual machines required for task t_m and data d_n are vm_m and vm_n. The capacity of compute node v_i and storage node v_j are C_i and C_j, respectively. The number of compute nodes and storage nodes are set to P and Q respectively. If the compute node that hosts task t_m and the storage node for hosting data d_n are v_i and v_j, respectively, $\delta_{m,i}^{cal} = 1, \delta_{n,j}^{store} = 1$, otherwise $\delta_{m,i}^{cal} = 0, \delta_{n,j}^{store} = 0$. Finally, the utilization U_i^{cal} of the compute node v_i and the utilization U_j^{store} of the storage node v_j are calculated by

$$U_i^{cal} = \sum_{m=0}^{M-1} \delta_{m,i}^{cal} * vm_m / C_i \tag{9}$$

and

$$U_j^{store} = \sum_{n=0}^{N-1} \delta_{n,j}^{store} * vm_n / C_j \tag{10}$$

The average utilization of all compute nodes and storage nodes, denoted as $\overline{U^{cal}}$ and $\overline{U^{store}}$, respectively which are calculated by

$$\overline{U^{cal}} = \sum_{i=0}^{P-1} U_i^{cal} / P \tag{11}$$

and

$$\overline{U^{store}} = \sum_{j=0}^{Q-1} U_j^{store} / Q \tag{12}$$

Then the average utilization variance of all compute nodes and storage nodes, denoted as $\widetilde{U^{cal}}$ and $\widetilde{U^{store}}$, are calculated by

$$\widetilde{U^{cal}} = \frac{1}{P} * \sum_{i=0}^{P-1} (U_i^{cal} - \overline{U^{cal}})^2 \tag{13}$$

and

$$\widetilde{U^{store}} = \frac{1}{Q} * \sum_{j=0}^{Q-1} (U_i^{store} - \overline{U^{store}})^2 \tag{14}$$

Finally, the average utilization variance $\widetilde{U}$ of all nodes is calculated by

$$\widetilde{U} = \frac{1}{2} * (\widetilde{U^{cal}} + \widetilde{U^{store}}) \tag{15}$$

3.4   Two-Factor Security Protection Model

The whole two-factor security protection model contains four entities: central authority (CA), data owners (DOs), users and meteorological cloud server (MCS).

- CA: A CA is considered to be a entity that possesses unlimited computing and storage capacity. Meanwhile, a CA is also a trusted party, and its tasks are to generate system parameters, manage users (i.e., enrolling users: distributing the secret key to every user) and distribute security devices (sensor cards).
- DOs: DOs are owners of data to be stored in MCS. All the data is encrypted by using CP-ABE. Finally, they upload the generated ciphertext to MCS.
- Users: In meteorological applications, forecasters, analysts, collectors and other staffs in the meteorological department are users. They can download the encrypted public data from MCS. If the users want to get the data, they firstly do decrypt by using their security devices and obtain the resulting primary ciphertext, then users with specific attributes can decrypt primary ciphertext by using their secret keys.
- MCS: It is not a credible entity. Concretely, MCS is honest-but-curious, which can honestly implement the assigned tasks and return corresponding results. However, it will also do its best to collect sensitive information. Generally, MCS is regarded as a party with unlimited computing power and storage space. In this paper, DOs upload the encrypted data (primary ciphertext) to MCS, then MCS uses the public information obtained from CA to encrypt primary ciphertext, resulting in secondary ciphertex.

The two-factor security protection model consists of five algorithms. The five algorithms are described separately as follows.

Setup: $(1^k) \longrightarrow (param, msk)$. The algorithm is run by CA. A security parameter k is taken as input. The algorithm outputs public parameters $param$ and master key msk.

Keygen and Security Device Distribution: $(param, msk, S) \longrightarrow (sk_S, epk_i, esk_i)$. The algorithm is run by CA. On inputting the public parameters $param$, the master secret key msk and the attribute set S that users possess, the algorithm outputs secret key sk_S, public information epk_i, and secret information esk_i of security device.

Primary Encryption: $(param, A, m) \longrightarrow C_1$. The algorithm is run by DOs. The input includes the public parameters $param$, the data m and attribute set A. The output is the primary ciphertext C_1.

Secondary Encryption: $(param, epk_i, C_1) \longrightarrow C_2$. The algorithm is run by MCS. The public parameters, public information epk_i of security device and primary ciphertext C_1 are taken as input. The algorithm outputs secondary ciphertext C_2.

Data Decryption: $(esk_i, sk_S, C_2) \longrightarrow m$. The algorithm is run by users. The input includes secret information esk_i of security device, secret key sk_S and secondary ciphertext C_2. The output is data m.

4   Method Design

In this section, NSDE is leveraged for obtaining the balanced data placement strategies for CPM. Specifically, the placement strategies are encoded to generate an initial population. Then, the mutation, crossover, and selection operations are sequentially conducted. Based on SAW and MDCM, the best solution is output as the final placement strategy. Finally, the specific two-factor data security protection mechanism is designed.

4.1   Encoding

In the encoding phase, the collaborative placement strategies for all tasks, intermediate result data, and the input data of workflow are encoded as the real numbers. Therefore, the placement strategies for all tasks and data can be encoded as a placement strategies set $X = \{X^T, X^{MD}, X^{OD}\}$, where $X^T = \{x_0^T, x_1^T, ..., x_m^T, ..., x_{M-1}^T\}$ represents the placement strategies of M tasks. $X^{MD} = \{x_0^{MD}, x_1^{MD}, ..., x_m^{MD}, ..., x_{M-1}^{MD}\}$ and $X^{OD} = \{x_0^{OD}, x_1^{OD}, ..., x_n^{OD}, ..., x_{N-1}^{OD}\}$ represent the placement strategies of M intermediate results and N input data of the workflow, respectively. And the placement position of these data must be storage nodes that do not store historical data in cloud. At the same time, there is a correspondence between X^T and X^{MD}. For example, data x_m^{MD} is the intermediate result data generated by task x_m^T.

4.2   Objective Functions

In this constrained multi-objective optimization problem, there are three objective functions: average data access time, total energy consumption, and load balancing of each node. The smaller the objective function values are, the better the solution is. However, we need to find a suitable solution that achieves the balance of the three objective functions. The calculation process of the three objective functions is shown as follows:

Average Data Access Time: For each task in task set TS, the storage time of intermediate result and the access time of required data of each task are calculated by formula (2), and the average data access time of all tasks is calculated by formula (4).

Total Energy Consumption: For each task in task set TS, we calculate the energy consumption of switches by formulas (6) and (7). Then, we calculate the energy consumption generated by switches during the execution of all tasks by formula (8).

Load Balancing: Firstly, we calculate the load of each node by formulas (9) and (10), then we calculate the total load balance variance of all compute nodes and all storage nodes by formulas (13) and (14), respectively. Finally the average load variance of all nodes is calculated by formula (15).

4.3   NSDE-Based Accquision of Collaborative Placement Strategies

NSDE algorithm is a multi-objective optimization algorithm based on population evolution. Therefore, we first need to initialize a population.

Initialization. The initial population whose size is NP can be expressed as $X = \{X_0, X_1, ..., X_i, ..., X_{NP-1}\}$, where X_i is the i-th individual, and represents a placement strategy. Encoding an individual $X_i = \{X_i^T, X_i^{MD}, X_i^{OD}\}$ has been introduced in the *encoding* section. If the number of nodes is P, each gene $x_{i,j}$ in each individual X_i randomly takes values between 0 and $P - 1$, and finally the initial population X is generated.

Based on the initial population, NSDE begins to perform mutation, crossover, and selection operations.

Mutation. Mutation operation refers to combining the difference vector of two individuals with the third individual to generate the mutation individual.

Therefore, firstly, we randomly select three individuals X_a, X_b, and X_c in the parent population X. Then, based on the mutation factor F which is generally taken in $[0, 1]$, the mutation individual H_i is calculated as follows:

$$H_i = X_a + F * (X_b - X_c) \tag{16}$$

Finally, we can generate a mutation population $H = \{H_0, H_1, ..., H_i, ..., H_{NP-1}\}$ whose size is also NP.

Crossover. Based on the mutation population H and the parent population X, we perform the *crossover* operation to generate a crossover population.

Firstly, we randomly select a gene $H_{i,j}$ from the mutation individual H_i, and retain it to the crossover gene $R_{i,j}$. Then, according to the crossover factor CR which is also generally taken in $[0, 1]$, we select other genes from the mutation individual H_i and the parental individual X_i to form the crossover individual R_i as follows:

$$R_{i,j} = \begin{cases} H_{i,j}, \text{j} = \text{rand}(0, 2\text{M} + \text{N} - 1) || \text{rand}(0, 1) \leq \text{CR}; \\ X_{i,j}, \text{rand}(0, 1) > \text{CR}; \end{cases} \tag{17}$$

Finally, we generate the crossover population $R = \{R_0, R_1, ..., R_{NP-1}\}$ whose population size is also NP.

Selection. In the selection phase, we need to select individuals from the parent population. Therefore, firstly, the parent population X and the crossover population R are merged into a population $Y = \{Y_0, Y_1, ..., Y_i, ..., Y_{2NP-1}\}$ whose size is $2NP$. Then, we perform the *fast non-dominated sorting* and the *crowding distance calculation* operations. During performing the *fast non-dominated sorting*, the objective functions of all individuals in population Y are evaluated by formulas (4), (8) and (15). All individuals are divided into multiple dominant layers $L_i(i = 0, 1, 2, ...)$. The objective function values of all individuals in the L_i layer are better than the individuals in the L_{i+1} layer, so all individuals in the L_i layer can completely dominate all individuals in the L_{i+1} layer. However, we still need to check whether each individual meets the privacy preservation constraint by formula (17). Only the individuals which meet the privacy preservation in the L_i layer are more likely to be retained to the next generation population than the individuals in the L_{i+1} layer. Furthermore, in the same dominating layer L_i, we perform the *crowding distance calculation* for each individual, the individuals meeting privacy preservation with better crowding distance can be preferentially retained to the next generation population X until the size of X is N.

Iteration. NSDE continuously performs mutation, crossover, and selection operations on population X, and multiple non-dominated optimal solutions are obtained finally.

4.4   Optimal Collaborative Placement Strategy Confirmation

When the termination condition of algorithm is reached, multiple non-dominated optimal solutions may be output. We still need to choose the optimal individual among them as the optimal collaborative placement strategy. Therefore, based on SAW and MDCM, we calculate the utility values of these solutions for the normalization of multiple indicators.

Based on SAW, we set three corresponding weights w_1, w_2 and w_3 as three targets, and the sum of w_1, w_2 and w_3 is equal to 1. The more important the objective function is, the larger the corresponding weight is. The specific calculation method is as follows:

If T^i, E^i and U^i represent the three objective function values of individual X_i respectively, T^{min}, T^{max}, E^{min}, E^{max}, U^{min} and U^{max} represent the minimum and maximum values of the three objective function values of all individuals. Therefore, the calculation of utility value v_i of individual X_i is as follows.

$$v_i = w_1 * \frac{T^{max} - T^i}{T^{max} - T^{min}} + w_2 * \frac{E^{max} - E^i}{E^{max} - E^{min}} + w_3 * \frac{U^{max} - U^i}{U^{max} - U^{min}} \quad (18)$$

where $w_1 + w_2 + w_3 = 1$.

Based on SAW and MDCM, we calculate the utility values of multiple optimal solutions. Finally, the placement strategy with the largest utility value is identified as the final optimal collaborative placement strategy.

4.5   Two-Factor Data Security Protection Mechanism

Setup. All public parameters and master key will be generated in the setup phase. These public parameters will be shared among all parties. The master key can only be kept by CA. The specific process of setup is as follows.

We define $\mathbb{G}_1$ and $\mathbb{G}_2$ as cyclic multiplicative groups of prime order p, and e: $\mathbb{G}_1^2 \rightarrow \mathbb{G}_2$ is the bilinear map. The algorithm chooses $g, g_2, h \in \mathbb{G}_1$, $\alpha, \beta \in_R Z_q^*$. Four hash functions are chosen as follows: $H_1 : \mathbb{G}_1 \rightarrow Z_q^*$, $H_2 : \{0,1\}^* \rightarrow Z_q^*$, $H_3 : \mathbb{G}_2 \rightarrow \{0,1\}^*$ and $H_4 : \{0,1\}^* \rightarrow \mathbb{G}_1$. Meanwhile, the algorithm sets $g_1 = g^\alpha$. There are n attributes in the mechanism. The attribute set can be denoted as $A = \{A_1, A_2, \ldots, A_i, \ldots, A_n\}_{1 \leq i \leq n}$. Each attribute A_i has multiple attribute values $V = \{v_1, v_2, \ldots, v_i, \ldots, v_m\}_{1 \leq i \leq m}$. The public parameters are published as $param = (k, q, g, g_1, g_2, h, e(g,g), H_1, H_2, H_3, H_4)$. The master key is set as $msk = \alpha$.

Keygen and Security Device Distribution. Firstly, CA will distribute a security device for every user according to his/her ID. Secondly, CA is responsible for generating the secret keys for the users. Users can use their own security devices and secret keys to decrypt a ciphertext. The specific process is as follows.

The CA chooses $z_i \in_R Z_q^*$, and sets the public information of the security device as $epk_i = g^{z_i}$, and its corresponding secret information as $esk_i = z_i$. Finally, CA distributes security devices for every user and shares epk_i with the MCS. CA computes

$$\tau_i = H_4(s)^{-H_2(\beta||i)}, v_i = H_4(s)^{-H_2(\alpha||i)} \tag{19}$$

The secret key is $sk_S = (s, \tau_i, v_i)$, where s is the mapping of user attributes to strings. Attribute set of each user is mapped to the a unique string. S is the attributes that users possess.

Primary Encryption. DOs encrypt data and send the encrypted data to MCS. Knowing public parameters $param$, the data $m \in \{0,1\}^*$ and attribute set A. The process of primary encryption is as follows.

The algorithm computes $c_1 = m \cdot \alpha_A^k$, $c_2 = g^k$, $c_3 = \beta_A^k$, $c_4 = A$, and defines $\alpha_A = \prod \alpha_i$, $\beta_A = \prod \beta_i$. The primary ciphertext $C_1 = \{c_1, c_2, c_3, c_4\}$ is sent to MCS.

Secondary Encryption. After receiving the primary ciphertext from DOs, MCS will encrypt it again, resulting in secondary ciphertext. Knowing public parameters $param$, primary ciphertext and public information epk_i. The MCS encrypts $C_1 = \{c_1, c_2, c_3, c_4\}$ to secondary ciphertext as follows.

The algorithm chooses $\mu_1, \mu_2 \in_R \{0,1\}^*$, sets $r = H_2(\mu_1, \mu_2)$ and computes $c_5 = c_1 \oplus (\mu_1||\mu_2)$, $c_6 = (\mu_1||\mu_2) \oplus H_3(e(g,g)^r)$, $c_7 = (epk_i)^{r \cdot H_1(epk_i)}$, $c_8 = h^r$, $c_9 = H_4(c_5, c_6, c_7, c_8)^r$. At this point, secondary ciphertext is $C_2 = (c_2, c_3, c_4, c_5, c_6, c_7, c_8, c_9)$.

Data Decryption. When users need to decrypt ciphertext, security devices and keys are necessary. The decryption process is as follows.

Knowing $c_5 = c_1 \oplus (\mu_1 || \mu_2)$, so $c_1 = c_5 \oplus (\mu_1 || \mu_2)$. It is also known $c_6 = (\mu_1 || \mu_2) \oplus H_3(e(g,g)^r)$. As a result, the following formula can be obtained

$$c_1 = c_5 \oplus c_6 \oplus H_3(e(g,g)^r) \tag{20}$$

Since c_5 and c_6 are known, so users first use security devices to compute $e(g,g)^r$. The process is as follows

$$
\begin{aligned}
e(g,g)^r &= e(g,g^r) \\
&= e(g, epk_i^{\frac{r}{z_i}}) \\
&= e(g, epk_i^{r \cdot H_1(epk_i) \cdot \frac{1}{z_i \cdot H_1(epk_i)}}) \\
&= e(g, c_7^{\frac{1}{z_i \cdot H_1(epk_i)}})
\end{aligned}
\tag{21}
$$

By decryption of the users' security devices, c_1 can be obtained. Next, CA checks whether the attribute set S of users can satisfy A or not. If it is true, the CA computes $\tau_A = \prod \tau_i$, $v_A = \prod v_i$. The data can be decrypted as the following equation

$$m = \frac{c_1}{e(\tau_A \cdot v_A, g^k) \cdot e(H_4(s, \beta_A^k)} \tag{22}$$

4.6   Method Overview

In this paper, we aim to reduce average data access time, total energy consumption, optimize load balancing and protect data security. Therefore, the collaborative placement of machine learning workflows is modeled as a constrained multi-objective optimization problem. The security of two-factor data security protection mechanism is attributed to CP-ABE and public key encryption. In fact, the collaborative placement of machine-learning workflows and two-factor data security protection mechanism can be processed in parallel, namely, the two-factor security protection of data is completed while the machine-learning workflows are placed collaboratively. In other words, two-factor data security protection mechanism can be regarded as part of a collaborative placement method.

5   Comparison and Analysis of Experimental Results

In this section, in order to evaluate the performance of our proposed CPM method, we perform a series of experiments and compare them with two other common placement methods. In terms of data security, we compare the proposed mechanism with two other similar works in theory.

Table 1. Parameter settings.

Parameter	Value
Bandwidth of the edge layer	200 kb/s
Bandwidth between edge layer and aggregation layer	300 kb/s
Bandwidth between aggregation layer and core layer	400 kb/s
The forwarding rate of the switch	300 kb/s
The forwarding power of the switch	5 W

5.1 Parameters Setting and Comparison Methods

In this experiment, we model three different meteorological machine learning workflows separately. The settings of the used parameters are shown in Table 1. To show the performance of our proposed CPM intuitively, four other methods are employed for comparison analysis, which are elaborated as follows.

- Load-aware placement (LP). In LP, the tasks and data from the workflow are placed sequentially on the physical servers to achieve the goal of load balance.
- Access time aware placement (AP). In AP, the datasets are co-placed with the tasks that require the datasets for implementation in the same pod in priority.
- Attribute-based data sharing scheme [17]. In [17], encryption mechanism is only attribute-based encryption and does not support two-factor data security protection.
- Identity-based two-factor security protection scheme [19]. Because of identity-based encryption, the scheme does not support the security protection of public data.

5.2 Impact of Weight on Utility Value

In the experiment, to observe the variation of the utility value by altering weights, the three weights described in (18) are employed to adjust the proportion of the corresponding objective respectively. We adjust the value of w_1, and w_2 and w_3 are changed accordingly while w_2 and w_3 are set to the same value in this paper. Figure 3 shows the impact of the weight w_1 on the load balance and the access time metrics with different machine-learning workflows. It is intuitive from the 6 sub-figures in Fig. 3 that when the weight w_1 increases, the load balance variance becomes lower gradually, since w_1 represents the proportion of the load balance degree. Meanwhile, the energy consumption gets higher since the weight w_2 gets lower correspondingly.

5.3 Communication and Computational Cost Analysis

First of all, some notations used in efficiency analysis are defined as follows. $|\mathbb{G}_1|$ and $|\mathbb{G}_2|$ are utilized to denote the length of an element in groups $\mathbb{G}_1$ and

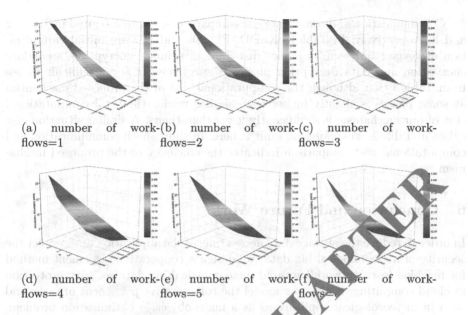

(a) number of work-flows=1

(b) number of work-flows=2

(c) number of work-flows=3

(d) number of work-flows=4

(e) number of work-flows=5

(f) number of work-flows=6

Fig. 3. The impact of the weight w_1 on the load balance and the access time metrics with different machine-learning workflows.

Table 2. Communication cost comparison.

Schemes	Ours	[17]	[19]
Secret key length	$2|\mathbb{G}$	$3|Z_q^*|$	$2|\mathbb{G}_1|$
Security device length	$\mathbb{G}_1| + |Z_q^*|$	$\perp$	$2|\mathbb{G}_1| + 2|Z_q^*|$
Primary ciphertext length	$(|m| + 2)|\mathbb{G}_1|$	$|ck|$	$6|\mathbb{G}_1| + 4l$
Secondary ciphertext length	$(|m| + 5)|\mathbb{G}_1| + |*|$	$|\mathbb{G}_1| + |\mathbb{G}_2|$	$3|\mathbb{G}_1|+|\mathbb{G}_2| + 4l$

Table 3. Computational cost comparison.

Phase	Ours	[17]	[19]
KSDD	$7EXP_1 + 4H$	$12EXP_1 + 2EXP_2 + H$	$4EXP_1$
PE	$3EXP_1$	EM	$2EXP_1 + EXP_2 + PA + 3H$
SE	$3EXP_1 + EXP_2 + 4H$	$4EXP_1 + EXP_2 + 2H$	$3EXP_1 + EXP_2 + PA + 3H$
DD	$7EXP_1 + 2PA + 3H$	$PA + 2EXP_2$	$9EXP_1 + 2PA + 3H$

$\mathbb{G}_2$, l denotes the length of security parameter, ck denotes the key length of a symmetric encryption algorithm, $|Z_q^*|$ denotes the length of an element in Z_q^*. $|m|$ and $|*|$ denote the length of data m and arbitrary 01 string, respectively. PA, EXP_1, EXP_2, and H are utilized to denote the cost of a bilinear pairing, an exponentiation in $\mathbb{G}_1$, an exponentiation in $\mathbb{G}_2$ and a hash function, respectively. EM and DM are utilized to denote the cost of symmetric encryption and decryption, respectively.

Communication and computational comparison are demonstrated in Tables 2 and 3, respectively. In Table 3, KSDD, PE, SE and DD are initial capitalization of keygen and security device distribution, primary encryption, secondary encryption and data decryption phases, respectively. It is not difficult to see from Table 3 that although the computational cost of the proposed mechanism at some phases is slightly higher than similar works, the total computational cost of our mechanism is significantly lower than theirs. A similar situation also exists in Table 2. Therefore, we omit it here. In short, both communication and computational cost comparison indicates the efficiency of the proposed mechanism.

6   Conclusion and Future Work

In order to reduce the average data access time of the application and protect the security of meteorological big data, we design a cooperative placement method for machine learning workflows and meteorological big data security protection in cloud computing. Firstly, we model the collaborative placement of tasks and data in meteorological applications as a multi-objective optimization problem. Secondly, we analyze and construct the average data access time model, total energy consumption model and load balancing model, and optimize the multi-objective problem using NSDE algorithm. Simultaneously, an efficient two-factor data security protection mechanism has been considered into the collaborative placement method. Finally, the effectiveness of our proposed method is verified by comparison and analysis of multiple sets of experiments.

Based on the work done in this paper, we would continue to optimize the placement of tasks, enhance data security, constantly update our method based on actual performance of the proposed method in this paper, achieve the perfect combination of rational placement of resources and data security protection.

References

1. Wang, X., Yang, L.T., Liu, H., Deen, M.J.: A big data-as-a-service framework: state-of-the-art and perspectives. IEEE Trans. Big Data **4**(3), 325–340 (2017)
2. Yu, Z., Tian, X., Qiu-Yu, L., Zhao-Guang, P., Si-Jie, L., Qing-Lai, G.: Research on key technologies of cloud energy management for wide area integrated energy internet. In: 2018 2nd IEEE Conference on Energy Internet and Energy System Integration (EI2), pp. 1–6. IEEE (2018)
3. Herbst, J.: A machine learning approach to workflow management. In: López de Mántaras, R., Plaza, E. (eds.) ECML 2000. LNCS (LNAI), vol. 1810, pp. 183–194. Springer, Heidelberg (2000). https://doi.org/10.1007/3-540-45164-1_19
4. Kleine Deters, J., Zalakeviciute, R., Gonzalez, M., Rybarczyk, Y.: Modeling PM2. 5 urban pollution using machine learning and selected meteorological parameters. J. Electr. Comput. Eng. **2017**, 14 (2017)
5. Kim, H., Kim, Y.: An adaptive data placement strategy in scientific workflows over cloud computing environments. In: NOMS 2018–2018 IEEE/IFIP Network Operations and Management Symposium, pp. 1–5. IEEE (2018)

6. Deng, S., Huang, L., Taheri, J., Zomaya, A.Y.: Computation offloading for service workflow in mobile cloud computing. IEEE Trans. Parallel Distrib. Syst. **26**(12), 3317–3329 (2015)

7. Wang, X., Wang, W., Yang, L.T., Liao, S., Yin, D., Deen, M.J.: A distributed HOSVD method with its incremental computation for big data in cyber-physical-social systems. IEEE Trans. Comput. Soc. Syst. **5**(2), 481–492 (2018)

8. Ren, X., London, P., Ziani, J., Wierman, A.: Joint data purchasing and data placement in a geo-distributed data market. In: ACM SIGMETRICS Performance Evaluation Review, vol. 44, pp. 383–384. ACM (2016)

9. Teng, F., Deng, D., Yu, L., Magoulès, F.: An energy-efficient VM placement in cloud datacenter. In: 2014 IEEE International Conference on High Performance Computing and Communications, 2014 IEEE 6th International Symposium on Cyberspace Safety and Security, 2014 IEEE 11th International Conference on Embedded Software and Systems (HPCC, CSS, ICESS), pp. 173–180. IEEE (2014)

10. Shen, Z., Lee, P.P.C., Shu, J., Guo, W.: Encoding-aware data placement for efficient degraded reads in XOR-coded storage systems. In: 2016 IEEE 35th Symposium on Reliable Distributed Systems (SRDS), pp. 239–248. IEEE (2016)

11. Xiong, R., Luo, J., Dong, F.: Optimizing data placement in heterogeneous hadoop clusters. Cluster Comput. **18**(4), 1465–1480 (2015)

12. Xiao, Y., Zhang, J., Ji, Y.: Energy efficient placement of baseband functions and mobile edge computing in 5G networks. In: 2018 Asia Communications and Photonics Conference (ACP), pp. 1–3. IEEE (2018)

13. Liu, Z., et al.: A data placement strategy for scientific workflow in hybrid cloud. In: 2018 IEEE 11th International Conference on Cloud Computing (CLOUD), pp. 556–563. IEEE (2018)

14. Gu, R., Huang, T., Xue, S., Ruan, L.: A big data placement method based on NSGA-III in meteorological cloud platform. EURASIP J. Wirel. Commun. Netw. **2019**, 1 (2019)

15. Gaggero, M., Caviglione, L.: Model predictive control for energy-efficient, quality-aware, and secure virtual machine placement. IEEE Trans. Autom. Sci. Eng. **99**, 1–13 (2018)

16. Zhao, J., Mortier, R., Crowcroft, J., Wang, L.: Privacy-preserving machine learning based data analytics on edge devices. In: Proceedings of the 2018 AAAI/ACM Conference on AI, Ethics, and Society, pp. 341–346. ACM (2018)

17. Wang, S., Liang, K., Liu, J.K., Chen, J., Yu, J., Xie, W.: Attribute-based data sharing scheme revisited in cloud computing. IEEE Trans. Inf. Forensics Secur. **11**(8), 1661–1673 (2016)

18. Peng, X., Qianhong, W., Wang, W., Susilo, W., Domingo-Ferrer, J., Jin, H.: Generating searchable public-key ciphertexts with hidden structures for fast keyword search. IEEE Trans. Inf. Forensics Secur. **10**(9), 1993–2006 (2017)

19. Liu, J.K., Liang, K., Susilo, W., Liu, J., Xiang, Y.: Two-factor data security protection mechanism for cloud storage system. IEEE Trans. Comput. **65**(6), 1992–2004 (2016)

20. Xu, X., et al.: An IoT-oriented data placement method with privacy preservation in cloud environment. J. Netw. Comput. Appl. **124**, 148–157 (2018)

21. Ren, Y., Suganthan, P.N., Srikanth, N.: A novel empirical mode decomposition with support vector regression for wind speed forecasting. IEEE Trans. Neural Netw. Learn. Syst. **27**(8), 1793–1798 (2014)

A Lightweight Certificateless User Authentication Scheme for Mobile Environment

Alzubair Hassan[1]([✉]), Rafik Hamza[1], Vittor Gift Mawutor[2],
Akash Suresh Patil[1], and Fagen Li[2]

[1] School of Computer Science and Cyber Engineering,
Guangzhou University, Guangzhou 51006, People's Republic of China
alzubairuofk@gmail.com
[2] Center for Cyber Security, School of Computer Science and Engineering,
University of Electronic Science and Technology of China, Chengdu 611731, China

Abstract. Nowadays, smartphone applications are the most widespread in our daily lives. These applications raised several security concerns such as authentication, key agreement, and mutual authentication. Accordingly, the researchers have been presented several user authentication schemes based on the identity-based cryptography (IBC) and certificateless cryptography (CLC). Smartphones considered as limited resources devices, thus, it needs lightweight protocols. However, the existing schemes are suffering from high computational costs especially the one that depends on CLC. In this paper, a lightweight certificateless user authentication scheme based on the elliptic curve cryptography (ECC) is introduced. The proposed scheme has the lowest computation costs comparing with the existing certificateless user's authentication protocols. Furthermore, The proposed scheme is secure under the computational Diffie-Hellman (CDH) Problem and the elliptic curve discrete logarithm problem (ECDLP). Indeed, the proposed scheme is suitable to use in the mobile client-server environment and the Internet of things (IoT) applications.

Keywords: User authentication · Key agreement ·
Certificateless cryptography · Elliptic curve cryptography

1 Introduction

It is an undeniable fact that many applications have been introduced to make life more comfortable. Many of these applications are network applications and therefore run in the client-server environment. In the client-server environment, powerful computers called servers provide services and resources to the client devices such as personal computers, laptops and mobile devices. Service providers are able to offer services and resources through these network applications via network [14].

© Springer Nature Switzerland AG 2019
X. Chen et al. (Eds.): ML4CS 2019, LNCS 11806, pp. 112–122, 2019.
https://doi.org/10.1007/978-3-030-30619-9_9

Recent upsurge of mobile environment has in turn increased the demand for network resources and services. These requests have and still being satisfied through the development of mobile applications. Mobile client-server environment contains several applications such as online payment, banking, shopping, and social network applications. These mobile devices have the problem of low computational power and battery limitation. This lead to a major drawback concerning the mobile devices capabilities. Also, the development of these mobile applications has not only help to solve much problem of the demand for network resources and services, but has also introduced other security issues. Therefore, the user authentication and key agreement are important in these applications [10].

By using the user authentication protocol, it easy to ensure that the system dealing with the authorized user. Otherwise, the system will give the service to an unauthorized user which is a danger. There is a need also for key agreement protocol to let the communicating parties (client and server) agree on a key that could be used to secure the communication in the future and the integrity. Many user authentication and key agreement schemes have been proposed and designed followed by the effect of Lamport scheme [13]. However, many of these authentication and key agreement schemes are insecure against many malicious attacks such as a forgery attack and replay attack. Also, many of these schemes are not suitable for mobile clients with low computational capabilities since many of them have high computational costs. From the above-mentioned issues, the mobile client-server environment requires secure user authentication and key agreement protocols. This paper proposes a lightweight certificateless user authentication scheme using elliptic curve cryptography (ECC). The proposed scheme has the lowest computation costs comparing with the existing certificateless user's authentication protocols. According to the security analysis, the proposed scheme is secure under the computational Diffie-Hellman (CDH) Problem and the elliptic curve discrete logarithm problem (ECDLP).

This paper presented as follows. The related works are discussed in Sect. 2. The preliminaries are given in Sect. 3. The proposed scheme is explained in Sect. 4. The result and discussion are introduced in Sect. 5. Finally, the conclusions are shown in Sect. 6.

2 Related Work

Over the years, many user authentication and key agreement protocols have been introduced for mobile client-server environment. These protocols have different authentication credentials. Before we move on to the different works done in this direction of security, we first want to mention the first basic key agreement protocol known as the Diffie-Hellman key agreement protocol [4]. This protocol has been modified in many ways to be able to provide implicit key authentication, which means, only the licit parties can be able to calculate the session key.

Previously, in order to develop an authentication and key agreement protocol, the Public Key Infrastructure (PKI) was employed, but this was very expensive with regards to the storage and distribution. In order to curb this problem of the PKI, Shamir [16] introduced the identity-based cryptography (IBC). This scheme was not practical due to integer factorization. Boneh and Franklin [2] introduced an identity-based encryption protocol which sparked the idea of client-server protocols.

In 2006, Das et al. [3] proposed an identity-based remote client authentication scheme which was pairing based with smart cards. Goriparthi et al. [7] was able to prove that the scheme of Das *et al.* [3] was not secured against a forgery attack. This means that, the authentication process of the scheme can easily be passed by an adversary. Based on the forgery attack weakness of the above scheme, two different improved schemes were proposed. The first scheme was proposed by Fang and Huang [5] to overcome the forgery attack in [3]. After that, Giri and Srivastava [6] discovered that Fang and Huang' scheme could also not overcome a type of forgery attack and also offline attack. Giri and Srivastava [6] went further to propose another scheme. Their scheme was an improved scheme which could withstand the forgery attack. The scheme made use of public key encryption on smart cards. This made the bilinear pairing operation on the identity-based encryption to utilize more time.

Tseng *et al.* [20] proved that Giri and Srivastava' scheme has a very high computational cost for smart cards possessing low computing capabilities. Tseng et al. [21] presented a more secured pairing-based authentication scheme for wireless clients with smart cards. The proposed scheme provided better performance and could also withstand the forgery attack. Apart from the proposal and the proof, Tseng *et al* [20] showed that the schemes in [3] and [6] were not able to provide mutual authentication. In 2010, Yoon and Yoo [23] proposed a user authentication and key exchange protocol for mobile client-server environment based on Wu *et al.*'s scheme [22] to improve the performance of their scheme. He [11] proposed an efficient user authentication key agreement protocol based on bilinear pairing suitable for mobile client-server environment. He claimed his protocol gives better performance than that of [22] and [11]. In 2013, Sun et al. [18] mentioned that most of the identity-based remote user authentication protocols have an inherent weakness since the server knows all the private keys of clients, therefore very vulnerable to inside attack and also, most of them could not provide user anonymity and perfect forward secrecy. They further went ahead to proposed a novel user authentication protocol for a mobile client-server environment. Recently, Tsai et al. [19] proved that the protocol of Sun et al. could not overcome the inside attack proposed by them. The server in the authentication protocol of Sun et al. could not verify the validity of a user's partial public key.

It is a clear notion that all the identity-based protocols have the inherent key escrow problem. To overcome this issue, Certificateless user authentication protocol can be proposed. Accordingly, all the schemes employed certificateless cryptography (CLC) should be resisted to the adversaries TYPE I and TYPE II as mentioned in [1]. Adversary TYPE I can replace the users' public key, but he/she cannot access the master key of the key generator center (KGC). The adversary TYPE II owns the KGC's master key, but he/she nevertheless can't substitute the public key of the users. In order to solve the key escrow problem, In 2017, Hassan et al. [8] proposed a certificateless user authentication protocol which was able to solve the key escrow problem. They claimed their scheme is secure against both adversary TYPE I and TYPE II. However, their protocol is not secured against the adversary TYPE II. In order to solve this security issue, Hassan *et al.* [9] proposed another certificateless user authentication protocol for the mobile client-server environment. This scheme proved to be secured and resistant to the adversaries TYPE I and TYPE II, but it has high computational cost due to the use of bilinear pairing. This paper proposes a lightweight protocol which is built on the CLC using ECC to reduce the computational costs in the previous works.

3 Preliminaries

Here, the elliptic curve cryptography and the hardness assumptions are introduced to use later in our proposed scheme.

1. **Elliptic curve cryptography:**
   It is known the elliptic curve clarified on prime field $\mathbb{F}_p$. Allow $\mathbb{E}(\mathbb{F}_p)$ indicates an elliptic curve $\mathbb{E}$ over a prime finite field $\mathbb{F}_p$, which is explained by the following an equation

$$y^2 = x^3 + ax + b \tag{1}$$

   While $a, b \in \mathbb{F}_p$ and with $\Delta = 4a^3 + 27b^2 \neq 0$. The curve compose of all the points in $\mathbb{E}(\mathbb{F}_p)$ with the point at infinity $\mathcal{O}$. The reader can refer to [12].

2. **The elliptic curve discrete logarithm problem ECDLP:**
   An elliptic curve $\mathbb{E}$ defined over a finite field $\mathbb{F}_q$ is given. Where $P \in \mathbb{E}(\mathbb{F}_q)$ is a point in $\mathbb{E}$ with order n as well as there is a point $Q = lP$ where $0 \leqslant l \leqslant n-1$. It is hard to determine l.

3. **The computational Diffie-Hellman (CDH) Problem:**
   If we have $\mathbb{G}$ is a base point of $\mathbb{E}(\mathbb{F}_p)$ and $P, xP, yP \in \mathbb{G}$.Then, the $xyP \in \mathbb{G}$ could not be computed due to its difficulty.

4 The Proposed Protocol

We have used the work that presented in [12] to design our scheme. Certificateless cryptography with bilinear paring has been used to design the user authentication protocols. However, these protocols have high computational costs. To overcome this problem, we employed CLC with ECC to design a lightweight user authentication and key agreement protocol. In the proposed protocol, the server plays the role of the KGC. The server generates the partial private key for the client, then the client select secret value to prepare the full private key. Accordingly, we have the concept of the CLC used in this protocol. Our proposed protocol compose of the following:

4.1 Setup

- *Setup* (1^λ): The server plays the KGC. The server uses λ as security parameter while the public parameters generate as follows:
  1. A set of elliptic curve ($\mathbb{E}$) domain parameters $D = \{q, \mathbb{F}_q, n, a, b, h\}$ are used in our protocol.
  2. The server picks his master secret key $s \in_R \mathbb{Z}_q^*$ and compute the corresponding master public key $P_{pub} = sP$.
  3. Select Two cryptographic secure hash functions $H_1 : \{0,1\}^* \times \{0,1\}^* \times \mathbb{G} \times \mathbb{G} \to \mathbb{Z}_q^*$, $H_2 : \{0,1\}^* \times \{0,1\}^* \times \mathbb{G} \times \mathbb{G} \times \mathbb{Z}_q^* \to \mathbb{Z}_q^*$.
  4. Publish the public parameters $\{D, \mathbb{G}, P, P_{pub}, H_1, H_2\}$ as general.

4.2 Key Extract

In this phase, the public and partial private keys are generated by the server as follows:

1. The client sends his identity ID_c to the server ID_s, then the server uses his secret value s and the set of $\mathbb{E}$ domain parameters to compute the user's partial private key $R_{ID_c} = sP$.
2. After receiving R_{ID_c}, the client selects his secret value $x_{ID_c} \in \mathbb{Z}_q^*$ to compute his full private key (R_{ID_c}, x_{ID_c}) and the public key $PK_{ID_c} = x_{ID_c}P$.

4.3 User Authenticated Key Exchange

1. After the client received the keys from the server, starts communicating with the server as follows:
   (a) Select $1 \le k \le n-1$.
   (b) Compute $kP = (x_1, y_1)$.
   (c) Compute $\varsigma = x_1 \bmod n$. if $\varsigma = 0$ then go step (a).
   (d) Choose $\varphi \in_R \mathbb{Z}_q^*$ and Compute $M = \varphi P$. Then, the client sends ID_c and M to the server.
2. The sever reacts as follows after received ID_c and M correctly:
   (a) Select $\beta \in \mathbb{Z}_q^*$. Then, $T = \beta P$ and $R_1 = \beta M$ are computed.
   (b) Compute $h_{ID_c} = H_1(ID_c, ID_s, R_{ID_c}, R_1)$.
   (c) Return T as well as h_{ID_c} to the client.
3. Since T and h_{ID_c} are received correctly, the client calculates the following equations:
   (a) Compute $R_2 = \varphi T$.
   (b) Check whether the received h_{ID_c} its equal to $H_1(ID_c, ID_s, R_{ID_c}, R_2)$.
   (c) Compute $S = k^{-1}(h_{ID_c} + x_{ID_c}\varsigma) \bmod n$. If $S = 0$ then go to step 1.
   (d) Here, the session key is computed as follow $sk = H_2(ID_c, ID_s, R_{ID_c}, R_2, h_{ID_c})$. Then, ς and S are sent to the server.
4. Finally, the server verifies from the validity of ς and S which are received from the client as follows:
   (a) Verify that ς and S are Integer in the internal $[1, n-1]$.
   (b) Compute $w = S^{-1} \bmod n$.

(c) Compute $u_1 = h_{ID_c}w \bmod n$.

(d) Compute $u_2 = \varsigma w \bmod n$.

(e) Compute $X = u_1 P + u_2 PK_{ID_c}$. If $X = \mathcal{O}$ then reject the client. Otherwise, Compute $v = x_1 \bmod n$ where $X = (x_1, y_1)$. Accept the client if and only if $v = \varsigma$.

(f) Here, the session key is computed as follow $sk = H_2(ID_c, ID_s, R_{ID_c}, R_1, h_{ID_c})$ (Fig. 1).

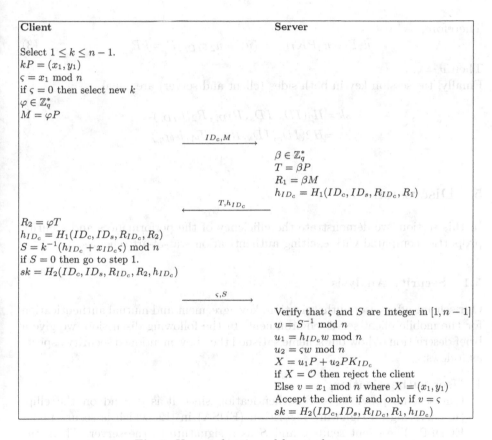

Fig. 1. User authenticated key exchange

4.4 The Correctness of Our Protocol

This subsection describes how the proposed scheme is free of error. Given $T = \beta P$ and $M = \varphi P$, the proposed scheme is correct due to

$$R_2 = \varphi T = \varphi\beta P = \beta\varphi P = \beta M = R_1 \tag{2}$$

In addition, given ς and S to the server. Then $S = k^{-1}(h_{ID_c} + x_{ID_c}\varsigma) \bmod n$. It can be written

$$
\begin{aligned}
k &\equiv S^{-1}(h_{ID_c} + x_{ID_c}\varsigma) \\
&\equiv S^{-1}h_{ID_c} + S^{-1}x_{ID_c}\varsigma \\
&\equiv wh_{ID_c} + wx_{ID_c}\varsigma \\
&\equiv u_1 + u_2 x_{ID_c} \pmod n
\end{aligned}
$$

Therefore,

$$ u_1 P + u_2 PK_{ID_c} = (u_1 + u_2 x_{ID_c})P = kP \tag{3} $$

Then $v = \varsigma$.

Finally, the session key in both sides (client and server) are equal.

$$
\begin{aligned}
sk &= H_2(ID_c, ID_s, R_{ID_c}, R_2, h_{ID_c}) \\
&= H2(ID_c, ID_s, R_{ID_c}, R_1, h_{ID_c})
\end{aligned}
$$

5   Discussion

In this section, we demonstrate the efficiency of the performances and security properties compared with exciting authentication stat-of-art schemes.

5.1   Security Analysis

Our scheme offers user authentication, key agreement and mutual authentication for the mobile client-server environment. In the following discussion, we give a brief description of how our scheme satisfied the abovementioned security aspects as follows:

1. **User authentication:**
   Our scheme provides user authentication since it is depend on the elliptic curve digital signature algorithm (EDSA) in [12] which is secure under ECDLP. The client sends ς and S as a signature to the server. Then, the server needs to verify from the client by ensuring that ς and S are an integer in $[1, n-1]$. Adversary can not forge the signature due to the ECDLP.
2. **Key agreement:**
   The proposed scheme provide the key agreement which can be used for the future communication between both client and server. To get the session key, the adversary needs to solve the CDH problem in sk. The key agreement is $sk = H_2(ID_c, ID_s, R_{ID_c}, R_2, h_{ID_c}) = H_2(ID_c, ID_s, R_{ID_c}, R_1, h_{ID_c})$. The adversary cannot get access to the key agreement due to the CDH problem in R_2 and R_1.

3. **Mutual authentication:**
   Our scheme enjoys mutual authentication and it is secure under CDH. The server can be sure that he is communicated with the right client by computing T and $h_{ID_c} = H_1(ID_c, ID_s, R_{ID_c}, R_1)$ in the server side. Then, the server sends T and the value of h_{ID_c} to the client to compute R_2 and $H_1(ID_c, ID_s, R_{ID_c}, R_2)$ as a value of h_{ID_c}. If a client gets the right value of the h_{ID_c}, then the server authenticates from the client. Otherwise, the server is communicated by the wrong client. The adversary cannot compromise the h_{ID_c} and T due to the CDH.

5.2   Performance Analysis

We conduct the performances evaluation regarding the security properties, the computational cost and the communication overhead of the proposed scheme compared with the existing protocols. The comparisons are done with He's scheme [11] (symbolize it by HDE), Hassan *et al.*'s scheme [9] (symbolize it by AHC). We represent a bilinear pairing operation time by T_{pr}, multiplication in $\mathbb{G}_1$ time by T_{mu}, inversion operation time by T_{inv}, addition in $\mathbb{G}_1$ time by T_d and hash function time by T_h.

The basis of our quantitative analysis is based on Scott*et al.*'s experimental results [15] as introduced in Table 1. From their experiment, Pentium IV with speeds 3 GHz, was employed to simulate the server. The Philips HiPersmart card provided a 32-bit RISC MIPS, 256 KB flash memory, 16 KB RAM and a maximum clock speed of 36 MHz was used to simulate the client. Their experiment considered the security level of the Ate pairing system, and employed an elliptic curve $\mathbb{E}$ over a finite field $\mathbb{F}_p$, with $p = 512$ bits and a large prime order $q = 160$ bits.

Table 1. Computation cost at client side and server side

	T_{pr}	T_{mu}	T_d	T_{inv}	T_H
Server	3.16 ms	1.17 ms	< 0.1 ms	< 1 ms	0.01 ms
Client	0.38 s	0.13 s	< 0.1 s	< 0.01 s	< 0.001 s

Table 2. Computational costs

	HDE [11]	AHC [9]	Ours
Client-time	$3T_m + 3T_h + T_{inv}$	$5T_{mu} + T_{ad} + 4T_h$	$5T_{mu} + 3T_d + 2T_h + T_{inv}$
Processing-time	0.266 s	0.754 s	0.962 s
Server-time	$T_{pr} + 2T_m + 2T_d + 3T_h$	$2T_{pr} + 4T_{mu} + 2T_d + 6T_h$	$T_{mu} + T_d + 2T_h + T_{inv}$
Processing-time	9.26 ms	11.26 ms	2.29 ms

The theoretical analysis is introduced to calculate the computational cost in Table 2. As a result, we find that the proposed scheme has the lowest computational cost in server side and the reasonable cost in the client side compared with the existing protocols [9,11]. Hence, the proposed scheme has the advantage of working with mobile-based applications and IoT environment due to the use of the ECC scheme. In Table 3, we use ✓ to express that a scheme enjoys specified security properties, as well as ✗ to express that a scheme does not enjoy the specified security properties. Table 3 gives a comparison based on the security properties.

Table 3. Security properties

	HDE [11]	AHC [9]	Our protocol
Mutual authentication	✓	✓	✓
Key agreement	✓	✓	✓
Resistance to forgery attack	✓	✓	✓
Perfect forward-secrecy	✗	✓	✓
No key escrow problem	✗	✓	✓
Based ECC	✗	✗	✓

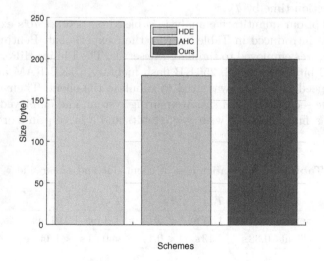

Fig. 2. Communication cost

To get the communication overhead, we compute the transformed elements between the client and server in all the schemes by using the following notation. Let $|ID| = \frac{80}{8} = 10$ bytes and employing the curve with $q = \frac{160}{8} = 20$ bytes, where the size of $\mathbb{G}_1$ is 1024 bits. Here, the size of $\mathbb{G}_1$ reduced to 65 bytes by using the compression method in [17].

The communication cost for He [11], Hassan *et al.* [9], and our scheme are shown as $|ID| + 2|\mathbb{Z}_q^*| + 2|\mathbb{G}_1| = 10 + 2 \times 20 + 3 \times 65 = 245$ bytes, $|ID| + 2|\mathbb{Z}_q^*| + 2|\mathbb{G}_1| = 10 + 2 \times 20 + 2 \times 65 = 180$ bytes and $|ID| + 3|\mathbb{Z}_q^*| + 2|\mathbb{G}_1| = 10 + 3 \times 20 + 2 \times 65 = 200$ bytes, respectively (see Fig. 2).

6 Conclusion

This paper presented a lightweight user authentication protocol with a key agreement and mutual authentication. The proposed scheme employed certificateless cryptography to solve the key escrow problem of identity-based cryptography, as well as the elliptic curve cryptography to reduce the computational and communication costs. Our protocol is secure under the hard assumptions CDH and ECDL problems. Indeed, Our protocol is fitting for both the mobile and IoT applications in client-server environments.

References

1. Al-Riyami, S.S., Paterson, K.G.: Certificateless public key cryptography. In: Laih, C.-S. (ed.) ASIACRYPT 2003. LNCS, vol. 2894, pp. 452–473. Springer, Heidelberg (2003). https://doi.org/10.1007/978-3-540-40061-5_29

2. Boneh, D., Franklin, M.: Identity-based encryption from the weil pairing. SIAM J. Comput. **32**(3), 586–615 (2003)

3. Das, M.L., Saxena, A., Gulati, V.P., Phatak, D.B.: A novel remote user authentication scheme using bilinear pairings. Comput. Secur. **25**(3), 184–189 (2006)

4. Diffie, W., Hellman, M.: New directions in cryptography. IEEE Trans. Inf. Theory **22**(6), 644–654 (1976)

5. Fang, G., Huang, G.: Improvement of recently proposed remote client authentication protocols (2006)

6. Giri, D., Srivastava, P.: An improved remote user authentication scheme with smart cards using bilinear pairings. IACR Cryptology ePrint Arch. **2006**, 274 (2006)

7. Goriparthi, T., Das, M.L., Negi, A., Saxena, A.: Cryptanalysis of recently proposed remote user authentication schemes. IACR Cryptology ePrint Arch. **2006**, 28 (2006)

8. Hassan, A., Eltayieb, N., Elhabob, R., Li, F.: A provably secure certificateless user authentication protocol for mobile client-server environment. In: Barolli, L., Zhang, M., Wang, X. (eds.) EIDWT 2017. LNDECT, vol. 6, pp. 592–602. Springer, Cham (2017). https://doi.org/10.1007/978-3-319-59463-7_59

9. Hassan, A., Eltayieb, N., Elhabob, R., Li, F.: An efficient certificateless user authentication and key exchange protocol for client-server environment. J. Ambient Intell. Humaniz. Comput. **9**(6), 1713–1727 (2018)

10. Hassan, A., Omala, A.A., Ali, M., Jin, C., Li, F.: Identity-based user authenticated key agreement protocol for multi-server environment with anonymity. Mobile Netw. Appl. **24**(3), 890–902 (2019)

11. He, D.: An efficient remote user authentication and key agreement protocol for mobile client-server environment from pairings. Ad Hoc Netw. **10**(6), 1009–1016 (2012)

12. Johnson, D., Menezes, A., Vanstone, S.: The elliptic curve digital signature algorithm (ECDSA). Int. J. Inf. Secur. **1**(1), 36–63 (2001)

13. Lamport, L.: Password authentication with insecure communication. Commun. ACM **24**(11), 770–772 (1981)

14. Odelu, V., Das, A.K., Kumari, S., Huang, X., Wazid, M.: Provably secure authenticated key agreement scheme for distributed mobile cloud computing services. Future Gener. Comput. Syst. **68**, 74–88 (2017)

15. Scott, M., Costigan, N., Abdulwahab, W.: Implementing cryptographic pairings on smartcards. In: Goubin, L., Matsui, M. (eds.) CHES 2006. LNCS, vol. 4249, pp. 134–147. Springer, Heidelberg (2006). https://doi.org/10.1007/11894063_11

16. Shamir, A.: Identity-based cryptosystems and signature schemes. In: Blakley, G.R., Chaum, D. (eds.) CRYPTO 1984. LNCS, vol. 196, pp. 47–53. Springer, Heidelberg (1985). https://doi.org/10.1007/3-540-39568-7_5

17. Shim, K.A., Lee, Y.R., Park, C.M.: EIBAS: an efficient identity-based broadcast authentication scheme in wireless sensor networks. Ad Hoc Netw. 11(1), 182–189 (2013)

18. Sun, H., Wen, Q., Zhang, H., Jin, Z.: A novel remote user authentication and key agreement scheme for mobile client-server environment. Appl. Math. Inf. Sci. 7(4), 1365 (2013)

19. Tsai, J.L.: Comments on a novel user authentication and key agreement scheme. IACR Cryptology ePrint Arch. 2014, 115 (2014)

20. Tseng, Y.M., Wu, T.Y., Wu, J.D.: A mutual authentication and key exchange scheme from bilinear pairings for low power computing devices. In: 31st Annual International Computer Software and Applications Conference (COMPSAC 2007), vol. 2, pp. 700–710. IEEE (2007)

21. Tseng, Y.M., Wu, T.Y., Wu, J.D.: A pairing-based user authentication scheme for wireless clients with smart cards. Informatica 19(2), 285–302 (2008)

22. Wu, T.Y., Tseng, Y.M.: An efficient user authentication and key exchange protocol for mobile client-server environment. Comput. Netw. 54(9), 1520–1530 (2010)

23. Yoon, E., Yoo, K.: A new efficient id-based user authentication and key exchange protocol for mobile client-server environment. In: 2010 IEEE International Conference on Wireless Information Technology and Systems, pp. 1–4. IEEE (2010)

Detection of GPS Spoofing Attack on Unmanned Aerial Vehicle System

Chen Liang[1], Meixia Miao[2], Jianfeng Ma[3], Hongyan Yan[4], Qun Zhang[1], Xinghua Li[3(✉)], and Teng Li[3]

[1] Institute of Information and Navigation,
Air Force Engineering University, Xi'an, Shaanxi, China
[2] National Engineering Laboratory for Wireless Security, Xi'an,
University of Posts and Telecommunications, Xi'an, Shaanxi, China
[3] School of Cyber Engineering, Xidian University, Xi'an, Shaanxi, China
xhli1@mail.xidian.edu.cn
[4] School of Computer Science, Guangzhou University, Guangzhou, China

Abstract. Most of the existing GPS spoofing detection schemes are vulnerable to the complex generative GPS spoofing attack, and require additional auxiliary equipments and extensive signal processing capabilities, leading to defects such as low real-time performance and large communication overhead which may not be available for the unmanned aerial vehicle (UAV, also known as drone) system. Motivated by the limitations of prior work, we propose a GPS spoofing detection scheme that requires minimal prior configuration and employs information fusion based on the GPS receiver and inertial measurement unit (IMU). We use a real-time model of tracking and calculating to derive the current location of the drones which are then contrasted with the location information received by the GPS receiver to judge whether the UAV system is under spoofing attack. Experiments show that, while the accuracy meets the requirements of detection, the proposed method can accurately determine whether the system is attacked within 8 s, with a detection rate of 98.6%. Compared with the existing schemes, the performance of real-time detecting is improved in our method while the detection rate is ensured. Even in our worst-case, we detect GPS spoofing attack within 28 s after the UAV system starts its mission.

Keywords: UAV · Drone · GPS spoofing · Attack detection

1 Introduction

UAV technology plays an important role in dealing with natural disasters, material distribution, film and television shooting, and social security incidents. A latest market report[1] indicates that, as of 2018, the global UAV market revenue has reached US$20.71 billion. It is expected that the market will grow at a compound annual growth rate of 14.15%, and will reach US$52.3 billion in 2025.

---

[1] http://www.avascent.com/2018/02/think-bigger-large-unmanned-systems-and-the-next-major-shift-in-aviation/.

© Springer Nature Switzerland AG 2019
X. Chen et al. (Eds.): ML4CS 2019, LNCS 11806, pp. 123–139, 2019.
https://doi.org/10.1007/978-3-030-30619-9_10

Recently, with the development of technologies such as software radio, GPS has become an indispensable part of the UAV navigation system, but suffered from destructive security threats [1,2]. For a UAV system, GPS is an extremely important sensor that provides accurate location information and reduces or even eliminates the cumulative errors of the IMU. In the case of GPS and IMU integrated navigation, the navigation accuracy and reliability of the drone have been greatly improved. However, once the GPS sensor is deceived or attacked, the data collected by the IMU will be false, and the UAV cannot resolve the current flight status, resulting in that the UAV could not fly stably according to the original trajectory, or even collide or crash [3].

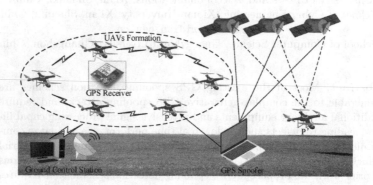

Fig. 1. Schematic diagram of GPS spoofing. The attacker records the real GPS signal, then adds a delay, or generates a GPS spoofing signal of a specific location and time through a specific program, then forwards the processed signal to the GPS receiver of the UAVs Formation member (the current location is P), positioning the drone to the wrong location P'.

GPS spoofing is a major security threat to GPS currently, it is to make the GPS receiver of the attacked target receive a false GPS signal by forging or replaying the GPS signal so that the target GPS receiver can resolve a wrong location and time information [4–7], as shown in Fig. 1. GPS spoofing can be divided into two types from the generation of the deceptive signals [8]: (1) Transmitting GPS spoofing is to record real GPS signals, plus a certain delay, and then send them to the target GPS receiver through signal simulator or transponder, so that the attacked target can resolve the wrong location and time information; (2) Generative GPS spoofing is relatively more complicated. Attackers usually extract location, time, satellite ephemeris and other information from real signals, align the carrier of false GPS signals with real GPS spoofing signals, then generate GPS deception signals of specific location and time through specific programs, and transmit them to the target GPS receiver through matrix antenna, so that the GPS receiver can calculate the wrong location and time information.

In this regard, the scientific community has put forward several detection schemes to deal with GPS spoofing. However, existing research usually have the following problems:

(1) The method of detecting GPS spoofing based on the physical layer charac-teristics of GPS signals can be applied to most UAV systems, but it can only detect simple transmitting GPS spoofing, which is often helpless for more elaborate generative GPS spoofing schemes. For example, when attackers use multiple GPS transmitters to transmit specific satellite GPS signals [9], or change the frequency of GPS signals dynamically in the process of spoofing, these detection methods will not work because the Doppler shift of different satellite signals no longer has the same changing rules.

(2) Most detection schemes based on cryptography apply symmetric cryptog-raphy. Although its computational complexity is low, key management and distribution is a difficult problem. Traditional public key cryptography can solve the key management problem, while this technology relies excessively on the ground public key infrastructure (PKI) system. In the UAV system, the nodes move at high speed and the network topology changes dynamically, it is hard to guarantee that the drones can obtain GPS public key certificates from the ground PKI system in real time. Moreover, this method needs to upgrade the existing UAV system, which will increase the communication overhead and calculation processing overhead of messages, resulting in that the real-time acquisition of location information by UAV group members is greatly reduced, and lead to the yaw of the drones.

At the same time, since the wireless medium does not have a complete and rapidly observable boundary, if some of the drone nodes are shielded or interfered by the signal, they have been blocked or flew away from the network. The schemes above are unable to obtain the flight information of these group members in time and will be powerless when the system is attacked by GPS spoofing attack. Therefore, this paper starts with the data communication between the groups through the communication link inherent in the UAV system [10]. Driven by the increasing threat and the lack of realistic short-term solutions, a lightweight active GPS spoofing detection scheme is proposed. The main contributions are as follows:

(1) We extract the data (such as location and speed of the drone) transmitted by IMU to the ground control station (GCS) [11], and place the processing of these information on the GCS. By this way to realize GPS spoofing detection, we do not need to update GPS infrastructure equipment, GPS receiver, and GPS signal format, which effectively improves the detection efficiency, and also helps to solve the positioning deviation caused by GPS signal shielding or interference.

(2) Combined with the classical multi-point positioning technology, a GPS spoofing detection scheme based on regional positioning algorithm is designed. The UAVs formation infers the location of formation members in real-time through the interaction of communication data between them, and compares the calculated data with the original position information received by the GPS receiver of the UAV, so that the group members can quickly determine whether they are deceived. At the same time, since the UAV sys-tem no longer detects and locates the real position of the group members by

directly measuring and analyzing the GPS signals received by the receiver and their characteristics, the scheme can detect common transmitting GPS spoofing attacks simultaneously. It can also effectively deal with more complex generated GPS spoofing attacks.

(3) When the number of the UAVs formation is small, the communication data generated between the group members is insufficient, and it is difficult to implement the GPS spoofing detection scheme by combining the multi-point positioning algorithm. In this case, using the flight characteristics and direction finding principle of the drone itself, the real-time positioning and tracking of the single target UAV is carried out, then whether the drone is suffered by GPS spoofing attacks is judged.

The structure of this paper is as follows: Sect. 2 mainly introduces the existing GPS spoofing detection schemes. Section 3 put forward our solutions. In Sect. 4, numerous simulations and experiments are carried out and analyzed. Section 5 is devoted to the conclusions.

2   Related Work

2.1   GPS Spoofing Detection Scheme Based on Physical Layer Characteristics of GPS Signals

Based on the principle of interference detection, Psiaki Lab [12] proposed a GPS spoofing detection scheme based on the direction-of-arrival (DOA) induction. The angle of arrival of the signal is judged by the change of carrier phase resolution signal between different antennas, so as to distinguish whether the current target is attacked by GPS spoofing. However, if the attacked target can only receive two GPS signals, or if the GPS spoofing system is deployed in the direction of the satellite-to-target connection, GPS spoofing cannot be detected effectively only by analyzing the direction of arrival of the signal. He et al. [13] proposed a GPS spoofing detection scheme based on signal distortion detection. Because the initial phase and C/A code of GPS signal are relatively stable at each modulation level, the GPS receiver uses different strategies to track the amplitude intensity of the access signal. When the target is deceived, the false signal generated by the attacker is fused with the original satellite signal on the GPS receiver. Users can be warned based on a transient observable peak signal at this time. However, this method can detect the attack only when the target receives the GPS spoofing signal for a very short period of time. When the spoofing signal tends to stabilize, it is difficult to detect whether the system is deceived.

2.2   GPS Spoofing Detection Scheme Based on Cryptography

Wesson et al. [14] defined and evaluated the concept of GNSS signal authentication with a statistically based probability model, incorporating digital signatures into scalable GPS civilian navigation signals. Bonior et al. [4] proposed a

GPS communication signal protection scheme based on quantum key distribution (QKD). During the communication process, the GPS clock is transmitted through two or more trusted entities (Beacons) connected by QKD to ensuring the positioning of the GPS. [15,16] are also some symmetric cryptography based detection schemes, which are generally trade-offs or optimizations of encryption protocols in various GPS signal streams. However, cryptography based GPS spoofing detection schemes usually require manufacturers or users to make changes in the physical structure of the GPS signal broadcasting mode, which increases communication overhead and has a certain degree of influence on the real-time performance of the UAV system. At the same time, it is difficult to cope with the transmitting GPS spoofing attack because the encryption method cannot effectively detect the signal replays.

There are also some spoofing detection schemes [17–20], which locate the drones by auxiliary positioning methods, and compare the target location information obtained by assistant positioning method with the unauthorized location information received by the target GPS receiver, to judge whether the target is attacked by GPS spoofing. For example, the multi-station arrival time based positioning method [21], the conventional time difference based positioning method [22], and the frequency difference based positioning method [23], etc., they have the advantages of long-range, good concealment performance and high positioning accuracy [24], but these methods require each auxiliary station to be in motion relative to the target to be detected, and cannot detect low-speed or stationary targets. For the UAV system, it's usually necessary to perform common missions such as hovering and low-speed flight. If the UAV system suffered from attacks such as GPS spoofing and no-fly zone deception, these methods cannot provide effective and accurate location information for UAV systems.

Therefore, this paper proposes an active GPS spoofing detection method for the specific situation and demands of the UAV system. In our scheme, with adding as little auxiliary equipment as possible, the UAV position information can be resolved in real-time and actively by extracting relevant data from UAV communication links and the inherent inertial navigation device of the UAV, and compared with the positioning information received by GPS receiver. In this case, the system can senses whether the group members are attacked at the first time of the GPS spoofing, thus effectively ensuring the safe flight of UAV.

3   Our Proposed Scheme

We consider each drone in the UAV system as an aerial motion platform, and propose a time difference based positioning method. This method not only overcomes the limitations of traditional positioning methods, achieves three-dimensional positioning of the UAVs in the mission, but also lets UAVs in the system can acquire the location information of all the other units. Thus, the UAV system can actively detect and judge the GPS spoofing attack when using UAV to carry out the flight mission, so as to ensure the safe implementation of the flight mission.

3.1 Multiple UAVs Formation

In the case of a UAVs formation, when the UAV U needs to judge whether it has been deceived, it sends a self-positioning request to the GCS and other drones around. After receiving the request, each of them uploads a position information packet with a time stamp to the GCS, then the GCS calculates the current position of the UAV U through a geometric algorithm. Ideally, after the UAV U sends the self-localization request, we need only three UAVs in the formation to respond to calculate the position of the UAV U.

(1) Obtain Location Information of the GCS. After the UAVs formation took off, the GCS sent a self-positioning request to any three of the drones. After receiving the request, the three drones (recorded as A, B, C) upload position information data packets with time stamps to the GCS respectively. The GCS receives the data packets uploaded by the three drones A, B, and C at $T_i(i = 1, 2, 3)$, then performs BPSK demodulation and Gold Code decoding. According to time $\Delta\tau$ of signal coding and modulation, the arrival time $t_i(i = 1, 2, 3)$ of decoded echoes from drone A, B and C is corrected, the transmission time $t_i + \Delta\tau(i = 1, 2, 3)$ and coordinate $(x_i, y_i, z_i)^T(i = 1, 2, 3)$ recorded in the data packets uploaded by these three UAVs are obtained, and the three-dimensional location information of the GCS itself is calculated through TOA algorithm. That is, the intersection point $(x_0, y_0, z_0)^T$ of three hemispheres are obtained by solving Eq. (1).

$$\rho_i = c\left[T_i - (t_i + \Delta\tau)\right] + n_i, \ i = 1, 2, 3 \tag{1}$$

Where $\rho_i = \sqrt{(x_0 - x_i)^2 + (y_0 - y_i)^2 + (z_0 - z_i)^2}$; c indicates the communication signal transmission speed; $n_i(i = 1, 2, 3)$ is the measurement noise.

(2) Calculate the Location of the Target Srone. Then, the three-dimensional position of the target is determined by the single branch intersection principle of three bilobal hyperboloids. The double-leaf hyperboloid represents the set of points that reach a constant difference between the two intersections. We take the position of the GCS as a common focus of the three two-leaf hyperboloids, and the UAV A, B and C as the other three focuses respectively. The distance difference between the UAV U scattering echo and the UAV A, B, C is fixed. In space, three hyperboloids with only one branch are formed. These three hyperboloids with only one branch form two spatial curves. When these two spatial curves intersect, this point is the position of the UAV U. As shown in Fig. 2, the specific steps are as follows:

(1) When the UAV A, B, and C upload data to the GCS, the GCS will also generate scattering signals to A, B, and C. The time $t_{ai}(i = 1, 2, 3)$ when the scattering signal reaches the three drones will also be recorded by the sensor, thus resulting in positioning errors. Therefore, this arrival time data needs to be excluded.

Calculate the clock time $E = |T_i - t_i - \Delta\tau| - |t_i - T_{A0}| \ (i = 1, 2, 3)$ received by the GCS from UAV A, B and C. Given a $\varepsilon(\varepsilon > 0, \varepsilon \to 0)$, if $E \leq \varepsilon$, it is the time $t_i = t_{ai}(i = 1, 2, 3)$ when the scattered signal from the GCS arrives at the

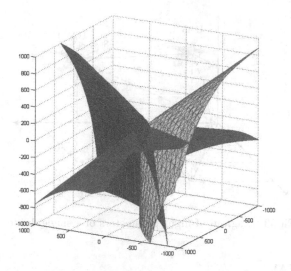

Fig. 2. The UAV U selects 3 other UAVs with the shortest communication time nearby to locate and draw three hyperboloids.

A, B and C, and eliminate this data; if $E \leq \varepsilon$, the time t_i is the time when the scattered signal from UAV U reaches A, B and C.

(2) It is known that the time t_0 when the scattering echo of the UAV U arrives at the GCS and the position coordinate $(x_0, y_0, z_0)^T$ of the GCS. After the time $t_i(i = 1, 2, 3)$ when the drone U scatters back to the drones A, B and C and the position coordinate $(x_i, y_i, z_i)^T (i = 1, 2, 3)$ of them are obtained, the coordinate $(x_U, y_U, z_U)^T$ of drone U is calculated by solving the nonlinear equations of the following Eq. (2).

$$\begin{cases} r_0 = \sqrt{(x_U - x_0)^2 + (y_U - y_0)^2 + (z_U - z_0)^2} \\ r_i = \sqrt{(x_U - x_0)^2 + (y_U - y_0)^2 + (z_U - z_0)^2} \quad , (i = 1, 2, 3) \\ \Delta r_i = r_i - r_0 = c(t_i - t_0) + \omega_i \end{cases} \quad (2)$$

Since we only need to judge whether the UAV is subject to GPS spoofing and do not need to be accurately positioned, it can be assumed that the ω_i is a Gaussian white noise with a variance of σ^2, and a mean of 0.

Given a decision threshold tsh_1, the drone U compares the coordinate(x_U, y_U, z_U) with the original GPS coordinate information received by the GPS receiver, and calculates the Euclidean distance $l(x, y, z)$ between the two. If $l(x, y, z) < tsh_1$, it means that the drone U is currently operating according to the predetermined trajectory; if $l(x, y, z) > tsh_1$, it indicates that the drone U has suffered a GPS spoofing attack.

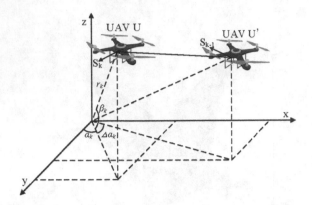

Fig. 3. Diagram of flight parameters of a single drone.

3.2 Single UAV

When the UAV U needs to judge whether it is deceived or not, it sends a self-positioning request to formation members nearby group members, and the number of responding drones around is less than 3, the number of drones in the formation is too small to realize the detection scheme in Sect. 3.1. At this time, we adopt the method of combining relevant angle and angle change rate to conduct real-time regional positioning and tracking of the target drone. Only the location information of the target to be detected is considered, and the location information is compared with the original GPS signal received by the system at any time to determine whether the target drone is currently attacked by GPS spoofing. As shown in Fig. 3. At this point, the position of the GCS is taken as the coordinate origin. Since it is only necessary to discuss whether the UAV U is attacked by GPS spoofing, the accuracy of the positioning allows a certain degree of error. After eliminating the effects of atmospheric disturbances, the target motion model of the UAV U can be described by the uniform motion model with a acceleration disturbance. After the UAV U took off, the communication signal with a period of T_r is carried out between the GCS and the UAV U (in general, only the estimation of the signal repetition period T_{ro} can be obtained, and T_{ro} is constantly updated), and the observed value is recorded every N pulses. $\Delta T_r = T_r - T_{ro}$ is taken as the estimation deviation and added into the state variable of the UAV U for calculation.

The state vector of time k is taken as $S_k = (x_k, y_k, z_k, x_{Uk}, y_{Uk}, z_{Uk}, \Delta T_{rk})^T$, and the GCS is taken as the coordinate origin, then the state equation of the UAV U is:

$$S_{k+1} = \Phi_{k+1|k} S_k + W_k \tag{3}$$

In the equation, $\Phi_{k+1|k} = \begin{pmatrix} I_{3\times3} & TI_{3\times3} & 0_{3\times1} \\ 0_{4\times3} & I_{4\times4} \end{pmatrix}$ is a state transition matrix, $W_k = \left(\omega_{xk}T_0^2/2, \omega_{yk}T_0^2/2, \omega_{zk}T_0^2/2, \omega_{xk}T_0, \omega_{yk}T_0, \omega_{zk}T_0, 0\right)^T$ is a measurement noise, and can be approximated as a Gaussian white noise with a mean of 0 and a variance of $Q_k \delta_{\eta k}$ ($T_0 = NT_{ro}$ is the observation time).

The azimuth angle α_k, the pitch angle β_k, the azimuth change rate $\Delta \alpha_k$ (which can be obtained by a phase interferometer) of the UAV U and the one-way arrival time T_{Ak} of the communication signal is recorded every time T_0 interval of the GCS. When the UAV U moves, the radial distance between it and the GCS changes, thus,

$$\begin{cases} \Delta T_{Ak} = T_{Ak} - T_{Ak-1} \\ T_{Ai} = r_i/c \end{cases} \tag{4}$$

Where r_i is the radial distance from the UAV U to the GCS at time T_{Ai}, and $r_i = \sqrt{x_i^2 + y_i^2 + z_i^2}$, c is the propagation speed of the communication signal. Since T_r is a constant, and a constant value T_{ro} is obtained every k time intervals, and $\Delta T_r = T_r - T_{ro}$, so the ΔT_{rk} does not change from time $k-1$ to time k. Take the derivative of both sides of the azimuth formula $\Delta \alpha_k = (x'_k y_k + x_k y'_k)/(x_k^2 + y_k^2)$ to get $\alpha_k = \arctan(x_k/y_k)$, and obtain a nonlinear measurement equation,

$$\begin{cases} \alpha_k = \arctan(x_k/y_k) + \delta_{\alpha k} \\ \beta_k = \arctan\left(z_k \Big/ \sqrt{x_k^2 + y_k^2}\right) + \delta_{\beta k} \\ \Delta \alpha_k = (x'_k y_k + x_k y'_k)/(x_k^2 + y_k^2) + \delta_{\alpha k} \\ \Delta T_{Ak} = (r_k - r_{k-1})/c + NT_{rok} + NT_{rk} + \delta_{tk} \end{cases} \tag{5}$$

Next, combining the kinematics principle of the particle and the motion information of the target, the state of the UAV U is solved. When the relative displacement between the UAV U and the GCS occurs, the radial distance r, the azimuth α and the pitch angle β change with time. Take the visual orthogonal coordinate system $(e_r, e_\alpha, e_\beta)^T$, where e_r is determined, e_α and e_β are the directions of increase of the angles α and β respectively. Then the motion state of the UAV U can be described as

$$\begin{aligned} r &= r e_r \\ v &= r' e_r + r e'_r \end{aligned} \tag{6}$$

The velocity vector in the e_r direction is $v_{er} = \omega e_r$, where $\omega = -\alpha' e_z + \beta' e_\alpha$ and $e_z = \cos\beta \cdot e_\beta + \sin\beta \cdot e_r$, it can be obtained that,

$$\begin{aligned} v &= r' e_r + r e'_r = r' e_r + r\alpha' \cos\beta \cdot e_\alpha + r\beta' e_\beta \\ &= r' e_r + V_{Ho} e_\alpha + V_{Ve} e_\beta \end{aligned} \tag{7}$$

In the equation, V_{Ho} and V_{Ve} are the horizontal tangential and vertical tangential velocity components of the UAV U in the visual coordinate system, $V_{Ho} = r\alpha' \cos\beta$ is known, $V_{Ho} = v_x \cos\alpha - v_y \sin\alpha$ is known through the kinematics principle. After obtaining the velocity information of the UAV U in the rectangular coordinate system, the radial distance r from the UAV U to the GCS can be obtained, there is,

$$r = (v_x \cos\alpha - v_y \sin\alpha)/\alpha' \cos\beta \tag{8}$$

After ranging, due to the correlation between angular measurements and velocity estimation errors, a non-linear filtering algorithm is used to obtain the position of the target through the geometric principle combined with angle measured values α and β, and to realize real-time tracking and recording of the flight path of the UAV U. Giving a decision threshold tsh_2, the UAV U compares this radial distance with the radial distance r_0 calculated from the original GPS coordinate information received by the system GPS receiver. If $|r - r_0| < threshold_2$, it indicates that the UAV U is currently operating normally according to the predetermined trajectory. If $|r - r_0| > threshold_2$, it indicates that the target has been attacked by GPS spoofing.

4   Evaluation

In order to verify the feasibility of the scheme, this paper conducts a positioning and tracking of the UAVs formation through simulation experiments. The flight speed of each unit of the UAVs formation is known in these experiments. In order to simplify the simulation process without loss of generality, the UAV is regarded as a uniform sphere, and it is assumed that the location of each unit in the UAVs formation is trusted before the time m. And during the communication process of positioning between the drone and the GCS, the two are in a relatively static state.

In the simulation experiment of the UAVs formation, our proposed method detects the GPS spoofing attack by locating the target UAV. Therefore, we use the geometrical dilution of precision (GDOP) to measure the detection accuracy of the proposed GPS spoofing detection technology, i.e., $GDOP = \sqrt{tr(\mathbf{P})}$, where $\mathbf{P}$ is the covariance matrix of the positioning error; $tr(\cdot)$ is the trace of the covariance matrix $\mathbf{P}$. Take the derivative of both sides of the following equation,

$$\begin{cases} r_0 = \sqrt{(x_U - x_0)^2 + (y_U - y_0)^2 + (z_U - z_0)^2} \\ r_i = \sqrt{(x_U - x_0)^2 + (y_U - y_0)^2 + (z_U - z_0)^2} \quad , (i = 1, 2, 3) \\ \Delta r_i = r_i - r_0 = c(t_i - t_0) + \omega_i \end{cases}$$

In order to facilitate the solution, it is recorded as $c_{ix} = \frac{\partial r_i}{\partial x} = \frac{x - x_i}{r_i}$, $c_{iy} = \frac{\partial r_i}{\partial y} = \frac{y - y_i}{r_i}$, $c_{iz} = \frac{\partial r_i}{\partial z} = \frac{z - z_i}{r_i}$ Finished out:

$$let \mathbf{C} = \begin{bmatrix} c_{1x} - c_{0x} & c_{2x} - c_{0x} & c_{3x} - c_{0x} \\ c_{1y} - c_{0y} & c_{2y} - c_{0y} & c_{3y} - c_{0y} \\ c_{1z} - c_{0z} & c_{2z} - c_{0z} & c_{3z} - c_{0z} \end{bmatrix},$$

$d\Delta \mathbf{r} = [d\Delta r_1, d\Delta r_2, d\Delta r_3]^T$, $d\mathbf{x} = [dx, dy, dz]$, $d\omega = [d\omega_1, d\omega_2, d\omega_3]^T$ then $d\Delta \mathbf{r} = \mathbf{C} d\mathbf{x} + d\omega$ The errors of arrival time measurement of the GCS are included in the process of time difference measurement. In the experiment, it is assumed that the noise errors of each Δr_i are irrelevant, and the least square method is chosen to solve the problem. The covariance matrix of the positioning error of the target UAV is:

$$P = E\left[\mathbf{dxdx}^T\right]$$
$$= E\left[\left(\mathbf{C}^T\mathbf{C}\right)^{-1}\mathbf{C}^T\mathbf{dxdx}^T\mathbf{C}\left(\mathbf{C}^T\mathbf{C}\right)^{-T}\right]$$
$$= \left(\mathbf{C}^T\mathbf{C}\right)^{-1}\mathbf{C}^T\mathbf{dxdx}^T\mathbf{C}\left(\mathbf{C}^T\mathbf{C}\right)^{-T}$$

The GDOP factor is:

$$GDOP = \sqrt{\mathrm{d}x^2 + \mathrm{d}y^2 + \mathrm{d}z^2}$$
$$= \sqrt{tr\left(E\left[\mathbf{dxdx}^T\right]\right)} = \sqrt{tr(\mathbf{P})}$$

Simulation 1. The time difference measurement error is set as 10 ns. In the experiment, it was set that there were 5 UAVs performing missions in the UAVs formation, all of which were controlled by the GCS and operated in accordance with the predetermined flight trajectory. The UAV U was attacked by GPS spoofing at 30 s after takeoff. The method proposed in Sect. 3.1 was used for 1000 Monte Carlo simulations. The flight trajectory of the target is shown in Fig. 4.

Taking time $t = 120$ s as an example, the coordinate of the intersection point in Fig. 2 is (58.4, 4.7, 153.2), which is the real-time position calculated by the UAV U through the method in this paper. The error between the real position and the intersection point is about 2 m.

Giving that the altitude of the target is 150 m, in the experimental environment of Simulation 1, the GDOP of target positioning is shown in Fig. 5. When the measurement error of time difference is 10 ns, the positioning error of the target is about 7.71 m, and the maximum positioning accuracy can reach 0.67 m near the center of the coverage area of the GCS. In the real scene, it can accurately determine whether the target is attacked by GPS spoofing

Simulation 2. Using the parameters setting in Simulation 1, the experiment was carried out on a single UAV, and 1000 Monte Carlo simulations were performed using the proposed method. The flight path of the target to be detected is shown in Fig. 6. It can be seen from the simulation results that the real-time trajectory of the target calculated by this method has strong credibility. After giving the appropriate decision conditions, it can accurately determine whether the target drone has been attacked by GPS spoofing.

In the environment of simulating the flight mission of a single drone, assuming that the measurement error of time difference increases from 2 ns to 20 ns, we conduct 1000 Monte Carlo experiments for each case, and use $bias(\theta) = E\left[\hat{\theta}\right] - \theta$ to measure the estimation deviation in x, y and z directions, then calculate the root mean square error (RMSE). Figure 7 shows the RMSE under different time measurement errors. Through calculation, it is concluded that the estimated RMSE of x, y and z components of the target position can reach CRLB, which are within the acceptable range and meet the requirements of GPS spoofing detection. It is pointed out that the estimated RMSE error of the z component

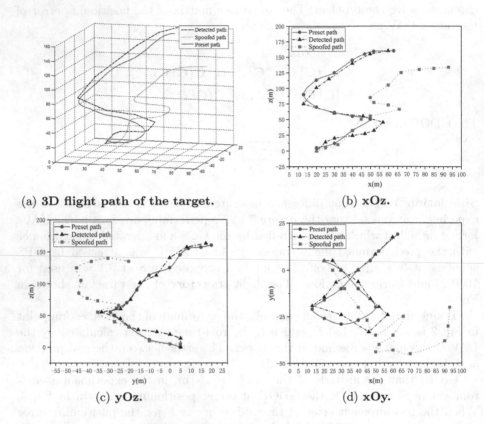

(a) **3D flight path of the target.**   (b) **xOz.**

(c) **yOz.**   (d) **xOy.**

Fig. 4. Flight trajectory of the target

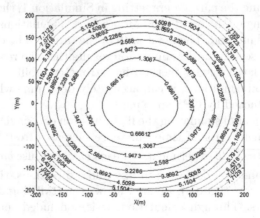

Fig. 5. Positioning GDOP of the drone at the height of target.

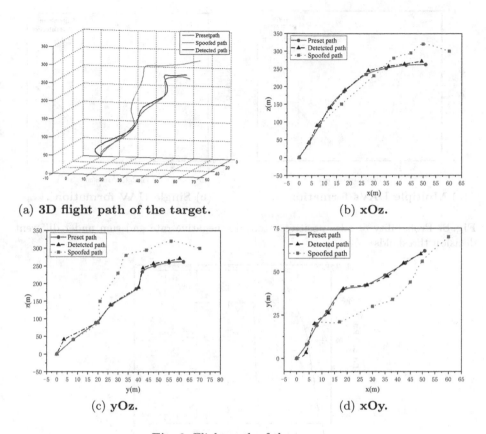

(a) **3D flight path of the target.**

(b) **xOz.**

(c) **yOz.**

(d) **xOy.**

Fig. 6. Flight path of the target.

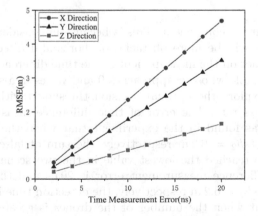

Fig. 7. RMSE of target position under different time difference measurement error.

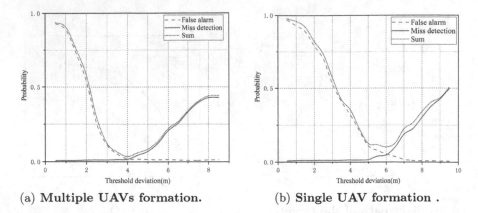

(a) **Multiple UAVs formation.**   (b) **Single UAV formation .**

Fig. 8. Probability of false positive rate, false negative rate and sum under different decision thresholds

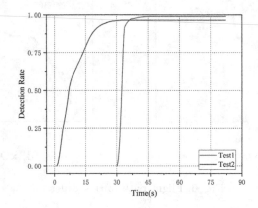

Fig. 9. Detection time.

is less than the x and y component. This is because in consideration of the real environment, there will be more obstacles on horizontal direction, which will have a certain impact on the measurement of the time difference, we arranged a Gaussian noise variable whose σ approaches 0 and varies in a small range.

In Fig. 8, we explore the optimal decision thresholds with minimum false alarm rate and miss rate. The error of time difference measurement was set as 20 ns, and it was found in the experiment that when the thresholds were $tsh_1 = 4.1$ m and $tsh_2 = 6.2$ m respectively, the sum of false alarm rate and missing alarm rate reached the lowest value in the two scenarios. In the case where the time difference measurement error is 20 ns and the thresholds are $tsh_1 = 4.1$ m and $tsh_2 = 6.2$ m respectively, the detection time is given in Fig. 9. It can be seen that when the number of the drones is greater than 4, it can be stably detected within 8 s after the system is spoofed, and the detection rate can reach 98.6%. When the number of the drones is less than 4, it will take

28 s to keep track of the target to detect whether the target is attacked by GPS spoofing, and the detection rate can reach 96.7%.

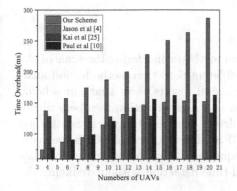

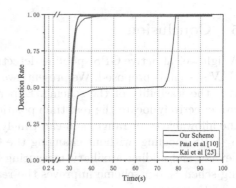

Fig. 10. Comparison of effective communication time overhead

Fig. 11. Comparison of detection time

In the same simulation environment, we compare the scheme of this paper with the existing schemes [4,10,25]. [26] points out that when the time cost of communication link in the UAV system exceeds 100ms, the measurability of relevant parameters will usually decline, and the flight quality of the UAV cannot be guaranteed when it is about 250–300 ms.

Firstly, we analyze the relationship between the time cost of one effective communication of the UAV system in each scheme and the number of formation members. It can be seen from the Fig. 10, in the GPS spoofing detection scheme based on cryptography [4], the communication overhead will seriously affect the normal operation of the UAV system with the increase of formation members; Jansen et al. [25] proposed the Crowd-GPS-Sec based GPS spoofing scheme to counter GPS spoofing attacks by means of broadcasting. Therefore, the change of formation members has no obvious impact on the communication link of UAV system. The experimental results show that when the number of drones increases, the time cost of the primary effective communication of UAVs in our scheme increases, but it does not affect the measurement of the related parameters. Our scheme can still effectively resist GPS spoofing attack in this case, and is better than the detection scheme based on the physical layer characteristics of GPS signals proposed by Hamelmann et al. [10].

Then, we compare the detection rate of each scheme and the required detection time when the UAV system is attacked. In the specific experiment, we set the number of UAVs formation members to 5, the simulation results are shown in Fig. 11. When the UAV system is spoofed, our scheme can detect the spoofing attack faster than others. The detection rate is slightly lower (about 0.2%) than the GPS detection scheme proposed by Kai et al., but their detection scheme based on Crowd-GPS-Sec need to take about 82 s to integrate the location information of all members of the system and broadcast it to the formation to achieve stable detection of GPS spoofing attacks. The experimental results show that the scheme can greatly improve the real-time detection of GPS spoofing attacks while ensuring the effectiveness of detection.

5   Conclusion

A lightweight active GPS spoofing detection method considering the scale of the UAV system is proposed. We present two different detection methods, and analyses the feasibility of the scheme. Experimental results show that our scheme can effectively locate the real-time position of UAVs formation members within the allowable error range, and can timely detect whether the system is attacked by GPS spoofing, without changing the GPS infrastructure and GPS receiving device, and adding auxiliary measuring equipment. Compared with the existing schemes, our scheme improves the real-time detection without reducing the detection rate.

Acknowledgment. This work were supported by National Natural Science Foundation of China (Grant Nos. U1708262, U1736203, 61772173, 61672413).

References

1. Psiaki, M.L., Humphreys, T.: Protecting GPS from spoofers is critical to the future of navigation. IEEE Spectrum. http://spectrum.ieee.org/telecom/security/protecting-gps-from-spoofers-is-critical-to-the-future-of-navigation. Accessed 29 July 2016
2. Amirtha, T.: Satnav spoofing attacks: why these researchers think they have the answer. ZDNet. http://www.zdnet.com/article/satnav-spoofing-attacks-why-these-researchers-think-they-have-the-answer. Accessed 27 Mar 2017
3. Kugler, L.: Why GPS spoofing is a threat to companies, countries. Commun. ACM **60**(9), 18–19 (2017)
4. Bonior, J., Evans, P., Sheets, G., et al.: Implementation of a wireless time distribution testbed protected with quantum key distribution. In: 2017 IEEE Wireless Communications and Networking Conference, pp. 1–6. IEEE, San Francisco (2017)
5. Psiaki, M.L., O'Hanlon, B.W., Bhatti, J.A., et al.: GPS spoofing detection via Dual-Receiver correlation of military signals. IEEE Trans. Aerosp. Electron. Syst. **49**(4), 2250–2267 (2013)
6. Yangy, K., Luoz, Z.-Q.: Robust target localization with multiple sensors using time difference of arrivals. In: Radar Conference, pp. 1–6. IEEE, Rome (2008)
7. Jansen, K., Tippenhauer, N.O., Pőpper, C.: Multi-receiver GPS spoofing detection: error models and realization. In: Annual Conference on Computer Security Applications, pp. 237–250. ACM, California (2016)
8. Tippenhauer, N.O., Pőpper, C., Rasmussen, K.B., Capkun, S.: On the requirements for successful GPS spoofing attacks. In: Computer and Communications Security, pp. 75–86. ACM, Illinois (2011)
9. Jansen, K., Schafer, M., Lenders, V., Pőpper, C., Schmitt, J.: POSTER: localization of spoofing devices using a Large-scale air traffic surveillance system. In: Asia Conference on Computer and Communications Security, pp. 914–916. ACM, Abu Dhabi (2017)

10. Hamelmann, P., Vullings, R., Mischi, M., et al.: An extended Kalman filter for fetal heart location estimation during Doppler-based heart rate monitoring. IEEE Trans. Instrum. Measur. 1–11 (2018)
11. Jafarnia-Jahromi, A., Broumandan, A., Nielsen, J., Lachapelle, G.: GPS vulnerability to spoofing threats and a review of antispoofing techniques. Int. J. Navig. Obs. **2012**, 1–16 (2012)
12. Psiaki, M.L., Humphreys, T.E., Stauer, B.: Attackers can spoof navigation signals without our knowledge. Here's how to fight back GPS lies. IEEE Spectr. **53**(8), 26–53 (2016)
13. He, L., Li, W., Guo, C., Niu, R.: Civilian unmanned aerial vehicle vulnerability to GPS spooing attacks. In: International Symposium on Computational Intelligence and Design, pp. 212–215. IEEE, Hangzhou (2015)
14. Wesson, K.D., Rothlisberger, M., Humphreys, T.E.: Practical cryptographic civil GPS signal authentication. Navigation **59**(3), 177–193 (2012)
15. O'Hanlon, B.W., Psiaki, M.L., Bhatti, J.A., et al.: Real-time GPS spoofing detection via correlation of encrypted signals. Navigation **60**(4), 267–278 (2013)
16. Kerns, A.J., Wesson, K.D., Humphreys, T.E.: A blueprint for civil GPS navigation message authentication. In: Position, Location and Navigation Symposium, pp. 262–269. IEEE, Monterey (2014)
17. Tang, Y., Hu, Y., Cui, J., et al.: Vision-Aided multi-UAV autonomous flocking in GPS-denied environment. IEEE Trans. Ind. Electron. **66**(1), 616–626 (2019)
18. Humphreys, T.E.: Detection strategy for cryptographic GNSS anti-spoofing. IEEE Trans. Aerosp. Electron. Syst. **49**(2), 1073–1090 (2013)
19. Yin, S., Zhao, Y., Li, L.: Resource allocation and basestation placement in cellular networks with wireless powered UAVs. IEEE Trans. Veh. Technol. **68**(1), 1050–1055 (2019)
20. Psiaki, M.L., Humphreys, T.E.: GNSS spoofing and detection. Proc. IEEE **104**(6), 1258–1270 (2016)
21. Zhang, Z., Trinkle, M., Qian, L., Li, H.: Quickest detection of GPS spoofing attack. In: Military Communications Conference, pp. 1–6. IEEE, Orlando (2012)
22. Chan, Y.-T., Ho, K.: A simple and efficient estimator for hyperbolic location. IEEE Trans. Sig. Process. **42**(8), 1905–1915 (1994)
23. Ho, K.O., Lu, X., Kovavisaruch, L.: Source localization using TDOA and FDOA measurements in the presence of receiver location errors: analysis and solution. IEEE Trans. Sig. Process. **55**(2), 684–696 (2007)
24. Yang, K., An, J.P., Bu, X.Y., Sun, G.C.: Constrained total least-squares location algorithm using Time-Difference-of-Arrival measurements. IEEE Trans. Veh. Technol. **59**(3), 1558–1562 (2010)
25. Jansen, K., Schäfer, M., Moser, D., et al.: Crowd-GPS-Sec: leveraging crowdsourcing to detect and localize GPS spoofing attacks. In: Security and Privacy, pp. 1018–1031. IEEE, San Francisco (2018)
26. Fadlullah, Z.M., Takaishi, D., Nishiyama, H., et al.: A dynamic trajectory control algorithm for improving the communication throughput and delay in UAV-aided networks. IEEE Netw. **30**(1), 100–105 (2016)

SwipeVLock: A Supervised Unlocking Mechanism Based on Swipe Behavior on Smartphones

Wenjuan Li[1,2], Jiao Tan[3], Weizhi Meng[1,4(✉)], Yu Wang[1], and Jing Li[1]

[1] School of Computer Science, Guangzhou University, Guangzhou, China
weme@dtu.dk
[2] Department of Computer Science, City University of Hong Kong,
Kowloon, China
[3] KOTO Research Center, Macao, China
[4] Department of Applied Mathematics and Computer Science,
Technical University of Denmark, Lyngby, Denmark

Abstract. Smartphones have become a necessity in people's daily lives, and changed the way of communication at any time and place. Nowadays, mobile devices especially smartphones have to store and process a large amount of sensitive information, i.e., from personal to financial and professional data. For this reason, there is an increasing need to protect the devices from unauthorized access. In comparison with the traditional textual password, behavioral authentication can verify current users in a continuous way, which can complement the existing authentication mechanisms. With the advanced capability provided by current smartphones, users can perform various touch actions to interact with their devices. In this work, we focus on swipe behavior and aim to design a machine learning-based unlock scheme called SwipeVLock, which verifies users based on their way of swiping the phone screen with a background image. In the evaluation, we measure several typical supervised learning algorithms and conduct a user study with 30 participants. Our experimental results indicate that participants could perform well with SwipeVLock, i.e., with a success rate of 98% in the best case.

Keywords: User authentication · Behavioral biometric · Swipe behavior · Smartphone security · Touch action

1 Introduction

With the revolution of information technology, mobile devices like smartphones have become prevalent in people's lives. More users are willing to store private information on their devices and use them to process some sensitive information for mobility and convenience [27,50]. However, this also makes smartphones a major target by cyber-criminals [31]. If attackers get the phone and unlock it successfully, then they can easily steal all sensitive data. Thus, there is a

© Springer Nature Switzerland AG 2019
X. Chen et al. (Eds.): ML4CS 2019, LNCS 11806, pp. 140–153, 2019.
https://doi.org/10.1007/978-3-030-30619-9_11

demanding requirement for implementing user authentication mechanisms to prevent unauthorized access.

Up to now, the most widely adopted authentication approach is still based on textual passwords. For example, iPhones use PIN code to protect the devices, but it may suffer many invasions, e.g., recording attacks [31]. In real-world applications, users have multiple accounts and may choose easy-to-remember passwords due to the multiple password inference [28] and limitation of long term memory [49]. Some research studies like [3,48] revealed that this situation may become even worse under existing state-of-the-art attacks. For example, the report from SplashData showed that the most frequently used password in 2018 is "123456" [39].

As an alternative, graphical passwords (GP) were developed to enhance the authentication process, since many studies like [30,36] identified that people could remember images better than string passwords. There are many GP schemes in the literature. For instance, Jermyn *et al.* [14] introduced DAS (draw-a-secret) that requires users to draw their passwords on a 2D grid. Wiedenbeck *et al.* [47] developed *PassPoints* that allows creating users' credentials by clicking on some locations on an image. In practice, GP schemes are not widely adopted by mobile devices, but there exists a typical application called *Android unlock patterns*, which requires users inputting correct patterns to unlock their phones in a grid size of 3×3 points [2,7]. For authentication, users have to recall the pattern registered during the enrollment.

However, Android unlock patterns may be vulnerable to many attacks in real-world usage, as users can only choose a pattern with 4 dots at least and 9 dots at most. This makes Brute-force attack feasible because the total number of possible patterns is only 389,112 [1]. In addition, it also suffers recording attacks [31] and charging attacks [25,26] (i.e., the phone screen can be captured by attackers). As a result, there is a great demand to enhance the security of such unlocking mechanism.

Contributions. Many existing research studies have shown that combining behavioral biometric could provide an additional security layer to safeguard the Android unlock patterns [7,17,52]. For example, De Luca et al. [7] showed how to combine behavioral biometric with unlock patterns using dynamic time warping (DTW). Motivated by this, in this work, we advocate the merit of enhancing authentication with behavioral biometric, and develop SwipeVLock, a swipe behavior-based unlock mechanism on smartphones. In our scheme, users can choose a background image and a location on the image to swipe their finger. The contributions of this work can be summarized as follows.

- We design SwipeVLock, a phone unlocking scheme that verifies users based on how they swipe the touchscreen. For enrollment, users have to choose one background image and one location, and then register their swipe behavior. This mechanism is transparent without additional hardware on smartphones. We also test several typical supervised learning algorithms for authentication.
- In the user study, we involve a total of 30 common phone users to evaluate the performance of SwipeVLock. Based on the collected data and users' feedback,

it is found that our scheme can provide good usability in practice. SwipeVLock can be considered as one alternative to complement existing solutions.

Road Map. The rest of this paper is structured as follows. Section 2 introduces related authentication schemes based on either graphical passwords or touch behavioral biometric. Section 3 describes our scheme of SwipeVLock in detail. In Sect. 4, we conduct a user study with 30 participants and analyze the collected data. We discuss some open challenges and conclude our work in Sects. 5 and 6.

2 Related Work

This section introduces related studies regarding graphical passwords schemes and touch behavioral authentication.

2.1 Authentication Based on Graphical Password

Graphical passwords have been researched over decades. There are three major types for a traditional GP scheme [4,29,42]: recognition-based scheme, pure recall-based scheme and cued recall-based scheme.

- *Recognition-based scheme.* This kind of scheme (e.g., [6,32]) needs users to remember and recognize several images. Taking *PassFaces* [32] as a typical example, it requires users to figure out human faces for user authentication.
- *Pure recall-based scheme.* This type of scheme requires users to generate a pattern on an image. For example, Jermyn *et al.* [14] introduces *DAS* ('draw-a-secret'), in which users have to create their passwords on a grid. Android unlock pattern (AUP) mechanism belongs to this type, asking users to swipe their finger to input a correct pattern and unlock the device. It is indeed a modified version of Pass-Go [44], in order to fit a small touchscreen. AUP has some rules, i.e., it defines a valid pattern with 4 dots at least and 9 dots at most, within a grid of 3×3 points on smartphones.
- *Cued recall-based scheme.* Such schemes require users to create a pattern on an image or more images. Taking a typical system of *PassPoints* [47] as an example, it needs users to remember five points on one image in an order. Then Chiasson *et al.* [5] introduced Persuasive Cued Click-Points (PCCP), in which users have to pick a point on a sequence of background images.

In addition to the above major schemes, existing GP schemes are more integrated. For example, with the aim of enhancing the password space, world map has been proposed as the background image, in which users can choose a location worldwide [11,38]. Based on this idea, Sun *et al.* [43] designed *PassMap* that requires users to choose two locations (in an order) on a world map. Then Thorpe *et al.* [45] introduced *GeoPass* that only requires users to select one location. The previous study showed that there is no significant difference between the selection of one or two locations [29]. Meng [22] designed *RouteMap*, a map-based scheme that demands users to create a route on a world map.

Similar to textual passwords, graphical passwords may also suffer the issue of multiple password interference. Meng *et al.* [28] investigated this issue with 60 participants between textual passwords and map-based passwords under six account scenarios. They found that participants in the map-based graphical password scheme could perform better than the textual password scheme in both short-term (one-hour session) and long term (after two weeks) password memorability tests.

To further enhance the performance of graphical passwords, there is a balance should be made between security and usability. A set of hybrid GP schemes were also developed in the literature, like click-draw based GP scheme [17]. Some relevant GP studies could be referred but not limited to [8,9,13,16–20,23,24,27,51].

2.2 Touch Behavioral Authentication

With the advent of touchscreen, touch dynamics has become popular on smartphones. Fen *et al.* [10] developed a finger gesture-based authentication system on touchscreen devices, reaching a FAR of 4.66% and a FRR of 0.13% based on a random forest classifier. Meng *et al.* [17] validated the feasibility of touch behavioral authentication on smartphones, where they designed scheme with 21 features and achieved an average error rate of around 3% based on a combined classifier of PSO-RBFN. Frank *et al.* [12] developed *Touchalytics*, a touch behavioral authentication scheme with 30 features, and reached a median equal error rate of around 4% (one week after the enrollment phase).

Up to now, more touch behavioral authentication schemes have been proposed [21]. Zheng *et al.* [53] researched users' tapping behaviors on a passcode-enabled smartphone, and achieved an averaged equal error rate of nearly 3.65% by using a one-class algorithm. Smith-Creasey and Rajarajan [37] achieved an equal error rate of 3.77% by means of a stacked classifier approach. Sharma and Enbody [41] studied how users interact with the application interface, and achieved a mean equal error rate of 7% for user authentication based on the SVM-based ensemble classifier. Shahzad *et al.* [40] researched users' particular behavior and designed an authentication scheme based on how users input a gesture or a signature, such as velocity, device acceleration, and stroke time.

3   Design of SwipeVLock

The purpose of our proposed SwipeVLock is to complement existing unlocking mechanisms on smartphones, through involving touch behavioral authentication. Figure 1 shows the basic design of SwipeVLock with three major steps.

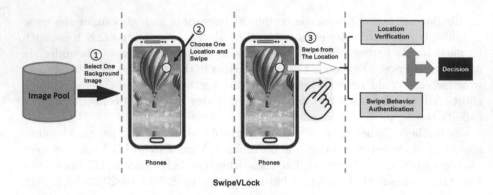

Fig. 1. SwipeVLock: (1) Step1: select one background image from a pool; (2) Step2: choose one location on the background image; and (3) Step3: swipe from the selected location to unlock the phone.

SwipeVLock Enrollment. Users have to select one background image from an image pool, with different themes such as fruits, cartoon characters, sport, landscape, food, buildings, transportation, people, etc. Then, users can choose one location as the starting point and then swipe the screen from this selected location.

SwipeVLock Verification. For authentication, users have to select the same background image from the pool, and swipe the screen from the same location on the image. The authentication process can be regarded to be successful, if and only if both image location and swipe behavior are verified by our scheme.

SwipeVLock Framework. Figure 2 depicts how to realize SwipeVLock. In this work, our scheme employs a supervised learning-based framework to help model users' touch behavior. When users swipe the screen, SwipeVLock will extract the touch features from swipe behavior and train the classifier. The classifier mainly generates a normal profile based on the swipe behavior, and compares it with the current swipe features. A decision will be output in the end.

On the other hand, SwipeVLock can compare the image location with the stored location in the database. If there is a match, then it is considered to be successful. In particular, we set the error tolerance to a 21×21 pixel box around the selected location. This selection is based on the previous work like [29,45]. For example, *GeoPass* [45] proved that an error tolerance of 21×21 pixel is usable in practice.

Swipe Features. In this work, based on the previous studies [7,12,24], we consider some common and typical touch features that can be used to model swipe behavior: the coordinates of location (XY), touch pressure, touch size, touch time, and touch speed.

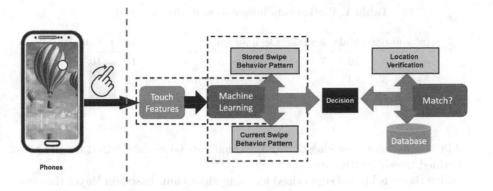

Fig. 2. Detailed authentication processes for SwipeVlock.

- *Coordinates of location.* Our scheme records the location coordinates on the selected image. Intuitively, users may have their own selection preference, making the location different from others.
- *Touch pressure.* With the increasing capability of smartphones, current screen sensors are able to identify the values of touch pressure, which can be used to model users' touch behavior.
- *Touch duration.* This feature can be computed by measuring the time difference between touch press-down and touch press-up. It is a common feature that can be used to distinguish different users, i.e., some users may press longer while some may press shorter.
- *Touch speed.* Intuitively, swipe behavior can be treated as a swift touch movement. Based on [24], suppose a swipe action starts from (x1, y1) and ends at (x2, y2), if we know relevant time of occurrence *T1* and *T2*, then we can calculate the touch speed according to Eq. (1).

$$Touch\ Speed = \frac{\sqrt{(x2 - x1)^2 + (y2 - y1)^2}}{T2 - T1} \tag{1}$$

4 User Study

To investigate the performance of our scheme, we perform a user study with 30 participants who are regular Android phone users. The detailed information is shown in Table 1. In particular, we have 17 males and 13 females who aged from 18 to 45. Most of them are students in addition to business people, university staff and faculty members. A \$20 gift voucher was provided to each participant.

Supervised Learning. As mentioned in Fig. 2, SwipeVLock uses supervised learning algorithms to help verify users. In this work, we consider the following classifiers as a study: Decision tree (J48), Naive Bayes, SVM and Back Propagation Neural Network (BPNN). These are the typical and popular classifiers in the literature.

Table 1. Participants information in the user study.

Information	Male	Female	Occupation	Male	Female
Age <25	10	7	Students	13	10
Age 25–35	4	4	University Faculty&Staff	2	2
Age 35–45	3	2	Business People	2	1

- J48 is a decision tree classifier [33], which can label data based on the pre-trained tree-like structure.
- Naive Bayes is kind of supervised learning algorithms based on Bayes theorem by assuming conditional independence between every pair of features given the value of the class variable [34].
- BPNN is a kind of neural network classifier [35], which uses a differentiable transfer function at each network node and then uses error back-propagation process to modify the internal network weights after each training round.
- Support Vector Machine (SVM) [15] is a linear model for both classification or regression challenges, by generating a line or a hyperplane that separates the data into classes.

To avoid any bias during classifier implementation, we adopted WEKA platform, which is an open-source machine learning collection in Java [46]. We used the default settings for all classifiers in the study. Below are two metrics used to evaluate the performance of our scheme.

- False Acceptance Rate (FAR): indicates the percent of how many intruders are classified as normal users.
- False Rejection Rate (FRR): indicates the percent of how many legitimate users are classified as intruders.

Study Steps. In the study, we first introduced our objectives to all participants and demonstrated what kind of data would be collected. Each participant could get one Android phone (Samsung Galaxy Note) and before the experiment, each of them has three trials to get familiar with the scheme. Then we randomly divided participants into two groups. In particular, Group-A was asked to perform the experiment in our lab, while the participants in Group-B could set their SwipeVLock in the lab and keep using the phone outside. Below are the detailed study steps.

- *Group1.* Participants in this group were required to complete the experiment in the lab.
  - Step 1. Creation phase: participants have to create their credentials according to SwipeVLock' steps.
  - Step 2. Confirmation phase: participants should confirm the password by verifying both the image location and swipe behavior for 10 times (used for classifier selection). Participants could modified their credentials if they fail or want to change it.

- Step 3. Distributed memory: participants were provided one paper-based finding tasks to distract them for 15 min.
- Step 4. Login phase: participants should swipe to unlock the phone for 10 trials. The system recorded all the data for analysis.
- Step 5. Feedback form: participants should respond to several questions in a *feedback form* regarding our scheme usage.
- Step 6. Retention. After three days, participants were asked to return and unlock the phone for 10 times in our lab.
- Step 7. Participants have to finish another *feedback from* regarding our scheme usage.

- *Group2.* Participants in this group could create their SwipeVLock credentials in the lab, and then keep using the phone outside the lab.
  - Step 1. Creation phase: participants have to create their credentials according to SwipeVLock' steps.
  - Step 2. Confirmation phase: participants should confirm the password by verifying both the image location and swipe behavior for 10 times (used for classifier selection). Participants could modified their credentials if they fail or want to change it.
  - Step 3. Distributed memory: participants were provided one paper-based finding tasks to distract them for 15 min.
  - Step 4. Login phase: participants should swipe to unlock the phone for 10 trials. The system recorded all the data for analysis.
  - Step 5. Feedback form: participants should respond to several questions in a *feedback form* regarding our scheme.
  - Step 6. Retention. Participants could keep the phone and try to unlock the phone at last once each day. After three days, participants were asked to return and unlock the phone for 10 times in our lab.
  - Step 7. Participants have to finish another *feedback from* regarding our scheme.

Study Results. In the confirmation phase, we could collect 150 trials in the login phase for each Group1 and Group2. We used 60% of them as training data and the rest as testing data (with a cross-validation mode). The performance of different classifiers is depicted in Table 2. It is found that SVM could achieve a smaller error rate than other classifiers, i.e., it could reach an AER of 4.1% and 4.45% in Group1 and Group2, respectively. In contrast, BPNN could reach an AER of around 7%, while J48 & NBayes may cause an AER over 10%.

In this case, we used SVM as the classifier in SwipeVLock. Table 3 shows the successful unlock trials for login phase and retention phase in Group1 and Group2.

- *Login phase.* It is observed that participants in both groups could perform well with a success rate of 97.3% (Group1) and 95.3% (Group2), respectively. The errors were mainly caused by behavioral deviation, i.e., some participants may perform a swipe too fast.

Table 2. The performance of different classifiers under different groups.

Group1	J48	NBayes	SVM	BPNN	Group2	J48	NBayes	SVM	BPNN
FAR (%)	9.7	12.4	3.7	6.8	FAR (%)	10.6	11.5	4.1	6.8
FRR (%)	10.3	10.3	4.5	7.2	FRR (%)	11.3	12.2	4.8	7.6
AER (%)	10.0	11.35	4.1	7.0	AER (%)	10.95	11.85	4.45	7.2

Table 3. Success rate in the login and retention phase for Group1 and Group2.

Login	Group1	Group2
Success rate	146/150 (97.3%)	143/150 (95.3%)
Retention	Group1	Group2
Success rate	132/150 (88%)	147/150 (98%)

– *Retention phase.* After three days, it is found that participants in Group2 performed much better than those in Group1. This is because participants in Group2 could keep the phone and practice the unlocking behavior. Some participants reported that they might unlock the phone 16 times a day, making their swipe behavior more stable.

It is interesting to notice there are fewer errors caused by location selection, indicating that the error tolerance is suitable in practical usage. Further, our results validate that more practice can make the touch behavior more stable, which is in-line with the observations in [24]. For the retention phase in Group2, participants achieved a success rate of 98%, which is promising in real-world applications.

User Feedback. During the study, we gave two feedback forms to each participant regarding the scheme usage. Ten-point Likert scales were used in each feedback question, where 1-score indicates strong disagreement and 10-score indicates strong agreement. Several key questions and scores are summarized in Table 4.

– *Group1.* Most participants were satisfied with the usage of SwipeVLock, resulting in a score of over 8.5 on average for each question. We informally interviewed 10 of them, and they believed this is an easy-to-use unlock mechanism.
– *Group2.* The participants in Group2 provided a higher score than Group1, i.e., 9.1 vs. 8.7 for the third question. The reason may be due to that the participants in this group could keep the phone and try it for three days. We also informally interviewed 12 of them, and found that they had fun of using this mechanism. Most of them have an interest to use it in their own phones.

Table 4. Major questions and average scores received from the user study.

Questions (Group1)	Average scores
1. I could easily create a credential under SwipeVLock	8.8
2. The time consumption for SwipeVLock creation is acceptable	8.5
3. I could easily login to the system	8.7
Questions (Group2)	Average scores
1. I could easily create a credential under SwipeVLock	9.0
2. The time consumption for SwipeVLock creation is acceptable	8.7
3. I could easily login to the system	9.1

Though users' feedback is a subjective way of evaluating the scheme performance, it still provides valuable comments on our scheme. For instance, in the study, we received many positive answers, which can support and motivate the development of SwipeVLock, i.e., some participants are willing to use our mechanism on their own phones. We consider that our scheme could become a promising alternative to complement existing unlock mechanisms on smartphones.

5 Discussion

In the user study, we obtain promising results on the usage of our scheme. However, our work is still an early study to explore the performance of SwipeVLock, there are many challenges and limitations.

– *Time consumption.* In this work, we did not investigate the time consumption, as it normally takes less than 10 s. Most participants also satisfied with the login time in our feedback forms. In our future work, we plan to perform a larger study to explore this issue.
– *Image selection.* The first step of SwipeVLock is to select one background image from a pool (i.e., with 10 images). Intuitively, users have their own preference and are likely to choose a different image. However, with more users, it is unclear whether there would be a bias. This is an interesting topic in our future work.
– *Location selection.* The second step of SwipeVLock is to choose a location on the selected image. Similar to the image selection, it is also an interesting topic to investigate whether there is a selection bias, and explore which part of image is most likely to be selected.
– *More participants.* In this work, we mainly involved 30 participants in the study. In our future work, we plan to recruit more participants with diverse background to validate our results. In addition, it is also an interesting topic to investigate the difference between right handed and left handed participants, and check the observations.

- *Advanced attacks.* Our focus in this work is to investigate the performance of SwipeVLock, we did not consider some adversarial scenarios, where an attacker may get the phone and try to unlock it. This is an important topic in our future work, i.e., exploring the effect of recording attacks and mimic attacks.
- *Multi-touch behavior.* At this stage, our scheme only considers a swipe action with single finger, while it is an interesting topic to investigate the performance by using two fingers.
- *Phone type.* In this work, we mainly used one type of Android phone in the user study, while it could be an interesting topic to explore whether phone models may affect the scheme performance. This is also an open challenge for existing authentication schemes.
- *Machine leaning.* Supervised learning algorithms are widely adopted when designing a user authentication scheme [21]. In this work, we considered some common and popular machine learning schemes to model users' behavior. Our future work plans to involve more diverse learning algorithms, e.g., ensemble algorithms, and to investigate the effect of feature distance approaches.
- *Comparison with other schemes.* Our study focuses on evaluating the performance of SwipeVLock itself, while we plan to consider a comparison with similar schemes in future. For example, we can include some existing graphical password schemes, behavioral schemes or hybrid schemes. This is an open challenge in this area, as there lacks a unified platform for comparison.

6   Conclusion

Unlock mechanisms like Android unlock patterns are an important security tool to protect smartphones from unauthorized access, but attackers can still compromise the phone via various attacks like shoulder surfing, recording attacks and charging attacks. As a result, there is an increasing need to enhance the security of unlock mechanisms. In this work, motivated by this issue, we develop SwipeVLock, a swipe behavior-based unlock scheme with a supervised framework on smartphones, which requires users to choose one background image and a location to perform a swipe action. A successful trial should have both successful location selection and swipe verification. In our user study, we involved a total of 30 participants and investigated their performance like success rate. Our results demonstrate that participants could reach a success rate of 98% in the best scenario. Most participants also provide positive feedback on the practical usage of SwipeVLock.

Acknowledgments. We would like to thank the participants for their hard work in the user study. This work was partially supported by National Natural Science Foundation of China (No. 61802077).

References

1. Aviv, A.J., Gibson, K., Mossop, E., Blaze, M., Smith, J.M.: Smudge attacks on smartphone touch screens. In: Proceedings of the 4th USENIX Conference on Offensive Technologies, pp. 1–7. USENIX Association (2010)
2. Berkeley Churchill, Unlock Pattern Generator (2013). https://www.berkeleychurchill.com/software/android-pwgen/pwgen.php
3. Bonneau, J.: The science of guessing: analyzing an anonymized corpus of 70 million passwords. In: Proceedings of the 2012 IEEE Symposium on Security and Privacy, pp. 538–552 (2012)
4. Chiasson, S., Biddle, R., van Oorschot, P.C.: A second look at the usability of click-based graphical passwords. In: Proceedings of the 3rd Symposium on Usable Privacy and Security (SOUPS), pp. 1–12. ACM, New York (2007)
5. Chiasson, S., Stobert, E., Forget, A., Biddle, R.: Persuasive cued click-points: design, implementation, and evaluation of a knowledge-based authentication mechanism. IEEE Trans. Dependable Secure Comput. 9(2), 222–235 (2012)
6. Davis, D., Monrose, F., Reiter, M.K.: On user choice in graphical password schemes. In: Proceedings of the 13th Conference on USENIX Security Symposium (SSYM), pp. 151–164. USENIX Association, Berkeley (2004)
7. De Luca, A., Hang, A., Brudy, F., Lindner, C., Hussmann, H.: Touch me once and i know it's you!: implicit authentication based on touch screen patterns. In: Proceedings of CHI, pp. 987–996. ACM (2012)
8. Dirik, A.E., Memon, N., Birget, J.C.: Modeling user choice in the passpoints graphical password scheme. In: Proceedings of the 3rd Symposium on Usable privacy and security (SOUPS), pp. 20–28. ACM, New York (2007)
9. Dunphy, P., Yan, J.: Do background images improve "draw a secret" graphical passwords? In: Proceedings of the 14th ACM Conference on Computer and Communications Security (CCS), pp. 36–47 (2007)
10. Feng, T., et al.: Continuous mobile authentication using touchscreen gestures. In: Proceedings of the 2012 IEEE Conference on Technologies for Homeland Security (HST), pp. 451–456. IEEE (2012)
11. Fox, S.: Future Online Password Could be a Map (2010). http://www.livescience.com/8622-future-online-password-map.html
12. Frank, M., Biedert, R., Ma, E., Martinovic, I., Song, D.: Touchalytics: on the applicability of touchscreen input as a behavioral biometric for continuous authentication. IEEE Trans. Inf. Forensics Secur. 8(1), 136–148 (2013)
13. Gołofit, K.: Click passwords under investigation. In: Biskup, J., López, J. (eds.) ESORICS 2007. LNCS, vol. 4734, pp. 343–358. Springer, Heidelberg (2007). https://doi.org/10.1007/978-3-540-74835-9_23
14. Jermyn, I., Mayer, A., Monrose, F., Reiter, M.K., Rubin, A.D.: The design and analysis of graphical passwords. In: Proceedings of the 8th Conference on USENIX Security Symposium, pp. 1–14. USENIX Association, Berkeley (1999)
15. LIBSVM - A Library for Support Vector Machines. https://www.csie.ntu.edu.tw/~cjlin/libsvm/
16. Lin, D., Dunphy, P., Olivier, P., Yan, J.: Graphical passwords & qualitative spatial relations. In: Proceedings of the 3rd Symposium on Usable Privacy and Security (SOUPS), pp. 161–162 (2007)
17. Meng, Y.: Designing click-draw based graphical password scheme for better authentication. In: Proceedings of the 7th IEEE International Conference on Networking, Architecture, and Storage (NAS), pp. 39–48 (2012)

18. Meng, Y., Li, W.: Evaluating the effect of tolerance on click-draw based graphical password scheme. In: Chim, T.W., Yuen, T.H. (eds.) ICICS 2012. LNCS, vol. 7618, pp. 349–356. Springer, Heidelberg (2012). https://doi.org/10.1007/978-3-642-34129-8_32

19. Meng, Y., Li, W.: Evaluating the effect of user guidelines on creating click-draw based graphical passwords. In: Proceedings of the 2012 ACM Research in Applied Computation Symposium (RACS), pp. 322–327 (2012)

20. Meng, Y., Li, W., Kwok, L.-F.: Enhancing click-draw based graphical passwords using multi-touch on mobile phones. In: Janczewski, L.J., Wolfe, H.B., Shenoi, S. (eds.) SEC 2013. IAICT, vol. 405, pp. 55–68. Springer, Heidelberg (2013). https://doi.org/10.1007/978-3-642-39218-4_5

21. Meng, W., Wong, D.S., Furnell, S., Zhou, J.: Surveying the development of biometric user authentication on mobile phones. IEEE Commun. Surv. Tutor. 17(3), 1268–1293 (2015)

22. Meng, W.: RouteMap: a route and map based graphical password scheme for better multiple password memory. In: Qiu, M., Xu, S., Yung, M., Zhang, H., et al. (eds.) Network and System Security. LNCS, vol. 9408, pp. 147–161. Springer, Cham (2015). https://doi.org/10.1007/978-3-319-25645-0_10

23. Meng, W.: Evaluating the effect of multi-touch behaviours on android unlock patterns. Inf. Comput. Secur. 24(3), 277–287 (2016)

24. Meng, W., Li, W., Wong, D.S., Zhou, J.: TMGuard: a touch movement-based security mechanism for screen unlock patterns on smartphones. In: Manulis, M., Sadeghi, A.-R., Schneider, S. (eds.) ACNS 2016. LNCS, vol. 9696, pp. 629–647. Springer, Cham (2016). https://doi.org/10.1007/978-3-319-39555-5_34

25. Meng, W., Lee, W.H., Liu, Z., Su, C., Li, Y.: Evaluating the impact of juice filming charging attack in practical environments. In: Kim, H., Kim, D.-C. (eds.) ICISC 2017. LNCS, vol. 10779, pp. 327–338. Springer, Cham (2018). https://doi.org/10.1007/978-3-319-78556-1_18

26. Meng, W., Fei, F., Li, W., Au, M.H.: Harvesting smartphone privacy through enhanced juice filming charging attacks. In: Nguyen, P., Zhou, J. (eds.) ISC 2017. LNCS, vol. 10599, pp. 291–308. Springer, Cham (2017). https://doi.org/10.1007/978-3-319-69659-1_16

27. Meng, W., Li, W., Kwok, L.-F., Choo, K.-K.R.: Towards enhancing click-draw based graphical passwords using multi-touch behaviours on smartphones. Comput. Secur. 65, 213–229 (2017)

28. Meng, W., Li, W., Lee, W.H., Jiang, L., Zhou, J.: A pilot study of multiple password interference between text and map-based passwords. In: Gollmann, D., Miyaji, A., Kikuchi, H. (eds.) ACNS 2017. LNCS, vol. 10355, pp. 145–162. Springer, Cham (2017). https://doi.org/10.1007/978-3-319-61204-1_8

29. Meng, W., Lee, W.H., Au, M.H., Liu, Z.: Exploring effect of location number on map-based graphical password authentication. In: Pieprzyk, J., Suriadi, S. (eds.) ACISP 2017. LNCS, vol. 10343, pp. 301–313. Springer, Cham (2017). https://doi.org/10.1007/978-3-319-59870-3_17

30. Nelson, D.L., Reed, V.S., Walling, J.R.: Pictorial superiority effect. J. Exp. Psychol.: Hum. Learn. Mem. 2(5), 523–528 (1976)

31. Nyang, D., et al.: Two-thumbs-up: physical protection for pin entry secure against recording attacks. Comput. Secur. 78, 1–15 (2018)

32. Passfaces. http://www.realuser.com/

33. Quinlan, J.R.: Improved use of continuous attributes in C4.5. J. Artif. Intell. Res. 4(1), 77–90 (1996)

34. Rennie, J.D.M., Shih, L., Teevan, J., Karger, D.R.: Tackling the poor assumptions of Naive Bayes text classifiers. In: Proceedings of the 20th International Conference on Machine Learning, pp. 616–623 (2003)

35. Rumelhart, D., Hinton, G., Williams, R.: Learning representations by back-propagating errors. Nature **323**, 533–536 (1986)

36. Shepard, R.N.: Recognition memory for words, sentences, and pictures. J. Verbal Learn. Verbal Behav. **6**(1), 156–163 (1967)

37. Smith-Creasey, M., Rajarajan, M.: A continuous user authentication scheme for mobile devices. In: Proceedings of the 14th Annual Conference on Privacy, Security and Trust (PST), pp. 104–113 (2016)

38. Spitzer, J., Singh, C., Schweitzer, D.: A security class project in graphical passwords. J. Comput. Sci. Coll. **26**(2), 7–13 (2010)

39. SplashData Inc., The Worst Passwords of 2018. https://www.teamsid.com/splashdatas-top-100-worst-passwords-of-2018/

40. Shahzad, M., Liu, A.X., Samuel, A.: Behavior based human authentication on touch screen devices using gestures and signatures. IEEE Trans. Mob. Comput. **16**(10), 2726–2741 (2017)

41. Sharma, V., Enbody, R.: User authentication and identification from user interface interactions on touch-enabled devices. In: Proceedings of the 10th ACM Conference on Security and Privacy in Wireless and Mobile Networks (WiSec), pp. 1–11 (2017)

42. Suo, X., Zhu, Y., Owen, G.S.: Graphical passwords: a survey. In: Proceedings of the 21st Annual Computer Security Applications Conference (ACSAC), pp. 463–472. IEEE Computer Society (2005)

43. Sun, H., Chen, Y., Fang, C., Chang, S.: PassMap: a map based graphical-password authentication system. In: Proceedings of AsiaCCS, pp. 99–100 (2012)

44. Tao, H., Adams, C.: Pass-Go: a proposal to improve the usability of graphical passwords. Int. J. Netw. Secur. **2**(7), 273–292 (2008)

45. Thorpe, J., MacRae, B., Salehi-Abari, A.: Usability and security evaluation of GeoPass: a geographic location-password scheme. In: Proceedings of the 9th Symposium on Usable Privacy and Security (SOUPS), pp. 1–14 (2013)

46. Weka: Machine Learning Software in Java. https://www.cs.waikato.ac.nz/ml/weka/

47. Wiedenbeck, S., Waters, J., Birget, J.-C., Brodskiy, A., Memon, N.: Passpoints: design and longitudinal evaluation of a graphical password system. Int. J. Hum.-Comput. Stud. **63**(1–2), 102–127 (2005)

48. Weir, M., Aggarwal, S., Collins, M., Stern, H.: Testing metrics for password creation policies by attacking large sets of revealed passwords. In: Proceedings of CCS, pp. 162–175 (2010)

49. Yan, J., Blackwell, A., Anderson, R., Grant, A.: Password memorability and security: empirical results. IEEE Secur. Priv. **2**, 25–31 (2004)

50. Yang, Y., Guo, B., Wang, Z., Li, M., Yu, Z., Zhou, X.: BehaveSense: continuous authentication for security-sensitive mobile apps using behavioral biometrics. Ad Hoc Netw. **84**, 9–18 (2019)

51. Yu, X., Wang, Z., Li, Y., Li, L., Zhu, W.T., Song, L.: EvoPass: evolvable graphical password against shoulder-surfing attacks. Comput. Secur. **70**, 179–198 (2017)

52. Zhao, X., Feng, T., Shi, W., Kakadiaris, I.A.: Mobile user authentication using statistical touch dynamics images. IEEE Trans. Inf. Forensics Secur. **9**(11), 1780–1789 (2014)

53. Zheng, N., Bai, K., Huang, H., Wang, H.: You are how you touch: user verification on smartphones via tapping behaviors. In: Proceedings of the 2014 International Conference on Network Protocols (ICNP), pp. 221–232 (2014)

An Enumeration-Like Vector Sampling Method for Solving Approximate SVP

Luan Luan$^{(\boxtimes)}$ (ID), Chunxiang Gu, and Yonghui Zheng

Henan Key Laboratory of Network Cryptography Technology, Zhengzhou, China
lunaluan9555@gmail.com

Abstract. Lattice reduction with random sampling is a kind of randomized heuristic algorithm for solving approximate Shortest Vector Problem (SVP). In this paper, we propose a lattice vector sampling method for solving approximate SVP. Firstly, we apply enumeration techniques into vector sampling using natural number's representation (NNR), enlightened by discrete pruning. Secondly, to find optimal parameters for the enumeration-like sampling method, we study the statistical properties of a structured candidate vector set, and give a parameter calculation strategy for minimizing the sampling time. This new sampling method is a universal framework that can be embedded into most of the sampling-reduction algorithms. The experimental result shows that sampling reduction algorithm with the new sampling method embedded runs faster than the original Restricted Reduction (RR) algorithm within 90 dimensions.

Keywords: Public-key cryptosystem · Shortest vector problem · Lattice reduction · Enumeration

1 Introduction

A lattice $\mathcal{L}$ is all the integral combinations of n linear independent vectors $\mathbf{b}_1, \ldots, \mathbf{b}_n \in \mathbb{R}^{m \times n}$, and these vectors are called a basis of $\mathcal{L}$. Lattice is a useful tool for analyzing public key cryptosystem [15] such as knapsack public key system [20] and RSA [6,8]. Lattice-based cryptography is also widely believed to resist quantum computer attacks, which called a lot of researches in this field. NIST launched a post-quantum crypto project in 2016 and the half candidate algorithms are lattie-based. For reasons of practical implementation, the researches of lattice problem are mainly focused on integer lattices, namely $\mathbf{B} = [\mathbf{b_1}, \ldots, \mathbf{b_n}] \in \mathbb{Z}^{m \times n}$.

One of the most important topic in lattice theory is computational problems of lattice. The hardness of these problems becomes the foundation of many lattice-based public key system, and studying the computational complexity of these problems is an interesting part of computational theory. Two of the famous computational problems on lattice are:

© Springer Nature Switzerland AG 2019
X. Chen et al. (Eds.): ML4CS 2019, LNCS 11806, pp. 154–172, 2019.
https://doi.org/10.1007/978-3-030-30619-9_12

1. Shortest vector problem (SVP): Given a lattice basis $\mathbf{B} \in \mathbb{Z}^{m \times n}$, find a nonzero vector $\mathbf{Bx}\,(\mathbf{x} \in \mathbb{Z}^n \backslash \{\mathbf{0}\})$ such that $\|\mathbf{Bx}\| \leq \|\mathbf{By}\|$ for any other $\mathbf{y} \in \mathbb{Z}^n \backslash \{\mathbf{0}\}$.
2. Closest Vector Problem (CVP): Given a lattice basis $\mathbf{B} \in \mathbb{Z}^{m \times n}$ and a target vector $\mathbf{t} \in \mathbb{Z}^m$, find an integer vector $\mathbf{x} \in \mathbb{Z}^n$ such that $\|\mathbf{Bx} - \mathbf{t}\| \leq \|\mathbf{By} - \mathbf{t}\|$ for any other $\mathbf{y} \in \mathbb{Z}^n$.

The CVP was proved to be NP-complete by van Emde Boas in 1981 [9] and the SVP was proved in 1998 by Ajtai under randomized reduction. Many lattice-based cryptosystems are based on these two problems, and cracking the cryptosystem is reduced to solving SVP or CVP on high dimension lattice. Therefore, the algorithms solving the two main problems are quite important for the research community.

The approximate version of SVP and CVP also calls widely concern and are also useful in cryptanalysis [17].

1. Approximate SVP: Given a lattice basis $\mathbf{B} \in \mathbb{Z}^{m \times n}$, find a nonzero vector $\mathbf{Bx}\,(\mathbf{x} \in \mathbb{Z}^n \backslash \{\mathbf{0}\})$ such that $\|\mathbf{Bx}\| \leq \gamma \lambda_1$, where λ_1 is the length of the shortest vector.
2. Approximate CVP: Given a lattice basis $\mathbf{B} \in \mathbb{Z}^{m \times n}$ and a target vector $\mathbf{t} \in \mathbb{Z}^m$, find an integer vector $\mathbf{x} \in \mathbb{Z}^n$ such that $\|\mathbf{Bx} - \mathbf{t}\| \leq \gamma \|\mathbf{By} - \mathbf{t}\|$ for any other $\mathbf{y} \in \mathbb{Z}^n$.

The parameter $\gamma \geq 1$ is called *approximation factor*, and we denote it by *apfa*. The hardness of approximate SVP depend on it approximation factor. It is proved that approximate SVP to within factors $2^{(\log n)^{1/2-\epsilon}}$ is NP-hard. For larger factor such as $\sqrt{n/\log n}$, approximate SVP is not believed to be NP-hard anymore [13,15]. In 2010, Darmstadt University launched a project of SVP-challenge, aiming at finding the solutions to approximate SVP in various dimension with fixed approximation factor $\gamma = 1.05$ [1].

For solving SVP and approximate SVP, a number of algorithms for solving the shortest vector problem (SVP) on lattice have been proposed, and the ideas of these algorithms are mainly divided to three types:

Enumeration. Enumeration is to exhaustive search following a structure called "enumeration tree" of lattice vectors on a well-reduced lattice basis, and sometimes combined with pruning method. The classical enumeration algorithm is believed to have time complexity of $2^{\mathcal{O}(n \log n)}$, but polynomial (even linear) space complexity [12]. The pruning strategies dramatically optimize the performance of enumeration in practice while the probability of success is reduced [4,11].

Sieving. The key idea of sieving is to sample some vectors in a hypersphere with radius R and reduce the radius step by step by vectors reduction under certain condition. Sieving algorithm usually has both time and space complexity of $2^{\mathcal{O}(n)}$, such as classical AKS sieve [3], NV sieve [16], etc. There were no practical sieving algorithms showing higher efficiency than enumeration until HashSieve

[5] and LD Sieve [14] were proposed. Recently, Martin Albrecht and Leo Ducas find solutions to the SVP challenge on dimension 155 and 157 [1] using sieving algorithm and lattice reduction.

Lattice Reduction with Random Sampling. It was first proposed by Schnorr in 2003 [18], and refined by Buchmann, Ludwig [7], Kashiwabara, Fukase and Teruya [10,19]. The main routine of sampling-reduction is to sample short vectors on lattice "heuristically", and then reduce the lattice basis by inserting the very short vector into lattice basis and run LLL or BKZ. The procedure runs iteratively until a target vector is found. Kenji Kashiwabara and Tadanori Teruya solved the approximate SVP problem of 150 dimension in 2017, and update their 152-dimensional record in 2018.

In 2017, Aono *et al.* [4] proposed lattice enumeration with discrete pruning, generalizing the strategies of Fukase *et al.* [10]. Discrete pruning has more rigorous theoretical analysis on success probabilities and running times than random sampling, but random sapling method still shows good practicality in solving SVP, especially suitable for massive parallelization, which revealed by Fukase and Teruya's high-dimensional SVP challenge records. However, there are still some unsettled details in random sampling such as the construction of candidate set and parameter selection.

In the rest of this paper, we focus on the random sampling reduction, and try to give both theoretical analysis and practical details of random sampling method, under some assumptions. In Sect. 2, we give a brief summary and explanation of Schnorr's sampling algorithm and Fukase-Kashiwabara algorithm. In Sect. 3, we propose a new vector sampling method embedding enumeration technology into sampling algorithm, enlightened by discrete pruning [4]. In Sect. 4, we establish a probability model of the structured candidate vector set, and give parameters calculating algorithm to find optimal parameters for sampling short vector in the candidate vector set. In Sect. 5, we embed the enumeration-like sampling method into lattice reduction algorithm, and give practical implementation to compare with RR algorithm.

2 Preliminary

2.1 Lattice

Given a series of linear independent vectors $\mathbf{B} = [\mathbf{b}_1, \ldots, \mathbf{b}_n] \in \mathbb{R}^{m \times n}$, the lattice is defined as a set $L(\mathbf{B}) = \{\mathbf{B}\mathbf{x}, \mathbf{x} \in \mathbb{Z}^n\}$, and n is called the dimension of L. A lattice is full-dimensional when $m = n$. Lattice has many basis. For any two bases $\mathbf{B}_1, \mathbf{B}_2$ of the same lattice, there is a unique unimodular matrix $\mathbf{U}$ such that $\mathbf{B}_1 = \mathbf{B}_2\mathbf{U}$. For reasons of practical implementation (data storage and computing with limited precision) and for solving SVP challenge [1], in this paper, we mainly study the full-dimensional integer lattice, namely, $\mathbf{B} \in \mathbb{Z}^{n \times n}$.

The determinant of a lattice is defined by $\det(L(\mathbf{B})) = \sqrt{\det(\mathbf{B}^T\mathbf{B})} = \prod_{i=1}^{n} \|\mathbf{b}_i^*\|$, where $\mathbf{b}_i^*$ is the orthogonalized vector of $\mathbf{b}_i$. It is easy to see that the determinant of lattice is an invariant which is independent of the choice of basis.

The length of shortest vector is denoted by λ_1, and Minkowski's first theorem implies that in a lattice Λ, $\lambda_1 < \sqrt{n} \cdot \det(\Lambda)^{\frac{1}{n}}$. A better estimation named Gaussian Heuristic [11] is defined by $\mathrm{GH}(L) = \frac{1}{\sqrt{\pi}} \Gamma\left(\frac{n}{2} + 1\right)^{\frac{1}{n}} \det(L)^{\frac{1}{n}}$. In fact, $\mathrm{GH}(L)$ is exactly the radius of an n-dimensional ball whose volume is $\det(L)$. In SVP challenge [1], given a lattice basis $\mathbf{B} \in \mathbb{Z}^{n \times n}$, the challenger is required to submit a vector $\mathbf{x}$ such that $\|\mathbf{Bx}\| \leq 1.05\,\mathrm{GH}(L)$.

For a lattice basis $\mathbf{B} = [\mathbf{b}_1, \dots \mathbf{b}_n]$, the corresponding Gram-Schmidt orthogonalized basis $\mathbf{B}^* = [\mathbf{b}_1^*, \dots \mathbf{b}_n^*]$ is defined by $\mathbf{b}_i^* = \mathbf{b}_i - \sum_{j=1}^{i-1} \mu_{i,j} \mathbf{b}_i^*$ with $\mu_{i,j} = \frac{\langle \mathbf{b}_i, \mathbf{b}_j^* \rangle}{\langle \mathbf{b}_j^*, \mathbf{b}_j^* \rangle}$. Using orthogonalization we can define orthogonal projection. Let $\pi_i : \mathbb{R}^n \to span(\mathbf{b}_1, \dots, \mathbf{b}_i)^{\perp}$ be the i-th orthogonal projection, such that $\pi_i(\mathbf{v}) = \mathbf{v} - \sum_{j=1}^{i-1}(\langle \mathbf{v}, \mathbf{b}_j^* \rangle / \|\mathbf{b}_j^*\|^2)\mathbf{b}_j^*$. Actually if we write lattice vector $\mathbf{v}$ in the form of $\mathbf{v} = \sum_{i=1}^{n} u_i \mathbf{b}_i^*$, then $\pi_i(\mathbf{v}) = \sum_{j=i}^{n} u_j \mathbf{b}_j^*$.

We can use orthogonalized basis to analyze the shortest vector problem. Given a lattice vector $\mathbf{v} = \sum_{i=1}^{n} u_i \mathbf{b}_i^*$, then $\|\mathbf{v}\|^2 = \sum_{i=1}^{n} |u_i|^2 \|\mathbf{b}_i^*\|^2$. In order to find a very short vector, there are two methods one can take:

1. Decreasing μ_i to $|\mu_i| \leq \frac{1}{2}$ for $i = 1, \dots, n$. Given a vector $\mathbf{v} = \sum_{j=1}^{n} \mu_j \mathbf{b}_j^* \in L$ and an integer μ, for a certain index i, then vector $\mathbf{v}' = \mathbf{v} - \mu\,\mathbf{b}_i = \sum_{j=1}^{n} \mu_j' \mathbf{b}_j^*$ satisfies $|\mu_i'| \leq \frac{1}{2}$ if $|\mu - \mu_i| \leq \frac{1}{2}$. This method called "size reduced" is widely used in many reduction algorithms such as LLL and BKZ.
2. Shortening $\mathbf{b}_i^*$. We can find a very short vector $\mathbf{b} \in L(\mathbf{b}_i, \dots, \mathbf{b}_n)$ to minimize $\|\pi_i(\mathbf{b})\|^2 = \sum_{j=i}^{n} \mu_j^2 \|\mathbf{b}_j^*\|^2$ by replacing $\mathbf{b}_i$ with $\mathbf{b}$. A key idea of sampling method is to choose the vector $\mathbf{b}$ in a suitable subset $S_i \subset L(\mathbf{b}_i, \dots, \mathbf{b}_n)$. Schnorr mentioned that the various reduction algorithms differ by the choice of S_i [18].

Both classical enumeration and sieving algorithms only consider one case, simply enumerating/searching vectors in the origin or projection lattice without changing the lattice basis during the whole algorithm. However, sampling reduction method takes both cases into consideration, which is believed to have better performance on high dimension SVP.

2.2 Random Sampling Reduction (RSR) Algorithm

In the research of lattice problem, an important assumption is about the property of well-reduced basis. Given an LLL or BKZ-reduced basis, the basis is size-reduced and each $\mathbf{b}_i^*$ is a relatively short vector in the i-th orthogonal complement span$(\mathbf{b}_1, \dots, \mathbf{b}_n)$, also denoted by $\pi_i(L) = \{\pi_i(\mathbf{v}) | \mathbf{v} \in L\}$. Then the basis generally meets the following assumption:

Assumption 1 (Geometry Series Assumption, GSA). *Given an LLL-reduced or BKZ-reduced basis $\mathbf{B}$ and its corresponded orthogonalized basis $\mathbf{B}^*$, then $\left\{\|\mathbf{b}_i^*\|^2\right\}_{i=1}^{n}$ can be regarded as a geometric series. i.e., there exists $q \in \left[\frac{3}{4}, 1\right)$, s.t. $\|\mathbf{b}_i^*\|^2 / \|\mathbf{b}_1\|^2 = q^{i-1}$ for $i = 1, \dots, n$.*

If the lattice basis conforms to GSA, then given a lattice vector $\|\mathbf{v}\|^2 = \sum_{j=1}^{n} |u_j|^2 \|\mathbf{b}_j^*\|^2$, it is believed that if the vector is very short, then $|v_i|$ is more likely to be small when the index i is small.

Based on GSA, Schnorr proposed the heuristic idea of random sampling. Let $1 \le u < n$ be a constant. Then in Schnorr's strategy, the candidate lattice vectors $\mathbf{v} = \sum_{j=1}^{n} u_j \mathbf{b}_j^*$ should satisfy:

$$|\mu_i| = \begin{cases} \frac{1}{2}, & i < n - u \\ 1, & n - u \le i < n \end{cases}, \quad \mu_n = 1.$$

In Schnorr's random sampling algorithm SHORT [18], the algorithm iteratively samples vector $\mathbf{v}$ shorter than $\mathbf{b}_1$, and then insert $\mathbf{v}$ into the basis to execute lattice reduction algorithm (LLL or BKZ), until a basis with $\|\mathbf{b}_1\| \le \gamma \text{GH}(L)$ is found.

Schnorr proposed an assumption on the distribution of μ_i to simplify the analysis on sampling method's performance:

Assumption 2 (Randomness Assumption, RA). *The Gram-Schmidt coefficients u_j of the generated vectors $\mathbf{v} = \sum_{j=1}^{n} u_j \mathbf{b}_j^*$ are uniformly distributed in $\left[-\frac{1}{2}, \frac{1}{2}\right]$ for $i < n - u$ and in $[-1, 1]$ for $n - u \le i < n$. For a given vector $\mathbf{v}$, u_j $(j = 1, \ldots, n-1)$ are statistically independent, and for two distinct vectors $\mathbf{v}, \mathbf{v}'$, u_j and u_j' are statistically independent for any $j = 1, \ldots, n-1$.*

Under GSA and RA, Schnorr gave the relationship between parameter setting and success probability. The vector sampled by their algorithm follows a certain probability distribution [18]. Schnorr's Random Sampling Reduction (RSR) algorithm also enlightened many other studies in random sampling such as Buchmann's best bound analysis on random sampling algorithm [7], and Fukase's restricted reduction algorithm [10].

2.3   Restricted Reduction (RR) Algorithm

The restricted reduction algorithm (RR) proposed by Fukase and Kashiwabara generalized Schnorr's random sampling strategy. The key idea of RR is using a short representation of lattice vector which is called "natural number representation" (NNR) to sample candidate vectors.

Definition 1 (The Natural Number Representation). *Given a lattice basis $\mathbf{B}$ and a lattice vector $\mathbf{v} = \sum_{j=1}^{n} u_j \mathbf{b}_j^*$. The natural number representation of $\mathbf{v}$ is a natural number vector $\mathbf{z} = (z_1, \ldots, z_n) \in \mathbb{N}^n$, such that $u_j \in \left(-\frac{z_j+1}{2}, -\frac{z_j}{2}\right]$ or $\left(\frac{z_j}{2}, \frac{z_j+1}{2}\right]$.*

The NNR is a bijection between lattice vector and natural number vector. The proof is given in [10]. Then the F-K algorithm samples short vectors in a candidate set $V_B(\mathbf{s}, \mathbf{t}) \in L$:

Definition 2. $V_B(\mathbf{s}, \mathbf{t}) = \{\mathbf{v} \in L(\mathbf{B}) : \mathbf{d}(\mathbf{v}) \leq \mathbf{s}, \mathbf{w}(\mathbf{v}) \leq \mathbf{t}\}$, where $d_i(\mathbf{v}) = \#\{z_j(\mathbf{v}) = i, 1 \leq j \leq n\}$, $w_i(\mathbf{v}) = n - \min\{j : z_j(\mathbf{v}) = i\} + 1$ and for some $c \in \mathbb{Z}_+$ such that $\mathbf{s}, \mathbf{t} \in \mathbb{N}^c$.

The parameter $\mathbf{s}$ defines the upper bounds of times that each natural number $1, 2 \ldots$ shows in vector $\mathbf{z}$. And vector $\mathbf{t}$ puts restriction on the index where each natural number first shows in the vector. For lattice vectors in $V_B(\mathbf{s}, \mathbf{t})$, their corresponding NNR vectors always have "heavy tail" and "light head".

Notice that $V_B(\mathbf{s}, \mathbf{t})$ is a subset of L, and depends on lattice basis $\mathbf{B}$. We denote its corresponding NNR vector set as $Z(\mathbf{s}, \mathbf{t}) = \{\mathbf{z} \in \mathbb{N}^n\}$ which only depends on parameter $\mathbf{s}$ and $\mathbf{t}$.

Fukase and Kashiwabara introduce a concept "G-S sum" denoted by $GSS = \sum_{j=1}^{n} \|\mathbf{b}_j^*\|^2$, and explain that a lattice basis with shorter GS sum may have higher probability of finding short vectors in $V_B(\mathbf{s}, \mathbf{t})$. Based on this heuristic analysis, they design a reduction algorithm aiming at decreasing G-S sum of basis.

In order to control the G-S sum goes down, they put up with a definition *insertion index* [10]:

Definition 3 (insertion index). *Let* $\mathbf{B}$ *be a lattice and* $\mathbf{v} \in L(\mathbf{B})$*, and* $\delta \in \mathbb{R}$ *with* $\delta \leq 1$*. The insertion index* $h_\delta(\mathbf{v}) = \min\{j : \|\pi_j(\mathbf{v})\|^2 < \delta\|\mathbf{b}_j^*\|^2\}$*.*

Their is a restriction index ℓ growing from 1 to an upper bound ℓ_{max} during the reduction procedure of RR algorithm. The targeting vector in each round is restricted by insertion index such that $h_\delta(\mathbf{v}) \geq \ell$. When the ℓ-th basis vector $\mathbf{b}_l$ is not changed, the ℓ grows up to $\ell + 1$. The whole algorithm repeats until a very short vector $(< 1.05 GH(L))$ is found.

3 Applying Enumeration to Vector Sampling

In this section we introduce a more efficient way to find short vectors in sampling algorithm based on the work of Fukase *et al.* [10] and Aono *et al.* [4].

3.1 Natural Number Representation (NNR)

Before introduce the key idea of out method, we first give some analysis on natural number representation.

Our first result is about the symmetry of NNR vectors, namely, the relationship between $z(\mathbf{v})$ and $z(-\mathbf{v})$. According to the definition and bijection relationship, the conclusion shows as follows:

Theorem 1 (symmetry of NNR vectors). *Given two lattice vectors* $\mathbf{v}_1 = \mathbf{B}\mathbf{x}_1, \mathbf{v}_2 = \mathbf{B}\mathbf{x}_2$ *and their corresponding NNR vector* $\mathbf{z}_1 = \mathbf{z}(\mathbf{v}_1), \mathbf{z}_2 = \mathbf{z}(\mathbf{v}_2)$*. If* $\mathbf{x}_1 = -\mathbf{x}_2$ *and denote the last non-zero component of* $\mathbf{x}_1$ *by* x_t*, w.l.o.g., let* $x_t > 0$*, then the NNR vectors satisfy*

$$\left\lceil \frac{z_t(\mathbf{v}_1)}{2} \right\rceil = \left\lceil \frac{z_t(-\mathbf{v}_2)}{2} \right\rceil$$

and $z_t(\mathbf{v}_1)$ is odd.

Proof. Given lattice vector $\mathbf{v}_1 = \mathbf{B}\mathbf{x} = \mathbf{B}^*\mathbf{u}$ with $u_j = \frac{\langle \mathbf{v}, \mathbf{b}_j^* \rangle}{\langle \mathbf{b}_j^*, \mathbf{b}_j^* \rangle} = \sum_{i=j}^{n} \mu_{i,j} x_i$. If the last non-zero component of $\mathbf{x}$ is x_t, then $u_t = \sum_{i=t}^{n} \mu_{i,t} x_i = x_t$ must be an non-zero integer and for all $j > t$, $u_j = 0$, therefore $z_j(\mathbf{v}) = 0$. Since $u_t = x_t$ is a non-negative integer, its natural number representation $z_t = 2x_t - 1$ is odd; if $x_t < 0$ then $z_t = -2x_t$ is even. Under both condition, $\lceil \frac{z_t}{2} \rceil$ are the same. $\square$

In our sampling method, the last component of the NNR vector should be non-even. Then if a vector $\mathbf{v}$ is found during sampling, then $-\mathbf{v}$ will not be calculated again.

Another relationship between lattice vector and NNR vector is the value of length. Under randomness assumption (RA), Given a lattice basis $\mathbf{B}$, any NNR vector $\mathbf{z}$ has a corresponding lattice vector $\mathbf{v}$ with expected value

$$E[\|\mathbf{v}\|^2] = \frac{1}{12} \sum_{j=1}^{n} (3z_j^2 + 3z_j + 1)\|\mathbf{b}_j^*\|^2 \tag{1}$$

and variance

$$Var[\|\mathbf{v}\|^2] = \sum_{j=1}^{n} (\frac{z_j^2}{48} + \frac{z_j}{48} + \frac{1}{180})\|\mathbf{b}_j^*\|^4 \tag{2}$$

See the proof in [4,10].

3.2 A New Structure of Candidate Vector Set

We first define a simple structure of candidate NNR vector set.

Definition 4. *Given any integer vector $\bar{\mathbf{z}} = (\bar{z}_1 \ldots, \bar{z}_n) \in \mathbb{N}^n$, NNR vector set $S(\bar{\mathbf{z}})$ is defined as $S(\bar{\mathbf{z}}) = \{\mathbf{z} \in \mathbb{N}^n : 0 \leq z_i \leq \bar{z}_i, i = 1, \ldots, n\}$, and $\bar{\mathbf{z}}$ is called "template vector". If lattice basis $\mathbf{B}$ is given, the corresponding lattice vector set is denoted by $S_B(\bar{\mathbf{z}})$.*

One thing to note is that this definition has no dependence on GSA. In next section we will prove that for any NNR vector set of this shape, the corresponding lattice vector length in it will follows an asymptotically normal distribution.

Generally speaking, if the basis is an LLL-reduced or BKZ-reduced, the orthogonal basis conforms to this assumption. Thus, for a lattice vector $\|\mathbf{v}\|^2 = \sum_{j=1}^{n} |u_j|^2 \|\mathbf{b}_j^*\|^2$ to be very small, $|v_i|$ needs to be small especially for small i. The vector's corresponding NNR vector also has this property. We give a special construction of $S(\bar{\mathbf{z}})$ below, which heuristically shows a relationship with GSA.

Definition 5. *Given a vector $\mathbf{t} \in \mathbb{N}^{c+1}$ such that $t_0 = 0 < t_1 < \ldots < t_c = n$, let*

$$Z(\mathbf{t}) = \{\mathbf{z} \in \mathbb{N}^n : for\ t_j < i \leq t_{j+1}, 0 \leq z_i \leq j,$$
$$where\ j = 0, \ldots, c-1\ and\ i = 1, \ldots, n\},$$

and there always exists a "template vector" $\bar{\mathbf{z}}$ correspond to $Z(\mathbf{t})$ such that $Z(\mathbf{t}) = S(\bar{\mathbf{z}})$. Actually, for $j = 0, \ldots, c$ and $t_j < i \leq t_{j+1}$, $\bar{z}_i = j$.

For any $\mathbf{t}$, it generates a unique "template vector" $\bar{\mathbf{z}}$ of $Z(\mathbf{t})$. The parameter $\mathbf{t}$ puts restrictions on the location where natural numbers first shows in the NNR vector $\mathbf{z}$.

3.3   Sampling Vectors in Candidate Set Using Enumeration

Under randomness assumption (RA), for any given NNR vector, its corresponding lattice vector $\mathbf{v}$ in lattice $L(\mathbf{B})$ has an expected value of square length $E[\|\mathbf{v}\|^2]$ defined by Eq. 1. $E[\|\mathbf{v}\|^2]$ is a good way to estimate the length of a vector in linear time $\mathcal{O}(n)$. More specifically, it needs about $M(2n) + 2n$ time ($M(\cdot)$ denotes the time of multiplication operation) to estimate one vector's length, and if the NNR vector is quite "sparse", the time can be much more shorter. But Algorithm 1 in [10] indicates that complexity of computing a real lattice vector's length is about $\mathcal{O}(M(1.5n^2))$, and the main cost is generated in the last step when calculating the lattice vector representation $\mathbf{v} = \mathbf{Bx}$.

Since using NNR vector to estimate the length of lattice vector is of high efficiency, in the rest part of the paper, we denote

$$ f(\mathbf{z}) \triangleq E[\|\mathbf{v}\|^2] = \frac{1}{12} \sum_{j=1}^{n} (3z_j^2 + 3z_j + 1)\|\mathbf{b}_j^*\|^2 \qquad (3) $$

as a *quick-estimating function* for $\|\mathbf{v}\|^2$.

As a pre-computation procedure of the original RR algorithm, all the NNR vectors $\mathbf{z} \in V_{\mathbf{B}}(\mathbf{s}, \mathbf{t})$ are sorted by value $f(\mathbf{z})$ from small to large, and the first N NNR vectors are kept in memory. However, sorting a very large set $V_{\mathbf{B}}(\mathbf{s}, \mathbf{t})$ with size $O(2^n)$ is impractical since the time complexity and space is a polynomial of $\#V_{\mathbf{B}}(\mathbf{s}, \mathbf{t})$. Besides, the parameter N is experiential. They set $N = 5 \times 10^7$ in their implementation without precise explanation.

We put up with a new sampling method to solve the problem. We embed the candidate set into our enumeration-like sampling algorithm as a boundary condition, in another word, a pruning method. Our algorithm enumerates NNR vectors in a given $Z(\mathbf{t})$. In any layer of the enumeration tree, if the current node does not satisfy the condition $\mathbf{z} \notin Z(\mathbf{t})$, then the branch should be cut off from the tree. It is more practical than the "sorting-selecting" way, because the spatial complexity of enumeration is only $O(poly(n))$ where n is lattice dimension, while the sorting algorithm, as mentioned above, needs a space of approximately $O(poly(2^n))$ to store all the vectors.

The pseudocode of the enumeration-like sampling algorithm is given in Appendix A.

This algorithm is a universal framework that can be embedded into any lattice sampling-reduction algorithm such as RSR and RR, by modifying the pruning method. Generally speaking, the conditional control statement $\mathbf{z} \in Z(\mathbf{t})$ can be replaced by any other pruning method.

However, there are questions remain to be explained, and most important one is parameter selection. Different $\mathbf{t}$ and R may influence the running time.

4 Statistical Analysis and Parameter Selection

Given a lattice basis $\mathbf{B}$, the NNR vector set $Z(\mathbf{t})$ generates a lattice vector set over $\mathbf{B}$ denoted by $V_B(\mathbf{t})$. In this section, we will analyze the statistical properties of candidate NNR vector set $Z(\mathbf{t})$ and corresponding $V_B(\mathbf{t})$, and give the parameters optimization strategy.

In this section, for a given parameter $\mathbf{t}$, we use the equivalent representation "template vector" $\bar{\mathbf{z}}$ for convenience, namely, using the notation $S(\bar{\mathbf{z}})$ and $S_B(\bar{\mathbf{z}})$ to represent $Z(\mathbf{t})$ and $V_B(\mathbf{t})$ respectively.

4.1 Distribution of Candidate Vectors

Before we study the statistical properties of candidate vector set $S(\bar{\mathbf{z}})$ and its corresponding $S_B(\bar{\mathbf{z}})$, some necessary theorems [4] are given below.

Lemma 1. *Let X be a random variable uniformly distributed over $[a, b]$, then the expectation value of X^2 is $E(X^2) = \frac{a^2 + b^2 + ab}{3}$ and variance $V(X^2) = \frac{4}{45}a^2 - \frac{1}{45}a^3 b - \frac{2}{15}a^2 b^2 - \frac{1}{45}a^3 b + \frac{4}{45}b^4$.*

Lemma 2 (Lyapunov Central Limit Theorem). *Suppose $\{X_1, X_2, \ldots\}$ is a sequence of independent random variables, each with finite expected value μ_i and finite variance σ_i^2. If there exists $\delta > 0$ such that*

$$\lim_{n \to \infty} \frac{1}{B_n^{2+\delta}} \sum_{k=1}^{n} E|X_k - \mu_k|^{2+\delta} = 0 \tag{4}$$

where $B_n^2 = \sum_{k=1}^{n} \sigma_k^2$, then $\sum_{k=1}^{n} \frac{X_k - \mu_k}{B_n}$ converges in distribution to a standard normal random variable as n goes to infinity, i.e.:

$$\frac{1}{B_n} \sum_{k=1}^{n} (X_k - \mu_k) \xrightarrow{d} N(0, 1) \tag{5}$$

Given a lattice basis $\mathbf{B}$ and a template vector $\bar{\mathbf{z}}$, the two variances can define an NNR vector set $S(\bar{\mathbf{z}})$ and a corresponding lattice vector set $S_B(\bar{\mathbf{z}})$. For $\mathbf{v} \in S_B(\bar{\mathbf{z}})$ and $\|\mathbf{v}\|^2 = \sum_{j=1}^{n} |u_j|^2 \|\mathbf{b}_j^*\|^2$, since $z_j(\mathbf{v}) < \bar{z}_j$ for each $j = 1, \ldots, n$ and therefore $0 \le |u_j| \le \frac{\bar{z}_j + 1}{2}$. If Random Assumption (RA) holds, then for all $j = 1 \ldots n$, $|u_j|$ can be regarded as independent random variables uniformly distributed over $\left[0, \frac{\bar{z}_j + 1}{2}\right]$. According to Lemma 1, the expectation value of $|u_j|^2$ is

$$E_j = \frac{1}{12}(\bar{z}_j + 1)^2 \tag{6}$$

and variance value

$$V_j = \frac{1}{180}(\bar{z}_j + 1)^4 \tag{7}$$

Since $\|\mathbf{v}\|^2$ is a linear combination of those random variables $|u_j|^2$, it can also be regard as a random variable. Then we have a theorem on the distribution of $\|\mathbf{v}\|^2$ over $S_B(\bar{\mathbf{z}})$:

Theorem 2. *If there exists $C_1 \in \mathbb{R}$ such that $\mathrm{vol}\,(L) = \prod_{j=1}^{n} \|\mathbf{b}_j^*\| < C_1$ for any n, and there exists $C_2 \in \mathbb{R}$ such that $\|\mathbf{t}\|_\infty < C_2$ for any n-dimensional lattice vector set $S_B(\overline{\mathbf{z}})$, then for $\mathbf{v} \in S_B(\overline{\mathbf{z}})$ with $\|\mathbf{v}\|^2 = \sum_{j=1}^{n} |u_j|^2 \|\mathbf{b}_j^*\|^2$:*

$$\frac{1}{\sigma}\left(\|\mathbf{v}\|^2 - \mu\right) \xrightarrow[n\to\infty]{d} N(0,1) \tag{8}$$

with $\sigma^2 = \sum_{j=1}^{n} V_j \|\mathbf{b}_j^*\|^4$ and $\mu = \sum_{j=1}^{n} E_j \|\mathbf{b}_j^*\|^2$.

Proof. It can be proved that the case satisfies the Lyapunov condition with $\delta = 1$. Let $X_i = |u_i|^2 \|\mathbf{b}_i^*\|^2$, $\sigma_i^2 = V_i^2 \|\mathbf{b}_i^*\|^4$ and $\mu_i = E_i \|\mathbf{b}_i^*\|^2$ in Lemma 2, and we have $B_n^2 > \frac{n}{180} \sim \mathcal{O}(n)$ and $\sum_{j=1}^{n} \mu_j < C_1^2 C_2^2\, n \sim \mathcal{O}(n)$. Then let $\delta = 1$ and the left side of Eq. 4 is equal to $\frac{\mathcal{O}(n^2)}{\mathcal{O}(n^{2/3})} = \mathcal{O}(1/\sqrt{n}) \to 0$, according to Lemma 2 we have

$$\frac{1}{\sigma}\left(\|\mathbf{v}\|^2 - \mu\right) = \frac{1}{\sigma}\sum_{k=1}^{n}\left(|u_k|^2\|\mathbf{b}_k^*\|^2 - E_k\|\mathbf{b}_k^*\|^2\right) \xrightarrow{d} N(0,1) \qquad \square \tag{9}$$

As we mentioned in Sect. 3.2, the candidate vector set $Z(\mathbf{t})$ we used in the enumeration-like sampling method is a special construction of $S(\overline{\mathbf{z}})$, and therefore the relevant conclusions still hold for $V_B(\mathbf{t})$:

Corollary 1. *If there exists $C_1 \in \mathbb{R}$ such that $\mathrm{vol}\,(L) = \prod_{j=1}^{n} \|\mathbf{b}_j^*\| < C_1$ for any n, and there exists $C_2 \in \mathbb{R}$ such that $\|\mathbf{t}\|_\infty < C_2$ for any n-dimensional lattice vector set $V_B(\mathbf{t})$ with template vector $\overline{\mathbf{z}}$, then for $\mathbf{v} \in V_B(\mathbf{t})$ with $\|\mathbf{v}\|^2 = \sum_{j=1}^{n} |u_j|^2 \|\mathbf{b}_j^*\|^2$:*

$$\frac{1}{\sigma}\left(\|\mathbf{v}\|^2 - \mu\right) \xrightarrow[n\to\infty]{d} N(0,1) \tag{10}$$

with $\sigma^2 = \sum_{j=1}^{n} V_j \|\mathbf{b}_j^*\|^4$ and $\mu = \sum_{j=1}^{n} E_j \|\mathbf{b}_j^*\|^2$.

To verify the theorem and its corollary, we choose two sets of parameters in 150 and 180 dimensional lattice and sample 500000 vectors in each candidate set $V_B(\mathbf{t})$. The comparison of $\|\mathbf{v}\|^2$ obtained by sampling with the theoretical normal distribution in Theorem 1 is shown in Fig. 1. The histogram shows the frequency distribution of experimental observation, and the curve is the theoretical normal distribution.

The experimental result seems to be consistent with the theoretical conclusion. Unfortunately, in both of the 150 and 180 dimensional cases, Kolmogorov–Smirnov test rejects the null hypothesis at level $\alpha = 0.05$, indicating that the frequency distribution of $\|\mathbf{v}\|^2$ we observed differs from a normal distribution with high probability.

This inconsistency has an explanation. In practice, $\mathrm{vol}\,(L)$ does not always have an upper bound C_1 as assumed in Theorem 1. In fact, the n-dimensional lattice L provided by SVP challenge [1] has $\mathrm{vol}\,(L)$ growing super-exponentially with respect to n. Since n is not too large in practical implementation and therefore the $\mathrm{vol}\,(L)$ can be bounded by a C_1 large enough, we heuristically assume

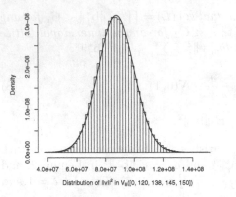 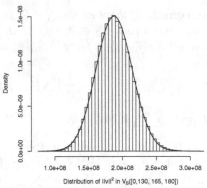

Fig. 1. The distribution of $\|\mathbf{v}\|^2$ in different candidate set $V_B(\mathbf{t})$

that for any n-dimensional random lattice basis with $n \gtrsim 50$, the distribution of $\|\mathbf{v}\|^2$ in $S_B(\overline{\mathbf{z}})$ approximately follows $N(\mu, \sigma^2)$.

From Theorem 1 we can calculate the probability of sampling a short lattice vector in $V_B(\mathbf{t})$ has an estimated value:

$$p(A) \triangleq Pr\left(\|\mathbf{v}\|^2 \le A\right) = \frac{1}{\sigma\sqrt{2\pi}} \int_{-\infty}^{A} \exp\left[-\frac{(x-\mu)^2}{2\sigma^2}\right] dx \qquad (11)$$

For a given basis $\mathbf{B}$ and a certain NNR vector $\mathbf{z}$, the expectation value $E\left[\|\mathbf{v}\|^2\right]$ can be regarded as a quick-estimating function of the real length $\|\mathbf{v}\|^2$ and is denoted by $f(\mathbf{z}) = \frac{1}{12}\sum_{j=1}^{n}(3z_j^2 + 3z_j + 1)\|\mathbf{b}_j^*\|^2 = \sum_{j=1}^{n}\left(\frac{1}{4}(z_j + \frac{1}{2})^2 + \frac{1}{48}\right)\|\mathbf{b}_j^*\|^2$.

If a vector $\mathbf{z}$ is uniformly sampled from $S(\overline{\mathbf{z}})$, which implies that z_j is uniformly distributed over discrete values $0, \ldots, \overline{z}_j$ and all z_j are mutual independent, then $f(\mathbf{z})$ can also be regarded as a random variable.

Let

$$f_j(x) = \left(\frac{1}{4}(x + \frac{1}{2})^2 + \frac{1}{48}\right)\|\mathbf{b}_j^*\|^2 \qquad (12)$$

then we have

$$E(f(\mathbf{z})) = \sum_{j=1}^{n} \frac{1}{\overline{z}_j + 1} \sum_{i=0}^{\overline{z}_j} f_j(i) \qquad (13)$$

and variance value

$$V(f(\mathbf{z})) = \sum_{j=1}^{n} \frac{1}{\overline{z}_j + 1} \sum_{i=0}^{\overline{z}_j} \left[f_j(i) - \frac{1}{\overline{z}_j + 1}\sum_{k=0}^{\overline{z}_j} f_j(k)\right]^2 \qquad (14)$$

The expectation and variance values are easy to calculate if basis $\mathbf{B}$ and candidate set $S(\overline{\mathbf{z}})$ is given. And we can prove that the distribution of value $f(\mathbf{z})$ with $\mathbf{z}$ sampled from $S(\overline{\mathbf{z}})$ converges to normal distribution under certain conditions.

The conclusion and proof are same with Theorem 1 and we will not describe it in detail here. We also compare the histograms obtained by sampling with theoretical norm distribution curves provided by Eqs. (13) and (14) (see Fig. 2). We also heuristically assume that for any n-dimensional random lattice basis with $n \gtrsim 50$ and for $\mathbf{z} \in Z(\mathbf{t})$, the distribution of $f(\mathbf{z})$ approximately follows a normal distribution $N(E(f(\mathbf{z})), V(f(\mathbf{z})))$.

4.2   Parameter Selection Strategy

In Schnorr's sampling algorithm, the targeting vector in candidate set satisfies $\|\mathbf{v}\|^2 < \delta \|\mathbf{b}_1\|^2$. In our sampling model, the probability that finding a vector such that $\|\mathbf{v}\|^2 < \delta \|\mathbf{b}_1\|^2$ is $p(\delta \|\mathbf{b}_1\|^2)$ defined in Eq. (11). Then it is expected to randomly sample $N = \frac{1}{2\,p(\delta \|\mathbf{b}_1\|^2)}$ vectors in $V_B(\mathbf{t})$ to find a targeting vector, where the coefficient in denominator is due to the symmetry of lattice vectors.

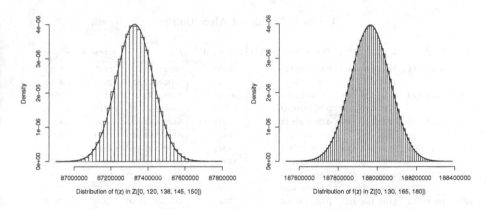

Fig. 2. The distribution of $f(\mathbf{z})$ when $\mathbf{z}$ is sampled from $Z(\mathbf{t})$

We can use our enumeration method to heuristically increase the successful rate, in another word, decrease the sampling amount N to save time. Considering the quick-estimating function $f(\mathbf{z}) = \sum_{j=1}^{n} \left(\frac{1}{4}(z_j + \frac{1}{2})^2 + \frac{1}{48} \right) \|\mathbf{b}_j^*\|^2$, which implies that for $\mathbf{v} \in V_B(\mathbf{t})$ and its corresponding $\mathbf{z} \in Z(\mathbf{t})$, the smaller $f(\mathbf{z})$ is, the shorter $\|\mathbf{v}\|^2$ is expected to be. In practice, randomly choosing N vectors from $V_B(\mathbf{t})$ needs to choose N vectors from $Z(\mathbf{t})$ and then map them into lattice vectors. The algorithm is given in Appendix A.

This algorithm outputs a roughly estimation of the enumeration radius R. Using R we can control the sampling procedure to find the smallest $\frac{1}{p(\delta \|\mathbf{b}_1\|^2)}$ vectors in NNR candidate set. However in practice, many other factors should be taken into consideration. One question is that in candidate set $Z(\mathbf{t})$, $f(\mathbf{z})$ has a minimum value $\frac{1}{12} \sum_{j=1}^{n} \|\mathbf{b}_j^*\|^2$ corresponding to $\mathbf{z} = \mathbf{0}$. When $R < \frac{1}{12} \sum_{j=1}^{n} \|\mathbf{b}_j^*\|^2$, no vector can be sampled out, but in this case, probability p is relatively high and finding a target vector is easy, we can just enlarge R a little to guarantee that the sampling algorithm can continue.

We apply the parameter selection algorithm on high dimension to see the theoretical and practical results. It shows that in high dimension, our algorithm not only give an theoretical upper bound of sampling amount, and even has better result in practice. We applied the algorithm to different dimensional lattice and using different parameters. The lattice bases are generated by the C program on [1] with seed 0, and are all BKZ-20 reduced.

In Table 1, $\|\mathbf{b}_1\|^2$ are directly obtained by the reduced basis, and we choose different $\mathbf{t}$ to test our algorithm. The value $p = Pr(\|\mathbf{v}\|^2 < \|\mathbf{b}_1\|^2)$, expected sample amount N and output R is directly calculated by theoretical value. Then we use the algorithm output R as the parameter of enumeration-like sampling Algorithm 1, and we list the actual sampling amount when Algorithm 1 finds the first target lattice vector $\mathbf{v}$ such that $\|\mathbf{v}\|^2 < \|\mathbf{b}_1\|^2$. The table shows that in the enumeration-like sampling procedure, the first target vector is always found earlier than reaching the theoretical estimation N.

Table 1. Results of Algorithm 2

n	$\|\mathbf{b}_1\|^2$	$\mathbf{t}$	$Pr(\|\mathbf{v}\|^2 < \|\mathbf{b}_1\|^2)$	Expected N	R	Actual N	$\frac{min\|\mathbf{v}\|^2}{\|\mathbf{b}_1\|^2}$
140	39226111	[115 130 136]	0.000246722	4053	69025155.27	1995	0.8303
		[110 130]	0.00024104	4149	69059667.85	2083	0.8303
145	34495520	[110 136 142]	0.000009906	100949	75730820.62	80419	0.9960
		[110 140]	0.000010232	97733	75618150.70	79816	0.9960
150	51276487	[125 140 146]	0.000532548	1878	84922647.92	1136	0.8265
		[120 140]	0.000524222	1908	84923582.07	1190	0.8265
155	51537003	[120 145 152]	0.000071214	14042	98728124.49	13340	0.9141
		[120 148]	0.000072322	13827	98729111.79	20000	0.8078
160	71289521	[130 150 156]	0.000370468	2699	122347973.70	1668	0.8161
		[125 150]	0.000366028	2732	122345526.74	2083	0.7682
165	109181313	[130 156 162]	0.000488326	2048	188897231.50	1000	0.7816
		[130 158]	0.000489816	2042	188614310.10	1309	0.8322
170	77704714	[130 160 166]	0.000155746	6421	140157767.60	12500	0.8896
		[134 166]	0.00016018	6243	140156366.02	3846	0.9036

Considering an extreme case where $p(\delta\|\mathbf{b}_1\|^2)$ is too small, the number of vectors $N = \frac{1}{2\,p(\delta\|\mathbf{b}_1\|^2)}$ might be very close to, or even larger than $\#Z(\mathbf{t})$, which makes the sampling procedure meaningless(invalid). This remains a question to look into.

If the algorithm fails to find a targeting vector in the enumeration sampling procedure, Schnorr and Fukase gave their solutions that taking i-th orthogonal projection into consideration. In the extension version of Schnorr's algorithm [18], vectors such that $\|\pi_i(\mathbf{v})\|^2 < \delta\|\mathbf{b}_i^*\|^2$ can be inserted to basis and execute a BKZ or LLL reduction. In Fukase's algorithm, they proposed the concept "insertion index" in Definition 3 and enforce to insert the targeting vector in order.

5 Experimental Results and Conclusion

Based on Schnorr's framework, We embedded the enumeration-like sampling method (see Algorithm 1) into lattice reduction algorithm. The main routine, Algorithm 3, is given in Appendix A.

5.1 Experiment Result

We implement Fukase's RR algorithm and Algorithm 3 on a server computer with a 2.10GHz Intel Xeon CPU(E5-2620) with 64GB RAM, and we executed our program on single thread. Our program used the NTL library [2] and the lattice bases are generated by SVP challenge [1] with seed 0. Here we compare the time consumptions of the two algorithms in Tables 2 and 3.

Table 2. Results of RR algorithm

n	Parameters	CPU time (sec)	Norm	$apfa$
66	$s = [65\ 16\ 3]$, $t = [66\ 28\ 6]$	148	2173.046	1.033
70	$s = [69\ 16\ 3]$, $t = [70\ 30\ 8]$	30179	2232.389	1.046
74	$s = [73\ 18\ 4]$, $t = [74\ 30\ 6]$	381848	2281.597	1.035

We tried our best to optimize and the original RR algorithm described in [10] and build the program. We did not use parallel programming technology and therefore computation capability is relatively limited, our result may not be the best performance that RR algorithm can achieve. We did not apply RR algorithm on higer dimension(>74) since it might need to run several days.

Table 3. Results of Algorithm 3

n	Parameters	CPU time (sec)	Norm	$apfa$
66	$t = [0\ 38\ 60\ 66]$	1516	2173.046	1.041
70	$t = [0\ 40\ 62\ 70]$	2334	2205.844	1.034
74	$t = [0\ 44\ 68\ 74]$	6384	2312.38	1.049
78	$t = [0\ 40\ 72\ 74\ 78]$	113388	2192.766	0.968
82	$t = [0\ 46\ 76\ 78\ 82]$	133847	2374.588	1.025
86	$t = [0\ 71\ 83\ 86]$	73320	2429.330	1.023
90	$t = [0\ 50\ 82\ 86\ 90]$	298260	2468.856	1.018

According to the results, our algorithm runs generally faster than RR algorithm, although the structure of candidate vector sets are different and not comparable. During the running of the programs, we find that our program ran faster in the first several iterations because the size of candidate vector set is adjusted according to the lattice basis, which made the lattice basis reduced efficiently at the beginning.

Besides, we compare the single-thread running time of our algorithm with some single-thread SVP challenge records provided by the authors in their comments [1]. We show the comparison in Fig. 3. The efficiency of our algorithm is higher than some classical sieving and very closed to the records made by other algorithms such as lattice reduction, enumeration with other methods and so on.

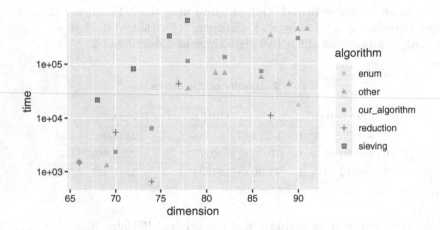

Fig. 3. Our algorithm vs. SVP challenge records

5.2   Conclusions and Further Work

Sampling-reduction method is believed to be efficient in solving high dimensional shortest vector problem. It can continuously optimize lattice basis by sampling and inserting short vectors. During the whole algorithm, the probability of finding a very short lattice vector increases step by step.

We put up with a new sampling reduction method for solving SVP, and get rid of the hard restriction of Schnorr's Random Sampling Reduction algorithm, and also have better theoretical support than Fukase's Restricted Reduction algorithm. Our Enumeration-like Sampling algorithm can be generally embedded into various sampling reduction frameworks. We proved the distribution of vector length in our candidate set converges to normal distribution under some reasonable assumptions, which make it easy to calculate the sampling parameters and adjust parameters according to different goals.

In our research, there are several problems remain considering:

1. The relationship between G-S sum and success rate. Fukase pointed out [10, 21] that basis with smaller G-S sum have higher probability of finding very short lattice vector, and we have a similar conclusion in Sect. 4 that the

expectation value of vector length is related to a weighted sum of $\|\mathbf{b}_i^*\|^2$. How to control the G-S sum efficiently decreasing in the iteration of algorithm is a meaningful and important problem.

2. Multiprocess implementation. There are mainly two ways to parallelize the sampling reduction algorithms. One is parallel sampling, but it can only accelerate in constant speed. Another is to using different basis in different process. It can raise the success rate but every process has heavy work to do. A better parallelization strategy was done perfectly by [19], and they achieved 150 dimensional SVP challenge using their sophisticated extension version of RR algorithm. Their ideas inspired us to exploit more special properties of lattice basis in our algorithm.

Appendix A   The Pseudocode of Algorithms

Algorithm 1. Enumeration-Sampling($\mathbf{B}, Z(\mathbf{t}), R$)

Input:
    B: lattice basis $\mathbf{B} = [\mathbf{b}_1, \ldots, \mathbf{b}_n]$ and its orthogonal basis $\mathbf{B}^* = [\mathbf{b}_1^*, \ldots, \mathbf{b}_n^*]$;
    t: parameters of the candidate NNR vector set $Z(\mathbf{t})$
    $R \in \mathbb{R}$.

Output:
    All NNR vectors $\mathbf{z} \in Z(\mathbf{s}, \mathbf{t})$ such that $f(\mathbf{z}) = \frac{1}{12} \sum_{j=1}^n (3z_j^2 + 3z_j + 1)\|\mathbf{b}_j^*\|^2 < R$.

1: $z_2 = \ldots = z_n = f_{n+1} = 0$ // Initialize nodes
2: **for** $k = n$ **to** 2 **do**
3:     $f_k \leftarrow f_{k+1} + \frac{1}{12}(3z_k^2 + 3z_k + 1)\|\mathbf{b}_k^*\|^2$ // Initialize function value (at each layer)
4: **end for**
5: $k \leftarrow 1$ // Search from the last component as the root of the enumeration tree
6: $z_1 \leftarrow 1$
7: $\mathbf{z}' = (z_1', \ldots z_n')$
8: **while** *true* **do**
9:     **for** $k = n$ **to** 1 **do**
10:       $f_k \leftarrow f_{k+1} + \frac{1}{12}(3z_k^2 + 3z_k + 1)\|\mathbf{b}_k^*\|^2$ // Update function value
11:       $z_k' \leftarrow z_{n-k+1}$ // Reverse the tree to obtain NNR vectors
12:     **end for**
13:     **if** $f_k < R$ **and** $\mathbf{z}' \in Z(\mathbf{t})$ **then**
14:       **if** $k = 1$ **then**
15:         output $\mathbf{z}'$
16:         $z_k \leftarrow z_k + 1$
17:       **else**
18:         $k \leftarrow k - 1$
19:         $z_k \leftarrow 0$
20:       **end if**
21:     **else if** $f_k > R$ **and** $\mathbf{z}' \in Z(\mathbf{t})$ **then**
22:       $k \leftarrow k + 1$
23:       **if** $k = n + 1$ **then**
24:         exit   // No more vectors

```
25:      else
26:          z_k ← z_k + 1
27:      end if
28:  else
29:      z_k ← z_k − 1
30:      k ← k + 1
31:      if k = n + 1 then
32:          exit                                           // No more vectors
33:      else
34:          z_k ← z_k + 1
35:      end if
36:  end if
37: end while
```

Algorithm 2. CalculateParameter($\mathbf{B}, \mathbf{t}, LEN$)

Input:

$\mathbf{B}$: lattice basis $\mathbf{B} = [\mathbf{b}_1, \ldots, \mathbf{b}_n]$ and its orthogonal basis $\mathbf{B}^* = [\mathbf{b}_1^*, \ldots, \mathbf{b}_n^*]$;

$\mathbf{t}, \overline{\mathbf{z}}$: parameters of the candidate NNR vector set $Z(\mathbf{t})$ and its template vector;

LEN: targeting squared length of random sampling. In Schnorr's algorithm, let $LEN = \delta \|\mathbf{b}_1\|^2$;

Output:

$R \in \mathbb{R}$: upper bound of enumeration in Algorithm 1.

1: calculate $E_j = \frac{1}{12}(\overline{z}_j + 1)^2$ and $V_j = \frac{1}{180}(\overline{z}_j + 1)^4$ for $j = 1, \ldots, n$;

2: calculate $\sigma^2 = \sum_{j=1}^{n} V_j \|\mathbf{b}_j^*\|^4$ and $\mu = \sum_{j=1}^{n} E_j \|\mathbf{b}_j^*\|^2$;   // distribution parameters in $V_B(\mathbf{t})$

3: calculate $p = Pr(\|\mathbf{v}\|^2 < LEN)$ using formula 11;

4: calculate $E(f(\mathbf{z}))$ and $V(f(\mathbf{z}))$ using formula 13 and 14;   // distribution parameters in $Z(\mathbf{t})$

5: Look up table to find z_α such that $Pr(X < z_\alpha) = \frac{1}{p\#Z(\mathbf{t})}$, $X \sim N(0, 1)$;

6: $R = E(f(\mathbf{z})) + z_\alpha \sqrt{V(f(\mathbf{z}))}$;

7: **return** R;

Algorithm 3. Lattice Reduction With Enumeration-like Sampling

Input:

$\mathbf{B}$: A BKZ-reduced n-dimensional lattice basis;

$\mathbf{t}, \overline{\mathbf{z}}$: Parameters of the candidate NNR vector set $Z(\mathbf{t})$ and its template vector;

δ;

Output:

A lattice vector $\mathbf{v}$ with $\|\mathbf{v}\| \leq 1.05 \, GH(L)$;

```
1:  while ture do
2:      V_B(t) ← ∅;
3:      R ← CalculateParameter(B, t, δ‖b_1‖²);
4:      generate NNR vector set S ← Enumeration-like Sampling(B, Z(t), R);
5:      for all z ∈ S do
6:          v ← GenerateLatticeVector(B, z);
7:          V_B(t) ← V_B(t) ∪ v;
8:      end for
9:      for all v ∈ V_B(t) do
10:         calculate ‖v‖²;
```

11:     **if** $\|\mathbf{v}\| \leq 1.05\,\mathrm{GH}(L)$ **then**
12:         **return** $\mathbf{v}$;
13:     **end if**
14:     calculate $h_\delta(\mathbf{v})$;
15:   **end for**
16:   $\mathbf{v}_0 \leftarrow$ the smallest vector by lexicographical order $(h_\delta(\mathbf{v}), \|\mathbf{v}\|^2)$;
17:   $\mathbf{B} \leftarrow \mathrm{BKZ}([\mathbf{b}_1, \ldots, \mathbf{b}_{h_\delta(\mathbf{v}_0)-1}, \mathbf{v}_0, \mathbf{b}_{h_\delta(\mathbf{v}_0)}, \ldots, \mathbf{b}_n])$;
18: **end while**

References

1. http://www.latticechallenge.org/svp-challenge/
2. http://www.shoup.net/ntl/
3. Ajtai, M., Kumar, R., Sivakumar, D.: A sieve algorithm for the shortest lattice vector problem. In: Proceedings of the Thirty-Third Annual ACM Symposium on Theory of Computing, pp. 601–610. ACM (2001)
4. Aono, Y., Nguyen, P.Q.: Random sampling revisited: lattice enumeration with discrete pruning. In: Coron, J.-S., Nielsen, J.B. (eds.) EUROCRYPT 2017. LNCS, vol. 10211, pp. 65–102. Springer, Cham (2017). https://doi.org/10.1007/978-3-319-56614-6_3
5. Becker, A., Ducas, L., Gama, N., Laarhoven, T.: New directions in nearest neighbor searching with applications to lattice sieving. In: Proceedings of the Twenty-Seventh Annual ACM-SIAM Symposium on Discrete Algorithms, pp. 10–24. Society for Industrial and Applied Mathematics (2016)
6. Boneh, D., et al.: Twenty years of attacks on the RSA cryptosystem. Not.-Am. Math. Soc. **46**, 203–213 (1999)
7. Buchmann, J., Ludwig, C.: Practical lattice basis sampling reduction. In: Hess, F., Pauli, S., Pohst, M. (eds.) ANTS 2006. LNCS, vol. 4076, pp. 222–237. Springer, Heidelberg (2006). https://doi.org/10.1007/11792086_17
8. Coppersmith, D.: Finding small solutions to small degree polynomials. In: Silverman, J.H. (ed.) CaLC 2001. LNCS, vol. 2146, pp. 20–31. Springer, Heidelberg (2001). https://doi.org/10.1007/3-540-44670-2_3
9. van Emde Boas, P.: Another NP-complete problem and the complexity of computing short vectors in a lattice. Tecnical report, Department of Mathmatics, University of Amsterdam (1981)
10. Fukase, M., Kashiwabara, K.: An accelerated algorithm for solving SVP based on statistical analysis. J. Inf. Process. **23**(1), 67–80 (2015)
11. Gama, N., Nguyen, P.Q., Regev, O.: Lattice enumeration using extreme pruning. In: Gilbert, H. (ed.) EUROCRYPT 2010. LNCS, vol. 6110, pp. 257–278. Springer, Heidelberg (2010). https://doi.org/10.1007/978-3-642-13190-5_13
12. Kannan, R.: Improved algorithms for integer programming and related lattice problems. In: Proceedings of the Fifteenth Annual ACM Symposium on Theory of Computing, pp. 193–206. ACM (1983)
13. Khot, S.: Hardness of approximating the shortest vector problem in lattices. J. ACM (JACM) **52**(5), 789–808 (2005)
14. Laarhoven, T.: Sieving for shortest vectors in lattices using angular locality-sensitive hashing. In: Gennaro, R., Robshaw, M. (eds.) CRYPTO 2015. LNCS, vol. 9215, pp. 3–22. Springer, Heidelberg (2015). https://doi.org/10.1007/978-3-662-47989-6_1

15. Micciancio, D.: Lattice-based cryptography. In: van Tilborg, H.C.A., Jajodia, S. (eds.) Encyclopedia of Cryptography and Security, pp. 713–715. Springer, Boston (2011). https://doi.org/10.1007/978-1-4419-5906-5_417

16. Nguyen, P.Q., Vidick, T.: Sieve algorithms for the shortest vector problem are practical. J. Math. Cryptol. **2**(2), 181–207 (2008)

17. Regev, O.: On lattices, learning with errors, random linear codes, and cryptography. J. ACM (JACM) **56**(6), 34 (2009)

18. Schnorr, C.P.: Lattice reduction by random sampling and birthday methods. In: Alt, H., Habib, M. (eds.) STACS 2003. LNCS, vol. 2607, pp. 145–156. Springer, Heidelberg (2003). https://doi.org/10.1007/3-540-36494-3_14

19. Teruya, T., Kashiwabara, K., Hanaoka, G.: Fast lattice basis reduction suitable for massive parallelization and its application to the shortest vector problem. In: Abdalla, M., Dahab, R. (eds.) PKC 2018. LNCS, vol. 10769, pp. 437–460. Springer, Cham (2018). https://doi.org/10.1007/978-3-319-76578-5_15

20. Van Hoeij, M.: Factoring polynomials and the Knapsack problem. J. Number Theory **95**(2), 167–189 (2002)

21. Yasuda, M., Yokoyama, K., Shimoyama, T., Kogure, J., Koshiba, T.: Analysis of decreasing squared-sum of gram-schmidt lengths for short lattice vectors. J. Math. Cryptol. **11**(1), 1–24 (2017)

Secure Multiparty Learning from Aggregation of Locally Trained Models

Xu Ma[1,2(✉)], Cunmei Ji[2], Xiaoyu Zhang[1], Jianfeng Wang[1], Jin Li[3], and Kuan-Ching Li[4]

[1] State Key Laboratory of Integrated Service Networks (ISN), Xidian University, Xi'an, China
{xma,jfwang}@xidian.edu.cn, moliyanyan@163.com
[2] School of Software, Qufu Normal University, Qufu, China
jicm2015@qfnu.edu.cn
[3] School of Computer Science and Educational Software, Guangzhou University, Guangzhou, China
lijin@gzhu.edu.cn
[4] School of Computer Science and Information Engineering, Providence University, Taichung, Taiwan
kuancli@pu.edu.tw

Abstract. In this paper, we propose a new protocol for secure multiparty learning *(SML)* from the aggregation of locally trained models, by using homomorphic proxy re-encryption and aggregate signature techniques. In our scheme, we utilize the method of secure verifiable computation delegation to privately generate labels for auxiliary unlabeled public data. Based on the labeled dataset, a central entity can learn a global learning model without direct access to the local private datasets. The generalization performance of *SML* is excellent and almost equals to the accuracy of the model learned from the union of all the parties' datasets. We implement *SML* on MNIST, and extensive analysis shows that our method is effective, efficient and secure.

Keywords: Aggregate signature · Proxy re-encryption · Multiparty learning · Computation delegation

1 Introduction

Advances in machine learning in recent years have transformed the solutions of many data-driven applications due to its superior performance, such as speech recognition [11], image classification [13] and self-driving car [19], etc. Generally, the learning model is trained from a large amount of data and can later be used for inference, and the generalization capability of a leaning model is greatly affected by the volume and quality of the training data. However, the data used for training is always quite sensitive; therefore, collecting and holding large

© Springer Nature Switzerland AG 2019
X. Chen et al. (Eds.): ML4CS 2019, LNCS 11806, pp. 173–182, 2019.
https://doi.org/10.1007/978-3-030-30619-9_13

amount of such sensitive data by one machine learning service provider creates high privacy risks to the data subject, whereas it is required for users to benefit from such services [1].

The aforementioned problem motivates plenty of work on secure multiparty machine learning, such as privacy-preserving decision tree [14], logistic regression [21], linear regression [9], etc. The main idea of these solutions is to utilize secure multiparty computation (SMC) or fully homomorphic encryption to process the whole dataset directly during the training process, which incurs high computation overhead. Hamm et al. [12] extended multiparty learning based on the ensemble of local classifiers and differentially privacy. In this strategy, the local classifiers are collected by a trusted entity who uses the classifier ensemble to generate labels for auxiliary unlabeled data. Then, the labeled data are used to train a new global classifier. Finally, a differentially private global classifier is released using output perturbation method [6]. Although the finally released global classifier is secure against the malicious adversary, the protocol cannot protect the privacy of the local classifiers, since it assumes that the local classifiers are firstly collected by a "trusted" entity. As pointed out from recent attacks against machine learning [10], private training data can be recovered with high probability from the models. Such attacks can be implemented by analyzing the internal parameters of the model directly, which is known as while-box attack. Alternatively, the attacks can also proceed by repeatedly querying the model in a black-box manner to gather data for further analysis; therefore, the method proposed in [12] cannot be applied in privacy sensitive applications.

Some other relevant research tried leveraging outsourcing computation [7,8] to improve the efficiency of privacy-preserving multiparty learning. Zhang et al. [22] proposed a cloud computing based privacy-preserving single-layer perceptron training scheme that supports batch patterns training and verification for the training results. To solve the problem of information leakage in [20], Ma et al. [16] proposed a privacy-preserving aggregation protocol to share the parameters privately during the training process using additive homomorphic encryption. In privacy-preserving neural network prediction, the first scheme which can be implemented on the encrypted data was proposed by Barni et al. [3]. However, during the prediction procedure the data provider has to decrypt the ciphertext for each node, which introduces high communication overhead and significant information leakage about the neural network model. Ma et al. [15] proposed the first non-interactive neural network prediction scheme using two non-colluding servers and additive homomorphic encryption.

1.1   Our Contributions

- We propose a novel scheme *SML* based on verifiable computation delegation, which enables mutually distrust parties to learn a global model privately from the aggregation of mixed locally trained models. The core of *SML* is a secure and verifiable aggregation protocol which is used to generate the labels for the auxiliary public unlabeled data.

- We use homomorphic proxy re-encryption to realize secure aggregation of the encrypted labels encrypted under multiple keys, and the aggregate signature is used to realize the verifiability of the aggregated results returned from the malicious cloud server.
- We evaluate *SML* comprehensively with MNIST, and the results show that it is practically effective and efficient. The accuracy performance of the global model shows great improvement compared to the averaged accuracy of locally trained models (Fig. 1).

Organization. Section 2 formally describe the system model and security definitions. In Sect. 3, we then proceed to give a concrete construction of our proposed scheme, and the security proof and efficiency analysis are presented in Sect. 4. In Sect. 5 we evaluate the effectiveness and efficiency of our protocol, and finally we conclude the paper in Sect. 6.

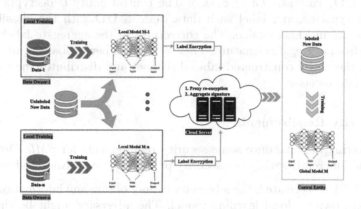

Fig. 1. Framework of secure multiparty learning based on the local models

2   System Model and Security Definitions

2.1   System Model

Definition 1. A secure multiparty machine learning scheme from aggregation of the local models *SML = (Setup, LabGen, LabAgg, GloTra)* consists of four algorithms defined below.

- *Setup*(1^κ): On input the security parameter κ, the setup algorithm is run by the data owner, the cloud server and the central entity to generate their own public/secret key pairs (pk, sk), respectively. Noting that the proxy re-encryption key $rk_{i \to \mathcal{C}}$, for $1 \le i \le n$ is generated privately by $\mathcal{O}_i$, $\mathcal{S}$ and $\mathcal{C}$ together.

- *LabGen*(M_i, **UD**): Assuming that each data owner already has a learning model M_i. Given a new unlabeled dataset **UD** $= \{ud_1, ud_2, \cdots, ud_m\}$, this algorithm is run by each data owner to generate the label $Lab_{i,j} = M_i(ud_j)$, the corresponding label encryption $\mathbf{Enc}(pk_i, Lab_{i,j})$ and label signature $\mathbf{Asig}(sk_i, Lab_{i,j})$, where $1 \leq i \leq n$ and $1 \leq j \leq m$. Finally, the label encryptions are sent to the cloud server who will re-encrypt and aggregate the encryptions into the ciphertext of the label summation. And the signatures are firstly sent to the data owner $\mathcal{O}_n$ who computes the aggregate signature σ that will be transferred to the central entity.

- *LabAgg*($\mathbf{Enc}(pk_i, Lab_{i,j}), rk_{i \to \mathcal{C}}$): On input the label encryptions from all the data owners, and the proxy re-encryption keys the label aggregation algorithm is run by the cloud server to convert the label encryptions from each data owner into the label encryption of the central entity $\mathbf{Enc}(pk_\mathcal{C}, Lab_{i,j})$. Then, the ciphertexts are aggregated into one ciphertext $\mathbf{Enc}(pk_\mathcal{C}, Lab_j)$ based on the property of additive homomorphism.

- *GloTra*(**UD**, $\mathbf{Enc}(pk_\mathcal{C}, Lab_j), \sigma, sk_c$): The central entity $\mathcal{C}$ decrypts all the label encryptions, and label each data item in **UD** with the classification that has the maximum value. The correctness of the aggregate label can be verified from aggregate signature. Then, $\mathcal{C}$ trains a new global learning model M from the newly constructed labeled dataset and distributes the model to all the data owners.

2.2   Security Requirements

In the following, we introduce some security requirements for *SML*. Obviously, *SML* should inherently satisfy two security properties, i.e., privacy and accuracy.

Privacy: A *SML* is private if the adversary cannot obtain any information about the any data owner's local learning model. The adversary might be the cloud server, the central entity, or other data owners. Specifically, we assume that the cloud server is malicious, but the central entity and data owners are honest-but-curious. Moreover, our scheme works in a non-collusion model.

Accuracy: A *SML* is accurate if the prediction accuracy of the global model M output by *GloTra*() is better than the averaged accuracy of all the individual locally-learning models M_i, for $1 \leq i \leq n$.

3   Construction of *SML*

In this section, we propose a concrete *SML* scheme based on proxy re-encryption [4] and aggregate signature [5].

- *Setup*(1^κ): Let κ be the security parameter. Let $\mathbb{G}_1$, $\mathbb{G}_2$, and $\mathbb{G}_T$ be three multiplicative cyclic groups of prime order p, where p is a large secure prime, and g_1, g_2 be generators of $\mathbb{G}_1$ and $\mathbb{G}_2$, respectively.

- For each data owner $\mathcal{O}_i$, randomly selects $sk_i = x_i \xleftarrow{R} \mathbb{Z}_p^*$ and computes the public key $pk_i = g^{x_i}$. In addition, a full-domain hash function $h : \{0,1\}^* \rightarrow \mathbb{G}_2$ is employed to generate signatures on arbitrary messages $msg \in \{0,1\}^*$.
- The cloud server $\mathcal{S}$ and central entity $\mathcal{C}$ also generate their private and public keys in the same way, output (pk_s, sk_s) and (pk_c, sk_c).
- For $1 \leq i \leq n$, generate the proxy re-encryption keys $rk_{i \rightarrow \mathcal{C}}$ as follows: (1) $\mathcal{S}$ randomly selects $r_i \xleftarrow{R} \mathbb{Z}_p^*$ and sends it to $\mathcal{O}_i$; (2) $\mathcal{O}_i$ computes $x_i^{-1}r_i$ and sends it to $\mathcal{C}$. (3) $\mathcal{C}$ computes $x_c x_i^{-1} r_i$ and sends it to $\mathcal{S}$; (4) $\mathcal{S}$ computes $rk_{i \rightarrow \mathcal{C}} = r_i^{-1} x_c r_i x_i^{-1} = x_c x_i^{-1}$.

- $LabGen(\mathsf{M}_i, \mathbf{UD})$: Assuming that each data owner $\mathcal{O}_i$ already has a learning model M_i. Given a new unlabeled dataset $\mathbf{UD} = \{ud_1, ud_2, \cdots, ud_m\}$, $LabGen()$ firstly generates the label $Lab_{i,j} = \mathsf{M}_i(ud_j)$, for $1 \leq i \leq n$ and $1 \leq j \leq m$, where $Lab_{i,j}$ is a vector of λ elements and λ represents the output size of model M_i. Each element of $Lab_{i,j}$ might be $0/1$ (for max voting) or a real number represents the confidence for a classification (for summation voting and weighted voting). The label encryption (signature) is an encryption (signature) vector composed of the encryption (signature) of each element of $Lab_{i,j}$. For simplicity, we $\mathbf{Enc}(Lab_{i,j})$ or $\mathbf{Asig}(Lab_{i,j})$ to represent the encryption vector or the signature vector. The details are described as follows:

For $1 \leq i \leq n$ and $1 \leq j \leq m$:
- **Encryption.** (1) $\mathcal{O}_i$ randomly selects $r_{i,j} \xleftarrow{R} \mathbb{Z}_p^*$; (2) $\mathcal{O}_i$ computes $c_{i,j} = g_1^{Lab_{i,j}+r_{i,j}}$, and $c'_{i,j} = g_1^{x_i r_{i,j}}$; (3) $\mathbf{Enc}(Lab_{i,j}) = (c_{i,j}, c'_{i,j})$.
- **Signature.** (1) $\mathcal{O}_i$ randomly selects $r'_{i,j} \xleftarrow{R} \mathbb{Z}_p^*$ and computes $h_{i,j} = h(r'_{i,j}, Lab_{i,j})$; (2) the signature is computed as $\mathbf{Asig}(Lab_{i,j}) = g_2^{Lab_{i,j}} h_{i,j}^{x_i}$.
- $\mathbf{Enc}(Lab_{i,j})$, $h_{i,j}$ and $\mathbf{Asig}(Lab_{i,j})$ are sent to $\mathcal{S}$, $\mathcal{C}$, and $\mathcal{O}_n$, respectively. When $\mathcal{O}_n$ has received all the signatures from $n-1$ data owners, an aggregate signature σ is computed and sent to the central entity $\mathcal{C}$:

$$\sigma = \prod_{i=1}^{n} \mathbf{Asig}(Lab_{i,j}) = \prod_{i=1}^{n} g_2^{Lab_{i,j}} h_{i,j}^{x_i}$$

$$= g_2^{\sum_{i=1}^{n} Lab_{i,j}} \prod_{i=1}^{n} h_{i,j}^{x_i} = g_2^{Lab_j} \prod_{i=1}^{n} h_{i,j}^{x_i}$$

- $LabAgg(\mathbf{Enc}(Lab_{i,j}), rk_{i \rightarrow \mathcal{C}})$: The cloud server aggregates the label encryptions for ud_j from all the data owners into one ciphertext $\mathbf{Enc}(Lab_j)_c$ of the central entity. Lab_j represents the aggregated label for ud_j, that is, $Lab_j = \sum_{i=1}^{n} Lab_{i,j}$. In the following subsection, we will describe the details about the aggregation.
  - $\mathcal{S}$ uses the proxy re-encryption key $rk_{i \rightarrow \mathcal{C}}$ to convert the label encryptions $\mathbf{Enc}(Lab_{i,j})$ for each data owner into label encryptions of the central entity $\mathbf{Enc}(Lab_{i,j})_c$. For $1 \leq i \leq n, 1 \leq j \leq m$,

$$\mathbf{Enc}(Lab_{i,j})_c = (c_{i,j}, (c'_{i,j})^{rk_{i \rightarrow \mathcal{C}}}) = (g_1^{Lab_{i,j}+r_{i,j}}, g_1^{x_c r_{i,j}})$$

- As the above encryption satisfies additive homomorphism, so $\mathcal{S}$ can aggregate all the ciphertext into:

$$\mathbf{Enc}(Lab_j)_c = \prod_{i=1}^{n} \mathbf{Enc}(Lab_{i,j})_c = (\prod_{i=1}^{n} g_1^{Lab_{i,j}} g_1^{r_{i,j}}, \prod_{i=1}^{n} g_1^{x_c r_{i,j}})$$

$$= (g_1^{\sum_{i=1}^{n} Lab_{i,j}} g_1^{\sum_{i=1}^{n} r_{i,j}}, g_1^{x_c \sum_{i=1}^{n} r_{i,j}})$$

$$= (g_1^{Lab_j} g_1^{\sum_{i=1}^{n} r_{i,j}}, g_1^{x_c \sum_{i=1}^{n} r_{i,j}})$$

– $GloTra(\mathbf{UD}, \mathbf{Enc}(Lab_j)_c, \mathbf{Asig}(Lab_{i,j}), h_{i,j}, sk_c)$: The central entity $\mathcal{C}$ decrypts the label encryption, verifies its correctness using the aggregate signature σ. Then, $\mathcal{C}$ trains a new global learning model M using the new labeled dataset. The details are described as follows:
  - Decrypts all the label encryptions $\mathbf{Enc}(Lab_j)_c$ using secret key sk_c.
  - Verifies the correctness of Lab_j

$$e(g_1, \sigma) = e(g_1, g_2^{Lab_j} \prod_{i=1}^{n} h_{i,j}^{x_i}) = e(g_1, g_2^{Lab_j}) e(g_1, \prod_{i=1}^{n} h_{i,j}^{x_i})$$

$$= e(g_1, g_2^{Lab_j}) \prod_{i=1}^{n} e(g_1^{x_i}, h_{i,j}) = e(g_1, g_2^{Lab_j}) \prod_{i=1}^{n} e(pk_i, h_{i,j})$$

- If the above equation holds, $\mathcal{C}$ accepts Lab_j and constructs a new dataset with $(ud_j, v(ud_j))$, for $1 \leq j \leq m$, where $v(ud_j)$ is the corresponding classification for ud_j, generated by simply selecting the classification with the most votes or highest score among all the items of Lab_j. That is,

$$v(ud_j) = argmax_k \, Lab_{j,k}$$

where $Lab_{j,k}$ represents the k-th item of Lab_j.
- $\mathcal{C}$ trains the global learning model M with $(ud_j, v(ud_j))$, for $1 \leq j \leq m$.

4   Security and Efficiency Analysis

4.1   Security Analysis

Theorem 1. *The proposed SML scheme satisfies the security requirement of privacy.*

Proof: Based on the security definition of privacy, we prove the theorem by contradiction. Assume there exist PPT adversaries $\mathcal{A}_1$ and $\mathcal{A}_2$ that have a non-negligible advantage ϵ in the experiment $\mathbf{Exp}_{\mathcal{A}_1, \mathcal{A}_2}^{SML}[\mathsf{M}, \kappa]$, then we can use $\mathcal{A}_1$ or $\mathcal{A}_2$ to build an efficient algorithm B to break the underlying proxy re-encryption scheme or aggregate signature. As what has been proven in [4] and [5] that if there exist a PPT adversary $\mathcal{A}$ that have a non-negligible advantage in breaking the proxy re-encryption (aggregate signature), then $\mathcal{A}$ can be further used to solve the computational Diffie-Hellman (computational co-Diffie-Hellman) problem.

Table 1. Computation and computation efficiency analysis

	Computation	Communication
Data Owner	$I+M+m(4E+H+M)$	$(4m+1)|p|$
Cloud Server	$mnE+2m(n-1)M$	$2(mn+m+n)|p|$
Central Entity	$m[(n+1)(P+M)+2I+E]$	$2(mn+m)|p|$

Table 2. Efficiency comparison

Scheme	Privacy	Computation (data owner)	Communication (data owner)	Accuracy (MNIST)
[20]	Gradient leakage	$O(|M|)$	$O(|M|)$	92%
[18]	Local model prediction leakage	$O(|\mathbf{UD}|)$	$O(|\mathbf{UD}|)$	98%
[17]	Secure against honest-but-curious adversary	$O(|M|)$	$O(|M|)$	98%
[2]	Secure against honest-but-curious adversary	$O(|M|)$	$O(|M|)$	98%
Ours	Secure against malicious adversary	$O(|\mathbf{UD}|)$	$O(|\mathbf{UD}|)$	98%

[a] $|M|$ denotes the size of learning model M, and $|\mathbf{UD}|$ denotes the size of the unlabeled dataset $\mathbf{UD}$. Generally, $|\mathbf{UD}|$ is much smaller than $|M|$.
[b] Representation of the abbreviations: Secret sharing (SS), oblivious transfer (OT), homomorphic encryption (HE), proxy re-encryption (PRE), aggregate signature (AS), garbled circuits (GC).

4.2 Efficiency Analysis

Table 1 shows the cryptography related computation and communication overhead of the data owner, the cloud server and the central entity. We denote by E, M and I to represent an exponentiation, a multiplication and an inversion in the group $\mathbb{G}_1$(or $\mathbb{G}_2$, $\mathbb{G}_T$) respectively, by P the computation of one pairing and by H a hashing operation. The additions are omitted in the table. n is the number of participants and m is the volume of unlabeled dataset. Note that we assume there already exists a local learning model for each data owner, so we omit the data owner's computation for training the local model. In addition, we use $Pred$ to represent one prediction computation overhead given an input data to the learning model and $Tra(D)$ the training computation overhead when given a dataset D. Table 2 shows the computation comparison of our scheme with the previous related work.

5   Experimental Evaluation

5.1   Effectiveness Evaluation

The experiments are implemented by Kersas 2.2.4 language, Tensorflow 1.4.1 back-end on the machine running Ubuntu 16.4 with 2 Tesla P100 GPUs. The training and testing samples are 60 K and 10K, respectively. The volume of unlabeled dataset is set to be 2K. Firstly, we compare the performance of SML with different label-generating methods: (1) Vote: labeling using max voting; (2) Sum: labeling using classification probability summation; (3) Weighted_sum: labeling using weighted summation. Figure 2 shows that weighted_sum performs a little better than vote and sum when all the local models are bad, where "bad" denotes the models with accuracy less than 70%. In the subsequent experiments, we choose weighted_sum as the label-generating method for our scheme SML. Intuitively, we can expect batch learning to perform better and individual learning to perform worse than SML. To simulate various real applications, we set the percentage of bad local models $P = 0, 0.5$ and 1.0 (Figs. 3, 4 and 5).

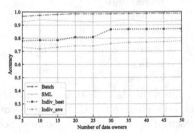

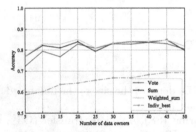

Fig. 2. Performance comparison of different label-generating method

Fig. 3. Performance comparison with $P = 0\%$.

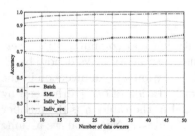

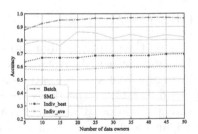

Fig. 4. Performance comparison with $P = 50\%$

Fig. 5. Performance comparison with $P = 100\%$.

5.2 Efficiency Evaluation

All our experiments are implemented by C programming language and the Pairing-Based Cryptography (PBC) library on Linux machine running Ubuntu 14, which is with Intel dual core i7, 2.5 GHz CPU and 16 GB RAM, and we simulate all the parties on this machine. The computation cost of each data owner is linearly related with the volume of the unlabeled dataset. The average computation time for each data item is about 10 ms. For the computation cost of the cloud server, we set the number of participants from 5 to 50, and set the data volume of the unlabeled dataset from 1000 to 5000. It requires about 2500 s for the cloud server to complete all the computation when given 5000 unlabeled data items and 50 participants. In real applications, this time consumption can be greatly cut down using powerful cloud server and running the scheme in parallel. The computation efficiency of the central entity can also be improved in parallel computation mode. As for the communication cost of the data owner, the cloud server and the central entity. The data volume is set from 1000 to 5000. For simplification, the number of data owners is set to be 50. As analysed in Table 1, the communication cost of each data owner is linearly related with the data volume. Particularly, when the data volume is 5000 and $|p| = 1024$, the communication cost of the data owner is 2.5 MB. As for the interaction between the cloud server and central entity, the communication cost reaches about 64 MB when data volume is 5000 and the number of data owners is 50.

6   Conclusion

In this work, we propose a secure multiparty learning scheme via the aggregation of locally trained models. Our scheme provides a secure and more efficient aggregation method to construct a global model from private local models. We mainly use proxy re-encryption and aggregate signature techniques to realize the security requirement of privacy and verifiability. Our experiment results show that our proposed scheme outperforms the state-of-the-art and is practical in real-world applications.

References

1. Alipanahi, B., Delong, A., Weirauch, M.T., Frey, B.J.: Predicting the sequence specificities of DNA-and RNA-binding proteins by deep learning. Nat. Biotechnol. **33**(8), 831 (2015)
2. Aono, Y., Hayashi, T., Wang, L., Moriai, S.: Privacy-preserving deep learning via additively homomorphic encryption. IEEE Trans. Inf. Forensics Secur. **13**(5), 1333–1345 (2018)
3. Barni, M., Orlandi, C., Piva, A.: A privacy-preserving protocol for neural-network-based computation. In: Proceedings of the 8th Workshop on Multimedia and Security, pp. 146–151. ACM (2006)
4. Blaze, M., Bleumer, G., Strauss, M.: Divertible protocols and atomic proxy cryptography. In: Nyberg, K. (ed.) EUROCRYPT 1998. LNCS, vol. 1403, pp. 127–144. Springer, Heidelberg (1998). https://doi.org/10.1007/BFb0054122

5. Boneh, D., Gentry, C., Lynn, B., Shacham, H.: Aggregate and verifiably encrypted signatures from bilinear maps. In: Biham, E. (ed.) EUROCRYPT 2003. LNCS, vol. 2656, pp. 416–432. Springer, Heidelberg (2003). https://doi.org/10.1007/3-540-39200-9_26
6. Chaudhuri, K., Monteleoni, C., Sarwate, A.D.: Differentially private empirical risk minimization. J. Mach. Learn. Res. **12**(Mar), 1069–1109 (2011)
7. Chen, X., Li, J., Ma, J., Tang, Q., Lou, W.: New algorithms for secure outsourcing of modular exponentiations. IEEE Trans. Parallel Distrib. Syst. **25**(9), 2386–2396 (2014)
8. Chen, X., Li, J., Weng, J., Ma, J., Lou, W.: Verifiable computation over large database with incremental updates. IEEE Trans. Comput. **65**(10), 3184–3195 (2016)
9. Du, W., Han, Y.S., Chen, S.: Privacy-preserving multivariate statistical analysis: linear regression and classification. In: Proceedings of the Fourth SIAM International Conference on Data Mining, pp. 222–233 (2004)
10. Fredrikson, M., Jha, S., Ristenpart, T.: Model inversion attacks that exploit confidence information and basic countermeasures. In: Proceedings of the 22nd ACM SIGSAC Conference on Computer and Communications Security, pp. 1322–1333. ACM (2015)
11. Graves, A., Mohamed, A.R., Hinton, G.E.: Speech recognition with deep recurrent neural networks. In: IEEE International Conference on Acoustics, Speech and Signal Processing, pp. 6645–6649 (2013)
12. Hamm, J., Cao, Y., Belkin, M.: Learning privately from multiparty data. In: Proceedings of the 33nd International Conference on Machine Learning, pp. 555–563 (2016)
13. Krizhevsky, A., Sutskever, I., Hinton, G.E.: Imagenet classification with deep convolutional neural networks. Commun. ACM **60**(6), 84–90 (2017)
14. Lindell, Y., Pinkas, B.: Privacy preserving data mining. J. Cryptol. **15**(3), 177–206 (2002)
15. Ma, X., Chen, X., Zhang, X.: Non-interactive privacy-preserving neural network prediction. Inf. Sci. **481**, 507–519 (2019)
16. Ma, X., Zhang, F., Chen, X., Shen, J.: Privacy preserving multi-party computation delegation for deep learning in cloud computing. Inf. Sci. **459**, 103–116 (2018)
17. Mohassel, P., Zhang, Y.: SecureML: a system for scalable privacy-preserving machine learning. In: Proceedings of the 2017 38th IEEE Symposium on Security and Privacy (SP), pp. 19–38. IEEE (2017)
18. Papernot, N., Abadi, M., Erlingsson, U., Goodfellow, I., Talwar, K.: Semi-supervised knowledge transfer for deep learning from private training data. arXiv preprint arXiv:1610.05755 (2016)
19. Ren, S., He, K., Girshick, R., Sun, J.: Faster R-CNN: towards real-time object detection with region proposal networks. In: Proceedings of the Advances in Neural Information Processing Systems, pp. 91–99 (2015)
20. Shokri, R., Shmatikov, V.: Privacy-preserving deep learning. In: Proceedings of the 22nd ACM SIGSAC Conference on Computer and Communications Security, pp. 1310–1321. ACM (2015)
21. Slavkovic, A.B., Nardi, Y., Tibbits, M.M.: Secure logistic regression of horizontally and vertically partitioned distributed databases. In: Workshops Proceedings of the 7th IEEE International Conference on Data Mining, pp. 723–728 (2007)
22. Zhang, X., Chen, X., Wang, J., Zhan, Z., Li, J.: Verifiable privacy-preserving single-layer perceptron training scheme in cloud computing. Soft. Comput. **22**(23), 7719–7732 (2018)

Data-Driven Android Malware Intelligence: A Survey

Junyang Qiu[1](✉), Surya Nepal[2], Wei Luo[1], Lei Pan[1], Yonghang Tai[3],
Jun Zhang[4], and Yang Xiang[4]

[1] School of Information Technology, Deakin University, Melbourne, Australia
{qiuju,wei.luo,l.pan}@deakin.edu.au
[2] Data61, CSIRO, Sydney, Australia
surya.nepal@data61.csiro.au
[3] School of Physics and Electronic Information, Yunnan Normal University,
Kunming, China
taiyonghang@ynnu.edu.cn
[4] School of Software and Electrical Engineering, Swinburne University of Technology,
Melbourne, Australia
{junzhang,yxiang}@swin.edu.au

Abstract. Android has dominated the smartphone market and become
the most popular mobile operating system. This rapidly increasing market share of Android has contributed to the boom of Android malware
in numbers and in varieties. There exist many techniques which are
proposed to accurately detect malware, e.g., software engineering-based
techniques and machine learning (ML)-based techniques. In this paper,
our main contributions are threefold: We reviewed the existing analysis techniques for Android malware detection; We focused on the code
analysis based detection techniques under the ML frameworks; We gave
the future research challenges and directions about Android malware
analysis.

Keywords: Android malware detection · Static analysis ·
Dynamic analysis · Hybrid analysis · Feature extraction ·
Machine learning · Code obfuscation

1 Introduction

The Android mobile devices continue to dominate the global mobile market,
with about 86.8% market share in the third quarter of 2018 according to the
statistical information published by *IDC Corporate*[1]. Almost eight out of ten
people worldwide use an Android mobile phone because they are cheap to buy[2].
Android has become the most popular operating system without a doubt. Due to
the fact that Android is an open source operating system, thus users can easily

---

[1] https://www.idc.com/promo/smartphone-market-share/os.
[2] https://www.gdatasoftware.com/.

© Springer Nature Switzerland AG 2019
X. Chen et al. (Eds.): ML4CS 2019, LNCS 11806, pp. 183–202, 2019.
https://doi.org/10.1007/978-3-030-30619-9_14

download and install a wide variety of applications from both official (*Google Play*[3]) and third-party (e.g., *WanDouJia*[4], *AnZhi*[5]) app stores (Currently there are approximately 2.6 million Android apps available at *Google Play*[6]). However, along with Android's popularity and its openness, Android mobile device users have become the most attractive targets of cyber criminals as the number of malicious apps has skyrocketed at an alarming rate. Figure 1 presents the number of Android malware samples being detected per year from 2012 to 2018[7]. It is estimated that almost 12,000 new Android malware samples being detected per day in 2018. Besides, the number of Android malware families has reached about 1,200 [62]. In addition, the sophisticated Android malware samples may be implemented with various strategies (e.g., code obfuscation, encryption) to evade detection.

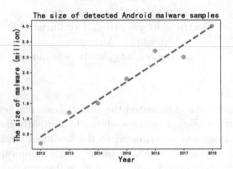

Fig. 1. The number of Android malware samples detected per year from 2012 to 2018.

To preserve a clean and safe ecosystem for Android users, both the academic researchers and the security vendors have invested enormous effort to design effective techniques to defend against Android malware samples or further categorize them into specific malware families [5,25,27,32,42,47,52,83,86,87]. Generally, the existing techniques for malware detection can be roughly divided into three categories [6]. The first one is called static analysis technique, which inspects the disassembled source code to find any potential suspicious functionalities without executing the application. The second one is the dynamic analysis technique, also called behaviors analysis technique. Dynamic analysis executes the given application in an isolated environment (e.g., sandbox, simulator, virtual machine), then monitors and traces its behaviors. The combination of static analysis and dynamic analysis is the third category called hybrid analysis technique [6].

---

[3] https://play.google.com/store.

[4] https://www.wandoujia.com/.

[5] http://www.anzhi.com/.

[6] https://www.appbrain.com/stats/number-of-android-apps.

[7] https://www.gdatasoftware.com/.

To provide a detailed review about Android malware detection, in this paper, our contributions are threefold: Firstly, we reviewed the existing Android malware detection techniques (including static, dynamic and hybrid techniques) as well as the advantages and disadvantages of each technique. Secondly, in the defender's perspective, targeting the Android code analysis, we introduced the machine learning based Android malware detection framework. We provided an overview of the framework, and then the involved techniques and challenges were reviewed in detail. In addition, we share our views of future potential research directions about the Android malware analysis.

The remaining of this paper is structured as follows. Section 2 presented the research status of Android malware detection. In Sect. 3, the Machine Learning framework for Android malware detection was reviewed. The future research direction and conclusion about this paper were given in Sects. 4 and 5, respectively.

2 Traditional Software Engineering Based Android Malware Analysis

A large number of Android malware analysis methods are built on traditional software engineering technique. Generally, software engineering technique can be roughly divided into three categories: Static code analysis, dynamic behavior analysis, and hybrid analysis. In this Section, we briefly review these three categories.

2.1 Static Code Analysis

The static code analysis is performed by disassembling and analyzing the source code of the given Android applications without executing it [79]. The static code analysis can be further categorized into signature based technique, permission based technique, the Dalvik bytecode-based technique, and the hybrid static analysis technique.

Signature-Based Technique

The signature involved methods are high efficiency and have been widely used by commercial malware detection products. The key building block of signature technique is to generate robust and accurate signatures based on the specific strings or semantic patterns in the source code [26]. Zheng et al. [85] designed DroidAnalytics, a signature-based analysis system which automatically collected Android malware samples, produced signatures, retrieved the information, and associated the malware samples based on a similarity score. Feng et al. proposed Apposcopy, a novel semantics-based approach for detecting a common class of Android malware samples that steals users' privacy data [26]. In [27], Feng et al. further implemented ASTROID, a system for automatically generating semantic Android malware signatures from very few malicious samples within a malware family. The core idea underlying ASTROID was to look for a Maximally Suspicious Common Subgraph that was shared between all the known malicious samples within an Android malware family [37].

Permission-Based Technique

To ensure the security of the Android operating system, the permission management plays an indispensable role in governing the access privilege [23]. The software authors must declare the requested permissions in the *AndroidManifest.xml* file. Thus, the core idea of permission-based technique is focusing on analyzing the requested sensitive or suspicious permissions to identify the potential malware samples. In 2009, Enck et al. proposed Kirin as a security service for Android analysis [22]. Without complicated and boring code inspection process, Kirin provided practical light-weight certification of Android applications at the installation time using the meaningful security rules to hinder malware samples. ASEDS was created using the Security Distance model to evaluate the risk level of specific combination of permissions [67]. Wu et al. provided a static analysis to extract the permissions related to the APT call traces from *Android-Manifest.xml* [74]. In 2013, PUMA was designed to perform Android malware detection using the permission usage features [57].

Dalvik Bytecode-Based Technique

Android software is usually developed using Java and compiled into Java bytecode. To execute more efficiently, the Java bytecode is optimized to Dalvik bytecode *classes.dex*. The *classes.dex* bytecode contains abundant semantic information, e.g., API calls, data flows, which is related to the application behaviors. The main idea of Dalvik bytecode-based technique is to disassemble the binary code and then analyze the source code to identify the Android malicious samples. A significant tool was Soot[8] originally designed by the Sable Group of McGill University. Soot can translate the Android applications into several intermediate representations, such as *Baf, jimple, Shimple*, and *Grimp*. An improved version of Soot, called Dexpler was presented in [10]. A robust and light-weight system called DroidAPIMiner was implemented to detect Android malware [1]. DroidAPIMiner extracted the API related semantic information (such as critical API calls, their package level information, and parameters) within the bytecode to represent Android samples. In 2017, HinDroid was proposed using the structured heterogeneous information network to represent the Android applications [32]. An approach named MaMaDroid was presented to detect Android malware by modeling the sequences of API calls as Markov chains [42].

Hybrid Static Analysis Technique

Some works have been conducted to extend the hybrid static analysis by analyzing both the *AndroidManifest.xml* file as well as disassembled *classes.dex* code. In [58], Sato et al. parsed various types of features (including permissions, intent filters, process names and the number of redefined permissions) to characterize

---

[8] https://sable.github.io/soot/.

the pattern of Android malicious samples. In 2014, Arp et al. proposed a lightweight method named Drebin to detect Android malware samples directly on the device [5]. Drebin extracted 4 types of feature sets from *AndroidManifest.xml* and other 4 feature sets from disassembled *classes.dex* files to characterize the Android applications. Arzt et al. designed a novel and accurate static taint analysis tool named FlowDroid in [7]. Different from the previous approaches, to reduce the false alarm rate, FlowDroid modeled Android's lifecycle or callback methods.

In summary, the static analysis techniques are efficient since they target the source code of the Android software. However, an increasing number of Android malicious samples have been obfuscated or encrypted using various tricks to evade detection [38, 66, 79]. Under this circumstance, it is difficult to disassemble the binary bytecode and detect the malicious samples accurately. Besides, the static analysis will overestimate the code execution paths. In addition, static analysis techniques are often accompanied by high false positive rate.

2.2 Dynamic Behavior Analysis

Dynamic behavior analysis is conducted by monitoring and tracing the behaviors of Android application during the execution to determine whether it is malicious or not [15].

In 2014, an efficient, system-wide Android dynamic analysis system Taint-Droid was proposed to track the flow of sensitive data [21]. An improved version of TaintDroid named Droidbox was introduced in [19]. Portokalidis et al. proposed an alternative dynamic approach [49]. This approach performed the malware detection task on the remote servers in the cloud while the execution of Android software on the device was mirrored in virtual machine environments. In 2011, a crowdsourcing-based dynamic analysis approach was proposed to detect Android malware samples [15]. The detector was embedded in an integrated framework to collect different behavior traces of the candidate applications from a crowdsourcing system. The crowdsourcing strategy made it possible to capture real behaviors traces of a large number of applications. Shabtai et al. presented a dynamic host-based Android malware detection framework in [60].

Another dynamic analysis platform for Android named DroidScope, which could reconstruct Linux OS level and Java Dalvik level semantic information simultaneously and seamlessly was presented in [77]. To perform large-scale Android applications analysis, Rastogi et al. implemented an automatic dynamic analysis framework for Android named AppsPlayground [54]. AppsPlayground integrated various automatic detection or exploration techniques (e.e., a taint analysis tool [21], a kernel-level system call monitoring) to construct an effective dynamic analysis platform. Reina et al. implemented CopperDroid [55], a tool built on QEMU [12] to automatically analyze the out-of-box dynamic behaviors of Android malicious samples. In 2014, AirBag, a client-side approach that leveraged light-weight operating system level virtualization was presented to enhance the safety of the Android platform and to facilitate the defense capability against

Android malware [73]. Backes et al. introduced a genetic and extensible Android Security Framework (ASF) in [9].

In summary, the dynamic behavior analysis can easily discover the malicious behaviors that may miss out by static code analysis. Besides, it is effective in combating code encryption or obfuscation techniques [66,79]. However, the code coverage rate of dynamic behaviors analysis is lower than that of the static code analysis, thus it tends to miss some code sections that will be executed or triggered at certain time or scenarios (e.g., the advanced Android malware may hide or stop their malicious behaviors once they detect the virtual environment, the malicious activities may be triggered only at night). In addition, dynamic analysis techniques cost more computational resources.

2.3 Hybrid Analysis

The hybrid analysis technique combines both the static code analysis and the dynamic behaviors analysis. In other words, it not only analyses the source code of Android applications but also monitors the behaviors while the applications are actually executed [11].

In 2010, a system named AASandbox (Android Application Sandbox) was proposed to perform a hybrid analysis to automatically detect Android malicious samples [14]. In the static analysis part, AASandbox disassembled the *classes.dex* bytecode into the intermediate *Smali* code and then pre-checked the code that may imply malicious code segments. In the dynamic analysis part, the candidate Android applications were executed in the emulator for the behavior inspection. A comprehensive investigation for the detection of Android malware samples from both official and third-party stores using the hybrid analysis technique was presented in [86]. Firstly, a permission-based footprinting method was proposed to detect known-family malware samples. Then to detect the unknown malware samples, a heuristics-based filtering method was designed to identify the specific inherent behaviors of unknown malware families. In 2012, Zheng et al. addressed the challenging issue about how to activate the sensitive behaviors of Android applications in [84]. A hybrid analysis was proposed to uncover the UI-based trigger conditions through automated interactions. First of all, the static analysis was used to discover the expected activity switch paths by constructing Function Call and Activity Call Graphs. Then the dynamic analysis was performed to traverse each UI element and to investigate the UI interaction paths towards the sensitive APIs. Furthermore, the produced trigger conditions of the proposed approach could facilitate the existing dynamic tools, such as TaintDroid [21], to automatically identify the corresponding sensitive behaviors.

Another novel hybrid analysis system named Mobile-Sandbox was presented in [61]. Mobile-Sandbox employed specific techniques to track calls to native APIs (e.g., C/C++). In the static analysis, the *AndroidManifest.xml* and binary *classes.dex* were disassembled and analyzed to determine whether the candidate Android applications were performing potential suspicious permissions or intents. Then these applications were executed in the sandbox to log all behaviors including native API calls. EvoDroid [41] and A5 (Automated Analysis of

Adversarial Android Applications) [68] were two hybrid analysis systems similar to Mobile-Sandbox [61], which also utilized the static analysis to traverse all possible activity path to guide the further dynamic analysis. In [2], Afonso et al. conducted a large-scale hybrid analysis of Android applications in the wild to investigate how applications use the native code.

To address the code obfuscation issue, Rasthofer et al. presented HAR-VESTER to capture run time values from Android applications, even from those highly obfuscated advanced Android malware [53]. HARVEST could boost the recall of the existing analysis tools, such as the dynamic tool TaintDroid [21] and the static tool FlowDroid [7].

A generic Android input generator named IntelliDroid was proposed in [72]. IntelliDroid could be configured to generate inputs specific for a dynamic analysis system. Two techniques were employed to activate the targeted APIs with the injected inputs: identifying event chains and device-platform interface input injection. In addition, combining IntelliDroid with dynamic analysis tool Taint-Droid [21] was able to provide better performance than FlowDroid [7].

In summary, the hybrid analysis technique exploits the advantages of static and dynamic analysis techniques. It not only captures the semantic structural information from the source code of Android applications but also tracks their running behaviors. Therefore, the hybrid analysis technique is able to adapt to code obfuscation while increasing the code coverage rate. However, hybrid analysis consumes expensive resources, and it requires a longer time to produce the analysis results [66,79]. Thus the usability of hybrid analysis is limited in a practical deployment.

3 Machine Learning Involved Android Malware Analysis

Given the soaring number of Android applications from both official and third-party stores, security experts or vendors have to inspect them in a short period to figure out their purposes or capabilities. Then the corresponding countermeasures will be provided based on the inspection results [61]. Thus it is necessary to accelerate the malware analysis process with little or even no human interventions. The Machine Learning techniques, which have been widely used in many cyber security areas [34,40,51,63,71,75,82], open the door for an alternative perspective to effectively and automatically identify or classify Android malicious samples. This section reviews the Android malware analysis methods using machine learning methods. Figure 2 presents the general framework of machine learning based malware analysis. The framework mainly consists of four steps: First of all, collecting the raw Android applications (including both benign and malicious samples) and setting up the ground truth (malicious/benign or specific family class). Second, performing feature engineering to extract informative features to characterize Android application samples. Third, training machine learning models for the following malware detection or classification. Fourth, predicting the candidate samples, evaluating the model and explaining the results. In the following, we will review the related works based on each step of the framework.

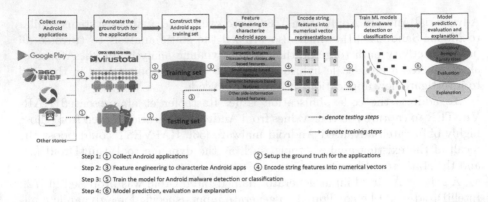

Step 1: ① Collect Android applications   ② Setup the ground truth for the applications

Step 2: ③ Feature engineering to characterize Android apps   ④ Encode string features into numerical vectors

Step 3: ⑤ Train the model for Android malware detection or classification

Step 4: ⑥ Model prediction, evaluation and explanation

Fig. 2. The general Machine Learning framework for binary Android malware detection or multi-class family classification.

3.1   Raw Android Application Data Collection

Collect Raw Android Applications

The raw Android applications can be downloaded from various sources, e.g., the official Google Play store and the alternative third-party app stores (such as WanDouJia, AnZhi). For large-scale and up-to-date access to Android applications, it is necessary to implement specific crawlers for different Android application stores to automatically browse, retrieve, and download applications into repository [4,39].

However, there exist many challenges in crawling Android applications [4]. Firstly, different app stores have specific policies to limit or forbid the crawling of applications. For example, without a verified Google account, users cannot download any Android applications from Google Play. In addition, a valid account is allowed to download a limited number of applications in a given time from one IP address. Secondly, during the application downloading process, the crawlers have to be adapted to the updates of the stores. For example, if the application stores change the structure of the HTML pages, then a new analysis of the web pages is required to revise the crawling scripts. Thirdly, for a given application, it is difficult to download its previous versions. Most stores only provide the latest version of applications. Thus, it is hard to guarantee that all versions of the applications have been downloaded [39].

Annotate the Ground Truth of Applications

Reliable ground truth data is essential for evaluating the effectiveness of the malware analysis approaches. When the raw Android applications have been downloaded, the next step is to annotate the ground truth (identify the malicious samples or further assign a family class to them) to construct the training set. Most of the malware labeling works employed the state-of-the-art open-source online scanning service VirusTotal[9] to annotate the labels for Android applications. VirusTotal incorporates more than 70 anti-virus tools and URL/domain blacklisting services to provide a comprehensive analysis report for each uploaded sample. Give a candidate Android application, the detailed ground truth annotation steps are as follows: First of all, determining whether the application is malicious or not using the majority voting strategy based on the results of different anti-virus tools in VirusTotal. Second, if the candidate application is malicious, we can further assign it a family class based on the returned analysis results of different anti-virus tools. However, there exists the inconsistent family naming issue from different anti-virus tools. Thus it is challenging to assign an accurate family class to the candidate malware sample.

Currently, there were two state-of-the-art works focusing on the Android malware family class annotation. The first piece of work was based on the dominant keyword algorithm [69]. First of all, the keywords from each of the detection reports of anti-virus tools were extracted. Then the generic keywords were filtered out. Finally, the rest keywords were counted to identify the dominant keyword, which was thus considered as the family name. The second piece of work was AVclass proposed in [59]. AVclass utilized new techniques to address three issues: normalization, removal of generic tokens, and alias detection. Thus AVclass was able to generate the most likely family names for a massive number of Android malware samples based on the detection reports of selected anti-virus tools.

3.2 Feature Engineering for Application Representation

The key building block in machine learning involved methods is feature engineering. Extracting the informative and robust features to represent Android applications is critical to the effectiveness and reliability of the models. In general, the common features used to characterize Android applications can be roughly divided into four categories: *AndroidManifest.xml* based semantic features. Disassembled *classes.dex* based semantic features. Intermediate *Smali* opcode based features. Fourth, the dynamic behaviors based features and other side-information based features.

AndroidManifest.xml-Based Features

Each Android application package contains the *AndroidManifest.xml* file. This file presents the essential information of the application, such as *Hardware components*, *Requested permissions*, *App components*, and *Filtered intents*. The stored information in this file can be parsed efficiently through static analysis [5]. Table 1 shows the detailed information of the features that can be extracted from *AndroidManifest.xml* to characterize Android samples.

Disassembled classes.dex-Based Features

The Android application package is usually implemented using Java programming language and then compiled into *classes.dex* bytecode for its execution

---

[9] https://www.virustotal.com/.

Table 1. The detailed information of the features that can be parsed from *Android-Manifest.xml*.

Feature subset	Detailed description of the feature subset
Requested permission	Android apps will request permissions for accessing critical resources during installation
App components	Android apps can declare many components, for instance, Service, Activity, Broadcastreceiver, ContentProvider
Filtered intents	Android apps use intent filters to appoints the operations it can perform and the data type it can manipulate
Hardware components	Apply specific hardware or a series of particular hardwares may imply potential security or privacy risks

in the Dalvik virtual machine. The *classes.dex* bytecode contains the comprehensive semantic knowledge about the critical API calls and data access within an application [5]. Besides, the *classes.dex* bytecode can be efficiently disassembled and parsed to represent Android applications. Table 2 shows the detailed descriptions of the low-level features that can be captured through disassembling *classes.dex*. Some high-level graph features, e.g., control flow graph [8,78], API dependency graph [83], code property graph [76], and inter-component call graph [25,28] can also be extracted from *classes.dex*.

Table 2. The detailed information of the low-level features that can be captured from *classes.dex*.

Feature subset	Detailed description of the feature subset
Suspicious API calls	The suspicious API calls represent the potential malicious actions of malware
Restricted API calls	The restricted API calls reveal the critical capability of Android applications
Used permissions	The restricted API calls will be used to decide and match the requested or indeed used permissions
Network addresses	The network addresses appeared in the source codes are related to potential botnet attacks or suspicious websites

Intermediate Smali Opcode-Based Features

Smali code is the intermediate but interpreted code between Java and Dalvik virtual machine. All the *Smali* codes follow a set of grammar specifications. The *classes.dex* can be disassembled into a set of *Smali* format files. Each *Smali* file represents a single class containing all the methods within the class and each method contains human-readable Dalvik instructions. Each instruction can be parsed into a single opcode and multiple operands [36]. To reduce the noise and improve efficiency, the common Dalvik instructions can be further categorized into 7 core instruction sets while discarding the operands as shown in Table 3. Then n-grams features can be extracted from the opcode sequences of all the classes of an Android application.

Table 3. The descriptions of the 7 types of *Smali* opcode instruction sets.

Instruction type	The involved instructions
Move (M)	move, move/from16, move/16, move-wide, move-wide/from16, move-wide/16, move-object, move-object/from16, move-object/16, move-result, move-result-wide, move-result-object, move-exception
Return (R)	return-void, return, return-wide, return-object
Goto (G)	goto, goto/16, goto/32
If (I)	if-eq, if-ne, if-lt, if-ge, if-gt, if-le, if-eqz, if-nez, if-ltz, if-gez, if-gtz, if-lez
Get (T)	aget, aget-wide, aget-object, aget-boolean, aget-byte, aget-char, aget-short, iget, iget-wide, iget-object, iget-boolean, iget-byte, iget-char, iget-short, sget, sget-wide, sget-object, sget-boolean, sget-byte, sget-char, sget-short
Put (P)	aput, aput-wide, aput-object, aput-boolean, aput-byte, aput-char, aput-short, iput, iput-wide, iput-object, iput-boolean, iput-byte, iput-char, iput-short, sput, sput-wide, sput-object, sput-boolean, sput-byte, sput-char, sput-short
Invoke (V)	invoke-virtual, invoke-super, invoke-direct, invoke-static, invoke-interface, invoke-virtual/range, invoke-super/range, invoke-direct/range, invoke-static/range, invoke-interface-range, invoke-direct-empty, invoke-virtual-quick, invoke-virtual-quick/range

Dynamic Behaviors-Based Features

The dynamic analysis tools can track abundant behaviors information of Android applications during actual execution. These behaviors information, e.g., file or network operations, information leaks can be efficiently parsed to represent Android applications. Table 4 lists the 10 common dynamic behavior feature set that can be used to characterize Android application samples [24].

Other Side-Information-Based Features

In addition to the features extracted directly from the static or dynamic analysis, other side-information-based features can also be parsed to characterize Android applications [20,56,87]. Zhu et al. proposed a method named FeatureSmith to automatically engineering features for malware detection by mining the security literature [87]. The natural language techniques were employed for mining Android documents (e.g. scientific or academic papers) and for representing and retrieving the semantic information about malware. Besides, the metadata, such

Table 4. The detailed introduction of 10 common dynamic behavior feature sets.

Dynamic behavior	Detailed description of the behavior
File operations	Scanning the file-system to retrieve sensitive data or creating external files to store the data
Network operations	Receiving bot commands from C& C servers or fetching malicious payloads from malicious websites
Cryptographic operations	Encrypting root exploits, targetd premium SMS number, critical methods, malicious payloads or URLs to evade detection
Information leaks	Collecting sensitive data (IMEI, account credentials, SMS, contact lists) and sending them to remote server
Dexclass load	Loading malicious payloads from app's assets, from another app or from remote system at running
Phone calls	Making phone calls stealthily without users' awareness
Sent SMS	Causing financial charges to infected devices by subscribing premium-rate services
Receiver actions	Malware usually exploits system events to trigger malicious payloads, while receivers are good indicators of system events
Service start	Malicious behaviors usually perform in background processes contained in Android's service components
System calls	System calls show how applications request services from operating system's kernel

as the profile information of Android applications or the profile of application developers can also be parsed to represent Android applications [45]. Furthermore, the software complexity metrics, e.g., the *Chidamber and Kemerer Metrics Suite* [17] and *McCabe's Cyclomatic Complexity* [43], can be employed to characterize Android application samples [13,50].

3.3   Model Training for Malware Detection or Classification

In this step, the machine learning models will be trained for Android malware detection or classification. Currently, both traditional machine learning models (e.g., Support Vector Machine [5], Random Forest [42], K-Nearest Neighbors [42]) and deep learning models (e.g., Deep Neural Networks [31,80,81], Convolutional Neural Networks [33]) have been applied to malware analysis. In addition, for a specific malware detection issue, some particular machine learning algorithms were also employed. For example, in [32], to aggregate different similarities between Android applications, multi-kernel learning [65] was applied to automatically learn the weights of different similarity perspectives.

3.4   Model Prediction, Evaluation, and Explanation

In this step, the trained machine learning model will be used to detect or classify the candidate Android applications in the wild. Generally, there is no ground truth data available for the Android samples in the wild. To evaluate the effectiveness of the proposed approach, it is common to divide part of the labeled Android applications as the testing set to validate the efficiency and efficacy of the model.

Since Android malware detection or family attribution are class-imbalanced classification problem, thus *Accuracy* along is far from enough to comprehensively evaluate the effectiveness of the models, more metrics, e.g., *Recall*, *Precision* or *F1-score* should be introduced. In practice, an effective machine learning based malware detection or classification approach should work with high accuracy as well as high efficiency. Generally, the efficiency refers to prediction time, because in most cases the training process can be finished offline. Therefore training time may not be a key challenge in the Android malware analysis while prediction time is really important especially the trained model is deployed on the mobile devices with limited computation resources.

Android malware samples constantly evolve over time. Thus it is important that the proposed approach is able to adapt to the evolution or population drift of malware (e.g., code obfuscation or encryption). *Adaptiveness* is a metrics used to explore whether malware detectors are able to learn fresh patterns while unlearning the obsolete patterns of malicious samples with time evolving [46].

In practice, an Android malware detection method must not only identify malicious samples but also offer explanations for the corresponding detection results [5]. The existing works provided different explanation granularity [5,16,27]. For example, in [5], the explanation consisted of a ranked list of features most indicative of malicious behavior and the corresponding weights reflecting their relative contribution to the detection results. In [27], the explanation results could locate the malicious components and the corresponding suspicious metadata (e.g., sensitive data leaked by the component).

4   Possible Future Research Directions

In this section, we briefly present the future research directions of Android malware detection. It is known that malware detection is a fundamental and indispensable topic in Cyber Security area. Researchers, as well as security vendors have invested a considerable amount of time and money to address this topic. And Machine learning techniques have been applied to Android malware detection for almost ten years. The future research directions will focus on fine-grained analysis, the details are as follows:

Firstly, as mentioned in the previous section, the source code of Android applications can be regarded as a special format natural language text, thus the Natural Language Processing (NLP) techniques can be employed to facilitate the detection performance. Besides, the NLP technique can be employed to better capture the semantic meanings within and between Android applications [48].

Therefore, the combination of Android malware detection and NLP technique will be a promising research direction [3].

Secondly, it has been shown that lots of detection methods or commercial tools are good at detecting specific type or family of malware. However, the detection performance is unsatisfactory when extending to other types of malware. Besides, the detection approaches are necessary to adapt to different versions of the same malware across various versions of the device OS. To address this issue, Transfer Learning may be a potential future direction [70].

Thirdly, concept drift in Android malware detection is a serious issue whereby models trained using older malware are not able to detect newer malware with confidence. Thus identifying such antiquated detection models accurately and timely is vital to the final performance. Traditional ML framework shown in Fig. 2 had to re-train frequently to adapt to the latest landscape of malware. To address this issue, online learning techniques can be introduced to fight against concept drifting by updating the model continuously and efficiently with the most recent malware examples [29,35,46].

Fourthly, inspired by the breakthroughs of Deep Learning in image classification, machine translation and natural language processing [18,30], Deep Learning has been introduced to malware detection and achieved satisfactory performance [44,80]. It can be expected that the latest Deep Learning models will continue to be a potential approach for malware detection.

Essentially, Android malware detection can be regarded as a class-imbalanced classification problem. The number of malware is far less than the number of benign applications. However, to the best of our knowledge, there are few works targeting the imbalance characteristic of Android malware detection issue. Thus, the cost-sensitive classification approaches, which has been shown effective in tackling class-imbalanced problems, may be a future research focus [64].

5   Conclusion

Android malware detection is a fundamental and systematic research topic in cyber security. It has been widely studied by both academic communities and security corporations. Meanwhile, machine Learning technique has also been applied to Android malware detection for nearly ten years. However, there also exist several challenges and difficulties in Android malware analysis area. In this survey, the research status of Android malware detection was presented. On the first, like other surveys, we reviewed the traditional software engineering based Android malware analysis techniques (static, dynamic and hybrid techniques). Our main focus is the Machine Learning framework for Android malware detection. We presented the detailed introduction of each part of the Machine Learning framework. Then, we gave the possible research directions about Android malware detection. In the end, we concluded the full survey.

References

1. Aafer, Y., Du, W., Yin, H.: DroidAPIMiner: mining API-level features for robust malware detection in Android. In: Zia, T., Zomaya, A., Varadharajan, V., Mao, M. (eds.) SecureComm 2013. LNICSSITE, vol. 127, pp. 86–103. Springer, Cham (2013). https://doi.org/10.1007/978-3-319-04283-1_6
2. Afonso, V.M., et al.: Going native: using a large-scale analysis of Android apps to create a practical native-code sandboxing policy. In: NDSS. The Internet Society (2016)
3. Allamanis, M., Barr, E.T., Devanbu, P.T., Sutton, C.A.: A survey of machine learning for big code and naturalness. ACM Comput. Surv. **51**(4), 81:1–81:37 (2018)
4. Allix, K., Bissyandé, T.F., Klein, J., Traon, Y.L.: Androzoo: collecting millions of Android apps for the research community. In: MSR, pp. 468–471. ACM (2016)
5. Arp, D., Spreitzenbarth, M., Hubner, M., Gascon, H., Rieck, K.: DREBIN: effective and explainable detection of Android malware in your pocket. In: 21st Annual Network and Distributed System Security Symposium, NDSS 2014, San Diego, California, USA, 23–26 February 2014 (2014)
6. Arshad, S., Shah, M.A., Khan, A., Ahmed, M.: Android malware detection & protection: a survey. Int. J. Adv. Comput. Sci. Appl. **7**(2), 463–475 (2016)
7. Arzt, S., et al.: FlowDroid: precise context, flow, field, object-sensitive and lifecycle-aware taint analysis for Android apps. In: ACM SIGPLAN Conference on Programming Language Design and Implementation, PLDI 2014, Edinburgh, United Kingdom, 09–11 June 2014, pp. 259–269 (2014)
8. Atici, M.A., Sagiroglu, S., Dogru, I.A.: Android malware analysis approach based on control flow graphs and machine learning algorithms. In: 2016 4th International Symposium on Digital Forensic and Security (ISDFS), pp. 26–31. IEEE (2016)
9. Backes, M., Bugiel, S., Gerling, S., von Styp-Rekowsky, P.: Android security framework: extensible multi-layered access control on Android. In: Proceedings of the 30th Annual Computer Security Applications Conference, ACSAC 2014, New Orleans, LA, USA, 8–12 December 2014, pp. 46–55 (2014)
10. Bartel, A., Klein, J., Traon, Y.L., Monperrus, M.: Dexpler: converting Android dalvik bytecode to jimple for static analysis with soot. In: Proceedings of the ACM SIGPLAN International Workshop on State of the Art in Java Program analysis, SOAP 2012, Beijing, China, 14 June 2012, pp. 27–38 (2012)
11. Baskaran, B., Ralescu, A.: A study of Android malware detection techniques and machine learning. In: Proceedings of the 27th Modern Artificial Intelligence and Cognitive Science Conference 2016, Dayton, OH, USA, 22–23 April 2016, pp. 15–23 (2016)
12. Bellard, F.: QEMU, a fast and portable dynamic translator. In: Proceedings of the FREENIX Track: 2005 USENIX Annual Technical Conference, Anaheim, CA, USA, 10–15 April 2005, pp. 41–46 (2005)
13. Beyer, D., Fararooy, A.: A simple and effective measure for complex low-level dependencies. In: ICPC, pp. 80–83. IEEE Computer Society (2010)
14. Bläsing, T., Batyuk, L., Schmidt, A., Çamtepe, S.A., Albayrak, S.: An Android application sandbox system for suspicious software detection. In: 5th International Conference on Malicious and Unwanted Software, MALWARE 2010, Nancy, France, 19–20 October 2010, pp. 55–62 (2010)
15. Burguera, I., Zurutuza, U., Nadjm-Tehrani, S.: Crowdroid: behavior-based malware detection system for Android. In: Proceedings of the 1st ACM Workshop Security and Privacy in Smartphones and Mobile Devices, SPSM 2011, Co-Located with CCS 2011, Chicago, IL, USA, 17 October 2011, pp. 15–26 (2011)

16. Chen, K., et al.: Finding unknown malice in 10 seconds: mass vetting for new threats at the Google-play scale. In: USENIX Security Symposium, pp. 659–674. USENIX Association (2015)
17. Churcher, N.I., Shepperd, M.J.: Comments on "a metrics suite for object oriented design". IEEE Trans. Softw. Eng. **21**(3), 263–265 (1995)
18. Costa-jussà, M.R., Allauzen, A., Barrault, L., Cho, K., Schwenk, H.: Introduction to the special issue on deep learning approaches for machine translation. Comput. Speech Lang. **46**, 367–373 (2017)
19. Desnos, A., Lantz, P.: DroidBox: an Android application sandbox for dynamic analysis. Technical report, Lund University, Lund, Sweden (2011)
20. Dumitras, T.: Automatic feature engineering: learning to detect malware by mining the scientific literature (2017)
21. Enck, W., et al.: TaintDroid: an information-flow tracking system for realtime privacy monitoring on smartphones. In: Proceedings of the 9th USENIX Symposium on Operating Systems Design and Implementation, OSDI 2010, Vancouver, BC, Canada, 4–6 October 2010, pp. 393–407 (2010)
22. Enck, W., Ongtang, M., McDaniel, P.D.: On lightweight mobile phone application certification. In: Proceedings of the 2009 ACM Conference on Computer and Communications Security, CCS 2009, Chicago, Illinois, USA, 9–13 November 2009, pp. 235–245 (2009)
23. Enck, W., Ongtang, M., McDaniel, P.D.: Understanding Android security. IEEE Secur. Priv. **7**(1), 50–57 (2009)
24. Feng, P., Ma, J., Sun, C., Xu, X., Ma, Y.: A novel dynamic Android malware detection system with ensemble learning. IEEE Access **6**, 30996–31011 (2018)
25. Feng, Y., Anand, S., Dillig, I., Aiken, A.: Apposcopy: semantics-based detection of Android malware through static analysis. In: Proceedings of the 22nd ACM SIGSOFT International Symposium on Foundations of Software Engineering, pp. 576–587. ACM (2014)
26. Feng, Y., Anand, S., Dillig, I., Aiken, A.: Apposcopy: semantics-based detection of Android malware through static analysis. In: Proceedings of the 22nd ACM SIGSOFT International Symposium on Foundations of Software Engineering, (FSE-22), Hong Kong, China, 16–22 November 2014, pp. 576–587 (2014)
27. Feng, Y., Bastani, O., Martins, R., Dillig, I., Anand, S.: Automated synthesis of semantic malware signatures using maximum satisfiability. In: 24th Annual Network and Distributed System Security Symposium, NDSS 2017, San Diego, California, USA, 26 February–1 March 2017 (2017)
28. Feng, Y., Wang, X., Dillig, I., Lin, C.: EXPLORER: query- and demand-driven exploration of interprocedural control flow properties. In: OOPSLA, pp. 520–534. ACM (2015)
29. Gama, J., Zliobaite, I., Bifet, A., Pechenizkiy, M., Bouchachia, A.: A survey on concept drift adaptation. ACM Comput. Surv. **46**(4), 44:1–44:37 (2014)
30. Hinton, G., et al.: Deep neural networks for acoustic modeling in speech recognition: the shared views of four research groups. IEEE Sig. Process. Mag. **29**(6), 82–97 (2012)
31. Hou, S., Saas, A., Chen, L., Ye, Y.: Deep4maldroid: a deep learning framework for Android malware detection based on Linux kernel system call graphs. In: WI Workshops, pp. 104–111. IEEE Computer Society (2016)

32. Hou, S., Ye, Y., Song, Y., Abdulhayoglu, M.: HinDroid: an intelligent Android malware detection system based on structured heterogeneous information network. In: Proceedings of the 23rd ACM SIGKDD International Conference on Knowledge Discovery and Data Mining, Halifax, NS, Canada, 13–17 August 2017, pp. 1507–1515 (2017)

33. Hsien-De Huang, T., Kao, H.-Y.: R2–D2: color-inspired convolutional neural network (CNN)-based Android malware detections. In: 2018 IEEE International Conference on Big Data (Big Data), pp. 2633–2642. IEEE (2018)

34. Jiang, J.J., Wen, S., Yu, S., Xiang, Y., Zhou, W.: Identifying propagation sources in networks: state-of-the-art and comparative studies. IEEE Commun. Surv. Tutor. **19**(1), 465–481 (2017)

35. Jordaney, R., et al.: Transcend: detecting concept drift in malware classification models. In: 26th USENIX Security Symposium, USENIX Security 2017, Vancouver, BC, Canada, 16–18 August 2017, pp. 625–642 (2017)

36. Kang, B., Yerima, S.Y., McLaughlin, K., Sezer, S.: N-opcode analysis for Android malware classification and categorization. In: 2016 International Conference on Cyber Security and Protection of Digital Services (Cyber Security), pp. 1–7. IEEE (2016)

37. Li, C.M., Manyà, F.: MaxSAT, hard and soft constraints. In: Handbook of Satisfiability, pp. 613–631 (2009)

38. Li, L., et al.: Static analysis of Android apps: a systematic literature review. Inf. Softw. Technol. **88**, 67–95 (2017)

39. Li, L., et al.: Androzoo++: collecting millions of Android apps and their metadata for the research community. CoRR, abs/1709.05281 (2017)

40. Liu, L., de Vel, O.Y., Han, Q., Zhang, J., Xiang, Y.: Detecting and preventing cyber insider threats: a survey. IEEE Commun. Surv. Tutor. **20**(2), 1397–1417 (2018)

41. Mahmood, R., Mirzaei, N., Malek, S.: EvoDroid: segmented evolutionary testing of Android apps. In: SIGSOFT FSE, pp. 599–609. ACM (2014)

42. Mariconti, E., Onwuzurike, L., Andriotis, P., Cristofaro, E.D., Ross, G.J., Stringhini, G.: MaMaDroid: detecting Android malware by building Markov chains of behavioral models. In: 24th Annual Network and Distributed System Security Symposium, NDSS 2017, San Diego, California, USA, 26 February–1 March 2017 (2017)

43. McCabe, T.J.: A complexity measure. IEEE Trans. Softw. Eng. **2**(4), 308–320 (1976)

44. McLaughlin, N., et al.: Deep Android malware detection. In: Proceedings of the Seventh ACM on Conference on Data and Application Security and Privacy, CODASPY 2017, Scottsdale, AZ, USA, 22–24 March 2017, pp. 301–308 (2017)

45. Muñoz, A., Martín, I., Guzmán, A., Hernández, J.A.: Android malware detection from Google play meta-data: selection of important features. In: CNS, pp. 701–702. IEEE (2015)

46. Narayanan, A., Chandramohan, M., Chen, L., Liu, Y.: Context-aware, adaptive, and scalable Android malware detection through online learning. IEEE Trans. Emerg. Top. Comput. Intell. **1**(3), 157–175 (2017)

47. Narayanan, A., Chandramohan, M., Chen, L., Liu, Y.: A multi-view context-aware approach to Android malware detection and malicious code localization. Empirical Softw. Eng. **23**(3), 1222–1274 (2018)

48. Nguyen, T.D., Nguyen, A.T., Phan, H.D., Nguyen, T.N.: Exploring API embedding for API usages and applications. In: Proceedings of the 39th International Conference on Software Engineering, ICSE 2017, Buenos Aires, Argentina, 20–28 May 2017, pp. 438–449 (2017)
49. Portokalidis, G., Homburg, P., Anagnostakis, K., Bos, H.: Paranoid Android: versatile protection for smartphones. In: Twenty-Sixth Annual Computer Security Applications Conference, ACSAC 2010, Austin, Texas, USA, 6–10 December 2010, pp. 347–356 (2010)
50. Protsenko, M., Müller, T.: Android malware detection based on software complexity metrics. In: Eckert, C., Katsikas, S.K., Pernul, G. (eds.) TrustBus 2014. LNCS, vol. 8647, pp. 24–35. Springer, Cham (2014). https://doi.org/10.1007/978-3-319-09770-1_3
51. Qiu, J., Luo, W., Nepal, S., Zhang, J., Xiang, Y., Pan, L.: Keep calm and know where to focus: measuring and predicting the impact of Android malware. In: Gan, G., Li, B., Li, X., Wang, S. (eds.) ADMA 2018. LNCS (LNAI), vol. 11323, pp. 238–254. Springer, Cham (2018). https://doi.org/10.1007/978-3-030-05090-0_21
52. Qiu, J., Luo, W., Pan, L., Tai, Y., Zhang, J., Xiang, Y.: Predicting the impact of Android malicious samples via machine learning. IEEE Access 7, 66304–66316 (2019)
53. Rasthofer, S., Arzt, S., Miltenberger, M., Bodden, E.: Harvesting runtime values in Android applications that feature anti-analysis techniques. In: NDSS. The Internet Society (2016)
54. Rastogi, V., Chen, Y., Enck, W.: AppsPlayground: automatic security analysis of smartphone applications. In: Third ACM Conference on Data and Application Security and Privacy, CODASPY 2013, San Antonio, TX, USA, 18–20 February 2013, pp. 209–220 (2013)
55. Reina, A., Fattori, A., Cavallaro, L.: A system call-centric analysis and stimulation technique to automatically reconstruct Android malware behaviors. In: EuroSec, April 2013
56. Sabottke, C., Suciu, O., Dumitras, T.: Vulnerability disclosure in the age of social media: exploiting Twitter for predicting real-world exploits. In: USENIX Security Symposium, pp. 1041–1056. USENIX Association (2015)
57. Sanz, B., Santos, I., Laorden, C., Ugarte-Pedrero, X., Bringas, P.G., Álvarez, G.: PUMA: permission usage to detect malware in Android. In: Herrero, Á., et al. (eds.) International Joint Conference CISIS 2012-ICEUTE 2012-SOCO 2012 Special Sessions. AISC, vol. 189, pp. 289–298. Springer, Heidelberg (2012). https://doi.org/10.1007/978-3-642-33018-6_30
58. Sato, R., Chiba, D., Goto, S.: Detecting Android malware by analyzing manifest files. Proc. Asia-Pac. Adv. Netw. 36(23–31), 17 (2013)
59. Sebastián, M., Rivera, R., Kotzias, P., Caballero, J.: AVCLASS: a tool for massive malware labeling. In: Monrose, F., Dacier, M., Blanc, G., Garcia-Alfaro, J. (eds.) RAID 2016. LNCS, vol. 9854, pp. 230–253. Springer, Cham (2016). https://doi.org/10.1007/978-3-319-45719-2_11
60. Shabtai, A., Kanonov, U., Elovici, Y., Glezer, C., Weiss, Y.: "Andromaly": a behavioral malware detection framework for Android devices. J. Intell. Inf. Syst. 38(1), 161–190 (2012)
61. Spreitzenbarth, M., Freiling, F.C., Echtler, F., Schreck, T., Hoffmann, J.: Mobile-sandbox: having a deeper look into Android applications. In: SAC, pp. 1808–1815. ACM (2013)

62. Suarez-Tangil, G., Stringhini, G.: Eight years of rider measurement in the Android malware ecosystem: evolution and lessons learned. CoRR, abs/1801.08115 (2018)
63. Sun, N., Zhang, J., Rimba, P., Gao, S., Zhang, L.Y., Xiang, Y.: Data-driven cyber-security incident prediction: a survey. IEEE Commun. Surv. Tutor. **21**(2), 1744–1772 (2019)
64. Sun, Y., Kamel, M.S., Wong, A.K.C., Wang, Y.: Cost-sensitive boosting for classification of imbalanced data. Pattern Recogn. **40**(12), 3358–3378 (2007)
65. Sun, Z., Ampornpunt, N., Varma, M., Vishwanathan, S.: Multiple kernel learning and the SMO algorithm. In: Advances in Neural Information Processing Systems, pp. 2361–2369 (2010)
66. Tam, K., Feizollah, A., Anuar, N.B., Salleh, R., Cavallaro, L.: The evolution of Android malware and Android analysis techniques. ACM Comput. Surv. **49**(4), 76:1–76:41 (2017)
67. Tang, W., Jin, G., He, J., Jiang, X.: Extending Android security enforcement with a security distance model. In: 2011 International Conference on Internet Technology and Applications, pp. 1–4. IEEE (2011)
68. Vidas, T., Tan, J., Nahata, J., Tan, C.L., Christin, N., Tague, P.: A5: automated analysis of adversarial Android applications. In: SPSM@CCS, pp. 39–50. ACM (2014)
69. Wei, F., Li, Y., Roy, S., Ou, X., Zhou, W.: Deep ground truth analysis of current Android malware. In: Polychronakis, M., Meier, M. (eds.) DIMVA 2017. LNCS, vol. 10327, pp. 252–276. Springer, Cham (2017). https://doi.org/10.1007/978-3-319-60876-1_12
70. Weiss, K.R., Khoshgoftaar, T.M., Wang, D.: A survey of transfer learning. J. Big Data **3**, 9 (2016)
71. Wen, S., Haghighi, M.S., Chen, C., Xiang, Y., Zhou, W., Jia, W.: A sword with two edges: propagation studies on both positive and negative information in online social networks. IEEE Trans. Comput. **64**(3), 640–653 (2015)
72. Wong, M.Y., Lie, D.: IntelliDroid: a targeted input generator for the dynamic analysis of Android malware. In: NDSS. The Internet Society (2016)
73. Wu, C., Zhou, Y., Patel, K., Liang, Z., Jiang, X.: AirBag: boosting smartphone resistance to malware infection. In: 21st Annual Network and Distributed System Security Symposium, NDSS 2014, San Diego, California, USA, 23–26 February 2014 (2014)
74. Wu, D., Mao, C., Wei, T., Lee, H., Wu, K.: DroidMat: Android malware detection through manifest and API calls tracing. In: Seventh Asia Joint Conference on Information Security, AsiaJCIS 2012, Kaohsiung, Taiwan, 9–10 August 2012, pp. 62–69 (2012)
75. Wu, T., Wen, S., Xiang, Y., Zhou, W.: Twitter spam detection: survey of new approaches and comparative study. Comput. Secur. **76**, 265–284 (2018)
76. Yamaguchi, F., Golde, N., Arp, D., Rieck, K.: Modeling and discovering vulnerabilities with code property graphs. In: IEEE Symposium on Security and Privacy, pp. 590–604. IEEE Computer Society (2014)
77. Yan, L., Yin, H.: DroidScope: seamlessly reconstructing the OS and Dalvik semantic views for dynamic Android malware analysis. In: Proceedings of the 21th USENIX Security Symposium, Bellevue, WA, USA, 8–10 August 2012, pp. 569–584 (2012)
78. Yang, C., Xu, Z., Gu, G., Yegneswaran, V., Porras, P.: DroidMiner: automated mining and characterization of fine-grained malicious behaviors in Android applications. In: Kutyłowski, M., Vaidya, J. (eds.) ESORICS 2014. LNCS, vol. 8712, pp. 163–182. Springer, Cham (2014). https://doi.org/10.1007/978-3-319-11203-9_10

79. Ye, Y., Li, T., Adjeroh, D.A., Iyengar, S.S.: A survey on malware detection using data mining techniques. ACM Comput. Surv. **50**(3), 41:1–41:40 (2017)
80. Yuan, Z., Lu, Y., Wang, Z., Xue, Y.: Droid-sec: deep learning in Android malware detection. In: ACM SIGCOMM 2014 Conference, SIGCOMM 2014, Chicago, IL, USA, 17–22 August 2014, pp. 371–372 (2014)
81. Yuan, Z., Lu, Y., Xue, Y.: Droiddetector: Android malware characterization and detection using deep learning. Tsinghua Sci. Technol. **21**(1), 114–123 (2016)
82. Zhang, J., Xiang, Y., Wang, Y., Zhou, W., Xiang, Y., Guan, Y.: Network traffic classification using correlation information. IEEE Trans. Parallel Distrib. Syst. **24**(1), 104–117 (2013)
83. Zhang, M., Duan, Y., Yin, H., Zhao, Z.: Semantics-aware Android malware classification using weighted contextual API dependency graphs. In: Proceedings of the 2014 ACM SIGSAC Conference on Computer and Communications Security, Scottsdale, AZ, USA, 3–7 November 2014, pp. 1105–1116 (2014)
84. Zheng, C., et al.: SmartDroid: an automatic system for revealing UI-based trigger conditions in Android applications. In: SPSM@CCS, pp. 93–104. ACM (2012)
85. Zheng, M., Sun, M., Lui, J.C.S.: Droid analytics: a signature based analytic system to collect, extract, analyze and associate Android malware. In: 12th IEEE International Conference on Trust, Security and Privacy in Computing and Communications, TrustCom 2013/11th IEEE International Symposium on Parallel and Distributed Processing with Applications, ISPA 2013/12th IEEE International Conference on Ubiquitous Computing and Communications, IUCC-2013, Melbourne, Australia, 16–18 July 2013, pp. 163–171 (2013)
86. Zhou, Y., Wang, Z., Zhou, W., Jiang, X.: Hey, you, get off of my market: detecting malicious apps in official and alternative Android markets. In: 19th Annual Network and Distributed System Security Symposium, NDSS 2012, San Diego, California, USA, 5–8 February 2012 (2012)
87. Zhu, Z., Dumitras, T.: FeatureSmith: automatically engineering features for malware detection by mining the security literature. In: Proceedings of the 2016 ACM SIGSAC Conference on Computer and Communications Security, Vienna, Austria, 24–28 October 2016, pp. 767–778 (2016)

Semantically Secure and Verifiable Multi-keyword Search in Cloud Computing

Lili Zhang[1,2(✉)], Wenjie Wang[3], and Yuqing Zhang[1,3,4(✉)]

[1] National Key Laboratory of Integrated Services Networks, Xidian University,
Xi'an 710071, China
lillyzh@126.com

[2] Henan International Joint Laboratory of Cyberspace Security Applications,
Information Engineering College, Henan University of Science and Technology,
Luoyang 471023, China

[3] National Computer Network Intrusion Protection Center,
University of Chinese Academy of Sciences, Beijing 100049, China
zhangyq@ucas.ac.cn

[4] State Key Laboratory of Information Security Institute of Information Engineering,
Chinese Academy of Sciences, Beijing 100093, China

Abstract. In cloud computing model, the data are usually encrypted before outsourced to the cloud server, which protects the data privacy, but also leaves keyword searches over ciphertext data a challenging problem. A keyword search scheme over encrypted data should achieve both index privacy and query privacy; moreover, verification of search results is desirable because the incorrectf results can be returned owing to system defects or the cloud server's motivation to save computation recourses. Many multi-keyword search schemes have been proposed; however, few of these schemes are verifiable and adaptively index-hiding and adaptively query-hiding. In this paper, a semantically secure multi-keyword search scheme is constructed, which is adaptively index-hiding and adaptively query-hiding, also supports the correctness verification of search results. We provide a detailed performance comparison and give a thorough security proof by a sequence of games. The combined results demonstrate that our scheme is secure and practical.

Keywords: Privacy-preserving search · Cloud computing ·
Search results verification · Semantically secure

1 Introduction

As a new computing paradigm, cloud computing can provide enormous computing and storage resources and enable users to conveniently access the computing resources with high efficiency and saved overhead. Attracted by the powerful and appealing advantages of cloud services, a lot of people and companies encrypt

X. Chen et al. (Eds.): ML4CS 2019, LNCS 11806, pp. 203–223, 2019.
https://doi.org/10.1007/978-3-030-30619-9_15

their data and outsource them to cloud servers. However, data outsourcing actually may lead to various security problems. To solve the search over the encrypted data, searchable encryption (SE) came into being. In SE schemes, the data owner usually generates an index according to document collection and then uploads the encrypted documents set and the encrypted index to the remote server. Upon receiving the trapdoor associated with query keywords, the server performs the search over the searchable index and returns the matching documents. In the last decade, SE has been widely researched, however, the existing SE schemes have the following problems.

(1) In many existing SE schemes, "1" or "0" authorization model [1–5] is utilized and the data owner is responsible for authorization operation. "1" or "0" authorization model means the eligible users are/ aren't given a secret key which enables the user to execute any query of his choice. Such an authorization model may leak the sensitive information of the user. Therefore, a user should be only allowed to search for partial keywords set. The data owner is responsible for the authorization means the data owner checks whether the user is eligible, such that the data owner is desired to be constantly online, which is impractical.
(2) In many existing SE schemes [1–6], the verification function of search results isn't equipped. However, in practice, the cloud server may return incorrect results due to system faults or motivation to save computation recourses. Thus, a mechanism to verify the correctness of the search results by the users is desirable.
(3) In the existing SE schemem, Few schemes are semantically secure. Informally, semantic security means that an adversary can't get related information about target data, even though it can adaptively obtain plaintext-ciphertext pairs.

In this paper, we apply the predicate encryption(PE) for inner products to achieve multi-keyword search over the encrypted data. However, we observe that the existing SE schemes [6–8] based on PE are only selectively secure, which means that when the security is proved, paitial challenge ciphertext information must be given before the public parameters are given to the adversary. We remove the restriction by applying the PE and the dual system encryption method. We construct a semantically secure multi-keyword search scheme, which supports the search results verification and be adaptively index-hiding and query-hiding. In our scheme, we introduce a trusted authority (TA), which takes charge of authorization and generating keys. Our contributions are concluded below.

1. A trusted authority (TA) is introduced into our system, which is in charge of generating keys and authorization. Thus, our scheme overcomes the disadvantages of "0" or "1" authorization model, in addition, the data owner isn't needed to be always online.
2. A semantically secure and verifiable multi-keyword scheme is proposed. The proposed scheme is adaptively index-hiding and adaptively query-hiding against chosen plaintext attack (CPA), moreover, it supports validation of the correctness of the search results.

3. A theoretical performance comparison and thorough security proof are made. The combined results demonstrate that the proposed scheme is secure and practical.

2   Related Work

On the basis of the keywords number in the query, SE mechanism can fall into single keyword SE and multi-keyword SE.

As single-keyword search [2–9] doesn't providing more accurate search results, many multi-keyword search schemes have been proposed. Hwang et al. [10] proposed a public key cryptography (PKC)-based conjunctive keyword search scheme. Some works [7,11] such as applied PE model to enhance the query expression and realize conjunctive and disjunctive search. Okatoma et al. [8] constructed a hierarchical predicate encryption (HPE) scheme, providing hierarchical delegation. The schemes [7,8] are selectively index-hiding against CPA attack, which means when index security was proven, partial challenge ciphertext information must be given before the adversary is given the public system parameters. Applying dual system encryption and predicate encryption(PE), Lewko et al. [13] realized multi-keyword search scheme, which is proved to be adaptively index-hiding against CPA attack, which means that the adversary with the capacity of obtaining adaptively plaintext-ciphertext pairs can't infer partial information about the index. However, the above PKC-based schemes can't address query privacy owing to the dictionary attack. Based on HPE [8], Li et al. [6] achieved secure keyword searches on encrypted data, supporting range query and subset query. They addressed query privacy by inserting a random number in the processing of generating ciphertext. Their scheme was selectively index-hiding and selectively query-hiding against CPA. In the symmetrical scenarios, Golle et al. [5] first constructed the conjunctive keyword search scheme. Afterwards, Ballard et al. [14] also presented the conjunctive keyword search schemes. Shen et al. [12] proposed a predicate only encryption scheme, which was selectively index-hiding and selectively query-hiding against CPA. Since this scheme was constructed on bilinear groups of composite order, it needed large computation overhead. Zhang et al. [4] constructed Multi-attribute Tree (MAT)-based index structure and improved the search efficiency of the scheme in [3]. These two schemes were index-hiding and query-hiding against known plaintext attack(KPA). Lai et al. [16] presented a semantically secure search scheme to achieve association rule mining, however, it only addressed the problem of single keyword search, moreover, all of the above schemes utilized "honest-but-curious" model, in which the server can returns the correct search results by the protocol, however, in practice the cloud server can return incorrect search results owing to the intention to save computational resources, therefore, verification of search results is desirable.

A variety of verification methods of search results have been proposed in the plaintext database scenarios [17]. The Merkle hash tree as well as cryptographic signature are utilized to build a tree structure for authentication. However, they didn't the privacy protection.

In the encrypted data search scenario [18], Wang et al. [19] used a hash chain to construct a verification structure, however, their scheme only achieved single-keyword search. Sun et al. [20] used a Merkle hash tree and cryptographic signature to create a verifiable multi-dimensional b-tree. However, Sun's method is only suitable for text search and it can't be directly used in our scenario, because in their method the index construction is based on term frequency. Chen et al. [21] designed a minimum hash sub-tree, and utilized it and cryptographic signature to achieve the correctness and freshness verification of search results. However, none of the above-mentioned schemes are semantically secure.

Based on the properties of bilinear pairs and Lagrange polynomials, Li et al. [22] proposed a method of constructing reciprocal mapping. They applied reciprocal mapping to construct a PKC-based searchable encryption scheme, which was adaptively index-hiding against CPA attack. But this scheme couldn't achieve query privacy; moreover, this scheme wasn't equipped with the results verification. Lai et al. [16] proposed a fully secure ciphertext search scheme, which was adaptively index-hiding and adaptively query-hiding, meaning that the adversary with the capacity of obtaining adaptively plaintext-ciphertext pairs can't infer partial information about index and query, however, this scheme only achieved verification of single-keyword search.

3   Preliminaries

3.1   DPVS

Dual Pairing vector spaces (DPVS) [8] is a tuple (q, G, G_T, g, V, A, e), here q is a prime, G and G_T are cyclic groups of order q, $V := \overbrace{G \times \ldots \times G}^{N}$ over F_q is N-dimensional vector space, $A = (a_1, \ldots, a_N)$ is canonical basis of V, here $a_i := (\overbrace{1, \ldots, 1}^{i-1}, g, \overbrace{1, \ldots, 1}^{N-1})$, $e : V \times V \to G_T$ is a bilinear pairing. DPVS satisfies the following conditions.

1. e is a polynomial-time bilinear pairing operation, satisfying $e(aP, bQ) = e(P, Q)^{ab}$, if $e(P, Q) = 1$, for all $Q \in V$, and $P = 0$, where $a, b \in F_q$, $P = (p_1, \ldots, p_N) \in V$, $Q = (q_1, \ldots, q_N) \in V$.
2. For all i and j, the equation $e(a_i, a_j) = e(g, g)^{\varphi_{i,j}}$ holds, if $i = j$, then $\varphi_{i,j} = 1$; otherwise, $\varphi_{i,j} = 0$.

3.2   Predicate Encryption

In inner product predicate encryption(PE) [7], every attribute is associated with a vector $\overrightarrow{X}$ and each predicate $f_{\overrightarrow{Y}}$ is associated with a vector $\overrightarrow{Y}$. The equation $f_{\overrightarrow{Y}}(\overrightarrow{X}) = 1$ holds iff $\overrightarrow{X}.\overrightarrow{Y} = 0$. In this paper, we takes a class of predicates $F = \left\{ f_{\overrightarrow{Y}} \middle| \overrightarrow{Y} \in F_q^n \right\}$. Iff $\overrightarrow{X}.\overrightarrow{Y} = 0$, $f_{\overrightarrow{Y}}(\overrightarrow{X}) = 1$.

3.3 Index and Predicate Vectors Representation

In inner product predicates encryption, each index is represented by an index vector and each query is represented by a query vector. According to [7], we can represent the index and query in vector form for keyword conjunctive search by first converting them into polynomial forms and then converting to vectors. For example, for the conjunctive keyword query:

$$(A_1 = w_1) \wedge (A_2 = w_2) \ldots, \wedge (A_d = w_d),$$

here d represents the number of the attributes, A_i represents the ith attribute and w_i represents the query keyword according to the ith attribute, index and query vector can be represented by the following steps.

(1) Convert the query to polynomial forms:
$p(A_1, A_2, \ldots, A_d) = r_1(A_1 - k_1) + r_2(A_2 - k_2) +, \ldots, +r_{d-1}(A_{d-1} - k_{d-1}) + (A_d - k_d)$,
where $r_i \in F_q (1 \leq i \leq d - 1)$.

(2) The index vector is denoted as $\overrightarrow{X} = (A_1, A_2, \ldots, A_d, 1)$, where A_i should be replaced by the attribute value of the ith attribute of the index.

(3) The query vector is represented as $\overrightarrow{Y} = (r_1, r_2, \ldots, r_{d-1}, 1, -(r_1 k_1 + r_2 k_2 + r_{d-1} k_{d-1} + k_d))$.

3.4 Notations

Letters m, d and n represent the number of the data documents collection, the number of the attributes in each index and the length of the index vector respectively. $c \leftarrow A(a, b)$ means running an algorithm A which takes as inputs (a, b) and outputing c. $s \xleftarrow{R} S$ denotes that s is uniformly at random selected from the collection S. $GL(N, F_q)$ denotes the linear group of degree N over F_q, $F : \mathrm{Keys}(F) \times \mathrm{D} \rightarrow \mathrm{R}$ represents a mapping whose domain is D and the range is R. $\mathrm{Keys}(F)$ is the keys set of F. $F(K, x)$ is also denoted by $F_K(x)$. $\varsigma_{bpg}(1^\lambda)$ represents the bilinear map generation algorithm. ς_{ob} is a random orthonormal bases generation algorithm.

$\varsigma_{ob}(1^\lambda, N) : (q, g, \mathrm{G}, \mathrm{G}_T, \mathrm{V}, \mathrm{A}, e) \leftarrow \varsigma_{dpvs}(1^\lambda, N)$

$Z = (z_{i,j}) \xleftarrow{R} GL(N, F_q)$,

$(t_{i,j}) = (Z^T)^{-1}$,

$b_i = \sum_{j=1}^{N} z_{i,j} a_j (i = 1, \ldots, N), B = (b_1, \ldots, b_N)$,

$b_i^* = \sum_{j=1}^{N} t_{i,j} a_j (i = 1, \ldots, N), B^* = (b_1^*, \ldots, b_N^*)$,

$Return$ $(q, g, \mathrm{G}, \mathrm{G}_T, \mathrm{V}, \mathrm{A}, e, \mathrm{B}, \mathrm{B}^*)$.

B, B^* and e satisfy $e(b_i^*, b_j^*) = e(g, g)^{\delta_{i,j}}$, for all i and j, $if i = j, \delta_{i,j} = 1$, otherwise $\delta_{i,j} = 0$. B, B^* are dual orthonormal bases of vector space.

3.5 Assumptions

Assumption 1: n-eDDH Assumption

$\varsigma_\beta^{n-eDDH}(1^\lambda) : param_G = (q, G, G_T, g, e) \leftarrow \varsigma_{bpg}(1^\lambda),$

$k \xleftarrow{R} F_q - \{0\}, w, h_i, r_i \xleftarrow{R} F_q, for\ i = 1, \ldots, n,$

$X_0 := g^{kw}, X_1 \leftarrow G,$

$T = (g, g^k, \{g^{w+h_1r_1}, g^{r_i}, g^{h_i}\}_{1 \le i \le n}, \{g^{r_ih_j}\}_{1 \le i \ne j \le n}),$

$Return(param_G, T, X_\beta).$

n-eDDH assumption is that given $(param_G, T, X_\beta)$, a probabilistic polynomial-time(PPT) adversary **A** guesses $\beta \in \{0, 1\}$. For any PPT adversary A, the advantage for this assumption is Adv_A^{n-eDDH}.

$Adv_A^{n-eDDH} = |\Pr[A(param_G, T, X_0) = 1] - \Pr[A(param_G, T, X_1) = 1]|$

Adv_A^{n-eDDH} is negligible. See the reference [13] for details.

Assumption 2

$(q, g, G, G^T, e, V, B, B^*) \leftarrow \delta_{ob}(1^\lambda, 2n + 3),$

$\widehat{B} = (b_1, \ldots, b_n, b_{2n+1}, b_{2n+3}), \widehat{B^*} = (b_1^*, \ldots, b_n^*, b_{2n+1}^*, b_{2n+2}^*),$

$T = (q, g, G, G^T, e, V, B, B^*),$

$i, j = 1, \ldots n,$

$\varepsilon_1, \varepsilon_{2,i} \leftarrow F_q, \chi \xleftarrow{R} F_q - \{0\}, \mu_{i,j} \xleftarrow{R} GL(n + 1, F_q)$

$d_{0,i} = \varepsilon_1 b_i + \varepsilon_{2,i} b_{2n+3}\ (\beta = 0),$

$d_{1,i} = \varepsilon_1 b_i + \chi \sum_{j=1}^n u_{i,j} b_{n+j} + \varepsilon_{2,i} b_{2n+3}\ (\beta = 1),$

Assumption 2 is that given $(T, \{d_{\beta,i}\}_{(1 \le i \le n)})$, a PPT adversary guesses $\beta = 0$ or $\beta = 1$. The advantage of a PPT adversary A for Assumption 2 is as follows:

$Adv_A^{AP_2} = \left| \Pr[A(T, \{d_{0,i}\}_{i=1,\ldots,n}) = 1] - \Pr[A(T, \{d_{1,i}\}_{i=1,\ldots,n}) = 1] \right|$

$ADV_A^{Ap_2}(\lambda)$ is equal to $ADV_A^{n-eDDH}(\lambda)$, which has been proved in [13].

Assumption 3

$(q, g, G, G^T, e, V, B, B^*) \leftarrow \delta_{ob}(1^\lambda, 2n + 3),$

$\widehat{B} = (b_1, \ldots, b_n, b_{2n+1}, b_{2n+3}), \widehat{B^*} = (b_1^*, \ldots, b_n^*, b_{2n+1}^*, b_{2n+2}^*),$

$T = (q, g, G, G^T, e, V, B, B^*),$

$i, j = 1, \ldots n,$

$w, \gamma_i \xleftarrow{R} F_q, \chi, \tau \xleftarrow{R} F_q - \{0\}$

$u_{i,j} \xleftarrow{R} GL(n, F_q), (z_{i,j}) = ((u_{i,j})^{-1})^T,$

$k_{0,i}^* = wb_i^* + +r_i b_{2n+2}^* (\beta = 0),$

$k_{1,i}^* = wb_i^* + \tau \sum_{j=1}^n z_{i,j} b_{n+j}^* + r_i b_{2n+2}^* (\beta = 1),$

$d_i = \varepsilon b_i + \chi \sum_{j=1}^n u_{i,j} b_{n+j},$

Assumption 3 is that given $(T, \{d_i, k_{\beta,i}^*\}_{(1 \le i \le n)})$, a PPT adversary guesses $\beta = 0$ or $\beta = 1$. The advantage of a PPT A for Assumption 3 is as follows:

$Adv_A^{AP_3} = \left| \Pr[A(T, \{d_i, k_{0,i}^*\}_{(1 \le i \le n)}) = 1] - \Pr[A, (T, \{d_i, k_{1,i}^*\}_{(1 \le i \le n)}) = 1] \right|.$

$ADV_A^{Ap_3}(\lambda)$ is equal to $ADV_A^{n-eDDH}(\lambda)$, which has been proved in [13].

Assumption 4

Assumption 4 is the same as Assumption 3 except that $\{d_i\}_{i=1,\ldots,n}$ aren't given to the adversary when the adversary guesses $\beta \in \{0, 1\}$. Specifically, Assumption 4 is to guess $\beta = 0$ or $\beta = 1$, given $(T, \{k_{\beta,i}\}_{(1 \le i \le n)})$. The advantage of A for Assumption 4 is defined as:

$$Adv_A^{AP_4} = \left| \Pr[A(T, \{k_{0,i}^*\}_{(1 \le i \le n)}) = 1] - \Pr[A, (T, \{k_{1,i}^*\}_{(1 \le i \le n)}) = 1] \right|$$

Assumption 5

Assumption 5 is the same as Assumption 2 except that additional $\{k_i^*\}_{i=1,\ldots,n}$ along with $(T = (q, g, G, G^T, e, V, B, B^*), \{d_{\beta,i}\}_{(1 \le i \le n)})$, are given to the adversary in game when guessing $\beta = 0$ or $\beta = 1$. Specifically, Assumption 5 is a PPT adversary guesses $\beta \in \{0, 1\}$, given $(T, \{d_{\beta,i}, k_i^*\}_{(1 \le i \le n)})$, where $D, \{d_{\beta,i}\}_{(1 \le i \le n)}$ are the same as that in Assumption 2. $h_i^* = wb_i^* + \tau \sum_{j=1}^{n} z_{i,j} b_{n+j}^*$, where $w \xleftarrow{R}$ $F_q, \tau \xleftarrow{R} F_q^*, (z_{i,j}) = ((u_{i,j})^{-1})^T$, For a PPT A, the advantage for Assumption 5 is defined as:

$$Adv_A^{AP_5} = \left| \Pr[A(T, \{d_{0,i}, k_i^*\}_{(1 \le i \le n)},) = 1] - \Pr[A(T, \{d_{1,i}, k_i^*\}_{(1 \le i \le n)}) = 1] \right|.$$

4 Problem Formulation

4.1 System Architecture

The system architecture comprises the data owner, the trusted anthority(TA), the cloud server, the user.

Data Owner: It encrypts the searchable index vector and a huge amount of data collection, sends them to the cloud server. About document encryption, it is beyond the focus of this paper.

TA: TA is responsible for generating and managing system keys and authorizing the search privileges to the query users. When receiving a trapdoor request for the query Q from a user, TA judges whether this user is allowed or not by the predefined authorization rules. TA will authorize the search privileges to the user if the attributes values of the user satisfy the preestablished authorization rules. Users' attribute values can be certified by the credentials signed TA. TA is generally governmental institution and assumed to be trusted.

Cloud Server: It stores the encrypted index and document set from the data owner. Receiving the trapdoor, it performs the search over the encrypted index and returns the matching results to the user.

Data User: After submitting the query request, the qualified user can receive the trapdoor associated with the query keywords and submits the trapdoor to the cloud server.

4.2 Security Goals

Firstly, we will give some related definitions.

Chosen Plaintext Attack Model: The main idea of the CPA model is that the attacker is allowed to request ciphertext for multiple selected plaintext messages. That is, the attacker **A** is allowed to interact freely with the encryption oracle, which can be thought of as a "black box" and encrypts message selected by **A** with the private key.

Adaptively Index-Hiding Against CPA: A SE scheme is adaptively index-hiding against CPA if for any PPT adversary **A**, the advantage of winning index privacy game is negligible.

Adaptively Query-Hiding Against CPA: A SE scheme is adaptively query-hiding if for any PPT adversary **A**, the advantage of winning the query privacy game is negligible.

Unforgeability of the Results: Unforgeability needs to ensure that under chosen plaintext attack model, the cloud server is unable to forge a valid proof to let the data owner believe that an index contains all the query keywords which it actually does not contain. Note: index privacy game and query privacy game will be described in the security proof part of the scheme.

The security goals are: (1) Adaptively index-hiding against CPA; (2) Adaptively query-hiding against CPA; (3) Unforgeability of the search results.

5 The Proposed Schemes

5.1 Construction of Our Scheme

The proposed scheme is mainly comprised of five phases: system initialization, encryption of the documents and index, generation of the trapdoor, secure search in cloud server and verification at data user site.

1. System Initialization
System Initialization mainly generate the system keys and consists of the following two steps.

(1) TA runs $Setup(1^\lambda, 2n + 3)$ to generate public key PK, private keys SK_2.
   $Setup(1^\lambda, 2n + 3) : (q, g, \mathrm{G}, \mathrm{G}_T, \mathrm{V}, \mathrm{A}, e, \mathrm{B}, \mathrm{B}^*) \leftarrow \zeta_{ob}(1^\lambda, 2n + 3)$,
   $\widehat{B} = (\mathrm{b}_1, \dots \mathrm{b}_n, \mathrm{b}_{2n+1}, \mathrm{b}_{2n+3})$,
   Define pseudorandom function $F : \{0,1\}^{L_k} \times \{0,1\}^{L_r} \rightarrow F_q$ $satisfying$ $2^{l_k} \leq q$,
   Return $PK = (q, g, \mathrm{G}, \mathrm{G}_T, \mathrm{V}, e, F, \widehat{B})$, $SK_2 = (K_2, B^*)$.
(2) TA and data owner apply the Diffie-Hellman key exchange protocol to generate $SK_1 = (s, K_1)$. Let **A** and **B** debote TA and the data owner.

- **A** selects elements a_1, a_2 uniformly at random from $[1, q - 1]$, and computes $g_{a_1} \leftarrow g^{a_1}(mod q), g_{a_2} \leftarrow g^{a_2}(mod q)$, and sends g_{a_1}, g_{a_2} to **B**;

- **B** selects elements b_1, b_2 uniformly at random from $[1, q-1]$, and computes $g_{b_1} \leftarrow g^{b_1}(modq), g_{b_2} \leftarrow g^{b_2}(modq)$ and sends g_{b_1}, g_{b_2} to **A**;
- computes $s = g_{b_1}^{a_1}(modq), K_1 = g_{b_2}^{a_2}(modq)$;
- computes $s = g_{a_1}^{b_1}(modq), K_1 = g_{a_2}^{b_2}(modq)$, $SK_1 = (s, K_1)$. (s, K_1) is shared by TA and the data owner.

2. Encryption of the Index
The encrypted index is generated according to the following steps.

(1) The data owner converts each index I_i into the index vectors $\overrightarrow{X_i} = \{x_{i1}, \ldots, x_{in}\}$ by the representative method of index vector.
(2) The data owner runs index encryption algorithm $EncIndex(PK, SK_1, \overrightarrow{X_i})$ to generate the encrypted index.
$EncIndex(SK_1, \overrightarrow{X_i}) : DID_i \xleftarrow{R} \{0,1\}^{l_r}, \varepsilon_1, \varepsilon_2 \xleftarrow{R} F_q,$
$\alpha_i = F_{K_1}(DID_i)$, DID_i is the identifier of the document d_i.
$$C_{\overrightarrow{X_i}} = s(\varepsilon_1(\sum_{j=1}^{n} x_{i,j}b_i) + \alpha_i b_{2n+1} + \varepsilon_2 b_{2n+3}),$$
$Return(\alpha_i, C_{\overrightarrow{X_i}})$, $C_{\overrightarrow{X_i}}$ is the ciphertext of $\overrightarrow{X_i}$.
(3) The date owner sends $(\alpha_i, C_{\overrightarrow{X_i}})(1 \leq i \leq m)$ to the cloud server.

3. Generation of the Trapdoor
The processing of generating the trapdoor is as follows.

(1) TA converts the query Q to the query vector $\overrightarrow{Y} = \{y_1, y_2, \ldots, y_n\}$, according to the representation method of the query vector.
(2) TA runs the trapdoor generation algorithm $GenTrapdoor(SK, \overrightarrow{Y})$ to generate the trapdoor $TD_{\overrightarrow{Y}}$.
$GenTrapdoor(SK, \overrightarrow{Y}) : \rho_1, \rho_2, \theta_1, \theta \xleftarrow{R} F_q,$
$\gamma_i = F_{K_2}(KID_i), \gamma = \gamma_1 \cdot \gamma_2, \ldots, \gamma_{d-1} \cdot \gamma_d,$

When the user doesn't care the jth attribute; we define $\gamma_j = 1(1 \leq j \leq d)$,

$$K_1^* = s^{-1}(\rho_1(\sum_{i=1}^{n} y_i b_i^*) + \rho_2 b_{2n+2}^*), K_2^* = s^{-1}(\theta_1(\sum_{i=1}^{n} y_i b_i^*) + \gamma b_{2n+1}^* + \theta_2 b_{2n+2}^*),$$

$Return(\gamma, TD_{\overrightarrow{Y}}), where \ TD_{\overrightarrow{Y}} = (K_1^*, K_2^*).$
(3) TA sends $(\gamma, TD_{\overrightarrow{Y}})$ to the user.

4. Secure Search in Cloud Server
The cloud server excutes the search and sends the results to the user.

(1) The cloud server runs query algorithm $Query(C_{\overrightarrow{X_i}}, K_1^*)$.

$$Query(C_{\overrightarrow{X_i}}, K_1^*) = e(C_{\overrightarrow{X_i}}, K_1^*)$$
$$= e(s(\varepsilon_1(\sum_{j=1}^{n} x_{i,j}b_j + \alpha_i b_{2n+1} + \varepsilon_2 b_{2n+3}), s^{-1}((\rho_1(\sum_{i=1}^{n} y_i b_i^*) + \rho_2 b_{2n+2}^*)))$$

If $\overrightarrow{X_i}.\overrightarrow{Y} = 0$, this algorithm returns 1, Otherwise, it returns 0. That output is 1 means that the index I_i contains all the keywords in Q.

(2) To convince the user that index I_i contains all the query keywords in the query Q, the cloud server generates a proof $pf_i = e(C_{\overrightarrow{X_i}}, K_2^*)$.

(3) The cloud server sends $((\alpha_1, pf_1), (\alpha_2, pf_2), \ldots)$ to the user.

5. Verification of the Search Results

For each search result (α_i, pf_i), the query user runs the verification algorithm $Verify(\gamma, \alpha_i, pf_i)$ to verify the correctness of search results.

$$Verify(\gamma, \alpha_i, pf_i) : \text{vari} = e(g, g)^{\alpha_i \gamma},$$

If $pf_i = vari$, it returns 1, Otherwise, it returns 0.

5.2 Proof of Correctness

Proof of the Search Correctness: $Query(C_{\overrightarrow{X_i}}, K_1^*) = e(C_{\overrightarrow{X_i}}, K_1^*)$

$$= e(s(\varepsilon_1(\sum_{j=1}^{n} x_{i,j} b_j + \alpha_i b_{2n+1} + \varepsilon_2 b_{2n+3}), s^{-1}((\rho_1(\sum_{i=1}^{n} y_i b_i^*) + \rho_2 b_{2n+2}^*)))$$

$$= e(g, g)^{s.s^{-1} \varepsilon_1 \rho_1 \sum_{j}^{n} x_{i,j} y_j} = e(g, g)^{\varepsilon_1 \rho_1 \sum_{j}^{n} x_{i,j} y_j}$$

If $\sum_{j=1}^{n} x_{i,j}.y_j = \overrightarrow{X_i}.\overrightarrow{Y} = 0$, then $e(C_{\overrightarrow{X_i}}, K_1^*) = 1$.

Proof of the Correctness for the Verification of the Research Eesults:

$$pf_i = e(C_{\overrightarrow{X_i}}, K_2^*)$$

$$= e(s(\varepsilon_1(\sum_{j=1}^{n} x_{i,j} b_i) + \alpha_i b_{2n+1} + \varepsilon_2 b_{2n+3}), s^{-1}(\theta_1(\sum_{i=1}^{n} y_i b_i^*) + \gamma b_{2n+1}^* + \theta_2 b_{2n+2}^*))$$

$$= e(s(\varepsilon_1(\sum_{j=1}^{n} x_{i,j} b_i), s^{-1} \theta_1(\sum_{i=1}^{n} y_i b_i^*)).e(s\alpha_i b_{2n+1}, s^{-1} \gamma b_{2n+1}^*)$$

$$= e(g, g)^{ss^{-1} \varepsilon_1 \theta_1 \sum_{j=1}^{n} x_{i,j}.y_j} .e(g, g)^{ss^{-1} \alpha_i \gamma}$$

If $\overrightarrow{X_i}.\overrightarrow{Y} = 0$, then $pf_i = e(g, g)^{\alpha_i \gamma}$. So $\overrightarrow{X_i}.\overrightarrow{Y} = 0, verify(\gamma, \alpha_i, pf_i) = 1$.

6   Performance Comparison

We compare our scheme with the similar schemes [6,13,16], in terms of security and basic functionality, as shown in Table 1.

From Table 1, scheme of Li et al. [6] is selectively index-hiding and query-hiding against CPA. The scheme in [13] is adaptively index-hiding, but query-

Table 1. Performance comparison of the schemes (1)

	LYC [6]	LOS [13]	LLD [16]	Our scheme
Index privacy	Selectively index-hiding against CPA	Adaptively index-hiding against CPA	Adaptively index-hiding against CPA	Adaptively index-hiding against CPA
Query privacy	Selectively query-hiding against CPA	/	Adaptively query-hiding against CPA	Adaptively query-hiding against CPA
Verification	No	No	Yes	Yes
MKS or SKS	MKS	MKS	SKS	MKS

privacy cannot be achieved in [13]. Search results verification is not supported in [6] and [13]. The scheme in [16] and our scheme are adaptively index-hiding and query hiding, however, the scheme in [16] only achieves the single keyword search (SKS)and our scheme can achieve the multi-keyword search (MKS) and verification.

We compare our scheme with the schemes in [13,16], which can achieve adaptively security in terms of storage and computation overhead, as shown in Table 2.

Let m and n denote the number of the documents and the length of the index vector, $|G|$ denote the size of an element in G, $|F_q|$ denote the size of an element in F_q, P denote one pair operation on $e : G \times G \to G_T$, M denote an exponentiation operation (point multiplication).

Encrypted Index Size: In our scheme, we consider $(\alpha_i, C_{\overrightarrow{X_i}})$ size as the encrypted index size, which is $|F_q| + (2n + 3)|G|$; the size of the encrypted index in [16] is $l_k + (2n + 5)|G|$, where l_k represents the size of the document identifier, and the size of the encrypted index in [13] is $(2n + 3)|G|$.

Trapdoor Size: In our scheme, the size refers to the size of (γ, K_1^*, K_2^*), and it is $|F_q| + (2n+3)|G| + (2n+3)|G|$, Similar to our scheme, the size of the trapdoor in [16] refers to the size of (SID, K_1^*, K_2^*), and is $l_k + (2n+5)|G| + (2n+5)|G|$, here l_k is the size of SID. For the scheme [13] we consider two situations: hierarchy and no hierarchy.

Key Generation Time: In our scheme and the scheme in [13,16], the overhead of generating key is generating B and B^*. Although in the our scheme and the scheme in [13], $\widehat{B}$ is used. To computer $\widehat{B}$, we must first computer B). The total overhead of generating B and B^* is $2N^2M$ (our scheme and [13]: $N = 2n + 3$; [16]: $N = 2n + 5$. To avoid the weakness of using "0" and "1" authorization model, we introduce the TA. When TA and the data owner establish the shared keys, Diffie–Hellman key exchange protocol is used, introducing $4M$ computation overhead. Therefore the total overhead of generating keys is $2.(2n + 3)^2 M + 4M$.

Index Encryption Time: When generating the encrypted index, the basic operation is to encrypt the index. In our scheme, to achieve the verification of the results, our scheme carries F function over the identifier information over the document. So, the total computation overhead of generating the encrypted index is $F+(n+4)(2n+3)M$. Similarly, this type of overhead in [16] is $F+(n+4)(2n+5)M$. The scheme in [13] don't have the verification functionality and its overhead of generating the encrypted index is $(n+3)(2n+3)M$.

Trapdoor Generation Time: In our scheme and [16], the time of generating the trapdoor conclude the time of generating (K_1^*, K_2^*) and the time of running F function. For the scheme in [13], we consider two situations: hierarchy and no hierarchy.

Search Time: To our scheme and the scheme [16], we consider the time of searching m documents and time of generating a proof. However, the scheme in [13] has the function of verification, therefore this scheme in [13] don't need to generate the proof.

From Table 2, we can see that the efficiency of our scheme is slightly less than the efficiency of the scheme [13] without authorization function. However, in terms of trap size, index generation and trapdoor generation, our scheme is superior to [13] with authorization. From Table 2, our scheme is superior to the [16] in storage overhead and computation overhead. Combined results show that our scheme is secure and practical.

Table 2. Performance comparison of the schemes (2)

	LOS [13]	LLD [16]	Our scheme
Encrypted index size	$(2n+3)\,|G|$	$l_k + (2n+5)\,|G|$	$|F_q| + (2n+3)\,|G|$
Trapdoor size	No hierarchy: $(2n+3)|G|$ Hierarchy: $[1+2+(n-u_l)]\cdot$ $(2n+3)|G|$	$l_k+2(2n+5)|G|$	$|F_q|+2(2n+3)|G|$
Key generation	$2(2n+3)^2M$	$2(2n+5)^2M$	$2(2n+3)^2M + 4M$
Index encryption	$(n+3)(2n+3)M$	$(n+4)(2n+5)M$ $+F$	$(n+4)(2n+3)M$ $+F$
Trapdoor generation	No hierarchy: $(n+3)(2n+3)$M Hierarchy: $[(u_l+l+1)$ $+(l+1)(u_l+l+1)$ $+(n-u_l)(u_l+l+2)]$ $\cdot(2n+3)M$	K_1^*: $((n+3)(2n+5))\,M$ K_2^*: $((n+4)(2n+5))\,M$ $+ F$	K_1^*: $((n+3)(2n+3)))\,M$ K_2^*: $((n+4)(2n+3))\,M$ $+ xF$
Search	m(2n+3)P	Search: m(2n+5)P Proof: (2n+5)P	Search: m(2n+3)P Proof: (2n+3)P

7   Conclusion

In this paper, based on the inner product predicate encryption and dual system encryption, we propose a semantically secure multi-keyword search scheme with both index privacy and query privacy. Our scheme is adaptively index-hiding and adaptively query-hiding. Our scheme also is equipped with the capacity of verifying the authenticity of search results. Moreover, our scheme overcomes the disadvantages of traditional "0" or "1" authorization and the data owner is required to be always online by introducing the trusted authority. At last, We make a theoretical performance comparison and thorough security proof by a sequence of games. Combined results show that our scheme is secure and practical.

Acknowledgement. National Key Research and Development Program of China (2016YFB0800703), Chinese National Natural Science Foundation (*Grant U*1836210, Grant 61572460, Grant 61772174 and Grant 61370220), in part by the National Information Security Special Projects of theNational Development and Reform Commission of China under Grant (2012)1424, and in part by the Open Project Program of the State Key Laboratory of Information Security under Grant 2017-ZD-01.

Appendix A.1 Dual System Encryption

The scheme security is proved by dual system encryption, in which both ciphertext and keys present two states: standard and semi-functional. The trapdoor generated by *GenTrapdoor* is called the normal trapdoor, and the encrypted index generated by *EncIndex* is called the standard ciphertext. We define the semi-function index ciphertext and the semi-function trapdoor, which are only employed in the proof of the scheme.

We use $C_{\overrightarrow{X}}^{norm}$ to denote the normal index ciphertext of $\overrightarrow{X}, (K_1^{*(norm)},$ $K_2^{*(norm)})$ to denote the normal trapdoor of $\overrightarrow{Y}$, $C_{\overrightarrow{X}}^{semi}$ to denote the semi-functional index ciphertext of $\overrightarrow{X} = \{x_1, \ldots, x_n\}$.

$$C_{\overrightarrow{X_i}}^{norm} = s(\varepsilon_1(\sum_{j=1}^{n} x_{i,j}b_i) + \alpha_i b_{2n+1} + \varepsilon_2 b_{2n+3})$$

$$K_1^{*(norm)} = s^{-1}(\rho_1(\sum_{i=1}^{n} y_i b_i^*) + \rho_2 b_{2n+2}^*), K_2^{*(norm)} = s^{-1}(\theta_1(\sum_{i=1}^{n} y_i b_i^*) + \gamma b_{2n+1}^* + \theta_2 b_{2n+2}^*)$$

We use $C_{\overrightarrow{X}}^{semi}$ to denote the semi-functional index ciphertext of $\overrightarrow{X} = \{x_1, \ldots, x_n\}$.

$$C_{\overrightarrow{X}}^{semi} = s(\varepsilon_1(\sum_{i=1}^{n} x_i b_i) + \sum_{j=1}^{n} u_j b_{n+j} + \alpha b_{2n+1} + \varepsilon_2 b_{2n+3}) = s(\varepsilon_1 \overrightarrow{X}, \overrightarrow{U}, \alpha, 0, \varepsilon_2)B$$

$\overrightarrow{U} = (u_1, \ldots, u_n), u_j(1 \le j \le n) \leftarrow F_q$, others are the same as those in $C_{\overrightarrow{X}}^{norm}$.

We use $(K_1^{*(semi)}, K_2^{*(semi)})$ to denote the semi-functional trapdoor of $\overrightarrow{Y} = \{y_1, \ldots, y_n\}$.

$$K_1^{*(semi)} = s^{-1}(\rho_1(\sum_{i=1}^{n} y_i b_i^*) + \sum_{i=1}^{n} v_i b_{n+i}^* + \rho_2 b_{2n+2}^*) = s^{-1}(\rho_1 \overrightarrow{Y}, \overrightarrow{V}, 0, \rho_2, 0)B^*$$

$$K_2^{*(semi)} = s^{-1}(\theta_1(\sum_{i=1}^{n} y_i b_i^*) + \sum_{i=1}^{n} w_i b_{n+i}^* + \gamma b_{2n+1}^* + \theta_2 b_{2n+2}^*) = s^{-1}(\theta_1 \overrightarrow{Y}, \overrightarrow{W}, \gamma, \theta_2, 0)B^*$$

where $\overrightarrow{V} = (v_1, \ldots, v_n), v_j (1 \le j \le n) \leftarrow F_q$ and $\overrightarrow{W} = (w_1, \ldots, w_n), w_i (1 \le i \le n) \leftarrow F_q$, other parameters are the same as those in $K_1^{*(norm)}$ and $K_2^{*(norm)}$.

If $\overrightarrow{X}.\overrightarrow{Y} = 0$, we can observe that

$$e(C_{\overrightarrow{X}}^{norm}, K_1^{*norm}) = e(C_{\overrightarrow{X}}^{semi}, K_1^{*(norm)}) = e(C_{\overrightarrow{X}}^{norm}, K_1^{*(semi)}) = 1 \in_T$$

$$e(C_{\overrightarrow{X}}^{norm}, K_2^{*(norm)}) = e(C_{\overrightarrow{X}}^{semi}, K_2^{*(norm)}) = e(C_{\overrightarrow{X}}^{norm}, K_2^{*(semi)}) = e(g,g)^{\alpha\gamma}$$

$$e(C_{\overrightarrow{X}}^{semi}, K_1^{*(semi)}) = e(g,g)^{\varepsilon_1 \rho_1 \overrightarrow{X}.\overrightarrow{Y}}.e(g,g)^{\overrightarrow{U}.\overrightarrow{V}} \qquad (1)$$

$$e(C_{\overrightarrow{X}}^{semi}, K_2^{*(semi)}) = e(g,g)^{\varepsilon_1 \theta_1 \overrightarrow{X}.\overrightarrow{Y}}.e(g,g)^{\overrightarrow{U}.\overrightarrow{W}}.e(g,g)^{\alpha\gamma}. \qquad (2)$$

$e(C_{\overrightarrow{X}}^{semi}, K_2^{*(semi)}) = e(g,g)^{\varepsilon_1 \theta_1 \overrightarrow{X}.\overrightarrow{Y}}.e(g,g)^{\overrightarrow{U}.\overrightarrow{W}}.e(g,g)^{\alpha\gamma}$ are uniformly and independently distributed over G_T. From the Formula (1) and (2), we can observe that the decryption fails when the semi-functional ciphertext is decrypted with the semi-functional key.

Appendix A.2 The Proof of the Scheme Security

Index privacy game: it is a game between the challenger B and the PPT adversary A. This game is also called game 0.

1. B executes $Setup(1^\lambda)$ to generate PK and secret keys $SK = \{SK_1, SK_2\}$, and PK is given to the adverdary. The private key is safely kept and SK_1 is also safely kept by the data owner. Note B generates SK_1 by acting as both parties in the the Diffie-Hellman key exchange protocol.
2. A may adaptively issue queries, where each query can be ciphertext query or trapdoor query. On the j-th ciphertext query, A issues an index vector $\overrightarrow{X_j}$ and receives the corresponding ciphertext $C_{\overrightarrow{X_j}} \leftarrow EncIndex(SK, \overrightarrow{X_j})$. On the j-th trapdoor query, A issues a query vector $\overrightarrow{Y_j}$ and receives the corresponding trapdoor $TD_{\overrightarrow{Y_j}} \leftarrow GenTrapdoor(SK, \overrightarrow{Y_j})$.
3. A issues two challenge index vectors $(\overrightarrow{X^0}, \overrightarrow{X^1})$, subject to the restriction $\overrightarrow{X}^{(0)}.\overrightarrow{Y} \neq 0$ and $\overrightarrow{X}^{(1)}.\overrightarrow{Y} \neq 0$ for the entire query vector $\overrightarrow{Y}$ issued by A. B randomly chooses a random bit $b \in \{0,1\}$, A is given $C_{\overrightarrow{X}^{(b)}} \leftarrow EncIndex(SK, \overrightarrow{X}^{(b)})$.

4. A may continue to submit additional queries as in step (2), with the same restriction as that in step 3.
5. A outputs one bit b' , and it will win the game if $b' = b$.

Game 1: A really random function substitutes F_{K_1} in game 0, which has the same range and domain.

Game 2: A really random function substitutes F_{K_2} in game 1, which has the same range and domain.

Game 3: Semi-functional challenge ciphertext for the index is given to the adversary.

Game 4-t: the challenge index ciphertext is semi-functional, and the first t trapdoors are semi-functinal.

Game 5: The challenge index ciphertext and all the trapdoors are semi-functional.

Theorem 1. If the advantages for Assumptions 2 and 3 are negligible, then the proposed scheme is adaptively index-hiding against CPA.

Proof: In game 5, since the index ciphertext and trapdoor are semi-functional, so for any PPT adversary, he can't attain any advantage in game 5. So, if the index privacy game can be proved to be computationally indistinguishable with the game 5, then we also prove the advantage for the original index privacy is negligible. Below we will prove that the index privacy game and game 5 are computationally indistinguishable by 5 lemmas.

Lemma 1. Game0 and game 1 is computationally indistinguishable.

Proof. For convenience of proving of Lemma 1, we construct a PPT machine **B** that uses the adversary **A** to distinguish pseudorandom function and random function. The processing is as follows. (1) **B** returns the system public parameters $PK = (q, G, G_T, g, V, e, \widehat{B})$ to **A** and keeps $SK = (r, K_1, K_2, B^*)$.

(2) **A** issues a ciphertext query on the attribute vector $\overrightarrow{X}$ to **B**, **B** queries its oracle on DID (the identifier of $\overrightarrow{X}$) and set the result as α. When $f = F_{K_1}$, then $\alpha = F_{K_1}(DID)$, otherwise, α is distributed uniformly at random. As response, **B** answers a ciphertext $C_{\overrightarrow{X}} = r(\varepsilon_1(\sum_{i=1}^{n} x_i b_i) + \alpha b_{2n+1} + \varepsilon_2 b_{2n+3})$, where $\varepsilon_1, \varepsilon_2 \in F_q$ uniformly at random.

(3) **A** issues a query, **B** answers a normal trapdoor computed by using B^* and K_2.

(4) When **B** gets the challenge index vector $(\overrightarrow{X^0}, \overrightarrow{X^1})$, **B** chooses a random bit $b \in \{0, 1\}$, and sends a ciphertext index $C_{\overrightarrow{X^b}} = s(\varepsilon_1(\sum_{i=1}^{n} x_i^b b_i) + \alpha b_{2n+1} + \varepsilon_2 b_{2n+3})$.

(5) **A** and **B** continues to operate as the step (2) and (3). In fact, when $f = F_{K_1}$, B has simulated game 0, when f is random function with the domain $D = (0, 1)^{l_t}$ and the range $R = F_q$, and then B simulated game 1.

(6) **A** outputs bit b', if $b' = b$, which means that **A** can distinguish game 0 from game 1, then **B** can distinguish pseudorandom function and random function, which contradicts with the property of the pseudorandom function. Therefore, game 0 and game 1 are computationally indistinguishable.

Lemma 2. Game1 and game 2 is computationally indistinguishable.

We omit this proof of the Lemma 2, because it is similar to proof of Lemma 1.

Lemma 3. Assuming the advantage for Assumption 2 is negligible, and then game 2 and 3 are computationally indistinguishable.

Proof. For convenience of proving of this lemma, we construct a PPT machine **B** that uses the adversary **A** against Assumption 2.

After receiving Assumption 2 instance $(q, G, G_T, g, e, V, \widehat{B}, \widehat{B^*}, \{d_{\beta,i}\}_{(1 \leq i \leq n)}$, **B** tries his best to decide $\beta = 1$ or $\beta = 0$. **B** runs **A** to break Assumption 2. The processing is as follows.

(1) **B** returns the system public parameters $PK = (q, G, G_T, g, V, e, \widehat{B})$ to **A** and keeps $SK = (s, K_1, K_2, B^*)$.

(2) **A** submits a ciphertext query on the index vector $\overrightarrow{X}$, **B** answers a normal ciphertext $C_{\overrightarrow{X}} = s(\varepsilon_1(\sum_{i=1}^{n} x_i b_i) + \alpha b_{2n+1} + \varepsilon_2 b_{2n+3})$ omputed by $\widehat{B}$ and S.

(3) **A** issues a trapdoor query on all the query keywords, **B** answers a normal trapdoor computed by $\widehat{B^*}$ and S .

(4) Getting the challenge index vector $(\overrightarrow{X^0}, \overrightarrow{X^1})$, **B** selects a random bit $b \in \{0,1\}$, parses $\overrightarrow{X^b} = \{x_1^b, \ldots, x_n^b\}$, and computes $C_{\overrightarrow{X^b}} = s(\sum_{i=1}^{n} x_i^b d_{\beta,i} + \alpha' b_{2n+1})$, where $\alpha' \in F_q$ uniformly at random.

(5) **A** continues to adaptively submit additional queries as in steps (2) and (3).

When $\beta = 0$, then $C_{\overrightarrow{X^b}} = r(\sum_{i=1}^{n} x_i^b d_{0,i} + \alpha' b_{2n+1}) = r(\varepsilon_1 \sum_{i=1}^{n} x_i^b b_i + \alpha' b_{2n+1} + (\sum_{i=1}^{n} x_i^b \varepsilon_{2,i}) b_{2n+3})$, **B** has simulated game 2.

When $\beta = 1$, then $_{\overrightarrow{X^b}} = r(\sum_{i=1}^{n} x_i^b d_{1,i} + \alpha' b_{2n+1}) = r(\varepsilon_1 \sum_{i=1}^{n} x_i^b b_i + \sum_{i=1}^{n} (\sum_{t=1}^{n} \rho x_t^b u_{t,i}) b_{n+i} + \alpha' b_{2n+1} + (\sum_{i=1}^{n} x_i^b \varepsilon_{2,i}) b_{2n+3})$, **B** has simulated game 3.

(6) **A** outputs bit b', if $b' = b$, which means that **A** can distinguish game 3 and game 2, then **B** can decide $\beta = 0$ or 1. This means that **B**'s advantage of breaking Assumption 2 is non-negligible. This contradicts $ADV_A^{Ap_2}(\lambda) = ADV_A^{n-eDDH}(\lambda)$, which has been proved in []. Therefore, if the advantage for Assumption 2 is negligible, game 3 and game 2 are computationally indistinguishable.

Lemma 4. Assuming the advantage for Assumption 3 is negligible, then game 4-(t-1) and game 4-t are computationally indistinguishable for $1 \leq \vartheta \leq t$. where ϑ denotes the number of trapdoor queries the adversary makes.

Proof. To For the sake of proving this Lemma 4, we construct a PPT machine **B** that uses the adversary **A** against Assumption 3.

Receiving $(q, G, G^T, g, e, V, \widehat{B}, \widehat{B}^*, \{h^*_{\beta,i}, d_i\}_{(1 \leq i \leq n)})$, **B** tries to decide if $\beta = 0$ or 1. **B** runs **A** as a subroutine to break Assumption 3. The processing is as follows.

(1) **B** returns the system returns the system Parameter $PK = (q, G, G_T, g, V, e, \widehat{B})$ to **A**, and keeps $SK = (s, \widehat{B}^*)$.

(2) **A** issues a ciphertext query for the index vector $\overrightarrow{X}$, **B** answers a normal ciphertext $C_{\overrightarrow{X}} = s(\varepsilon_1(\sum_{i=1}^{n} x_i b_i) + \alpha b_{2n+1} + \varepsilon_2 b_{2n+3})$ computed by s and $\widehat{B}$.

(3) **A** issues the ν-th trapdoor query on the query vector $\overrightarrow{Y} = \{y_1, \ldots, y_n\}$, **B** answers query ciphertext according to the following rules.

If $1 \leq v \leq k-1$, **B** creates a semi-functional trapdoor for $\overrightarrow{Y} = \{y_1, \ldots, y_n\}$ by using s and B*.

If $v > k$, **B** answers a normal trapdoor by using s and B*.

If $v = k$, **B** calculates $K^*_1 = s^{-1}(\rho(\sum_{i=1}^{n} y_i h^*_{\beta,i}) + \rho' b^*_{2n+2}), K^*_2 = s^{-1}(\theta(\sum_{i=1}^{n} y_i h^*_{\beta,i}) + \eta' b^*_{2n+1} + \theta' b^*_{2n+2})$, where $\rho, \rho', \theta, \theta', \eta' \in F_q$ uniformly at random.

(4) Getting the challenge attribute vector $(\overrightarrow{X^0}, \overrightarrow{X^1})$, **B** selects a random bit $b \in \{0,1\}$, parses $\overrightarrow{X^b} = \{x^b_1, \ldots, x^b_n\}$. **B** chooses $\varepsilon_2', \alpha' \in F_q$ and $DID \in \{0,1\}^{l_t}$ uniformly at random, computes $\alpha = F_{K_1}(FID), C_{\overrightarrow{X^b}} = r(\sum_{i=1}^{n} x^b_i d_i + \alpha' b_{2n+1} + \varepsilon_2' b_{2n+3})$, **B** sends $(\alpha, C_{\overrightarrow{X^b}})$ to **A**.

(5) **A** continues to adaptively issue additional queries as in steps (2) C(3).

In fact, when $\beta = 0$, **B** has simulated game 4-(t-1). when $\beta = 1$, then **B** simulated game 4-t.

(6) **A** outputs b', if $b' = b$, which means that **A** can distinguish game 4-(t-1) and game 4-t, then **B** can decide $\beta = 0$ or 1. This means that **B**'s advantage for Assumption 2 is non-negligible. This conflicts $ADV^{Ap3}_A(\lambda) = ADV^{n-eDDH}_A(\lambda)$, which has been proved in []

So game 4-(t -1) and game 4-t are computationally indistinguishable.

Lemma 5. Game 4-ϑ and game 5 are essentially equivalent.

Proof. For convenience of proving of Lemma 5, we prove distribution $(\{k^{(j)*}\}_{i=1,\ldots,x}, \{C_{\overrightarrow{X}}^{(j)}\}_{j=1,\ldots,y} \, C_{\overrightarrow{X}}^*)$ in game 4-ϑ and that in Game 5 are equivalent, where x and y denote the number of ciphertext queries and trapdoor queries the adversary issues, respectively.

Set $d_i = b_i, d_{n+i} = b_{n+i} - \sum_{s=1}^{n} z_{i,s} b_s - \theta_i b_{2n+1} (i = 1, \ldots, n), d_{2n+i} = b_{2n+i} (i = 1, 2, 3),$

Set $D := (d_1, \ldots, d_{2n+3}), D^* := (d_1^*, \ldots, d_{2n+3}^*)$.

In the game 4-t, the trapdoor $k^{(j)*}$ for the j-th$(1 \le j \le \vartheta)$ query, the index ciphertext $C_{\overrightarrow{X}}^{(j)}$ for the first j$(1 \le j \le x)$ index, and the challenge ciphertext $C_{\overrightarrow{X}}^*$ can be represented by B and B^* as follows. $k^{(j)*} = (k_1^{(j)*}, k_2^{(j)*})$

$$K_1^{(j)*} = s^{-1}(\rho_1^{(j)}(\sum_{i=1}^{n} y_i^{(j)} b_i^*) + \sum_{i=1}^{n} v_i^{(j)} b_{n+i}^* + \rho_2^{(j)} b_{2n+2}^*)$$

$$K_2^{(j)*} = s^{-1}(\theta_1^{(j)}(\sum_{i=1}^{n} y_i b_i^*) + \sum_{i=1}^{n} w_i^{(j)} b_{n+i}^* + \gamma^{(j)} b_{2n+1}^* + \theta_2^{(j)} b_{2n+2}^*),$$

$$C_{\overrightarrow{X}}^{(j)} = s(\varepsilon_1^{(j)}(\sum_{i=1}^{n} x_i^j b_i) + \alpha^{(j)} b_{2n+1} + \varepsilon_2^{(j)} b_{2n+3})$$

$$C_{\overrightarrow{X}}^* = s(\varepsilon_1^*(\sum_{i=1}^{n} x_i^* b_i) + \sum_{i=1}^{n} u_i b_{n+i} + \alpha^* b_{2n+1} + \varepsilon_2^* b_{2n+3})$$

We notice that $(\{k^{(j)*}\}_{j=1,\ldots,x}, \{C_{\overrightarrow{X}}^{(j)}\}_{j=1,\ldots,y}, C_{\overrightarrow{X}}^*)$ can be represented by D and D^*.

$$K_1^{(j)*} = s^{-1}(\rho_1^{(j)}(\sum_{i=1}^{n} y_i^{(j)} b_i^*) + \sum_{i=1}^{n} v_i^{(j)} b_{n+i}^* + \rho_2^{(j)} b_{2n+2}^*)$$

$$= s^{-1}(\rho_1^{(j)}(\sum_{i=1}^{n} y_i^* d_i^*) + \sum_{t=1}^{n} v_t^{(j)'} d_{n+t}^* + \rho_2^{(j)} d_{2n+2}^*)$$

where is $v_t^{(j)'} = v_t^{(j)} - \rho_1^{(j)} \sum_{i=1}^{n} y_i^{(j)} z_{t,i}$ uniformly and independly distributed.

$$K_2^{(j)*} = s^{-1}(\theta_1^{(j)}(\sum_{i=1}^{n} y_i b_i^*) + \sum_{i=1}^{n} w_i^{(j)} b_{n+i}^* + \beta^{(j)} b_{2n+1}^* + \theta_2^{(j)} b_{2n+2}^*)$$

$$= s^{-1}(\theta_1^{(j)}(\sum_{i=1}^{n} y_i d_i^*) + \sum_{t=1}^{n} w_t^{(j)'} d_{n+t}^* + \beta^{(j)} d_{2n+1}^* + \theta_2^{(j)} d_{2n+2}^*)$$

where $w_t^{(j)'} = w_t^{(j)} - \theta_1^{(j)} \sum_{i=1}^{n} y_i^{(j)} z_{t,i} - \beta^{(j)} \theta_t$ are uniformly and independently distributed

$$C_{\overrightarrow{X}}^{(j)} = s(\varepsilon_1^{(j)}(\sum_{i=1}^{n} x_i^j b_i) + \alpha^{(j)} b_{2n+1} + \varepsilon_2^{(j)} b_{2n+3}) = s(\varepsilon_1^{(j)}(\sum_{i=1}^{n} x_i^j d_i) + \alpha^{(j)} d_{2n+1} + \varepsilon_2^{(j)} d_{2n+3}),$$

$$C_{\overrightarrow{X}}^* = s(\varepsilon_1^*(\sum_{i=1}^{n} x_i^* b_i) + \sum_{i=1}^{n} u_i b_{n+i} + \alpha^* b_{2n+1} + \varepsilon_2^* b_{2n+3}),$$

$$= s(\sum_{t=1}^{n} \varepsilon_x d_t + \sum_{i=1}^{n} u_i d_{n+i} + \alpha_x d_{2n+1} + \varepsilon_2^* d_{2n+3})$$

$\varepsilon_x = \varepsilon_1 x_t^* + \sum_{i=1}^{n} u_i z_{i,t}, \alpha_x = \alpha^* + \sum_{i=1}^{n} u_i \theta_i$ are uniformly and independently distributed.

Therefore, $(\{k^{(j)}\}_{i=1,\ldots,y}, \{C_{\overrightarrow{X}}^{(j)}\}_{j=1,\ldots,x}, C_{\overrightarrow{X}}^*)$ can be represented as trapdoor and index ciphertext with two methods, in Game 4-ϑ over bases B, B^*) in Game 5 over bases D, D^*). Thus, Game 4-ϑ can be conceptually changed to Game 5.

In conclusion, if the function is paseudorandom function and the advantages for Assumptions 2 and 3 are negligible, the index privacy game and game 5 are computationally indistinguishable. Moreover, any PPT adversary has no advantage for game 5. At this point, Theorem 1 is proved.

Index privacy game game 0: it is the origal query privacy game between the challenger **B** and the adaversary **A**. We describe the original query privacy game can be described by the similar method with the original index privacy game.

Theorem 2. If the advantages for Assumptions 4 and 5 are negligible, then the proposed scheme is adaptively query-hiding against CPA.

The proof ofthe Theorem 2 is similar to the proof of the Theorem 1.

Appendix A.3 The Proof of Unforgeability of the Results

Theorem 3. The proposed scheme achieves unforgeability of the results.
Aftering receiving the trapdoor $TD_{\overrightarrow{Y}} = (K_1^*, K_2^*)$, the cloud server searches all the encrypted index and sends $((\alpha_1, pf_1), (\alpha_2, pf_2), \ldots)$ to the user, where pf_i is the proof that d_i with the DID_i matches with Q. $pf_i = e(C_{\overrightarrow{X_i}}, K_2^*)$

$$= e(s(\varepsilon_1(\sum_{j=1}^{n} x_{i,j} b_i) + \alpha_i b_{2n+1} + \varepsilon_2 b_{2n+3}), s^{-1}(\theta_1(\sum_{i=1}^{n} y_i b_i^*) + \gamma b_{2n+1}^* + \theta_2 b_{2n+2}^*))$$

$$= e(s(\varepsilon_1(\sum_{j=1}^{n} x_{i,j} b_i), s^{-1} \theta_1(\sum_{i=1}^{n} y_i b_i^*)).e(s\alpha_i b_{2n+1}, s^{-1} \gamma b_{2n+1}^*)$$

$$= e(g,g)^{ss^{-1} \varepsilon_1 \theta_1 \sum_{j=1}^{n} x_{i,j}.y_j}.e(g,g)^{ss^{-1} \alpha_i \gamma}$$

$$= e(g,g)^{\varepsilon_1 \theta_1 \sum_{j=1}^{n} x_{i,j}.y_j}.e(g,g)^{\alpha_i \gamma}$$

If $\overrightarrow{X_i}$ matchs with $\overrightarrow{Y} = (y_1, \ldots, y_n)$, then $\overrightarrow{X_i}.\overrightarrow{Y} = 0$, i.e., $\sum_{j=1}^{n} x_{i,j}.y_j = 0$, then $pf_i = e(C_{\overrightarrow{X_i}}, K_2^*) = e(g,g)^{\alpha_i \gamma}$, here $\alpha_i = F_{K_1}(DID_i), \gamma = \gamma_1, \ldots, \gamma_d, \gamma_i = F_{K_2}(KID_i)$ Otherwise, pf_i are uniformly and independently distributed in G_T. So, If $\overrightarrow{X_i}$ doesnt matchs with $\overrightarrow{Y} = (y_1, \ldots, y_n)$, the probability that an adversary outputs $pf_i = e(g,g)^{\alpha_i \gamma}$ is negligible. So, we prove that the proposed scheme achieves unforgeability of the results.

References

1. Boneh, D., Di Crescenzo, G., Ostrovsky, R., Persiano, G.: Public key encryption with keyword search. In: Cachin, C., Camenisch, J.L. (eds.) EUROCRYPT 2004. LNCS, vol. 3027, pp. 506–522. Springer, Heidelberg (2004). https://doi.org/10.1007/978-3-540-24676-3_30
2. Song, D., Perrig, A.: Practical techniques for searches on encrypted data. In: Proceeding of the IEEE Symposium on Security and Privacy, (S&P 2000), Berkeley, USA, pp. 3–10 (2000)
3. Zhang, L.L., Zhang, Y.Q., Liu, X.F., Quan, H.Y.: Efficient conjunctive keyword search over encrypted medical records. J. Softw (in Chin.) 27(6), 1577–1591 (2015)
4. Zhang, L.L., Zhang, Y.Q., Ma, H.: Privacy-preserving and dynamic multi-attribute conjunctive keyword search over encrypted cloud data. IEEE Access 6(1), 34214–34225 (2018)
5. Golle, P., Staddon, J., Waters, B.: Secure conjunctive keyword search over encrypted data. In: Jakobsson, M., Yung, M., Zhou, J. (eds.) ACNS 2004. LNCS, vol. 3089, pp. 31–45. Springer, Heidelberg (2004). https://doi.org/10.1007/978-3-540-24852-1_3
6. Li, M., Yu, S., Cao, N., Lou, W.J.: Authorized private keyword search over encrypted data in cloud computing. In: Proceeding of the International Conference on Distributed Computing Systems (ICDCS), Minneapolis, MO, USA, pp. 383–392 (2011)
7. Katz, J., Sahai, A., Waters, B.: Predicate encryption supporting disjunctions, polynomial equations, and inner products. In: Smart, N. (ed.) EUROCRYPT 2008. LNCS, vol. 4965, pp. 146–162. Springer, Heidelberg (2008). https://doi.org/10.1007/978-3-540-78967-3_9
8. Okamoto, T., Takashima, K.: Hierarchical predicate encryption for inner-products. In: Matsui, M. (ed.) ASIACRYPT 2009. LNCS, vol. 5912, pp. 214–231. Springer, Heidelberg (2009). https://doi.org/10.1007/978-3-642-10366-7_13
9. Wang, C., Ren, K., Yu, S., Mahendra, K., Urs, R.: Achieving usable and privacy-assured similarity search over outsourced cloud data. In: Proceedings of the IEEE INFOCOM, Orlando, FL, USA (2012)
10. Hwang, Y.H., Lee, P.J.: Public key encryption with conjunctive keyword search and its extension to a multi-user system. In: Takagi, T., Okamoto, T., Okamoto, E., Okamoto, T. (eds.) Pairing 2007. LNCS, vol. 4575, pp. 2–22. Springer, Heidelberg (2007). https://doi.org/10.1007/978-3-540-73489-5_2
11. Boneh, D., Waters, B.: Conjunctive, subset, and range queries on encrypted data. In: Vadhan, S.P. (ed.) TCC 2007. LNCS, vol. 4392, pp. 535–554. Springer, Heidelberg (2007). https://doi.org/10.1007/978-3-540-70936-7_29
12. Shen, E., Shi, E., Waters, B.: Predicate privacy in encryption systems. In: Reingold, O. (ed.) TCC 2009. LNCS, vol. 5444, pp. 457–473. Springer, Heidelberg (2009). https://doi.org/10.1007/978-3-642-00457-5_27
13. Lewko, A., Okamoto, T., Sahai, A., Takashima, K., Waters, B.: Fully secure functional encryption: attribute-based encryption and (hierarchical) inner product encryption. In: Gilbert, H. (ed.) EUROCRYPT 2010. LNCS, vol. 6110, pp. 62–91. Springer, Heidelberg (2010). https://doi.org/10.1007/978-3-642-13190-5_4
14. Ballard, L., Kamara, S., Monrose, F.: Achieving efficient conjunctive keyword searches over encrypted data. In: Qing, S., Mao, W., López, J., Wang, G. (eds.) ICICS 2005. LNCS, vol. 3783, pp. 414–426. Springer, Heidelberg (2005). https://doi.org/10.1007/11602897_35

15. Waters, B.: Dual system encryption: realizing fully secure IBE and HIBE under simple assumptions. In: Halevi, S. (ed.) CRYPTO 2009. LNCS, vol. 5677, pp. 619–636. Springer, Heidelberg (2009). https://doi.org/10.1007/978-3-642-03356-8_36

16. Lai, J., Li, Y., Deng, R.: Towards semantically secure outsourcing of association rule mining on categorical data. Inf. Sci. **267**, 267–286 (2014)

17. Li, F., Hadjieleftheriou, M., Kollios, G., Reyzin, L.: Dynamic authenticated index structures for outsourced databases. In: Proceedings of the SIGMOD, New York, USA, pp. 121–132 (2013)

18. Fu, A.M., Yu, S., Zhang, Y.Q.: NPP: a new privacy-aware public auditing scheme for cloud data sharing with group users. IEEE Trans. Big Data (2017). https://doi.org/10.1109/TBDATA.2017.2701347

19. Wang, C., Ren, K., Yu, S., Mahendra, K., Urs, R.: Achieving usable and privacy-assured similarity search over outsourced cloud data. In: Proceedings of the IEEE INFOCOM, Orlando, FL, USA (2010)

20. Sun, W., et al.: Privacy-preserving multi-keyword text search in the cloud supporting similarity-based ranking. In: Proceedings of the ASIACCS, Hangzhou, China, pp. 71–82 (2013)

21. Chen, C., Zhu, X., Shen, P., Hu, J., Guo, S.: An efficient privacy-preserving ranked keyword search method. IEEE Trans. Parallel Distrib. Syst. **27**(4), 951–963 (2016)

22. Li, X.X., Hua, L.F., Song, C.G.: Public key generation with multi-keyword search. J. Xidian U. **42**(5), 20–26 (2015)

Content Recognition of Network Traffic Using Wavelet Transform and CNN

Yu Liang, Yi Xie[✉], Xingrui Fei, Xincheng Tan, and Haishou Ma

School of Data and Computer Science,
Guangdong Key Laboratory of Information Security, Sun Yat-sen University,
Guangzhou 510275, China
xieyi5@mail.sysu.edu.cn

Abstract. With the development of the Internet, the content types of
the network traffic become more and more diverse, including video, news,
music, image and so on. Traffic identification plays an important role in
network management, security defense and performance optimization.
Traditionally, the network traffic analysis focuses on the protocol identification and application classification, which has been well studied in
the past two decades. However, as a large number of existing general
protocols and legal applications can be abused to hide and transmit the
data of different content types, illegal content may penetrate the traffic
analysis system, and lead to inefficient network management and cause
potential risks for internal networks. Different from the traditional work
on the identification of the protocols or applications, in this paper, we
propose a new method for recognizing the content types for the network
traffic. The proposed method is based on two technologies including the
wavelet transform and CNN. The wavelet transform is exploited to process the time-frequency signals of the observed network traffic that is
further classified by the CNN. Experiment results are presented to validate the performance of the proposed scheme.

Keywords: Content recognition · Network traffic ·
Wavelet transform · CNN

1 Introduction

Network traffic analysis is generally regarded as the classification of network
traffic or the identification of network application in the past few decades. This
area is fundamental to modern network management, security systems and the
environments for cloud computing [1].

To handle network traffic classification or identification, several traditional
methods have been applied including the port-based predication method and the

---

Supported by the Natural Science Foundation of Guangdong Province, China (No.
2018A030313303).

X. Chen et al. (Eds.): ML4CS 2019, LNCS 11806, pp. 224–238, 2019.
https://doi.org/10.1007/978-3-030-30619-9_16

payload-based prediction method. The port-based method exploits the relationship between the network application and the transport-layer ports registered at Internet Assigned Numbers Authority (IANA). Although this method is efficient and simple, it becomes more and more inaccurate recently due to the dynamic ports applied by more applications, and at the same time, this method is exposed to the risk of being maliciously exploited by criminals. The payload-based methods which are also known as Deep Packet Inspection (DPI) solve the risk to some extent. These methods first extract information from the packets of the network traffic, including port, IP address and the information of the application layer, and then the applications or protocols can be identified by the signatures in the payload [2]. However, the methods require the upgrade of application signatures over time, and cannot be used in the classification of encrypted applications. These problems hinder the further applying of the payload-based method. Due to the limitation of the port-based and payload-based methods, the statistics-based methods attract more attention, which use the statistical information of packets to identify applications [3]. However, the success of the statistics-based method highly depends on the handcrafted features driven by the domain-expert. The analyses of network traffic have been promoted by these work greatly. But there are also some problems expected to be solved. For example, most previous studies assume that one type of services or content is only related to one application or protocol. Starting from this assumption, if the applications or protocols are identified, the content or service can be identified. But unfortunately the assumption is not always true at all time in reality, the reason is that the information is encapsulated for delivery in modern network. That means different types of content or services may be delivered through the same application or protocol. For instance, in the Web, the HTTP or HTTPs can be used to deliver many different types of content or services, such as video, image, music, news and so on. And many applications can accept or deliver different types of content or services. Obviously, only identifying the application or protocol for the network traffic is not enough for more efficient network management and enhancing network security.

To tackle this potential risk and provide another perspective for network management, instead of studying the identification of applications and protocols, we propose a new method to recognize the types of the content or services in this paper. The proposed method is inspired by the different time-varying characteristics for the different network traffic of different content types. More specifically the content type of the traffic impacts the inherent mode and attributes of the traffic to some extent, therefore, some properties of the unobservable content can be reflected by the time-varying characteristics of the traffic. Based on the above ideas, we propose to integrate the Wavelet transform [4] and the CNN to identifying the content type of the network traffic. The wavelet has been applied in many areas requiring signal processing successfully [5,6]. In their work, the wavelet is exploited to extract the feature from the analysed signal, and features are utilized for classification or identification. These methods use the wavelet to detect the changes in the spectral components of the corresponding signals and extract the features. In the field of signal processing, the Fourier transform (FT) is widely applied. However, it is known that the Fourier transform is not suitable for extracting both time domain and frequency domain features simultaneously. In addition, the FT is better at analyzing stationary signals, but the signals above are generally nonstationary. These signals mentioned above generally consist of brief high-frequency components closely spaced in time, accompanied by long lasting, low-frequency components closely spaced in frequency. The wavelet methods are considered more appropriate for analyzing such signals than the FT. As for the network traffic, obviously the traffic is usually nonstationary. In our method, we preprocess the network traffic, and generate the virtual signal corresponding to the traffic. Then the virtual signals are processed by the wavelet transform to extract time-frequency information. Finally, the CNN is applied to grasp the relationship between the time-frequency information obtained by processing the time-varying traffic, so we can identify the content types of the network traffic.

The rest of the paper is organized as follows. Related works are reviewed in Sect. 2. In Sect. 3 the rationale and implementation of our method are presented. Section 4 presents the experiments and the result. Finally, Sect. 5 concludes the paper.

2   Related Work

In the past several decades, there are many methods proposed to deal with the internet traffic classification, including port-based methods, payload-based methods and statistics-based methods [7]. The port-based methods become inaccurate gradually. There are several reasons, first of all, lots of applications begin to use the same specific protocols, such as HTTP which is used by many types of traffic, the next is that more and more applications start to avoid using well known ports along with the use of dynamic ports [8]. The payload-based methods well known as DPI also attract many researchers' attention [9]. The sticking points of these methods are the application signature and the packet payload. Bujlow et al. [9], the author indicates that DPI is traditionally regarded as the most accurate technique for the network traffic classification, and they compare six DPI-based tools for different scenes. The HTTP application traffic produced by the Web is identified for the hybrid HTTP/non-HTTP traffic, and the information of HTTP header like content-type is exploited to identify applications [10]. The payload information is also used in [11] to identify the content types, including Text, Picture, Audio, Video, Compressed and so on. The method does not use the port number, but it has to resort to the payload of any packet of the traffic. So it is also faced with some trouble. For example, the payload methods cannot be applied to the identification of encrypted traffic. Furthermore, because the method has to exploit the information in the payload, privacy issues cannot be ignored [12].

The statistics-based methods are generally used in conjunction with Machine Learning algorithms. These methods exploit packet and flow level characteristics, which also extract a vector of features to describe the flow. Moore et al. [8]

indicate that the accuracy of the traditional method based on flow classification is low. They use a Naive Bayesian estimator to classify flows, more specifically, the training data used in their method is manually classified according to the content of the traffic, and then the labeled feature vectors can be input into a supervised Naive Bayes classifier. The Bayesian classifier they used is improved. Combining with the kernel density estimation theory, they break the Gaussian assumption, and with the help of Fast Correlation-Based Filter (FCBF) [13], the dimensionality of the features is reduced. Zhang and Chen [14] combine K-means with Random Forest to tackle the problem of zero-day applications with sufficient accuracy. Logistic regression is used to classify the network traffic in [15], and they try to use a non-convex Capped-$\ell 1, \ell 1$ as the regularizer to learn a set of shared features in traffic data. In order to handle the problem of unknown applications, a bag-of-words is introduced to represent the content of clusters which is built by the statistics-based features in [16], Based on their payload content, similar traffic clusters are aggregated by the latent semantic analysis. Wang et al. [17] suggest that the quality for only applying clustering algorithms such as K-means and EM for the task is far from satisfaction. Therefore, more researchers begin to focus on combining unlabeled traffic with labeled traffic or correction information. Kumar et al. [18] propose a new method based on multiple trained cluster models. This method is a semi-supervised clustering based on multi-training clustering models. They use multiple sets of the traffic attributes to train many models simultaneously, and then select a group of selection strategies for classification considering all the output of each model. In order to improve the performance for the small size of training data, Zhang et al. [19] propose a semi-supervised framework incorporating correlated information into the classification process through the bag-of-flow model.

Recently, some approaches based on deep learning (DL) have appeared. Shi et al. [20] focus on choosing the optimal and the most steady features for the traffic classification. This approach is based on deep learning (DL) and feature selection. With the help of deep learning, the high dimension and non-uniformity of the flow can be well handled. Wang et al. [12] used a CNN-based representation method to identify malicious traffic. Representation learning methods make it possible to learn features automatically from the raw data. It can help solve the problem of extracting features manually. The method takes each byte of the binary traffic file as a pixel image, and then inputs the data into CNN for classification. Lotfollahi et al. [21] propose applying Deep Packet scheme to describe and identify network traffic. This method uses deep learning architecture, such as Auto-encoders which is a widely used in feature extracting and 1D-CNN which can catch the relationships of the adjacent traffic bytes. This approach can not only identify unencrypted network traffic but also encrypted traffic. Lopez-Martin et al. [22] propose a method to classify network traffic by combining RNN and CNN. They take advantage of features extracted from the packet in the flow life time, and then a time series of the feature vectors is built for each flow. After labeling each flow, the data can be learned. They use LSTM which is a variant model of RNN and easier to train. They view the time series of the feature vectors as images, the data preprocessed by the CNNs can be input into the LSTM. They discuss the architecture obtained by combining RNN and CNN and the impact of the packets studied in the flow on the result. The method based on deep learning (DL) is also used for the mobile encrypted traffic classification in [23]. They compare different DL techniques in the mobile traffic classification scenario, from the viewpoint of Traffic view, Types of Input data, DL architecture, and the set of performance measures.

Overall, the above studies have improved the performance of the network traffic classification, but the problems still exist. The statistics-based methods identify the network traffic according to the statistic information extracted from the traffic. However the information related to the time characteristics is generally ignored, so do some of existing methods based on DL, and the computational complexity of some DL methods is high. Moreover, the content types of the network traffic are rarely researched. Those may prevent the further improvement in performance for the network traffic classification and network management. In this paper, we combine the Wavelet transform with the CNN to handle the problem for the identification of content types.

3   Proposed Method

3.1   Rationale

In this section, we introduce the proposed scheme used in this paper. During the data transmission, the content type of communication data is one of the important factors driving and determining the mode of network transmissions and characteristics of network traffic. Therefore, the characteristics of the network traffic can reversely reveal the communication data of the specific content type. From the perspective of the network layer (IP layer), communication data of different content types present different transferring characteristics. And the transferring characteristics are embodied in the IP traffic. If the different content type data can be represented by the transferring characteristics of the IP traffic, the content type of the traffic can be identified by identifying the IP traffic. Since the collected data packets of IP traffic have the nature of the time series and time series can be regarded as a virtual signal triggered by the data of the traffic, so we intend to extract features of the triggered virtual signal and distinguish the IP traffic by exploiting the signal processing method. In the processing, we extract frequency-domain features of the signal and preserve the time-domain features simultaneously. The time-frequency features are exploited to depict the network traffic formed by different content type data. Eventually, the features of signals are grasped with the help of learning algorithms, and the virtual signal obtained from the unknown content type can be identified.

As shown in Fig. 1, two kinds of square blocks represent the IP packet including the direction information, where the pure black square block indicates the upstream packet and another indicates the downstream packet respectively. The two kinds of packets form the time series of the network traffic. In the preprocessing stage, we construct an abstractly generalized representation of the

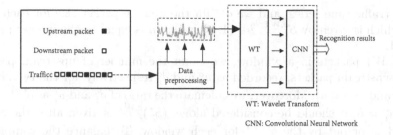

Fig. 1. The proposed classification structure.

IP traffic of a specific content type by processing the original time series with the window. The data processed in different windows triggers various signals. Therefore, the time series processed with the window can be regarded as the process of data triggering signals, and the network traffic of different content types can be classified according to the signals triggered by the data. Generally, to classify or identify signals, we have to process the signals first to obtain the features (frequency-domain features or time-domain features) that can characterize the signals. Traditionally, only the frequency-domain features of the signals are extracted, which results in the loss of the time-domain information. In order to extract the features of the frequency and time domain simultaneously, we exploit the Wavelet transform to process the signal obtained. Compared with the traditional signal processing methods (FT or STFT), the Wavelet transform also has much more advantages in frequency resolution and time resolution. The time-frequency information of the signal processed with the Wavelet transform can well describe the characteristics related with the signal, and we can identify the traffic of the unknown content according to the time-frequency information of the signal obtained. Considering that the representation of the time-frequency information is represented by the wavelet coefficients and the adjacent coefficients are correlated, that promotes us to think of the time-frequency information as image information and to identify signals by image recognition methods. Therefore, we intend to exploit the convolutional neural network (CNN) to identify the image obtained from the time-frequency information to achieve signal recognition. The main idea behind this approach is that data of different content types trigger different signals with various signal characteristics. Therefore, the characteristics of signals can be grasped by learning algorithms, and the content type of invisible instance can be correctly identified.

3.2 Formulation

On the basis of the above considerations, we can set $C = \{1,...,|C|\}$ as the content type of the network traffic captured from the Internet. We also set $S^c = \{S_1^c, \ldots, S_{N_c}^c\}$ as the network traffic packet size time series of the type $c \in C$ traffic, and N_c is the number of packets for type c. The direction of the packet is given by D^c. And we set a non-overlapping window $W1$ to preprocess the IP traffic time series, and we obtain the average packet size for each window, which is given by $S_i^{c,W1}$, $i \in (1, n)$, where n is equal to the integer part of $N_c/W1$.

For $W1$ packets in a window, we count the number of upstream packets and downstream packets, recorded as u_i^c and d_i^c respectively, for the type $c \in C$ traffic, and $i \in (1, n)$. Moreover, we calculate the ratio of d_i^c and u_i^c as $q_i^{c,W1}$, and when $u_i^c = 0$, it should be considered alone. $(S^*)_i^{c,W1}$ is given after the $S_i^{c,W1}$ zoomed in or out by the $q_i^{c,W1}$ for each window. To balance the complexity and performance, another window $W2$ is set to obtain the sub-sequence of the full traffic time series. Then $(S^*)_{W2}^{c,W1}$ can be got. For the data in $W2$, they trigger various signals, and $(S^*)_{W2}^{c,W1}$ can be input into the CWT as a signal. The coefficients of the scale M and time s can be obtained and given by

$$W_{S_*}^{\psi}(\tau, M) = \frac{1}{\sqrt{|M|}} \int (S^*)_{W2}^{c,W1} \psi^* \left(\frac{s-\tau}{M} \right) ds \qquad (1)$$

Finally, the wavelet coefficient matrixes for the type c network traffic can be represented by $(M \times W2)^c$.

3.3　Algorithms

Considering a specific traffic with the content type c, the direction of the packet is given by

$$D^c = \begin{cases} 1 \\ -1 \end{cases} \qquad (2)$$

where if the network traffic packet is upstream, we set $D^c = 1$, and if downstream, we set $D^c = -1$. The average packet size for the i-th window and type c is given by

$$S_i^{c,W1} = \frac{\sum_{k=i*W1+1}^{(i+1)*W1} S_k^c}{W1}, \quad i \in (1, n), \quad c \in C \qquad (3)$$

and we can obtain $S^{c,W1} = \{S_1^{c,W1}, \ldots, S_n^{c,W1}\}$, where n is equal to the integer part of $N_c/W1$. The ratio of u_i^c and d_i^c is given by

$$q_i^{c,W1} = \begin{cases} \frac{d_i^c}{u_i^c}, \, for \quad u_i^c \neq 0. \\ d_i^c, \, for \quad u_i^c = 0. \end{cases}, \quad i \in (1, n), \quad c \in C \qquad (4)$$

when $u_i^c = 0$, we set $q_i^{c,W1} = d_i^c$, which can describe the upstream and downstream situation in the window approximately. After that, we obtain $Q^{c,W1} = \{q_1^{c,W1}, \ldots, q_n^{c,W1}\}$. Finally, we let

$$(S^*)_i^{c,W1} = S_i^{c,W1} \times q_i^{c,W1}, \quad i \in (1, n), \quad c \in C \qquad (5)$$

And we get the time series $(S^*)^{c,W1} = \{(S^*)_1^{c,W1}, \ldots, (S^*)_n^{c,W1}\}$, which can also be regarded as the time series signal and the time series obtained is processed by the Wavelet transform. As mentioned before, for the full network traffic, n is relatively big, which makes it hard to learn the parameters. Thus we intend to consider the sub-sequence of the time series in order to achieve the balance between the complexity and performance without losing much accuracy. So we set another overlapping window $W2$ to deal with $(S^*)^{c,W1}$. The moving step of the window is 2. Then, the sub-sequence is input into the CWT with the Biorthogonal basic function. The coefficient matrix $P^c = (M \times W2)^c$ for type c can be obtained as

$$
P^c = \begin{bmatrix} W_{S^*}^\psi(\tau, M)_{1,1}^c & W_{S^*}^\psi(\tau, M)_{1,2}^c & \cdots & W_{S^*}^\psi(\tau, M)_{1,W2}^c \\ W_{S^*}^\psi(\tau, M)_{2,1}^c & W_{S^*}^\psi(\tau, M)_{2,2}^c & \cdots & W_{S^*}^\psi(\tau, M)_{2,W2}^c \\ \vdots & \vdots & \ddots & \vdots \\ W_{S^*}^\psi(\tau, M)_{M,1}^c & W_{S^*}^\psi(\tau, M)_{1,2}^c & \cdots & W_{S^*}^\psi(\tau, M)_{M,W2}^c \end{bmatrix} \tag{6}
$$

where the M and $W2$ is the scale and the window applied. After the Wavelet transform under M scale, many $M \times W2$ matrixes about the wavelet coefficients are obtained. The correlation of the adjacent wavelet coefficients inspires us to regard the matrixes as images. Therefore, the matrixes obtained above are normalized and given by

$$
P_{j,k}^c = \left(\frac{W_{S^*}^\psi(\tau, M)_{j,k}^c - min(W_{S^*}^\psi(\tau, M)_{j,:}^c)}{max(W_{S^*}^\psi(\tau, M)_{j,:}^c)) - min(W_{S^*}^\psi(\tau, M)_{j,:}^c)} \right)_{M \times W2} , c \in C \tag{7}
$$

and $j \in (1, M), k \in (1, W2)$. Finally, the matrixes are set to $0\tilde{\ }255$ by $P_c^{c,k} = P^{c,k} \times 255$. According to our analyses in Sect. 3.1, the final matrixes can be regarded as the gray images. Then they can be identified by the CNN, which has been applied in image recognition maturely.

3.4   Implementation

The proposed method can be applied in many network locations in reality, such as backbone links, and server-side. The framework of the implementation is shown in Fig. 2 in detail. It can be described in three parts: data preprocessing, Wavelet transform, training and recognition.

Firstly, from the network traffic, we extract the IP packet size and obtain the IP traffic time series of packet size. Then the data preprocessing module divides the time series with the fixed non-overlapping window size and step. The average packet size of the window is further zoomed in and out with $q_i^{c,W1}$. The time series $(S^*)^{c,W1}$ can be obtained, and then it is divided with fixed window size $W2$ and step 2. After that, the sub time series which can be seen as a virtual signal can be obtained, the Wavelet transform is applied to the signal, which helps us get the time-frequency information. After normalizing, the image obtained is mapped to the content type, and all images of each content type are labeled.

Secondly, as long as the labeled training dataset is prepared, they are applied to train the CNN. The CNN is trained with the SGD, which makes the training

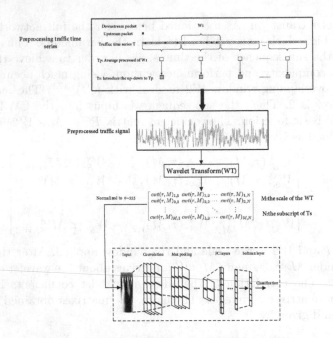

Fig. 2. The framework for implementation.

procedure converge faster and better. The CNN includes two convolutional layers and two pooling layers, and the output of the last pooling layer is input into Full-connection layer. Finally the softmax layer is combined with layers above.

Thirdly, after the model has been trained, the parameters of CNN have been learned. The testing dataset obtained after the data preprocessing is further classified by the CNN.

4 Experiment

We conduct experiments to evaluate the performance of the proposed method based on the real dataset of the network traffic.

4.1 Dataset Description

The network traffic used in this experiment is generated by the Web based on HTTP or HTTPs. It is made up with six most popular content types shown in Table 1, including video, image, music, news, trading, and live video traffic. The video traffic is captured from the online movie. The images come from the browsing images process on the Web. The music consists of the playing of many songs. The news is collected when we read the news online. The trading is captured when browsing the information of products. Different from the video, the live video traffic is the most popular content type recently, and it comes from the real-time live broadcast room online. In the following experiment, we consider both directions of the traffic. And we filter out those packets with the same 3-tuple (server IP address, Sever port, Protocol) that are relatively unrelated with the traffic. For each training dataset and testing dataset, we disrupt them when we train or test the model. All the experiment run on a general computer configured with Intel Core i7 CPU at 3.60 GHz and 32G RAM.

Table 1. Composition of the dataset

Content types	Number of packets
Video	20646
Image	192879
Music	2015891
News	44372
Trading	567507
Live video	296122

4.2 The Signal Feature

For packets of the window $W1$, we consider the packet size and the number of upstream and downstream packets. We do not apply more information, because the information can achieve the desired recognition performance. However, we focus on the selection of the window W1 and W2. The best combination of $W1$ and $W2$ is determined in this Section.

In the data preprocessing part, we exploit the Wavelet transform to process $(S^*)^{c,W1}$ which are regarded as virtual signals. With the help of signal processing method, the time-frequency information of signals is obtained simultaneously, which helps correlate the signals with the content types. Other features of the packets may be studied in future work to further improve the performance.

4.3 Evaluation Metrics

We apply Accuracy and Kappa coefficient to evaluate the overall performance of a classifier, and use the Precision and Recall to evaluate the performance of each class traffic. The Kappa coefficient is statistic which measures the inter-rater agreement for categories. The definitions of the above metrics are shown in Eqs. (8)–(11).

$$Accuracy = \frac{\sum_{c=1}^{|C|} TP_c}{\sum_{c=1}^{|C|} (TP_c + FN_c)} \tag{8}$$

$$Precision_c = \frac{TP_c}{TP_c + FP_c} \tag{9}$$

$$Recall_c = \frac{TP_c}{TP_c + FN_c} \tag{10}$$

$$Kappa = \frac{Accuracy - p_e}{1 - p_e} \tag{11}$$

where p_e is given by $p_e = (\sum_{c=1}^{|C|} a_c \times b_c)/(|C| \times |C|)$, and a_c represents the number of real samples of the c-th class, b_c represents the number of samples belonging to the c-th class.

4.4   Parameters Configuration

In addition to the CNN parameter learned, there are some parameters that cannot be obtained by learning, such as the window $W1$ and $W2$. Here we analyze the value via experiments. In Table 2, we show the classification accuracy of CNN for various parameter combinations of $(W1, W2)$. Five experiments conducted in each case are averaged.

Table 2. The Accuracy for different combination of $W1$ and $W2$

(%)	W1 = 1	W1 = 4	W1 = 8	W1 = 12	W1 = 16
W2 = 100	67.8	76.7	84.4	86.6	87.4
W2 = 200	89.3	91.8	91	91.8	90.9
W2 = 300	91.7	95.6	92.5	96.6	93.4
W2 = 400	89.3	97.1	94.8	94	97.3
W2 = 500	94.4	97.4	93.2	95.6	99.5

The result shows that the size of window $W1$ and $W2$ may be helpful for making the classification accuracy better. Figure 3 indicates the basics of our selection of $W1$ and $W2$. Although the best selection is to set $W1 = 16$ and $W2 = 500$, the gray image size is 100×500 and the computing complexity is very high. From Fig. 3(a), we can see that increasing $W1$ form 1 to 4 improves the performance a lot, and from Fig. 3(b), we see that increasing $W2$ form 100 to 300 also makes the result better.

In order to study the impact of $W1$ and $W2$ on the performance, we calculate the accuracy increment in consideration of the windows. In Table 2, we obtain the Accuracy matrix. Therefore, the accuracy increment along with $W1$ for each $W2$ and the accuracy increment along with $W2$ for each $W1$ are given as follows:

$$Increment_{W1} = \frac{Accuracy_{i(j+1)} - Accuracy_{ij}}{4 \times j}, \quad i \in (1,5), \quad j \in (1,4) \tag{12}$$

$$Increment_{W2} = \frac{Accuracy_{(i+1)j} - Accuracy_{ij}}{i+1}, \quad i \in (1,4), \quad j \in (1,5) \tag{13}$$

where i represents the selection of $W2$, and j represents the selection of $W1$, e.g. $i = 1$ and $j = 1$ represent $W2 = 100$ and $W1 = 1$, and so on. In Fig. 5, we give the trend of the accuracy increment for each case. Obviously, we can see that setting $W1 = 4$ leads to surprising performance improvement in Fig. 5(a). In Fig. 5(b), setting $W2 = 200$ or $W2 = 300$ both improve the performance, but the performance under $W2 = 200$ is not satisfactory.

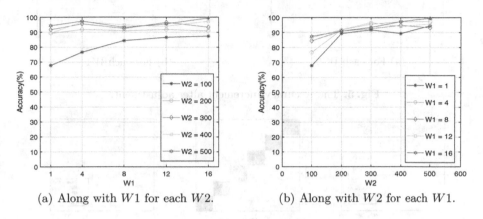

(a) Along with $W1$ for each $W2$.   (b) Along with $W2$ for each $W1$.

Fig. 3. The Accuracy change.

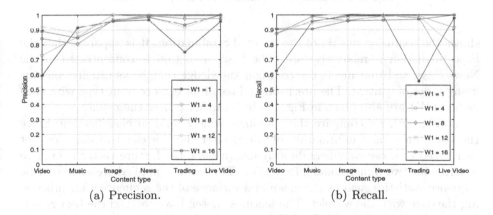

(a) Precision.   (b) Recall.

Fig. 4. The Precision and Recall for each content type with $W2 = 300$.

Therefore, to balance the data size required, complexity and performance, we let $W1 = 4$ and $W2 = 300$. In that scenario, we get a better result without losing too much accuracy. In Fig. 6(a), we also evaluate the Kappa coefficient. When we set $W1 = 4$ and $W2 = 300$, the Kappa coefficient is 0.943, where we can judge that the result of the classification is almost perfect agreement [24]. Figure. 6(b)

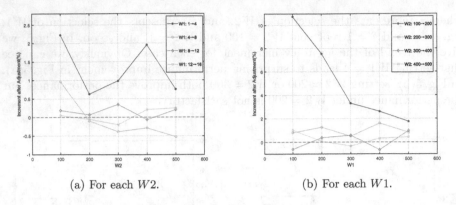

(a) For each $W2$.   (b) For each $W1$.

Fig. 5. The Accuracy increment after adjustment.

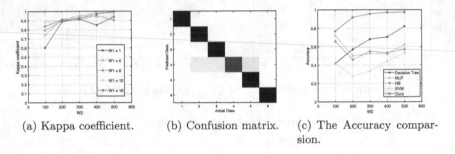

(a) Kappa coefficient.   (b) Confusion matrix.   (c) The Accuracy comparison.

Fig. 6. Comprehensive evaluation of the performance.

shows the confusion matrix of the selected combination. It is apparent that the false prediction is relatively rare. The false prediction is concentrated in the News class, and that meets the common knowledge that News usually contains many types of content. The precision and recall for each content type with each value of $W1$ are also given in Fig. 4, which further proves the result.

In Fig. 6(c), we compare the classifiers widely used in classification. Since the two-dimensional information obtained after the Wavelet transform cannot be applied to those classifiers directly except ours, the feature vector is built to describe the two-dimensional information. The features applied are some specific sequence statistics such as the mean and variance of the sequence after processing the data with the wavelet. The features chosen have reached the best result. The result shows that: (i) the CNN can better handle the sequence after processing the data with the wavelet. (ii) the CNN classifier performs more stable performance than others, which promotes us to do further researches using this scheme.

5 Conclusion

In this paper, we propose a new method to recognize the types of content for the network traffic. We regard the packets of the network traffic as the signal, which makes the method almost unrelated with the TCP port number and the protocol of the application layer. That suggests that the method can be applied to the encrypted and unencrypted traffic at the same moment. In our work, we introduce the Wavelet transform to process the network traffic signal, which can reserve the characteristics of the time-varying signal. The time-frequency information of the signal can be obtained simultaneously. Considering the correlation of the adjacent elements' information obtained from the traffic, we decide to exploit the CNN to learn the relationship of the time-frequency information. The time-frequency information matrixes are regarded as the gray images, which can be input into the CNN experting in image recognition. The accuracy of multi-classification classifier reaches 95.8% fully considering the data size and complexity. The Kappa coefficient is 0.943, which shows the result of the classification is almost a perfect agreement. Although, the previous work has proved the feasibility of the proposed method, we notice that there exist some disadvantages, e.g. the data size required. For further research, we intend to introduce more information of the packet such as the packet inter-arrival time, which allows us to use multiple channels CNN for making up for the disadvantages.

References

1. Wang, Y., Xiang, Y., Zhang, J., Zhou, W., Xie, B.: Internet traffic clustering with side information. J. Comput. Syst. Sci. **80**(5), 1021–1036 (2014)
2. Ertam, F., Avci, E.: Classification with intelligent systems for internet traffic in enterprise networks. Int. J. Comput. Commun. Instrum. Engg. (IJCCIE) **3** (2016). ISSN 2349-1469
3. Nguyen, T.T.T., Armitage, G., Branch, P., Zander, S.: Timely and continuous machine-learning-based classification for interactive IP traffic. IEEE/ACM Trans. Network. **20**(6), 1880–1894 (2012)
4. Daubechies, I.: The wavelet transform, time-frequency localization and signal analysis. IEEE Trans. Inf. Theory **36**(5), 961–1005 (1990)
5. Qian, K., Ren, Z., Pandit, V., Yang, Z., Zhang, Z., Schuller, B.: Wavelets revisited for the classification of acoustic scenes. In: Proceedings of the DCASE Workshop, Munich, Germany, pp. 108–112 (2017)
6. Khushaba, R.N., Kodagoda, S., Lal, S., Dissanayake, G.: Driver drowsiness classification using fuzzy wavelet-packet-based feature-extraction algorithm. IEEE Trans. Biomed. Eng. **58**(1), 121–131 (2011)
7. Sun, G., Liang, L., Chen, T., Xiao, F., Lang, F.: Network traffic classification based on transfer learning. Comput. Electr. Eng. **69**, 920–927 (2018)
8. Moore, A.W., Zuev, D.: Internet traffic classification using Bayesian analysis techniques. In: ACM SIGMETRICS Performance Evaluation Review, Vol. 33, pp. 50–60. ACM (2005)
9. Bujlow, T., Carela-Español, V., Barlet-Ros, P.: Independent comparison of popular DPI tools for traffic classification. Comput. Netw. **76**, 75–89 (2015)

10. Bujlow, T., Riaz, T., Pedersen, J.M.: Classification of HTTP traffic based on C5.0 machine learning algorithm. In: 2012 IEEE Symposium on Computers and Communications (ISCC), pp. 000882–000887. IEEE (2012)
11. Wang, Y., Zhang, Z., Guo, L.: Traffic classification beyond application level: identifying content types from network traces. In: Proceedings of the 2011 ACM Symposium on Applied Computing, pp. 540–541. ACM (2011)
12. Wang, Y., An, J., Huang, W.: Using CNN-based representation learning method for malicious traffic identification. In: 2018 IEEE/ACIS 17th International Conference on Computer and Information Science (ICIS), pp. 400–404. IEEE (2018)
13. Yu, L., Liu, H.: Feature selection for high-dimensional data: a fast correlation-based filter solution. In: Proceedings of the 20th International Conference on Machine Learning (ICML 2003), pp. 856–863 (2003)
14. Zhang, J., Chen, X., Xiang, Y., Zhou, W., Jie, W.: Robust network traffic classification. IEEE/ACM Trans. Netw. (TON) 23(4), 1257–1270 (2015)
15. Li, D., Guyu, H., Wang, Y., Pan, Z.: Network traffic classification via non-convex multi-task feature learning. Neurocomputing 152, 322–332 (2015)
16. Zhang, J., Xiang, Y., Zhou, W., Wang, Y.: Unsupervised traffic classification using flow statistical properties and IP packet payload. J. Comput. Syst. Sci. 79(5), 573–585 (2013)
17. Wang, Y., Xiang, Y., Zhang, J., Zhou, W., Wei, G., Yang, L.T.: Internet traffic classification using constrained clustering. IEEE Trans. Parallel Distrib. Syst. 25(11), 2932–2943 (2014)
18. Kumar, A., Kim, J., Suh, S.C., Choi, G.: Incorporating multiple cluster models for network traffic classification. In: 2015 IEEE 40th Conference on Local Computer Networks (LCN), pp. 185–188. IEEE (2015)
19. Zhang, J., Xiang, Y., Wang, Yu., Zhou, W., Xiang, Y., Guan, Y.: Network traffic classification using correlation information. IEEE Trans. Parallel Distrib. Syst. 24(1), 104–117 (2013)
20. Shi, H., Li, H., Zhang, D., Cheng, C., Cao, X.: An efficient feature generation approach based on deep learning and feature selection techniques for traffic classification. Comput. Netw. 132, 81–98 (2018)
21. Lotfollahi, M., Zade, R.S.H., Siavoshani, M.J., Saberian, M.: Deep packet: a novel approach for encrypted traffic classification using deep learning. arXiv preprint arXiv:1709.02656 (2017)
22. Lopez-Martin, M., Carro, B., Sanchez-Esguevillas, A., Lloret, J.: Network traffic classifier with convolutional and recurrent neural networks for internet of things. IEEE Access 5, 18042–18050 (2017)
23. Aceto, G., Ciuonzo, D., Montieri, A., Pescapé, A.: Mobile encrypted traffic classification using deep learning. In: 2018 Network Traffic Measurement and Analysis Conference (TMA), pp. 1–8. IEEE (2018)
24. Landis, J.R., Koch, G.G.: The measurement of observer agreement for categorical data. Biometrics 33(1), 159–174 (1977)

Compositional Information Flow Verification for Inter Application Communications in Android System

Xue Rao[(✉)], Ning Xi[(✉)], Jing Lv[(✉)], and Pengbin Feng[(✉)]

Xidian University, Xi'an, China
{xrao,lvj}@stu.xidian.edu.cn, nxi@xidian.edu.cn, pbfeng@outlook.com

Abstract. Inter-component communication (ICC) is commonly used in Android for information exchange among different components/apps. However, it also brings severe challenges to information flow security. When data is transferred and processed, the diversity of different security mechanisms in various apps make data more vulnerable to leakage. Although there are several analysis approaches on security verification on inter-component information flow, repetitive verification on the same component during complex interactions increases the overhead, which would affect task execution efficiency and consume more energy. Therefore, we propose a compositional information flow security verification approach, which improves efficiency by separating the intra-app and inter-app analysis and verification process. The experiment and analysis show that our method is more effective than traditional global approaches.

Keywords: Android system · Information flow model ·
Inter-Component Communication · Compositional verification

1 Introduction

The current android operating system allows users to run many applications developed by third-party independent developers, which are available in android app markets. In addition, multiple applications can communicate and exchange data by inter-component communication (ICC). ICC is the key mechanism of communication between applications in android, which enriches the functions of android applications, such as WeChat, which can access health data for ranking. Unfortunately, while ICC enhances user functionality, it can be exploited by malicious software to threaten user privacy. Indeed, researchers have shown that android apps frequently collect and use users' private data without their prior consent [17].

When applications communicate with each other, it is more prone to data leakage [1,3]. Existing information flow analysis methods mainly include static analysis, dynamic analysis and machine learning analysis. In addition, there are

© Springer Nature Switzerland AG 2019
X. Chen et al. (Eds.): ML4CS 2019, LNCS 11806, pp. 239–252, 2019.
https://doi.org/10.1007/978-3-030-30619-9_17

some methods that combine the previous methods, such as hybrid (combining dynamic and static) analysis methods.

The static analysis method decompile the .APK file of each app, and then perform static taint analysis on the decompiled code to find out the data leakage path, such as flowDroid [4], IIFDroid [8], DroidSate [10], DroidGuard [14] and so on. They can analyze all the application's resources or codes to achieve high coverage on code. However, they lack an actual execution path and face critical challenges in the presence of code obfuscation [22], loading dynamic code [15], reflection calls [23], native code [24], and multithreading issues. The dynamic analysis method detects the privacy leakage within an application by executing the application in a real or virtual device, such as Mobile-sandbox [16], Taint-Droid [6] and ScanDroid [12]. They can observe actual execution trace and tackle code obfuscation and dynamic code loading. However, code coverage is limited by dynamic analysis methods because it cannot execute all possible traces in one time. As a result, the private data leakage vulnerabilities which exist in the uncovered codes will be missed. Moreover, current malware can recognize dynamic monitors as the analyzed app executes, causing the app to pose as a benign program in these situations [25]. In order to solve the challenges of static analysis and dynamic analysis, some hybrid solutions are proposed. For example, HybriDroid [9] present a novel hybrid approach aims to automatically find privacy leakages in a given app set.

In addition, in recent years, with the development of artificial intelligence algorithms, it has become a trend to combine information flow analysis with artificial intelligence. Machine learning is a branch of artificial intelligence mainly treating information flow analysis as a classification problem. By analyzing the differences in features between benign applications and malicious applications, the features with statistical differences are selected, and then trained to classify [26–31]. In the feature extraction stage, static analysis method is generally used to extract features. [32] makes use of the similarity analysis of android application features of multiple dimensions to obtain the relevant rules of multiple dimensions of android application. [33] automatically learns security/privacy-related behaviors by analyzing user comments based on machine learning. In order to extract API data dependencies, [34] conducts context-sensitive, flow-sensitive and inter-process data flow analysis. [35] proposes a semantic-based feature extraction and detection method for malicious code, which extracts the key behaviors of malicious code and the dependencies between behaviors. The advantages of machine learning analysis are low implementation overhead and simple operation. The disadvantage is that it is influenced by the difference of training applications and the selection of characteristics. Besides, the current machine learning approach does not support analysis of inter-apps.

Most above analysis methods can be used for the analysis on the information flow within a single component or application. In addition, many researches are proposed for information flow analysis on the inter-communication between different components [2,7,11,18,19]. IccTA [2] combines multiple applications into one and performs intra-app analysis on the combined one. Covert [7] is a tool for analyzing vulnerabilities across applications that allows incremental analysis of applications while they are being installed, updated, or deleted. MR-Droid [19] empirically assesses ICC risks and tests for high-risk pairs. However, most of these approaches works in a global way, in which they analyze the flows across multiple components by modeling them as one combined entity. In other words, the whole model must be remodeled even if there is a little change on one component. And it would cost many efforts but with little benefits. Besides, flows in the unchanged component or application will be reverified during the analysis, which causes the additional verification load on mobile devices.

In order to reduce the overhead of verifying compositional information flow security, this paper presents a compositional approach to automatically verify security of information flow across multiple components or applications. This paper presents the following original contributions:

(1) We define a formal model on individual application and sequential composite applications combined by inter-component communication for information flow analysis.
(2) We make the formal security constraints on information flow for each participant across multiple applications.
(3) We propose a compositional information flow verification approaches for secure inter-app communication among applications in android.

The rest of the paper is structured as follows. Section 2 presents the motivation examples for this study. Sections 3 and 4 defines the formal models and propose a security theorem for compositional information flow which verify with the verification framework in Sect. 5. Section 6 evaluates our methodology and Sect. 7 is conclusion.

2   Motivating Example

To illustrate our approach, we provide a concrete example of information transmission among different android's apps through Inter-Component Communication (ICC). Android provides a flexible application level message known as Intent for communications between components. The example includes three apps. App_1 contains $GetDataActivity$ which obtains the user's sensitive data such as phone number, e-health record and so on, which is shown in LIST1. App_2 contains $ForwardActivity$, which receives sensitive data (user's movement steps) from intent message $MSteps$ and forwarding it to App_3 by intent message $Fsteps1$. App_2 is shown in LIST2. App_3 contains $ReceiveDataActivity$ which is responsible for receiving intent message and sends the data to a remote server which can exploit it at will.

LIST 1 : App_1: send an intent to transmit data

```
1   public class GetDataActivity extends AppCompatActivity {
2       protected void onCreate(Bundle savedInstanceState) {
3           ...
```

```
4          sp = getSharedPreferences("User", Context.MODE_WORLD_READABLE);
5             SharedPreferences.Editor edit = sp.edit();
6             edit.putString("Value",meditText1.getText().toString().trim());
7                edit.commit();
8                String value = sp.getString("Value","Null");
9                ...
10               Intent MSteps = new Intent();
11               Bundle bundle = new Bundle();
12                MSteps.setAction("com.example.second");
13                bundle.putString("params3", value);
14               MSteps.putExtra("bundle", bundle);
15               startActivity(MSteps);
16        }
17      }
```

LIST 2:*App₂*: receive an intent and send an intent to transmit data

```
1   public class ForwardActivity extends AppCompatActivity {
2    protected void onCreate(Bundle savedInstanceState) {
3     ...
4     final Intent Rsteps1 = getIntent();//source
5
6     button.setOnClickListener(new View.OnClickListener() {
7       public void onClick(View v) {
8         ...
9             Intent Fsteps1 = new Intent();
10            Bundle bundle1 = new Bundle();
11            Fsteps1.setAction("com.example.three");
12            String value1 = text.getText().toString();
13            bundle1.putString("para",value1);
14           Fsteps1.putExtra("bundle",bundle1);
15            Fsteps1.putExtra("para",value1);
16            startActivity(Fsteps1);//sink
17      });
18    }
```

Listing 3: *App₃*: receives an intent

```
1   public class ThreeActivity extends AppCompatActivity {
2   protected void onCreate(Bundle savedInstanceState) {
3       ...
4          final Intent Rsteps2 =getIntent(); //source
5          Bundle bundle = intent.getBundleExtra("bundle");
6          final String value = bundle.getString("para");
7          text.setText(value);
8          ...
9     }
10   }
```

More specifically, from line 4 to line 9 in LIST 1, *GetDataActivity* edits a e-health record and stores it in SharedPreferences which is a lightweight storage class on the Android platform. From line 10 to line 15, *GetDataActivity* sets the action of Intent, then gets the stored e-health data and subsequently sends it to *ForwardActivity* through an Intent message. The Intent filter which is defined in the Manifest file of *App2* is responsible for receiving this Intent message and handle it. Likewise, *ForwardActivity* gets an Intent and receives users movement step data of the message from *GetDataActivity* (On line 4 in *App2*). From line 9 to 16, *ForwardActivity* sets the type of Intent and sends an Intent message to *ReceiveDataActivity*. In *ReceiveDataActivity*, it gets the Intent message and receives the data.

In this example, if *App3* is malicious software or is monitored by an attacker, the sensitive data in *App1* may be leaked to the attacker even though the information flow is secure in *App1* and *App2*.

3 Android Application Model

In Android system, an application is composed by components which are described in a special file called Manifest. There are four kinds of components, i.e., activity, service, content provider and broadcast receiver. Activities construct user interface of an app. Each app may have multiple activities representing different screens of the application to the user. Services do not have user interface but perform time-consuming tasks in the background. Content providers act analogous to a database and provide access to a constructed set of data. Broadcast receivers listen to global events.

Referring to the android application model described in [7], an app model can be formally defined as follows.

Definition 1. *A model for an android app is a tuple $A_i = <C_i, I_i, IF_i, Sec_i>$ $1 \leq i \leq n$, where*

C_i is a set of components represent as $C_i = \{ c_1, c_2, \ldots, c_m \}$, and each c_j ($j < m$) is a component of A_i. Each component contains a series of methods for executing the required functions. We use M_i to represent the set of methods that used in application A_i.

I_i is a set of event messages called intents that can be used for both intra-and inter-app communications. Here we use $In_{i,j}$ to represent an intent message set from Application A_i to Application A_j where $In_{i,j} \subset I_i$.

IF_i is a set of Intent filters. Each intent filter is attached to a component and responsible for filtering implicit intents.

Sec_i is the set of security properties of all methods in A_i.

Different applications can cooperate with each other to fulfill different user's requirements through ICC. This paper studies a simplified type of inter-application communications, i.e., sequential inter-application communication. And we call these applications as sequential composite applications. Sequential composite applications is composed by a set of applications $A_1, A_2, \ldots, A_n$ which communicates with each other in a sequential way. According to the characteristics of sequential composite application, its model can be defined as follow.

Definition 2. *The composite apps A_c can be represented as a tuple $A_c = <AC, CI, CIF>$. where*

AC is a sequential group of apps in which each app has only one predecessor and one successor.
CI is a collection of all intents using for communication between A_i and A_{i+1}.
CIF is the set of all Intent filters from all the applications used as the entry point for the adjacent application communications.

Based on the above definition of the composite application model, the model of the example in Sect. 2 can be extracted as A_c. $AC = \{App_1, App_2, App_3\}$, where, $App_1 = <\{GetDataActivity\}, \{Msteps\}, \{Interfilters\}>$. Each intent is shown in bold in the code in Sect. 2. *Interfilters* are defined in the corresponding application Manifest file.

4 Secure Information Model for Composite Application in Android

4.1 Security Label Model

As a device for storing and processing data, android phone contains a lot of sensitive information, such as e-health, contacts, and so on. According to the different sensitivity of information, we use multi-level security model to describe the security properties of data.

By referring to [20], security label model can be defined as a lattice $(SL, \geq)$, where SL is a finite set of security levels that is orderly by $\geq$.

We define a function $g : M_i \rightarrow sl$ to represent the security level of each method in application A_i. Based on the security label model, security property in A_i can be represented by the security level on the methods.

4.2 Information Flow in Intra-app

For intra-app information flows, we use static analysis technique [4] to analyze them. In one application's component, there are source methods that are responsible for accessing sensitive data such as phone numbers and sink methods that are responsible for outputting data [5]. During the execution of the application, data are received by different sources, processed by methods in component, and finally outputted by different sinks, which constructs different data prorogation paths. And we can define the information flow within an intra-app as follows.

Definition 3. *The information flow of android's app A_i can be represented as a tuple $flow = <source, sink>$ where, $source, sink \in M_i$.*

Based on the above description, we define $Flow_i = \{<source, sink>| source, sink \in M_i, i \in N\}$ as the set of all flows in A_i.

Combining with the multi-level security model, $sl(source)$ and $sl(sink)$ are used to represent the security levels of sources and sinks. According to the definition of non-interference [13], the security of information flow in a intra-app can be formally defined as follows.

Definition 4. *The information flows in application A_i are secure if it satisfies that for $\forall source, sink \in M_i$, $sl(source) > sl(sink)$, there is no existence of information flow from source to sink, namely $<source, sink> \notin Flow_i$.*

4.3   Secure Information Flow in Composite Applications

Considering sequential group apps $A_1, A_2, \ldots, A_n$, when applications communicates with each other by intents, data are passed from the *sink* method of one component in A_i to the *source* method of component in A_{i+1}, which forms an inter-app information flow across multiple applications. And the following apps $A_j(j > i)$ may leak data despite the information flow in A_i is secure. The Fig. 1 shows the intra and inter flows in our example in Sect. 2.

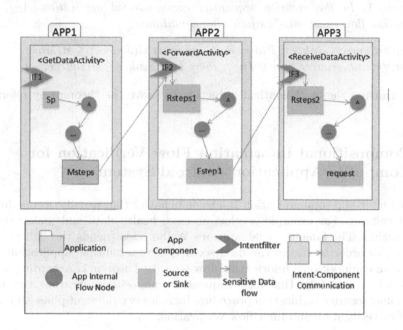

Fig. 1. Composite information flow

For sequential composite application A_C, the definitions of inter-app information flow can be given as follows.

Definition 5. *For $\forall source_i \in M_i$, $\forall sink_j \in M_j$, there is a inter flow $flow_{i,j} = <source_i, sink_j>$ from A_i to A_j, if they satisfy one of the following conditions.*

(1) For $i = j - 1$, there $\exists sink_i \in M_i$, $source_j \in M_j$ that satisfy $<sink_i, source_j> \in In_{i,j}$.

(2) For $i \neq j - 1$, $\exists A_k, 1 < k < j$; $\exists source_k \in M_k, \exists sink_{k+1} \in M_{k+1}$, and they satisfy that $\exists flow_{i,k} = <source_i, sink_k>, \exists flow_{k+1,j} = <source_{k+1}, sink_j>$ and $\exists <sink_k, source_{k+1}> \in In_{k,k+1}$.

According to the above description of the inter-app information flow, we use $Flow_{inter}$ to represent the set of all inter-app information flows in the sequential composite applications where $Flow_{inter} = \bigcup_{0 \le i,j \le n} flow_{i,j}$.

Then we can obtain the following definition on secure information flow in composite application.

Definition 6. *The information flows in sequential composite application A_C are considered secure iff it satisfies that for each $A_i \in A_C$, for $\forall source_i \in M_i, \forall sink_j \in M_j (i \leq j)$, there is no existence of information flow $source_i$ to $sink_j$, namely $<source_i, sink_j> \notin Flow_i \cup Flow_{inter}$.*

Based on the composite information flow security definition above, we can obtain the following theorem.

Theorem 1. *In the security sequential combinatorial application $A_C s$, the information flow must satisfies following conditions.*

(1) For $\forall <source, sink> \in Flow_i$ in A_i, there is $sl(source) \leq sl(sink)$.
(2) For $\forall <sink_i, source_{i+1}> \in In_{i,j}$, there is $sl(sink_i) \leq sl(source_{i+1})$.

We can use the mathematical induction to prove the theorem by referring to [20].

5   Compositional Information Flow Verification for Composite Application Android System

Android inter-app communication is a basic behavior that usually occurs during system running. For example, wechat accesses health data and makes statistical ranking. The famous social software Weibo adds friends through visiting contacts. In order to ensure the data security across multiple applications, we propose an compositional information flow security Theorem 1. According to the Theorem 1, we can infer that for a sequential composite application, the information flow security verification procedure includes two different phases, i.e., the intra-flow verification and inter-flow verification.

5.1   Intra Flow Verification in Single Application

In the process of intra-flow verification, we first use the flowdroid tool [4] to obtain the application's sensitive information flow. Then each flow is verified according to condition (1) in Theorem 1. If the flows in the application is valid, the certificate is generated which can be used for the inter flow verification to avoid the repeated verification. The certificate includes all essential information for inter flow verification, e.g., the security level on each source and sink method and so on. The procedure for flow validation and certificate generation is shown in Algorithm 1.

After successful verification, the generated certificate will be stored in the database. This procedure can be executed during the application is going to be installed on the system at the first time. And only secure ones can obtain the certificates while the others are not allowed to be installed. The counterexample will also be return to users.

Algorithm 1. Intra-app verification & certificate set-up

Input: $A_i =< C_i, I_i, IF_i, Sec_i >$Apk file
Output: $Ce =< i, It, sl >$, true, false

1: use flowdroid anaysis apk file to get the set of intra flow $FlowResult$
2: **for** each flow $f \in FlowResult$ **do**
3:     get security level $sl(source)$ and $sl(sink)$ from Sec_i
4:     **if** $(sl(source) > sl(sink))$ **then**
5:         break
6:     **else**
7:         n++
8:     **end if**
9: **end for**
10: **if** $(n < |FlowResult|)$ **then**
11:     **return** false
12: **else**
13:     generate the certificate Ce base on I_i, Sec_i
14:     signature(Ce, CA)
15:     **return** true
16: **end if**

5.2 Compositional Flow Verification for Inter-application Communications

According to the condition (2) in Theorem 1, the security on the inter-app flows can be ensured by verification on the inter flows between the adjacent applications. The compositional verification algorithm is as follows.

In the compositional verification process, the certificate is obtained first and then the adjacent application's inter-flows are verified. If the validation is successful, the result is returned to the user. Otherwise, return counterexample of an insecure flow.

6   Implementation and Evaluation

This paper mainly studies the compositional application's information flow security verification approach. In this section, we experimentally compare the verification time overhead of our approach with the global verification approach. Our approach has been described in Sect. 5. The global approach first uses ApkCombiner [21] to combine multiple applications into one, and then use flowdroid [4] for information flow analysis and verification. The basic experiment configuration is shown in Table 1 and verification results are shown in Figs. 2 and 3. In Table 1, the Applications number refers to the number of applications tested, and Combined applications number refers to the number of compositional applications formed.

Algorithm 2. Compositional verification approach

Input: A_i, A_{i+1}
Output: true, false, leakagepath

1: get Ce_i and Ce_{i+1}
2: **for** each intent $in \in Ce_i \cdot It$ **do**
3:     get security level of $sink_i$ and $source_{i+1}$ from Ce_i and Ce_{i+1}
4:     **if** $(sl(sink_i) > sl(source_{i+1}))$ **then**
5:         $leakagepath = < sink_i, source_{i+1} >$
6:         break
7:     **else**
8:         n++
9:     **end if**
10: **end for**
11: **if** $(n < |Ce_i \cdot It|)$ **then**
12:     output leakagepath
13:     **return** false
14: **else**
15:     **return** true
16: **end if**

Table 1. Basic configuration

General	
Testing tools	ApkCombiner, Flowdroid, Our approach
Application	
Applications form	apk files
Applications number	3, 6, 9, 12, 15, 18
Combined applications number	1, 8, 27, 64, 125, 216
Inter-app communications number	1, 2, 3, 4, 5, 6, 7

Figures 2 and 3 show that the verification time of the global method is much higher than that of our approach. The reason is that when the communication among different applications changes, the global approach needs to reverify all the flows in the whole composite application. On the contrary, our approach only needs to verify the relevant inter flows between the applications according to certificate, which saves lots of costs on the reverification on intra flows in the same application. Besides, our compositional verification algorithm is easy to extend. With the increasing number of steps n, we only need to verify the additional flows between A_n and A_{n+1} to ensure the security of the composite application.

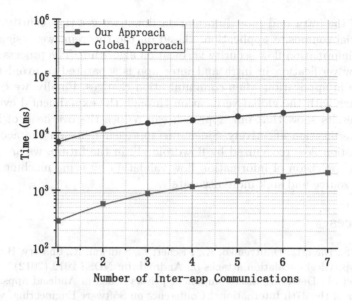

Fig. 2. The verification time increases with the inter-app communication number

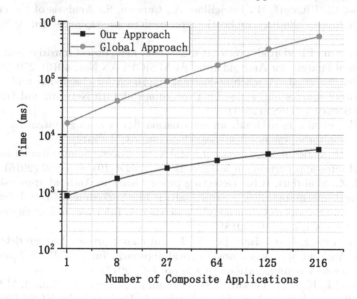

Fig. 3. Verification time increases with the number of composite applications

7   Conclusion

ICC is used to communicate among multiple applications, which may cause leakage on users' sensitive data. In this paper, we design the formal model of android application and sequential composite applications by ICC. Then, through the analysis of the intra and inter information flows, we get the security theorem on sequential composite application. Based on the theorem, we design a compositional information flow security verification algorithm. The process of information flow verification in intra and inter app is separated to avoid repeated verification in application when communication changes. Finally, we compared our approach with the global verification through the experimental evaluation. And the results show that our approach can reduce the overhead of information flow verification effectively. Since our approach relies on the accuracy of the information flow recognized by flowdroid [4], in the future, we are going to improve the precision of information flow validation by using machine learning to identify source and sink more accurately.

References

1. Bugiel, S., Davi, L., Dmitrienko, A., Fischer, T., Sadeghi, A., Shastry, B.: Towards taming privilege-escalation attacks on Android. In: NDSS 2012 (2012)
2. Li, L., et al.: Detecting inter-component privacy leaks in Android apps. In: Proceedings of the 37th International Conference on Software Engineering, vol. 1, pp. 280–291 (2015)
3. Marforio, C., Ritzdorf, H., Francillon, A., Capkun, S.: Analysis of the communication between colluding applications on modern smartphones. In: ACSAC 2012 (2012)
4. Arzt, S., et al.: FlowDroid: precise context, flow, field, object sensitive and lifecycle-aware taint analysis for Android apps. ACM SIGPLAN Not. **49**(6), 259–269 (2014)
5. Rasthofer, S., et al.: A machine-learning approach for classifying and categorizing Android sources and sinks. In: Proceedings of 14th Network and Distributed System Securit (NDSS) (2014)
6. Enck, W., et al.: TaintDroid: an information flow tracking system for real-time privacy monitoring on smartphones. Commun. ACM (2014)
7. Bagheri, H., Sadeghi, A., Garcia, J., Malek, S.: Covert: compositional analysis of Android inter-app permission leakage. IEEE TSE **41**(9), 866–886 (2015)
8. Bohluli, Z., Shahriari, H.R.: Detecting privacy leaks in Android apps using inter-component information flow control analysis. In: Proceedings of 15th International ISC (Iranian Society of Cryptology) Conference on Information Security and Cryptology (ISCISC), pp. 1–6 (2018)
9. Chen, H., Leung, H.-F., Han, B., Su, J.: Automatic privacy leakage detection for massive Android apps via a novel hybrid approach. In: 2017 IEEE International Conference on Communications (ICC), pp. 1–7 (2017)
10. Gordon, M.I., Kim, D., Perkins, J.H., Gilham, L., Nguyen, N., Rinard, M.C.: Information flow analysis of Android applications in DroidSafe. In: NDSS (2015)
11. Bosu, A., Liu, F., Yao, D., Wang, G.: Collusive data leak and more: large-scale threat analysis of inter-app communications. In: ASIACCS (2017)
12. Fuchs, A.P., Chaudhuri, A., Foster, J.S.: ScanDroid: automated security certification of Android applications. Technical report, Department of Computer Science, University of Maryland, College Park (2009)
13. Goguen, J.A., Meseguer, J.: Security policies and security models. In: 1982 IEEE Symposium on Security and Privacy, pp. 11–20. IEEE (1982)
14. Bagheri, H., Sadeghi, A., Jabbarvand, R., Malek, S.: Automated dynamic enforcement of synthesized security policies in Android. Technical report (2015)

15. Poeplau, S., Fratantonio, Y., Bianchi, A., Kruegel, C., Vigna, G.: Execute this! Analyzing unsafe and malicious dynamic code loading in Android applications. In: NDSS 2014, no. February, pp. 23–26 (2014)

16. Spreitzenbarth, M., Freiling, F., Echtler, F., Schreck, T., Hoffmann, J.: Mobile-sandbox: having a deeper look into android applications. In: Proceedings of the 28th Annual ACM Symposium on Applied Computing, pp. 1808–1815. ACM, Coimbra (2013)

17. Zhou, Y., Jiang, X.: Dissecting android malware: characterization and evolution. In: 2012 IEEE Symposium on Security and Privacy (SP), pp. 95–109. IEEE (2012)

18. Jing, Y., Ahn, G.-J., Doupe, A., Yi, J.H.: Checking intent-based communication in Android with intent space analysis. In: ASIACCS (2016)

19. Liu, F., Cai, H., Wang, G., Yao, D., Elish, K.O., Ryder, B.G.: MR-Droid: a scalable and prioritized analysis of inter-app communication risks. In: 2017 IEEE Security and Privacy Workshops (SPW), pp. 189–198 (2017). 10.11999JEIT140902

20. Xi, N., Ma, J., Sun, C., Shen, Y., Zhang, T.: Distributed information flow verification framework for the composition of service chain in wireless sensor network. Int. J. Distrib. Sens. Netw. **2013**, 10 (2013)

21. Li, L., Bartel, A., Bissyandé, T.F., Klein, J., Traon, Y.L.: ApkCombiner: combining multiple Android apps to support inter-app analysis. In: Federrath, H., Gollmann, D. (eds.) SEC 2015. IAICT, vol. 455, pp. 513–527. Springer, Cham (2015). https://doi.org/10.1007/978-3-319-18467-8_34

22. Harrison, R.: Investigating the effectiveness of obfuscation against Android application reverse engineering. Royal Holloway University of London, RHUL-ISG-2015-7 (2015)

23. Ghosh, S., Tandan, S.R., Lahre, K.: Shielding Android application against reverse engineering. Int. J. Eng. Res. Technol. **2**(6), 2635–2643 (2013)

24. Protsenko, M., Mller, T.: Protecting Android apps against reverse engineering by the use of the native code. In: 12th International Conference on Trust and Privacy in Digital Business, Valencia, Spain, pp. 99–110 (2015)

25. Strazzere, T.: DEX education 201: anti-emulation. In: HITCON 2013 (2013)

26. Wolfe, B., Elish, K.O., Yao, D.D.: Comprehensive behavior profiling for proactive Android malware detection. In: Chow, S.S.M., Camenisch, J., Hui, L.C.K., Yiu, S.M. (eds.) ISC 2014. LNCS, vol. 8783, pp. 328–344. Springer, Cham (2014). https://doi.org/10.1007/978-3-319-13257-0_19

27. Wu, D.J., Mao, C.H., Wei, T.E., Lee, H.M., Wu, K.P.: DroidMat: Android malware detection through manifest and API calls tracing. In: Proceedings of the Asia Joint Conference on Information Security (Asia JCIS), pp. 62–69 (2012). https://doi.org/10.1109/AsiaJCIS.2012.18

28. Gascon, H., Yamaguchi, F., Arp, D., Rieck, K.: Structural detection of Android malware using embedded call graphs. In: Proceedings of the ACM Workshop on Artificial Intelligence and Security (AISEC), pp. 45–54 (2013). https://doi.org/10.1145/2517312.2517315

29. Chakradeo, S., Reaves, B., Traynor, P., Enck, W.: MAST: triage for market-scale mobile malware analysis. In: Proceedings of the ACM Conference on Security and Privacy in Wireless and Mobile Networks (WISEC), pp. 13–24 (2013). https://doi.org/10.1145/2462096.2462100

30. Aafer, Y., Du, W., Yin, H.: DroidAPIMiner: mining API-level features for robust malware detection in Android. In: Zia, T., Zomaya, A., Varadharajan, V., Mao, M. (eds.) SecureComm 2013. LNICST, vol. 127, pp. 86–103. Springer, Cham (2013). https://doi.org/10.1007/978-3-319-04283-1_6

31. Arp, D., Spreitzenbarth, M., Hubner, M., Gascon, H., Rieck, K.: DREBIN: effective and explainable detection of Android malware in your pocket. In: Proceedings of the 21th Annual Symposium on Network and Distributed System Security (NDSS 2014) (2014). https://doi.org/10.14722/ndss.2014.23247
32. Zhang, X.Y., Zhang, G., Shen, L.W., Peng, X., Zhao, W.Y.: Similarity analysis of multi-dimension features of Android application. Comput. Sci. **43**(3), 199–205, 219 (2016). (in Chinese with English abstract). https://doi.org/10.11896/j.issn.1002-137X.2016.03.037
33. Kong, D.G., Cen, L., Jin, H.X.: AUTOREB: automatically understanding the review-to-behavior fidelity in Android applications. In: Proceedings of the 22nd ACM Conference on Computer and Communications Security (CCS 2015), pp. 530–541 (2015). https://doi.org/10.1145/2810103.2813689
34. Zhang, M., Duan, Y., Feng, Q., Yin, H.: Towards automatic generation of security-centric descriptions for Android apps. In: Proceedings of the 22nd ACM Conference on Computer and Communications Security (CCS 2015), pp. 518–529 (2015). https://doi.org/10.1145/2810103.2813669
35. Wang, R., Feng, D.G., Yang, Y., Su, P.R.: Semantics-based malware behavior signature extraction and detection method. Ruanjian Xuebao/J. Softw. **23**(2), 378–393 (2012). https://doi.org/10.3724/SP.J.1001.2012.03953. (in Chinese with English abstract), http://www.jos.org.cn/1000-9825/3953.htm

A Blackboard Sharing Mechanism
for Community Cyber Threat Intelligence
Based on Multi-Agent System

Yue Lin[1,2], He Wang[1,2], Bowen Yang[1,2], Mingrui Liu[1,2], Yin Li[1,2],
and Yuqing Zhang[2,1(✉)]

[1] School of Cyber Engineering, Xidian University, Xi'an, Shaanxi, China
liny@nipc.org.cn, hewang@xidian.edu.cn, xmkrui@gmail.com,
{bwyang,liyin}@stu.xidian.edu.cn
[2] National Computer Network Intrusion Protection Center,
University of Chinese Academy of Sciences, Beijing, China
zhangyq@ucas.ac.cn

Abstract. In the process of increasing cybersecurity attack and defense confrontation, there is a natural asymmetry between the offensive and defense. The Cyber Threat Intelligence (CTI) sharing mechanism is an effective means to improve the emergency-response ability of the protection party. However, currently, there are no effective sharing schemes in the community network to facilitate cross-sector threat intelligence sharing. This paper presents a collaborative threat intelligence sharing mechanism based on the blackboard model, which can be used to identify potential risks, prevent cyber attacks at an early stage, and facilitate community incident response. According to the China National Standard "Cyber security threat information format", we divide threat intelligence sharing into routine and attack-specific threat intelligence sharing. Also, we design an attack-specific threat intelligence sharing module based on the blackboard model and describe the sharing process. Finally, we design the blackboard monitoring mechanism as a Multi-Agent System (MAS) to realize many tasks in the sharing process. Our scheme is illustrated by several CTI sharing scenarios in the community.

Keywords: CTI · Threat intelligence sharing · Blackboard ·
Monitoring mechanism · MAS

1 Introduction

The current offensive and defensive in cyberspace is an "asymmetric" war. In recent years, new attacks represented by 0 day vulnerability utilization, APT and social engineering emerge one after another [1–3]. In contrast, traditional security protection is mostly in a passive state, and in the face of new threats and attacks, defense and detection have little effect [4]. Given this situation, Cyber Threat Intelligence (CTI) sharing emerges at a historical moment, which

© Springer Nature Switzerland AG 2019
X. Chen et al. (Eds.): ML4CS 2019, LNCS 11806, pp. 253–270, 2019.
https://doi.org/10.1007/978-3-030-30619-9_18

strengthens the collaboration and mutual assistance of all information systems to improve threat detection and emergency response capability of all parties. However, the current cybersecurity situation is unbalanced, in which the need for shared threat intelligence exceeds the development of threat intelligence sharing mechanisms. In response to this problem, how threat intelligence is shared and exchanged is still an issue that needs to be studied and explored.

Besides, the threat intelligence is not only beneficial at the government level but also necessary for cross-sector sharing in the community. Generally, a community consists of all of the entities within a geographical region, including local government, academics, and industry organizations [5]. Many cyber threats are difficultly detected and identified through a single sector. By correlating shared intelligence in the community, a more efficient approach can be developed to identify potential risks and prevent cyber threats at an early stage. Based on the above objectives, Zhao et al. [6] proposed a group-centric collaborative information sharing framework, which provides a good idea for the design and improvement of the sharing scheme. However, there are two inadequacies in the design of this scheme: (1) the shared information has a narrow focus and lacks a standard data format; (2) it lacks an authentication mechanism to solve the trust problem between sharing participants. To solve the above problems, we add the latest threat intelligence format specification—"Cyber security threat information format" into the sharing mechanism, which provides a structured and universal framework for expressing CTI, and use the blackboard model to realize the fine-grained access control and identity authentication.

In recent years, the blackboard model has been widely used in knowledge sharing fields. Because of its good interactivity and collaboration, it becomes a central component in the construction of the decision system [7–11]. The literature [12] proposed an Incident Handling System (IHS), which allows the collaborative interaction between incident handling steps implemented using the blackboard pattern. The establishment of a Multi-Agent System also requires the blackboard model [13,14], especially for intelligent systems with dynamic, uncertain, and complex tasks, which provides a flexible and efficient communication method between Agents. Also, the application of the blackboard model includes e-learning [15,16], network management [17], etc., which are not described here in detail.

Therefore, this paper proposes a multi-cooperation community CTI sharing model. We rely on the extended Group-centric Secure Information Sharing (g-SIS) model in [6] and modify it. At the same time, we will add the extended blackboard model as a sharing module in the Collaboration Group to realize threat intelligence sharing through the interaction with a blackboard. The specific contributions of this paper are as follows:

– In the sharing process, we use the "Cyber security threat information format" as a standardized description of threat intelligence currently used in China, which makes up for the inadequacies (1). According to different types of threat intelligence components, the sharing method is divided into routine and attack-specific threat intelligence sharing to achieve sharing flexibility.

- We adopt a blackboard model based on the "registration-feedback" mechanism, which can refine the access control of the sharing Participants to the threat intelligence about specific attack activities. At the same time, the added security verification function can avoid identity falsification to improve the inadequacies (2).
- We design the monitoring mechanism in the blackboard sharing module as a Multi-Agent System. The interaction among agents in this system can solve the concurrent problems of threat intelligence sharing, eliminate the disadvantages of a single system, and improve the execution efficiency of tasks. It fully reflects the possibility of combining artificial intelligence with threat intelligence sharing.

The rest of the paper is organized as follows. In Sect. 2, we introduce the current development status of CTI sharing and relevant academic research in recent years, pointing out the design flaw of threat intelligence sharing. In Sect. 3, we introduce the overall architecture of the blackboard sharing model for CTI and the contents of each part. In Sect. 4, we put forward the community CTI sharing framework, designing the blackboard model in Sect. 3 as an attack-specific threat intelligence sharing module. Also, we describe the entire sharing process and the design of the blackboard monitoring mechanism in detail. Section 5 takes "WannaCry" blackmail worm as a practical example to describe the possible scenario of threat intelligence sharing. Section 6 discusses innovation and future work; then Sect. 7 concludes the paper.

2   Related Work

In the face of sophisticated cyber threats, we need a new paradigm to detect and defend these cyber threats, to effectively establish situational awareness of cybersecurity. However, much of this work is carried out by CNCERT[1], and the sharing of threat intelligence across sectors is rare. The United States is the earliest country to carry out the threat information construction at the government level, in recent years, the US government has continued to invest much energy in cybersecurity policy legislation and to promote cybersecurity information sharing between the federal government and the private sectors [4]. However, in practice, secure information sharing is usually achieved through unique and informal relationships [18]. Typically, CNCERT acts as a national focal point, coordinating and aggregating security incident reports through E-mail, instant messaging, file exchange/storage, VoIP, IRC, Web, and other communication channels [19]. The problem with these information-sharing services is that the organizations directly share information with government entities to a centralized location. What is lacking is collaboration among different organizations in the same sector or across different sectors in a community [6].

In the academic research of CTI sharing, most of the inchoate content aimed at the needs and motivations, problems and challenges of information sharing, trying to find ways to solve these problems and put forward some feasible

---

[1] https://www.cert.org.cn; July 2019

opinions and suggestions [20–23]. With the development of research, more and more summative investigation literature about security information sharing has emerged. Serrano et al. [24] analyzed four challenges in network security information sharing: legal issues, support for different ontologies, information sharing for different communities and uncertain management issues, and proposed technical solutions with the help of current advanced technologies. Skopik et al. [25] provided a structured overview of the dimensions of cybersecurity information sharing. Goodwin et al. [26] used Microsoft's years of experience in infrastructure security management to present a historical background on information sharing and described the classification of information sharing in terms of models, methods, and mechanisms. Finally, they provided feasible suggestions for collaborative information sharing and exchange. For the specific sharing content and network security in various countries, some threat intelligence sharing platforms [27,28] have also been launched. Standards bodies and similar organizations have also issued a series of standards on how to build security information-sharing networks, among which the typical examples are the NIST guide "Guide to Cyber Threat Inform Sharing" [29] and ENISA document "Cyber Security Information Sharing: An Overview of Regulatory and non-regulatory Approaches" [30], etc. While these recommendations represent essential work, but they are not complete, and essential parts are still missing. For example, the current recommendations mostly take an architectural view and ignore guidance on the operational aspects of enabling secure information sharing. For these potential and complex network systems, the techniques and processes required to maintain situational awareness have received little attention.

3 Blackboard Sharing Model Overview

We take the blackboard model as an appropriate design pattern for attack-specific threat intelligence sharing (see Fig. 1) because it provides information sharing components that enable participants to work together, which will be briefly introduced in Sect. 3.1. We classify threat intelligence sharing according to the national standard "Cyber security threat information format" to achieve a more flexible and efficient cyber-threat defense, which will be briefly introduced in Sect. 3.2. To realize the multi-function characteristics of the blackboard monitoring mechanism, we design it as MAS, which will be briefly introduced in Sect. 3.3.

3.1 Blackboard Model

Hayes-Roth introduced blackboard architecture in 1985 [31], which is an extension of the expert system [32]. The blackboard model consists of knowledge sources (KSs), blackboard, and controller (The controller is referred to as a monitoring mechanism in the following). The blackboard model introduces a shared data structure called blackboard as global memory. Entities working independently on the blackboard are called knowledge sources that have specific knowledge in different domains. The control flow depends on the current

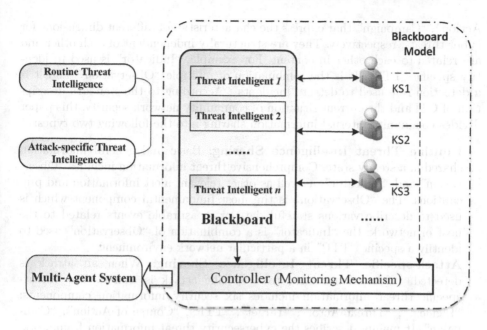

Fig. 1. Blackboard sharing model overview

state of the blackboard and is monitored by the monitoring mechanism. The goal of the blackboard model is to decompose a complex problem into more feasible sub-problems. In the process of solving the problem, KSs always modify the blackboard, and the final result is produced by these KSs cooperatively.

The blackboard model is chosen because of its prominent advantages. As an efficient and universal knowledge storage and processing tool, the blackboard can record the state information and intermediate results generated in the process of problem-solving. Also, it can dispatch and manage the communication and knowledge transfer between KSs, showing unique advantages in the extensive capacity knowledge processing.

3.2 CTI Sharing Type

"Information security technology–Cyber security threat information format" [33] is the expression specification of threat intelligence issued by China National Standardization Management Committee in October 2018, which is used to standardize the modeling, analysis, and exchange of CTI. The standard provides a structured and universal framework for expressing CTI, which can improve the accuracy, interoperability and automatic processing efficiency of intelligence, and can adequately support the automation of cyber threat management processes and applications. To make the standard adapt to a variety of independent scenarios, it early considered scalability in the design process.

The framework consists of eight primary components which are "Observation", "Indicator", "Incident", "Threat Actor", "Target", "TTP", "Course of

Action", "Campaign" that express the characteristics of different dimensions for cyber threats, respectively. They are structurally independent of each other and are related to each other in content. For example, "Indicator" is used to identify specific "TTP". It is the combination of multiple "Observation", and it is a detection rule used to detect "Incidents". According to the standard description of CTI and the current situation of community network security, this paper divides community internal information sharing into the following two types:

- **Routine Threat Intelligence Sharing:** Basic and general information shared in a steady state. Comprehensive threat information includes "Observation" and "Indicator", as well as other relevant alert information and precautions. The "Observation" is the most fundamental component which is used to describe various stateful data or measurable events related to the host or network; the "Indicator" is a combination of "Observation" used to identify a specific "TTP" in a particular network environment.
- **Attack-specific Threat Intelligence Sharing:** When an attack is detected, information related to a specific attack is shared. The threat-specific threat information includes six security information components: "Incident", "Threat Actor", "Target", "TTP", "Course of Action", "Campaign". It mainly describes the cybersecurity threat information framework, including cyber threats, network intrusions, security incidents, vulnerabilities, technical impacts, potential consequences, risk assessments, response activities, responsiveness, mitigation strategies, etc.

3.3 Multi-Agent System

Multi-Agent System (MAS) is a collection composed of multiple Agents. Its goal is to divide large and complex systems into small, connected, and easy-to-manage systems. MAS is an essential branch of Distributed Artificial Intelligence (DAI).

As a whole of distributed problem solving, MAS has the following characteristics: (1) the data is distributed or scattered; (2) the computing process is asynchronous, concurrent or parallel; (3) each Agent has incomplete information and problem-solving ability, there is no global control; (4) Agents can interact, dynamically self-organize, coordinate and cooperate with each other, thus significantly improving their ability to solve problems.

Compared with the traditional single system, the cooperative working ability of MAS improves the efficiency of task execution, and it is easy to extend and upgrade. Moreover, MAS can accomplish distributed tasks that cannot be accomplished by a single system [34].

4   Community Threat Intelligence Sharing Framework Based on the Blackboard Model

In the traditional threat intelligence sharing, both sides communicate directly. Once a large number of entities need to share information for a common goal, the traditional method may be very inefficient. A natural and effective way to facilitate the sharing of information between more entities is to group information and participants.

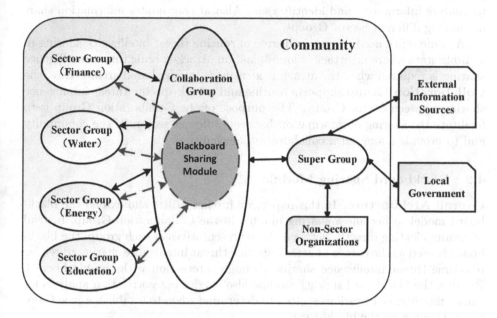

Fig. 2. Threat intelligence sharing framework based on the blackboard model

The Group-centric Secure Information Sharing (g-SIS) model [35] is an access control model that aggregates users and information in a grouped manner. In the g-SIS model, participants join and leave groups; meanwhile, threat intelligence is added or removed from groups. Participants gain access to the information within the group through membership. The framework is a flexible sharing framework suitable for highly dynamic environments, such as security incident response or threat intelligence real-time sharing. In this paper, a community threat intelligence sharing framework based on the blackboard is proposed, and g-SIS is selected as the overall architecture to realize community CTI sharing requirements (see Fig. 2). We designed with the extended g-SIS model, which introduces different types of groups and different inter-group relationships. We also added an extended blackboard model to achieve attack-specific threat intelligence sharing through the interaction between the group representatives and the blackboard.

4.1 Collaborative Threat Intelligence Sharing Entity

In this framework, community threat intelligence sharing entities include **Sector Groups**, **Non-Sector Organizations**, and **Super Group** [6]. Each entity plays different roles in community CTI sharing. For example, Non-Sector Organizations can provide valuable information for cybersecurity situational awareness within the community. The Super Group is generally composed of experts in the field of cybersecurity, who are responsible for assisting the Collaboration Group to analyze information and identify risks. Also, it coordinates information sharing among different Sector Groups.

A community needs a certain degree of routine threat intelligence sharing in a stable state where no attack is found, and an attack-specific threat intelligence sharing is required when the attack is identified. In our shared architecture, the **Collaboration Group** supports routine and attack-specific threat intelligence sharing between Sector Groups. The purpose of the Collaboration Group is to facilitate the sharing of information between different sectors of the community and to provide a long-term collaboration mechanism.

4.2 Blackboard Sharing Module

Overall Architecture. In this paper, we further utilize and extend the blackboard model to become a sharing module in the Collaboration Group. Instead of communicating directly between the representatives of each group, the blackboard is used as the carrier of attack-specific threat intelligence sharing to realize real-time threat intelligence sharing through interaction with the blackboard. Besides, the blackboard sharing module also carries out correlation analysis for threat intelligence of various sectors to determine when to establish a new Campaign Domain on the blackboard.

The overall structure of the Blackboard Sharing Module is shown in Fig. 3. The following is the relevant definition of this module:

Φ: The collection of Participants, that is, representatives of various Sector Groups and Super Group members who participate in the threat intelligence sharing of a specific attack.

$$\Phi = \{P_1, P_2, \cdots, P_n\} \tag{1}$$

B: Blackboard, which is a collection of Campaign Domains. Campaign Domain covers information about a cyber threat in cyberspace and is a set of components of threat intelligence. That is, the Campaign Domain can record information such as "Observation", "Indicator", "Incident", "Threat Actor", "Target", "TTP", "Course of Action" and "Campaign". The definition and format of the Campaign Domain depend on the scalability of the standard threat intelligence model. The components defined in the threat intelligence model are optional. They can be used independently or in any combination. Thus, the Campaign Domain provides a flexible extension mechanism for the blackboard.

$$B = \{D_1, D_2, \cdots, D_m\} \tag{2}$$

Register: Blackboard registration mechanism. When the Participant needs to publish or access information about a Campaign Domain on the blackboard, it must register in the monitoring mechanism.

$$Register = \{\langle P_{j_1}, D_{i_1}\rangle, \langle P_{j_2}, D_{i_2}\rangle, \cdots, \langle P_{j_k}, D_{i_k}\rangle\}, \langle P_{j_k}, D_{i_k}\rangle \in \Phi \times B \quad (3)$$

where, $\langle P_{j_k}, D_{i_k}\rangle$ means that the Participant P_{j_k} is registered in the Campaign Domain D_{i_k}.

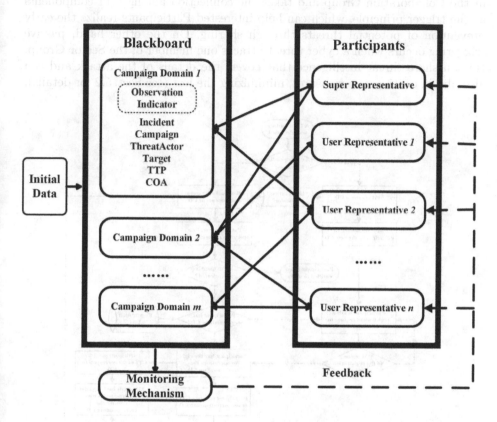

Fig. 3. The overall structure of the blackboard sharing module

Feedback: Blackboard feedback mechanism. According to the following rules:

$$if\ Changed(D_i)$$

$$then\ \forall P_j, \langle P_j, D_i\rangle \in Register, F(P_j, D_i)$$

where, $Changed(D_i)(1 \le i \le m)$ indicates that the Campaign Domain D_i has been modified or updated, and $F(P_j, D_i)$ indicates feedback to the Participant P_j that the Campaign Domain D_i in the blackboard has been modified or updated.

Attack-Specific Threat Intelligence Sharing Process. Before the cyber threat is identified, the Participant within the Collaboration Group can share the routine threat intelligence, current warning, and defense content in order to maintain an excellent situational awareness order (see Sect. 5.1 for details). This paper divides the situations that can trigger attack-specific threat intelligence sharing into active and passive triggering. On the one hand, active triggering relies on the association analysis of information collected from each Sector Group in the Collaboration Group and takes the connection among CTI components as the trigger principle, which can help interested Participants realize the early prevention of potential threats through sharing. On the other hand, passive triggering occurs when a cyber threat attacks one member of the Sector Group. He can share threat intelligence that covers the details of the attack and can also obtain contingency measures, minimizing the loss (see Sect. 5.2 for details).

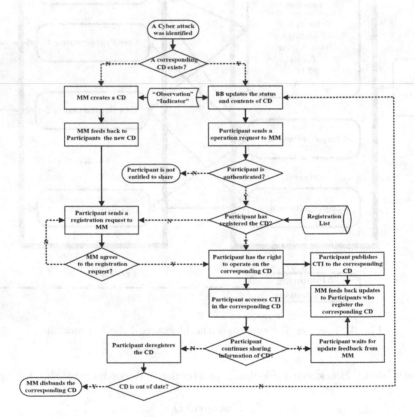

Fig. 4. Participants share the threat intelligence through the attack-specific threat intelligence sharing process, where CD, MM, BB respectively refer to Campaign Domain, Monitoring Mechanism, and blackboard.

The attack-specific threat intelligence sharing process is shown in Fig. 4. During the sharing process, firstly, the Participant needs to apply for authentication. If the verification is passed, Participants can then register the Campaign Domains they are interested in on the blackboard. After the blackboard monitoring mechanism agrees, the Participants can publish and access the content of the Campaign Domain when a special attack is confirmed. The blackboard monitoring mechanism is responsible for the consistency problem after the Campaign Domain updates. Once the information of a Campaign Domain on the blackboard is changed, the blackboard monitoring mechanism notifies the Participants that have registered in the Campaign Domain. This process is called feedback. This interaction between the Participants and the blackboard is called a "registration-feedback" mechanism. The Participant updates its known threat intelligence to a specific Campaign Domain in the blackboard so that the information can be perceived by other Participants registered in the same Campaign Domain. In this way, threat-specific information sharing is achieved through blackboard.

It can be seen that in the entire attack-specific sharing process, the blackboard monitoring mechanism is the core of the shared module. The monitoring mechanism is a software agent with information processing and decision-making capabilities, which can control shared content to achieve corresponding functions and support collaboration and sharing among Participants. The monitoring mechanism acts as a proxy for monitoring and managing the blackboard, also assigns shareable resources to the Campaign Domain. In general, the blackboard monitoring mechanism is the intermediary that the Participants can access the blackboard and the control mechanism of the blackboard.

Monitoring Mechanism. To realize the functions provided by the blackboard monitoring mechanism, we chose Agent technology, which is well adapted to the concurrency and dynamic design of the threat intelligence sharing process.

According to the Multi-Agent System, the functional architecture we designed for the blackboard monitoring mechanism is shown in Fig. 5. Each Participant is assigned to an artificial Agent, that is, the **Personal Agent**. In the system, the Personal Agent replaces human behavior by executing all user requests, which must first pass through itself, then retransmit to other Agents, and finally return the response to the user. On the other hand, the monitoring mechanism must ensure the authentication and access control of the Participant, and manage the related sharing operations of the Participant, so different artificial Agents implement the above functions:

- **Authentication Agent:** It is necessary to carry out authentication, which can prevent the identity forgery of the Participant, that is, all accesses of the Participants to the blackboard must first pass security verification. For example, a Participant can ensure that information comes from a credible one by using a certificate authority to generate credentials for a Participant.
- **Interaction Agent:** Interaction Agent manages the interaction between different agents in the system and the blackboard. All Agents must access the blackboard through an Interaction Agent.
- **Registration & Revocation Agent:** The Participant cannot have unlimited access to the Campaign Domains, so they should be given sharing permissions. Through the conditional request of the Participant, the access authority of the corresponding Campaign Domain is specified or revoked for the Participant, and a registration list of Campaign Domains is maintained.

- **Feedback Agent:** To ensure that the threat intelligence in the blackboard is consistent with that owned by the registered Participant, the Feedback Agent needs to feedback the updates of the blackboard content. Thus, the Participant can obtain a real-time perception of the information on the blackboard, and realize the "registration-feedback" mechanism together with the Registration & Revocation Agent.
- **Creation & Disbandment Agent:** This Agent receives the command of the Collaboration Group administrator, and conducts the creation of a new Campaign Domain or the disbandment of an outdated one. According to the different threat "Campaigns", the threat intelligence is classified, and Participants can purposefully share information by creating different Campaigns domains.

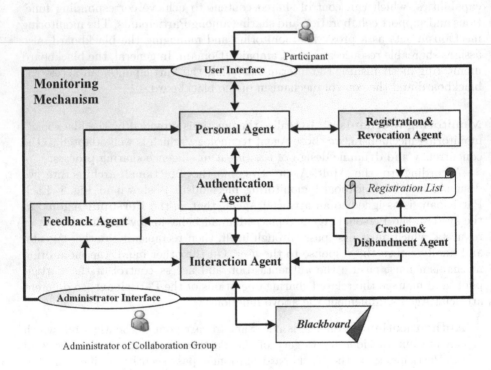

Fig. 5. The blackboard monitoring mechanism

In addition to coordinating and managing routine threat intelligence sharing in the Collaboration Group, the administrator of the Collaboration Group also assists the Creation & Disbandment Agent to decide when to create or dismiss specific Campaign Domains based on the request of the Participants. Generally, the administrator of the Collaboration Group is selected by the security department of the local government in the community to ensure the safe and healthy operation of the monitoring mechanism.

5   Description of Threat Intelligence Sharing Scenario

In order to make the proposed scheme more precise, this paper will provide several possible application scenarios for threat intelligence sharing, further illustrating the design of the threat intelligence sharing framework. Our sharing framework focuses more on important issues at the level of abstraction, allowing communities to carry out based on their specific needs and realities.

Since the collection, aggregation, and analysis of information are not the focus of this paper, we assume that each group has tools and methods to collect and aggregate information. At the same time, there is a sufficient correlation analysis mechanism to determine whether there is a potential threat in the community. (For example, if a large amount of "Observation" from all the Sector Groups meets the "Indicator" for a particular attack on files, processes or registries, they can be judged that they constitute a threat to the community.) Also, Collaboration Groups should have guidelines that allow members to match the threat intelligence they want to share with existing Campaign Domains according to the characteristics and descriptions defined by each Campaign Domain.

Based on the above assumptions, we take the "WannaCry" worm virus [33] as an attack case, and introduce several possible scenarios for threat intelligence sharing.

5.1   Routine Threat Intelligence Sharing

The first scenario is simple, assuming that the Super Group receives an alert message about an SMB vulnerability from another community. The Super Group members will share this information and provide particular "Course of Action (COA)", such as providing a patch for the vulnerability to the Collaboration Group cg so that the members of the Sector Group can be aware of the vulnerability and protect their Sector Group from the attack. In the Collaboration Group, members of the Sector Group will issue threat intelligence containing warnings and resources to their group if they believe their group is related to the vulnerability.

5.2   Attack-Specific Threat Intelligence Sharing

Defense Against Threats. If the user u_1 in (Energy) Sector Group sg_1 detects that a specific domain name "http://www.iuqerfsodp9ifjaposdfjhgosurij faewrwe-rgwea.com" exists in the URL access record, thinking the abnormal URL access record may pose a potential threat. To prevent related attacks, he may wish to share this threat information in sg_1. Based on the predefined Sector Group guidelines, information including URL access and DNS essential records should be structured in a standard threat intelligence format and shared in sg_1 as "Observation" threat intelligence. Other members of sg_1 can read this intelligence and take precautions when necessary, such as strengthening the monitoring of this anomaly.

In this scenario, we assume that no relevant threats are found in the community, and aggregated threat intelligence will be shared with the Collaboration Group cg based on predefined community guidelines. Suppose that within a specified time interval, another user u_2 detects file information named "t. wncry", and user u_3 detects abnormal scanning behavior of 445 File Sharing port, both of whom share the intelligence in sg_1 in threat intelligence standard format. This intelligence will be aggregated and correlated in sg_1; then the aggregated threat intelligence may prompt the user u_{rep1} to generate a new "Observation" intelligence. u_{rep1} is a representative member of sg_1 and also a member of cg. The aggregated intelligence will be shared into the cg by u_{rep1}.

The Collaboration Group cg will correlate all threat intelligence collected from other Sector Groups and analyze this information to determine if there is a potential threat to the community. When each "observation" collected meets the "indicators" of the "WannaCry" worm virus (For example, the parameters of relevant files, registry and process are changed), it can be determined that the community may be infected by "WannaCry". Collaboration Group administrator will create a Campaign Domain cd_1 for "WannaCry" on the blackboard through the blackboard monitoring mechanism, which can provide detailed information on upcoming attacks and provide references to potentially affected Sector Group members, further sharing attack-specific threat intelligence through the Campaign Domain. The Super Group representative in cg will provide prevention strategies or mitigation plans for the registered users by sharing threat intelligence like "COA", "Threat Actor" and "Target" in cd_1 in order to assist with information analysis and incident response. The members who register cd_1 can publish the preventive measures, mitigation plans, and other resources about cd_1 to their groups. For other unregistered cg members, the alarm information and routine threat information can be shared with them.

In this simple scenario, the attack is low-level, and no specific attack attempts occur in the community. This scenario reflects that the community can realize defense against attack through the sharing of threat intelligence.

Emergency Response to Threats. Suppose that the "WannaCry" blackmail worm attacks user u_4 in the (Education) Sector Group sg_2. He wants to report information about the worm and get an efficient and real-time emergency response. According to the predefined community guideline, he needs to share threat intelligence that covers the details of the attack, including "Campaign", "TTP", "Threat Actor", "Incident", "Indicator" and other threat intelligence standard components.

The representative u_{rep2} in sg_2, (also a member of the Collaboration Group), will examine the existing Campaign Domains in the blackboard of Collaboration Group cg. Assume that in the cg, the report about the "WannaCry" worm has been received from the Sector Group sg_3. Through the correlation analysis, the Campaign Domain cd_2 has been created on the blackboard for the new threat attack on port 445. u_{rep2} can apply to the blackboard monitoring mechanism to register cd_2 and publish relevant intelligence to cd_2 after the registration. The representatives of Super Group can help mitigate and respond to this situation by sharing resources such as "COA" on cd_2, and they can provide appropriate recommendations for Sector Groups that have previously reported this attack but have not been compromised.

If there is no Campaign Domain associated with "WannaCry", u_{rep2} can request cg to create a new Campaign Domain. Based on the severity and extent of the attack, and by analyzing or correlating previously received threat intelligence, the cg administrator will authorize the blackboard monitoring mechanism to create a new Campaign Domain cd_3. u_{rep2} can share the relevant threat information by registering cd_3 and obtain valid references. Similarly, relevant recommendations such as "COA" will also be provided. After u_{rep2} obtains the corresponding disposal measures, it will post the intelligence in sg_2 so that the infected user u_4 can implement the response measures as soon as possible to minimize the loss.

6 Discussion

6.1 Innovation

In this paper, the g-SIS framework is still adopted as a whole to realize the sharing of threat intelligence among multiple parties in the community, retaining its advantages in data access control and adapting to the dynamic changing environment. On this basis, we rely on the national standard "Cyber security threat information format". According to the correlation between threat intelligence components, we divide the sharing ways into routine and attack-specific threat intelligence sharing, which makes attack prevention and incident response more flexible and efficient.

Besides, we utilize the blackboard model to solve collaborative threat intelligence sharing. In essence, the cross-sector threat information sharing in the community is a process of multiparty cooperation and joint problem solving, which completely conforms to the usage scenario of the blackboard model. Using the blackboard model based on "registration-feedback", the access control of the Participant to threat intelligence can be refined to specific attack activities. Besides, the added security verification function can prevent the identity of the malicious attacker from forging and can solve the trust problem between the Participants.

Finally, we propose that MAS is a meritorious solution for distributed function realization of the blackboard monitoring mechanism. It can be seen that we have added additional functions based on the original blackboard monitoring mechanism. The previous single system architecture cannot solve the concurrency problem of threat intelligence sharing, and cannot satisfy the premise that the Participants are unlimited by time and place. Therefore, MAS can not only eliminate the disadvantages of a single system but also improve the efficiency of task execution. Moreover, according to the extensible characteristics of MAS, the function of the blackboard monitoring mechanism can be upgraded and extended.

6.2 Further Work

The first task we need to do in our future work is to design thoughtful and complete interactive details for Participants and the blackboard (such as secure authentication and encrypted communication). On this basis, it is necessary to analyze possible security problems like collusion attacks and privacy protection, which highlights the feasibility and security of the scheme.

Also, we are working on implementing the proposed blackboard monitoring mechanism on the JADE (Java Agent Development Framework) platform. On the other hand, we plan to carry out practical experimental verification of the proposed model in the actual threat intelligence sharing scenario to highlight the strengths of the sharing model to consolidate and its weak points to correct.

7 Conclusion

This paper presents a cooperative threat intelligence sharing framework based on the blackboard model, which can be used to improve community cybersecurity. According to the national standard "Cyber security threat information format", we divide threat intelligence sharing into routine and attack-specific threat intelligence sharing. We use the blackboard model to realize attack-specific threat intelligence sharing and describe the sharing process. Finally, we design the blackboard monitoring mechanism as MAS to realize many tasks in the sharing process. We illustrate our model using information sharing scenarios in the community. Although our model still needs many steps in practice, it provides a broad and clear development idea for the combination of threat intelligence sharing and artificial intelligence.

Acknowledgements. The National Key R&D Program China (2018YFB0804701), The National Natural Science Foundation of China (No. U1836210,No. 61572460), The Open Project Program of The State Key Laboratory of Information Security (2017-ZD-01), The National Information Security Special Projects of National Development and Reform Commission of China [(2012)1424].

References

1. Chen, P., Desmet, L., Huygens, C.: A study on advanced persistent threats. In: De Decker, B., Zúquete, A. (eds.) CMS 2014. LNCS, vol. 8735, pp. 63–72. Springer, Heidelberg (2014). https://doi.org/10.1007/978-3-662-44885-4_5
2. Verizon: 2019 data breach investigations report. https://enterprise.verizon.com/resources/reports/dbir/
3. Kaspersky: APT trends report Q1 2019. https://securelist.com/apt-trends-report-q1-2019/90643/
4. Yang, P., Wu, Y., Cu, L., Liu, B.: Overview of threat intelligence sharing technologies in cyberspace. Comput. Sci. **45**(6), 9–18 (2018). (in Chinese)
5. Zhao, W., White, G.: A collaborative information sharing framework for community cyber security. In: 2012 IEEE Conference on Technologies for Homeland Security (HST), pp. 457–462. IEEE (2012)

6. Zhao, W., White, G.: Designing a formal model facilitating collaborative information sharing for community cyber security. In: 2014 47th Hawaii International Conference on System Sciences, pp. 1987–1996. IEEE (2014)
7. Agarwal, R., Prasad, K.: A blackboard framework for the design of group decision support systems. Behav. Inf. Technol. **13**(4), 277–284 (1994)
8. Straub, J., Reza, H.: The use of the blackboard architecture for a decision making system for the control of craft with various actuator and movement capabilities. In: 2014 11th International Conference on Information Technology: New Generations, pp. 514–519. IEEE (2014)
9. Zhang, Y., Zhang, L., Du, Z.: Distributed blackboard decision-making framework for collaborative planning based on nested genetic algorithm. J. Syst. Eng. Electron. **26**(6), 1236–1243 (2015)
10. Liu, J., Zhang, Y.: A collaborative task decision-making method based on blackboard framework. Fire Control & Command Control **42**(11), 43–48 (2017) (in Chinese)
11. Chu, H.D.: A blackboard-based decision support framework for testing client/server applications. In: 2012 Third World Congress on Software Engineering, pp. 131–135. IEEE (2012)
12. Herold, N., Kinkelin, H., Carle, G.: Collaborative incident handling based on the blackboard-pattern. In: Proceedings of the 2016 ACM on Workshop on Information Sharing and Collaborative Security, pp. 25–34. ACM (2016)
13. Silva, O., Garcia, A., Lucena, C.: The reflective blackboard pattern: architecting large multi-agent systems. In: Garcia, A., Lucena, C., Zambonelli, F., Omicini, A., Castro, J. (eds.) SELMAS 2002. LNCS, vol. 2603, pp. 73–93. Springer, Heidelberg (2003). https://doi.org/10.1007/3-540-35828-5_5
14. He, L., Li, G., Xing, L., Chen, Y.: An autonomous multi-sensor satellite system based on multi-agent blackboard model autonomiczny wieloczujnikowy system satelitarny oparty na wieloagentowym modelu tablicowym. EKSPLOATACJA I NIEZAWODNOSC **19**(3), 447 (2017)
15. Jurado, F., Redondo, M.A., Ortega, M.: Blackboard architecture to integrate components and agents in heterogeneous distributed elearning systems: an application for learning to program. J. Syst. Softw. **85**(7), 1621–1636 (2012)
16. Huang, M.J., Chiang, H.K., Wu, P.F., Hsieh, Y.J.: A multi-strategy machine learning student modeling for intelligent tutoring systems: based on blackboard approach. Library Hi Tech **31**(2), 274–293 (2013)
17. Prem Kumar, G.: Integrated network management using extended blackboard architecture. Ph.D. thesis (2013)
18. US DHS Cyber Security R&D Center: a roadmap for cybersecurity research. Technical report, DHS (2009)
19. ENISA: Practical guide/roadmap for a suitable channel for secure communication: secure communication with the certs & other stakeholders. Technical report, ENISA (2011)
20. Kampanakis, P.: Security automation and threat information-sharing options. IEEE Secur. Priv. **12**(5), 42–51 (2014)
21. Vázquez, D.F., Acosta, O.P., Spirito, C., Brown, S., Reid, E.: Conceptual framework for cyber defense information sharing within trust relationships. In: 2012 4th International Conference on Cyber Conflict, CYCON 2012, pp. 1–17. IEEE (2012)
22. Haass, J.C., Ahn, G.J., Grimmelmann, F.: ACTRA: a case study for threat information sharing. In: Proceedings of the 2nd ACM Workshop on Information Sharing and Collaborative Security, pp. 23–26. ACM (2015)

23. Sandhu, R., Krishnan, R., White, G.B.: Towards secure information sharing models for community cyber security. In: 6th International Conference on Collaborative Computing: Networking, Applications and Worksharing, CollaborateCom 2010, pp. 1–6. IEEE (2010)
24. Serrano, O., Dandurand, L., Brown, S.: On the design of a cyber security data sharing system. In: Proceedings of the 2014 ACM Workshop on Information Sharing & Collaborative Security, pp. 61–69. ACM (2014)
25. Skopik, F., Settanni, G., Fiedler, R.: A problem shared is a problem halved: a survey on the dimensions of collective cyber defense through security information sharing. Comput. Secur. **60**, 154–176 (2016)
26. Goodwin, C., et al.: A framework for cybersecurity information sharing and risk reduction. Microsoft (2015)
27. Mutemwa, M., Mtsweni, J., Mkhonto, N.: Developing a cyber threat intelligence sharing platform for South African organisations. In: 2017 Conference on Information Communication Technology and Society (ICTAS), pp. 1–6. IEEE (2017)
28. Wagner, C., Dulaunoy, A., Wagener, G., Iklody, A.: MISP: the design and implementation of a collaborative threat intelligence sharing platform. In: Proceedings of the 2016 ACM on Workshop on Information Sharing and Collaborative Security, pp. 49–56. ACM (2016)
29. Johnson, C., Badger, M., Waltermire, D., Snyder, J., Skorupka, C.: Guide to cyber threat information sharing. Technical report, National Institute of Standards and Technology (2016)
30. Bedrijfsrevisoren, D., De Muynck, J., Portesi, S.: Cyber security information sharing: an overview of regulatory and non-regulatory approaches. ENISA (2015)
31. Hayes-Roth, B.: A blackboard architecture for control. Artif. intell. **26**(3), 251–321 (1985)
32. Waterman, D.: A Guide to Expert Systems. Pearson, London (1986)
33. Cai, L., et al.: Information security technology-Cyber security threat information format. Technical report, China Electronics Standardization Institute (2018)
34. Zhang, B.: Research on multi-agent system and its classical problems. http://bokekeji.blogchina.com/3046743.html
35. Krishnan, R., Niu, J., Sandhu, R., Winsborough, W.H.: Group-centric secure information-sharing models for isolated groups. ACM Trans. Inf. Syst. Secur. (TISSEC) **14**(3), 23 (2011)

A Lightweight Secure IoT Surveillance Framework Based on DCT-DFRT Algorithms

Rafik Hamza$^{(\boxtimes)}$, Alzubair Hassan, and Akash Suresh Patil

School of Computer Science and Cyber Engineering, Guangzhou University,
Guangzhou, China
Rafik.hamza@hotmail.com

Abstract. In this paper, we propose an energy-efficient surveillance framework for real-time video processing. The proposed framework guarantees the confidentiality of important frames and transfers them for a real-time decision. First, we extract the keyframes from the surveillance video using a lightweight summarization technique based on a fast histogram-clustering approach. Then, we employ an enhanced discrete cosine transform (DCT) compression technique to reduce the size of the extracted key frames. Finally, the cryptosystem encrypts these keyframes using a lightweight image encryption scheme based on discrete fractional random transform (DFRT) and Chen chaotic system. The proposed framework is fast and ensures real-time processing. Furthermore, this framework has the ability to reduce the transmission cost, and storage required during transmitting the video surveillance.

Keywords: Data compression · Data encryption · DFRT · DCT ·
Keyframes · Surveillance video

1 Introduction

IoT systems have large operating costs and produce huge amounts of data, especially upon storage using third-party like cloud systems. Images and video required a large-scale processing power to extract the information from data. To deal with computational complexity, the researchers propose several contributions including data compression and video summarization techniques [1,2]. Generally, these techniques deal with the problem of efficient management of massive data and reduce the data dissemination to remote IoT centers. However, most of these techniques present several security problems and lack to robustness analysis. For instance, Muhammad et al. [2] proposed a symmetric encryption scheme to secure IoT surveillance systems. However, this technique cannot resist against noise and cropping attacks. In case losing a single pixel of the encrypted image, this will make retrieving of the plain image impossible.

The researchers have proposed different techniques to reduce the volume of data such as compression [1], blockchain [3] and video summarization techniques

© Springer Nature Switzerland AG 2019
X. Chen et al. (Eds.): ML4CS 2019, LNCS 11806, pp. 271–278, 2019.
https://doi.org/10.1007/978-3-030-30619-9_19

[4,5]. The purpose from using these techniques is to extract only informative frames and forward these data for processing in real time. Video summarization techniques select a subset of the images and create a brief video contain the relevant information of the video data [6,7]. Video compressions reduce the size of the video bits by identifying and removing statistical redundancy [8]. Indeed, video compression requires low computation power, resulting in decreased bandwidth and storage requirement.

To tackle the above-mentioned issues, we propose an efficient and secure image encryption-compression framework for IoT surveillance systems based on discrete fractional random transform. The main contribution of this work is using dynamic keys encryption instead of static block cipher comparing to state-of-art schemes [9–11]. The encrypted data are probabilistic which means that encrypting same data will produce different encrypted data (using same secret-keys and cipher algorithm). The proposed framework contains three steps. First, a video summarization is employed to reduce the images and video redundancy [4]. Second, we use an image coding to compress the extracted frames from step one. Finally, the proposed framework encrypts the compressed keyframes using a fast and secure image encryption scheme based on the discrete fractional random transform and Chen chaotic system. The nonlinear map employed to produce two keys. First, a permutation key to shift the pixels of the image. Second, a random matrix employed in discrete fractional random transform. Taking into consideration the various requirements of constrained surveillance devices, the proposed framework can be suitable for IoT-based surveillance systems.

The rest of the paper is organized as follows. Section 2 presents the proposed framework. Section 3 presents brief experimental results. Finally, a conclusion and future directions in Sect. 4.

2   Proposed Framework

In this part, a fast keyframe extraction based on an automatic video summarization technique is proposed. Our framework contains three parts that guarantee a fast and secure transmission of informative frames upon real-time. First, by eliminating video redundancy and select the informative frames using a video summarization. Followed by the compression technique to reduce the frames size from the extracted video. Finally, the framework encrypts the video using a lightweight encryption scheme. The proposed work minimize the analysing time to scan surveillance video for irregular events including fire detection by a surveillance camera, and unusual activities. The cryptosystem ensures the confidentiality of extracted frames prior to transmission.

2.1   Video Summarization Technique

Generally, a surveillance video contains various frames represent different scenes. However, some scenes content fewer activities for a long time such as gas pipelines surveillance in the desert. Sometimes, the scenes could contain a considerable

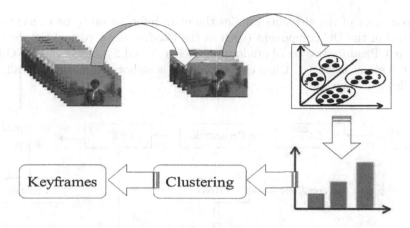

Fig. 1. The proposed summary method includes the following steps: pre-sampling, frames representation, clustering, and identify the keyframes.

amount of activities for shorter duration like in a case of leak detection for oil and gas pipelines. Thus, it is required to employ extra layers techniques to discard the irrelevant frames in the input video, minimizing the bandwidth requirements. Several works have been proposed to extract keyframes based on different techniques [4]. Some works have extracted keyframes using color spaces such as YUV. Figure 1 shows the steps of the proposed summarization framework.

2.2 A Lightweight Cryptosystem

The following points illustrate the steps of image compression-encryption Cryptosystem based on PNRG chaotic system and DFRT. The nonlinear cycle shift operation controlled by a Chen chaotic system is used for diffusion.

First, we compress the extracted keyframes using fractional cosine transform used in JPEG system [12]. The keyframe, denoted by I, is transformed into spectrum via the fractional cosine transform. We employ a secure and fast pseudo random number algorithm [13] to produce the random matrix of discrete fractional random transform (DFRT) [9]. The final encrypted image, denoted as D, is obtained after applying the discrete fractional random transform, where the fractional order is the key of DFRT. To make it easier for the readers, we illustrate the steps of the proposed cryptosystem as Fig. 2 shown.

Step 1. Load the original image and the secret keys. A color keyframe extracted is encrypted using the proposed cryptosystem in Sect. 2 by reshaping the RGB matrices [N, M, 3] into two-dimensional formats [3*N, M]. Followed by the compression-encryption steps.

Step 2. The original image is transformed into spectrum by the fractional cosine transform. The cryptosystem applies DCT on one-dimensional matrix.

The front part of the elements implies the main information to be encrypted is contained in the DC component (such as the low-frequency part of the image).

Step 3. Produce two set of random numbers (S_1 and S_2) based on PRNG [13] using the secret keys. The Chen chaotic system is elaborated mathematically by the following equations

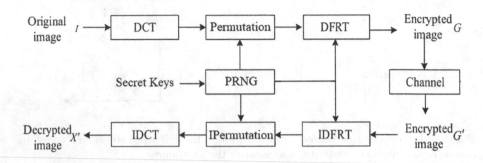

Fig. 2. Image compression-encryption algorithm based on PRNG and DFRT

Step 4. Perform permutation process based on index sort of the generated sequences from PRNG. So, each sequence will shift the plaintext using the a random indexes of the generated chaotic numbers.

Step 5. Perform a discrete fractional random transform, where the fractional order is the key of DFRT [11]. The discrete fractional random transform of a two dimensional signal I is

$$E_R = H^\alpha I (H^\alpha)^T. \tag{1}$$

E_R is the kernel transform of DFRT.

$(H^P)^T$ is the transpose of (H^P).

α is the fractional order.

The transform kernel is random due to the from of randomized matrix I generated from S_1.

The kernel transform (H^P) is defined as:

$$H^\alpha = \Gamma D^\alpha (\Gamma)^T. \tag{2}$$

where Γ is the eigenvector basis. While, Γ^T is the transpose of Γ. $\Gamma(\Gamma^T) = I.D^P$ is an $N \times N$ diagonal matrix.

$$\mathbf{D}^\alpha = \mathrm{diag}\left\{1, \exp\left(-\frac{i2\pi\alpha}{T}\right), \exp\left(-\frac{i4\pi\alpha}{T}\right), \ldots, \exp\left[-\frac{i2(N-1)\pi\alpha}{T}\right]\right\} \tag{3}$$

where positive number T is the period of DFRT.

$$E = \frac{P + P^t}{2}. \tag{4}$$

The transform kernel of DFRT is random which results from the randomness of matrix. The obtained image is denoted as an encrypted image. Figure 2 shows the structure of the proposed work based on PRNG and DFRT.

3   Simulation Results

The experimental results are presented in this section. Simulations and analysis on various grayscale images have been performed on a Matlab (R2017b) platform. The proposed framework is tested using a set of video dataset [1]. We evaluate the security of the proposed framework using different dataset (such as SIPI database) and some standard testing images such as Cameraman and Lenna images. We use the following values ($x_0 = -1.2$, $y_0 = 0.7$, $z_0 = 14$, $a = 35, b = 3$, and $c = 28$) as secret keys for the proposed cryptosystem.

3.1   Security Analysis

The proposed cryptosystem relies on the initial values and controlling paramcters in Chen chaotic system as secret keys. The key space in this case is computed based on the sensibility to initial values and controlling parameters (x_0, y_0, z_0, a, b, and c) of Chen map. According to the evolution, these keys are sensitive enough to change the sequence from PRNG with any difference equal to or large than 10^{-15}. Hence, the key space for each generated sequences is computed to be more than $10^{90} \simeq 2^{300}$. The key space can be 2^{600}, if the user choose to produce S_1 and S_2 using different secret keys. The size of a key space should be large enough to resesit the exhaustive attacks e.g brute force [14]. Additionally, Table 1 shows that the proposed cryptosystem has larger Key space compared to other recent state-of-art schemes [10,11].

Table 1. Key space comparison.

Algorithm	Proposed algorithm	Gong et al. [11]	Zhou et al. [10]
Key space	2^{300}	2^{187}	2^{300}

Figure 3 shows the summarized frames from an original video, subsequently the compressed frames, and finally encrypted frames. The simulation also proves that the proposed work can ensure a high level of security against different attacks such as exhaustive search to find the secret keys. Due to the fact that the proposed framework is extremely sensitive to the chosen secret keys, any adjustment will change completely the encryption process. For example, Fig. 4 shows the attempts to decrypt the encrypted image using different secret keys set. The values have been chosen closely to the original secret keys. This test demonstrates that the proposed cryptosystem can withstand against different attacks.

Fig. 3. Summarized frame, compressed, and encrypted. Finally, decrypted frame

Fig. 4. Decrypted keyframes with incorrect keys (differ by a tiny value)

3.2   Compression Ratio

As known, image compression ratio measures the relative reduction in the image size representation given by the compression technique. The most common procedure to compute compression ratio is the division of uncompressed size by compressed size. In this work, compression ratio (CR) is defined as the following equation illustrates (5).

$$CR = \frac{\text{Size of Original Data}}{\text{Size of Compressed Data}} \tag{5}$$

Since the proposed framework relies directly on DCT compression, the compression rate is computed based on the quality factor and DCT performance. In this work, we assume quality factor is 60, which allows us to compress the data and maintains the image quality. Table 2 shows the performances of compressed images from SIPI Image database[1]. The compression rate of the proposed cryptosystem is around 3.5, archiving good performances. This means that our proposed method reduced the data size, storage, and bandwidth requirements in processing, and communication.

---

[1] http://sipi.usc.edu/database/.

Table 2. CR of the proposed cryptosystem

Image name	Compression ratio	Image name	Compression ratio
Airplane	3.29	Clock	3.06
Moon surface	3,79	Resolution chart	3.24
Airplane	3.32	Chemical plant	3,19
Aerial	3.21	Couple	3,11

4 Conclusion

In this paper, a fast and secure framework is proposed for surveillance systems. The extraction method of keyframes uses K-means clustering based on HSV Histograms. Then, we propose a fast and efficient cryptosystem to guarantee the keyframes confidentiality during the transmission over the public networks. A DCT algorithm is used to compress the extracted frames and discrete fractional random transform is employed to achieve fast and secure image encryption scheme. Chen chaotic map is employed to produce two keys. A permutation key to shift the pixels of the image and a random matrix which has been employed in discrete fractional random transform. The proposed cryptosystem is experimentally tested from different perspectives, showing excellent performances and results. The results demonstrate superiority of the proposed work compared to state-of-art techniques. Furthermore, the proposed cryptosystem guarantees fast and secure transmission of the important keyframes to data centers, reducing the requirements of communication bandwidth and energy, the analysing time, and efforts to make the appropriate decisions.

References

1. Taj-Eddin, I.A.T.F., Afifi, M., Korashy, M., Hamdy, D., Nasser, M., Derbaz, S.: A new compression technique for surveillance videos: evaluation using new dataset. In: 2016 Sixth International Conference on Digital Information and Communication Technology and its Applications (DICTAP), pp. 159–164. IEEE (2016)
2. Muhammad, K., Hamza, R., Ahmad, J., Lloret, J., Wang, H., Baik, S.W.: Secure surveillance framework for IoT systems using probabilistic image encryption. IEEE Trans. Ind. Inform. **14**(8), 3679–3689 (2018)
3. Patil, A.S., Tama, B.A., Park, Y., Rhee, K.-H.: A framework for blockchain based secure smart green house farming. In: Park, J.J., Loia, V., Yi, G., Sung, Y. (eds.) CUTE/CSA -2017. LNEE, vol. 474, pp. 1162–1167. Springer, Singapore (2018). https://doi.org/10.1007/978-981-10-7605-3_185
4. Jiaxin, W., Zhong, S., Jiang, J., Yang, Y.: A novel clustering method for static video summarization. Multimed. Tools Appl. **76**(7), 9625–9641 (2017)
5. Hamza, R., Muhammad, K., Lv, Z., Titouna, F.: Secure video summarization framework for personalized wireless capsule endoscopy. Pervasive Mob. Comput. **41**, 436–450 (2017)

6. Rochan, M., Ye, L., Wang, Y.: Video summarization using fully convolutional sequence networks. In: Ferrari, V., Hebert, M., Sminchisescu, C., Weiss, Y. (eds.) ECCV 2018. LNCS, vol. 11216, pp. 358–374. Springer, Cham (2018). https://doi.org/10.1007/978-3-030-01258-8_22

7. Hamza, R., Yan, Z., Muhammad, K., Bellavista, P., Titouna, F.: A privacy-preserving cryptosystem for IoT E-healthcare. Inf. Sci. (2019). https://doi.org/10.1016/j.ins.2019.01.070. ISSN: 0020-0255

8. Babu, R.V., Tom, M., Wadekar, P.: A survey on compressed domain video analysis techniques. Multimed. Tools Appl. **75**(2), 1043–1078 (2016)

9. Liu, Z., Zhao, H., Liu, S.: A discrete fractional random transform. Opt. Commun. **255**(4–6), 357–365 (2005)

10. Zhou, N., Dong, T., Wu, J.: Novel image encryption algorithm based on multiple-parameter discrete fractional random transform. Opt. Commun. **283**(15), 3037–3042 (2010)

11. Gong, L., Deng, C., Pan, S., Zhou, N.: Image compression-encryption algorithms by combining hyper-chaotic system with discrete fractional random transform. Opt. Laser Technol. **103**, 48–58 (2018)

12. Wu, H., Sun, X., Yang, J., Zeng, W., Wu, F.: Lossless compression of JPEG coded photo collections. IEEE Trans. Image Process. **25**(6), 2684–2696 (2016)

13. Hamza, R.: A novel pseudo random sequence generator for image-cryptographic applications. J. Inf. Secur. Appl. **35**, 119–127 (2017)

14. Zhang, M., Tong, X.: A new algorithm of image compression and encryption based on spatiotemporal cross chaotic system. Multimed. Tools Appl. **74**(24), 11255–11279 (2015)

Interpretable Encrypted Searchable Neural Networks

Kai Chen[1], Zhongrui Lin[2], Jian Wan[2], and Chungen Xu[1(✉)]

[1] School of Science, Nanjing University of Science and Technology, Nanjing, China
{kaichen,xuchung}@njust.edu.cn
[2] School of Computer Science and Engineering, NJUST, Nanjing, China
{zhongruilin,wanjian}@njust.edu.cn

Abstract. In cloud security, traditional searchable encryption (SE) requires high computation and communication overhead for dynamic search and update. The clever combination of machine learning (ML) and SE may be a new way to solve this problem. This paper proposes interpretable encrypted searchable neural networks (IESNN) to explore probabilistic query, balanced index tree construction and automatic weight update in an encrypted cloud environment. In IESNN, probabilistic learning is used to obtain search ranking for searchable index, and probabilistic query is performed based on ciphertext index, which reduces the computational complexity of query significantly. Compared to traditional SE, it is proposed that adversarial learning and automatic weight update in response to user's timely query of the latest data set without expensive communication overhead. The proposed IESNN performs better than the previous works, bringing the query complexity closer to $O(\log N)$ and introducing low overhead on computation and communication.

Keywords: Searchable encryption · Searchable neural networks ·
Probabilistic learning · Adversarial learning · Automatic weight update

1 Introduction

The frequent and massive disclosure of private data has drawn the growing attention of the public to the *cyberspace security*. Meanwhile, *cloud storage* services are increasingly attracting individuals and enterprises to outsource data into cloud server with the rapid development of *cloud computing*. Unfortunately, outsourcing data into cloud server may reveal the privacy of data [10,14]. In *cloud security*, *searchable encryption* (SE) has received widespread attention as it protects the privacy of outsourced data and prevents sensitive information from leaking [5]. However, traditional SE [1,3,6,8–10,12–14] requires high computation and communication overhead to enable *dynamic search* and *dynamic update*, which makes SE still unable to satisfy user's experience and requirements of the actual application adequately. Actually, *machine learning* (ML) can provide intelligent and efficient means yet the current popular ML only supports

© Springer Nature Switzerland AG 2019
X. Chen et al. (Eds.): ML4CS 2019, LNCS 11806, pp. 279–289, 2019.
https://doi.org/10.1007/978-3-030-30619-9_20

plaintext data training and can not satisfy the special requirements of encrypted cloud data. Therefore, it is necessary to discuss the cross-fusion problem of ML and SE, and introduce intelligence and high-efficiency into SE.

SE has been continuously developed since it was proposed [8], and *multi-keyword ranked search* scheme is recognized as excellent [5]. Cao et al. [1] first discussed privacy-preserving multi-keyword ranked search over encrypted cloud data (MRSE) for single data owner model, and established strict privacy requirements. They first used *asymmetric scalar-product preserving encryption* (ASPE) [12] to obtain the *similarity score* of the query vector and the index vector. In this way, cloud server can retrieve *top-k* documents that are most relevant to the data user's query request. However, since matrix operations require high computation overhead, MRSE is not suitable for practical application scenario. For the purpose of managing the keyword dictionary dynamically and improving system performance, Li et al. [6] proposed efficient multi-keyword ranked query over encrypted data in cloud computing (MKQE) based on MRSE, which owns a low overhead index construction algorithm and a novel trapdoor generation algorithm. However, it still has no major breakthrough in improving search efficiency when the data set is large. To achieve *dynamic search*, Xia et al. [13] provided a secure and dynamic multi-keyword ranked search scheme over encrypted cloud data (EDMRS) to support dynamic operation in SE. For tree-based index structures, search efficiency is improved by the greedy depth-first search (GDFS) algorithm and parallel computing. Regrettably, the search efficiency of ordinary balanced binary tree they used gradually decreases and tends to linear search efficiency when migrating to multiple data owners model with large amount of differential data. Moreover, maintaining such an index tree is not flexible and efficient. Guo et al. [3] discussed secure multi-keyword ranked search over encrypted cloud data for multiple data owners model (MKRS_MO) and designed a heuristic weight generation algorithm based on the relationships among keywords, documents and owners (KDO). They considered the correlation among documents and the impact of documents' quality on search results. Experiments on the real-world data set showed that MKRS_MO is better than the schemes using traditional $TF \times IDF$ keyword weight model [9]. However, the fly in the ointment is that the operations of calculating index similarity in MKRS_MO may lead to "curse of dimensionality", which limits the availability of the system. Last but not least, they ignored the secure solution in *known background model* [1] (*threat model* for measuring the ability of cloud server to evaluate private data and the risk of revealing private information in SE system).

For the first time, this paper proposes *interpretable encrypted searchable neural networks* (IESNN) to explore *intelligent SE*. Based on the *neural network*, we propose *sorting network* and employ *probabilistic learning* to obtain the query ranking for encrypted searchable index. To be specific, firstly it performs a sufficient amount of random queries (obey *uniform distribution*) and then calculates the sum of the inner product of each index vector and all random query vectors. Finally it sorts the index vectors according to the match scores from high to low. Therefore, the probabilistic ranking of the index is close to the ranking in the actual query, which reduces the computational complexity of the query significantly. Moreover, *probabilistic query* with computational complexity close to $O(\log N)$, is used to retrieve *top-k* documents. In order to achieve secure weight update without revealing private information to "semi-trusted" cloud server [10,14], we propose *searching adversarial network* and *weight update network* in an encrypted cloud environment. Specifically, in order to respond to user's timely query of the latest data set, we employ *adversarial learning* [2] and *optimal game equilibrium* to make the probabilistic ranking of the index close to its popular ranking. Furthermore, we combine *backpropagation neural network* [4] with *discrete Hopfield neural network* [7] to enable *automatic weight update*. It is worth mentioning that the update operations are done in the cloud, which means there is no expensive communication overhead. So we can use IESNN for model training and intelligent system implementation. On the one hand, it introduces intelligence into the SE system, which improves user's experience and reduces system overhead. On the other hand, training data sources for ML can be derived from ciphertext. It means that data mining based on ciphertext analysis can not only obtain results consistent with plaintext analysis but also strengthen the intensity of data privacy protection. The comparison among several previous typical schemes and ours is described in Table 1.

Table 1. Comparison of related works.

Item	MRSE [1]	MKRS_MO [3]	MKQE [6]	EDMRS [13]	IESNN
High-precision query	√	√	√	√	√
Privacy-preserving query	√	×	√	√	√
Automatic weight update	×	×	×	×	√
High-quality ranked search	×	√	√	×	√
Efficient multi-keyword search	√	√	√	√	√
Flexible dynamic maintenance	×	×	×	×	√

Our main contributions are summarized as follows:

(1) Towards *intelligent SE* by combining popular ML with traditional SE effectively;
(2) We employ *probabilistic learning* method to achieve *maximum likelihood searching* and improve search efficiency significantly;
(3) We use IESNN to implement *flexible dynamic operation and maintenance* in an encrypted cloud environment.

The remainder of this paper is organized as follows: Sect. 2 describes the SE model. Section 3 describes the details of IESNN and its performance tests. Section 4 discusses our solution and its implications.

2 Searchable Encryption Model

2.1 System Model

The system model proposed in this paper consists of three parties, is depicted in Fig. 1, and the specific description is as follows:

Data owners (DO): DO are responsible for building searchable index and original IESNN, encrypting the data and sending them to cloud server.

Data users (DU): DU are consumers of cloud services. Once the license is granted, they can retrieve the encrypted cloud data.

Cloud server (CS): CS is considered "semi-trusted" in SE [10,14]. It provides cloud service, including running authorized access controls, performing searches for encrypted cloud data based on query requests, returning *top-k* documents to DU and enabling dynamic operation and maintenance with IESNN.

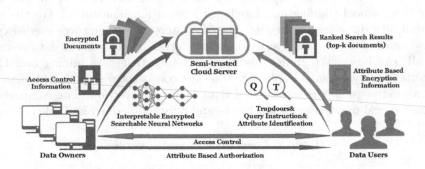

Fig. 1. The basic architecture of searchable encryption system

2.2   System Framework

Setup: Based on privacy requirements in *known background model* [1], DO_i determines the size N_i of dictionary D_i, the number U_i of pseudo-keyword, sets the parameter $V_i = U_i + N_i$. For all data owners $DO = \{DO_1, \ldots, DO_m\}$, we have $V = \{V_1, \ldots, V_m\}$, $U = \{U_1, \ldots, U_m\}$, $N = \{N_1, \ldots, N_m\}$.

KeyGen(V): DO generate secret key $SK = \{SK_1, \ldots, SK_s\}$, where $SK_i = \{S_i, M_{i,1}, M_{i,2}\}$, $M_{i,1}$ and $M_{i,2}$ are two invertible matrices with the dimension $V_i \times V_i$ and S_i is a random V_i-length vector.

Extended-KeyGen(SK_i, Z_i): For *dynamic search* [6], if Z_i new keywords are added into the i-th dictionary D_i (belongs to D_i), the DO_i generates a new $SK_i' = \{S_i', M_{i,1}', M_{i,2}'\}$, two invertible matrices $M_{i,1}'$ and $M_{i,2}'$ with the dimension $(V_i + Z_i) \times (V_i + Z_i)$, and a new $(V_i + Z_i)$-length vector S_i'.

BuildIndex(I, SK): In order to reduce the possibility that "semi-trusted" cloud server [10,14] evaluates the private data successfully, DO first build searchable indexes for documents and obtain the weighted index vectors, and then fill index vectors with random pseudo-keywords (obey *Gaussian distribution*) and obtain secure index vectors with high privacy protection strength [1]. Finally they use secure index vectors to build IESNN and send IESNN to CS (specific example: DO_i "splits" index vector I_i into two random vectors

$\{I_{i,1}, I_{i,2}\}$. Specifically, if $S_i[t] = 0$, $I_{i,1}[t] = I_{i,2}[t] = I_i[t]$; else if $S_i[t] = 1$, $I_{i,1}[t]$ is a random value, $I_{i,2}[t] = I_i[t] - I_{i,1}[t]$. DO_i encrypts I_i as $\widetilde{I}_i = \{M_{i,1}^T I_{i,1}, M_{i,2}^T I_{i,2}\}$ with SK_i).

Trapdoor(Q, SK): DU send query request (query keywords and k) to DO. DO generate query $Q = \{Q_1, \dots, Q_m\}$ (where Q_i is a weighted vector with dimension V_i) and calculate the trapdoor $T = \{T_1, \dots, T_m\}$ using SK and send T to DU (specific example: DO_i "splits" query vector Q_i into two random vectors $\{Q_{i,1}, Q_{i,2}\}$. Specifically, if $S_i[t] = 0$, $Q_{i,1}[t]$ is a random value, and $Q_{i,2}[t] = Q_i[t] - Q_{i,1}[t]$; else if $S_i[t] = 1$, $Q_{i,1}[t] = Q_{i,2}[t] = Q_i[t]$. Finally, DO_i encrypts Q_i as $T_i = \{M_{i,1}^{-1} Q_{i,1}, M_{i,2}^{-1} Q_{i,2}\}$ with SK_i).

Query(T, k, I): DU send trapdoors, query instruction and attribute identification to CS. CS performs searches based on the query, and returns *top-k* documents to DU.

3 Interpretable Encrypted Searchable Neural Networks

3.1 Maximum Likelihood Searching

We employ *inner product similarity* [11] to quantitatively evaluate the effective similarity between the query vector and the index vector. As illustrated in Fig. 2 (for an intuitive understanding, it shows the unencrypted network), in *sorting network*, it performs a sufficient amount of random queries (obey *uniform distribution*: $X \sim (-\sigma\sqrt{3}, \sigma\sqrt{3})$, that is $f(x) = \frac{1}{2\sigma\sqrt{3}}, x \in [-\sigma\sqrt{3}, \sigma\sqrt{3}]$), and then calculates the sum of the inner product $\sum_{j=1}^{m} I_i^T \cdot Q_j$ of each index vector and all random query vectors with formula 1. Finally it sorts the index vectors according to the match scores from high to low. Therefore, the index ranking obtained by *probabilistic learning* is close to the ranking in the actual query.

$$Score = \widetilde{I}_i \cdot T_i = \{M_{i,1}^T I_{i,1}, M_{i,2}^T I_{i,2}\} \cdot \{M_{i,1}^{-1} Q_{i,1}, M_{i,2}^{-1} Q_{i,2}\} = I_i^T \cdot Q_i \qquad (1)$$

We implement the proposed scheme using Python in Windows 10 operation system with Intel Core i5 Processor 2.40 GHz and test its efficiency on a real-world document set (IEEE INFOCOM publications, including 400 papers and 2,000 keywords). The *probabilistic query* algorithm based on the probabilistic ranking of encrypted searchable index brings the query complexity closer to $O(\log N)$. As shown in Fig. 3, when retrieving the same number of *top-k* documents, *probabilistic query* performs better than the related works that based on tree search [3,13] and matrix operation [1,6]. As the ordered feature of the balanced binary tree is not guaranteed in the index tree and the query based on matrix operation needs to traverse all indexes to retrieve *top-k* documents, the number of retrieved indexes is far more than the number of retrieved documents.

3.2 Adversarial Learning

Adversarial network works when the probabilistic ranking of the index deviates from the index ranking in the actual query result. As shown in Fig. 4, it employs

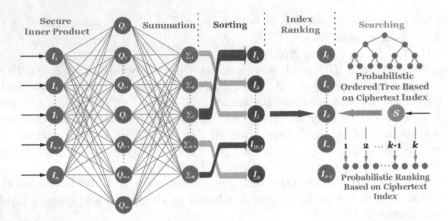

Fig. 2. Sorting network

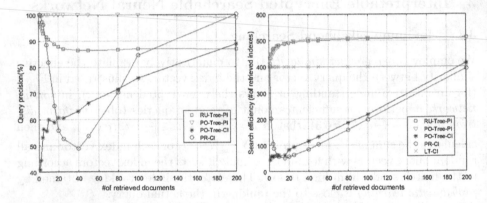

Fig. 3. Performance testing of multiple query algorithms. {The *query precision* and *search efficiency* for different numbers of retrieved documents with the same document collection (400) and dictionary (2,000). It requires an average of 100 experimental results to measure performance of the following subjects: random unordered tree based on plaintext index (RU-Tree-PI) [3,13], probabilistic ordered tree based on plaintext index (PO-Tree-PI), probabilistic ordered tree based on ciphertext index (PO-Tree-CI), probabilistic ranking based on ciphertext index (PR-CI), linear traversal based on ciphertext index (LT-CI) [1,6]. The number of retrieved *top-k* documents is the factor of 400: $k = 1, 2, 4, 5, 8, 10, 16, 20, 25, 40, 50, 80, 100, 200$. Note: the nodes of the tree are also included in the number of retrieval indexes. According to the experimental results, *probabilistic query* can significantly improve the search efficiency. When k takes a specific interval value, the query precision is high or low. It is because that the probabilistic ranking of the index vector is not strictly ordered, and the query is random. Therefore, when the query vector is very "unpopular", the query precision will become lower, and when the query vector is "popular", the query precision and search efficiency will perform well.}

optimal game equilibrium to make the probabilistic ranking of the index close to its popular ranking (described by formula 2, $p_i(x)$ and $p_q(y)$ are the *probability distributions* of the index ranking and query result, respectively).

$$\min_{S} \max_{A} V(A, S) = \mathbb{E}_{x \sim p_i(x)}[\log A(x)] + \mathbb{E}_{y \sim p_q(y)}[\log(1 - A(S(y)))] \quad (2)$$

Inspired by *generative adversarial networks* (GAN) [2] and *self-attention generative adversarial networks* (SAGAN) [15] but different from GAN and SAGAN, *searching adversarial networks* (SAN) do not require complex gradient calculations and extensive iterative training. As a matter of fact, SAN only require simple residual calculations and index sorting floating steps. Specifically, after completing the query, the ranked search result list is feedback to *adversarial network* in SAN. *Adversarial network* calculates the residual before and after the weight change of the index corresponding to *top-k* documents, and calculates the relative floating of the index ranking of the feedback result (i.e. new index ranking) and the original index ranking. Finally, SAN send the results of the calculation (the residual of the weights) and the index ranking changes to the *weight update network* as a target for index update (see Fig. 5 for details).

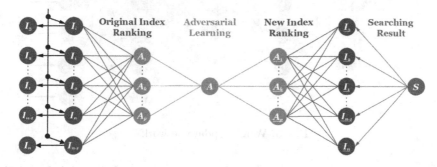

Fig. 4. Searching adversarial networks

3.3   Automatic Weight Update

As illustrated in Fig. 5, in order to achieve *automatic weight update* and respond to users' queries for the latest data sets in a timely manner, *weight update network* (WUN) combines *backpropagation neural network* (BPNN) [4] with *discrete Hopfield neural network* (DHNN) [7]. In WUN, the update of index weights uses vector and matrix operations to approximate the actual increments, which has the characteristics of local homomorphism for ciphertext operations and plaintext operations. For instance, considering index vector $I_\alpha = [\alpha_1, \ldots, \alpha_n]^T$, query vector $Q_\gamma = [\gamma_1, \ldots, \gamma_n]^T$, and two invertible matrices $M = (a_{ij})_{n \times n}$ and $M^{-1} = (b_{ij})_{n \times n}$. The *update principle* of ciphertext index is as follows:

Matrix and vector multiplication: $I_\alpha^T M = [\sum\limits_{i=1}^{n} \alpha_i a_{i1}, \ldots, \sum\limits_{i=1}^{n} \alpha_i a_{in}], M^{-1} Q_\gamma =$
$[\sum\limits_{j=1}^{n} b_{1j} \gamma_j, \ldots, \sum\limits_{j=1}^{n} b_{nj} \gamma_j];$ *Secure inner product calculation:* $I_\alpha^T M \cdot M^{-1} Q_\gamma =$
$I_\alpha^T \cdot Q_\gamma = \sum\limits_{i=1}^{n} \alpha_i \gamma_i;$ *Index vector update:* $(I_\alpha^T + \Delta I_\alpha^T)M = [\sum\limits_{i=1}^{n} (\alpha_i +$
$\Delta \alpha_i) a_{i1}, \ldots, \sum\limits_{i=1}^{n} (\alpha_i + \Delta \alpha_i) a_{in}] \approx [\sum\limits_{i=1}^{n} \alpha_i a_{i1} + \Delta \beta_1, \ldots, \sum\limits_{i=1}^{n} \alpha_i a_{in} + \Delta \beta_n] =$
$I_\alpha^T M + \Delta I_\alpha^T M;$ *Inner product approximation:* $(I_\alpha^T + \Delta I_\alpha^T)M \cdot M^{-1} Q_\gamma \approx (I_\alpha^T M +$
$\Delta I_\beta^T M) \cdot M^{-1} Q_\gamma = I_\alpha^T \cdot Q_\gamma + \Delta I_\beta^T \cdot Q_\gamma = \sum\limits_{i=1}^{n} \alpha_i \gamma_i + \sum\limits_{i=1}^{n} \Delta \beta_i \gamma_i.$

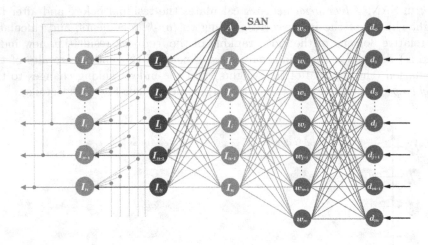

Fig. 5. Weight update network

Asynchronous Work Mode of WUN: The update task from SAN to WUN is only updating the weight of an index, while other indexes still retain their original weight. i.e.

$$I_j(t+1) = \begin{cases} sgn[net_j(t)], j = i \\ I_j(t), \qquad j \neq i \end{cases}, I_j(t+1) = \begin{cases} satlins[net_j(t)], j = i \\ I_j(t), \qquad\quad j \neq i \end{cases} \quad (3)$$

Synchronous Work Mode of WUN: The synchronous work mode is parallel, i.e. the weights of all indexes are all changed in one update. The adjustment of the weight is determined according to the current input value. The weight update is complete and the weight of an index continues to be used for the next update. When the weight of each index is stabilized, the work ends.

$$\begin{cases} I_j(t+1) = sgn[net_j(t)], \qquad j = 1, 2, \ldots, n \\ I_j(t+1) = satlins[net_j(t)], j = 1, 2, \ldots, n \end{cases} \quad (4)$$

When updating an index, the schemes [3,13] employ tree-based index need to update the index vector itself (leaf node of index tree) and its corresponding other data (parent node of leaf node). Moreover, in order to achieve *dynamic search*, the current schemes [1,3,6,9,13] need to download the ciphertext index from the cloud, update its plaintext after local decryption, and finally upload the new ciphertext index to the cloud. In comparison, our solution only needs to update the index vector in the cloud with touching a smaller amount of data and introduce low overhead on computation and communication.

3.4 Overall Operation and Maintenance of IESNN

As shown in Fig. 6, IESNN consist of *sorting net, adversarial net, searching net* and *weight update net*. Except that the initial index weight needs to be generated by data owners, the rest of automatic update operations ("add, delete, change and investigate" operations of index) are all completed in an encrypted cloud environment. The system forms a "query-learning-update-learning-query" *self-attention* [15] loop and an "automatic operation and maintenance" mechanism. *Dynamic operation and maintenance* of SE system are almost entirely done in cloud server. On the one hand, implementing *dynamic operation and maintenance* in an encrypted cloud environment not only improves the usability and flexibility of SE system, but also enhances the strength of privacy protection. On the other hand, when it is necessary to update the index in cloud server, compared with traditional SE [1,3,6,9,13], our solution eliminates the need to rebuild the index locally and upload a new index to cover the old index stored in the cloud, which introduces low overhead on computation, communication and local storage.

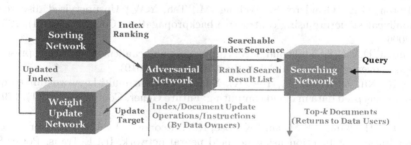

Fig. 6. The overall composition of IESNN

4 Discussion

In this paper, we discuss the cross-fusion problem of ML and SE, and propose IESNN. We creatively combine popular ML with traditional SE, which is committed to exploring *intelligent SE*. We employ *probabilistic learning* method to generate *sorting network* that is trained by a sufficient amount of random queries, which makes a contribution to achieve *maximum likelihood searching* and bring the query complexity closer to $O(\log N)$. It means that exploiting ML to optimize the query is effective in an *uncertain system*, even better than special construction methods. Obviously, traditional query algorithms based on matrix operations and tree searching are not optimistic in big data environments because high dimensional data processing can lead to "curse of dimensionality" and even system crashes. Implementing *flexible dynamic operation and maintenance* in an encrypted cloud environment with IESNN that reduces communication overhead, protects data privacy and leverages cloud computing well.

Acknowledgment. This work was supported by "the Fundamental Research Funds for the Central Universities" (No. 30918012204) and "the National Undergraduate Training Program for Innovation and Entrepreneurship" (Item number: 201810288061). NJUST graduate Scientific Research Training of 'Hundred, Thousand and Ten Thousand' Project *"Research on Intelligent Searchable Encryption Technology"*.

References

1. Cao, N., Wang, C., Li, M., Ren, K., Lou, W.: Privacy-preserving multi-keyword ranked search over encrypted cloud data. IEEE Trans. Parallel Distrib. Syst. **25**(1), 222–233 (2014)
2. Goodfellow, I.J., et al.: Generative adversarial networks. CoRR abs/1406.2661 (2014)
3. Guo, Z., Zhang, H., Sun, C., Wen, Q., Li, W.: Secure multi-keyword ranked search over encrypted cloud data for multiple data owners. J. Syst. Softw. **137**(3), 380–395 (2018)
4. Hinton, G.E., Osindero, S., Welling, M., Teh, Y.W.: Unsupervised discovery of nonlinear structure using contrastive backpropagation. Cogn. Sci. **30**(4), 725–731 (2006)
5. Kumar, D.V.N.S., Thilagam, P.S.: Approaches and challenges of privacy preserving search over encrypted data. Inf. Syst. **81**, 63–81 (2019)
6. Li, R., Xu, Z., Kang, W., Yow, K., Xu, C.: Efficient multi-keyword ranked query over encrypted data in cloud computing. Future Gener. Comp. Syst. **30**(1), 179–190 (2014)
7. Park, J.H., Kim, Y.S., Eom, I.K., Lee, K.Y.: Economic load dispatch for piecewise quadratic cost function using hopfield neural network. IEEE Trans. Power Syst. **8**(3), 1030–1038 (1993)
8. Song, D.X., Wagner, D.A., Perrig, A.: Practical techniques for searches on encrypted data. In: IEEE S & P 2000, pp. 44–55. IEEE Computer Society (2000)
9. Sun, W., et al.: Verifiable privacy-preserving multi-keyword text search in the cloud supporting similarity-based ranking. IEEE Trans. Parallel Distrib. Syst. **25**(11), 3025–3035 (2014)
10. Wang, C., Wang, Q., Ren, K., Lou, W.: Privacy-preserving public auditing for data storage security in cloud computing. In: INFOCOM 2010, pp. 525–533 (2010)
11. Witten, I.H., Moffat, A., Bell, T.C.: Managing Gigabytes: Compressing and Indexing Documents and Images, 2nd edn. Morgan Kaufmann, Burlington (1999)
12. Wong, W.K., Cheung, D.W., Kao, B., Mamoulis, N.: Secure KNN computation on encrypted databases. In: ACM SIGMOD 2009, pp. 139–152. ACM (2009)

13. Xia, Z., Wang, X., Sun, X., Wang, Q.: A secure and dynamic multi-keyword ranked search scheme over encrypted cloud data. IEEE Trans. Parallel Distrib. Syst. **27**(2), 340–352 (2016)

14. Yu, S., Wang, C., Ren, K., Lou, W.: Achieving secure, scalable, and fine-grained data access control in cloud computing. In: INFOCOM 2010, pp. 534–542. IEEE (2010)

15. Zhang, H., Goodfellow, I.J., Metaxas, D.N., Odena, A.: Self-attention generative adversarial networks. In: ICML 2019, pp. 7354–7363. PMLR (2019)

Game Theory Based Dynamic Defense Mechanism for SDN

Deming Mao[1,2], Shuwen Zhang[1(✉)], Ling Zhang[1], and Yu Feng[1]

[1] China Electronic Technology Cyber Security Co., Ltd.,
Chengdu 610041, Sichuan, China
zhngsf@yeah.net
[2] Northwestern Polytechnical University, Xi'an 710072, Shanxi, China

Abstract. Many efforts have been down on tackling the network security issues using game theory, especially studying the dynamic defense mechanism. They mostly concentrated on the traditional networks, while omitting the advantages of SDN (software-defined networks). In this paper, we formulate a new defense framework for SDN, which adopts multistage dynamic defense strategies with the help of a quantization method of attack. The defender may find the behaviors of a particular attacker and make an adaptive response. This framework seeks to support the defender to interact with an attacker following the initial deployment of cyber defenses. Finally, we conduct evaluations to verify the effectiveness of the framework and method proposed in the paper. In the future, we will further study how to improve the defense capability of those critical nodes in SDN, enable more sophisticated responses to attacker behaviors, and improve the defensive situation.

Keywords: Software-defined network (SDN) · Multistage dynamic game · Cyber Deception · New cyber security · Adaptive defense

1 Introduction

Traditional networks are rigid and inflexible because of their large scale and complex technical system. There is basically no information interaction interface between the security devices and applications running on the network that they are in a state of separation from each other, these make it unable to effectively deal with the endless attacks [1, 2]. The emergence of SDN (software-defined network) provides a new light for cyber security defense, supporting more defense mechanisms designed by cyber defender and enabling the dynamic resilience [3, 4].

In the process of network attack and defense, the defender's role is notoriously unfair since a defender aims to prevent intrusions at every possible location, and the attacker only needs to discover and exploit a single vulnerability in order to breach defenses [5]. This kind of target confrontation and relationship non-cooperation are the embodiment of the game [6]. In addition, while many techniques have been developed to increase the speed and accuracy of detecting adversarial activity with the aim of making a defender's job easier, beyond a priori hardening of systems, less research has been done on techniques to make the attacker's job fundamentally more difficult. The

© Springer Nature Switzerland AG 2019
X. Chen et al. (Eds.): ML4CS 2019, LNCS 11806, pp. 290–303, 2019.
https://doi.org/10.1007/978-3-030-30619-9_21

use of game theory for cyber defense can add more uncertainty by dynamically adjusting defense strategies and masking true information. This further impacts the decision-making of attackers, causing them to waste both time and effort [7]. Therefore, designing an effective defense mechanism for SDN based on attack and defense game is the practical need and important direction in the field of cyber security [8, 9].

There have some researches on cyber defense based on game theory, which can be classified into two aspects [10, 11]. One is that network attack and defense game is employed for the prediction of attack behaviors or when and how strategies should be adopted by cyber defender. However, the game models in these researches are mostly static method, which cannot reflect the interactive and multistage characteristics of network confrontation. Kayode et al. proposed a non-zero and deterministic game to analyze the security of computer networks, and the probability that the network may be attacked can be obtained according to a given attack strategy or response strategy [12]. Zhang et al. improved the quantization method of attack and defense strategies, using the non-cooperative and static game to select the optimal defense strategy based on attack prediction [13]. Jiang et al. asserted that network attack and defense confrontation is a two-person, zero-sum, and static game, where cyber security assessment and defense strategy selection are studied [14]. Carin et al. developed a static attack and defense game for the effectiveness analysis of critical infrastructure security protection strategies [15]. Wang et al. used the stochastic game to study the security evaluation of the target network and defense strategy selection [16]. Gueye et al. analyzed the game relationship between virus designers, data tamper and defenders, giving a choice of defense strategies [17].

Another is that researchers used the incomplete information and dynamic game to characterize the uncertainties with in the process of the network attack and defense. Compared with the complete information and static game, it is more in line with the reality of network attack and defense. However, the dynamic multistage division method is not reasonable and feasible, with not considering the effect of motivation and deception on cyber defense. Liu et al. analyzed the characteristics of attack and defense confrontation in the context of dynamic target defense, proposing the selection method of optimal defense strategy under different security situations based on incomplete information and dynamic game [18]. Zhang et al. used the signal game to describe the dynamic attack and defense process with incomplete information constraints, and quantitatively described the signal attenuation [19]. Lin et al. formulated a dynamic defense game to solve the problem of uncertain change on attack intention and attack strategy [20].

Although some achievements have been made in the above researches, they are all concentrated on the traditional network and fail to character the cyber security issues under the SDN architecture. Therefore, we study that dynamic defense mechanism for SDN to protect the key nodes based on game theory, formulating a multistage game by using the architectural advantages of SDN, in which deceptive behaviors of cyber defender in different stages were considered. This is important for defenders, since as the dynamic adjustment of defense strategies can reduce the chances of SDN key nodes being attacked, improving the security of SDN.

2 Dynamic Defense Mechanism for SDN

We design a dynamic defense mechanism for SDN based on game theory to solve the problem that static defense mechanism in the existing methods cannot describe the uncertain and continuous change in the process of the network attack and defense. The framework is shown in Fig. 1. The protected object is the target to be attacked, that is, the key node in the network. SDN controller is the core of dynamic defense mechanism, including a monitoring timer and multistage dynamic game, where the monitoring timer is responsible for switching between different game stages by setting a fixed time period or sensing the security state of the SDN. Based on that, multistage game is used to dynamic transformation of defense strategies according to the behaviors of cyber attackers, considering the influence of cyber defender's deceptive behaviors on attacker's decision making and cyber defense effects in different game stages.

Additionally, in our model we define the game object as SDN controller and network host. The actual situation of network attack and defense is that when cyber attacker is limited by its own technology and knows less about the related information of cyber defender. It is wise to use exploratory attacks, such as port scanning to collect further defense information. Correspondingly, defenders must implement cyber defense in a targeted manner to ensure cyber security. From this perspective, attack and defense confrontation is a multi-round process. Therefore, dynamic defense mechanism for SDN can be described as an interaction process between SDN controller and network host through various individual strategies, and making a decision that how cyber defender adapts the optimal defense strategies based on the attacker's potential actions and their expected defense utility.

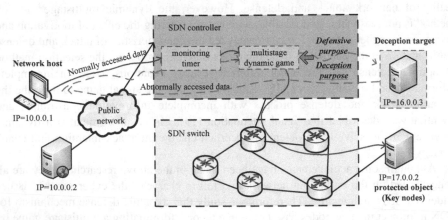

Fig. 1. Dynamic defense mechanism for SDN based on game theory

3 Multistage Dynamic Game for SDN

Attack and defense confrontation in SDN environment is non-cooperative, incomplete information, multistage and dynamic game process. In our model and analysis, we use the well-known definitions of improved Bayesian game, imperfect information, incomplete information, information sets, and perfect Bayesian equilibrium. We define cyber attackers as the leader of the game, similarly, cyber defenders as the follower of the game. We define defenders for two purposes, namely defensive purposes and deceptive purposes, which differentiate our model from traditional game theory models. In particular, we differentiate between a player's perception of possible motivations, deceptions, and payoffs of the game.

3.1 Formal Definition of Multistage Dynamic Game

We first give a formal definition of our multistage dynamic game for SDN (MDGS), in the following, all sets are finite.

Definition 1. $MDGS = (S, N, \Theta, T, U, P, \widetilde{P})$ consists of the following:

S is the number of stages of MDGS, $S = \{1, 2, \ldots, n\}$. The current stage of MDGS is represented by MDGS(S), which is determined by the monitoring timer deployed on the SDN controller.

$N = (N_A, N_D)$ is a set of players, N_A indicates the cyber attacker, and the same notation is used for N_D indicated the cyber defender.

$\Theta = (\Theta_A, \Theta_D)$ is a type space of attacker and defender, according to different attack capabilities, attackers can be divided into several types as $\Theta_A = (\theta_1, \theta_2, \ldots, \theta_h)$. The probability distribution of Θ_A is the common knowledge of attackers and defenders, and the type of the defender is $\Theta_D = (\eta)$.

$T = (T_A, T_D)$ is a strategy space of attackers and defenders, and attack strategy profile is a tuple expressed as $T_A = \{a_1, a_2, \ldots, a_i\}$, similarly as $T_D = \{d_1, d_2, \ldots, d_j\}$. A strategy is a complete description of one or more moves to take in all contingencies.

A tuple $U = (U_A, U_D)$ of utility functions for each player. The utility $U_i(\theta)$ is a numerical score representing the payoff to player i of the type of θ.

P is the prior beliefs of attacker's type, $P = (p_1, p_2, \ldots, p_h)$ represents the defender's initial judgment on the attacker's type θ.

$\widetilde{P}$ is the posterior beliefs of attacker's type, $\widetilde{P} = \widetilde{P}(\theta_h | a_i)$ represents the defender's correction for the prior beliefs P by using Bayesian rule after observing the attacker's strategy a_i.

3.2 Strategy Benefits Quantization

Strategy benefits quantization of cyber attacker and cyber defender is the key to realize MDGS. Whether the quantization is reasonable directly affects the effect of cyber defense [21]. We first propose the following quantitative method for cyber attackers.

Definition 2. AR (Attack Reward) is the income of cyber attacker after a successful attack. It is generally expressed by the system losses, that is, sum of SDD (System Direct Damage) and SID (System Indirect Damage).

We define SDD as ID (Integrity Damage), AD (Availability Damage), and CD (Confidentiality Damage), drawing on three basic attributes of information security. Therefore, SDD can be expressed as Eq. (1).

$$SDD = \lambda * (w_1 * ID + w_2 * AD + w_3 * CD) \tag{1}$$

The coefficient λ is a numerical score between 0 and 10, representing the danger degree of a certain type of attack strategy, which can be determined according to the attack classification method of MIT Lincoln Laboratory [22]. w_1, w_2 and w_3 respectively represent weighting preferences of different networks for ID, AD and CD, and $w_1 + w_2 + w_3 = 1$.

SID is a numerical score between 0 and 100, representing the system indirect damage after a certain attack strategy, such as life length reduced degradation of performance and quality of service declined.

Definition 3. AC (Attack Cost) is a numerical score between 0 and 100, representing the cost of cyber attacker using an attack strategy. It usually measured by economics, time, hardware and software resources, human resources, and professional knowledge required to discover and invade system. For different levels of attackers, the cost of attacking the same network is different. The higher the level, the lower the attack cost.

We now define the following quantitative method as an extension of regular method that allows us to formulate deception in the framework of game theory. Specifically, we introduce the concept of Cyber Deception Reward (CDR) to demonstrate the importance of deceptive strategies for cyber defenders.

Definition 4. DR (Defense Reward) is the income of cyber defender after taking a defense strategy against a certain attack, including DDR (Direct Defense Reward) and CDR (Cyber Deception Reward). Therefore, a formal definition of DR can be expressed as Eq. (2).

$$DR = DDR + CDR = \eta(\theta, a, d) * SDD + \mu(\theta, a, d) * SID + CDR \tag{2}$$

We define DDR as the system losses reduced by the implementation of a defense strategy, that is, the reduction of SDD and SID.CDR defined an income that cyber defender deploying deceptive strategies, such as honeypots to detect an attacker and obtain information on the attacker's intentions, manners and actions. Moreover, the attacker observes a system without being able to detect its real type and is uncertain whether to attempt to compromise the system. CDR can be divided into three levels according to the degree of deception, 1st-CDR belongs to 0 and 100, 2st-CDR belongs to 100 and 200, and 3st-CDR belongs to 200 and 300.

Defense strategy may be effective against a certain attack strategy, but it is invalid for other attack strategies. Therefore, we define $\eta(\theta, a, d)$ and $\mu(\theta, a, d)$ as the effectiveness that defender's strategy d against attacker's strategy a when attacker's type is θ, where $0 \le \eta(\theta, a, d) \le 1$ and $0 \le \mu(\theta, a, d) \le 1$.

Definition 5. DC (Defense Cost) represents the cost that cyber defender deploying a defense strategy, sum of OC (Operation Cost) and NC (Negative Cost). It can be expressed as Eq. (3).

$$DC = OC + NC = OC + \kappa(\theta, a, d) * AD \tag{3}$$

OC represents the cost of cyber defender deploying a defense strategy. It usually quantified by the occupancy rate of resources such as CPU, memory, storage, etc., and the average operation time. We define NC as the system availability is affected, such as the failure of the system to work properly or the quality of other services declined due to the implementation of the defense strategy. The coefficient $\kappa(\theta, a, d)$ is the degree of negative impact that defender's strategy d against attacker's strategy a when attacker's type is θ, where $0 \leq \kappa(\theta, a, d) \leq 1$.

Relying on expert experience and scoring, we define quantified scores for SDD and OC in different level, as shown in Tables 1 and 2.

Table 1. Quantified scores for SDD.

Different threat degrees of attack strategy	Quantified scores		
	ID	AD	CD
5st-level: Deadly threat to system	80	90	90
4st-level: Major threat to system	60	70	80
3st-level: Certain threat to system	40	50	60
2st-level: Mild threat to system	20	30	40
1st-level: Weakly threat to system	10	10	20

Table 2. Quantified scores for OC.

Different impact levels of defense strategy	Quantified scores
5st-level: Deadly impact on system	90
4st-level: Major impact on system	70
3st-level: Certain impact on system	50
2st-level: Mild impact on system	30
1st-level: Weakly impact on system	10

As defined and analyzed above, the payoff functions for cyber attacker can be expressed as Eq. (4).

$$U_A(\theta_h, a_i, d_j) = AR_{(\theta,i)} - AC_{(\theta,i)} - DR_{(\theta,i,j)} = (SDD_{(\theta,i)} + SID_{(\theta,i)})$$
$$-AC_{(\theta,i)} - (\eta(\theta_h, a_i, d_j) * SDD_{(\theta,i)} + \mu(\theta_h, a_i, d_j) * SID_{(\theta,i)}) - CDR_{(\theta,j)} \tag{4}$$

Similarly, the payoff functions for cyber attacker can be expressed as Eq. (5).

$$
\begin{aligned}
U_D(\theta_h, a_i, d_j) &= DR_{(\theta,i,j)} - DC_{(\theta,i,j)} - AR_{(\theta,i)} = (\eta(\theta_h, a_i, d_j) * SDD_{(\theta,i)} \\
&+ \mu(\theta_h, a_i, d_j) * SID_{(\theta,i)}) + CDR_{(\theta,j)} - (OC_{(\theta,j)} + \kappa(\theta_h, a_i, d_j) * AD_{(\theta,i)}) - AR_{(\theta,i)}
\end{aligned}
\tag{5}
$$

3.3 Game Rules

In MDGS we use the well-known theory of incomplete information and dynamic game. The dynamic game needs to know the game sequence of each player [23]. Harsanyi transformation is an effective method to simulate and deal with such incomplete information and dynamic game problems, by introducing a virtual participant "Nature", "Nature " first gives the attack type a prior belief, which can be obtained through historical experience or the average distribution. The defender constantly corrects the beliefs of attacker's type by observing the attack behaviors, for adjusting defense strategies. Briefly, game rules of our model are as following:

First, "Nature" selects a type θ_h from the attacker's type space Θ_A with a certain probability, where $\theta_h \in \Theta_A$. The attacker N_A knows θ_h, while the defender does not know, it has the prior belief of the attacker's type θ_h.

Second, attacker N_A selects a_i as the attack strategy from its strategy space T_A after observing the type θ_h.

Third, when defender N_D observes the strategy a_i adopted by N_A, it will first apply the Bayesian rule to get the posterior belief from prior belief, and then choose a defense strategy d_j from its strategy space T_D.

Fourth, utilities of both attacker and defender are calculated by $U_A(\theta_h, a_i, d_j)$ and $U_D(\theta_h, a_i, d_j)$.

Fifth, the condition for terminating the game is that the defender or attacker has reached their target.

3.4 Existence of Equilibrium Solutions

Before solving the equilibrium solution of game, it is first asserted that there must be an equilibrium solution in our model.

Theorem 1. The MDGS must have an equilibrium solution.

Proving as following: In MDGS, since $N = (N_A, N_D)$, $\Theta = (\Theta_A, \Theta_D)$ and $T = (T_A, T_D)$ are both finite sets, we can draw a conclusion that MDGS is a finite game. Fudenberg and Selten's research has shown that in any finite game, there is at least one equilibrium solution, possibly including a hybrid strategy. Therefore, Theorem 1 holds.

3.5 Perfect Bayesian Equilibrium Algorithm

The MDGS we formulated is an incomplete information dynamic game, and its equilibrium solution $EQ = (a^*(\theta_h), d^*(a_i), \tilde{p}^*(\theta_h|a_i))$ is refined perfect Bayesian equilibrium. We now proposed the perfect Bayesian equilibrium algorithm, defined in the following manner.

Step 1. Initializing the posterior belief $\tilde{p}(\theta_h|a_i)$ on each information set based on historical experience.

Step 2. Calculating the defender's optimal defense strategy $d^*(a_i)$. When defender observes the strategy a_i adopted by attacker, based on posterior belief $\tilde{p}(\theta_h|a_i)$, it will choose an optimal defense strategy $d^*(a_i)$ to maximize the expected utility U_D brought by the game. The formula is defined as Eq. (6).

$$d^*(a_i) = \arg\max_{d \in T_D} \sum_{\theta \in \Theta_A} \tilde{p}(\theta_h|a_i) U_D(\theta_h, a_i, d_j) \tag{6}$$

Step 3. Calculating the attacker's optimal attack strategy $a^*(\theta_h)$. The attacker θ foresees that the defender will make an optimal defense strategy $d^*(a_i)$ based on its own actions, so it can maximize his game payoff expectation U_A brought by the game, adopting an optimal attack strategy $a^*(\theta_h)$. The formula is defined as Eq. (7).

$$a^*(\theta_h) = \arg\max_{a \in T_A} U_A(\theta_h, a^*(\theta_h), d^*(a_i)) \tag{7}$$

Step 4. Calculating the perfect Bayesian equilibrium. Using the subgame Nash Equilibrium calculated in step 2 and step 3, the posterior belief $\tilde{p}^*(\theta_h|a_i)$ can be calculated by Bayesian rule based on priori belief $p_i = p(\theta_i)$. If $\tilde{p}^*(\theta_h|a_i)$ and $\tilde{p}(\theta_h|a_i)$ are not contradictory. Therefore, perfect Bayesian equilibrium solution can be named as Eq. (8).

$$EQ = (a^*(\theta_h), d^*(a_i), \tilde{p}^*(\theta_h|a_i)) \tag{8}$$

4 Example Scenario and Analysis

MDGS is carried out in a sequential manner, with considering the incomplete information and maximizing payoff in the whole game process. The optimal strategy in each stage of the game is not always the same, but is updated with the posterior belief. In comparison, this is more in line with the actual network attack and defense scenarios. Furthermore, we used the XX virus attack mode as an example for experimental verification and analysis.

4.1 Example Scenario

As an illustrative example, consider a SDN scenario in which the defender has pre-deployed honeypots on the network, and the attacker has just initiated a port scan of a particular system. They believe the system is a server containing possibly valuable information, and would like to break in to it. For purposes of simplicity, the illustrative scenario in this paper assumes the cyber attacker who has two types of high level and low level, and the XX virus is used to invade the target network, which can be abstracted as shown in Fig. 2.

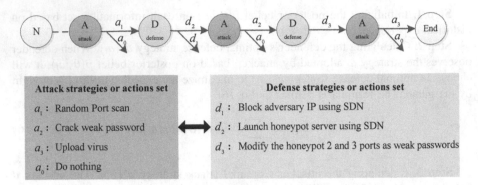

Fig. 2. A possible experimental scenario for SDN

When the defender observes the attacker's actions, there are two actions depending on the defense purpose, one is to directly limit packets form the ports, and the other is to deploy the honeypot to deceive the attacker [22].

4.2 Relevant Data Calculation

Referring to the existing literature [13, 19] and the strategy benefits quantification method in Sect. 3.2, the relevant data in experimental scenario are shown in Tables 3, 4, 5 and 6, in where the value of bold mark is the relevant parameter of the high level attacker, and the others are relevant parameter of the low level attacker.

Table 3. Reward and cost of attack strategy under different attacker's type.

Strategy	λ	ID	AD	CD	SDD	SID	AR	AC
a_1	**(4,3)**	**(10,10)**	**(10,10)**	**(20,20)**	**(48,36)**	**(5,5)**	**(53,41)**	**(40,50)**
a_2	**(6,5)**	**(20,20)**	**(50,50)**	**(80,80)**	**(264,220)**	**(15,10)**	**(279,230)**	**(60,75)**
a_3	**(10,9)**	**(40,40)**	**(90,90)**	**(90,90)**	**(700,630)**	**(50,40)**	**(750,670)**	**(50,80)**

Where $w_1 = 0.4$, $w_2 = 0.4$, $w_3 = 0.2$

Table 4. Values of $\eta(\theta, a, d)$, $\mu(\theta, a, d)$ and $\kappa(\theta, a, d)$ under different attacker's type.

	d_1	d_2	d_3
a_1	**(0.8,0.8,0.4)** (0.9,0.9,0.3)	**(0.7,0.7,0.3)** (0.8,0.8,0.2)	**(0.2,0.2,0.3)** (0.3,0.3,0.2)
a_2	**(0.3,0.3,0.4)** (0.3,0.3,0.4)	**(0.7,0.7,0.3)** (0.9,0.9,0.3)	**(0.4,0.4,0.4)** (0.5,0.5,0.3)
a_3	**(0.3,0.3,0.45)** (0.3,0.3,0.4)	**(0.4,0.3,0.4)** (0.6,0.6,0.35)	**(0.7,0.7,0.4)** (0.9,0.9,0.3)

Table 5. Values of CDR and OC under different attacker's type.

Defense strategy	Cyber Deception Reward (CDR)	Operation Cost (OC)
d_1	**(0,0)**	**(35,35)**
d_2	**(180,150)**	**(30,30)**
d_3	**(300,260)**	**(30,30)**

As defined and analyzed above, Payoff for both attacker and defender is obtained, as shown in Eq. (9). We can find that the sum of payment of attacker and defender is negative, meaning that each player needs to pay the price regardless of the outcome of network attack and defense confrontation, this is in line with the basic theory of information security.

$$
\begin{array}{cccc}
 & d_1 & d_2 & d_3 \\
a_1 & (-29.4,-49.6)(-45.9,-42.1) & (-24.1,-48.9)(-41.8,-40.2) & (2.4,-75.4)(-21.3,-60.7) \\
a_2 & (-44.7,-70.3)(-64,-66) & (-156.3,51.3)(-202,82) & (-72.6,-37.4)(-110,-10) \\
a_3 & (175,-305)(129,-280) & (105,-221)(-72,-69.5) & (-125,9)(-273,136)
\end{array}
\tag{9}
$$

4.3 Equilibrium Solution and Defense Decision

(1) When $S = 1$, it is the first game stage, namely MDGS (1).
The game tree of the first stage is obtained by using the Harsanyi transformation as shown in Fig. 3. Let $P = (p(\theta_1), p(\theta_2)) = (0.5, 0.5)$ be the prior belief of attacker's type selected by player "Nature". $p(a_i|\theta_h)$ representing the probability of using different attack strategies under different attacker's type, which can be obtained through historical experience and statistics, then calculating the posterior belief on different sets of information as $\tilde{p}(\theta_h|a_i)$. When defender observes the attack strategy a_1, the posterior belief of attacker's type (θ_1, θ_2) is $(\tilde{p}_1, 1 - \tilde{p}_1)$. Similarly as the posterior beliefs $(\tilde{p}_2, 1 - \tilde{p}_2)$ and $(\tilde{p}_3, 1 - \tilde{p}_3)$.

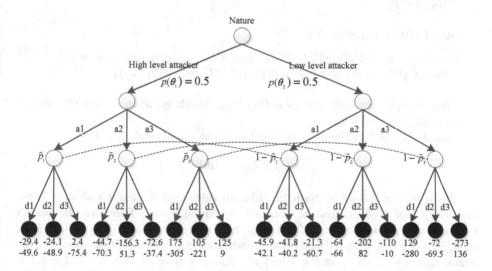

Fig. 3. Game tree of the first stage.

Step 1. The defender's optimal defense strategy set is calculated by the Eq. (10).

$$\max_{d \in T_D} \sum_{\theta \in \Theta_A} \tilde{p}(\theta_h|a_i) U_D(\theta_h, a_i, d_j) \tag{10}$$

When $a = a_1$,

$$\max_{(d_1,d_2,d_3)} \sum_{\theta_1,\theta_2} \tilde{p}(\theta_h|a_1) U_D(\theta_h, a_1, d_j) =$$
$$\max\{\tilde{p}(\theta_1|a_1) U_D(\theta_1, a_1, d_1) + \tilde{p}(\theta_2|a_1) U_D(\theta_2, a_1, d_1),$$
$$\tilde{p}(\theta_1|a_1) U_D(\theta_1, a_1, d_2) + \tilde{p}(\theta_2|a_1) U_D(\theta_2, a_1, d_2),$$
$$\tilde{p}(\theta_1|a_1) U_D(\theta_1, a_1, d_3) + \tilde{p}(\theta_2|a_1) U_D(\theta_2, a_1, d_3)\} \tag{11}$$
$$= \max\{\tilde{p}_1 * U_D(\theta_1, a_1, d_1) + (1 - \tilde{p}_1) * U_D(\theta_2, a_1, d_1), \tilde{p}_1 * U_D(\theta_1, a_1, d_2)$$
$$+ (1 - \tilde{p}_1) * U_D(\theta_2, a_1, d_2), \tilde{p}_1 * U_D(\theta_1, a_1, d_3) + (1 - \tilde{p}_1) * U_D(\theta_2, a_1, d_3)\}$$
$$= \max\{-7.5 * \tilde{p}_1 - 42.1, -8.7 * \tilde{p}_1 - 40.2, -14.7 * \tilde{p}_1 - 60.7\}$$

Where $\tilde{p}_1 = \tilde{p}(\theta_1|a_1) = \frac{\tilde{p}(\theta_1) * \tilde{p}(a_1|\theta_1)}{\tilde{p}(\theta_1) * \tilde{p}(a_1|\theta_1) + \tilde{p}(\theta_2) * \tilde{p}(a_1|\theta_2)} = 0.48$, then the optimal defense strategy $d^*(a_1) = d_2$ can be obtained by calculation. Similarly, when $a = a_2$ and $\tilde{p}_2 = \tilde{p}(\theta_1|a_2) = 0.38$, the optimal defense strategy $d^*(a_2) = d_2$.when $a = a_3$ and $\tilde{p}_3 = \tilde{p}(\theta_1|a_3) = 0.56$, the optimal defense strategy $d^*(a_3) = d_3$.

Step 2. The attacker's optimal attack strategy set is calculated by the Eq. (12).

$$\max_{a \in T_A} U_A(\theta_h, a(\theta_h), d^*(a_i)) \tag{12}$$

When $\theta = \theta_1$,

$$\max_{a_1,a_2,a_3} U_A(\theta_1, a(\theta_1), d^*(a_i)) =$$
$$\max\{U_A(\theta_1, a_1(\theta_1), d^*(a_1)), U_A(\theta_1, a_2(\theta_1), d^*(a_2)), U_A(\theta_1, a_3(\theta_1), d^*(a_3))\} \tag{13}$$
$$= \max\{U_A(\theta_1, a_1(\theta_1), d_2), U_A(\theta_1, a_2(\theta_1), d_2), U_A(\theta_1, a_3(\theta_1), d_3)\}$$

Then the optimal attack strategy $a^*(\theta_1) = a_1$. Similarly, when $\theta = \theta_2$, the optimal attack strategy $a^*(\theta_2) = a_1$.

Step 3. The perfect Bayesian equilibrium is calculated by the Eq. (14).

$$(a^*(\theta_h), d^*(a_i), \tilde{p}^*(\theta_h|a_i)) \tag{14}$$

Based on the sub-game Nash Equilibrium calculated in step 1 and step 2, the posterior belief $\tilde{p}^*(\theta_h|a_i)$ can be obtained by Bayesian rule. Therefore, the perfect Bayesian equilibrium solution of first stage $EQ_1 = \{(a_1, a_1), (d_2, d_2), \tilde{p}_1 = 0.48, \tilde{p}_2 = 0.38, \tilde{p}_3 = 0.56\}$ is a mixed equilibrium, indicating that when defender observes the attack strategy a_1, the posterior belief of attacker's type (θ_1, θ_2) is $(\tilde{p}_1, 1 - \tilde{p}_1) = (0.48, 0.52)$. The significance of this for the defender is to improve the probability inference that the attacker is a low level type.

Furthermore, we can explain the meaning of this equilibrium solution in two aspects: for attackers, since there is less information at the beginning of cyber-attack, no matter what type of attacker, the optimal attack strategy is usually adopting an exploratory attack, such as *port scanning*. For defenders, we consider the deception purpose, when observing the attacker has just initiated a port scan of the particular system, the optimal defense strategy may not to *block adversary IP*, but chooses to *launch honeypot server using SDN* for the purpose of deception.

(2) When $S = 2$, it is the second game stage, namely MDGS (2).
In our model for SDN environment, the monitoring timer is responsible for switching between different game stages. We will use the posterior belief of attacker's type in the first stage as the prior belief of attacker's type in second stage, that is $p(\theta_1) = 0.48$ and $p(\theta_2) = 0.52$. The game tree of second stage is revised to Fig. 4.

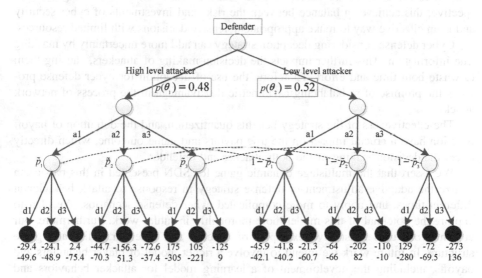

Fig. 4. Game tree of the second stage

Similarly, we can get the perfect Bayesian equilibrium solution of second stage $EQ_2 = \{(a_1, a_2), (d_2, d_2), \tilde{p}_1 = 0.46, \tilde{p}_2 = 0.37, \tilde{p}_3 = 0.54\}$, which is separation equilibrium, indicating that when defender observes the attack strategy a_1, the optimal defense strategy is d_2 and the posterior belief of attacker's type (θ_1, θ_2) is $(\tilde{p}_1, 1 - \tilde{p}_1) = (0.46, 0.54)$. However, if defender observes the attack strategy a_2, the optimal defense strategy is d_2 and the posterior belief of attacker's type (θ_1, θ_2) is $(\tilde{p}_1, 1 - \tilde{p}_1) = (0.37, 0.63)$. The significance of this for the defender is to improve the probability inference that the attacker is a low level type. In summary, the defender infers that the probability of the attacker being a low level type is further increased.

(3) Subsequent stage game.
Updating the value of $p(\theta_1)$ and $p(\theta_2)$ by using the posterior belief of attacker's type in the previous stage, the equilibrium solution of the stage will be obtained. This process will be repeated until the end of the game that the defender successfully tricks the attacker into the honeypot to protect the SDN key nodes, or the attacker was confused to achieve the target.

5   Conclusion and Future Work

In this work, we demonstrate a straightforward extension of cyber defense model through the use of game theory where the defender becomes aware of the identity of the attacker through their interaction with deception strategy, such as a honeypot and is therefore able to manipulate the true payoffs and game outcome using deception. Our work combines aspects of SDN, cyber security research, network-based deception techniques, and game theory. The main conclusions are as following:

The multistage dynamic game for SDN can automatically react to malicious behavior and evolve over time as attacks change, which allows the cyber defenders without to invest all the resources to deal with a potential attack. From a game perspective, this achieves a balance between the risks and investments of cyber security and is an effective way to make appropriate defensive decisions with limited resources.

Cyber defense considering deception strategy can add more uncertainty by masking true information. This further impacts the decision-making of attackers, causing them to waste both time and effort. Therefore, the use of deception for cyber defense provides the promise of re-balancing asymmetric disadvantage in the process of network attack.

The effectiveness of the strategy benefits quantization, and the definition of payoff function have a crucial impact on the true payoffs and game outcome, which directly affect the decision-making of the both attacker and defender.

We assert that the multistage dynamic game for SDN presented in this paper can realize the adaptive adjustment of defense strategy in response to attack behavior at different times, and apply to more complicated cyber defense scenarios. We plan to explore the potential of this model more thoroughly in future work. Furthermore, our current work uses illustrative examples of attacker and defender utility and game structure. In future work we intend to involve a richer model of player behaviors and payoffs, including the development of a learning model for attacker behaviors and utility.

References

1. La, Q.D., Quek, T.Q.S., Lee, J., et al.: Deceptive attack and defense game in honeypot-enabled networks for the internet of things. IEEE Internet of Things J. **3**(6), 1025–1035 (2016)
2. Wang, Q., Tai, W., Tang, Y., et al.: A two-layer game theoretical attack-defense model for a false data injection attack against power systems. Int. J. Electr. Power Energy Syst. **104**, 169–177 (2019)
3. Kreutz, D., Ramos, F., Verissimo, P.: Towards secure and dependable software-defined networks. In: Proceedings of the Second ACM SIGCOMM Workshop on Hot Topics in Software Defined Networking, pp. 55–60. ACM (2013)
4. Ahmad, I., Namal, S., Ylianttila, M., et al.: Security in software defined networks: a survey. IEEE Commun. Surv. Tutor. **17**(4), 2317–2346 (2015)
5. Fugate, S., Ferguson-Walter, K., Mauger, J., et al.: Game Theory for Adaptive Defensive Cyber Deception. Space and Naval Warfare Systems Center Pacific, San Diego, United States (2018)

6. Kovach, N.S., Gibson, A.S., Lamont, G.B.: Hypergame theory: a model for conflict, misperception, and deception. Game Theory **2**, 1–20 (2015)
7. Jajodia, S., Ghosh, A.K., Swarup, V., et al.: Moving Target Defense: Creating Asymmetric Uncertainty for Cyber Threats. Springer, New York (2011). https://doi.org/10.1007/978-1-4614-0977-9
8. Dabbagh, M., Hamdaoui, B., Guizani, M., et al.: Software-defined networking security: pros and cons. IEEE Commun. Mag. **53**(6), 73–79 (2015)
9. Akhunzada, A., Ahmed, E., Gani, A., et al.: Securing software defined networks: taxonomy, requirements, and open issues. Commun. Mag. **53**(4), 36–44 (2015)
10. Zhu, J.M., Wang, Q.: Analysis of cyberspace security based on game theory. Chin. J. Netw. Inf. Secur. **1**(01), 43–49 (2015)
11. Manshaei, M.H., Zhu, Q., Alpcan, T., et al.: Game theory meets network security and privacy. ACM Comput. Surv. (CSUR) **45**(3), 25 (2013)
12. Kayode, A.B., Babatunde, I.G., Israel, H.D.: DGM approach to network attacker and defender strategies. In: 2013 8th International Conference for Internet Technology and Secured Transactions (ICITST), pp. 313–320. IEEE (2013)
13. Zhang, H.W., Zhang, J., Han, J.H.: Defense strategies selection method based on non-cooperative game attack forecast. Comput. Sci. **43**(01), 195–201 (2016)
14. Jiang, W., Fang, B.X.: Defense strategies selection based on attack- defense game model. J. Comput. Res. Dev. **47**(12), 714–723 (2014)
15. Carin, L., Cybenko, G., Hughes, J.: Cybersecurity strategies: The queries methodology. Computer **41**(8), 20–26 (2008)
16. Wang, Y.Z., Lin, C., Cheng, X.Q., et al.: Analysis for network attack-defense based on stochastic game model. Chin. J. Comput. **33**(09), 1748–1762 (2010)
17. Gueye, A., Walrand, J.C.: Security in networks: a game-theoretic approach. In: Proceedings of the 47th IEEE Conference on Decision and Control Cancun, pp. 829–834 (2013). Springer, Mexico
18. Liu, J., Zhang, H.Q., Liu, Y.: Research on optimal selection of moving target defense policy based on dynamic game with incomplete information. Acta Electronica Sinica **46**(01), 82–89 (2018)
19. Zhang, H.W., Li, T.: Optimal active defense based on multistage attack-defense signaling game. Acta Electronica Sinica **45**(02), 431–439 (2017)
20. Lin, W.Q., Wang, H., Liu, J.H., et al.: Research on active defense technology in network security based on non-cooperative dynamic game theory. J. Comput. Res. Dev. **48**(02), 306–316 (2011)
21. Zhu, J., Song, B., Hang, Q.: Evolution game model of offense-defense for network security based on system dynamics. J. Commun. **35**(1), 54–61 (2014)
22. Pingree, L.: Emerging technology analysis: deception techniques and technologies create security technology business opportunities. Gartner Inc. (2015)
23. Tadelis, S.: Game Theory: An Introduction. Princeton University Press, Princeton (2014)

A Visualization-Based Analysis
on Classifying Android Malware

Rory Coulter[1], Lei Pan[2(✉)], Jun Zhang[1], and Yang Xiang[1]

[1] School of Software and Electrical Engineering,
Swinburne University of Technology, Hawthorn, VIC 3122, Australia
[2] School of Information Technology, Deakin University,
Geelong, VIC 3216, Australia
l.pan@deakin.edu.au

Abstract. Since the introduction of the Android mobile platform, the state of mobile malware has evolved in both attack sophistication and its ability to evade detection. Given the right combination of elements, the detection of malicious applications may be found among those that pose no threat, yet the threats that exist across these malware types reveal distinguishable attack characteristics. This paper investigates the benign and attacking characteristics. By plotting complex features into dendrograms, we propose a novel approach to visually distinguish Android apps. We visualize the complicated relationship and evaluate the effect of different text mining methods. Specifically, we employ machine learning techniques including feature reduction using Principle Component Analysis, and the Random Forest classifier, to compare eight different models. Using the Drebin dataset, we achieved an average accuracy of 95.83%.

Keywords: Artificial intelligence · Cyber security ·
Data driven cyber security · Machine learning · Malware detection

1 Introduction

The popularity of the Android platform, the ability of malware to easily find its way onto devices and other related security issues have been numerously reported [5,16]. Strikingly, more than 3 times as many applications existed in 2015 compared to 2014 which contained malware, a 230% increase [24]. A widespread release of remote access tools (RATs) were also observed in 2016 [18], and a significant majority share of threats for 2016 were dominated by ransomware types [13]. The rate and trends of Android malware are not subsiding; and the cycle between attacker release to mitigating techniques or research observation is still a game of catchup [28]. Another observable trend in the distribution of new malware is the increase of payload, or attack sophistication [17] and evolution in detection evasion [19], besides the introduction of some new attack types, i.e. ransomware, fundamental payload principles remain the same.

© Springer Nature Switzerland AG 2019
X. Chen et al. (Eds.): ML4CS 2019, LNCS 11806, pp. 304–319, 2019.
https://doi.org/10.1007/978-3-030-30619-9_22

The approach typically towards malware detection follows the identification of key features and uses a trained model to determine the nature of samples [23,30]. One noteworthy drawback is the dimensionality of the feature space which may grow too large, becoming unruly and over-saturated [22]. Furthermore, the process of triage is one that is left to the user, which in Bring Your Own Device (BYOD) domains may introduce threats into corporate or sensitive environments [16]. We therefore can assume that within these domains some precautionary actions would be initiated so that device access is granted by the ability to monitor, or assess the applications on user end devices, extracting the underlying structural elements of applications for identification, much like the original Drebin approach [3]. With the issue of obfuscation remaining prevalent and techniques sophisticated [1,6], we consider that features can be grouped according to different characteristics of malware behaviour [1]. Another noted issue is the aspect of providing a rapid response post-detection [22], with the time between malware exploit identification to patch a lengthy process from the path of Google to manufacturer to user [25].

The threat of zero-day, or undetected vulnerabilities and attacks remains an open issue for discussion. The predominate methods for malware classification is of a binary nature, identifying benign or malicious samples. To the best of our knowledge, this visualization-focused approach is novel for Android malware research and we seek in understanding the following research questions: (1) What is the influence of text indexing and sparsity may have? (2) Does Principle Component Analysis (PCA) effectively reduce the complexity and size of the feature space? We see this work as the starting point in addressing the discussed through a data-driven approach, in which the action of security defenses may be better organized or automated with elements of intrusion detection. This paper has the following key contributions:

1. We propose a data-driven malware analysis framework with a strong emphasis on visualization. By using dendrograms, we provide human analysts with instantaneous and intuitive insights of distance relationship deeply embedded in sparse matrices. This novel approach provides greater visual feedback and explainability to security professionals regarding the *why* of a classification.
2. We find a significant difference of classification accuracy due to various settings of text mining methods. Such methods are overlooked in the context of malware analysis. However, these text-mining methods are inevitable due to the nature of sparse data presented in the malware corpus. On the Drebin dataset, our empirical studies achieved an average accuracy of 95.83% by using a combination of Principal Component Analysis and Document Term Matrix in the full feature space. This combination out performs seven other text mining, sparsity and feature space reduction combinations, producing comparable results to [3] and [31] based on text mining alone.

The remaining sections are ordered as follows: Sect. 2 presents recent publications on malware analysis and summarizes the research gaps; Sect. 3 presents our data-driven approach with the emphasis on visualization; Sect. 4 provides the results obtained from the well-known Drebin dataset [3] with discussions; Sect. 6 concludes the paper.

2   Related Work

Unlike the other fields of study, the landscape of Android mobile malware does not contain an impartial or current representation dataset for researchers. The environment is rapidly changing and the malware itself is evolving very quickly. Many approaches are seen to better extend the ability of classifying benign or malicious applications, whilst lowering the risk of incorrect identification. Similarities in achieving this objective are shared with the approach of binary benign or malicious and/or multi-class family classification, the use of traditional machine learning approaches or contributing new and novel methods. Encapsulating many of these approaches is the Drebin Android malware dataset that was shared with the research community in 2012 [3]. According to Arp et al. [3], Support Vector Machine (SVM) was used with an overall accuracy of detection at 94%, and family-type detection of each of the top 20 sized malicious families at 93%. Furthermore, this contribution developed an application providing analysis with feedback to users regarding the natures of detected applications and features. Utilizing Random Forest (RF), Zhu et al. [31] presented FeatureSmith, training three classifiers of varying subsets of the Drebin dataset. Conversely to Drebin using all 8 features, FeatureSmith reduced the feature category to three: API, permission and intents. An accuracy of 92.5% was achieved with a false positive rate of 1%. A semantic network was constructed for feature selection based on literature [31].

Hou et al. [12] used APIs and supporting information from their code block or method association etc., through a meta-path multi-kernel approach using SVM. The approach constructed a similarity amongst samples achieving an accuracy of 98.6% [12]. Yuan et al. proposed DroidDetector for online deep learning combining both static and dynamic feature analysis achieving a 96.76% accuracy [29]. Online learning was continued with the framework named CASANDRA through novel graph kernel functions in behaviour identification and dependence graphs for context information. An accuracy of 89.92% was achieved for through the batch-training method [19]. For more up-to-date attack vectors, Maiorca et al. presented R-PackDroid concerned with ransomware [17]. Sole use of APIs and additional information were used with RF. While evaluating known and zero-day risks, Grace et al. invented RiskRanker aimed to measure the risk of an potential application for the threat of zero-day exploits. Applications are categorised based on a threat level risk that they may belong to a category of attack by firstly comparing the signatures, function call graphs, and then analysis of code loading and encryption functionality. While distantly similar in theme by associating the surrounding risk of an attack, focuses mainly on root-exploits for high risk applications and it is not concerned with the elements that define a given attack class [9]. A common drawback among these works is the lack of visualization that is essential for synthesizing knowledge. Analysis of the datasets is lacking, focusing on classification alone. Therefore we seek to obtain deeper knowledge surrounding Android malware.

The success or failure of a classifier is very much dependant on the quality of data used, with as best representation of the challenges ultimately see greater success [4]. Suarez-Tangil et al. [22] used semantic and statistical approaches titled DENDROID makes use of statistical analysis based on code semantic structures for the identification of Android malware families. Similar to our visualization, DENDROID makes use of distance measurements and hierarchical clustering to enable adaptation of the Vector Space Model for identification and evolution tracking [22]. Feng et al. [7] used a semantic based approach for static analysis in detecting malware and their family association. Analysis of data and control flows is linked with a specification language to determine new applications with an overall detection of 90% across many family types [7].

Wei et al. [26] sought to identify required permissions of an application based on the description given, like Drebin and FeatureSmith it too seeks to confer to uneducated users about the intent of a given application and the expected requested permissions, achieving an accuracy as high as 87%. A training set it used to build a relationship between applications and extracted keywords [26]. Like these approaches, most of the reviewed work fails to mention if at all the process behind their text mining steps. Therefore there is no suitable evaluation for the combination text mining influences for Android malware, we propose an empirical study to explicitly compare.

We can infer from the literature that features remain a powerful element to the aiding of malware detection. Furthermore we can see that overtime the data itself shifts with the evolution of new malware from the template to the sibling versions. The use of machine learning aids the discovery process, reducing time and effort compared to manual investigation. Regardless of the change in data, the process of our work, visualization, feature analysis, text mining comparisons are complemented by classification. Seeking new views of the data allows us to investigate unforeseen knowledge that classification helps support.

3   A Data-Driven Approach with Visualization Focus

3.1   System Overview

Typically within detection attempts, supervised learning employs the use of a categorical, or labelled variable which allows a classifier to establish a point of reference in building its model for classification. Any new samples that are interpreted are then matched. Unsupervised is not reliant on any labelled data, as one does not exist. In a sense of its true purpose, it groups, or classifies samples on its relationship or closeness to other samples [27]. A supervised training approach is employed with an unsupervised method for classification. Figure 1 presents our overall framework. Our framework can be used to classify malware samples through three phrases—visualization, text mining analysis, and classification evaluation.

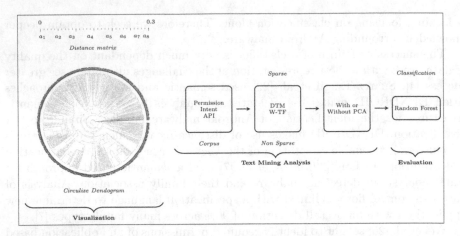

Fig. 1. Process Diagram: Visualization sees a distance matrix constructed and then visualized through a circularized dendrogram to enhance representation. Following this stage a corpus is created of APIs, permissions, and intents. Classification is compared for 8 models consisting of multiple combinations of indexing, sparsity and with or without the use of PCA. Random forest is used for classification.

Table 1 lists the 8 different text mining models we will investigate. We observe 8 different total combinations in combining indexing, sparsity and the use of PCA. The additional PCA comparison is included due to its maturity, and proven effectiveness to reduce complex feature spaces. The accuracy of these will be compared with the RF classifier. RF is selected partly due to its successful use with the Drebin dataset in [31], and the explainability of results. Table 1 provides an ID for each model, the approach elements and the factor combination that it contains.

Table 1. Classification approaches

Model	Approach in abbreviation	Technical methods
1	DTM N-S	DTM matrix, full feature space
2	Weighted N-S	W-TF matrix, full feature space
3	Weighted SPARSE	W-TF matrix, lowest featuring 0.5% feature space removed
4	DTM SPARSE	DTM matrix, lowest featuring 0.5% feature space removed
5	PCA Weighted SPARSE	PCA, W-TF matrix, lowest featuring 0.5% feature space removed
6	PCA DTM SPARSE	PCA, DTM matrix, lowest featuring 0.5% feature space removed
7	PCA Weighted N-S	PCA, W-TF matrix, full feature space
8	PCA DTM N-S	PCA, DTM matrix, full feature space

3.2   Drebin Dataset

The Drebin dataset [3] is comprised of 123,453 benign and 5,560 malicious Android applications collected between August–October 2012. Samples were sourced from the GooglePlay Store, Chinese and Russian equivalents, the Android Malware Genome Project, other Android websites, blogs and known malware forums. The original Drebin paper retrieved the inner structure of each sample application, providing a data set of the 5560 malicious samples. All samples within the dataset are used excluding premium SMS-based applications. This provides 129,013 benign and 5560 malicious samples. A ground truth is also provided identifying the malicious family of the given application. This labeling was originally conducted in the original Drebin experiment. The dataset is well understood and accepted within the research community, and therefore selected for use.

3.3 Labels and Features

The process of training classifiers walks a fine line, whereby the introduction of noise may unintentionally reduce the accuracy, yet too few may choke the necessary diversity to adequately distinguish good from bad. Thus machine learning results can be linked to the quality of the data and the ability to best present it as good representations encourage better results. Feature selections allows removing noise from data to better enable learning [2,4]. Both the approaches in [3] and [31] looked to filter the most appropriate features, i.e. $Permission_x$ and API_y. Following the approach of [31], where only API, Intent and Permission features were considered, this approach is followed, a sample is seen in Table 2. Unlike [3] and [31], the reduction of the feature space will not be wholly be considered, and all available features of these categories are used subject to sampling considering the variance of samples. We aim to compare the affect of applying either a Sparse or Non-Sparse (N-S) matrix to each approach, the sparse matrix is set at 0.5% of less frequent terms removed.

Table 2. Dataset & Text mining: The number of unique features per element is vast with each applications existing of many different combinations. The requirement for evaluating various text mining approaches is apparent.

Feature category	Unique entries	Common examples
API	21,305	getAccounts, restartPackage, startService
Permission	18,020	READ_SMS, RESTART_PACKAGE, WAKE_LOCK
Intent	5,747	LAUNCHER, BOOT_COMPLETED, VIEW

3.4 Indexing

A well established preprocessing step in text mining is in the representation of textual elements that are more significant to a machine [21]. For two of these methods, we will compare the impact they may have on the classification of benign or malicious applications. Of these, the main methods are the use of a term matrix or a weighted document frequency which we will consider an inverse frequency [14]. A clear distinction can be drawn between these two methods, where a term matrix is only concerned with the occurrence of a word in a document, a weighted term frequency is concerned with the importance of a word in a document, with respect to other participating documents. For enabling the classification of textual elements we initially create a corpus or a body of words for each of the applications used, we lower the case of words and also create a text document, no stop words or punctuation is removed, yet special, or reserved characters are removed.

Document Term Matrix (DTM). Text documents, or samples are read into an $M \times N$ matrix where an occurrence of a word is marked of either existing or not existing through binary representation. For the frequency of a given term i in document j, term frequency is defined as:

$$TF_{ji} = \frac{\text{Ocurrance of term}}{\text{Absence of term}} \tag{1}$$

Each word is arranged as a column, whilst each document or sample is arranged for each row. Herein a Document Term Matrix is denoted as a DTM.

Weight by Term Frequency–Inverse Document Frequency (W-TF). Like a Document Term Matrix in its layouts of words and samples and package requirement, a Weight by Term Frequency–Inverse Document Frequency matrix provides further steps than binary representation. For term frequency, $tf_{i,j}$, frequency occurrence is counted, $n_{i,j}$, for a term t_i in a document d_j. In need of normalization, the term frequency $tf_{i,j}$ is divided by $\Sigma_k n_{k,j}$. Inverse document frequency (idf) for a term t_i is defined as:

$$idf_i = \log_2 \frac{|D|}{|\{d \mid t_i \in d\}|} \tag{2}$$

where $|D|$ denotes the document totals, and $|\{d \mid t_i \in d\}|$ is the number of documents where the term t_i is represented. We can now define Term frequency–inverse document frequency as $tf_{i,j} \cdot idf_i$. Herein a Weight by Term Frequency–Inverse Document Frequency is denoted as a W-TF.

3.5   Visualization

The method for visualizing the hierarchical clustering of the distance matrix is done through the form of circularized dendrograms [8,11]. The method for using a distance matrix with clustering, and a dendrogram was shown positively for [22] in displaying the relationship and evolution of malware families, this approach is complementary in displaying the closeness samples. We have particularly chosen this circularized method for its ability to clearly display the cluster relationships, the ordering of samples in a way that is distinct whist retaining independence between interpretation. In interpreting the figures, the inner structure represents the cluster relationship as noted by its color, starting on the right and moving counter-clockwise vertically, whilst the outside leave represents the leaves, or samples and their closeness to one another, with the beginning leaves furthest from the end in similarity. The color of the leave furthermore represents their class types.

3.6 Principal Component Analysis (PCA)

Principal component analysis (PCA) is an unsupervised machine learning technique that allows a way in which high dimension data to be represented in a lower dimensional format. A large data space of variables which may share a relationship are then lineally uncorrelated into principal components. The resulting number of principle components is either equal or less than the original amount of observations. The process of this representation is done so that the first principle component holds the most variance in the data and so forth down for the second having the second most variance etc, orthogonal to the proceeding component [20]. We define x_i as a set of n column vectors of dimension D and the covariance matrix $\mathbf{C}_x$ respective of the data set as

$$\mathbf{C}_x = \sum_{i=1}^{n}(x_i - \boldsymbol{\mu}_x)(x_i - \boldsymbol{\mu}_x)^T \tag{3}$$

where $\boldsymbol{\mu}_x$ is the mean of the dataset:

$$\boldsymbol{\mu}_x = \frac{1}{n}\sum_{i=1}^{N} x_i \tag{4}$$

Principle components p are the eigenvectors e_i corresponding to the p largest eigenvalues, we choose p as $p < D$. Eigenvectors of $\mathbf{C}$ can be found by using singular value decomposition. The direction of variation is determined through the dominant eigenvectors, which is used in projecting the data into a p dimensional space, we can define this as:

$$W = [\boldsymbol{\mu}_1, \boldsymbol{\mu}_2, \ldots, \boldsymbol{\mu}_d] \tag{5}$$

Thus, $y = W^T x$ is defined as the projection of vector x and the corresponding covariance matrix $\mathbf{C}_y$ of the vectors y_i is:

$$\mathbf{C}_y = W^T \mathbf{C}_x W \tag{6}$$

The matrix of W maximizes the determinant of $\mathbf{C}_y$ for a given p.

3.7 Random Forest Classifier

Random Forest is mainly for classification or regression. An ensemble approach is undertaken where multiple decision trees are constructed during the training of the classifier through the method of building decision trees. Depending on the approach, the mode of classes is obtained for classification, and the mean prediction for regression. The approach to training typically is supervised, whilst predictions can be made through unsupervised means [15]. For training of the algorithm, bootstrapping aggregation is applied to the tree results, where a mode or mean is determined. The process of aggregating the tree results is applied. For a training set $X = \{x_1, \ldots, x_n\}$ with labels $Y = \{y_1, \ldots, y_n\}$, bagging is repeated B times, where a random sample is chosen for replacement of the training set and fit trees with respect to selected samples.

For $b \in \{1, \ldots, B\}$ samples and their replacement, n training samples from (X), (Y). We can refer to these as (X_b) and (Y_b), and for the classification or regression tree f_b on (X_b), (Y_b). For decision on new samples, $x\prime$ can be chosen by averaging the resulting predictions for all trees on $x\prime$. We can summarize as:

$$\hat{f} = \frac{1}{B} \sum_{b=1}^{B} \hat{f}_b(x\prime) \tag{7}$$

As an individual tree may suffer noise influence, training several tress on varied data allows a less influenced distribution in conjunction with aggregation. The random forest algorithm takes this process yet also selects a random sample of the feature space as to not rely on features that are prominent in the dataset.

4   Empirical Studies

4.1   Visualization

Distance Measurement and Hierarchical Clustering. In working towards a deeper understanding of attack characteristics, a distance matrix was clustered hierarchically where applications are placed structurally together, for the approach to clustering malware has shown to feature heavily on key features in recent years [10]. The result were displayed in a circularized dendrogram while clustering was repeated for a cluster size of 2 to 12 for the Binary approach. The clustering process requires a decision from the algorithm in which way a sub tree should go, with tighter clusters grouped to the left. Since there are $n - 1$ merges, there are $2^{(n-1)}$ ordering to the leaves.

Visualizing this result the leaves or outer ring of the dendrogram show the placement of applications based on their distance from one another, whilst the inner structure represents the trees of the clusters. Leaves that belong to a given cluster can be associated by their placement within a determined cluster color, Fig. 2 presents our initial result of 2 clusters for binary labeling. Reference point 2 and 3 reveals that only a small percentage of samples were separated into cluster 1, which displays a mix between classes. Point 1 is one of many sections where structurally there is a mix of classes in cluster 2, with malicious applications varying their positioning greatly.

Figure 3 has a cluster count increase to 7. Point 1 reveals a very early separation of initial clusters, with a larger distance up to cluster 5. Cluster 6 still

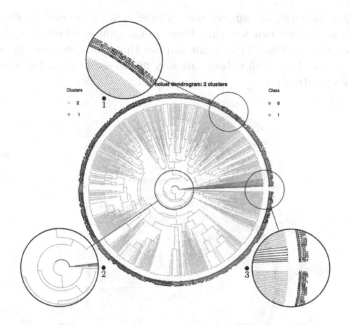

Fig. 2. Two cluster Dendrogram, Binary data: Moving counter-clockwise from point 3, the outer leaves represent the hierarchical positioning of samples based on their features. The interior tress display our cluster participation. We can observe that no clear positioning exists with the similarity of applications, there is a mix of red and blue leaves. We can also observe that only a small portion fall into cluster 1. (Color figure online)

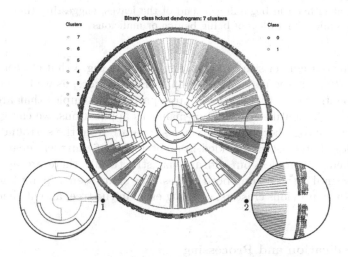

Fig. 3. Seven cluster Dendrogram, Binary data: The leaves will remain in the same position, but the cluster association has developed. A large portion still falls within cluster 7, which is a large mix of benign and malicious samples.

encompass the majority of samples with a brief split at the end. Even with this increase of clusters we can see that three main groups (clusters 4, 5, 6) contain the majority portion. This result implies that while we have good or bad applications, there may be a subset category where application purpose may be linked to this positioning.

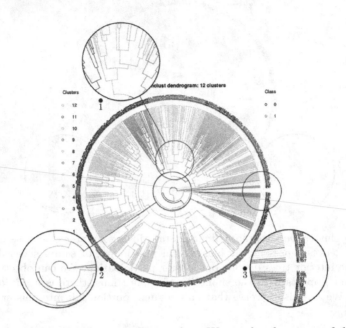

Fig. 4. Twelve cluster Dendrogram, Binary data: We see the placement of clusters have been placed at either the beginning or end of the leaves, suggesting that samples in cluster 8 are similar regardless of being benign or malicious

Increasing our cluster size to 12, we further see in Fig. 4 that cluster 8 (previously 6 and 2) holds the majority of samples. Furthermore, as we have increased cluster amounts there still remains a large portion of samples that are remain together. Point 3 identifies that of our malicious applications, we can group one subset efficiently together, but this remains separate from the surrounding same class samples. The clusters included in point 1 (4, 5, 6) further separates malicious and benign samples, but affirms that structurally there are applications which share similarities among both classes. The splits seen in point 2 follow the same pattern as previous clusters, splitting early in the tree, and at then at later stages.

4.2   Classification and Processing

Accuracy. Attack classification is compared against 8 different indexing and processing methods, we compare the overall accuracy and the TP, FP and Precision per class. 150 samples from each class are selected into 10 different subsets to be used for classification. These 10 sets are used per model and resulting confusion matrices are aggregated with each model being passed to the RF classifier, which was trained in a supervised fashion, and run as unsupervised for classification. The overall average accuracy per model can be seen in Table 3.

Table 3. Average accuracy of the 8 models

Model	Average accuracy
1 – DTM, N-S	90.33%
2 – W-TF, N-S	90.95%
3 – W-TF, S	93.00%
4 – DTM, S	93.00%
5 – PCA, W-TF, S	91.33%
6 – PCA, DTM, S	95.39%
7 – PCA, W-TF, N-S	91.89%
8 – PCA, DTM, N-S	95.83%

The Impact of indexing matrix style was shown to be impartial for models without PCA, and the use of a sparse matrix showed to increase accuracy by roughly 2%. Weighted and DTM indexing both achieved in the 90 per cents for accuracy for a N-S matrix, the increase was shown across both when sparsity in considered. The same effect can be observed with the use of PCA, yet rather with the indexing that has been applied. Weighted matrix models were seen to perform considerably lower than those that used a DTM, which is also in line with the models without the use of PCA. The best performing model seen in Table 3 is model 8, incorporating PCA, DTM, N-S matrix. Achieving an average accuracy of 95.83% and a best performing 97.78%. This result sees roughly a 5.5% increase over the same model with the use of PCA, and the second best model, 6, gain roughly a 2.4% increase. The influence of PCA can be identified among all measurements. Models that used a DTM saw an average 4% increase against those with W-TF with the inclusion of PCA, while those without achieved little improvement.

5   Discussion

5.1   Empirical Study Results

Our best performing model was comprised of DTM N-S with PCA. An average accuracy of 95.93% was achieved. The best two models both consisted of PCA, models 6 & 8, roughly 2% greater in accuracy. The original Drebin paper [3] achieved an accuracy of 94% and particularly 93% for family accuracy using SVM and a wider range of feature optimisation and training in comparison. The work of [31] also used a refined feature selection and training and the RF classifier, achieving a TPR of 92.5%. This result is noteworthy as optimal API, Permission and Intent features were selected from their semantic network. [12] used multi-kernel learning, concentrating on APIs and their relationship among themselves, achieving an accuracy of 98.6%. Among these approaches binary classification was employed. The addition of PCA reveals improvement in both accuracy over complete models. The improvement in these two classes in noteworthy as it may come down to the authors intent that separates benign or malicious applications with respect to the data they are requesting.

Empirically we find that several factors contribute to class accuracy, TP and FP rates between model approaches 1–4 and models 5–8, which are distinctly separated by the use of PCA. The use of PCA is seldom seen in conjunction with Android malware, for this approach of models 1–4, the sparsity of a matrix was shown to influence results most rather than the indexing type shown across all classes. Drawing any distinction regarding the indexing format, no distinct conclusions can be made, yet DTM is regarded stronger across classes than W-TF. For models 5–8 we can empirically observe that several factors complement one another. The indexing format of DTM is shown most influential across both sparsity types, while PCA is seen to improve the classification results. From these two models we can conclude that sparsity and to a lesser extent DTM are most influential for non PCA models, while DTM, N-S and PCA combine best allowing a wider feature dimension size.

5.2   Processing Techniques

Approaches to language processing techniques vary across similar works with a combination of DTM, W-TF and adjustments to sparsity. As to the best of our knowledge, no meaningful contributions were found in comparing approaches, we therefore aimed to examine language processing influences in Android malware detection. As identified, the inclusion of PCA showed significant due to the approach of this work as the entire feature space is considered, for approaches without the use of PCA we identified that sparsity was the majority factor. Indexing formats were negligible for a sparse matrix as seen with models 3 and 4, there is no difference across all metrics. Whilst with a N-S matrix the use of a DTM was complementary, out performing a W-TF matrix except for class 0 TP results.

For those methods that use PCA, we can identify that the inclusion of PCA yielded improvements across all metrics, we further identified that the indexing method has a greater impact compared to sparsity. A DTM was revealed as the complementary factor, out performing a W-TF matrix, which was lower across all classes in the used metrics. Use of PCA saw an improvement towards FPs in class 0 which remained high for approaches without PCA.

The application of applying a sparse matrix is common among research approaches for various reasons. The nuance of outlying features may help aid classification or increase noise among a wide feature space as they are outlying and rare regardless of their indication from benign or malicious applications. Furthermore the size of features space can grow significantly large, with even the Drebin dataset feature space being upwards of 70 GB when used with traditional machine learning algorithms like SVM. We observe like the majority of approaches that DTM and a sparse matrix is most complementary to processing for Android malware.

5.3 Visualization and Feature Identification

Visualization of attack association through class labels revealed what was expected regarding malware families, families are not uniform, nor is their functionality. It is then expected that after redefining the labeling based of visualization methods in Sect. 4.1 that accuracy and other metrics like FP would improve. This point therefore helps us understand that identifying families by similar semantic elements may results in unwanted FPs.

6 Conclusions

The attention towards malware detection is an issue that requires further investigation. The ability of new malware to evolve and remain hidden continues to plague users and security researchers. The combination of text mining processes and knowledge gained through visualization were evaluated within our research. Among these, we find the combination of DTM, N-S, and PCA most significant. Validated through the random forest classifier, an average accuracy of 95.83% was achieved. PCA furthermore helped increase the average accuracy of roughly 5%. In particular, the dendrograms used in this paper revealed the complex relations between features in the malware samples through visualization. Visualization suggests that the behavior of malware families should be examined further, as the samples are intermixed between benign and malicious classes. Semantic elements and the malware's author intention play a role in producing similar distances between these samples. Future work intends to compare the techniques used against, and with related work to investigate their effectiveness.

References

1. Ahmadi, M., Ulyanov, D., Semenov, S., Trofimov, M., Giacinto, G.: Novel feature extraction, selection and fusion for effective malware family classification. In: Proceedings of the Sixth ACM Conference on Data and Application Security and Privacy, CODASPY 2016, pp. 183–194. ACM, New York (2016). https://doi.org/10.1145/2857705.2857713
2. Armanfard, N., Reilly, J.P., Komeili, M.: Local feature selection for data classification. IEEE Trans. Pattern Anal. Mach. Intell. 38(6), 1217–1227 (2016). https://doi.org/10.1109/TPAMI.2015.2478471
3. Arp, D., Spreitzenbarth, M., Hubner, M., Gascon, H., Rieck, K., Siemens, C.: DREBIN: effective and explainable detection of android malware in your pocket. In: NDSS (2014)

4. Bengio, Y., Courville, A., Vincent, P.: Representation learning: a review and new perspectives. IEEE Trans. Pattern Anal. Mach. Intell. **35**(8), 1798–1828 (2013). https://doi.org/10.1109/TPAMI.2013.50
5. Coulter, R., Pan, L.: Intelligent agents defending for an IoT world: a review. Comput. Secur. **73**, 439–458 (2018)
6. Deshotels, L., Notani, V., Lakhotia, A.: DroidLegacy: automated familial classification of android malware. In: Proceedings of ACM SIGPLAN on Program Protection and Reverse Engineering Workshop 2014, PPREW 2014, pp. 3:1–3:12. ACM, New York (2014). https://doi.org/10.1145/2556464.2556467
7. Feng, Y., Anand, S., Dillig, I., Aiken, A.: Apposcopy: semantics-based detection of android malware through static analysis. In: Proceedings of the 22nd ACM SIGSOFT International Symposium on Foundations of Software Engineering, FSE 2014, pp. 576–587. ACM, New York (2014). https://doi.org/10.1145/2635868.2635869
8. Galili, T.: dendextend: an R package for visualizing, adjusting, and comparing trees of hierarchical clustering. Bioinformatics (2015). https://doi.org/10.1093/bioinformatics/btv428. http://bioinformatics.oxfordjournals.org/content/31/22/3718
9. Grace, M., Zhou, Y., Zhang, Q., Zou, S., Jiang, X.: RiskRanker: scalable and accurate zero-day android malware detection. In: Proceedings of the 10th International Conference on Mobile Systems, Applications, and Services, MobiSys 2012, pp. 281–294. ACM, New York (2012). https://doi.org/10.1145/2307636.2307663
10. Graziano, M., Canali, D., Bilge, L., Lanzi, A., Balzarotti, D.: Needles in a haystack: mining information from public dynamic analysis sandboxes for malware intelligence. In: 24th USENIX Security Symposium, USENIX Security 2015, pp. 1057–1072. USENIX Association, Washington, D.C. (2015). https://www.usenix.org/conference/usenixsecurity15/technical-sessions/presentation/graziano
11. Gu, Z., Gu, L., Eils, R., Schlesner, M., Brors, B.: Circlize implements and enhances circular visualization in R. Bioinformatics **30**, 2811–2812 (2014)
12. Hou, S., Ye, Y., Song, Y., Abdulhayoglu, M.: HinDroid: an intelligent android malware detection system based on structured heterogeneous information network. In: Proceedings of the 23rd ACM SIGKDD International Conference on Knowledge Discovery and Data Mining, KDD 2017, pp. 1507–1515. ACM, New York (2017). https://doi.org/10.1145/3097983.3098026
13. Labs, M.: State of malware report. https://www.malwarebytes.com/pdf/white-papers/stateofmalware.pdf. Accessed 15 July 2019
14. Li, B., Yan, Q., Xu, Z., Wang, G.: Weighted document frequency for feature selection in text classification. In: 2015 International Conference on Asian Language Processing (IALP), pp. 132–135, October 2015. https://doi.org/10.1109/IALP.2015.7451549
15. Liaw, A., Wiener, M.: Classification and regression by randomforest. R News **2**(3), 18–22 (2002)
16. Liu, L., De Vel, O., Han, Q.L., Zhang, J., Xiang, Y.: Detecting and preventing cyber insider threats: a survey. IEEE Commun. Surv. Tutor. **20**(2), 1397–1417 (2018)
17. Maiorca, D., Mercaldo, F., Giacinto, G., Visaggio, C.A., Martinelli, F.: R-PackDroid: API package-based characterization and detection of mobile ransomware. In: Proceedings of the Symposium on Applied Computing, SAC 2017, pp. 1718–1723. ACM, New York (2017). https://doi.org/10.1145/3019612.3019793
18. McAfee: McAfee labs 2017 threats predictions. https://www.mcafee.com/au/resources/reports/rp-threats-predictions-2017.pdf. Accessed 15 July 2019

19. Narayanan, A., Chandramohan, M., Chen, L., Liu, Y.: Context-aware, adaptive, and scalable android malware detection through online learning. IEEE Trans. Emerg. Top. Comput. Intell. **1**(3), 157–175 (2017). https://doi.org/10.1109/TETCI.2017.2699220
20. Narayanan, B.N., Djaneye-Boundjou, O., Kebede, T.M.: Performance analysis of machine learning and pattern recognition algorithms for malware classification. In: 2016 IEEE National Aerospace and Electronics Conference (NAECON) and Ohio Innovation Summit (OIS), pp. 338–342, July 2016. https://doi.org/10.1109/NAECON.2016.7856826
21. Plansangket, S., Gan, J.Q.: A new term weighting scheme based on class specific document frequency for document representation and classification. In: 2015 7th Computer Science and Electronic Engineering Conference (CEEC), pp. 5–8, September 2015. https://doi.org/10.1109/CEEC.2015.7332690
22. Suarez-Tangil, G., Tapiador, J.E., Peris-Lopez, P., Blasco, J.: DenDroid: a text mining approach to analyzing and classifying code structures in Android malware families. Expert Syst. Appl. **41**(4), 1104–1117 (2014). https://doi.org/10.1016/j.eswa.2013.07.106. http://www.sciencedirect.com/science/article/pii/S0957417413006088
23. Sun, N., Zhang, J., Rimba, P., Gao, S., Zhang, L.Y., Xiang, Y.: Data-driven cybersecurity incident prediction: a survey. IEEE Commun. Surv. Tutor. **21**(2), 1744–1772 (2018)
24. Symantec: Internet security threat report. https://www.symantec.com/content/dam/symantec/docs/reports/istr-21-2016-en.pdf. Accessed 15 July 2019
25. Vidas, T., Votipka, D., Christin, N.: All your droid are belong to us: a survey of current android attacks. In: WOOT, pp. 81–90 (2011)
26. Wei, M., Gong, X., Wang, W.: Claim what you need: a text-mining approach on android permission request authorization. In: 2015 IEEE Global Communications Conference (GLOBECOM), pp. 1–6, December 2015. https://doi.org/10.1109/GLOCOM.2015.7417472
27. Wu, S.X., Banzhaf, W.: The use of computational intelligence in intrusion detection systems: a review. Appl. Soft Comput. **10**(1), 1–35 (2010). https://doi.org/10.1016/j.asoc.2009.06.019. http://www.sciencedirect.com/science/article/pii/S1568494609000908
28. Xue, Y., et al.: Auditing anti-malware tools by evolving android malware and dynamic loading technique. IEEE Trans. Inf. Forensics Secur. **12**(7), 1529–1544 (2017). https://doi.org/10.1109/TIFS.2017.2661723
29. Yuan, Z., Lu, Y., Xue, Y.: DroidDetector: android malware characterization and detection using deep learning. Tsinghua Sci. Technol. **21**(1), 114–123 (2016)
30. Zhang, J., Xiang, Y., Wang, Y., Zhou, W., Xiang, Y., Guan, Y.: Network traffic classification using correlation information. IEEE Trans. Parallel Distrib. Syst. **24**(1), 104–117 (2012)
31. Zhu, Z., Dumitras, T.: FeatureSmith: automatically engineering features for malware detection by mining the security literature. In: Proceedings of the 2016 ACM SIGSAC Conference on Computer and Communications Security, pp. 767–778. ACM (2016)

Protecting the Visual Fidelity of Machine Learning Datasets Using QR Codes

Yang-Wai Chow[1]([✉]), Willy Susilo[1], Jianfeng Wang[2], Richard Buckland[3], Joonsang Baek[1], Jongkil Kim[1], and Nan Li[4]

[1] Institute of Cybersecurity and Cryptology, School of Computing and Information Technology, University of Wollongong, Wollongong, Australia
{caseyc,wsusilo,baek,jongkil}@uow.edu.au
[2] State Key Laboratory of Integrated Service Networks (ISN), Xidian University, Xidian, China
jfwang@xidian.edu.cn
[3] School of Computer Science and Engineering, University of New South Wales, Sydney, Australia
richardb@unsw.edu.au
[4] School of Electrical Engineering and Computing, University of Newcastle, Newcastle, Australia
nan.li@newcastle.edu.au

Abstract. Machine learning is becoming increasingly popular in a variety of modern technology. However, research has demonstrated that machine learning models are vulnerable to adversarial examples in their inputs. Potential attacks include poisoning datasets by perturbing input samples to mislead a machine learning model into producing undesirable results. Such perturbations are often subtle and imperceptible from a human's perspective. This paper investigates two methods of verifying the visual fidelity of image based datasets by detecting perturbations made to the data using QR codes. In the first method, a verification string is stored for each image in a dataset. These verification strings can be used to determine whether an image in the dataset has been perturbed. In the second method, only a single verification string stored and is used to verify whether an entire dataset is intact.

Keywords: Adversarial machine learning · Cyber security · QR code · Visual fidelity · Watermarking

1 Introduction

The popularity of Machine Learning (ML) has rapidly grown in recent years, and it has made its way into a variety of modern technology. ML techniques empower a range of diverse applications, including self-driving cars, network intrusion detection, speech recognition, and so on. However, research has demonstrated that ML models are vulnerable to adversarial examples in its inputs. The purpose of this is to use malicious inputs to fool a ML model into producing erroneous

© Springer Nature Switzerland AG 2019
X. Chen et al. (Eds.): ML4CS 2019, LNCS 11806, pp. 320–335, 2019.
https://doi.org/10.1007/978-3-030-30619-9_23

outputs [18]. This has given rise to a research field known as adversarial machine learning [3].

There are a number of different adversarial attacks that can be deployed against ML, for example, an adversary can poison a dataset by perturbing samples in the training data [3]. Over the years, researchers have examined and demonstrated the effectiveness of such poisoning attacks [2,19,23]. Adversarial attacks are a serious threat to the success of ML in practice, as small and subtle perturbations in the inputs can mislead a ML model into outputting incorrect predictions. In computer vision, such perturbations are often imperceptible to the human visual system [1].

This paper focuses on protecting image based datasets by verifying the visual fidelity of the data. Due to the ML necessity of requiring large amounts of training data, many ML models are trained using public datasets that are freely available online. These public datasets are often copied and distributed without any mechanism for protecting the integrity of the data. This makes these datasets vulnerable to alterations by an adversary.

To address this problem, this paper investigates two methods of verifying the visual fidelity of image based datasets by detecting perturbations in the data using QR codes. The advantage of the proposed methods is that a copy of the original dataset does not have to be used for verification. In the first method, a verification string is generated for each image in a dataset using a QR code. The size of a verification string is much smaller than the original image, and it can be used to verify the visual fidelity of the image. To verify image fidelity, a verification process is used to recover a QR code for each image. If the QR code is noisy or cannot be recovered using this verification process, this means that the dataset has been altered.

However, since this method requires a verification string for each image in a dataset, the storage requirement increases linearly with the number of images. While this is fine if storage space is not an issue, it may not be an attractive solution for applications with limited storage capacity. Therefore, a second method is proposed where only a single verification string is required, and can be used to verify the fidelity of images in an entire dataset. The limitation of the second method is that one cannot determine whether individual images have been altered, but only whether the dataset is intact or has been altered from the original.

Our Contribution. In this paper, we investigate the problem of protecting image based ML datasets against alteration by an adversary. The proposed methods attempt to provide mechanisms for verifying the visual fidelity of images in a dataset without the need to use the original dataset. To do this, we generate verification strings from the visual contents of the images and associate these with QR codes. The reason for using QR codes is due to its inherent data capacity and error correction properties, which are in-built in the QR code structure. We present two methods for creating verification strings and for verifying the fidelity of images. The advantage of the first method, which we named the Linear

Verification String (LVS) method, is that the fidelity of each image can be verified individually. However, this comes at the cost of higher storage requirements. The advantage of the second method, which we named the Aggregate Verification String (AVS) method, is that only a single verification string is required to determine whether an entire dataset is intact. Nevertheless, it does not allow for one to determine the visual fidelity of individual images.

2   Background

The proposed methods are based on several concepts, including the QR code structure, the Discrete Wavelet Transform (DWT), the Arnold transform and trapdoor permutation. This section presents a brief background to these concepts followed by a description of related work.

2.1   Preliminaries

QR Code. The Quick Response (QR) code is a two-dimensional (2D) barcode, which was invented by the company Denso Wave [7]. The purpose of using the QR code in this study is because the QR code structure has an inherent error correction mechanism. This mechanism enables QR codes to be correctly decoded even if part of it is corrupted.

A QR code is made up of light and dark modules, which are organized into function patterns and an encoding region [11]. The size and data capacity of a QR code is determined by its version and error correction level. There are forty different QR code versions and four error correction levels. These error correction levels are L (low), M (medium), Q (quartile) and H (high); these correspond to error tolerances of approximately 7%, 15%, 25% and 30%, respectively.

DWT. The Discrete Wavelet Transform (DWT) is a transform domain technique that is widely used in signal processing. For 2D images, it involves decomposing an image into frequency channels of constant bandwidth on a logarithmic scale [17]. An image is decomposed into four sub-bands, which are labeled LL (low-low), LH (low-high), HL (high-low) and HH (high-high). Sub-bands can be further decomposed and this process can continue until the desired number of levels is achieved. A depiction of how an image can be decomposed into two levels of DWT sub-bands is shown in Fig. 1. The LL sub-band contains most of the information of the original image [16]. As such, it represents the highest visual fidelity of an image, as the human visual system is more sensitive to its contents. Data from the LL_2 sub-band was used in experiments conducted in this study.

Arnold Transform. Adjacent pixels in images have a strong correlation to each other. The Arnold transform, shown in Eq. 1, is a invertible transform that

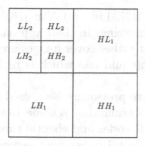

Fig. 1. Sub-bands of a two-level DWT.

can be used to disrupt the correlation between adjacent pixels [10]. An original image that undergoes a number of Arnold transform iterations results in a chaotic image. The reason for using this transform in this study is because image perturbations introduce noise to an image. Applying the Arnold transform to an image scrambles the pixels, and thus, scatters noise over the image. This increases the potential of being able to recover the QR code despite image perturbations.

$$\begin{bmatrix} x' \\ y' \end{bmatrix} = \begin{bmatrix} 1 & 1 \\ 1 & 2 \end{bmatrix} \begin{bmatrix} x \\ y \end{bmatrix} \quad \mod N \tag{1}$$

Trapdoor Permutation. Let D be a finite set. A permutation family Π over D specifies a randomized algorithm for generating (descriptions of) a permutation and its inverse, denoted as $(s,t) \xleftarrow{R} Generate$; an evaluation algorithm $Evaluate(s,\cdot)$; and an inversion algorithm $Invert(t,\cdot)$. We require that for all (s,t) produced by the algorithm $Generate$, $Evaluate(s,\cdot)$ be a permutation of D and $Invert(t, Evaluate(s,\cdot))$ be the identity map. A trapdoor permutation family is one way if it is hard to invert, given just the forward permutation description s. Formally, a trapdoor permutation family is (t,ϵ)-one way if no t-time algorithm $\mathcal{A}$ has advantage greater than ϵ. Hence,

$$\mathsf{Adv\ Invert}_{\mathcal{A}} \stackrel{def}{=} \Pr\left[x = \mathcal{A}(s, Evaluate(s,x)) : (s,t) \xleftarrow{R} Generate, x \xleftarrow{R} D\right],$$

where the probability is over the coin tosses of $Generate$ and $\mathcal{A}$.

2.2 Related Work

Researchers have previously proposed the use of QR codes for various applications in computer security. For example, for storing private and public information [22], secret sharing [5], visual cryptography [9], digital watermarking [6] and so on.

The methods proposed in this paper are related to zero-based watermarking. Unlike traditional watermarking techniques, which necessitates that a watermark be embedded within an image, zero-based approaches do not require the embedding of a watermark [12]. Liu and Yan [16] proposed a secret sharing scheme based on zero watermarking. In their approach, the watermark was not embedded within images, but rather cover images are used to create shares that are distributed to participants and one which is registered with a certification authority.

In addition, QR codes have previously been used in conjunction with watermarking. For instance, a watermarking scheme based on the combination of discrete cosine transform, QR codes and chaotic theory was proposed by Kang et al. [13]. In other work, a digital rights management technique for protecting documents by repeatedly inserting a QR code into the DWT sub-band of a document was investigated [4]. Various other QR code watermarking approaches have also been proposed [6,14,21].

Zero-based watermarking scheme using QR codes have also been proposed. As an example, an authentication method for medical images using zero watermarking and QR codes was devised. In this scheme, a patient's identification details and a link their data was encoded in the form of a QR code that serves as the watermark [20]. Similarly, Li et al. [15] proposed a QR code based zero watermarking scheme in conjunction with visual cryptography for authenticating identification photos.

3   Proposed Methods

Two proposed methods are described in this section. The first method allows for the verification of each image in a dataset. It provides a mechanism whereby a user can check whether individual images in a dataset have been perturbed. However, the first method comes at a cost of storing a verification string for each image. This may not be an appealing solution in situations where limited storage space is an issue. As such, the second method has a very low storage requirement, and provides a mechanism to verify whether an entire dataset is intact. Nevertheless, in the second method, while a user can determine if a dataset is not intact, the user cannot identify which of the images have been altered.

3.1   Method 1 - Linear Verification String (LVS) Method

The notion behind this method is to generate a verification string for each image in a dataset. Hence, we call it the *Linear Verification String (LVS)* method. The purpose of a verification string is to be able to ascertain whether an image has been altered from the original image. An advantage of generating a verification string is so that images in a dataset do not have to be compared with their respective original image. Moreover, the verification strings will require much less storage space when compared with the entire image dataset.

The motivation behind this approach is based on zero-based image watermarking [16]. Unlike traditional watermarking techniques that requires a watermark to be embedded within an image, zero-based approaches do not alter the image. This is in line with the objective of the proposed approach, which is to detect whether samples in a dataset have been altered.

Generating Verification Strings. Figure 2 gives an overview of the process used to generate verification strings for all the images in a dataset. It can be seen from the figure that to create the verification strings, a QR code that contains the secret message, S, and a key, K, for encryption is required. K is a random bit string, which can be generated in a number of different ways, for example, by using a pseudorandom number generator or by using the hash of a password. Encryption involves performing $S \oplus K$ for all modules in S. As such, the length of K must equal the number of modules in S. For instance, a QR code version 1 which consists of 21×21 modules requires the key to contain 441 random bits.

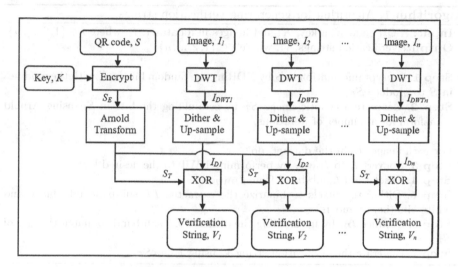

Fig. 2. Overview of the process to generate a verification string for each image in a dataset.

The purpose of performing encryption is so that an adversary will not be able to obtain any information about S from the verification strings. Arnold transform will then be performed on the encrypted secret, S_E, to scramble the pixels. The reason for doing this is to scatter any noise that may result from perturbations to an image over the entire image. The scrambled secret, S_T, will be used for creating the verification strings. Note from Fig. 2 that the same S_T can be used for all images, as this will avoid the necessity of having to generate multiple QR code messages and keys.

Each image in the dataset then undergoes the same process. Each image is decomposed into DWT components at the desired level, level 2 DWT was used in experiments in this paper. Note that color images will first have to be converted to greyscale. The LL sub-band, which represents the highest visual fidelity, will be binarized using a dithering process. The objective of dithering is to binarize the image into black and white bits (i.e. 0s and 1s), while maintaining the average grey level distribution. In the experiments, we adopted the Floyd-Steinberg dithering technique, an approach that is based on error diffusion [8].

After the dithering process, each image is upsampled using nearest neighbor sampling to match the size of S_T. The upsampling process is the reason why S can be of any size. Finally, a verification string, V_i, is produced for each image in the dataset by XORing S_T with the dithered and upsampled results.

The details of an algorithm to generate verification strings for all images in a dataset is provided in Algorithm 1. Inputs to the algorithm are a secret QR code, S, an encryption key, K, and all images in a dataset. The algorithm outputs a verification string for each image in the dataset.

Algorithm 1. Algorithm for generating verification strings.

Input: A QR code, S, a key, K, and images in a dataset, I_i, where $i \in \{1, 2, ..., n\}$.
Output: Verification strings, V_i, where $i \in \{1, 2, ..., n\}$

Step 1. Encrypt information in S by XORing the random bits in K with the modules in S to produce S_E.
Step 2. Generate a chaotic image S_T by scrambling the bits in S_E using Arnold transform for a number of iterations.

For each image, I_i, in the dataset, do
Step 3. Convert I_i to I_{DWTi} by performing DWT to the desired level.
Step 4. Exact the LL sub-band from I_{DWTi}.
Step 5. Dither the pixels to binarize the extracted LL sub-band into black and white bits (i.e. 0s and 1s).
Step 6. Produce I_{Di} by upsampling the dithered LL sub-band to match the size of S_T.
Step 7. Generate the verification string V_i using $I_{Di} \oplus S_T$.

Verifying Image Fidelity. The verification strings can be used to verify the visual fidelity of images in the dataset, and to determine whether any of the images were perturbed. An overview of this process is depicted in Fig. 3. Similar to the process of generating verification strings, each image in the dataset is decomposed into DWT components. The LL sub-band at the pre-determined level is dithered and upsampled using nearest neighbor sampling to match the size of the verification string. Each pair of these are XORed, i.e. $V_i \oplus I_{Di}$, to produce S'_{Ti}. Note that if an image was perturbed, $S'_{Ti} \neq S_T$ for that image.

To recover the QR code, Arnold transform is inversed and K is used for decryption to produce a recovered QR code for each image, S_{Ri}. If no images in the dataset were altered, the QR code can be recovered perfectly for all images in the dataset. However, if an image was perturbed, S_{Ri} for that image will result in a noisy QR code.

Algorithm 2 details the steps involved in verifying the fidelity of images in a dataset. The required inputs to the algorithm are the key, K, that was used for encryption, the verification strings and the images in the dataset. For each image in the dataset, the algorithm outputs the recovered QR code. The visual

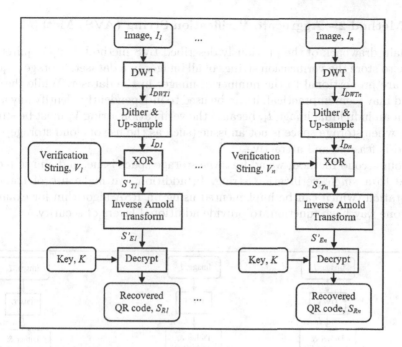

Fig. 3. Overview of the process to verify each image in a dataset.

Algorithm 2. Algorithm for verifying image fidelity.

Input: The key, K, verification strings, V_i, and images in a dataset, I_i, where $i \in \{1, 2, ..., n\}$.
Output: Recovered QR codes, S'_{Ri}, where $i \in \{1, 2, ..., n\}$

For each image, I_i, in the dataset, do
Step 1. Convert I_i to I_{DWTi} by performing DWT to the desired level.
Step 2. Exact the LL sub-band from I_{DWTi}.
Step 3. Dither the pixels to binarize the extracted LL sub-band into black and white bits (i.e. 0s and 1s).
Step 4. Produce I_{Di} by upsampling the dithered LL sub-band to match the size of S_T.
Step 5. Generate S'_{Ti} using $V_i \oplus I_{Di}$.
Step 6. Inverse the Arnold transform on S'_{Ti} to produce S'_{Ei}.
Step 7. Decrypt S'_{Ei} using K to recover the QR code, S_{Ri}.

---

fidelity of each image can be determined based on whether the resulting S_{Ri} is a clean or a noisy QR code. If S_{Ri} is noisy, a clean reconstructed the QR code can be obtained by averaging the black and white pixels per module. If there are more white pixels, the module should be white, and vice versa.

3.2   Method 2 - Aggregate Verification String (AVS) Method

The main drawback of the previously described LVS method, is its requirement to have to store the verification strings of all images in a dataset. Storage requirements are proportional to the number of images in the dataset. While the LVS method may seem impractical, it can be used to independently identify any alteration in an individual image I_i, because the verification string V_i must be stored. Hence, when storage space is not an issue (such as the use of cloud storage), this method is feasible and attractive.

In our second method, we address the storage space issue, and aim to reduce its size to a *single* verification string. In addition, we make use of trapdoor permutation (which can be implemented using an RSA algorithm for example) and a one way hash function, to provide additional layers of security.

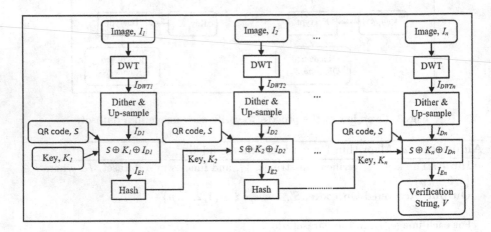

Fig. 4. Overview of the AVS method.

An overview of the AVS method is depicted in Fig. 4, and the algorithm is detailed in Algorithm 3. The initial process is similar to the LVS method. After the dithering process, we obtain I_{Di}, which will be XORed with the key K_i and the QR code S. Hence, $I_{Ei} \leftarrow S \oplus K_i \oplus I_{Di}$. However, unlike the LVS method, $K_i \xrightarrow{R} Evaluate(s, \cdot)$, where the input of the *Evaluate* algorithm is obtained from the hash value of the $I_{E(i-1)}$, which is the output of I_{Ei} from the previous image block. For the first image block, we can use the initial string, such as the hash value of S or any other initial vector. With this chained mechanism, the final output block will only comprise of a single verification string, V, regardless the number of images involved.

Algorithm 3. AVS algorithm.

Input: A QR code, S, the first key, K_1, and images in a dataset, I_i, where $i \in \{1, 2, ..., n\}$.

Output: A verification string, V

For each image, I_i, in the dataset, do

Step 1. Convert I_i to I_{DWTi} by performing DWT to the desired level.

Step 2. Extract the LL sub-band from I_{DWTi}.

Step 3. Dither the pixels to binarize the extracted LL sub-band into black and white bits (i.e. 0s and 1s).

Step 4. Produce I_{Di} by upsampling the dithered LL sub-band to match the size of S.

Step 5. Generate I_{Ei} using $S \oplus K_i \oplus I_{Di}$. If $i \neq 1$, $K_i = hash(I_{E(i-1)})$.

For the last image, I_n, output the verification string, $V = I_{En}$.

Furthermore, as we use trapdoor permutation in the construction, the verification will require the use of the $Invert(t, \cdot)$ algorithm, which cannot be executed without the value of the trapdoor. Therefore, when verifying the images in a dataset, if the QR code cannot correctly be recovered at any image block, this means that the image has been altered and the dataset is not intact. On the other hand, if the QR code can be recovered in all image blocks, the dataset is completely intact.

In summary, to highlight the differences between LVS and AVS, we have achieved a constant size output regardless the number of the image blocks in AVS. Furthermore, we enhance the security level from incorporating a symmetric encryption scheme in LVS with a trapdoor permutation algorithm in AVS.

4   Results and Discussion

An implementation of Algorithms 1 and 2 was implemented using the OpenCV library. This was tested using a number of test images. Figures 5 and 6 show examples of results obtained from the experiments. Additional results can be found in Figs. 7 and 8 in the Appendix section of this paper.

Figure 5(a) shows an example of S, i.e. a QR code containing a secret message. The QR code is of version 3, which contains 29×29 modules, with error correction level H. An example of S after encryption, i.e. S_E, is shown in Fig. 5(b). Figure 5(c) was produced by scrambling the bits in S_E using Arnold transform to generate S_T. Note that in line with Algorithm 1, the same S_T was used in the experiment to obtain the results shown in Figs. 6, 7 and 8. The test images were commonly used image processing test images; namely, the lena, peppers and mandrill images, respectively.

Fig. 5. Example of S, S_E and S_T (a) QR code containing secret message; (b) encrypted QR code; (c) result after Arnold transform.

Fig. 6. Example results for the 'lena' image (a) input image; (b) dithered LL_2 subband; (c) visual depiction of the verification string; (d) S_R after JPEG compression; (e) S_R after noise; (f) S_R after blurring; (g) reconstructed QR code from (d); (h) reconstructed QR code from (e); (i) reconstructed QR code from (f).

Results on the lena image are provided in Fig. 6. Figure 6(a) shows the input image, I. In Fig. 6(b), the LL_2 sub-band of Fig. 6(a) was dithered and the result was upsampled to match the size of S_T. A visual depiction of the verification string, V, that was generated as a result of XORing all bits in I_D with all bits in S_T is shown in Fig. 6(a). Note that this is stored as a bit string rather than as an image to conserve memory storage requirements.

The test image was then perturbed using three common techniques; namely, JPEG compression, noise and blurring. For JPEG compression, OpenCV JPEG compression with a value of 95% quality was used. Figure 6(d) shows the result of using the verification string to recover the QR code from the JPEG compressed image. Figure 6(g) in turn shows a clean QR code that was reconstructed from S_R shown in Fig. 6(d), the grey modules indicate incorrect modules in the reconstruction. To test perturbations resulting from noise, 5 random pixels in the test image were altered. Figure 6(e) and (h) show the recovered QR code and a reconstructed version, respectively. For the blurring test, Gaussian blurring was used with $\sigma = 0.5$. The recovered QR code after blurring and the reconstructed versions are shown in Fig. 6(f) and (i), respectively. Similar experiments using other test images are provided in the Appendix.

5   Conclusion

This paper investigates the problem of protecting image based ML datasets against alteration by an adversary. Two methods are presented in this paper; namely, the Linear Verification String (LVS) method and the Aggregate Verification String (AVS) method. The purpose of these methods is to provide a mechanism for verifying the visual fidelity of images in a dataset without the need to use the original dataset. In both methods, we generate verification strings from the visual contents of the images and associate these with QR codes. In the LVS method, a verification string is generated for each image in a dataset. For verification, a verification process is used whereby each verification string is used to verify the visual fidelity of individual images in the dataset. However, the drawback of the LVS method is that the storage requirement increases linearly with the number of images in a dataset. To solve this problem, we proposed the AVS method which only requires the use of a single verification string to verify whether an entire image dataset is intact. Nonetheless, in the AVS method, one can only ascertain whether the dataset has been altered, but cannot determine the visual fidelity of individual images.

Acknowledgment. The authors would like to acknowledge the support of the NSW Cybersecurity Network grant, the NUW Alliance grant and the National Natural Science Foundation of China (Nos. 61572382 and 61702401) that were awarded for this research.

Appendix

(a)   (b)   (c)

(d)   (e)   (f)

(g)   (h)   (i)

Fig. 7. Example results for 'peppers' image (a) input image; (b) dithered LL_2 subband; (c) visual depiction of the verification string; (d) S_R after JPEG compression; (e) S_R after noise; (f) S_R after blurring; (g) reconstructed QR code from (d); (h) reconstructed QR code from (e); (i) reconstructed QR code from (f).

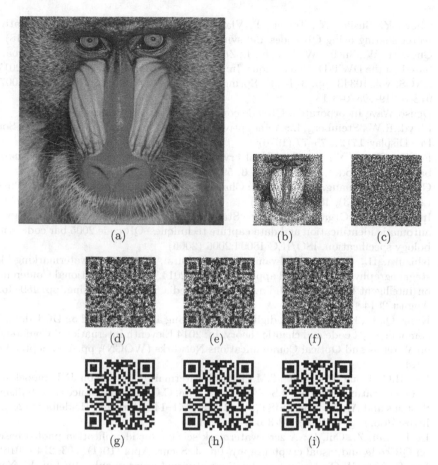

Fig. 8. Example results for 'mandrill' image (a) input image; (b) dithered LL_2 subband; (c) visual depiction of the verification string; (d) S_R after JPEG compression; (e) S_R after noise; (f) S_R after blurring; (g) reconstructed QR code from (d); (h) reconstructed QR code from (e); (i) reconstructed QR code from (f).

References

1. Akhtar, N., Mian, A.S.: Threat of adversarial attacks on deep learning in computer vision: a survey. IEEE Access **6**, 14410–14430 (2018)
2. Biggio, B., Nelson, B., Laskov, P.: Poisoning attacks against support vector machines. In: Proceedings of the 29th International Conference on Machine Learning, ICML 2012, vol. 2, pp. 1807–1814 (2012)
3. Biggio, B., Roli, F.: Wild patterns: ten years after the rise of adversarial machine learning. Pattern Recogn. **84**, 317–331 (2018)
4. Cardamone, N., d'Amore, F.: DWT and QR code based watermarking for document DRM. In: Yoo, C.D., Shi, Y.-Q., Kim, H.J., Piva, A., Kim, G. (eds.) IWDW 2018. LNCS, vol. 11378, pp. 137–150. Springer, Cham (2019). https://doi.org/10.1007/978-3-030-11389-6_11

5. Chow, Y., Susilo, W., Tonien, J., Vlahu-Gjorgievska, E., Yang, G.: Cooperative secret sharing using QR codes and symmetric keys. Symmetry 10(4), 95 (2018)
6. Chow, Y.-W., Susilo, W., Tonien, J., Zong, W.: A QR code watermarking approach based on the DWT-DCT technique. In: Pieprzyk, J., Suriadi, S. (eds.) ACISP 2017. LNCS, vol. 10343, pp. 314–331. Springer, Cham (2017). https://doi.org/10.1007/978-3-319-59870-3_18
7. Denso Wave Incorporated. QRcode.com. http://www.qrcode.com/en/
8. Floyd, R.W., Steinberg, L.: An adaptive algorithm for spatial greyscale. Proc. Soc. Inf. Display 17(2), 75–77 (1976)
9. Fu, Z., Cheng, Y., Yu, B.: Visual cryptography scheme with meaningful shares based on QR codes. IEEE Access 6, 59567–59574 (2018)
10. Guan, Z.-H., Huang, F., Guan, W.: Chaos-based image encryption algorithm. Phys. Lett. A 346(1–3), 153–157 (2005)
11. International Organization for Standardization: Information technology—automatic identification and data capture techniques–QR code 2005 bar code symbology specification. ISO/IEC 18004:2006 (2006)
12. Ishizuka, H., Echizen, I., Iwamura, K., Sakurai, K.: A zero-watermarking-like steganography and potential applications. In: 2014 Tenth International Conference on Intelligent Information Hiding and Multimedia Signal Processing, pp. 459–462, August 2014
13. Kang, Q., Li, K., Yang, J.: A digital watermarking approach based on DCT domain combining QR code and chaotic theory. In: 2014 Eleventh International Conference on Wireless and Optical Communications Networks (WOCN), pp. 1–7, September 2014
14. Lee, H.C., Dong, C.R., Lin, T.M.: Digital watermarking based on JND model and QR code features. In: Pan, J.S., Yang, C.N., Lin, C.C. (eds.) Advances in Intelligent Systems and Applications. SIST, vol. 21, pp. 141–148. Springer, Heidelberg (2013). https://doi.org/10.1007/978-3-642-35473-1_15
15. Li, D., Liu, Z., Cui, L.: A zero-watermark scheme for identification photos based on QR code and visual cryptography. Int. J. Secur. Appl. 10(1), 203–214 (2016)
16. Liu, F., Yan, W.Q.: Various applications of visual cryptography. In: Liu, F., Yan, W.Q. (eds.) Visual Cryptography for Image Processing and Security, pp. 127–143. Springer, Cham (2014). https://doi.org/10.1007/978-3-319-09644-5_5
17. Mallat, S.: A theory for multiresolution signal decomposition: the wavelet representation. IEEE Trans. Pattern Anal. Mach. Intell. 11(7), 674–693 (1989)
18. Papernot, N., McDaniel, P.D., Goodfellow, I.J., Jha, S., Celik, Z.B., Swami, A.: Practical black-box attacks against machine learning. In: Karri, R., Sinanoglu, O., Sadeghi, A., Yi, X. (eds.) Proceedings of the 2017 ACM on Asia Conference on Computer and Communications Security, AsiaCCS 2017, Abu Dhabi, United Arab Emirates, 2–6 April 2017, pp. 506–519. ACM (2017)
19. Rubinstein, B.I., et al.: Antidote: understanding and defending against poisoning of anomaly detectors. In: Proceedings of the 9th ACM SIGCOMM Conference on Internet Measurement, IMC 2009, pp. 1–14. ACM, New York (2009)
20. Seenivasagam, V., Velumani, R.: A QR code based zero-watermarking scheme for authentication of medical images in teleradiology cloud. Comput. Math. Methods Med. 2013(516465), 16 (2013)
21. Thulasidharan, P.P., Nair, M.S.: QR code based blind digital image watermarking with attack detection code. AEU - Int. J. Electron. Commun. 69(7), 1074–1084 (2015)

22. Tkachenko, I., Puech, W., Destruel, C., Strauss, O., Gaudin, J., Guichard, C.: Two-level QR code for private message sharing and document authentication. IEEE Trans. Inf. Forensics Secur. **11**(3), 571–583 (2016)
23. Xiao, H., Biggio, B., Brown, G., Fumera, G., Eckert, C., Roli, F.: Is feature selection secure against training data poisoning? In: 32nd International Conference on Machine Learning, ICML 2015, vol. 2, pp. 1689–1698 (2015)

Reinforcement Learning Based UAV Trajectory and Power Control Against Jamming

Zihan Lin[1], Xiaozhen Lu[1], Canhuang Dai[1], Geyi Sheng[1], and Liang Xiao[1,2](✉)

[1] Department of Communication Engineering,
Xiamen University, Xiamen, Fujian, China
lxiao@xmu.edu.cn
[2] National Mobile Communications Research Laboratory,
Southeast University, Nanjing, Jiangsu, China

Abstract. Unmanned aerial vehicles (UAVs) are vulnerable to jamming attacks that aim to interrupt the communications between the UAVs and ground nodes and to prevent the UAVs from completing their sensing duties. In this paper, we design a reinforcement learning based UAV trajectory and power control scheme against jamming attacks without knowing the ground node and jammer locations, the UAV channel model and jamming model. By evaluating the UAV transmission quality obtained from the feedback channel and the UAV channel condition, this scheme uses reinforcement learning to choose the UAV trajectory and transmit power based on the UAV location, signal-to-interference-and-noise ratio of the previous sensing data signal received by the ground node, and the radio channel state. Simulation results show that this scheme improves the quality of service of the UAV sensing duty given the required UAV waypoints and saves the UAV energy consumption.

Keywords: Unmanned aerial vehicle · Jamming · Trajectory control · Power control · Reinforcement learning

1 Introduction

Unmanned aerial vehicles (UAVs) have been widely used for sensing tasks such as the environment monitoring and military surveillance. However, the UAV sensing data transmission to the ground node is vulnerable to jamming attacks. By sending jamming signals to the ground node during the UAV transmission, a jammer aims to degrade the UAV sensing data reception at the ground node, drain the UAV battery and even prevent UAVs from carrying out the sensing duties for the prescribed waypoints, i.e., the area of interests [8].

Frequency hopping [9] and smart antenna [2] are critical techniques for UAVs to resist jamming attacks. The UAV trajectory control scheme as developed in [1] uses Isaacs' approach to choose the UAV trajectory against jamming attacks

© Springer Nature Switzerland AG 2019
X. Chen et al. (Eds.): ML4CS 2019, LNCS 11806, pp. 336–347, 2019.
https://doi.org/10.1007/978-3-030-30619-9_24

in a zero sum UAV pursuit evasion game. The UAV power control scheme in [13] formulates a Bayesian Stackelberg game and proposes an iterative algorithm with sub-gradient method to choose the UAV transmit power against jamming. However, these UAV jamming resistance schemes rely on the known UAV channel models and the jamming models, and their performance will be influenced by the accuracy and generalizability of the UAV knowledge on these models.

Reinforcement learning (RL) enables UAVs to optimize their communication policies via trials in the repeated UAV communication process against jamming. For instance, the UAV jamming resistance scheme (QPC) in [6] that uses Q-learning to optimize the UAV transmit power can improve the quality of the signals received by the ground node and save the UAV energy consumption against reactive jamming. However, this scheme does not consider the waypoints required by the UAV sensing task nor optimize the UAV trajectory in the sensing data transmission for the UAV sensing applications such as the environment monitoring.

In this paper, we present a RL based UAV trajectory and power control (RLTPC) scheme to resist jamming attacks. More specifically, by applying deep RL, this scheme enables a UAV to jointly optimize its trajectory and transmit power following the sensing task waypoint requirement. In this scheme, the UAV chooses the communication policy based on its current location, the next waypoint location in the sensing task and the signal-to-interference-and-noise ratio (SINR) of the previous sensing data signal received by the ground node in the dynamic game against jammers. Without relying on the channel model between the ground node and the jammer or the jamming model, this scheme applies a Multilayer Perceptron (MLP) to approximate the action-value function for the current UAV state. This scheme evaluates the quality of service (QoS) of the UAV sensing task via the feedback from the ground node, the UAV energy consumption in the previous sensing data transmission and the current distance to the target waypoint, and uses the resulting utility to select the future UAV communication policies against jamming. Simulations are performed for the UAV sensing task for given waypoints and the UAV chennel model given by [10]. The proposed UAV anti-jamming trajectory and power control scheme can significantly improve the QoS of the UAV sensing data transmission and save the UAV energy against smart jamming in comparison with the benchmark QPC in [6].

The remainder of this paper is organized as follows. The related work is reviewed in Sect. 2, and the UAV sensing and communication model is presented in Sect. 3. The UAV trajectory and power control scheme is proposed in Sect. 4, the simulation results are analyzed in Sect. 5, and the conclusion is drawn in Sect. 6.

2   Related Work

UAVs can apply the power control, trajectory planning and smart antenna techniques against jamming. For example, the anti-jamming evasion trajectory scheme as proposed in [1] formulates a UAV pursuit evasion game and uses the Isaacs' approach to obtain the saddle point strategy against jamming. The adaptive beam nulling anti-jamming scheme as proposed in [2] uses Kalman filter to estimate the jammer position and thus keeps the jamming signals in the null region of beamforming antenna. The power control based anti-jamming algorithm as designed in [13] applies the sub-gradient-based iterative algorithm to select the UAV transmit power with fixed UAV and jammer locations.

Reinforcement learning can be used to optimize the power control strategy, radio channel selection and discretized location planning in wireless networks. The RL based anti-jamming algorithm in [3] applies Q-learning to jointly optimize the jamming and anti-jamming radio channels in competing mobile networks. The deep RL based robot anti-jamming system as designed in [4] optimizes the radio channel and the mobility strategy to improve the SINR. The NOMA power allocation based anti-jamming game as formulated in [11] uses Dyna-Q to select the transmit power on the multiple antennas and uses hootbooting technique to reduce unnecessary exploration. The RL based anti-jamming scheme proposed in [6] selects the optimal discretized transmit power and location based on the previous jamming power and channel gains. The user-centric UAV anti-jamming algorithm as presented in [12] uses both RL and deep RL algorithms to optimize the UAV transmit power over a given number of radio channels.

3   System Model

We consider a UAV communication network in a three-dimensional space, consisting of a ground node, a legitimate UAV and a smart jammer. The UAV takes off and visits a series of M planned waypoints $\{W_m\}_{0 \leq m \leq M}$ at the scheduled times $\{nT\}_{0 \leq n \leq M}$ sequentially to execute some tasks such as point inspection, where T is the fixed interval time between two sensing duties. The time slot duration is shorter than the duration between sensing duties, so in the flight between two adjacent waypoints the UAV target waypoints are the same. During the flight, the UAV tries to adjust its trajectory to get closer to the ground node located at G to improve the quality of communication and arrive the next waypoint punctually as well. The maximum mobility of the UAV in x, y and z dimension in a time slot is V. The UAV senses the environment and transmits the sensing data such as photographs or sensor data to the ground node when it arrives at a planned waypoint [5,8] (Fig. 1).

At time k, the UAV is located at $l^{(k)}$ with a given target waypoint $W^{(k)}$. On the way to the next waypoint, the UAV transmits the sensing data of the previous waypoint to the ground node at the transmit power $p_U^{(k)}$ at time slot k. Meanwhile, the smart jammer located at J can sense the ongoing transmission and sends artificial noises at the power $p_J^{(k)}$ to interfere the UAV-to-ground transmission. The maximum power of the UAV and the jammer is denoted by P_U and P_J, respectively. Besides, the channel gain from the UAV and the jammer to the ground node is denoted by $h_U^{(k)}$ and $h_J^{(k)}$, respectively. The ground node sends

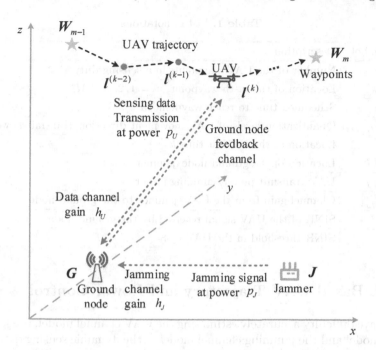

Fig. 1. Illustration of the anti-jamming communication network of a UAV located at $l^{(k)}$ with a sensing task that requests a UAV to carry out sensing tasks at M waypoints at time $k = nT$ with $1 \leq n \leq M$ and sends the sensing data to the ground node located at G during the flight to the next waypoint against a jammer located at J that sends jamming signals with power $p_J^{(k)}$ at time k.

a feedback message consisting of the SINR $\rho^{(k)}$ of the k-th data transmission to the UAV after receiving the data. The UAV then decides the location and transmit power at the next time slot based on the SINR of the last transmission and positioning information.

The UAV uses the probability that the SINR satisfies a minimum SINR threshold σ to evaluate the QoS, which can be denoted by $\mathbb{E}\left[\mathrm{I}\left(\rho^{(k)} > \sigma\right)\right]$. During the communication and flight process from the previous waypoint to the m-th waypoint, the UAV must find an optimal flight trajectory $\left\{l^{(k)}\right\}_{(m-1)T \leq k \leq mT}$ and determines the optimal transmit power at each location in the trajectory to achieve a better QoS of the sensing data. For simplicity, we assume that both the UAV and the jammer can use optical methods to get the location of each other [14]. The jammer can acquire the SINR of the signal from the UAV to the ground node using channel estimation. As the jammer is much closer to the ground node, we assume that the feedback channel from the ground node to the UAV cannot be jammed by the jammer.

The notations are summarized in Table 1 for easy reference.

Table 1. List of notations

Symbol	Description
M	Number of the UAV waypoints in a sensing duty
$\boldsymbol{W}_m$	Location of the m-th waypoint, $m = 1, 2, \cdots, M$
T_m	Scheduled time to reach waypoint m
$N_{x/y/z/p}$	Quantization levels of UAV movement direction/transmit power
$l^{(k)}$	Location of the UAV at time k
G/J	Location of the ground node/jammer
$p_{U/J}$	UAV transmit power/jamming power
$h_{U/J}^{(k)}$	Channel gain from the UAV/jammer to the ground node
$\rho^{(k)}$	SINR of the UAV signal received by the ground node
σ	SINR threshold in the UAV QoS

4   RL Based UAV Trajectory and Power Control

UAVs have difficulty accurately estimating the UAV channel model, the jamming attack model and the jamming channel model in the dynamic sensing data transmission game against smart jamming. Therefore, we propose a UAV trajectory and power control scheme based on deep reinforcement learning to resist jamming attacks. Based on the current UAV state that consists of the current UAV location, the UAV next waypoint and the UAV previous transmission quality according to the feedback from ground node, this scheme uses a deep Q-network [7] that combines reinforcement learning and deep learning techniques to choose the trajectory $\boldsymbol{x}_1^{(k)} \in [-V, V]^3$ and the transmit power $x_2^{(k)} \in [0, P_U]$ at each time slot in the dynamic sensing data transmission process against jamming.

As shown in Fig. 2, the UAV evaluates its current location vector $l^{(k)}$ that consists of the three-dimension UAV coordinates with the given M target waypoint $\boldsymbol{W}_m, 1 \leq m \leq M$, in the sensing duty. Based on the UAV transmission quality obtained from the ground node via the feedback channel, the UAV obtains the SINR of the previous sensing data signal received by the ground node $\rho^{(k-1)}$. The observed location $l^{(k)}$, the next waypoint $\boldsymbol{W}'$, and the previous sensing data SINR $\rho^{(k-1)}$ are used to form the state denoted by $\boldsymbol{s}^{(k)}$, i.e., $\boldsymbol{s}^{(k)} = \{l^{(k)}, \boldsymbol{W}', \rho^{(k-1)}\}$.

The UAV inputs the current state $\boldsymbol{s}^{(k)}$ to a small-scale neural network parameterized by $\boldsymbol{\theta}$, known as deep Q-network [7], to estimate the Q-values of the available trajectories and transmit powers in the action space $\mathcal{X}$, which is denoted by $Q\left(\boldsymbol{s}^{(k)}, \boldsymbol{x}; \boldsymbol{\theta}\right), \boldsymbol{x} \in \mathcal{X}$. The UAV can use the Q-values to choose an action $\boldsymbol{x}^{(k)} = \{\boldsymbol{x}_1, x_2\}$ including the movement direction on the x-, y- and z-axis $\boldsymbol{x}_1$ and the transmit power of sensing data x_2. Apparently, the UAV can choose the action with highest Q-value. However, this greedy strategy will lead to suboptimal trajectory and power control solutions due to the lack of trials of other actions. In piratical implementation, the ε-greedy policy is used in the selection of the

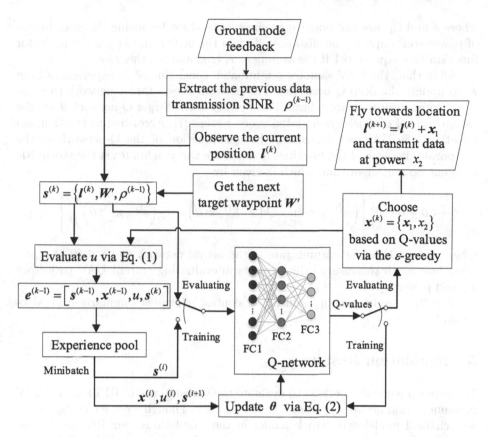

Fig. 2. Illustration of the RL based UAV trajectory and power control scheme.

communication policy $x^{(k)}$ to avoid the local maximum. In this way, the UAV keeps exploring the efficient jamming resistance polices by randomly choosing the other transmission policy with small probability ε instead of the policy that maximizes the Q-values at the sensing data transmission at the time step. The UAV collects the experience $e^{(k-1)} = \left\{ s^{(k-1)}, x^{(k-1)}, u^{(k-1)}, s^{(k)} \right\}$ and stores it into an experience pool denoted by $\mathcal{R} = \left\{ e^{(i)} \right\}_{1 \leq i \leq k-1}$.

The UAV flies toward the next location $l^{(k+1)} = l^{(k)} + x_1$, and transmits the sensing data at the power x_2 to the ground node on the way. The three dimensions of x_1 and the transmit power x_2 are quantized into N_x, N_y, N_z and N_p levels, respectively, as the Q-network cannot output continuous actions.

The UAV then evaluates the QoS satisfaction based on the threshold σ, uses the position sensor to measure the distance to the target waypoint, and evaluates its energy consumption based on the current battery level. The UAV utility is evaluated based on QoS satisfaction, energy consumption and distance to the target waypoint as follows,

$$u^{(k)} = \mathrm{I}\left(\rho^{(k-1)} > \sigma \right) - \delta \left(\left\| l^{(k)} - W' \right\|_2 \right) - C_U x_2, \qquad (1)$$

where δ and C_U are two positive coefficients used for balancing the punishment of power consumption and distance offset in the utility and $\mathrm{I}(\cdot)$ is the indicator function that equals to 1 if the argument is true and 0, otherwise.

After that, the UAV samples a minibatch consisting of N experiences from $\mathcal{R}$ to update the deep Q-networks. The network uses a target network to make the learning process more robust. The weights of the target Q-network $\hat{\boldsymbol{\theta}}$ are the frozen copy of $\boldsymbol{\theta}$ which are updated every τ steps [7]. According to the Bellman equation, the UAV can formulate the loss function of the Q-network as the temporal difference of the Q-values and update the weights $\boldsymbol{\theta}$ via the stochastic gradient descent algorithm, which is given by

$$\boldsymbol{\theta} \leftarrow \boldsymbol{\theta} + \alpha \nabla_{\boldsymbol{\theta}} \mathbb{E}\left[\left(u^{(i)} + \gamma \max_{\boldsymbol{x} \in \mathcal{X}} Q\left(\boldsymbol{s}^{(i+1)}, \boldsymbol{x}; \hat{\boldsymbol{\theta}}\right) - Q\left(\boldsymbol{s}^{(i)}, \boldsymbol{x}^{(i)}; \boldsymbol{\theta}\right)\right)^2\right], \quad (2)$$

where $\alpha \in (0, 1)$ is the learning rate of the neural network and $\gamma \in (0, 1]$ represents how much the future utility counts in evaluating current UAV trajectory $\boldsymbol{x}_1$ and power $\boldsymbol{x}_2$.

The RL based trajectory and power control scheme is summarized in Algorithm 1.

5   Simulation Results

We perform some simulations to evaluate the performance of RLTPC in a UAV communication network against a smart jammer. Though we use a certain wireless channel model and attack model in the simulations, our RL based UAV anti-jamming communication scheme can be adapted to any other UAV anti-jamming communication network as described in Sect. 3.

In the simulations, an orthogonal coordinate space as shown in Fig. 3 is considered. The UAV initially locates at the first waypoint $(0, 50, 30)$ m and uses the sensors such as the camera to obtain photographs and environment data. Then the UAV must fly to the next waypoint at $(40, 50, 30)$ m within 4 s and transmit the sensing data to the ground node located at $(0, 0, 0)$ m at a transmit power ranging from 0 to 4 W for every 1 s. This sensing and transmission process will be repeated on the other 4 waypoints from $(40, 50, 30)$ m to $(160, 50, 30)$ m. The UAV decides its trajectory to the next waypoint by choosing the UAV movement direction from current location. All the three dimensions of the movement direction are chosen from $\{-20, -10, 0, 10, 20\}$ m. The transmit cost of the UAV is $0.25\,\mathrm{W}^{-1}$ when evaluating the utility. The UAV can make 3 decisions between adjacent waypoints and samples 32 experiences from the experience pool in each update phase. The SINR of the UAV data signals must be larger than the threshold that is set as 15 dB to satisfy the QoS requirement.

During the UAV sensing data transmission, the UAV channel is under hilly and mountains channel settings. The UAV transmits the sensing data at C-band frequency 5.06 GHz. In the hilly environment, the path loss exponent is usually chosen as 1.7 similar to [10] and the UAV transmission signals will suffer from

---

Algorithm 1. RL based anti-jamming trajectory and power control scheme

Input: $\{W_m\}_{1 \leq m \leq M}$

1: Initialize γ, α, C_p, C_d, θ, $\hat{\theta} = \theta$, $\rho^{(0)}$ and $\mathcal{R} = \emptyset$
2: **for** $k = 1, 2, \cdots, MT$ **do**
3:      Observe the current location $l^{(k)}$
4:      Get the previous data transmission SINR $\rho^{(k-1)}$ from the ground node feedback
5:      $s^{(k)} = \left\{ l^{(k)}, W', \rho^{(k-1)} \right\}$
6:      Input $s^{(k)}$ to the Q-network to calculate the Q-values $Q\left(s^{(k)}, x; \theta\right), \forall x \in \mathcal{X}$
7:      Choose $x^{(k)}$ with the ε-greedy policy based on $Q\left(s^{(k)}, x; \theta\right)$
8:      Fly to $l^{(k+1)} = l^{(k)} + x_1$ and save the sensing data
9:      Send the sensing data at power x_2
10:     Caculate $u^{(k)}$ via Eq. (1)
11:     **if** $k > 1$ **then**
12:        Store $e^{(k-1)} = \left\{ s^{(k-1)}, x^{(k-1)}, u^{(k-1)}, s^{(k)} \right\}$ in $\mathcal{R}$
13:        Sample a minibatch of N experiences at random from $\mathcal{R}$
14:        Update θ via Eq. (2)
15:     **end if**
16: **end for**

---

a path loss of 119.7 dB at the reference distance 3.4 km with a large-scale log-normally distributed fading $X \sim N(0, 2.4\,\text{dB})$. So the instant channel gain of the UAV transmitting the sensing data to the ground node at location l can be calculated by

$$h_L = 10^{-(119.7+X)/10} \left(\frac{\|l\|_2}{3400} \right)^{-1.7}. \tag{3}$$

Besides, the Ricean fading channel is used to measure the small-scale fading because of the line-of-sight path. Thus the channel gain h_S caused by small-scale fading can be sampled from a Ricean distribution whose K-factor can be calculated by the linear fit equation in [10]. The total channel gain from the UAV to the ground node h_U consists of both the large-scale fading and the small-scale channel gains.

When the UAV is transmitting the sensing data to the ground node, a jammer located at (160, 0, 0) m will sense the transmission and send artificial noises to jam the ongoing transmission. The jammer chooses the jamming power p_J among 4 quantized power levels ranging from 10 mW to 100 mW according to the greedy strategy. Specifically, the jammer first evaluates its utility of all these available powers based on the expected QoS of the UAV data transmission and the power cost of itself, i.e.,

$$u_a = -\mathbf{I}\left(\rho^{(k)} > 15\,\text{dB}\right) - 10p_J, \tag{4}$$

and then chooses the power that maximizes the immediate utility.

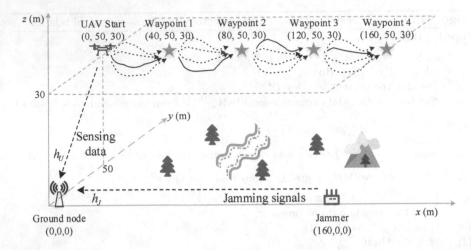

Fig. 3. Simulation settings of the UAV transmission for an UAV at 30 m height that carries out the sensing duties at 5 waypoints starting from (0, 50, 30) m to (160, 50, 30) m with the transmit power ranging from 0 to 4000 mW against a jammer that uses the greedy strategy to select its power from 0 to 100 mW.

We use the QPC scheme proposed in [6] as a benchmark, which considers the jamming power and channel gains as the state and uses Q-learning to decide the transmit power level $x_2 \in [0, 4]$ W. This scheme does not consider the trajectory of the UAV but only control the transmit power to address the jamming attack. We believe that we can further improve the QoS of the UAV sensing duties and save the energy consumption at the same time by jointly controlling the trajectory and transmit power in our proposed scheme.

The simulation results in Fig. 4 show that the proposed scheme RLTPC can improve the UAV sensing transmission QoS and save the UAV energy consumption. As shown in Fig. 4a, the RLTPC scheme improves the UAV QoS by 9.5% and saves the UAV energy consumption by 42.3% compared with the benchmark scheme QPC in [6] after convergence such as the 30000-th time slot. That is because the UAV with QPC cannot learn the complicated UAV-ground model and smart jamming strategies from the large continuous state space and the mobility of the UAV is not leveraged, which leads to lower QoS and higher energy consumption.

With higher QoS and lower energy consumption, RLTPC increases the UAV utility compared with QPC, as shown in Fig. 4c. For example, the UAV utility with RLTPC is 0.663 after 30000 time slots, which is about 99.5% higher than QPC. Besides, the convergence time of RLTPC reduces by 16.7% in comparison with QPC, because RLTPC uses the deep Q-network to optimize the UAV trajectory and power and applies experience replay technique to update the weights to save exploration time and thus reduces the learning required time and improves the UAV anti-jamming efficiency.

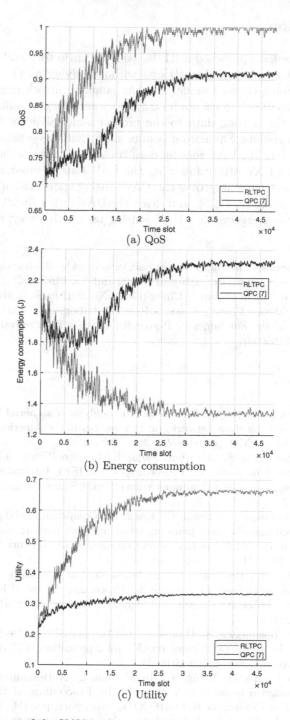

(a) QoS

(b) Energy consumption

(c) Utility

Fig. 4. Performance of the UAV in the sensing data transmission system against jamming attacks.

6   Conclusion

In this paper, we have proposed a RL based UAV trajectory and power control scheme to resist smart jamming attacks without relying on the UAV channel model, the jamming channel model and the jamming attack model. The UAV uses the deep Q-network to choose its trajectory and the transmit power for the transmission of the sensing data to the ground node following the predefined UAV sensing waypoints. Simulation results show that this scheme significantly increases the QoS of the UAV sensing data transmission, saves the UAV energy, and increases the UAV utility following the UAV sensing mission requirement. For instance, this scheme improves the UAV sensing transmission QoS by 9.5%, saves the UAV energy by 42.3%, and raises the UAV utility by 99.5%, compared with QPC after convergence in a UAV sensing task with 5 waypoints against a smart jammer.

Acknowledgements. This paper was in part supported by the National Natural Science Foundation of China (Grants No. 61671396 and No. 61971366), the Natural Science Foundation of Fujian Province, China (Grant No. 2019J01843), the open research fund of National Mobile Communications Research Laboratory, Southeast University (No. 2018D08) and the Fundamental Research Funds for the Central Universities of China (No. 20720190034).

References

1. Bhattacharya, S., Başar, T.: Game-theoretic analysis of an aerial jamming attack on a UAV communication network. In: Proceedings of the American Control Conference, Baltimore, MD, pp. 818–823, June/July 2010
2. Bhunia, S., Sengupta, S.: Distributed adaptive beam nulling to mitigate jamming in 3D UAV mesh networks. In: Proceedings of the IEEE International Conference on Computing Networking Communication (ICNC), Santa Clara, CA, pp. 120–125, January 2017
3. Gwon, Y., Dastangoo, S., Fossa, C., Kung, H.: Competing mobile network game: Embracing antijamming and jamming strategies with reinforcement learning. In: Proceedings of the IEEE Conference on Communication Network Security (CNS), National Harbor, MD, pp. 28–36, October 2013
4. Han, G., Xiao, L., Poor, H.V.: Two-dimensional anti-jamming communication based on deep reinforcement learning. In: Proceedings of the IEEE International Conference on Acoustics, Speech, and Signal Processing (ICASSP), New Orleans, LA, March 2017
5. Kingston, D., Rasmussen, S., Humphrey, L.: Automated UAV tasks for search and surveillance. In: IEEE Conference on Control Application (CCA), Buenos Aires, Argentina, pp. 1–8, September 2016
6. Lv, S., Xiao, L., Hu, Q., Wang, X., Hu, C., Sun, L.: Anti-jamming power control game in unmanned aerial vehicle networks. In: Proceedings of the IEEE Global Communication Conference (GLOBECOM), Singapore, pp. 1–6, December 2017
7. Mnih, V., et al.: Human-level control through deep reinforcement learning. Nature **518**(7540), 529–533 (2015)

8. Roldán, J.J., del Cerro, J., Barrientos, A.: A proposal of methodology for multi-UAV mission modeling. In: Proceedings of the IEEE Mediterranean Conference on Control Automation (MED), Torremolinos, Spain, pp. 1–7, June 2015

9. Shin, H., Choi, K., Park, Y., Choi, J., Kim, Y.: Security analysis of FHSS-type drone controller. In: Kim, H., Choi, D. (eds.) WISA 2015. LNCS, vol. 9503, pp. 240–253. Springer, Cham (2016). https://doi.org/10.1007/978-3-319-31875-2_20

10. Sun, R., Matolak, D.W.: Air–ground channel characterization for unmanned aircraft systems part II: Hilly and mountainous settings. IEEE Trans. Veh. Technol. **66**(3), 1913–1925 (2017)

11. Xiao, L., Li, Y., Dai, C., Dai, H., Poor, H.V.: Reinforcement learning-based NOMA power allocation in the presence of smart jamming. IEEE Trans. Veh. Technol. **67**(4), 3377–3389 (2018)

12. Xiao, L., Xie, C., Min, M., Zhuang, W.: User-centric view of unmanned aerial vehicle transmission against smart attacks. IEEE Trans. Veh. Technol. **67**(4), 3420–3430 (2018)

13. Xu, Y., et al.: A one-leader multi-follower Bayesian-Stackelberg game for anti-jamming transmission in UAV communication networks. IEEE Access **6**, 21697–21709 (2018)

14. Zhang, G., Wu, Q., Cui, M., Zhang, R.: Securing UAV communications via joint trajectory and power control. IEEE Trans. Wirel. Commun. **18**(2), 1376–1389 (2019)

A Fair and Efficient Secret Sharing Scheme Based on Cloud Assisting

Mingwu Zhang[1,2]($\boxtimes$), Xiao Chen[1], Gang Shen[1], and Yong Ding[2]

[1] School of Computer Science, Hubei University of Technology, Wuhan 430068, China
mzhang@hbut.edu.cn
[2] School of Computer Science and Information Security,
Guilin University of Electronic Technology, Guilin 541004, China

Abstract. In threshold secret sharing schemes, the secret s is divided into n shares by a dealer, such that learning t or more than t shares can reconstruct this secret, but knowing fewer than t shares cannot reveal any information about the secret s. In order to enhance the confidentiality of shares, reduce the participants' computational costs, and guarantee the fairness of secret reconstruction, this paper proposes a fair and efficient secret sharing scheme based on cloud assisting. Specifically, we represent the computational process of Shamir's scheme as a matrix operation and encrypt the shares by using a random one-dimensional matrix for guaranteeing the confidentially of shares. In addition, we employ cloud computation platform that assists to reduce the redundancy of reconstruction computation and participants' computational costs. To ensure the fairness of secret reconstruction, our scheme enables participants to recover their secret without revealing their share to the other participants, and ensure that only when all participants are honest, they can reveal the correct secret. The performance analysis demonstrates that the proposed scheme achieves a stronger level of security and a lower computational cost. We also provide the experimental results and show that the proposed approach is feasible and efficient compared with related works.

Keywords: Secret sharing · Fairness · Unconditional security · Matrix operations

1 Introduction

For the protection of cryptographic keys, Shamir [13] first proposed the notion of secret sharing scheme that is based on Lagrange interpolation polynomial, and

This work is supported by the National Natural Science Foundation of China under grants 61672010 and 61702168, the fund of Hubei Key Laboratory of Transportation Internet of Things (WHUTIOT-2017B001), and the Supported by Open Research Project of The Hubei Key Laboratory of Intelligent Geo-Information Processing (KLIGIP-2017A11), and Guangxi Key Laboratory of Cryptography and Information Security (GCIS201717).

© Springer Nature Switzerland AG 2019
X. Chen et al. (Eds.): ML4CS 2019, LNCS 11806, pp. 348–360, 2019.
https://doi.org/10.1007/978-3-030-30619-9_25

later Blakley [2] also gave a secret sharing construction that is based on hyper-plane geometry. The secret sharing scheme generally involves a distributor who has a secret s, a set of n shareholders, and more than t participants, which are a collection of subsets of shareholders, work together to reconstruct the secret. The secret sharing scheme is usually divided into algorithms: *share distribution* and *secret reconstruction*. In general, the threshold secret sharing scheme needs to satisfy two security requirements [13]: Firstly, the *correctness* requires that with knowledge of any t or more than t shares can recover the secret. Secondly, the *secrecy* requires that with knowledge of fewer than t shares cannot get any information about the secret s (t is threshold).

1.1 Related Work

The Shamir's (t, n) scheme in [13] is unconditionally secure since the scheme sat-isfies two security requirements. However, the scheme must guarantee the honest environments that the dealer must honestly distribute the secret during the share distribution phase and all shareholders should honestly correctly the shares dur-ing the reconstruction phase. It is remarkable that the illegitimate participant result in incorrect secret on the secret reconstruction phase and can also obtain some meaningful information about the secret. On the other hand, it is ineffi-cient in practical applications since it contains a lot of repetitive computations [9,19,20].

In order to prevent the cheat problem in threshold secret sharing, Chor *et al.* [3] proposed a notion of verifiable secret sharing (VSS), in which all shareholders are able to verify that shares was released by other shareholders in verifiable secret sharing scheme. For example, by using the non-interactive zero-knowledge in [11] and then obtains ac information-theoretic secure verifiable secret sharing. Harn and Lin [4] introduced new notions of strong t-consistency and strong VSS. Later, Araki [1] proposed a (t, n)-threshold secret sharing scheme that is capable of detecting the fact of cheating from $n - 1$ or less colluding participants. However, they require additional information and spend more processing time, which leads to high computational complexity.

For protecting the privacy of shares and secret, lots of secret sharing schemes that are based on some cryptographic assumptions, such as discrete logarithm problem [5,14], multi-party zero-knowledge interactive proof protocol [17] etc, however, the general encryption mechanisms will bring a lot of computational costs and inefficient. On the other hand, the original Shamir's scheme requires a large data expansion, and thus the scheme is inefficient for resource-constrained participants. In this work, we consider an assistant of cloud computing [6] into the protocol.

Cloud computing is a new paradigm in which computing resources such as processing, memory, and storage do not physically exist in the user's location [6, 18], and it can provide stronger computing capabilities for customers. However, outsourcing to the cloud is bound to produce some security and privacy issues [7,15,16]. Accordingly, the customer needs to encrypt/perturb input data prior to outsourcing to the cloud, and try to protect the privacy of output data.

In order to ensure that the encrypted data can be processed, and in which will not leak any original content, so the fully homomorphic encryption scheme has been proposed. However there is impractical and ineffective for fully homomorphic encryption scheme at present [8,10,12].

1.2 Our Contribution

In the paper, we are motivated to propose an efficient and secure solution for outsourcing the secret reconstruction computation to a public cloud that can achieve high efficiency with security. In this proposed scheme, we represent the processing of the Shamir's scheme as a matrix operation, then encrypt the participant's share by multiplying a random one dimension matrix. This achieves higher computational efficiency with strong security. Next, the cloud simply performs the preset operation and returns the computing result. The introduction of cloud computing is to reduce the redundancy of the reconstruction computation in Shamir's scheme and solve the problem of participants' insufficient computing power. After the participants receive the result returned by the cloud server, the participants can verify the validity of this result by using his/her secret share.

The main contributions of this paper are described as follows:

1. We propose a cloud-assistant computation to reduce the redundancy of the reconstruction computation in Shamir's scheme and allow a resource-constrained participant such as Internet-of-Thing node and wireless sensor to take part in the reconstruction.
2. We give a new scheme to securely outsource secret reconstruction computation to a public and semi-honest cloud server. That is, the proposed scheme guarantees that the cloud server cannot learn any meaningful information about the participants' private data.
3. The computation in our scheme is efficient, and the participants only need to perform simple operations, whose computational complexity of participants is less than Shamir's scheme. We give the experimental results to indicate that our scheme is efficient compared with related works.

1.3 Organization

The rest of this paper is organized as follows. Some preliminaries are introduced in Sect. 2. In Sect. 3, we propose the concrete scheme and take an example of this scheme. In Sect. 4, we analyze the correctness and security, and in Sect. 5 we give the experimental results and analysis. Finally, the conclusion is drawn in Sect. 6.

2 Preliminaries

In this section, we describe the limitation of Shamir's scheme and present a new system model. In addition, we introduce the framework of the proposed scheme.

2.1   Shamir (t, n)-Threshold Secret Sharing Scheme

Shamir's threshold secret sharing scheme is based on *Lagrange interpolation polynomial*, in which there exists n shareholders, i.e., $H = \{H_1, H_2, \cdots, H_n\}$, and a distributor (namely dealer) D, and the scheme consists of two phases that described as follow:

Share Distribution Phase. Distributor D randomly picks a polynomial $f(x)$ with degree $t-1$: $f(x) = a_0 + a_1 x + a_2 x^2 + \cdots + a_{t-1} x^{t-1}$, sets the secret $s = a_0$, where all coefficients $a_i \in \mathbb{F}_p = GF(p)$, $(i = 0, \cdots, t-1)$. The secret $s = a_0 \in GF(p)$. D at random selects n integer $\{x_1, x_2, \cdots, x_n\}$, $(x_i \neq x_j)$, corresponding n shareholders, and computes n shares $\{s_1, \cdots, s_n\}$, $s_i = f(x_i), (i = 1, \cdots, n)$. Finally, the distributor D sends each s_i to the corresponding shareholder H_i by a secure channel.

Secret Reconstruction Phase. Assume that $k(t \leq j \leq n)$ participants P_is want to reconstruct the secret s, i.e., $\{P_1, P_2, \cdots, P_j\} \subseteq H$. At first each participant P_j releases his share to the others, and then one of them can reconstruct the secret by calling the Lagrange interpolating formula as follow.

$$f(x) = \sum_{i=1}^{j} f(x_i) \left(\prod_{k=1, k \neq i}^{j} \frac{x - x_k}{x_i - x_k} \right) \pmod{p} \tag{1}$$

Finally, every participant obtain the secret by computing $s = f(0)$.

Actually, the computation of Shamir's secret share scheme can be regarded as the operation of the matrix: $y = Xa$, where a is a $t \times 1$ matrix, $a = [a_0 \ a_1 \ \cdots \ a_{t-1}]^T$, y is the $j \times 1$ matrix, $y = [y_1 \ y_2 \ \cdots \ y_n]^T$, and X is a $j \times t$ matrix, $X = \begin{bmatrix} 1 & x_1 & \cdots & x_1^{t-1} \\ 1 & x_2 & \cdots & x_2^{t-1} \\ \vdots & \vdots & & \vdots \\ 1 & x_n & \cdots & x_n^{t-1} \end{bmatrix}$.

Thus, the evaluation can be formally represented as follow:

$$\begin{bmatrix} y_1 \\ y_2 \\ \vdots \\ y_n \end{bmatrix} = \begin{bmatrix} 1 & x_1 & \cdots & x_1^{t-1} \\ 1 & x_2 & \cdots & x_2^{t-1} \\ \vdots & \vdots & & \vdots \\ 1 & x_n & \cdots & x_n^{t-1} \end{bmatrix} \times \begin{bmatrix} a_0 \\ a_1 \\ \vdots \\ a_{t-1} \end{bmatrix} \tag{2}$$

2.2   Limitation of Shamir's Scheme

Shamir's (t, n) threshold secret sharing only considers the scene that all participants are legitimate shareholders in the secret reconstruction phase. However, when more than t participants collude together to reconstruct secret and all shares are released asynchronously, an illegitimate participant can always release their fake secret share after obtaining a t valid secret share. As a result, the illegitimate, and thus the dealer can reconstruct the correct secret by using t valid secret shares. However, the legitimate participants will recover an incorrect secret by using a fake secret from an illegitimate participant. Thus, if anyone of t shareholders colludes together to reconstruct the secret, this scheme is insecure. Obviously, consider the largest number of participants, every participant performs exactly the same Lagrange interpolating formula to obtain the secret, and it shows that the local computation of Lagrange interpolating formula needs $O(n^2)$ times, and the total computational complexity is $O(n^3)$. It is easily to indicate that this scheme has a higher complexity and most redundant computation.

2.3   System Model and Assumptions

System Model. In this paper, our system model consists of a distributor D, n shareholders, j participants and a cloud server. The architecture of the proposed system is shown in Fig. 1.

- *Distributor*: The distributor D is an entity of absolute honesty that truthfully sends correct secret shares (x_i, y_i) and a secret key k to each shareholder in the share distribution phase.
- *Shareholders*: Each shareholder receive a valid share from the distributor in the share distribution phase.
- *Participants*: In the secret reconstruction phase, each of the participants encrypts corresponding share by using secret key k and then send the encrypted share to the cloud server. We consider participants as the following roles:

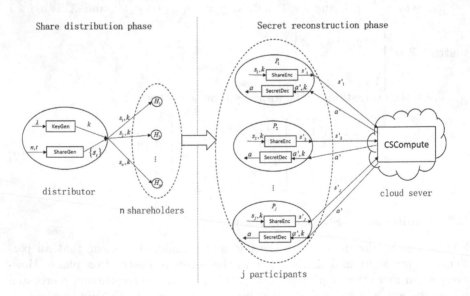

Fig. 1. Framework of the proposed system

1. **Legitimate participant:** The legitimate participant honestly executes the steps of the protocol.
2. **Outside adversary:** The outside adversary who does not have any valid share, but s/he can disguise themselves as legitimate participants to collect information and then identifies the secret.
3. **Inside adversary:** The inside adversary is also called legitimate participant, who obtains s/he own share, but releases a fake share to each other in secret reconstruction phase and thereby only s/he can obtain the secret correctly.

- *Cloud server*: The cloud server who honestly performs preset operations and returns the result to every participant. Finally, each of the participants decrypts the result to obtain the secret s with secret key k. We note that the cloud server is not completely trusted, who tries to learn any useful information about computation result about the secret.

Security Requirements. Our proposed scheme has the following requirements:

- The distributor is a completely credible entity who sends valid shares to legitimate shareholders via a secure channel in the secret distribution phase.
- The share of each shareholder is securely stored and confidential to the other shareholders.
- The cloud server is a semi-honest entity which honestly performs the operations and returns a trusted and correct result to every participant, but it wants to learn the meaningful information about secret.
- The scheme does not consider the collusion attacks between legitimate participants and cloud server.

2.4 Definition of the Proposed Scheme

The proposed scheme consists of the following algorithms:

- KeyGen(λ) $\longmapsto$ $\{k\}$. This algorithm takes a security parameter λ as input and generates a random secret key k, which will be used for encrypting the secret share and decrypting the result return by cloud server.
- ShareGen(n, t) $\longmapsto$ $\{s_i\}$. Taking as input n and t, this algorithm returns n secret shares $s_i = (x_i, y_i)$, for $i = 1, \cdots, n$.
- ShareEnc(s_i, k) $\longmapsto$ $\{s_i'\}$. Taking as input a secret key k and a secret share $s_i = (x_i, y_i)$, this algorithm encrypts the share (x_i, y_i), and returns encrypted share $s_i' = (x_i, y_i')$.
- CSCompute($s_1', s_2', \cdots, s_j'$) $\longmapsto$ $\{a'\}$. Taking j encrypted shares $s_1', s_2', \cdots, s_j'$ as input, this algorithm outputs a'.
- SecretDec(a', k) $\longmapsto$ $\{a\}$. Taking as input Decrypting a' and k, this algorithm returns a.

3 Concrete Construction

In this section, we present a novel scheme to solve the problem that balances the security and efficiency of secret sharing scheme. The specific scheme is presented as follows.

3.1 Share Distribution Phase

- KeyGen(λ)$\longmapsto\{k\}$. The distributor D takes a security parameter λ to generates a random $t \times 1$ vector $k = \begin{bmatrix} k_1 & k_2 & \cdots & k_t \end{bmatrix}^\mathrm{T}$. The vector k acts as the secret key that will be used for encrypting the secret share, and decrypting the result returned by cloud server.
- ShareGen(n, t) $\longmapsto\{s_i\}$. The distributor D opts a polynomial $f(x) = a_0 + a_1 x + a_2 x^2 + \cdots + a_{t-1} x^{t-1}$ with degree $t - 1$ randomly, and sets secret $s = a_0$, where all coefficients $a_i \in \mathbb{F}_p = GF(p)$, $(i = 0, \cdots, t-1)$. Then D at random selects n-integer $\{x_1, x_2, \cdots, x_n\}$, $(x_i \neq x_j; i, j = 1, \cdots, n; i \neq j)$, and computes $y_i = f(x_i)$. Let shares be $s_i = (x_i, y_i)$. Thus, the distributor D sends the share s_i and secret key k to corresponding shareholder H_i.

3.2 Secret Reconstruction Phase

Suppose that j participants $\{P_1, P_2, ..., P_j\} \subseteq H$ ($t \leq j \leq n$, $n < 2t$) take part in reconstructing the secret s, and their respective secret share is s_i.

- ShareEnc(s_i, k) $\longmapsto\{s_i{}'\}$. Each of the participants encrypts their share with secret key

$$y_i{}' = y_i + x_i k \tag{3}$$

$$y_i{}' = y_i + \begin{bmatrix} 1 & x_i & \cdots & x_i{}^{t-1} \end{bmatrix} \times \begin{bmatrix} k_1 \\ k_2 \\ \vdots \\ k_t \end{bmatrix}, \text{ and sends the encrypted share } s_i{}' = (x_i, y_i{}')$$

to cloud server, which can ensure the privacy of the share. Thus, the cloud server obtains j encrypted shares. i.e., $\{s_1{}', s_2{}', \cdots, s_j{}'\}$.
- CSCompute($s_1{}', s_2{}', \cdots, s_j{}'$)$\longmapsto\{a'\}$. After collecting at least j shares, the cloud server constructs two matrices as follows:

$$X = \begin{bmatrix} 1 & x_1 & \cdots & x_1{}^{t-1} \\ 1 & x_2 & \cdots & x_2{}^{t-1} \\ \vdots & \vdots & & \vdots \\ 1 & x_j & \cdots & x_j{}^{t-1} \end{bmatrix} \text{ and } y' = \begin{bmatrix} y_1{}' \\ y_2{}' \\ \vdots \\ y_j{}' \end{bmatrix}$$

And then compute:

$$a' = (X^\mathrm{T} X)^{-1} X^\mathrm{T} y' \tag{4}$$

Note that a' is a $t \times 1$ matrix, that is, $a' = \begin{bmatrix} a_0{}' & a_1{}' & \cdots & a_{t-1}{}' \end{bmatrix}^\mathrm{T}$
Thus, the cloud server outputs a' to each participant. In this step, the cloud server cannot obtain any meaningful information of secret (see Sect. 4.2 for proof).

- SecretDec(a', k) $\longmapsto$ $\{a\}$. After obtaining the result a' from the cloud server, each of the participants only need to perform a simple operation to decrypt the a' with secret key k:

$$a = a' - k \tag{5}$$

Note that a is a $t \times 1$ matrix that is composed of original polynomial's coefficients, $a = [a_0\ a_1\ \cdots\ a_{t-1}]^T$, therefore, every participants obtain the secret $s = a_0$.

3.3   Example

In this section, we give an example to describe the proposed scheme. In the example, we let the threshold t to be $t = 4$, and the number of participants j to be $j = 5$.

- Share distribution phase.
  - KeyGen(λ)$\longmapsto$$\{k\}$. Assume that the generated secret key k, $k = [5\ 3\ 8\ 10]$.
  - ShareGen(n, t) $\longmapsto$$\{s_i\}$. The distributor randomly opts a polynomial $f(x)$ where

$$f(x) = 7 + 4x + 8x^2 + 3x^3$$

  And the secret $s = 7$.
  Next, the distributor at random selects n integer $[9\ 8\ 5\ 4\ 10]$.
  Then it computes the corresponding function value:

$$[f(9)\ f(8)\ f(5)\ f(4)\ f(10)]$$
$$= [2878\ 2087\ 602\ 343\ 3847]$$

  Then the distributor sends $s_1 = (9, 2878)$ to P_1, $s_2 = (8, 2087)$ to P_2, $s_3 = (5, 602)$ to P_3, $s_4 = (4, 343)$ to P_4, $s_5 = (10, 3847)$ to P_5 with secret key k, respectively.
- Secret reconstruction phase.
  - ShareEnc(s_i, k) $\longmapsto$$\{s_i'\}$. Each of the participants encrypts their share with the secret key by using the Eq. 3. Therefore, $s_1' = (9, 10848)$, $s_2' = (8, 7748)$, $s_3' = (5, 2072)$, $s_4' = (4, 1128)$, $s_5' = (10, 14682)$, and then every participant sends the encrypted share s_i' to cloud server.
  - CSCompute(s_1', s_2', $\cdots$, s_j')$\longmapsto$$\{a'\}$. After receiving at least five shares,

the cloud server constructs two matrices: $X = \begin{bmatrix} 1 & 9 & 81 & 729 \\ 1 & 8 & 64 & 512 \\ 1 & 5 & 25 & 125 \\ 1 & 4 & 16 & 64 \\ 1 & 10 & 100 & 1000 \end{bmatrix}$ and $y' =$

$[1048\ 7748\ 2072\ 1128\ 14682]^T$ Then it computes:

$$a' = (X^T X)^{-1} X^T y' = [11\ 7\ 16\ 13]^T$$

Thus, the cloud server returns the result a' to every participant.

- SecretDec(a', k) $\longmapsto$ $\{a\}$. After obtaining the result a' from the cloud server, each of participants only need to perform a simple operation to decrypt the a' with secret key k:

$$a = a' - k = \begin{bmatrix} 7 & 4 & 8 & 3 \end{bmatrix}^{\mathrm{T}}$$

Notice that a is a $t \times 1$ matrix that is composed of original polynomial's coefficients. Thus, every participant obtains the secret $s = a_0 = 7$.

4   Analysis and Discussion

In this section, we theoretically analyze the correctness, security and computational complexity of the proposed scheme.

4.1   Correctness

Lemma 1. *For any matrix $M_{m \times n}$, its rank has following relation: $r(M) = r(MM^{\mathrm{T}}) = r(M^{\mathrm{T}}M)$.*

Theorem 1. *Our proposed scheme is correct.*

Proof. The correctness of scheme is guaranteed by Lemma 1. Note that X is a $j \times t$ ($j \geq t$) Vandermonde matrix, and the rank is $r(X) = t$. From Lemma 1, we have

$$r(X^{\mathrm{T}}X) = r(X) = t$$

and, $X^{\mathrm{T}}X$ is a $t \times t$ matrix. So the matrix $X^{\mathrm{T}}X$ is an invertible matrix.

Based on Eq. 2, we have $y = Xa$, and $X^{\mathrm{T}}y = X^{\mathrm{T}}Xa$, since $X^{\mathrm{T}}X$ is invertible matrix, then

$$(X^{\mathrm{T}}X)^{-1}X^{\mathrm{T}}y = a \tag{6}$$

Therefore, the secret reconstruction can be expressed as an above operation of the matrix.

Based on Eq. 3, we can integrate the encryption process of all participants into the following calculations:

$$y' = y + Xk \tag{7}$$

From Eqs. 6 and 7, we have

$$\begin{cases} a' &= (X^{\mathrm{T}}X)^{-1}X^{\mathrm{T}}y' \\ &= (X^{\mathrm{T}}X)^{-1}X^{\mathrm{T}}(y + Xk) \\ &= (X^{\mathrm{T}}X)^{-1}X^{\mathrm{T}}y + (X^{\mathrm{T}}X)^{-1}X^{\mathrm{T}}Xk \\ &= a + k \end{cases} \tag{8}$$

Equation 5 is satisfied, and the proof is completed.

The Eq. 8 is identical to the Eq. 6, and it's very hard to attract the attention of the cloud server. Finally, after receiving the results a' returned from the cloud server, all participants can recover secret s by performing the operations with secret key k, $a = a' - k$, and $a = \begin{bmatrix} a_0 & a_1 & \cdots & a_{t-1} \end{bmatrix}^{\mathrm{T}}$. Thus every participant get the secret $s = a_0$.

4.2   Security

Theorem 2. *Our proposed scheme is a perfect (t, n)-threshold secret sharing scheme.*

Proof. A (t, n)-threshold secret sharing scheme means that t participants or more than t participants working together can reconstruct the secret, but fewer than t participants cannot reveal any information about the secret s.

In our scheme, the participants submit shares s_i to cloud server in the reconstruction phase, and the cloud server constructs two matrix X and y', and computes $(X^T X)^{-1} X^T y = a$. However, when fewer t participants to reveal the secret, that is, $j \leq t$. From Lemma 1, we have $r(X^T X) = r(X) = j$, and matrix $X^T X$ is a $t \times t$ matrix, so the $X^T X$ is not an invertible matrix. Thus the cloud server will not be able to compute the invertible matrix. However, more than t participants can work together to reconstruct the secret correctly (See Sect. 4.1 for proof).

Theorem 3. *Our proposed scheme can guarantee the fairness in the secret reconstruction phase.*

Proof. For an inside adversary who owns a valid share, he releases a fake share to each other. As a result, only he/she obtains the correct secret. In our proposed scheme, if an inside adversary submits a fake secret share to the cloud server, which will lead to the cloud server compute the result incorrectly, and then the cloud server also returns a wrong result to every participant. Thus each of participant also recovers an erroneous secret. The any inside adversary cannot obtain a correct secret, and the legitimate participants can verify the validity of the result by substituting the share into the recovered polynomial and requires the cloud server to reconstruct the secret again.

For an outside adversary who does not carry a valid share, he/she tries to figure out the secret by disguising a legitimate participant to collect the information. In the proposed scheme, only legitimate participants have the secret key and corresponding secret shares, and there have no interaction between the participants. Therefore, the outside adversary is not able to obtain any meaningful information and figure out the secret.

Theorem 4. *In our proposed scheme, the cloud server is incapable of learning any meaningful information about the original polynomial, i.e. the secret s.*

Proof. In our scheme, the cloud server can obtain every participant's encrypted share $s_i' = (x_i, y_i')$ and can construct two matrices: X and y'. Then it computes $a' = (X^T X)^{-1} X^T y'$. The view of cloud server includes: x_i and y_i', then the cloud server can construct j equation $y_i' = y_i + k_1 + k_2 x_i + \cdots + k_t x_i^{t-1}$, $i = (1, 2, \cdots, j)$, but there have $2t$ unknown quantity $a_i, i = (0, 1, \cdots, t - 1)$, $k_m, m = (1, 2, \cdots, t)$ in equations, since j $(t \leq j \leq 2t)$. Thus the cloud server is not able to obtain these unknown quantities by solving the equations, in other words, it is impossible to learn any meaningful information about the secret.

5   Performance

As mentioned previously, in the original Shamir's (t, n)-threshold secret sharing scheme, each participant performs the Lagrange interpolation formula to obtain the secret, and it will incur $O(n^2)$ computational cost. The total computational complexity is $O(n^3)$. However, in our scheme, the participant only needs to compute $y_i' = y_i + x_i k$ (see Eq. 3) and $a = a' - k$ (see Eq. 5) for encrypting and decrypting the shares, which will spend $O(t)$ computation for any participant. In total, the computational complexity is $O(tn)$.

We now give the experiments to evaluate our proposed scheme that is implemented using Matlab R2016a on a PC with AMD Ryzen 5 2400G 3.6 GHz CPU and 8 GB memory.

Table 1. Notations in simulations

Notation	Remarks
t	Threshold of scheme
j	Number of participants
T_s	Total runtime of secret reconstruction in Shamir's scheme
T_l	Total runtime of ShareEnc, SecretDec at the participant
T_c	Runtime of CSCompute at the cloud sever

Table 2. Runtime of our scheme

t	j	T_s(ms)	T_l(ms)	T_c(ms)
5	5	0.096	0.025	0.109
5	6	0.175	0.030	0.181
5	7	0.243	0.034	0.260
5	8	0.272	0.037	0.285
50	50	0.970	0.050	1.010
50	60	1.370	0.054	1.450
50	70	1.480	0.069	1.510
50	80	1.590	0.073	1.650

We test five algorithms of the proposed scheme and also implement the Shamir's scheme. In Table 1, we briefly describe the notations in simulations, which include threshold, number of participants and running time in different stages.

The experimental results are given in Table 2, where the runtime (in millisecond, i.e., ms) is the average value of 30 runs. It is easily to see that, from Table 2, when threshold t is fixed, the time indices T_s, T_l, T_c increase with the increasing of the number of participants j. It is worthwhile that the participants' local computational cost T_l is far less than the runtime of the reconstruction phase in the original Shamir scheme T_s. That is, our scheme can reduce considerably the computational cost, which is derived from the proposed scheme to reduce the amount of redundant computation by outsourcing the cloud computing. In addition, if t is increased, the increasing rate of T_s is larger than that of T_l, which means when the threshold t is risen, which will not have a significant impact on participants in our scheme. Our proposed scheme is sufficient efficient in practice.

6   Conclusion

In this paper, we proposed a new scheme for securely outsourcing computation of secret reconstruction to a public cloud. In the proposed scheme, for guaranteeing the confidentially of shares, we covert the computational process of Shamir's scheme into a matrix operation, and encrypt the shares by multiplying a random one-dimensional matrix. Meaningfully, we employ the cloud to reduce the redundancy of reconstruction computation and participants computation costs. To guarantee the fairness of secret reconstruction, without releasing the share of the secret, our scheme can also reconstruct the secret efficiently. A comparative summary demonstrates that the proposed scheme is feasible and secure in practical application. Future research can focus on the identification of the cheater of the scheme and implement a multi-secret sharing scheme based on cloud assistant.

References

1. Araki, T.: Efficient (k, n) threshold secret sharing schemes secure against cheating from $n - 1$ cheaters. In: Pieprzyk, J., Ghodosi, H., Dawson, E. (eds.) ACISP 2007. LNCS, vol. 4586, pp. 133–142. Springer, Heidelberg (2007). https://doi.org/10.1007/978-3-540-73458-1_11
2. Blakley, G.R., et al.: Safeguarding cryptographic keys. In: AFIPS Conference Proceedings, vol. 48, pp. 313–317 (1979)
3. Chor, B., Goldwasser, S., Micali, S., Awerbuch, B.: Verifiable secret sharing and achieving simultaneity in the presence of faults. In: 26th Annual Symposium on Foundations of Computer Science (SFCS 1985), pp. 383–395. IEEE (1985)
4. Harn, L., Lin, C.: Strong (n, t, n) verifiable secret sharing scheme. Inf. Sci. **180**(16), 3059–3064 (2010)
5. Harn, L.: Efficient sharing (broadcasting) of multiple secrets. IEE Proc. - Comput. Digit. Tech. **142**, 237–240 (1995)
6. Kumar, K., Lu, Y.-H.: Cloud computing for mobile users: can offloading computation save energy? Computer **4**, 51–56 (2010)
7. Li, Y., Yu, Y., Min, G., Susilo, W., Ni, J., Choo, K.R.: Fuzzy identity-based data integrity auditing for reliable cloud storage systems. IEEE Trans. Dependable Secure Comput. **16**(1), 72–83 (2019)
8. Li, P., Li, J., Huang, Z., Gao, C.-Z., Chen, W.-B., Chen, K.: Privacy-preserving outsourced classification in cloud computing. Cluster Comput. **21**(1), 277–286 (2018)

9. Li, X., Zhu, Y., Wang, J., Liu, Z., Liu, Y., Zhang, M.: On the soundness and security of privacy-preserving SVM for outsourcing data classification. IEEE Trans. Dependable Secure Comput. **15**(5), 906–912 (2018)
10. Mahmood, Z.H., Ibrahem, M.K.: New fully homomorphic encryption scheme based on multistage partial homomorphic encryption applied in cloud computing. In: 2018 1st Annual International Conference on Information and Sciences (AiCIS), pp. 182–186. IEEE (2018)
11. Pedersen, T.P.: Non-interactive and information-theoretic secure verifiable secret sharing. In: Feigenbaum, J. (ed.) CRYPTO 1991. LNCS, vol. 576, pp. 129–140. Springer, Heidelberg (1992). https://doi.org/10.1007/3-540-46766-1_9
12. Rahman, M., Khalil, I., Alabdulatif, A., Yi, X.: Privacy preserving service selection using fully homomorphic encryption scheme on untrusted cloud service platform. Knowl.-Based Syst. **180**, 104–115 (2019)
13. Shamir, A.: How to share a secret. Commun. ACM **22**(11), 612–613 (1979)
14. Shao, J., Cao, Z.: A new efficient (t, n) verifiable multi-secret sharing (VMSS) based on YCH scheme. Appl. Math. Comput. **168**(1), 135–140 (2005)
15. Subashini, S., Kavitha, V.: A survey on security issues in service delivery models of cloud computing. J. Netw. Comput. Appl. **34**(1), 1–11 (2011)
16. Wei, L., et al.: Security and privacy for storage and computation in cloud computing. Inf. Sci. **258**, 371–386 (2014)
17. Vaikuntanathan, V., Vasudevan, P.N.: Secret sharing and statistical zero knowledge. In: Iwata, T., Cheon, J.H. (eds.) ASIACRYPT 2015. LNCS, vol. 9452, pp. 656–680. Springer, Heidelberg (2015). https://doi.org/10.1007/978-3-662-48797-6_27
18. Yu, Y., Li, H., Chen, R., Zhao, Y., Yang, H., Du, X.: Enabling secure intelligent network with cloud-assisted privacy-preserving machine learning. IEEE Netw. **33**(3), 82–87 (2019)
19. Zhang, M., Yao, Y., Li, B., Tang, C.: Accountable mobile e-commerce scheme in intelligent cloud system transactions. J. Ambient Intell. Humaniz. Comput. **9**(6), 1889–1899 (2018)
20. Zhang, M., Zhang, Y., Jiang, Y., Shen, J.: Obfuscating eves algorithm and its application in fair electronic transactions in public cloud systems. IEEE Syst. J. **13**(2), 1478–1486 (2019)

Secure and Fast Decision Tree Evaluation on Outsourced Cloud Data

Lin Liu[1], Jinshu Su[1,2(✉)], Rongmao Chen[1(✉)], Jinrong Chen[1],
Guangliang Sun[3], and Jie Li[1]

[1] School of Computer, National University of Defense Technology, Changsha, China
{liulin16,sjs,chromao}@nudt.edu.cn
[2] National Key Laboratory for Parallel and Distributed Processing,
National University of Defense Technology, Changsha, China
[3] National University of Defense Technology, Changsha, China

Abstract. Decision trees are famous machine learning classifiers which have been widely used in many areas, such as healthcare, text classification and remote diagnostics, etc. The service providers usually host a decision tree model on the cloud server and provide some classification service for clients to use such a model remotely. In such a scenario, the model is a valuable asset to the cloud which should not be disclosed to the clients, while the query data and classification results are private to the client. To solve such a problem, we propose several building blocks, i.e., secure comparison and secure polynomial calculation, in a two-cloud model. Based on these building blocks, we design a privacy-preserving decision tree evaluation scheme. Compared with the most recent works, our scheme can fully protect the tree model and clients' data privacy simultaneously. Besides, our scheme also supports offline service users which is essential to the system's scalability. Moreover, through theoretical analysis and real-world experimental test, it is oblivious that our scheme is quite efficient.

Keywords: Decision tree evaluation · Data security ·
Cloud Computing

1 Introduction

Predictive modeling has been proved to be an essential tool in practice by people and organizations, which has been used in many real-world scenarios, e.g., policy making, medicine, on-line diagnosis, banking. Nowadays, almost all the "Internet Giant", including Amazon, Google, Facebook, Alibaba and Tencent, are working on and use machine learning technology to build a predictive model. Usually, there are two phases. The first is the training phase, where a model is trained on a large dataset. The second is the evaluation phase, in which a classification label can be returned for the input data vector. The internet giants with the ability to collect massive data can train a more accurate predictive model on their

© Springer Nature Switzerland AG 2019
X. Chen et al. (Eds.): ML4CS 2019, LNCS 11806, pp. 361–377, 2019.
https://doi.org/10.1007/978-3-030-30619-9_26

cloud platform than normal individuals and organizations. With such a model, they can use it to provide classification as a kind of cloud service. In real-world setting, such typical machine learning prediction service requires the service users reveal their query data and corresponding classification label to the server. However, the query data and its corresponding classification result sometimes contain sensitive information. Thus, the service users may reluctant to use such a service for revealing this information to the server. One naive solution it to simply send the machine learning model to the client, who can run the evaluation phase locally. Unfortunately, such a model is a valuable asset to the company, which is trained by spending a great number of resources. Thus, leaking such a business secret to the others will greatly violate the company's interest. More importantly, the leakage of the machine learning model may even violate the laws and regulations such as Health Insurance Portability and Accountability Act (HIPAA) [1].

In this work, we mainly consider the security and privacy problems existing in the decision tree evaluation on the outsourced cloud data. Decision tree has been widely used in many research areas, e.g., disease diagnosis [2,3], credit-risk assessment [4] and text classification [5], which consists of a collection of decision nodes arranged in a tree structure. Early works focus on privacy-preserving training decision tree [6,7]. Recently, more and more researchers have started to study the privacy and security issues in the area of outsourced decision tree evaluation [8–10].

Motivating Scenario. In this work, we try to find a solution for privacy-preserving decision tree evaluation with high efficiency and security level. Here, we consider a cloud service provider which has trained a decision tree model and wants to use it to provide prediction service. In such a scenario, the following security and privacy issues should be considered.

1. Both the query vector and its corresponding classification label should be kept private from the cloud server and the other adversary.
2. The trained decision tree model should not be inferred to the client during the whole evaluation process.

Moreover, efficiency is also vital to such a scheme. The cloud should return the evaluation result to the client as soon as possible. Last but not least, supporting off-line service users is essential for the scalability of the system.

Our Contributions. In this paper, we design a privacy-preserving decision tree evaluation scheme in a two-cloud model. The contributions of this paper are three-fold, namely:

- We propose a novel secure comparison which is based on additively homomorphic cryptosystem and secret sharing. Compared with the existing works, our proposed protocol can reduce the communication round from $O(n)$ to $O(1)$.
- Based on the cryptographic blocks proposed, we construct a privacy-preserving decision tree scheme. Several real-world dataset experimental tests show the efficiency of our scheme.

- We show that our scheme can indeed achieve higher privacy level than most recent works [8–10]. And also, we fully prove the security of our scheme under the semi-honest mode.

Related Work. Privacy-preserving data mining was first considered by [6,7,11]. After that, several works have been proposed in this area [12–14]. Earlier works mainly consider how to securely construct a decision tree. The first work considering the private preserving decision tree evaluation was proposed by Brikell *et al.* [15], which was applied to a remote diagnosis system. In this work, both the homomorphic encryption and Garble Circuit (GC) [16] are used. The evaluation time of such a scheme is sublinear in the tree size, but the secure program itself and the communication cost are linear and hence is not efficient for large trees. Later, Barni *et al.* [17] improved this scheme by reducing costs by a constant factor. However, the communication cost is still linear.

Recently, Bost *et al.* proposed several privacy-preserving evaluation protocols including decision tree. In their scheme, a decision tree is represented as a polynomial whose output is the result of the classification label. The client and the server run an improved DGK comparison [18] to compare the attribute vector with the internal nodes of the tree. Finally, the server evaluates the polynomial through a fully homomorphic encryption system. However, the fully homomorphic encryption (FHE) is quite time-consuming. Therefore, it is not efficient enough for large tree applications. Wu *et al.* [9] improved it by using just an additive homomorphic encryption (AHE). The evaluation returns the index of the classification index. At the end of the protocol, the client needs to run an Oblivious Transfer (OT) [19] with the server to get the label. Tai *et al.* based the Wu *et al.*'s blueprint to make a significant improvement in efficiency. In their scheme, a decision tree is represented in the form of linear functions rather than a high-degree polynomial [10]. Cock *et al.* [20] proposed a privacy preserving decision tree evaluation scheme based on secret sharing (SS) in the commodity-based model. This scheme runs very fast with small trees but relatively slow to deal with large trees. Joye *et al.* [21] proposed a work also based on [9], but designed a new comparison protocol and improved the total number of comparison during the evaluations. Most recently, Tueno *et al.* [22] proposed a decision tree evaluation scheme by representing the tree as an array, which achieves sublinear complexity of the size of the tree. However, all the works proposed right now cannot protect the tree model perfectly, i.e., the number of the nodes or the depth of the tree may be leaked to the clients. Moreover, none of the works can support offline clients, meaning that during the evaluation process the clients need to communicate with the server and make some calculations on his own. Our work can truly protect the tree and supporting offline users simultaneously. We make a comparison with the most recent works in Table 1.

Table 1. Comparison summary

Algorithm	Support offline	Query privacy	Classification privacy	Cryptosystem	Model leakage
[8]	×	✓	✓	FHE	m
[9]	×	✓	✓	AHE, OT	m, d
[10]	×	✓	✓	AHE, OT	m
[20]	×	✓	✓	SS	m
[21]	×	✓	✓	AHE	m
[22]	×	✓	✓	GC, OT, ORAM	d
Ours	✓	✓	✓	SS, AHE	×

2   Preliminaries

In this section, we present several essential preliminary concepts of our scheme. The key notations used throughout this paper are introduced in Table 2.

Table 2. Notation used

Notations	Definition
pk	Public key of Paillier cryptosystem
$sk^{(1)}/sk^{(2)}$	Partial private key of Paillier cryptosystem
$\text{Enc}_{pk}(\cdot)$	Encryption with public key pk
$\text{PDec}_{sk^i}(\cdot)$	Partial Decryption with $sk^{(i)}$, $i = 1, 2$
$[\![x]\!]$	Ciphertext of x under Paillier cryptosystem
$\langle x \rangle$	Additive secret shares of x
$\langle x \rangle^A/\langle x \rangle^B$	Party A's/ B's additive secret share of x
$\|x\|$	Bit length of x
$\text{Add}(\cdot)$	Secure Addition
$\text{Mul}(\cdot)$	Secure Multiplication
$\text{Rec}(\cdot, \cdot)$	Reconstruction of the value of x
SC	Secure Comparison
SPC	Secure Polynomial Calculation
SDTE	Secure Decision Tree Evaluation

2.1   Decision Tree Evaluation

The decision tree is a frequently encountered machine learning method which is widely used in many classification and regression areas. A decision tree is a binary tree T, which contains m internal nodes, called decision nodes. An example of a decision tree is shown in Fig. 1. The leaf node of T is called a classification node which is associated with the classification label. We call the length of the longest path from the root to a leaf as the depth of a decision tree. Generally, a decision is usually not binary or complete. Nevertheless, each non-binary or non-complete tree can be transformed into a complete binary tree, by increasing the depth and introducing several dummy internal nodes [9]. Note that all the leaves of a dummy node have the same classification label. A decision tree with m internal nodes has a threshold vector $Y = \{y_1, y_2, \cdots, y_m\}$. We refer the vector feature received by a decision tree as $X = \{x_1, x_2, \cdots, x_n\}$. We associate each node in the tree with a Boolean function $f(x) = (x \geq y)$. For each dummy node, we associate it with a trivial Boolean function $f(x) = 0$. The value of the Boolean function decide the paths of the binary tree. If it is 1, we go to its left child else we go to its right child node. Starting from the root of a decision, we compare the internal node with the corresponding attribute value in X. When we reach a leaf node in this path, the corresponding classification value of this node can be outputted as the classification result of this vector X.

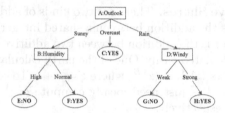

Fig. 1. Decision tree model

2.2 Paillier Cryptosystem with Distributed Decryption

Paillier encryption algorithm is a well known additively homomorphic cryptosystem [23]. recently, Hazay *et al.* designed a Paillier cryptosystem with distributed private keys [24]. In such a scheme, the private key is separated into two shares, i.e., $sk^{(1)}$, $sk^{(2)}$. The plaintext domain of such a cryptosystem is $\mathbb{Z}_N$, and the ciphertext space is $\mathbb{Z}_{N^2}$. The ciphertext of this scheme is denoted as $[\![x]\!]$. In the following, we use $\mathrm{Enc}_{pk}(\cdot)$ and $\mathrm{Dec}_{pk}(\cdot)$ to denote the encryption and decryption functions of this cryptosystem. Moreover, $\mathrm{PDec}_{sk^{(1)}}(\cdot)$, and $\mathrm{PDec}_{sk^{(2)}}(\cdot)$ are used to denote the partial decryption functions with partial private key $sk^{(1)}$ and $sk^{(2)}$. Given the ciphertext $[\![x]\!]$, the distributed decryption works as $[\![x']\!] \leftarrow \mathrm{PDec}_{sk^1}([\![x]\!])$ and $x \leftarrow \mathrm{PDec}_{sk^{(2)}}([\![x']\!])$.

The Paillier cryptosystem with distributed decryption is additively homomorphic, which means it has the following two properties:

1. **Homomorphic Addition:** Given two ciphertext, i.e, $[\![a]\!]$, $[\![b]\!]$, encrypted by the same public key pk, we easily get $\mathrm{Dec}([\![a]\!] \cdot [\![b]\!]) = a + b$.
2. **Scalar Multiplication:** Given the ciphertext $[\![x]\!]$ and a constant integer c, we can calculate $\mathrm{Dec}([\![x]\!]^c) = c \cdot x$. Specifically, when $c = N - 1$, it can be easily calculated $\mathrm{Dec}([\![x]\!]^{N-1}) = -x$, where $-x = N - x$.

More proofs of the correctness and semantic security of the Paillier cryptosystem with distributed decryption can be found in reference [24].

2.3 Additive Secret Sharing

Additive secret sharing scheme is a kind of secure multi-party computation scheme [16] proposed by Shamir [25]. In additive secret sharing scheme, an integer x from a ring $\mathbb{Z}_N$ is split into two additive shares. In the following, we use $\langle x \rangle$ to denote additive shares of x, and $\langle x \rangle^A$, $\langle x \rangle^B$ are used to denote the shares belong to party A and B. To reconstruct the value of x, a reconstruction function, i.e., $\texttt{Rec}(\cdot, \cdot)$ is needed. One of the two parties sends its share to the other, and the other calculates $x = \langle x \rangle^A + \langle y \rangle^B \pmod{N}$. In the following, for simplicity, we omit "mod N" in each calculation, even though all the calculations are with $\mathbb{Z}_N$.

Addition of Additive Shares. There are two kinds of addition to the additive shares. One of them is the addition between a shared integer $\langle x \rangle$ with a constant integer c; and the other is the addition between two additive shares, i.e., $\langle x \rangle$, $\langle y \rangle$. The former can be calculated easily. One of the party calculates $\langle z \rangle^A \leftarrow \langle x \rangle^A + c$, while the other just sets $\langle z \rangle^B \leftarrow \langle x \rangle^B$, where $z = x + c$. To compute the addition of $\langle x \rangle$, $\langle y \rangle$, the two parties just need locally compute $\langle z \rangle^A \leftarrow \langle x \rangle^A + \langle y \rangle^A$ and $\langle z \rangle^B \leftarrow \langle x \rangle^B + \langle y \rangle^B$ respectively.

Multiplication Triplets. Beaver proposed a method to compute the multiplication of two additively shared integers [26]. In such a scheme, a pre-computed arithmetic multiplication triple of the form $\langle c \rangle = \langle a \rangle \cdot \langle b \rangle$ is needed. The two parties compute $\langle e \rangle^A \leftarrow \langle x \rangle^A - \langle a \rangle^A$, $\langle e \rangle^B \leftarrow \langle x \rangle^B - \langle a \rangle^B$, $\langle f \rangle^A \leftarrow \langle y \rangle^A - \langle b \rangle^A$, and $\langle f \rangle^B \leftarrow \langle y \rangle^B - \langle b \rangle^B$ respectively. After that, they both run the $\texttt{Rec}(\cdot, \cdot)$ to reconstruct e and f. Then, party A and B calculate $\langle z \rangle^A \leftarrow f \cdot \langle a \rangle^A + e \cdot \langle b \rangle^A + \langle c \rangle^A$, $\langle z \rangle^B \leftarrow e \cdot f + f \cdot \langle a \rangle^B + e \cdot \langle b \rangle^B + \langle c \rangle^B$ respectively. Here, we stress that the pre-computed triples should be fresh for each multiplication. The generation of these triplets can be done offline. They can be distributed by the trusted third party or generated by the two parties through running Oblivious Transfer [19]. More details of the generation and distribution of these triplets can be found in reference [27].

3 System Model and Design Goal

3.1 System Model

Our scheme focuses on the privacy-preserving decision tree evaluation on the cloud data. In this scheme, we adopt a two-cloud model, namely Cloud Service Provider (CSP) and Evaluation Service Provider (ESP). The overall system model is shown in Fig. 2.

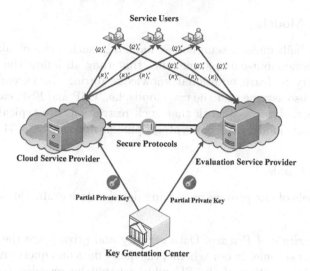

Fig. 2. System model

(1) **Key Generation Center:** The trusted Key Generation Center (KGC) is responsible for generating and managing both public and private keys for every party in our system. KGC also is responsible to split the private key into two shares and sends it to two clouds. After the key generation and distribution, KGC can remain offline.

(2) **Service Users:** Generally, Service Users (SU) is the decision tree evaluation service users in this scheme. The goal of SU is to find the classification result of his data vectors. Note that all the data uploaded are split into two additive shares, thus they can be given to CSP and ESP.

(3) **Cloud Service Provider:** In our scheme, we assume that the CSP has owned a pre-trained decision tree model. With such a model, it can provide classification service. Since the query data received are split into two shares. Only one share of query data is uploaded to CSP. Thus, the CSP should cooperate with ESP to fulfill the decision tree evaluation task.

(4) **Evaluation Service Provider:** In our scheme, the ESP mainly provide online computation service for SU and CSP. With the help of ESP, CSP and ESP can calculate the correct decision tree evaluation result.

Note that the Evaluator is an essential part in our system. On one hand, in additive secret share based schemes, two parties are needed to fulfill various computation tasks. On the other hand, the two-cloud model usually is capable of minimizing the interactions between the server users and cloud servers while one cloud cannot [28–30]. In our proposed scheme, SUs only send additive shares of queries and then remain offline until receiving the additive classification results. Moreover, we stress that all the entities involved should authenticate with each other before performing specific actions. In fact there are many works about the authentication [14,31,32]. For space limitation, we omit the details.

3.2   Threat Model

Our scheme is built under a semi-honest model. In such a model, all the entities involved are honest-but-curious, meaning that they all follow the rules of our scheme, but try to learn additional knowledge during the execution process. Moreover, we also assume that the two clouds, i.e., CSP and ESP, cannot collude with each other. Here we remark that such restrictions are typical and widely used in adversary model used in cryptographic protocols [28,33,34].

3.3   Design Goals

The design goals of our privacy-preserving decision tree evaluation are shown as follows:

(1) *Data Security and Privacy.* Data security and privacy are the prior design goals of our scheme. In our scheme, the query data and query result contains sensitive information of the SU which should be revealed to neither the CSP or ESP in our scheme. Moreover, the access pattern also should be protected. In addition, the decision tree is the property of CSP, which cannot be disclosed to ESP or SU.

(2) *Classification Result's Accuracy.* It is also really important that the classification accuracy must be guaranteed when applying the privacy-preserving strategy. Therefore, the proposed system should achieve the same accuracy compared with the non-privacy-preserving data mining system.

(3) *Efficiency.* Considering the real-time requirement of the online service, the decision tree evaluation process should be done as fast as possible. Therefore, the computation and communication overheads of ESP and CSP should be as small as possible.

(4) *Offline SUs.* Usually the SUs are resource-constrained in our scheme. After sending query data, they should be offline until receiving the classification result. Supporting offline SUs is a good way to minimize the computation and communication costs of them. Moreover, there are a great number of SUs in our scheme, supporting offline SUs is vital to the scalability of our scheme.

4   Privacy-Preserving Building Blocks

In this section, we mainly propose a secure comparison and secure polynomial calculation protocol. These building blocks are based on additive secret sharing and Paillier cryptosystem with distributed decryption. Both of them serve as the basic constructions of privacy-preserving decision tree evaluation scheme. In the following, we assume that CSP is the party A and ESP is the party B, i.e., $\langle \cdot \rangle^A$ belongs to CSP and $\langle \cdot \rangle^B$ belongs to ESP.

4.1 Secure Comparison

Suppose that the CSP and ESP have two additively shared integers $\langle x \rangle$, $\langle y \rangle$. Note that in this algorithm, $\|x\|, \|y\| \leq \|N\|/2 - 1$. Through running such a *Secure Comparison* (SC) protocol, they get the additive shares of the comparison result $\langle t \rangle$, where $t = (x \geq y)$. During the running of this protocol, nothing of the original data and the comparison result is leaked to CSP or ESP. We introduce our SC in Algorithm 1.

Algorithm 1. Secure Comparison (SC)

Input: CSP has $\langle x \rangle^A$, $\langle y \rangle^A$ and $sk^{(1)}$; ESP has $\langle x \rangle^B$, $\langle y \rangle^B$ and $sk^{(2)}$. A pre-computed arithmetic multiplication triple $\langle c \rangle = \langle a \rangle \cdot \langle b \rangle$.
Output: CSP outputs $\langle t \rangle^A$; ESP outputs $\langle t \rangle^B$.
1: ESP: $X^B \leftarrow \text{Enc}(2\langle x \rangle^B + 1)$, $Y^B \leftarrow \text{Enc}(2\langle y \rangle^B)$. Send X^B, Y^B to CSP.
2: CSP: $X^A \leftarrow \text{Enc}(2\langle x \rangle^A)$, $Y^A \leftarrow \text{Enc}(2\langle y \rangle^A)$. $X \leftarrow X^A \cdot X^B, Y \leftarrow Y^A \cdot Y^B$.
   Randomly pick $r_1, r_2 \in \mathbb{Z}_N$ and $\alpha \in \{0,1\}$, s.t., $\|r_1\| < \|N\|/2 - 1$. If $\alpha = 0$,
   $C \leftarrow X \cdot Y^{N-1}$; else $C \leftarrow Y \cdot X^{N-1}$. $D \leftarrow C^{r_1}$. Partial decrypt D as D', i.e,
   $D' \leftarrow \text{PDec}_{sk^{(1)}}(D)$, before sending it to ESP.
3: ESP: $d \leftarrow \text{PDec}_{sk^{(2)}}(D')$. If $d < N/2$, $\beta \leftarrow 1$; else $\beta \leftarrow 0$.
4: ESP: $\langle e \rangle^A \leftarrow \alpha - \langle a \rangle^A$, $\langle f \rangle^A \leftarrow \alpha - \langle b \rangle^A$.
5: ESP: $\langle e \rangle^B \leftarrow -\beta - \langle a \rangle^B$, $\langle f \rangle^B \leftarrow -\beta - \langle b \rangle^B$.
6: CSP& ESP: $e \leftarrow \text{Rec}(\langle e \rangle^A, \langle e \rangle^B)$, $f \leftarrow \text{Rec}(\langle f \rangle^A, \langle f \rangle^B)$.
7: CSP: $\langle t \rangle^A \leftarrow f \cdot \langle a \rangle^A + e \cdot \langle b \rangle^A + \langle c \rangle^A$.
8: ESP: $\langle t \rangle^B = e \cdot f + f \cdot \langle a \rangle^B + e \cdot \langle b \rangle^B + \langle c \rangle^B$.

In our SC, both the additive secret sharing scheme and Paillier cryptosystem with distributed decryption scheme are used. Firstly, CSP and ESP make a conversion from additive secret to Paillier cryptosystem ciphertext. Specifically, ESP computes $2(\langle x \rangle^B + 1)$, $2\langle y \rangle^B$ and then encrypts them as X^B and Y^B before sending them to CSP. At the same time, CSP also calculates $2\langle x \rangle^A$, $2\langle y \rangle^A$, and then encrypts them as X^A and Y^A. With X^A, Y^A, X^B and Y^B, CSP can easily compute $X \leftarrow X^A \cdot X^B, Y \leftarrow Y^A \cdot Y^B$, where $X = [\![2x + 1]\!]$, $Y = [\![2y]\!]$. Next, CSP picks two random integers from $\mathbb{Z}_N$, i.e., r_1, and $\alpha \in \{0,1\}$, where $\|r_1\| < \|N\|/2 - 1$. If $\alpha = 0$, CSP calculates $C \leftarrow X \cdot Y^{N-1}$, where $C = [\![2x + 1 - 2y]\!]$. Otherwise, CSP computes $C \leftarrow Y \cdot X^{N-1}$, where $C = [\![2y - (2x + 1)]\!]$. Then ,CSP also blinds C with r_1 through calculating $D \leftarrow C^{r_1}$ before sending it to cloud B. Note that, $D = [\![r_1(2x + 1 - 2y)]\!]$ or $D = [\![r_1(2y - 2x - 1)]\!]$. Finally, CSP partial decrypts it with $sk^{(1)}$ as D', and sends D' to ESP. Receiving D' from CSP, ESP decrypts it by the partial private key $sk^{(2)}$ as d and compares it with $N/2$. If $d < N/2$, ESP sets $\beta \leftarrow 1$. Otherwise, ESP sets $\beta \leftarrow 0$. Note that, after these steps in this SC protocol, $t = \alpha \oplus \beta$ is the final comparison result needed. Since $\alpha, \beta \in (0, 1)$, we can conclude $\alpha \oplus \beta = (\alpha - \beta)^2$. Let $\gamma = \alpha - \beta$. We can see $\langle \gamma \rangle$ as $\langle \gamma \rangle^A \leftarrow \alpha$ and $\langle \gamma \rangle^B = -\beta$. Therefore, CSP and ESP just needs to run a $\text{Mul}(\langle \gamma \rangle, \langle \gamma \rangle)$ to get the final comparison result. These multiplication steps are shown from line 4 to line 8 in Algorithm 1.

REMARK. In our SC, we mainly let the two clouds compare $r_1(2x + 1 - 2y)$ or $r_1(2y - 2x - 1)$ rather than directly compare $r_1(x - y)$. On one hand, if $x = y$, the decryption result obtained by ESP is 0. Thus, the comparison result is leaked to ESP. On the other hand, since x, y are integers, $x > y \Leftrightarrow 2x + 1 > 2y$ and $x < y \Leftrightarrow 2x + 1 < 2y$.

Discussion. Note that there are several works focusing on securely comparing two additive shared integers [35, 36]. Their works are just based on the secret sharing scheme. Thus, the communication rounds are about $O(n)$. However, in our scheme, CSP and ESP just need to communicate with each other in 3 rounds. We greatly reduce the communication rounds compared with references [35, 36].

4.2 Secure Polynomial Calculation

Polynomial is a combination of several elements' multiplications and additions. Since we have *Add* and *Mul* on the additive secret shares, we can easily get our *Secure Polynomial Calculation* (SPC) protocol. Such a SPC is also a series of Adds and Muls' combination. For example, if we want to compute $f(x, y, z) = a_1 x^{n_1} y^{m_1} z^{k_1} + a_2 x^{n_2} y^{m_2} z^{k_2} + \cdots + a_\lambda$, where x, y, z are shared by ESP and CSP, and $a_1, a_2, \cdots, a_\lambda$ are public constants. To solve such a problem, CSP and ESP calculate each monomial one by one, and then they run an Add on all the shared monomial to get the results. For each monomial, it is just a combination of several multiplications, and they just need to run Mul several times to get the additive shares of each monomial.

5   Privacy-Preserving Decision Tree Evaluation

With the building blocks proposed, we are ready to introduce the detailed scheme for our privacy-preserving decision tree evaluation. Our scheme consists of the following three stages: query vector issuing, secure decision tree evaluation and result recovering. Note that the modular N for the Paillier cryptosystem with distributed decryption is generated by KGC. Such an N is also used for the query data splitting. Thus, it also should be sent to SUs, before they issue their query to the CSP.

5.1   Query Request Issuing

Once receiving N from KGC, the multiple SUs are ready to split their query vectors. For a query vector $\boldsymbol{X} = \{x_1, x_2, \cdots, x_n\}$, the SU splits it into two additive shares through the following ways. The SU randomly chooses a set of integers r_i from $\mathbb{Z}_N$ where $i \in [1, n]$. Then, the SU sets $\langle x_i \rangle^A = r_i$, and $\langle x_i \rangle^B = x_i - r_i$. After these computations, the SU uploads $\langle \boldsymbol{X} \rangle^A$ to CSP and $\langle \boldsymbol{X} \rangle^B$ to ESP respectively. Here, we assume that the transmission channel between SUs with the CSP and ESP are secure which cannot be eavesdropped by $\mathcal{A}$.

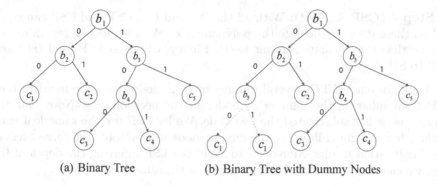

(a) Binary Tree   (b) Binary Tree with Dummy Nodes

Fig. 3. Binary decision tree

5.2 Secure Decision Tree Evaluation

In this stage, CSP and ESP cooperate with each other to obliviously evaluate the decision tree. We follow the idea of Bost *et al.* proposed that express the decision tree as a polynomial P [8]. The basic idea of such a P is that it is a sum of several terms, where each term is represented as a path from the root to one leaf node. If and only if the query vector is classified as the label c_i, the evaluation result of P is c_i. Therefore, the term corresponding to a path in the tree is the multiplication of the boolean variables on that path and the classification label at the leaf node. For example, the polynomial of the tree shown in Fig. 3(a) is
$P(b_1, b_2, b_3, b_4, c_1, c_2, \cdots, c_5) = (1 - b_1) \cdot (b_2 \cdot c_2 + (1 - b_2) \cdot c_1) + b_1 \cdot (b_3 \cdot c_5 + (1 - b_3)(c_4 + (1 - b_4) \cdot c_3)))$.

In our scheme, the decision tree model belongs to the CSP. Neither the ESP or the SU should learn anything about the tree structure. And the two clouds should also learn nothing about the query data and classification result. We illustrate the details of our *Secure Decision Tree Evaluation* (SDTE) as follows:

Step 1 (CSP): Suppose that the internal node of a tree is $Y = \{y_1, y_2, \cdots, y_m\}$. CSP adds some dummy node into the Y. Without loss of generality, we suppose that k dummy nodes are added. Then, CSP gets Y', where $Y' = \{y_1, y_2, \cdots, y_{m+k}\}$. Note that for the correctness of the evaluation result, all the dummy node goes to the same leaf node as the leaf node substituted by them. The tree with dummy nodes is shown in Fig. 3(b).

Step 2 (CSP): CSP chooses $m + k$ random integers α_i from $\mathbb{Z}_N$, and sets $\langle y_i \rangle^A = \alpha_i$ and $\langle y_i \rangle^B = y_i - \alpha_i$. CSP sends $\langle Y' \rangle^B$ to ESP. With the same way, CSP also splits all the c_i into two additive shares and send $\langle c_i \rangle^B$ to ESP. Note that, the two children of the dummy nodes are same. But here, we let CSP choose different random numbers to make it indistinguishable.

Step 3 (CSP & ESP): For each $\langle y_i \rangle$, CSP and ESP run a SC on it and its corresponding $\langle x_i \rangle$. Here we use b_i to denote the comparison results. Note that $\langle b_i \rangle$ is also secret shared by the two clouds. Neither the CSP nor the ESP knows these comparison results.

Step 4 (CSP & ESP): With all the $\langle b_i \rangle$ and $\langle c_i \rangle$, CSP and ESP can run a SPC on these data to calculate the polynomial P. Without loss of generality, we assume that the calculation result is $\langle r \rangle$. Finally, CSP and ESP send $\langle r \rangle^A$ and $\langle r \rangle^B$ to SU.

REMARK. In our **SDTE**, several dummy internal nodes are introduced to keep ESP from inferring the number of nodes in the decision tree. Note that the dummy node has substituted the leaf node. We let CSP use the same leaf node as the left and right children of the dummy node to guarantee the correctness of the classification results. Moreover, to avoid the ESP inferring the depth of the tree, we can introduce more dummy nodes in the same way.

5.3   Classification Result Reconstruction

After receiving the classification result shares, i.e., $\langle r \rangle^A$, $\langle r \rangle^B$, from CSP and ESP respectively, the SU can recover the label of his query vector X through local computation. That is, SU just computes $r \leftarrow \langle r \rangle^A + \langle r \rangle^B$.

6   Security Analysis

In this section, we first analyse the security of our building blocks and then our privacy-preserving decision tree evaluation scheme.

6.1   Security of Cryptographic Blocks

In this section, we prove the security of **SC** and **SPC**. Before that, we first present the definition of security in the semi-honest model [37].

Definition 1 (Security in the Semi-Honest Model [37]). *Let π denote the protocol and a_i, b_i be the input and output of party p_i computed in this protocol respectively. We also use $\Pi_i(\pi)$ to denote P_i's execution image of the protocol π. Then π is secure if $\Pi_i(\pi)$ can be simulated from a_i and b_i such that distribution of the simulated image is computationally indistinguishable from $\Pi_i(\pi)$ (More details can be found in [37]).*

From **Definition** 1, we can easily get that if a protocol is secure under the semi-honest model, its simulated execution image and the actual execution image should be computational indistinguishable. Usually, the data exchanged and the information calculated during the protocol running is included in the execution image of a protocol. Moreover, to prove the security of our protocols, the following lemmas can be used. For more details of the proofs of Lemma 1 and Lemma 2 can be found in reference [38].

Lemma 1. *[36,38] A protocol is perfectly simulatable if all its sub-protocols are perfectly simulatable.*

Lemma 2. *If r is a random integer uniformly chosen from $\mathbb{Z}_N$ and independent from any variable $x \in \mathbb{Z}_N$, $r + x$ is also uniformly random and independent from x.*

Theorem 1. *The SC proposed is secure under semi-honest model.*

Proof. As we have stated that from line 4 to line 8 in Algorithm 1, CSP and ESP cooperate with each other to run a Mul to get the final comparison result. Since the security of Mul have been proved in reference [26], we just need to prove other steps shown in Algorithm 1 is secure. In the following, we just give the execution image of the first three lines in Algorithm 1. Here, let the execution image of CSP be denoted by $\Pi_{CSP}(\text{SC})$ which is given by $\Pi_{CSP}(\text{SC}) = \{X^A, X^B, Y^A, Y^B, X, Y, C, \alpha, r_1, D, D'\}$. Note that α is a random numbers in $\mathbb{Z}_N$. We assume that $\Pi_{CSP}^S(\text{SC}) = \{X_0', X_1', Y_0', Y_1', X', Y', C', \alpha', r_1' D_0', D''\}$ where all the elements are randomly generated from $\mathbb{Z}_N$ except α', r_1', where α' is randomly chosen from $(0, 1)$ and r_1' is a random number whose bit length is smaller than $\|N\|/2 - 1$. Since Paillier cryptosystem with distributed decryption is a semantic secure encryption scheme [24], $X^A, X^B, Y^A, Y^B, X, Y, C, D, D'$ are computationally indistinguishable from $(X_0', X_1', Y_0', Y_1', X', Y', C', D_0', D'')$. Moreover, both α and α' are randomly chosen from $(0, 1)$, thus they are also computationally indistinguishable. Based on the above analysis, we can draw a conclusion that $\Pi_{CSP}(\text{SC})$ is indistinguishable from $\Pi_{CSP}^S(\text{SC})$.

Similarly, the execution image of ESP in this SC form line 1 to 3 is denoted as $\Pi_{ESP} = \{X^B, Y^B, D', d\}$, where $d = r_1(2x + 1 - 2y)$ or $d = r_1(2y - 2x - 1)$. The simulated image is $\Pi_{ESP} = \{X'', Y'', D', d'\}$, where all the elements are randomly chosen from $\mathbb{Z}_N$. Since Paillier cryptosystem with distributed decryption is semantic secure, $\Pi_{ESP}(\text{SC})$ is computationally indistinguishable from $\Pi_{ESP}^S(\text{SC})$.

According to Lemma 2, combining the above analysis, we can confirm that SC is secure under the semi-honest model.

Theorem 2. *The SPC is secure under semi-honest model.*

Proof. Our SPC is based on Add and Mul. Since the security of Add and Mul have been proved in reference [26], we can conclude that SPC is secure too.

6.2 Security of Privacy-Preserving Decision Tree Evaluation Scheme

Theorem 3. *The proposed privacy-preserving decision tree evaluation scheme is secure under semi-honest model.*

Proof. In the similar manner we can prove that our privacy-preserving decision tree evaluation scheme is secure under the semi-honest model firstly. In the first and third stage, the calculations are done locally by the SU. Thus, it is obviously secure. In the following, we mainly prove our SDET is secure under semi-honest model.

In Step 1 and Step 2, CSP just splits the internal nodes and the leaf nodes into two additive shares and sends one of the shares to ESP. Since one of the shares is a random number chosen from $\mathbb{Z}_N$, according to Lemma 1, the other share is random too. The other steps are based on our SC and SPC, which are proven to be secure under the semi-honest model. According to Lemma 2, we can conclude that our SDTE is secure under the semi-honest model.

7 Performance Analysis and Comparison

In this section, we evaluate the performance of our scheme.

7.1 Experiment Analysis

The performance evaluations of the proposed system are tested on two personal computers running Windows 8.1 with Intel Core i7-6700 CPU 3.40 GHz eight-core processor and 16 GB RAM memory. One of them acts as CSP and the other acts as ESP. We implement Pailier cryptosystem with distributed decryption by BigInteger Class in Java development kit, and using this to implement our computation protocols.

Table 3. Performance on Real-World Dataset (100-Times for Average, 80-bits Security Level)

Dataset	n	d	m	Time	Comm. Cost
Breast-cancer	9	8	12	0.532s	16.489 KB
Heat-disease	13	3	5	0.28s	6.89 KB
Housing	13	13	92	6.412s	136.419 KB
Credit-screening	15	4	5	0.352s	6.99 KB
Spambase	57	17	58	4.189s	83.692 KB

We test our privacy-preserving decision tree evaluation scheme on five datasets from the UCI repository[1] whose application domain including breast cancer diagnosis and credit rating classification. First, we train these dataset to get our decision tree by standard Matlab tools (**classregtree** and **Tree Bagger**).Note that we use the same dataset in reference [9]. The detailed experimental results are shown in Table 3. Compared with Wu *et al.*'s work, both the communication and computation costs of ours are much smaller.

---

[1] UC Irvine Machine Learning Repository https://archive.ics.uci.edu/ml/datasets. htm.

8   Conclusions

In this work, we proposed a privacy-preserving decision tree evaluation scheme on the outsourced cloud data. In our scheme, two-cloud model is used. During the evaluation process, nothing of the query data and classification result is leaked to either of the clouds. Moreover, the details of the tree are also kept secret to the service users. Besides, in our scheme, the service users do not need to take part in the evaluation, i.e, they just send a query and wait for the result. The experimental results show that our scheme is highly efficient. For the future, we plan to extend our work to support the random forest.

Acknowledgement. The work is supported by the National Key Research and Development Program under grant 2017YFB0802300, the National Natural Science Foundation of China (No. 61702541, No. 61702105), the Young Elite Scientists Sponsorship Program by CAST (2017QNRC001), the Science and Technology Research Plan Program by NUDT (Grant No. ZK17-03-46), and Guangxi Cloud Computing and Large Data Collaborative Innovation Center Project.

References

1. The health insurance portability and accountability act of privacy and security rules. http://www.hhs.gov/ocr/privacy
2. Singh, A., Guttag, J.V.: A comparison of non-symmetric entropy-based classification trees and support vector machine for cardiovascular risk stratification, pp. 79–82 (2011)
3. Azar, A.T., El-Metwally, S.M.: Decision tree classifiers for automated medical diagnosis. Neural Comput. Appl. **23**(23), 2387–2403 (2013)
4. Koh, H.C., Tan, W.C., Goh, C.P.: A two-step method to construct credit scoring models with data mining techniques. Int. J. Bus. Inf. **1**(1), 96–118 (2006)
5. Rago, A., Marcos, C., Diaz-Pace, J.A.: Using semantic roles to improve text classification in the requirements domain. Lang. Resour. Eval. **52**(3), 801–837 (2018)
6. Lindell, Y., Pinkas, B.: Privacy preserving data mining. In: Bellare, M. (ed.) CRYPTO 2000. LNCS, vol. 1880, pp. 36–54. Springer, Heidelberg (2000). https://doi.org/10.1007/3-540-44598-6_3
7. Agrawal, R., Srikant, R.: Privacy-preserving data mining. In: ACM SIGMOD Record, vol. 29, pp. 439–450. ACM (2000)
8. Bost, R., Popa, R.A., Tu, S., Goldwasser, S.: Machine learning classification over encrypted data. In NDSS, vol. 4324, p. 4325 (2015)
9. Wu, D.J., Feng, T., Naehrig, M., Lauter, K.: Privately evaluating decision trees and random forests. Proc. Priv. Enhanc. Technol. **2016**(4), 335–355 (2016)
10. Tai, R.K.H., Ma, J.P.K., Zhao, Y., Chow, S.S.M.: Privacy-preserving decision trees evaluation via linear functions. In: Foley, S.N., Gollmann, D., Snekkenes, E. (eds.) ESORICS 2017. LNCS, vol. 10493, pp. 494–512. Springer, Cham (2017). https://doi.org/10.1007/978-3-319-66399-9_27
11. Du, W., Zhan, Z.: Building decision tree classifier on private data. In IEEE International Conference on Privacy, Security and Data Mining (2002)
12. Ma, X., Chen, X., Zhang, X.: Non-interactive privacy-preserving neural network prediction. Inf. Sci. **481**, 507–519 (2019)

13. Ma, X., Zhang, F., Chen, X., Shen, J.: Privacy preserving multi-party computation delegation for deep learning in cloud computing. Inf. Sci. **459**, 103–116 (2018)
14. Yong, Y., Li, H., Chen, R., Zhao, Y., Yang, H., Xiaojiang, D.: Enabling secure intelligent network with cloud-assisted privacy-preserving machine learning. IEEE Netw. **33**(3), 82–87 (2019)
15. Brickell, J., Porter, D.E., Shmatikov, V., Witchel, E.: Privacy-preserving remote diagnostics. In: Proceedings of the 14th ACM Conference on Computer and Communications Security, pp. 498–507. ACM (2007)
16. Yao, A.C.-C.: How to generate and exchange secrets. In: 27th Annual Symposium on Foundations of Computer Science, pp. 162–167. IEEE (19860)
17. Barni, M., Failla, P., Kolesnikov, V., Lazzeretti, R., Sadeghi, A.-R., Schneider, T.: Secure evaluation of private linear branching programs with medical applications. In: Backes, M., Ning, P. (eds.) ESORICS 2009. LNCS, vol. 5789, pp. 424–439. Springer, Heidelberg (2009). https://doi.org/10.1007/978-3-642-04444-1_26
18. Damgard, I., Geisler, M., Kroigard, M.: Homomorphic encryption and secure comparison. Int. J. Appl. Crypt. **1**(1), 22–31 (2008)
19. Schneider, T., Zohner, M.: GMW vs. Yao? efficient secure two-party computation with low depth circuits. In: Sadeghi, A.-R. (ed.) FC 2013. LNCS, vol. 7859, pp. 275–292. Springer, Heidelberg (2013). https://doi.org/10.1007/978-3-642-39884-1_23
20. De Cock, M., et al.: Efficient and private scoring of decision trees, support vector machines and logistic regression models based on pre-computation. IEEE Trans. Dependable Secure Comput. **16**, 217–230 (2017)
21. Joye, M., Salehi, F.: Private yet efficient decision tree evaluation. In: Kerschbaum, F., Paraboschi, S. (eds.) DBSec 2018. LNCS, vol. 10980, pp. 243–259. Springer, Cham (2018). https://doi.org/10.1007/978-3-319-95729-6_16
22. Tueno, A., Kerschbaum, F., Katzenbeisser, S.: Private evaluation of decision trees using sublinear cost. Proc. Priv. Enhanc. Technol. **2019**(1), 266–286 (2019)
23. Paillier, P.: Public-key cryptosystems based on composite degree residuosity classes. In: Stern, J. (ed.) EUROCRYPT 1999. LNCS, vol. 1592, pp. 223–238. Springer, Heidelberg (1999). https://doi.org/10.1007/3-540-48910-X_16
24. Hazay, C., Mikkelsen, G.L., Rabin, T., Toft, T., Nicolosi, A.A.: Efficient RSA key generation and threshold Paillier in the two-party setting. J. Cryptol. **32**(2), 265–323 (2019)
25. Shamir, A.: How to share a secret. Commun. ACM **22**(11), 612–613 (1979)
26. Beaver, D.: Efficient multiparty protocols using circuit randomization. In: Feigenbaum, J. (ed.) CRYPTO 1991. LNCS, vol. 576, pp. 420–432. Springer, Heidelberg (1992). https://doi.org/10.1007/3-540-46766-1_34
27. Riazi, M.S., Weinert, C., Tkachenko, O., Songhori, E.M., Schneider, T., Koushanfar, F.: Chameleon: a hybrid secure computation framework for machine learning applications. In: Proceedings of the 2018 on Asia Conference on Computer and Communications Security, pp. 707–721. ACM (2018)
28. Liu, X., Choo, R., Deng, R., Lu, R., Weng, J.: Efficient and privacy-preserving outsourced calculation of rational numbers. IEEE Trans. Dependable Secure Comput. **15**, 27–39 (2016)
29. Elmehdwi, Y., Samanthula, B.K., Jiang, W.: Secure k-nearest neighbor query over encrypted data in outsourced environments. In: 2014 IEEE 30th International Conference on Data Engineering (ICDE), pp. 664–675. IEEE (2014)

30. Liu, L., et al.: Privacy-preserving mining of association rule on outsourced cloud data from multiple parties. In: Susilo, W., Yang, G. (eds.) ACISP 2018. LNCS, vol. 10946, pp. 431–451. Springer, Cham (2018). https://doi.org/10.1007/978-3-319-93638-3_25

31. Wang, D., Wang, P.: Two birds with one stone: two-factor authentication with security beyond conventional bound. IEEE Trans. Dependable Secure Comput. 15(4), 708–722 (2016)

32. Wang, D., Cheng, H., He, D., Wang, P.: On the challenges in designing identity-based privacy-preserving authentication schemes for mobile devices. IEEE Syst. J. 12(1), 916–925 (2016)

33. Liu, X., Deng, R.H., Choo, K.-K.R., Weng, J.: An efficient privacy-preserving outsourced calculation toolkit with multiple keys. IEEE Trans. Inf. Forensics Secur. 11(11), 2401–2414 (2016)

34. Nikolaenko, V., Weinsberg, U., Ioannidis, S., Joye, M., Boneh, D., Taft, N.: Privacy-preserving ridge regression on hundreds of millions of records. In: 2013 IEEE Symposium on Security and Privacy (SP), pp. 334–348. IEEE (2013)

35. Damgård, I., Fitzi, M., Kiltz, E., Nielsen, J.B., Toft, T.: Unconditionally secure constant-rounds multi-party computation for equality, comparison, bits and exponentiation. In: Halevi, S., Rabin, T. (eds.) TCC 2006. LNCS, vol. 3876, pp. 285–304. Springer, Heidelberg (2006). https://doi.org/10.1007/11681878_15

36. Huang, K., Liu, X., Fu, S., Guo, D., Xu, M.: A lightweight privacy-preserving CNN feature extraction framework for mobile sensing. IEEE Trans. Dependable Secure Comput. (2019)

37. Goldreich, O.: Foundations of Cryptography: Volume 2, Basic Applications. Cambridge University Press, Cambridge (2009)

38. Bogdanov, D., Laur, S., Willemson, J.: Sharemind: a framework for fast privacy-preserving computations. In: Jajodia, S., Lopez, J. (eds.) ESORICS 2008. LNCS, vol. 5283, pp. 192–206. Springer, Heidelberg (2008). https://doi.org/10.1007/978-3-540-88313-5_13

Who Activated My Voice Assistant?
A Stealthy Attack on Android Phones
Without Users' Awareness

Rongjunchen Zhang[1(✉)], Xiao Chen[1], Sheng Wen[1], and James Zheng[2]

[1] Swinburne University of Technology, Hawthorn, Australia
{rongjunchenzhang,xiaochen,swen}@swin.edu.au
[2] Macquarie University, North Ryde, Australia
james.zheng@mq.edu.au

Abstract. Voice Assistant (VAs) are increasingly popular for human-computer interaction (HCI) smartphones. To help users automatically conduct various tasks, these tools usually come with high privileges and are able to access sensitive system resources. A comprised VA is a stepping stone for attackers to hack into users' phones. Prior work has experimentally demonstrated that VAs can be a promising attack point for HCI tools. However, the state-of-the-art approaches require ad-hoc mechanisms to activate VAs that are non-trivial to trigger in practice and are usually limited to specific mobile platforms. To mitigate the limitations faced by the state-of-the-art, we propose a novel attack approach, namely Vaspy, which crafts the users' "activation voice" by silently listening to users' phone calls. Once the activation voice is formed, Vaspy can select a suitable occasion to launch an attack. Vaspy embodies a machine learning model that learns suitable attacking times to prevent the attack from being noticed by the user. We implement a proof-of-concept spyware and test it on a range of popular Android phones. The experimental results demonstrate that this approach can silently craft the activation voice of the users and launch attacks. In the wrong hands, a technique like Vaspy can enable automated attacks to HCI tools. By raising awareness, we urge the community and manufacturers to revisit the risks of VAs and subsequently revise the activation logic to be resilient to the style of attacks proposed in this work.

Keywords: Voice Assistant · Smartphone · Android ·
Software security · Systems security

1   Introduction

Voice assistants (VAs) have been widely used in smartphones, typically as human-computer interaction (HCI) mechanisms for device control and identity authentication. Popular examples from the market include Amazon Alexa [10], Samsung Bixby [29], Google Assistant [20], and Apple Siri [13]. Because

© Springer Nature Switzerland AG 2019
X. Chen et al. (Eds.): ML4CS 2019, LNCS 11806, pp. 378–396, 2019.
https://doi.org/10.1007/978-3-030-30619-9_27

human-beings are able to speak about 150 words per minute, which is much faster than typing, *e.g.*, roughly 40 words per minute on average, VAs are very useful to transform human speech into machine-actionable commands. This creates an easy-to-use design of smartphones, especially for those that need lots of inputs or for scenarios where 'hands-free' is mandatory (*e.g.*, making phone calls when driving). In order to support broad functionalities via voice, *e.g.*, sending text messages, making phone calls, browsing the Internet, playing music/videos, *etc.*, VAs are usually granted high-level privileges including dangerous permissions [28] (*e.g.*, ACCESS_COARSE_LOCATION, READ_CONTACTS).

Unfortunately, the VA technique is a double-edged sword. They not only bring great convenience to smartphone users, but also offer a backdoor for hackers to gain entrance into the mobile systems. Hackers can take advantage of VAs' required high privilege in accessing various applications and system services to steal users' private information like locations and device IDs [20], control smart home devices [4], forge emails, or even transfer money [5], *etc.* For example, after activating the Google Assistant with the keywords "OK Google", a hacker can further manipulate an episode of attacking voice that cheats the smartphone to send the user's location to a specific number via SMS with commands such as "send my location to 12345678" [20]. Given a list of VA-enabled functions [24], we can identify many potential attacks against users' smartphones.

Prior work has already demonstrated the feasibility of attacking smartphones via VAs [10,17,20,42]. The key to the successes of the approaches is to activate VAs in a stealthy manner. For example, Diao *et al.* [20] and Alepis *et al.* [10] utilise the Android inter-component communication (ICC) to wake up the VA. To be stealthy, they propose to launch attacks when smartphones are unattended or in the early morning (*e.g.*, 3 am). However, this approach requires to call a specific API ('ACTION_VOICE_SEARCH_HANDS_FREE'), which is only available in Google Assistant. This excludes the use of the approach in some brands like Huawei and Xiaomi, which provide custom VAs other than Google Assistant. Zhang *et al.* [42] propose using inaudible ultrasound to activate VAs. The attacking commands are undetectable by users but can be recognised by VAs on smartphones. However, this approach needs a special ultrasound generator on-site, which is not practical in the real world. There is another work under the same umbrella. Carlini *et al.* [17] apply adversarial machine learning technique to manipulate attacking sounds against voice recognition systems. This approach requires the hackers to have physical access to the targeting smartphones and run sound crafting processes iteratively. This premise is also impractical in most real-world scenarios.

In this paper, we propose a novel and practical stealthy attacking approach against voice assistants in Android phones, named Vaspy. It learns from the user's normal dialogue to craft the activation voice to the VA and leverages the built-in speaker to play and activate the VA. To be stealthy, the attack is triggered only at moments when the smartphone user is most likely to overlook the occurrence of activation voice. The idea of Vaspy comes from two practical facts: (1) the built-in speaker can be used to activate the VA of a phone [10];

and (2) the ringtone of a phone can be easily neglected by a user in a noisy environment.

We develop a proof-of-concept spyware based on Vaspy. The spyware disguises itself as a popular microphone controlled game to increase the chance of successful delivery to targeting Android phones[1]. The spyware records in/outbound calls and synthesises the activation keywords (*e.g.*, 'OK Google') using speech recognition and voice cloning [12] techniques. This operation is necessary as state-of-the-art VAs are resilient to unauthenticated voiceprints. The proof-of-concept spyware sheds light on two advantages of Vaspy: (1) since the attacking process only makes use of a common component in an Android phone (*e.g.*, the built-in speaker), Vaspy can be applied to most off-the-shelf Android phones that have built-in VAs; this breaks the limitations in prior work, which either requires a special equipment [17,42] or can only be applied to Google Assistant [10,20]; (2) Vaspy can employ machine learning techniques to analyse data collected from various on-board sensors; this helps Vaspy identify the optimal attacking time, making it stealthier compared to prior work [10,20].

Vaspy can be very dangerous to smartphone users, not only due to its stealthiness, but also because of its resilience to state-of-art anti-virus tools. We test the proof-of-concept spyware on VirusTotal [2], a widely adopted industrial anti-virus platform. We also test the spyware on three state-of-the-art learning-based Android malware detectors, namely Drebin [14], DroidAPIMiner [9], and MaMaDroid [33]. Results indicate that the spyware based on Vaspy can evade their detection. In fact, Vaspy seldom invokes sensitive APIs [6] and uses the VA as a puppet to carry out malicious activities, making it resilient to those anti-virus tools.

We summarise the contributions of this paper as follows.

- We propose a novel attacking approach called Vaspy, which can stealthily hack into Android phones via built-in VAs without users' awareness.
- We designed a context-aware module in Vaspy, making it stealthier compared to prior work. This module provides intelligent environment detection to identify the optimal time to launch attack, based on the data collected from various on-board sensors.
- We develop a proof-of-concept spyware based on Vaspy to evaluate the attack in a real-world empirical study. The empirical results show that users cannot detect the spyware and the spyware does not affect the performance of Android phones significantly. We also find that the spyware is resilient to typical anti-virus tools from both industry and academia.

The rest of this paper is organised as follows. Section 2 presents related works. Section 3 provides the details of the attacking model in Vaspy. Section 4 demonstrates the feasibility of Vaspy through a proof-of-concept spyware. The evaluation is presented in Sect. 5, followed by a discussion of some open issues in Sect. 6. Section 7 concludes this paper.

---

[1] This is only an example for delivery. There are many other social engineering methods to be used in the real world, *e.g.*, [40].

2 Related Work

2.1 Attacks to Smartphone VA

There are a few existing work designed to attack VAs. For example, Diao *et al.* [10,20] proposed an attacking method that made use of Android inter-component communication mechanism and built-in speaker. To be stealthy, Diao *et al.* [20] designed the attack to be triggered at 3 am, a time when smartphones were expected to be unattended (*e.g.*, users sleeping). A similar model to make the attack stealthy was adopted in Alepis *et al.*'s work [10]. However, these attacks require a specific API (Intent: 'ACTION_VOICE_SEARCH_HANDS_FREE'), which was only available in Google Assistant. This limits the use of their proposed attacking methods, *e.g.*, considering devices like Huawei's Xiao Yi and Xiaomi's Xiao Ai, which provide custom VAs for users. In addition, the stealthiness of the above methods is not complete. For example, the volume of activation voice (*e.g.*, 55±3 dB claimed in Table 4 of [20]) may be loud enough to wake the user, considering the quiet environment in the early morning [35].

There are some other attacking methods that focused on crafting special audio that could be recognised by smartphone VAs but not heard by human-beings [17,42]. For example, the idea of Nicholas *et al.* [17] was to obfuscate raw attack audio and make it sound like a noise. Based on adversarial machine learning techniques [15,38], the deliberately crafted audio could be recognised by smartphone VAs but was neglected by smartphone users as incomprehensible noise. In another example, Zhang *et al.* proposed using ultrasound [42], as its frequency is higher than the upper audible limit of human hearing. However, the approach of Nicholas *et al.* [17] requires access to the targeting voice recognition model as either a black-box or a white-box, in order to run audio crafting processes iteratively. Moreover, the approach of Zhang *et al.* requires a special instrument (*e.g.*, ultrasound generator) [42]. Both premises are impractical in most real-world scenarios.

There are also some works that specifically studied the attacks against speech recognition systems (*note*: a key part in VA) [30,36,41]. For example, Yuan *et al.* [41] embedded voice commands into a song that can be recognised as a complete sentence by the speech recognition system. Schönherr *et al.* [36] manipulated adversarial examples against speech recognition systems by crafting special audio signals based on psycho-acoustic hiding technique. Kumar *et al.* [30] explored interpretation errors made by Amazon Alexa and found that Amazon Alexa could make some permanent systematic errors. All these works focus on audio processing for attacks. However, in the proposed Vaspy, we mainly focus on the stealthier attacking behaviours such as identifying suitable attack time and making it imperceptible to users. The ideas of the above works can also be borrowed and integrated into our Vaspy to expand the attack range.

2.2   Context-Awareness Based on Smartphone Sensors

The success of Vaspy relies on activating VAs in a stealthy manner. This in turn relies on context-awareness that identifies the optimal attacking time according to the data collected from the smartphone's on-board sensors (*e.g.*, accelerometer, gyroscope, and ambient light sensor). In this subsection, we analyse similar works that also adopted context-awareness based on on-board sensors.

Silva *et al.* adopted a series of sensors in a smart home to predict human activities [19]. Wiese *et al.* collected sensor data to analyse where people keep their smartphones [39]. They achieved an 85% successful rate in determining if a smart phone was in a bag, in a pocket, out, or in hand. Liu *et al.* [32] proposed recognising PINs when users input them by keyboard to smart watches. They used the accelerometer to capture user's hand movement, and achieved high accuracy in keystroke inference. In another work, user's typing pattern was learned via accelerometer readings [34]. These patterns were then used to infer user's typing on the screen. Moreover, Ho *et al.* proposed a context-awareness algorithm that determined when and what information to present would not make flawless decisions on mobile devices with heavy communication traffic [27]. We can find many similar applications of context-awareness based on smartphone sensors, *e.g.*, [11,26,37].

Similar to prior work, Vaspy also uses context-awareness based on smartphone sensors. In this area, we reckon that there is no superiority among different context-awareness methods. Vaspy just integrates those that can increase the chance of successful attacking. The particular approach may be different when Vaspy is implemented in various proof-of-concept scenarios.

3   Attacking Model: Vaspy

The workflow of Vaspy is shown in Fig. 1. Vaspy's attacking approach includes two modules: (1) Activation Voice Manipulation and (2) Attacking Environment Sensing. The first module synthesises the commands (*e.g.*, 'OK Google') that are required to activate the VA. Because most popular VAs can differentiate the voice of genuine smartphone owners based on artificial intelligence technologies [16], the activation voice in Vaspy will be manipulated based on the targeted users' own voice.

There are mainly two approaches available for synthesising activation voice: (1) using users' voice recording to clone an activation voice [12]; and (2) extracting an activation voice form users' voice recordings. For the first approach, we can adopt voice cloning method [12] based on multi-speaker generative modelling [23] to generate the activation voice by a few users' own voice recordings. The method provides a trained multi-speaker model (fine-tuning) that takes a few audio-text pairs as input to simulate new speaker. This approach requires a text input to encode the cloned voice. Alternatively, the second approach adopts speech recognition techniques/tools such as Recurrent Neural Network (RNN) [25] to retrieve/synthesise the vocal pieces of those special words from users' own voice. This approach has been widely used in some commercial systems such as

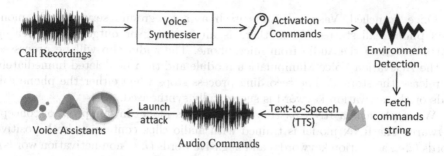

Fig. 1. The workflow of an example spyware based on Vaspy. Incoming/outgoing calls are monitored and recorded, and the activation voice is then synthesised. User's environment is monitored by built-in sensors to determine a suitable attacking occasion. When launching the attack, text commands can be retrieved from Firebase [7] and converted to speech by a built-in Text-to-Speech (TTS) module in the smartphone.

IBM Watson [1]. In Sect. 4, we implement an RNN-based method to synthesise users' voice in our proof-of-concept spyware, but alternative techniques/tools can also be integrated to Vaspy. In our implementation, the vocal corpus of special words can help craft the activation voice, e.g., 'OK' plus 'Google' producing 'OK Google' as a whole activation voice piece for Google Assistant. However, it can be very challenging when the targeted user seldom speaks these special words. In this case, Vaspy will synthesise the vocal pieces of the special words from syllables captured from users' voice [22], e.g., the first syllable of 'good' and the second syllable of 'single' can be concatenated to pronounce 'google'.

Once the activation commands are crafted, the second module will collect environment data such as light levels, noise levels, and motion states, via onboard sensors. Vaspy introduces machine learning techniques to decide an optimal time to launch the attack in a stealthy manner. The correctness of Vaspy's decisions is determined by the volume and quality of the contextual data collected to access the attacking environment. After the second module identifies a suitable attacking time, the synthesised activation voice is played, followed by prepared attacking commands (e.g., "send my location to 123456"), causing harm to the targeted smartphone user. After the activation, successive attacking commands can be easily delivered to the VAs to control the compromised phone.

4   Proof-of-Concept: A Spyware

4.1   Activation Voice Manipulation

We implement a proof-of-concept spyware in Android to evaluate Vaspy in a series of real-world scenarios. The spyware disguises itself as a microphone-controlled game. When a user starts playing the game, Vaspy will be activated in the background and stay active even if the game app is terminated.

Once launched, Vaspy registers itself as a foreground service[2] that monitors phone call status. When there is an incoming or outgoing call, Vaspy starts recording the audio from microphone. The audio clip will be processed by the Activation Voice Manipulation module and then be deleted immediately to release the storage. The recording process stops when either the phone call ends or the activation keyword is successfully synthesised.

We implement a RNN-based voice synthesis model in our proof-of-concept spyware. The RNN model is trained with audio clips containing both positive words (*i.e.*, activation keywords) and negative words (*i.e.*, non-activation words). Audio signals are converted into spectrograms which represent the spectrum of frequencies of the signals. Starting and ending frames of each activation keyword are labeled in the audio clips. The RNN is trained to extract activation words from audio clips. We implement the Gate Recurrent Unit as the core unit of our RNN [18]. There are 4500 and 500 audio clips used in training and testing, respectively. The accuracy on the testing set is 93.4%.

Note that in our prototype implementation, recorded audio clips must contain the activation keywords. However, this limitation can be removed by implementing voice cloning technique [12], which requires only a few voice recordings of arbitrary contents from the targeting user.

4.2 Attacking Environment Sensing

Environment data that decides whether to launch the attack is collected from smartphone on-board sensors. In particular, we extract the *movement intensity* features from accelerometer readings and the features of *environment variables* from microphone and light sensors readings. Since smartphones do not have built-in noise sensors, noise levels in decibel are calculated from the amplitude of the ambient sound that we gathered from microphone, according to $L_{dB} = 10 \, lg \left(\frac{A_1}{A_0} \right)^2$ wherein A_1 is the amplitude of the recorded sound, and A_0 is a standard amplitude that is usually set to one.

Movement intensity features describe an overall perspective of human behaviour state. We divide human behaviours into a series of states, including (1) the definite motion state, (2) the definite stationary state, and (3) the relative motion-stationary state. The sharp difference of readings between the definite motion state and the definite stationary state allows the classification model to recognise these behaviours with high accuracy. However, the activities that do not show an apparent fluctuation may confuse the classification model. Therefore, we define an intermediate, *i.e.*, a relative motion-stationary state, by which most of the confusing activities can be classified accurately. In this prototype, we use Random Forest as our classification model because RF does not directly output class labels but instead computes probabilities. We assign labels to the instances according to whether the probabilities of RF exceed a

---

[2] Android 9 disables background services from accessing user input and sensor data. Therefore, we use foreground service and hide the notification icon by making it transparent [3].

certain threshold. We label the motion state with the probability of over 60% and less than 40% as a definite motion state and a definite stationary state, respectively. We also label the motion state with the probability between 40% to 60% as a relative motion-stationary state. As the *movement intensity* features are categorical data, machine learning based algorithms cannot work with them directly. Therefore, we convert all the *movement intensity* features to numerical values using one-hot encoding. The definite motion state has been encoded to $[0, 1]$, the definite stationary state has been encoded to $[1, 0]$ and the relative motion-stationary state has been encoded to $[1, 1]$.

All collected sensors' data will be re-sampled in a frequency of 50 Hz and follow the Nearest Neighbour Interpolation principle [8], and merge with one hot encoded *movement intensity* features to built training matrices. The features of *environment variables* are used for the purpose of providing more specific details on the uncertain environmental factors, such as noise level and light intensity, which can also affect the decision about whether to launch a stealthy attack.

4.3   Post Attacks and Spyware Delivery

Once the environment detector determines to launch the attack, the synthesised activation voice is played via the speaker on the victim's phone. Meanwhile, the attacking commands (text format) are dynamically fetched from Firebase [10] and played via the smart phone's speaker using Android built-in Text-to-speech (TTS) service.

Three permissions are required in Vaspy, which are RECORD_AUDIO (to record the activation voice of the user), INTERNET (to dynamically fetch attacking commands from the Firebase server and interact with trained online model), and READ_PHONE_STATE (to monitor incoming/outgoing call status). Vaspy is disguised as a popular microphone-controlled game, so that it can legitimately request the RECORD_AUDIO permission. When a victim user plays the game, the player is required to blow or scream to the microphone to raise a rocket. (The snapshot of the game can be found in Appendix A). The game is very deceivable to teenagers or kids. In fact, the spyware can be delivered in other forms such as a malicious audio recorder. READ_PHONE_STATE and INTERNET permissions are very commonly requested by various Android games. There are 46 of the top 100 games on Google Play that requests the READ_PHONE_STATE permission, while all of the top 10 games request the INTERNET permission.

5   Evaluation

In this section, we evaluate the performance of our prototype spyware in terms of the attack success rate. The attack capabilities on the VAs from various vendors (*i.e.*, Google, Huawei, and Xiaomi) are also investigated. In addition, to examine its stealthiness, we evaluate the system overhead, and tested Vaspy against anti-virus tools/platforms.

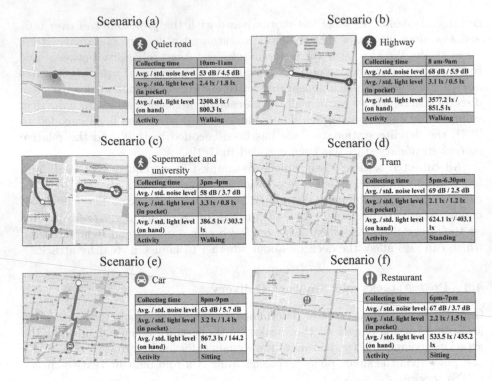

Fig. 2. Overview of the data collected in real-world scenarios.

5.1   Evaluation of the Attacking Environment Sensing Modulel

We evaluate the proposed attack on three VAs on four Android smartphones, including Google Assistant on Google Pixel 2 and Samsung Galaxy S9, Xiao Yi on Huawei Mate 8, and Xiao Ai on Xiaomi Mi 8. Smartphones are taken to various real-world scenarios for data collection. These scenarios include moving or stationary states, noisy or quiet environment, and putting a smartphone in pockets or holding it on hands. The example scenarios are shown in Fig. 2.

Each smartphone is carried by a participant for data collection. An audio piece of synthesised activation voice is stored in each smartphone. These activation voices are tested in advance to make sure that they can successfully activate the voices assistant on the smartphones. In every two minutes, the activation voice followed by one random attacking voice command (*e.g.*, "Send 'subscribe' to 1234567") is played via smartphone's built-in speaker. If the participant does not notice the voice command, and the command is successfully executed, we label this attack as success. Finally, the data we collected for training includes the readings from smartphone on-board sensors (*i.e.*, microphone, accelerometer, and ambient light sensor) and attack results (as label set).

We train a Random Forest with collected data, and evaluated the model based on Precision, Recall, and F1 Score. The results of 20-fold cross validation is presented in Table 1. It shows the proposed model is well-trained.

Table 1. Average accuracy performance

Invasion	Precision	Recall	f1-score
Unsuccessful	0.96	0.95	0.95
Successful	0.97	0.98	0.98
Avg	0.97	0.97	0.97

5.2 Evaluation of Real World Attack

We further evaluate the effectiveness of the attack in real-world scenarios in different times of a day. We Ten participants are recruited to carry one of the aforementioned smartphones to various real-world scenarios. Smartphone sensors collect real-time environment data, and feed it to the trained machine learning model. Then, a probability of whether to launch an attack is obtained. An attack will be triggered if the probability exceeds a threshold (*e.g.*, 80% in our experiment setting). We set up a restriction that in every two minutes, there will be at most one attack triggered. Figure 3 reports the sensors' readings and the output attacking probabilities in two typical scenarios (see Appendix C to find more scenarios), where "True" in the attack results indicates that the attack is triggered but not heard by the participant, while "False" represents that the attack is triggered and heard by the participants. "N/A" means that no attack is triggered in the time slot, so that it is excluded when calculating the success rate. We can see from Fig. 3 that the spyware based on Vaspy achieves 100% success rate in real world attack.

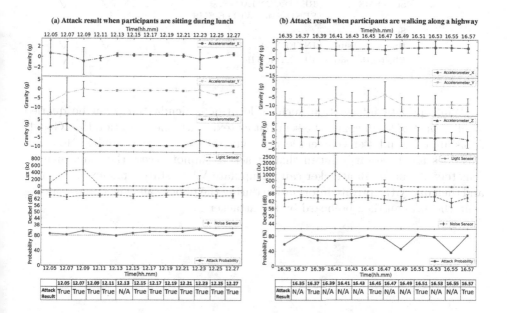

Fig. 3. Evaluation result of the attacking environment sensing.

5.3   Capability of Attack

After activating the VAs, the attackers may further acquire victim's private information, or conduct malicious activities on the infected smartphones, through remotely executing specific attacking commands.

In Table 2, we list and compare the potential attacks that can be launched on different VAs in victim smartphones, namely Google Assistant on Pixel 2, Xiao Yi on Huawei Mate 8, and Xiao Ai on Xiaomi Mi 8. We also listed the permissions required if the corresponding information are queried in an app. However, none of these permissions are required in the proposed attack, since VAs are naturally gained privilege to access such information.

Table 2. Post attack commands against VAs.

Category	Attack type	Permission(s) bypassed	Attack result against VAs		
			Google	Huawei	Xiaomi
Privacy leak	Query location	ACCESS_COARSE_LOCATION	√	√	√
	Share location	READ_CONTACTS, SEND_SMS, ACCESS_COARSE_LOCATION, WRITE_SMS	√	×	×
	Query calendar	READ_CALENDAR	√	√	√
	Share calendar	READ_CALENDAR, READ_CONTACTS, SEND_SMS, WRITE_SMS	×	×	×
Malicious activity	Phone Call	READ_CONTACTS, CALL_PHONE	√	√	√
	Send SMS	READ_CONTACTS, SEND_SMS, WRITE_SMS	√	√	√
	Send email	/	√	√	√
	Browse website	INTERNET	√	√	√
	Bluetooth control	BLUETOOTH	√	√	√

While private information such as location, calendar *etc.*, can be queried locally, most of them cannot be sent out as text, with one exception that Google Assistant can send user's current location via SMS to arbitrary number. However, this does not necessarily mean that attackers cannot access these information remotely. Actually, an attacker can manipulate VA to start a phone call to him, and then query the private information during the phone call. The audio response from the VA can then be heard by the attacker.

The malicious activities such as making phone calls to premium numbers, sending SMS, browsing malicious websites and so on, can be performed on all the VAs that we tested without requesting for any permissions.

Given the fact that VAs can be easily controlled by attackers to perform malicious activities as well as acquiring private information, we suggest that the vendors should rethink the privilege assigned to VAs.

5.4   Runtime Cost Analysis

We evaluate and analyse the runtime cost of the spyware because high runtime cost (*e.g.*, CPU, Memory) will reduce the stealthiness of the attack. We install the prototype spyware on Google Pixel 2, Huawei mate 8, Xiaomi Mi 8 and Samsung Galaxy S9. Since the spyware launches the attack in the four distinctive phases below, we evaluate each phase individually: P1 (Phone call state monitoring), P2 (Recording and synthesising activation command), P3 (Environment monitoring), and P4 (Attacking via a speaker).

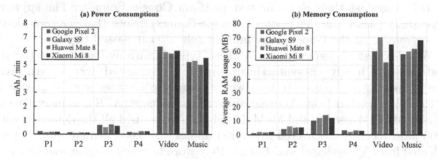

Fig. 4. Power and memory consumption of four phases: P1 (Phone call state monitoring), P2 (Recording and synthesising activation command), P3 (Environment monitoring), and P4 (Attacking via the speaker)

Power Consumption Analysis: Figure 4(a) reports the power consumption per minute for four attacking phases. We also compare the power consumption with playing 1080P video and music. The results show that in P1, P2, and P4, the power consumption per minutes on all Android phones are very low. P3 has the highest power consumption, which is approximately 0.8 mAh per minute. It is still negligible when compared with the scenarios such as playing video or listening to music, which consumes 6.1 mAh and 5.1 mAh per minute, respectively. We further reduce the frequency of collecting data from sensors in P3 from 50 Hz to 10 Hz. The power consumption decreases to 0.5 mAh, without affecting the success rate of the attack. The results suggest that the spyware consumes too little power to be noticed by the user.

Memory and CPU Analysis. Figure 4(b) shows the average RAM usage in the four processes. The average RAM usage in P1, P2, and P3 is less than 5 MB.

The P3 uses the highest memory (approximately 10 MB) because of sensor utilisation. Compared to the scenarios like playing video or listening to music, which consumes approximately 60 MB to 70 MB, the memory cost of our prototype spyware can hardly affect the performance of the hosting smartphone systems. Therefore, it is hard to be noticed by the user. We also evaluate the CPU cost. It is found that only P3 requires CPU, which consumes around 7% of the total capacity.

5.5   Resistance to Anti-Virus Tools

We test the spyware against industrial anti-malware tools as well as academic malware detection solutions.

For industrial anti-virus products, we test the spyware on VirusTotal (see Appendix B), as well as the top ten most popular anti-virus tools on Google Play, such as Norton Security and Antivirus, Kaspersky Mobile Antivirus, McAfee Mobile Security, and so on. None of them reported our spyware as malicious app. We also submit the spyware to Google Play store, where submitted apps are tested against their dynamic test platform Google Bouncer. The spyware successfully passes the detection of Google Bouncer. Note that we took down the spyware from the Google Play immediately after it passed the test.

We also test the spyware with three typical learning-based detectors in academia, which rely on syntactic features (e.g., requested permissions, presence of specific API calls, etc.), as well as semantic features (e.g., sequence of API calls) extracted from Android application package (APK), namely Drebin [14], DroidAPIMiner [9], and MaMaDroid [33]. We trained all the detectors with 5,000 most recently discovered malware samples and 5,000 benign apps that we collected from Virusshare[3] and Google Play store between August and October 2018, respectively. Our spyware is labeled as a benign app by all three detectors. The results show the resistance of the proposed attacking method to both industrial and academic malware detection tools.

6   Discussion

In this section, we will introduce the promising defence approaches for Vaspy and discuss the lessons from this work.

6.1   Defence Approaches for Vaspy

In this section, we demonstrate two possible defence approaches for Vaspy: (1) identifying the source of the voice commands; (2) continuous authentication for VAs.

---

[3] https://virusshare.com/.

(1) Identifying the source of the voice commands. In the proposed attack scenario, the voice commands are played via a speaker on a smartphone. New techniques [31] are able to locate the source of the sound, which can then determine whether the sound comes from the built-in speaker. The VA vendors can disable our attack by setting the VA to disregard any voice commands from the built-in speaker on its hosting smartphone.

(2) Continuous authentication for VAs. Feng *et al.* [21] propose a scheme that collects the body-surface vibrations of the user and matches with the speech signal received from a microphone. The VA only executes the commands that originate from the owner's voice. While it may successfully defend our attack, it also brings some inconvenience to the user. For example, users cannot activate the VA when they do not hold the smartphone. Actually, users tend to interact with VA when they are not able to touch the screen, such as the time when they are driving.

6.2 Lessons from This Work

This can be recognised as a vulnerability in the current VAs. Once the VAs are activated, they are able to change smartphone settings, and do malicious activities that require high level permission, such as sending SMS/emails and making phone calls. Due to the privileges it has to access system resources and private information. VAs can then be a stepping stone for the attackers to hack into the Android phones. More secure mechanisms will be implemented to improve the security of VAs, from either the research community or the VA vendors.

7 Conclusion

In this paper, we propose a smart and stealthy attack Vaspy targetting VAs on Android phones. With the new attack, an attacker can forge voice commands to activate the VA and launch a number of attacks, including leaking private information, sending forged Message or emails, and calling arbitrary numbers. An Attacking Environment Sensing module is built inside the Vaspy to choose an optimal attacking time and voice volume making the attack unnoticed by the users. We build a prototype spyware for Vaspy and evaluate the spyware with participants across various VAs on different Android phones. We demonstrate that Vaspy is able to launch attacks without being noticed by users. Moreover, our spyware cannot be detected by the state-of-art anti-malware tools from both industry and academia. We also propose a few potential solutions to detect our attack. This research work may inspire the researchers for Android phones to strengthen the security of VAs in general.

Appendix A The Snapshot of the Proof-of-Concept Spyware

(See Fig. 5).

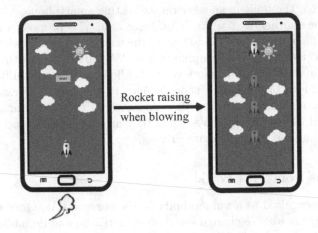

Rocket raising
when blowing

Fig. 5. The snapshot of the proof-of-concept spyware. After player clicking start button, the rocket will raise when player blows or scream to the microphone. The rising speed depends on the volume of sound that the microphone receives

Appendix B The Detection Result of VirusTotal

(See Fig. 6).

No engines detected this file

SHA-256   c8cfcb5b5033814ba619bf1b4b5742cad6b769fdd4a456343fa8dc3d361317dc
File name   app-release.apk
File size   2.39 MB
Last analysis 2018-09-25 10:32:04 UTC

0 / 60

Detection	Details	Relations	Community			
Ad-Aware	✅ Clean			AegisLab	✅ Clean
AhnLab-V3	✅ Clean			Alibaba	✅ Clean
ALYac	✅ Clean			Antiy-AVL	✅ Clean
Arcabit	✅ Clean			Avast	✅ Clean
Avast Mobile Security	✅ Clean			AVG	✅ Clean
Avira	✅ Clean			AVware	✅ Clean
Babable	✅ Clean			Baidu	✅ Clean
BitDefender	✅ Clean			Bkav	✅ Clean
CAT-QuickHeal	✅ Clean			ClamAV	✅ Clean
CMC	✅ Clean			Comodo	✅ Clean

Fig. 6. A snapshot of the detection result in VirusTotal

Appendix C   Evaluation Result of Other Typical Scenarios

(See Fig. 7).

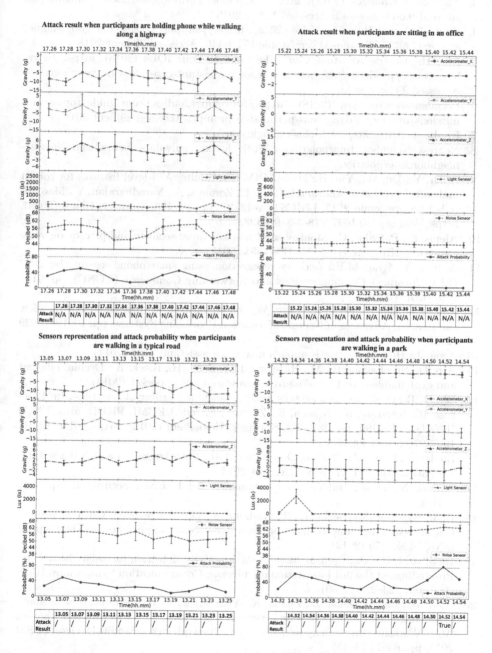

Fig. 7. Evaluation result of the attacking environment sensing.

References

1. IBM Watson. https://www.ibm.com/watson/. Accessed 28 Sept 2018
2. Virus Total. https://www.virustotal.com. Accessed 29 Sept 2018
3. Android 9 Changes (2018). https://developer.android.com/about/versions/pie/android-9.0-changes-all. Accessed 1 Apr 2019
4. Control Google Home by Voice (2018). https://support.google.com/googlehome/answer/7207759?hl=en-AU&ref_topic=7196346. Accessed 29 Sept 2018
5. Now the Google Assistant Can Take Care of Your IOUs (2018). https://www.blog.google/products/assistant/now-google-assistant-can-take-care-your-ious. Accessed 29 Sept 2018
6. Permissions Overview (2018). https://developer.android.com/guide/topics/permissions/overview#dangerous-permission-prompt. Accessed 29 Sept 2018
7. Firebase (2019). https://firebase.google.com
8. Nearest Neighbor Interpolation (2019). https://en.wikipedia.org/wiki/Nearest-neighbor_interpolation
9. Aafer, Y., Du, W., Yin, H.: DroidAPIMiner: mining API-level features for robust malware detection in Android. In: Zia, T., Zomaya, A., Varadharajan, V., Mao, M. (eds.) SecureComm 2013. LNICST, vol. 127, pp. 86–103. Springer, Cham (2013). https://doi.org/10.1007/978-3-319-04283-1_6
10. Alepis, E., Patsakis, C.: Monkey says, monkey does: security and privacy on voice assistants. IEEE Access 5, 17841–17851 (2017)
11. Anjum, A., Ilyas, M.U.: Activity recognition using smartphone sensors. In: 2013 IEEE Consumer Communications and Networking Conference (CCNC), pp. 914–919. IEEE (2013)
12. Arik, S., Chen, J., Peng, K., Ping, W., Zhou, Y.: Neural voice cloning with a few samples. In: Advances in Neural Information Processing Systems, pp. 10019–10029 (2018)
13. Aron, J.: How innovative is apple's new voice assistant, Siri? (2011)
14. Arp, D., Spreitzenbarth, M., Hübner, M., Gascon, H., Rieck, K.: Drebin: efficient and explainable detection of android malware in your pocket (2014)
15. Biggio, B., et al.: Evasion attacks against machine learning at test time. In: Blockeel, H., Kersting, K., Nijssen, S., Železný, F. (eds.) ECML PKDD 2013. LNCS (LNAI), vol. 8190, pp. 387–402. Springer, Heidelberg (2013). https://doi.org/10.1007/978-3-642-40994-3_25
16. Binder, J., Post, S.D., Tackin, O., Gruber, T.R.: Voice trigger for a digital assistant. US Patent App. 14/175,864, 7 August 2014
17. Carlini, N., et al.: Hidden voice commands. In: USENIX Security Symposium (2016)
18. Cho, K., Van Merriënboer, B., Bahdanau, D., Bengio, Y.: On the properties of neural machine translation: encoder-decoder approaches. arXiv preprint arXiv:1409.1259 (2014)
19. De Silva, L.C.: Multi-sensor based human activity detection for smart homes. In: Proceedings of the 3rd International Universal Communication Symposium, IUCS 2009, pp. 223–229 (2009)
20. Diao, W., Liu, X., Zhou, Z., Zhang, K.: Your voice assistant is mine: how to abuse speakers to steal information and control your phone. In: Proceedings of the 4th ACM Workshop on Security and Privacy in Smartphones & Mobile Devices, SPSM 2014, pp. 63–74 (2014)

21. Feng, H., Fawaz, K., Shin, K.G.: Continuous authentication for voice assistants. In: Proceedings of the 23rd Annual International Conference on Mobile Computing and Networking, MobiCom 2017, pp. 343–355 (2017)
22. Ganapathiraju, A., Hamaker, J., Picone, J., Ordowski, M., Doddington, G.R.: Syllable-based large vocabulary continuous speech recognition. IEEE Trans. Speech Audio Process. 9(4), 358–366 (2001)
23. Gibiansky, A., et al.: Deep voice 2: multi-speaker neural text-to-speech. In: Advances in Neural Information Processing Systems, pp. 2962–2970 (2017)
24. Google: What Can Your Google Assistant Do? (2018). https://assistant.google.com/explore?hl=en-AU. Accessed 29 Sept 2018
25. Graves, A., Mohamed, A., Hinton, G.: Speech recognition with deep recurrent neural networks. In: 2013 IEEE International Conference on Acoustics, Speech and Signal Processing (ICASSP), pp. 6645–6649. IEEE (2013)
26. Gross, M.: Context-aware computing: from neuroscience to mobile devices (2015)
27. Ho, J., Intille, S.S.: Using context-aware computing to reduce the perceived burden of interruptions from mobile devices. In: Proceedings of the SIGCHI Conference on Human Factors in Computing Systems, pp. 909–918. ACM (2005)
28. Kiseleva, J., et al.: Understanding user satisfaction with intelligent assistants. In: Proceedings of the 2016 ACM on Conference on Human Information Interaction and Retrieval, CHIIR 2016, pp. 121–130 (2016)
29. Knote, R., Janson, A., Eigenbrod, L., Söllner, M.: The what and how of smart personal assistants: principles and application domains for is research (2018)
30. Kumar, D., et al.: Skill squatting attacks on Amazon Alexa. In: 27th USENIX Security Symposium (USENIX Security 2018), pp. 33–47 (2018)
31. Liu, R., Cornelius, C., Rawassizadeh, R., Peterson, R., Kotz, D.: Poster: vocal resonance as a passive biometric. In: Proceedings of the 15th Annual International Conference on Mobile Systems, Applications, and Services, MobiSys 2017, pp. 160–160 (2017)
32. Liu, X., Zhou, Z., Diao, W., Li, Z., Zhang, K.: When good becomes evil: keystroke inference with smartwatch. In: Proceedings of the 22nd ACM SIGSAC Conference on Computer and Communications Security, CCS 2015, pp. 1273–1285 (2015)
33. Mariconti, E., Onwuzurike, L., Andriotis, P., De Cristofaro, E., Ross, G., Stringhini, G.: Mamadroid: detecting android malware by building Markov chains of behavioral models. arXiv preprint arXiv:1612.04433 (2016)
34. Marquardt, P., Verma, A., Carter, H., Traynor, P.: (sp)iPhone: decoding vibrations from nearby keyboards using mobile phone accelerometers. In: Proceedings of the 18th ACM Conference on Computer and Communications Security, pp. 551–562. ACM (2011)
35. Muzet, A.: Environmental noise, sleep and health. Sleep Med. Rev. 11(2), 135–142 (2007)
36. Schönherr, L., Kohls, K., Zeiler, S., Holz, T., Kolossa, D.: Adversarial attacks against automatic speech recognition systems via psychoacoustic hiding. arXiv preprint arXiv:1808.05665 (2018)
37. Shoaib, M., Bosch, S., Incel, O.D., Scholten, H., Havinga, P.J.: Fusion of smartphone motion sensors for physical activity recognition. Sensors 14(6), 10146–10176 (2014)
38. Szegedy, C., et al.: Intriguing properties of neural networks. arXiv preprint arXiv:1312.6199 (2013)
39. Wiese, J., Saponas, T.S., Brush, A.B.: Phoneprioception: enabling mobile phones to infer where they are kept. In: Proceedings of the SIGCHI Conference on Human Factors in Computing Systems, CHI 2013, pp. 2157–2166 (2013)

40. Xu, N., Zhang, F., Luo, Y., Jia, W., Xuan, D., Teng, J.: Stealthy video capturer: a new video-based spyware in 3G smartphones. In: Proceedings of the Second ACM Conference on Wireless Network Security, pp. 69–78. ACM (2009)
41. Yuan, X., et al.: CommanderSong: a systematic approach for practical adversarial voice recognition. In: 27th USENIX Security Symposium (USENIX Security 2018), pp. 49–64 (2018)
42. Zhang, G., Yan, C., Ji, X., Zhang, T., Zhang, T., Xu, W.: DolphinAttack: inaudible voice commands. In: Proceedings of the 2017 ACM SIGSAC Conference on Computer and Communications Security, CCS 2017 (2017)

Retraction Note to: A Cooperative Placement Method for Machine Learning Workflows and Meteorological Big Data Security Protection in Cloud Computing

Xinzhao Jiang, Wei Kong, Xin Jin, and Jian Shen

Retraction Note to:
Chapter "A Cooperative Placement Method for Machine
Learning Workflows and Meteorological Big Data Security
Protection in Cloud Computing" in: X. Chen et al. (Eds.):
Machine Learning for Cyber Security, **LNCS 11806,**
https://doi.org/10.1007/978-3-030-30619-9_8

The authors have retracted this chapter [1] because after publication they realized that the data set simulated in this paper was incorrectly selected in the experiment in Section 5. This resulted in serious errors in the meteorological workflows experimental results. Attempts at repeating the experiment with the appropriate data set failed due to other unknown errors.

In addition, the input in NSDE is inappropriate and flawed. As a consequence, it may result in unstable experiment results of meteorological workflows based on machine learning.

All authors agree to this retraction.

[1] Jiang, X., Kong, W., Jin, X., Shen, J.: A cooperative placement method for machine learning workflows and meteorological big data security protection in cloud computing. In: Chen, X., Huang, X., Zhang, J. (eds.) ML4CS 2019, LNCS, vol. 11806, pp. 94–111. Springer, Cham (2019). https://doi.org/10.1007/978-3-030-30619-9_8

The retracted version of this chapter can be found at
https://doi.org/10.1007/978-3-030-30619-9_8

Author Index

Printed in the United States
By Bookmasters